New Approaches
to the Study of Religic
2

D0771811

DISCARD

W
DE
G

New Approaches to the Study of Religion

Volume 2: Textual, Comparative, Sociological, and Cognitive Approaches

Edited by

Peter Antes, Armin W. Geertz, Randi R. Warne

Walter de Gruyter · Berlin · New York

Originally published as volume 43 in the series *Religion and Reason.*

♾ Printed on acid-free paper which falls within
the guidelines of the ANSI to ensure permanence and durability.

ISBN 978-3-11-020552-7

Library of Congress – Cataloging-in-Publication Data

A CIP catalogue record for this book is available from the Library of Congress.

Bibliographic information published by the Deutsche Nationalbibliothek

The Deutsche Nationalbibliothek lists this publication in the Deutsche Nationalbibliografie; detailed bibliographic data are available in the Internet at http://dnb.d-nb.de.

© Copyright 2008 by Walter de Gruyter GmbH & Co. KG, D-10785 Berlin
All rights reserved, including those of translation into foreign languages. No part of this book may be reproduced or transmitted in any form or by any means, electronic or mechanical, including photocopy, recording, or any information storage and retrieval system, without permission in writing from the publisher.

Printed in Germany
Cover design: Martin Zech

Contents

SHATFORD LIBRARY

AUG - 2010

1570 E. Colorado Blvd.
Pasadena, CA 91106

Section 6: Social Sciences

Section 7: Cognition and Cross-Cultural Psychology

Introduction

by

PETER ANTES, ARMIN W. GEERTZ, and RANDI R. WARNE

It is particularly fitting at the threshold of a new millennium to reflect back on what has transpired in academic approaches to the study of religion over the last two decades of the twentieth century. The summary of developments and achievements in our field presented here follows in the footsteps of two former publications, namely, Jacques Waardenburg's *Classical Approaches to the Study of Religion*, first published in 1973 (paperback edition 1999), and Frank Whaling's two volume edited work, *Contemporary Approaches to the Study of Religion*. Waardenburg's *Classical Approaches* provided scholars with a comprehensive survey of the academic field of religion from its inception as an academic discipline in the nineteenth century up until the end of World War II, and is marked by a phenomenological and textual emphasis that reflects the concerns that animated the field during that period. Whaling's *Contemporary Approaches*, covering the post World War II period up until the early 1980s, was subdivided into two volumes: *The Humanities* (1983) and *The Social Sciences* (1985), reflecting a shift of intellectual and scholarly terrain. While the former was comprised of a selection of texts chosen by the editor from works not initially intended for a publication on methodology, the latter presented articles on methodology explicitly solicited from various authors by the editor. Our present two volume publication, published like the preceding volumes in de Gruyter's *Religion and Reason* series, is a sequel to both, but as with the latter, all the contributions have been explicitly written for this publication. *New Approaches to the Study of Religion* thus completes the survey of the study of religion in the twentieth century with a focus on developments characteristic of its last two decades, i.e., the period from 1980 to the present.

Though many people in Western Europe and the Americas experienced a kind of a millennium fever at the turn of the twenty-first century, historians of religions know that the periodization of an era is rather arbitrary. A glance at different religious calendars confirms that neither Muslims nor Jews, Hindus nor Buddhists shared the tension of the transition from one century to another and even less so from one millennium to another. It is thus not surprising that in terms of methodological approaches, the end of a century of our era does not necessarily mean a turning point in the type of scholarly work being undertaken. What can be described here, therefore, is less a retrospective consideration of methods used, *per se*, than a consideration of the promise of new approaches that are currently being undertaken and need further methodological consideration.

The present two volume publication maps the methodological terrain in the scholarly study of religion in seven sections—as outlined below—with volume one covering regional, critical, and historical approaches; and volume two covering textual, comparative, sociological, and cognitive approaches.

A Survey of New Approaches in Various Parts of the World

Academic studies may seem to be universal in their methods and results. However, a closer look at what is actually being done shows that these studies are context-related in many respects: linguistically, politically, religiously, and culturally.

The linguistic setting is of major importance for determining what might be considered "new," particularly when considered in a world-wide context. Philippe Ariès' *History of Childhood* may serve as an example to illustrate the problem. The book was originally published in French in 1960, and launched an intense debate in the French-speaking world. A German translation was published in 1975, and led to vigorous debates similar to those undertaken in the French-speaking world fifteen years before. Within the German context, Ariès' thesis was something new, while the French were astonished to discover that Ariès was still being discussed in this way. What may be new in one context does not need to be so in another, or—put somewhat differently—academic debates do not need to be synchronic. Numerous and different levels of discussion may occur simultaneously in academic debate world-wide. Even though English is increasingly becoming the common language for academic publications, the diversity noted above is not well represented in respective journals and reviews because of the tendency for editors to work from their own frames of reference regarding "newness" and the established framework for debate, rather than documenting the full range of discussion being undertaken globally. It is necessary to highlight these context-related particularities to assess "new approaches" adequately.

There are also political reasons why academic discussions vary from one context to the other. This holds particularly true for Eastern Europe. The fall of the Berlin Wall in 1989 and the consequent end of communist rule over most of the countries in Eastern Europe produced new academic discussions in these regions. Many scholars were confronted with the methodological approaches of Western countries for the first time, and approaches that seemed outdated in the West were both welcome and fascinating in this new environment. For example, a strong interest in the phenomenology and psychology of religion has recently developed in the academic study of religion in Poland, and is, within that context, a genuine methodological innovation. The waning of Marxist ideology has also been paralleled by a decline in the currency of the neo-Marxist worldviews of the so-called Frankfurt School (Theodor W. Adorno, Max Horkheimer, Jürgen Habermas) in the West. The political landscape clearly shapes the academic enterprise in an important way. What is "new" and relevant is context-specific, with academic debate having become increasingly multifaceted so that it is nearly impossible to determine with any finality what is "new" on a world-wide scale.

However, political conditions alone are insufficient to describe extra-academic influences on the academic debate. Religious factors can also be decisive,[1] as consideration of research within Muslim contexts gives evidence. The contributions in this volume make clear that within the Muslim world a number of different approaches are possible, from a very religious one in the Arab world to a laicist approach in Turkey.

Linguistic, political, and religious factors are thus without doubt of great importance for determining what constitutes a "new approach" in the study of religion in various contexts. However these are all external to the study of religion as such, and shape its structure in that way. There is, however, an intrinsic argument for defining newness in the study of religion, one related to disciplinary barriers. Specifically, a widely approved method in one discipline may be totally unknown in another. A great deal of courage is often needed to introduce a method from one discipline into another. Moreover, it may take years for the new methods of one discipline to be adopted in others. This is particularly relevant to the study of religions if we consider the classical understanding of the "History of Religions." In Italy and France, the sociology and psychology of religion are not considered sub-disciplines of the field, while they are in German and Spanish contexts. The turn towards the humanities and the social sciences described in Whaling's *Contemporary Approaches to the Study of Religion* thus was far more easily and widely undertaken in Germany and Spain than in Italy and France.

The aim of a survey of new approaches in various parts of the world is to draw the reader's attention to these context-related realities of research in the study of religion. The goal is not to enumerate all the different studies that have been undertaken, or to itemize a list of important representative scholars. Rather, the task at hand is to provide an orientation that will allow the reader to put all these studies into a proper context, to clarify what is being done, and why it is being done in the way that it is. Each contribution that follows should

1 Cf. Marburg Revisited: Institutions and Strategies in the Study of Religion, ed. by Michael Pye, Marburg: diagonal-Verlag, 1989.

thus be considered in relation to its originating context, as an indicator of the state of the discipline therein.

We hope that the work in this section will inspire more (and much more detailed) studies in this area, for it is indeed a new field of research that begs for further study. Ideally, in future volumes of this kind, this section will be considerably enlarged and will encompass all relevant research areas of the discipline.

Critical Approaches

The next section is dedicated to critical approaches. "Critical" refers here to critical reflections that are relevant to the study of religion(s), although the arguments themselves stem from other disciplines. Critical arguments engage two main concerns: 1) the problem of the relationship between reality and the study of religion(s) and 2) the socio-psychological conditions of the researcher and their impact on the results of research.

Regarding the first, new approaches taken from philosophy and semantics strongly suggest that we have no immediate access to reality. The time when people explained truth as the equation between what things are and what is said about them (*adaequatio rei et intellectus*, in medieval terminology) has definitely passed. It is clear to most, if not all, philosophers and linguists that reality *per se*, or seen "objectively" (i.e. what things are), is beyond the reach of human intelligence. From this perspective, all so called "objectively true" statements are nothing but agreements between people and are, as such, only certain within a given context of people who are willing to accept the agreement. Meaning and truth claims are thus neither subjective nor objective, but intersubjective insofar as they express convictions shared by everyone within the group. Consequently, truth is much more the equation between intersubjective statements made within a particular group (*adaequatio intellectus ad intellectum*, to express it in terms analogous to the medieval claim) than it is a statement about reality, objectively known. This is of particular interest in the study of "religion," which is claimed to have a non-empirical dimension and is thus even less "objectively" accessible than the empirical data of other disciplines. The ongoing debate in philosophy and semantics about the relationship between reality and what is said about it thus has intriguing consequences for the discipline and needs to be widely engaged both generally and in relation to specific areas of investigation.

A second range of problems needs to be considered as well. The first critical approach questions the possibility of objective access to reality as such and suggests instead that all human knowledge is more "human" (i.e. intersubjective) rather than "objectively" true. The second suggests that human access to knowledge is further conditioned by different socio-psychological factors that influence research and have an impact on its results. Consequently, it is not only "objective reality" that is under debate but the neutrality of the researcher as well. For instance, it has now become clear that male dominated, androcentric studies have ignored, distorted, and elided knowledge by and about women. Feminist and gender-critical approaches have led to highly significant insights in areas which were hitherto un(der)investigated. It is therefore important to understand that the way we look at the world and the type of questions we ask in our work are conditioned by socio-psychological factors to a great extent, i.e. that we are all "located knowers" whose specificity of perspective is relevant to the kinds of studies we engage in and the conclusions we draw.

It is important to note that critical studies such as these are not relinquishing "objectivity" for open-ended relativism. Rather, they must be seen in the context of the general truth claims put forward by religions. Theoretical explanations in the studies of religion(s) do not lead to dogmas but to explanatory theories that need to be tested and can be rejected if proven flawed or otherwise inadequate to the task at hand. Changes are always possible, including revisiting theories from the past that may now appear to have greater relevance and/or applicability than when they were previously superseded. Such comings and goings further underline the relativity of newness, from another perspective, in the studies of religion(s).

Historical Approaches

Historical approaches characterize the historian of religion's work best. This section, however, goes beyond classical historical studies and is more innovative. Here the focus rests upon consideration of the religion under study as a construction of the describer in ongoing response to and exchange with the described cultural phenomenon. Jørn Borup's contribution on *Zen and the Art of Inverting Orientalism* in this volume concludes the following:

> Studying religion is not like looking through a window. It is necessary to see with glasses, to use models and maps to see religion not as a metaphysical truth to be perceived, but as a cultural phenomenon, itself a construction, a living reality. Though both constructivism and processes of relational interconnectedness are also keywords within Buddhist discourse, our "constructions" need not be in harmony with theirs. But ideally they need to be potentially reflecting each other. Though a mirror can be used for reflection and illumination, the images reflected in the mirror are not the thing itself. Historians of religion are not supposed to reveal a "truth," but to reflect on an always ongoing discourse about their truths—and on our own discourse.[2]

2 See page 482.

It is, consequently, the characteristic of "construction" that is relevant to all types of descriptions of religions. It is not only the fact that religions, in the history of religions, are seen from the outside and that the outsider's view might be different from an insider's, but rather that the "images reflected in the mirror" are to a large degree constructions generated out of the observer's own mind. This is perhaps less significant in cases of established traditions such as Buddhism (though some would disagree), but it is clearly the case for more general classifications of contentious topics such as new religions, new fundamentalisms and Western esotericism. Here, the first task of the researcher is to delineate the subject, determining what properly belongs to the field to be studied, and what ought be omitted. Thus shaped, the subject is submitted to more detailed study. Clearly, initial assumptions will implicitly shape the conclusions that may eventually be drawn. If, for example, one is convinced that fundamentalism is an important trend that is noticeable in all major religions at present, a list of elements will be established to prove its existence in each of them. If, on the contrary, one denies this basic thesis, the same elements will not be seen as sharing a cross-tradition commonality, but rather will be understood within the specific framework of the religious tradition itself. The same principle can be applied *mutatis mutandis* to new religions and Western esotericism. Different results will emerge, depending on the breadth or narrowness of the observer's conception of these phenomena. Studies in these fields are not "like looking through a window." Even the comparison with the image in the mirror is imprecise for, what is seen in the mirror is not the image of what is, so to speak, "the thing itself," but an image of the thing created in the observer's mind as the subject of study. All the elements put under scrutiny and the methods employed to that end are consequences of initial decisions made about content at the outset of the study.

Textual Approaches

This section—the opening section of volume two—addresses one of the most classical approaches in studies of religion. For decades the most prestigious type of study in the field of religion was textual analysis and translation, for which philological methods were the most appropriate. A continuing concern for this way of engaging the study of religion may seem to imply a certain stasis in the field. The present volume, however, shows that there are theoretical problems with translation that studies of religion need to take into account. A further problem is the context of the process of translation, and the implications this may have for the adequacy of the translation itself. A good example of the problem is the German tradition of using the German mystical vocabulary of the late Middle Ages to translate the key terms of Islamic mysticism, a practice that leaves the reader with the impression that religious experience in Islamic mysticism has striking parallels with that of German Christian mystics. What has not been noted in these translations is that these parallels were intentionally chosen by the translators, but are not necessarily justified parallels as such. Language dictionaries are the best examples of translating terms from one cultural or religious context into another without any debate on how legitimate these parallels might be for academic use in translations.

Another field in textual approaches is the use of electronic media in the study of sacred texts. There are methodological implications and interpretive consequences in this area as well that require further study.

Finally, literary theory deserves serious discussion in its possible application to the study of religion.

All this shows the importance of extra-disciplinary developments to textual approaches within the study of religion, and assessments of their relevance to it. It may be tempting for scholars to neglect these developments, on the assumption that textual approaches will always be the same. They may find it difficult to imagine that innovative methods might be introduced or have any effect on their traditional work with texts. There is all the more need, therefore, to underline the importance of progress in this field, and to invite scholars of our discipline to actively engage in ongoing discussion of these issues.

Comparative Approaches

The section on comparative approaches covers a variety of fields of application from classical concerns such as syncretism and ritual, to new areas of interest such as dance and human rights. In the former case the main focus is on new insights and developments within traditional subject areas, while in the latter case more emphasis is necessarily laid upon arguments for integrating such fields of research into the study of religion. Here, the case needs to be made that these new subjects are too important for and relevant to the study of religion to be ignored. Conversations with colleagues from other disciplines are imperative, so that their research enriches our own as ours may theirs. The new questions thus generated may spur reinvestigation of our own source material in light of these different perspectives, to fruitful results.

Social Sciences

The section on social sciences touches upon one of the most important fields of influence on the study of religion since World War II. This section contains a survey of advances in the sociology of religion, as well as more specific topics such as the reassessment of secularization theory, urbanization and religion, religion in the media, religion and law, and religion in diaspora. The latter topic signals important and innovative developments in vocabulary in the study of religion. The section on historical approaches made reference to neologisms in the study of religion insofar as the word "fundamentalism," originally used for a certain tendency in American Protestantism at the threshold of the twentieth century, has now become a general term for antimodern tendencies in all religions. A similar expansion of meaning is occurring with the word "diaspora" so that we currently speak of Muslim, Buddhist, Hindu diasporas in Europe and do not reserve the term for Jewish minorities in Europe nor—as in traditional Roman Catholic circles in Germany—for Catholic minorities in mainly Protestant areas of Germany.

It is important to note that such expansions of meaning occur first in public debate, and subsequently find entrance into academic circles without any debate on whether or not this new terminology should be employed. The crux is that common parlance becomes academic terminology without clarity of definition for the purpose of academic study, thus launching endless debates about its appropriate use. Establishing clear definitions at the outset, as is done in the natural sciences, would arguably help offset the proliferation of later debates about a term's descriptive value.

Cognition and Cross-cultural Psychology

The last section of volume two focuses on cognition and cross-cultural psychology. Both are well-developed research fields outside the study of religion but have a direct impact on studies of religion as well. It is therefore highly desirable to investigate these areas further to determine the usefulness of these approaches for academic studies of religion.

The various sections of the present volumes offer a wide range of approaches to the study of religion which are making, and can make, fruitful and important contributions to the study of religion. Each of these "lenses" has contributed significantly to the generation of knowledge within our field, signaling the fact that progress in academic studies depends deeply on methodological exchange with other disciplines. To encourage and advance this exchange is a key goal of this volume.

Bringing a work such as this to fruition would be impossible without a publisher's strong support. We, the editors, would like to thank de Gruyter Publishers for having accepted *New Approaches to the Study of Religion* for publication in de Gruyter's *Religion and Reason* series. We would also like to express our appreciation for the strong support of its general editor, Jacques Waardenburg, who was always there with help and advice as the volume progressed. We thank him in particular for his encouragement and hope that the results of these labors will be a volume that will be found useful by a wide range of scholars in religion across the globe. Last but not least, we greatly thank Dr. Karl-Heinz Golzio for compiling the indexes of both volumes.

Finally, we hope that our readership will be inspired to incorporate new approaches to the study of religion in their own work, developing and deepening studies in religion as a result.

Section 4

Textual Approaches

New Approaches to the Problem of Translation in the Study of Religion

by

ALAN WILLIAMS

1. Introduction: Is There a Problem of Translation?

Translation is so central an activity in the study of religion that it tends to be taken for granted by scholars and students alike. The very suggestion here that there may be a *problem* of translation may appear unnecessary and/or obvious: a translation, surely, is either faithful or unfaithful; it may be good, bad or indifferent as a piece of writing, but as a translation it either sinks or swims; to make a problem out of it is therefore unnecessary. There has been much theoretical work on translation in the past few decades, by linguists, literary theorists, philosophers, and others, which questions all such assumptions, and it is hoped religionists too will wish to join in consideration of these questions. A distinction should first be made between what is meant by the problem of *translation* (which is the subject discussed in this essay) and the problem of the activity of *translating*, the daily task of every working translator (which is not). The difference between these two terms is not absolute: theory affects practice and vice versa. Theorists in translation studies, however, are addressing a much greater context than that which is normally understood as the domain of translating. This has been expressed as a distinction

> between translation as a technical problem governed by formal conventions ... and translation as a political problem that mires us in the iniquities of cultural contact.[1]

Perhaps the notion of a "politics of translation" might also seem unwarranted, yet this is one of the conclusions to which theoreticians in several fields, including literary criticism, cultural studies and translation studies, have come in the past thirty years. The notion of an ideological and political agenda underlying the study of religion is under discussion in our field, and this debate should perhaps also consider the politics of translation.

---

1 Robinson 1993: 121.

Day-to-day problems of *translating* arise as the translator mediates the different features of the source and target[2] languages in question. Many textbooks are currently available to help the novice translator learn the discipline of translation through a systematic approach.[3] Yet, even when the translator is expert in the source and target languages, the problem of translation persists. A number of overarching, high-level questions continue to arise: what is the nature of translation? Is translation entirely a culturally constructed phenomenon? In the aftermath of deconstructionism, have we to face the radical questioning of what is the status of the source text vis à vis the translated text? Is something always lost from the "original" in translation? Is translation a kind of cultural theft? Can translation replace, or at least substitute, the "original"? What is untranslatable? And what about poetry? In the field of the study of religion, these questions of translation are all the more acute and as yet unanswered. What is forbidden to be translated? Are sacralized languages put into the service of a linguistic/cultural imperialism, as much as, perhaps even more than, as it is now affirmed, colonialist languages upheld and uphold state and cultural imperialism?

There is a danger of making the treatment of translation much too narrowly defined as a *linguistic* phenomenon, as indeed it was regarded in e.g. J.C. Catford's opening definition in *A Linguistic Theory of Translation*:

> Translation is an operation performed on languages: a process of substituting a text in one language for a text in another.[4]

Important as translation is in the study of religion, and far-reaching as the theoretical questions are, there has been a regrettable lack of interest in the subject. Most disciplines of the arts and humanities have similarly had little consideration for that invisible servant, the translator. The growth of a whole discipline of translation studies has demonstrated that whilst Catford's definition is in a narrow, linguistic sense, adequate, it is altogether insufficient for understanding the problematic nature of translation. In this essay I report and reflect on some of the developments made in thinking about translation, and ask how, given the peculiar nature of the field of religion, religionists may contribute to the general understanding of what we create when we translate.

---

2 The terms "source" and "target" are used here as they have become standard in translation studies as preferable to the more traditional terms "original" and "translated" (languages/texts, etc.).

3 E.g. Baker 1992.

4 Catford 1965: 1.

2. Translation and Scholarship: Subsidiary or Central?

The scholarly and student communities of Western universities, and the public at large, now require a ready and ever-expanding supply of translation. So why is translation, and translation theory, still regarded as a secondary research activity? The religionist is no stranger to translating and translation. More than any other field, perhaps, translation is an everyday activity for the student of religion. In doing research we may prefer to work with primary sources in the language of composition, i.e. without the intermediary of "translations," but we engage in our own translation as we read out of those primary sources. Many religionists come to the field from a background not of "theology" or "divinity," but of textual and historical studies in classical, semitic, Indo-Iranian and other ancient language groups, from modern, literary languages, or from disciplines of the social sciences where fieldwork demands interaction with another language and cultural context. Many readers will know that the labor and skill required to translate even a relatively short text are considerable: the effort is repaid, however, as translating affords a uniquely close look at a text—translation requires one to take both an analytical and synoptic view of the text. The translator has to focus on the fine balance between meaning and form, so much so that it is a primary paradigm of the analytical and heuristic process of academic work in the humanities: the struggle to find terms to reach over from one context to another. While the availability of texts either in the original or in reliable translation is a *sine qua non* of a good deal of work on religion, yet the academy often looks askance at the translator. The provision of translations is often downgraded to being considered merely auxiliary: it is deemed to be secondary to the primary academic work of linguistic and historical analysis and other forms of meta-level work. As Susan Bassnett reminds us, Hilaire Belloc summed up the problem of status in his 1931 Taylorian lecture *On Translation*, and his words are still applicable today:

> The art of translation is a subsidiary art and derivative. On this account it has never been granted the dignity of original work, and has suffered too much in the general judgment of letters. This natural underestimation of its value has had the bad practical effect of lowering the standard demanded and in some periods has almost destroyed the art altogether. The corresponding misunderstanding of its character has added to its degradation: neither its importance nor its difficulty has been grasped.[5]

When translation requires original linguistic and historical research, as, for example in the treatment of unpublished scriptures, that work is thereby afforded high academic prestige,[6] but the translation itself is seen almost as the by-

---

5 Hillaire Belloc 1931, quoted in Bassnett 1980: 2.

6 E.g. in my field of Iranian studies, for example, many great Iranists of the past to the present day including Bartholomae, Herzfeld, Nyberg, Henning, Humbach, Insler and

product of editing and establishing the *Urtext*. It is understandable, but nonetheless mistaken, that scholarly translation is regarded as a subsidiary outcome: prior to translation, so much groundwork of collation, decipherment, transcription and editing of manuscripts (which may be in poor, fragmentary condition) must be done. The mistake, however, is to see the work of studying and establishing the text as superior to and *separate* from, the act of translating. In fact the translation is the point of the scholarship, and therefore the scholar should be reflective about the very issues with which the field of translation studies grapple. Yet the latter is a field, which is, to put it politely, unrecognized by more traditional scholarly disciplines, including most in the study of religion.

An extreme form of the scholarly view of translation is one I have occasionally met in Iranian studies, that "real" scholars need not make translations at all: they need only edit and read the manuscript correctly "in the original." One translates as best one can the lexical items in the text according to established philological principles; if the resultant sentences do not make sense, well that is a problem for the reader, not for the text scholar. Translation, strictly speaking, then, is a popularizing distraction from the work of scholarship, not the main aim. The work of translation studies specialists overturns such narrowly conceived views of translation.

The linguistic problems of text scholars in their various fields are discussed in minutiae in learned monographs and journals the world over, and so no more generalizations about them will be made here. What is important to consider is how far scholars and students of religion think about the problems and dilemmas that confront translators. How far are we aware of developments in the study of translation in past decades? Do we still operate on unexamined assumptions about texts and translations? Are the gold standards of "fidelity" and "scientific accuracy" the most helpful guides towards the best kind of translation? Do the metaphors of previous centuries, of translator as civilizer or as servant of the "original text" still prevail? To what extent does the new self-consciousness prevailing in the post-modern, post-colonial academy pose new questions and demand new answers in respect of understanding the theory and practice of translation? Dogged refusal of academics in the study of religion to consider such questions could be construed as tantamount to a new form of cultural illiteracy, not merely academic conservatism and nostalgia for the standards of the better days of yore.

Kellens (to name but a few) have tried to solve the enigmas of the *Gāthās* of Zarathushtra, yet to this day no single scholarly or popular translation is generally accepted as entirely sound.

3. What is the Translator *Doing*? Examples of Translations and Issues Arising in Religious Texts in Translation

What do we nowadays understand the translator to be doing? The necessity of asking this is occasioned by the relative invisibility of the translator, in which professional translators often collude, as Lawrence Venuti says:

> Translators are always hard at work, but they are producing translations, not translation commentary, criticism, or theory; they appear as aesthetically sensitive amateurs or talented craftsmen, but not critically self-conscious writers who develop an acute awareness of the cultural and social conditions of their work. The contemporary translator is a paradoxical hybrid, at once dilettante and artisan. It is unfortunate that this is a prevalent representation, and more unfortunate still that many translators choose to live it out, since it will not help to make their activity more visible to readers: not only does it perpetuate the dubious idea that translation is foremost a practical activity, distinct from theorization, from reflection on the cultural and social implications of methodology, but it also participates in the cultural élitism fostered by class divisions in advanced capitalist societies, stigmatizing translation but likening it to manual as opposed to intellectual labor. [7]

Along with the invisibility of the translator lies the old doubt nurtured in the minds of certain writers who even question the *possibility* of translation. At the beginning of their 1998 book *Constructing Cultures* Susan Bassnett and André Lefevere, pioneers in translation studies, wonder at how the questions aimed at their subject have changed over twenty years:

> The most preposterous question was that of translatability or: 'is translation possible?' The question seems preposterous now because we have discovered the history of translation in the meantime, and that discovery enabled us to counter that question with another, namely: 'why are you interested in proving or disproving the feasibility of something that has been going on around most of the world for at least four thousand years?'[8]

Nevertheless, as they point out, in the post-war period, behind the questioning of translation, and the quest for an abstract and ultimate theory of translation, lay a hidden agenda: machine translation, which would replace the translator altogether in the way that technological advances were making other human workers and their skills redundant. In such a scheme of thinking the translator's presence is as obsolescent and unnecessary to the processing of texts as mental arithmetic of the accounting clerk in an age of electronic calculators. Yet, this has not happened, and is certainly not likely to happen in the foreseeable future in the case of translation of religious texts. Poetry is another stumbling block for "translation deniers." Again, Bassnett appeals for commonsense:

7 Venuti 1992: 1–2.
8 Bassnett/Lefevere 1998: 1.

> … there is a great deal of nonsense written about poetry and translation too, of which probably the best known is Robert Frost's immensely silly remark that 'poetry is what gets lost in translation', which implies that poetry is some intangible, ineffable thing (a presence? a spirit?) which, although constructed *in* language cannot be transposed *across* languages.[9]

There are positive reasons why students of religion, literature and history might consider taking a greater interest in what translators do when they translate, and even to contribute to a general theory which can be used as a guideline for the production of translations. The principal reason for them to take such an interest is succinctly expressed by Edwin Gentzler in his foreword to Bassnett and Lefevere's *Constructing Cultures*: "the study of translation *is* the study of cultural interaction." The authors make the point in various essays in their book that it is time for those interested in cultural interaction to turn towards the study of the praxis of translating in order to understand how complex manipulative textual processes take place.[10] Why do certain texts get selected for translation, whilst others remain untranslated? What is the role of the translator in the selection of texts, and what is the role of the editor, publisher, or, in the past, patron? What are the criteria for translation strategies, and how are the translations received by the readership in the target language? The point of all such questions is to raise an awareness of the fact that translation from the source text always takes place in a continuum and specific context of history, society and culture, and *not* in a void. The authors argue that until the 1970s, in spite of the arrival of deconstructionism in literary studies, discussion of translation still centered attention upon ideals of *definitive* translation, accuracy and faithfulness, and equivalence between literary and linguistic systems, which had not changed since the 1930s.[11]

There is another, more negative reason why the religionist should take an interest in translation. Translation may be seen as a precariously poised, unstable textual activity and entity. The attitude of the learned (secular and religious) critic has, in the past, been instrumental in intensifying the insecurity of translator and translation to the point where they have been treated as conjurors and tricksters, producing illusions of authentic originals—the *copy* of the original, not the real thing. This is particularly true when the accusation has issued from the precincts of religious hierarchies. The charismatic power of "original" syllables, incantations and other formulations of their religious texts is sacred and supposedly irreplaceable. Translation may be thought of as *traducing* holy scripture. Yet demand for translation is greater now than ever before. The role of the translator and translation is in need of reappraisal in a

9 Bassnett in ibid.: 57.

10 See Susan Bassnett's essay "The Translation Turn in Cultural Studies," ibid.: ch. 8.

11 Ibid.: 124.

global society, which is yet in fact dangerously divided by cultural difference and economic inequality: translation is an opportunity for meeting through linguistic difference, which itself is no longer a pretext for mutual incomprehension and enmity.

What evidence is there that, whilst hundreds of new and re-translations of texts in the study of religion are produced each year, there is any methodological reflection on translation in our field? Where are the monographs, articles and entries on theory and practice of translation in our learned journals and encyclopedias, considering, as has been suggested, that translating is an activity so central to the understanding of religion, and mistranslation so notoriously responsible for misunderstanding, in religious tradition and the modern academy alike? There are famous examples of problems of misunderstanding deriving from instances of lexical mistranslation. Best known of mistranslations in the Western canon are Jerome's Vulgate translation of Hebrew *almah* (Isaiah 7: 14) as "virgin" rather than "young woman" (and the consequent Christian cult of the *virgin mother* of Jesus); or his rendering of Hebrew *qaran 'or* (Exodus 34: 29 lit. "sent forth horns of light") as if Moses had returned from Mount Sinai with horns on his head, which "explains Michelangelo's statue of Moses and may account for the common superstition that Jews had horns growing out of their heads."[12] Whole scholarly monographs have been written on how mistranslation, linguistic distortion and development have given rise to fundamental theological conceptions, e.g. as Geza Vermes documents the genesis of the Christian language of the Son of God from Hebrew antecedents in his *Jesus the Jew*.[13] Beyond this kind of treatment of lexical mistranslation, however, lie questions and issues which as yet have not come center-stage into the study of religion. It is perhaps of interest to look at a selected range of twentieth century translations, taken in chronological order, to consider what the translator is doing. The selection is limited and determined by my own competence in a particular small corner of the study of religion, mainly that of the Indian and Iranian, Zoroastrian and Islamic traditions. A number of issues are also illustrated from personal experience with translating texts from these traditions.

1. One of the most prolific twentieth century translators of medieval works on Islamic mysticism ("Sufism") was Reynold A. Nicholson, formerly Professor of Arabic and Lecturer in Persian at the University of Cambridge, many of whose translations are still in print today, in various formats. His (slightly) abridged translation of the Persian prose Sufi classic *Kashf al-Mahjub* by Hujvīrī (d. circa 1075 C.E.) was first published in 1911, republished in a new edition in 1936, and remained in print, in paperback, until very recently. Nicholson's

12 Michael Alpert, "Torah Translation," in: Baker 1998: 269–70.

13 Vermes 1973.

eight page preface is terse, factual and technical—he gives no translation of the title ("revelation of veiled/hidden things")—yet he declares in his opening words that he hopes the translation

> will ... be found useful not only by the small number of students familiar with the subject at first hand, but also by many readers who, without being Orientalists themselves, are interested in the general history of mysticism and may wish to compare or contrast the diverse yet similar manifestations of the mystical spirit in Christianity, Buddhism and Islam.

Apart from the brief factual description of Hujviri's spiritual lineage and literary output, the briefest sketch of the contents of the book, and a few remarks about the manuscripts, Nicholson does not discuss his translation, either here or in the sparse footnotes which occasionally figure in the 420 pages of translation which follow. It seems that this translation is intended to be used *alongside* the Persian text, and indeed, even general readers had better learn Persian if they should wish to understand the translation! The role of the translator here is that of guide and expert teacher. The translation is from prose to prose, and the content is treated as information rather than as being of any particular literary merit.

2. Nicholson's most famous translation, that of the voluminous *Masnavī-ye Ma'navī* "The Spiritual Couplets," of Jalāluddīn Rūmī (d. 1273 C.E.) was first published in 1926 and has remained in print to this day, in spite of the fact that it is almost as unapproachable to the average general reader as the translation of the *Kashf al-Mahjub.* In the Introduction (of five pages) to the first two of the six books of the *Masnavī*, Nicholson explains the problem of translating it:

> The size of the *Mathnawī* is not the chief or the worst obstacle by which its translator is confronted. He at once finds himself involved in the fundamental difficulty, from which there is not escape, that if his translation is faithful, it must be to a large extent unintelligible, and that if he tries to make it intelligible throughout, he must often substitute for the exact rendering a free and copious paraphrase embodying matter which properly belongs to a commentary, though such a method cannot satisfy anyone who wants to understand the text and know what sense or senses it is capable of bearing. Therefore a complete version of the *Mathnawī* means, for scientific purposes, a faithful translation supplemented by a full commentary.[14]

Nicholson is here articulating a theory of translation which seems to be caricatured, if not summed up, in the oft-quoted quip of Roy Campbell, "Translations (like wives) are seldom faithful if they are in the least attractive."[15] Having helpfully given a brief description of four previous German and English translations, Nicholson declares that his own translation

14 Introduction in Nicholson 1911: xiii–xiv.

15 *Poetry Review*, June/July 1949.

> is intended primarily as an aid to students of Persian; it is therefore as exact and faithful as I can make it, but it does not attempt to convey the inner as distinguished from the outer meaning: that is to say, it gives the literal sense of the words translated without explaining either their metaphorical or their mystical sense. While these later senses have sometimes been indicated by words in brackets, I have on the whole adhered to the principle that translation is one thing, interpretation another, and that correct interpretation depends on correct translation, just as the most fertile source of misinterpretation is inability or neglect to translate correctly.[16]

This passage explains what quickly becomes apparent to the reader of Nicholson's translations of the *Masnavī*, that they are somewhat prosaic and lacking in poetical style, in spite of the fact that he says he has "attempted to preserve the idiomatic flavor of the original … ." Modern readers tend to find that the archaisms of his English (he uses "thou," "thee," "hast," "wert," etc.) are an annoyance rather than preserve any "idiomatic flavor," even more so when he resorts to Latin to "translate" passages he senses are too salacious to be made fully public. It is a slightly ironic characteristic of his translations that they are again probably more of an incentive to the reader to learn Persian so that the translation may be dispensed with. Moreover, the Persian verses are *over*-translated, i.e. the tensions and "knots" of the original poetry are flattened out into the prose rendering and accompanying glosses in parentheses. Nicholson's own attitude towards the text and its readers is a complex one, as is illustrated by a concluding remark:

> This is a translation for students of the text, but I venture to hope that it may attract others neither acquainted with Persia nor specially concerned with Sufism. To those interested in the history of religion, morals, and culture, in fables and folklore, in divinity, philosophy medicine, astrology and other branches of mediaeval learning, in Eastern poetry and life and manners and human nature, the *Mathnawī* should not be a sealed book, even if it cannot always be an open one.[17]

A fundamental problem of the *Masnavī* in modern translation is that it was meant to be *heard* and appreciated as a poetry of couplets, of which each half-line (*mesrā'*) is one 11-syllable length of a breath, and each couplet (Persian *masnavī*) is a complete syntactical unit. Nicholson's translation, by its very presentation, is conceived in large sections as alternating between elements of story and mystical discourse: in short, the literal, prose form which Nicholson chose for his translation is too monotonous for most readers to appreciate without recourse to the poetic colors and shifts of the original, which are largely expunged from the translation. A whole industry of "translation" and "Englishing" (!) of Jalāluddīn's poetry emerged, in the last twenty years of the twentieth century, centered in the USA, which reflects a modern American

16 Nicholson 1926: xv.

17 Ibid.: xvii.

appetite for the amalgam of poetry and "mysticism" that can be made out of "Rumi," as the Persian poet has become known there. The wide range of styles and markets catered to by such "translators," from the eighteenth century to the present day, has been usefully summarized by Franklin Lewis in a chapter of his recent study of Jalāluddīn Rūmī, entitled, tellingly, "Translations, Transpositions, Renditions, Versions and Inspirations."[18] Ironically, the very fullness and literalness of Nicholson's translation of the *Masnavī* have limited its appeal and indirectly caused the rash of retranslations, "Englishings" etc. about which Lewis has written. It is a monumental work, but a monument to something many readers have found has died in the translation.[19] In a sense, Jalāluddīn's *Masnavī*, and the history of its translation and reinterpretation, is a microcosm of many problems in translation studies and hence I have discussed it in greater length than other examples.

3. In 1984, Dick Davis published his translation of Fariduddīn 'Attār's *Manteq ut-Tayr*, "Conference of the Birds." This twelfth century Persian Sufi poem is analogous to the *Masnavī* of Jalāluddīn, though it is much shorter and simpler in conception. It is a sign of how the expectations of the modern, Western readership have changed over recent decades that Davis provides a substantial introductory essay (along with Afkham Darbandi) about the poetry of the text and translation (for the translation is done into verse), and one sees reflected the fact that Davis himself is a poet, and that his comments are intended to be helpful to the Western reader.[20] He notes that the stories are easier to render in English than the passages of commentary and religious exhortation—and, interestingly, the difficulty of translating the sustained use of the imperative mood in such passages. Davis translates the *masnavī* verse form into heroic couplets of rhymed iambic pentameters, "a form associated largely with the eighteenth century," and justifies this in terms of the proximity of the forms, and the advantages of the heroic couplet for "recitative"; he also argues that if it had been translated into free verse "all sense of tension, of struggle against a prevailing formality, would … be dissipated by the openness of the form." Davis informs us that his method of translation also owes something to the eighteenth century in that he has "followed, more or less, the guide-lines set out in Alexander Fraser Tytler's admirable *Essay on the Principles of Translation* (first

18 Lewis 2000: 564–615.

19 This is a sentiment expressed to me by many students and colleagues, both Western and Iranian. Yet, Nicholson is also held in very high regard in Iran: I was recently severely attacked in an Iranian newspaper for venturing to suggest in a lecture that a new translation of the *Masnavī* was timely because modern Western readers no longer find Nicholson's accessible.

20 Curiously, Davis is designated "Designer," and Darbandi "Contributor" on the Amazon.com website at the time of writing.

published in 1791), with particular reference to the chapters on verse translation."[21] The translator's emphasis on connecting with a recognized Western poetic tradition is marked. Unlike Nicholson, Davis saw fit to abridge the "Conference of the Birds." He omitted the invocation and epilogue (the first 600 and the last 500 couplets of the 5,000), presumably thinking that the religious prelude would only bore the Western, non-Muslim reader and because the epilogue "consists largely of self-praise and is a distinct anticlimax after a poem devoted to the notion of passing beyond the Self."[22] It is worth noting that Davis' strategies to approximate to the poetic form of the Persian original and to convey the sense of the original to the non-Western reader also led him to cut some of the poem as being unsuitable and perhaps misleading—i.e. his editorial instincts have an undiscussed intention of conveying the "spirit" of the original which requires it to be topped and tailed for the English reader. This translation is intended for the general reader and is not particularly "close" to the original, so that in an academic context with students having access only to this translation, it needs to be supplemented by a good deal of explanation of what has been paraphrased, glossed or left out from the original. This, then, provides an apt comparison with Nicholson's monumental translation of Jalāluddīn's *Masnavī*: it is not so "faithful," yet it is more poetically reminiscent of the original. Moreover, the audiences for which Nicholson and Davis composed their translations are, separated by some sixty years, markedly different in terms of their aesthetic tastes, knowledge and expectations.

4. Julie Scott Meisami's translation of the twelfth century poet Nizāmī Ganjavī's *Haft Paykar* ("The Seven Pictures")[23] is to be distinguished from the other works so far mentioned as not being Sufi, mystical or even "religious" at all, but rather of the courtly, romantic, literary genre. Nevertheless it is comparable to the foregoing as a translation by a modern, academic Western translator. The translator discusses previous versions of the *Haft Paykar* in English and other languages and declares:

> The present translation seeks to present Nizami's poem, as befits its importance in the Persian romance tradition, as a work of poetry first and foremost, and in a style approximating that of European romances.[24]

Unlike the other translations so far considered, Meisami has a section of her Introduction specifically as a "Note on the Translation," which is a most welcome consideration to the reader. Since she regards prose renderings, however competent, as tending to move the poem into the "storybook" genre, she uses

21 Attar 1984: 24.
22 Ibid.: 25.
23 Meisami 1995.
24 Ibid.: xxxviii.

an octosyllabic couplet verse form, "widely used in medieval narrative poetry in the West which is close in rhythm to the original and sufficiently flexible to prevent monotony," to render the "light," "festive" *khafīf* metre of the Persian. A further major feature of Meisami's translation is her attempt to retain as far as possible, though admittedly not consistently, the *aa bb cc* etc. rhyming scheme of the original. Most significantly, Meisami has taken account of the feature of enjambment: "end-stopped" lines tend to be complete statements, grammatically and syntactically (though not conceptually) independent of what precedes and follows, reflecting the fundamentally oral nature of Persian poetry which, though composed in writing, was intended to be heard aloud. It is perhaps this consideration of the oral character of Nizami's poem which brings this text to life for the modern reader. It is a fine example of specialist academic expertise brought to bear on a literary translation.

5. The recently published, first Western translation of the Indian Sufi mystical romance, *Madhumālatī*, by the sixteenth century poet Manjhan affords a means of moving over to the literature of the Subcontinent, yet remaining broadly in the Islamic world.[25] The translators of this enigmatic text provide a wealth of explanatory notes and a substantial bibliography. This translation from Awadhi, or eastern Hindavī, is the result of a collaborative project between Aditya Behl and Simon Weightman and a number of academic colleagues. Their enthusiasm for the subject is evident. In their Note on the Text the translators begin by stating "A famous dictum has it that one can never translate a poem, only rewrite it" (xlvii), and they say that they have aimed at recreating the poetic form while conveying the lexical sense of the poetry accurately, and they explain the metric form of the more than 500, six-couplet verses. In place of the complex prosody of the original, they use verse without rhyme. The translators seem to have gone to some pains to capture the "feeling" of the original, as they say: "since the texture of Manjhan's verse is polished, sweet and straightforward, the English used in the translation is equally light and unpretentious." It has to be left to eastern Hindavī specialists to say whether the translators have done linguistic justice to the source text, but the English appears to have achieved a suitably pleasing literary form, again, as in Meisami's translation of the *Haft Paykar*, combining a poetic sensitivity of tone with a light, oral and direct mood of address. Weightman adds a thirteen-page essay, complete with diagrams of Yogic symbolism, explaining his realization of a complex symmetrical Shattāri cosmological structure such as he finds in the *Madhumālatī*. Weightman intends that his Appendix will further the reader's understanding and appreciation of the poem in answer to a fundamental question, having calculated the structural symmetry of *Madhumālatī* and found that though it is

25 Behl/Weightman 2000.

present in the eastern Hindavī original it does not survive in the Persian and Dakkhani Urdu translations. He asks: "Such precision and proportionality cannot have been accidental and must have been deliberate on Manjhan's part. What is the explanation?"[26] His elucidations are an example of structural (as distinct from structural*ist*) analysis in the employ of interpretation. This translation is intended to be more than merely a conventional academic treatment, to judge by the translators' exhortation at the end of the introduction, after 46 pages of contextualizing the work:

> We would like to emphasize ... that the poem should be read and enjoyed as a *rasika* would read it, with an open heart and a sensibility open to the poem's suggestive power.[27]

The translators are thus enthusiasts and exegetes of their text, to a degree that is uncommon in academic circles but which, given the nature of the text, seems appropriate.

6. Patrick Olivelle's translation of the *Upanisads*, published in 1996, has to deal with several problems of translation particular to very ancient sources of the highest canonical status within a religion. First, as the substantial bibliography (of almost exclusively European publications) indicates, these texts have been much ploughed over by Western scholars, and they are indeed "some of the most important literary products in the history of Indian culture and religion" (xxiii). Olivelle considers it futile to try to discover a single doctrine or philosophy in the Upanisads, as he observes:

> Different theologians, philosophers and pious readers down the centuries both in India and abroad have discovered different 'truths' and 'philosophies' in them. That has been, after all, the common fate of scriptures in all religions. Even in the future, that is an enterprise best left to the readers themselves, and the prudent translator will try to step aside and not get in their way.[28]

Second, because of high antiquity and primary religious status of these texts, they are treated with immense scholarly respect by Olivelle, who also gives the general reader due consideration, for whom, after all, these translations are intended. His Introduction is substantial, on the social background, literary history, and ritual, cosmological and other aspects of the text, including a map of the geography of the Upanisads, and a diagram of the ritual sacrificial arena. Like Behl and Weightman, Olivelle provides a wealth of context for the reader, but also adds a Note on the Translation, which is particularly helpful in regard to this "living," sacred text and the many diverse problems of understanding

26 Ibid.: 229.

27 Ibid.: xlvi.

28 Olivelle 1996: xxiv.

and interpretation for their readers and, especially, for their translators. Olivelle reflects on the interpretive history of the texts, i.e. the multiple "native interpretations" of the Upanisads qua "living" sacred texts *vis à vis* modern translator's interpretations. His own position is reconstructive, with the intention of "illuminating the distant past of India":

> I want in my translation and notes to approximate, as far as our current knowledge permits, the understanding of these documents that their authors had and the meaning they desired to communicate to their contemporary audience.[29]

Olivelle states that his translation is not intended for philologists but for ordinary readers who have little or no access to the original Sanskrit. For such ordinary readers he provides over a hundred pages of closely written notes to the translations and useful cross-references between the texts. This new translation is a model of a new wave of generous and well-considered treatments of important non-Western sacred texts, which is incomparably more useful than, for example, the slender, volume of selected translations of Upanishads by Juan Mascaro and it signifies a wholly different relationship between the translator and "ordinary reader" from that of the mid-1960s.[30]

7. It has been left until this point to tackle the question of what is in many senses, the most problematic of texts for translators and academic commentators from Western academic traditions to deal with: the *Qur'ān*. As is well known, it has traditionally been considered illegitimate and indeed impossible, to translate the *Qur'ān*: it is believed to be divine in origin and inimitable by the human translator. The issue of the legitimacy of translation of the *Qur'ān* is different from that of its translatability. Both, however are matters of principle supported by the Qur'anic text itself. Not only *should* not the *Qur'ān* be translated, it is maintained that it *cannot* be translated, as its having been sent down from the divine world in Arabic is believed to be intrinsic to its being. Strictly speaking, any translation which is made is regarded not as a translation in the common sense of the word, but as a form of exegesis; hence if such is done, it is maintained, it should be done only by Muslims. These strictures have not prevented the making of many translations into Western languages since the Latin translation by Robert of Chester, sponsored by Peter the Venerable, Abbot of Cluny, in 1143 C.E. It remains, however, one of the most problematic of all texts to translate, not only because of the linguistic challenges it poses (which are considerable), but because of its status as inimitable, untranslatable, divine revelation. Western scholars, however have been far from daunted by the protective, reverential Muslim attitude towards their most holy scripture, and

29 Ibid.: lviii.
30 Juan Mascaró (1965), *The Upanishads*. London/New York: Penguin.

in some cases they have appeared to take extreme liberties with the text, such as, for example, Richard Bell, whose 1937 translation rearranged the *suras* of the *Qur'ān* in what he argued was the original chronological order. As with other, non-Muslim scriptures (e.g. Bible), one way of indicating that the translation is intended to be subordinate to the scriptural text is to place it in parallel to the original text on facing pages. Several translators have used this strategy, including Dawood (see below). A.J. Arberry avoided the prohibition of translation by announcing in the title his exegetical intention;[31] ironically, however, Arberry chose to experiment with stanza form of his translation, both in prosodic and visual styles, in order to emulate the quality of the original—which to the traditionalist viewpoint must have transgressed the spirit of the tradition, if not the letter. Another translation which has been very popular with Western readers is by N.J. Dawood. Dawood is unabashed about his intentions, and in a carefully phrased expression, even extols its virtues beyond the terms in which it would normally be considered by Muslims:

> In preparing this new translation it as been my aim to present the modern reader with an intelligible version of the Koran in contemporary English. It is my belief that the Koran is not only one of the greatest books of prophetic literature but also a literary masterpiece of surpassing excellence.[32]

Whereas previous translations failed to convey both the meaning and the rhetorical grandeur of the original by adhering to a rigidly literal rendering of Arabic idioms, he says, the *Qur'ān* contains many statements which lend themselves to more than one interpretation, and states: "I have taken great pains to reproduce these ambiguities wherever they occur." In his efforts to remain intelligible, he adheres to a prose medium, in short paragraphs which group together several verses. Dawood has abandoned the traditional arrangement of the suras for pragmatic not scholarly-historical reasons:

> … the new arrangement is primarily intended for the uninitiated reader who, understandably, is often put off by such mundane chapters as 'The Cow' or 'Women', which are traditionally placed at the beginning of the book.

More so than Dick Davis' slight foreshortening of the *Conference of the Birds*, then, Dawood's estimation of the Western audience's ability to tolerate the original sequence of the source text has led him to rearrange it radically. Dawood's version of the *Qur'ān* has remained in print and gone through many revisions, since 1956, making it one of the longest running modern translations. There is an irony in this, considering the Muslim proscription of translation, but this is mitigated perhaps by the fact that Dawood himself is a Muslim, is

31 A.J. Arberry (1955), *The Koran Interpreted*. London: Allen & Unwin.

32 "Introduction," in: N.J. Dawood (1956), *The Koran. A New Translation*. London/New York: Penguin.

duly reverential to the Arabic *Qur'ān*, and also that in recent years he has published a parallel text version, with the Arabic original opposite his translation.[33]

Over the course of the century considered, translations have changed along with everything else. In particular greater consideration is given for the public not conversant with the source language, and more contextualization is given. The representation of the source text, even when the target reader will not be able to read it directly, adds a dimension that is always missing if the text is absent (Zaehner's and Radhakrishnan's translations of Indian texts found favor among academics for this reason). The sense of the original may be preserved by other means than by actually printing the source text, but this has the unique advantage of juxtaposing source and target texts and offering the reader the option of scrutinizing both as they read the new translation.[34]

More particular points about academic translation of religious texts are best made with examples from experience of working with texts of different kinds. The first is concerned with the question of the "original" and how we may get caught among more than one "original." Some years ago I was working on an English translation of the early twentieth century monograph *El Islam Cristianizado* by the Spanish Arabist Miguel Asín Palacios.[35] Asín Palacios's work, written in his mature years, is a major study of the twelfth to thirteenth century C.E. Andalusian Sufi sheikh Muhyiddīn Ibn 'Arabī, and, though it has been superseded as a biographical study,[36] it still has great interest for the historian of religion for its particular approach. Having shown my draft translations of the first two parts of the book, on "The Life" and "The Spiritual Doctrine of Ibn 'Arabī," to academic colleagues, all, without exception, commented that it would not be sufficient just to translate Asín Palacios's third part, "Texts" (i.e. his translations of the Sufi sheikh's writings) but that I should translate afresh, from the Arabic, those same texts which Asín Palacios had translated, incorporating all the scholarly advances in knowledge which had been made in the intervening half-century, otherwise it would be of limited use as a work. Though I disagreed with the advice, I was discouraged and my translation did not see

33 *The Koran with Parallel Arabic Text* (1990). London/New York: Penguin Classics. On translatability of the *Qur'an* see further Hassan Mustapha "Qurān (Koran) translation," in: Baker 1998: 203–204. See also, in Part II of the same volume, articles by Saliha Paker and Ahmad Karimi Hakkak respectively on *Qur'an* and translation in Turkish and Persian tradition.

34 For an example of a scholarly translation of this type see Williams 1990, and of one intended for the general reader see my new translation of the first part of Jalāluddīn Rūmī's *Masnavī-ye Ma'navī* in Penguin Classics (forthcoming).

35 Asín Palacios 1931.

36 I.e. by works such as Claude Addas (1993), *Quest for the Red Sulphur: The Life of Ibn 'Arabī*. Cambridge: Islamic Texts Society.

the light of day. A little later I came across Bernard Dubant's French translation of the same work,[37] and found that he had done exactly as I had originally intended, i.e. he had made a literal French version of the whole work, including Asín Palacios's translations, so that it would be available to a new audience. When I saw it, I realized its value: without contributing anything discursive to the study of Ibn 'Arabī, Dubant had rendered the work appropriately, i.e. not just Asín Palacios's deliberations about the biography and doctrine of the great Sufi, but also his construal and understanding of the Arabic texts. Dubant's translation has not a single word of introduction or commentary added to Asín Palacios's original. The translator rendered a service to scholarship, and to the general reader, precisely by *not* introducing his own scholarship into his translation. This was a case where the twentieth century scholar's construction of Ibn 'Arabī was the *original* source, for which the thirteenth century Sufi's texts were, in a sense, *secondary* sources. This problem is a particular example of one that frequently confronts the modern editor of (for example) ancient religious texts, because so often those texts are part of a textual tradition which has itself included translation(s) in transmission.

The second example is taken from working on the ninth century C.E. books in Zoroastrian Pahlavi (Western Middle Iranian). These texts contain a genre of writing known in Pahlavi as *zand*, namely "commentary, explanation" upon the older Zoroastrian textual tradition both written and orally transmitted in the Avestan language. *Zand* is a term meaning both "translation" and "interpretation" or "exegesis," and often it is possible to detect in the Pahlavi text the outline of an Avestan substrate upon which the Pahlavi *zand* was based. The problem for the modern editor and translator is to decide to what degree one should correct the Pahlavi interpretation if it differs from modern understandings of the Avestan original (which in some cases still survive). The general problem which scholars face is: what is the role of the modern editor/translator? How radically, if at all, does one "repair" a text? This can be as apparently harmless as emending a manuscript by supplying an obvious missing word or phrase or deleting a gloss. When such "repair" is taken to an extreme, the question arises: what is the function of modern scholarly treatment?—what is the academic doing there in the first place?—especially if s/he is an outsider (or worst of all hostile) to the faith community of the scriptural tradition in question.

The third example gives an illustration of a form of the same problem which I had to deal with in editing and translating a ninth century C.E. Zoroastrian Pahlavi text.[38] The eighth of 65 chapters is on the subject of *xwēdōdah*, a Pahlavi term cognate with Avestan *x*^{v}*aētvadaθa-*. This term had previously been translated as "next-of-kin marriage" and even "incest" or "incestuous mar-

37 Asín Palacios 1984.

38 Williams 1990.

riage" by Western scholars. This subject had given rise to a minor scholarly controversy in academic literature (even extending to anthropological journals) and had caused great offence to some modern Zoroastrians, who objected to having their forebears accused of advocating incestuous relations. The *Pahlavi Rivāyat*, however incontrovertibly extols *xwēdōdah* as a great religious virtue and redeeming act, and research demonstrates that the term is used variously in Avestan and Pahlavi Zoroastrian texts to refer to a conjugal and marital act. My translation for the term, based on philological grounds, was "family marriage" and in a lengthy discussion[39] I argued that *xwēdōdah* was a case of urging the *extreme* in order to achieve the *mean*, namely endogamous marriage. A previous editor had omitted the whole chapter from his work, and it was even suggested to me that I do the same. In my book, a lengthy footnote explains the decision to include the chapter, followed by twelve pages of exegetical commentary. Such texts may make for uncomfortable reading for a modern religious community, and the academic translator has to come to a considered decision on how to proceed.

The idea that translation can have direct, even dire, consequences has been a practical experience of translators through the ages. We have not had to wait for deconstructionism and cultural studies in the post-modern academy to tell us that translators are in the thick of things. Looking back over the history of translation, Peter Fawcett puts the problem in its strongest terms in his article "Ideology and Translation":

> That translation was then and still is deeply implicated in religious ideology can be seen … also from the grisly fate of translators such as Tyndale in Britain … and Dolet in France … (both burnt at the stake), a fate mirrored in the twentieth century by the assassination of the Japanese translator of Salman Rushdie's *Satanic Verses* and the subsequent refusal by other publishers to produce a translation. And just as religion continues to grip translation output, so modern writers continue to project contemporary ideology onto earlier texts.[40]

It seems likely that many, if not most, who work on religious texts have similar anecdotes of problems encountered in the course of their work. It seems to be a logical step that discussion of such matters at a general theoretical level should take place in the study of religion in conjunction with translation studies specialists. The study of religious texts sometimes produces unique problems (e.g. that of the impossibility of translating what is regarded as the word of God) but usually its problems are instances of types found generally in other fields. In the penultimate section of this essay, attention is turned to general theories of translation.

39 Ibid., vol. 2: 126–37.

40 Peter Fawcett, "Ideology and Translation," in: Baker 1998: 109.

4. Translation Studies and Theories of Translation

In one sense the history of theorizing about translation in the last decades of the twentieth century, which led to the birth and growth of the field now known as translation studies, tells of a process of coming to terms with the realization that *we continue to project contemporary ideology on to earlier texts,* and the more we try to *stop doing* this, the more we *do* it. Translation studies is a discipline which helps producers and consumers of translations to come to terms with the real location of contemporary translation in the world, i.e. it is located *in* the world, not in some disembodied, ideal realm of "language" above and beyond culture, society, history and ideology. This is perhaps the reason why the study of translation was formerly seen as belonging exclusively to specialists in linguistics, and that a competent explanatory theory of translation must be a *linguistic* theory: this is no longer the case, and translation studies has broken free of those confines. The most succinct account of the development of theorization in this area is Edwin Gentzler's lucid and illuminating study *Contemporary Translation Theory.* Gentzler maintains an appropriately critical position throughout his survey (though he does not hide his enthusiasm for the possibilities opened up by translation studies as a discipline). He moves from the beginnings in the American translation workshop of the 1950s through the early attempts at scientific (linguistic) theories, to the beginnings of modern translation theory in the work of scholars from the Netherlands, Belgium, Czechoslovakia (as was), through polysystem theory from a group of Israeli scholars, to the establishment of translation studies as a discipline by scholars such as Bassnett and Lefevere in the 1970s and 1980s. Gentzler continues with a stimulating chapter on "Deconstruction," concluding with a brief, but up-beat, chapter on "The future of Translation Studies." I would also single out four other authors, here: Susan Bassnett and André Lefevere, who have made major contributions to the field both independently and jointly; Lawrence Venuti, whose works on rethinking translation in the light of postmodern thought are unsurpassed; and, in a more applied vein, Mona Baker. The latter's recently published *Routledge Encyclopedia of Translation Studies,*[41] co-edited with Kirsten Malmkjær, not only contains authoritative articles by a wide range of scholars on all principal areas of translation (including, it must be said, some on religious topics) and extensive bibliography, but it is especially valuable for also containing a very substantial descriptive catalogue of some 31 different national/ linguistic histories and traditions of translation from around the world.

As was suggested at the beginning of this essay, there are those in the study of religion, who think that making a discipline out of "translation studies" is as unnecessary as having a "committees committee." The attitude is

41 Baker 1998.

bolstered by a supposedly pragmatic and "commonsense" attitude, which would regard time spent thinking about translation theory as self-indulgent "navel-gazing." Yet those who are drawn to translation studies come as a result of practical experience of problems and perplexities. Leo Hickey, introducing an edited collection of essays, *The Pragmatics of Translation,* has articulated something of the theoretical complexity of what we do:

> ... it is now understood that translations do not simply 'say' in one language what somebody or some piece of writing has 'said' in another. Whatever translation is in its entirety, it [illegible] cultural and psychological aspects or elements, all of which are being studied nowadays as determining factors in whatever the translator does.[42]

Gentzler's 1993 work *Contemporary Translation Theories* is probably the best guide for the perplexed. Little has been written by religionists, at the level of survey and overview, on theoretical issues in the translation of texts from religion (though doubtless text scholars have to consider such matters in their praxis of translation). It seems not to be a subject which much exercises the minds of religionists in theoretical terms largely because, in the main, they do not speak about "translation" as an abstract subject, but rather as referring to their actual pieces of text. This is a quite different starting point from that of, say, the general editors of the *Translation Studies* series, Susan Bassnett and André Lefevere, when they write:

> Translation is, of course, a rewriting of an original text. All rewritings, whatever their intention, reflect a certain ideology and a poetics and as such manipulate literature to function in a given society in a given way. Rewriting is manipulation, undertaken in the service of power, and in its positive aspect can help in the evolution of a literature and a society. Rewritings can introduce new concepts, new genres, new devices, and the history of translation is the history also of literary innovation, of the shaping power of one culture upon another. But rewriting can also repress innovation, distort and contain, and in an age of ever increasing manipulation of all kinds, the study of the manipulative processes of literature as exemplified by translation can help us towards a greater awareness of the world in which we live.[43]

Religionists who doubt such possibilities for the study of translation need only read Gentzler's treatment of the genesis and evolution of the discipline from the 1960s to its maturity in the 1990s to be persuaded. Gentzler begins with the poets (perhaps Plato was right!). Poets of stature have often been drawn to render foreign language poetry through the medium of their own poetic voice: Ted Hughes and Seamus Heaney are two recent practitioners of this art, and in the 1960s, as Gentzler reminds us, quoting Ted Hughes himself, a whole generation of American poets was using literary translation as a vehicle for anti-

42 Hickey 1998: 1.

43 Bassnett/Lefevere, in the general editors' preface to Gentzler 1993: ix.

establishment aesthetic and political ideology.[44] However, much of the momentum for any nascent movement in terms of theory of translation seems to have come from a poet of a previous generation, namely Ezra Pound. Pound's theory was based upon a concept of energy in language, such that

> the words on the page, the specific details, were seen not simply as black and white typed marks on a page representing something else but as sculpted images—words engraved in stone. Such an approach allowed for more latitude for an individual translator's response; the translator was seen as an artist, and engraver or a calligrapher, one who moulds words. Pound is perhaps also the least understood translator and critic read by the current generation of translators in America.[45]

Pound wrote of the ways in which "language is charged or energized"—in *melopoeia, phanopoeia* and *logopoeia*: the musical, the visual, and verbal creative properties, the last of which includes the direct meaning and the play of the word in its context, which he defines as follows:

> *Logopoeia* does not translate; though the attitude of mind it expresses may pass through a paraphrase. Or one might say you can not translate it "locally," but having determined the original author's state of mind, you may or may not be able to find a derivative or an equivalent.[46]

So far from being vague and mystical, what Pound meant was that the author's state of mind could be determined by study of the language and context of the author, as Gentzler says:

> According to Pound's translation theory, meaning is not something abstract and part of a universal language, but something that is always already located in historical flux—the 'atmosphere' in which that meaning occurs. To unpack that meaning, one has to know the history and reconstruct the atmosphere/milieu in which that meaning occurred.[47]

The reason for Gentzler's including Pound in his account of contemporary translation theories is that just as Pound used translation as a tool in his cultural struggle against prevailing literary tastes in Victorian/Edwardian times, so too did Euro-American translators of the 1960s and 1970s use translation in their own counter-cultural movement. Gentzler admits to a preference for Pound's taste in translation but adds that, in terms of taste, what was revolutionary and innovatory in Pound's era had now become mainstream. Moreover, for the linguistic purist, the unthinkable happened:

> License has been given to allow translators to intuit good poems from another language without knowledge of the original language or the culture, and, as long as they

44 Gentzler 1993: 9.

45 Ibid.: 19.

46 "How to Read," in: *Polite Essays* (1937): 170; quoted in Gentzler 1993: 23–24.

47 Ibid.: 27.

> have some poetic sensibility and good taste, now governed by plain speech and lack of adornment, their translations are accepted ... Foreign language facility does not seem to be a requirement for entrance to a workshop: poetic sensibility and an ability to write well in English are the most important criteria.[48]

Such an approach is, admittedly problematic for the academic scholar who works with "source" languages. Though Pound's name was frequently invoked to lend authority to the modernist approach, he cannot after all be held to blame for this tendency, which is perhaps better ascribed rather to a naiveté and lack of systematization in the circles of the American workshops. Part of the reason for the lack of systematization was the pragmatic nature of what translators were doing: they practiced translation, but did not articulate in theoretical terms what they were doing. In such a climate a need was felt for a more objective approach to translation. Gentzler discusses the work of the Bible translator and theoretician of a new translation science, Eugene Nida, in conjunction with the work of Noam Chomsky, whose work, quips Gentzler, came literally as a "Godsend" for Nida.[49] Nida was and has remained a major figure in the theory and practice of translation to this day, mainly because of the field in which he worked, as Gentzler explains:

> Bible translating has generated more data in more languages than any other translation practice: it enjoys a longer history, has reached more people in more diverse cultures, and has involved more translators from different backgrounds than any other translation practice. In generic terms as well, Bible translating has touched all fields, for within the text one finds passages of poetry and prose, narrative and dialogue, parables and laws. The sheer quantity of examples and breadth of scope have made Bible translation a necessary part of any study on the theory of translation. However, in terms of its theoretical contribution it too can be viewed in terms similar to the practical anecdotal approach characteristic of American literary translation theory.[50]

Noam Chomsky had published his *Syntactic Structures* in 1957, before Nida produced his *Message and Mission* (1964); Nida had read (according to Gentzler)[51] a mimeographed version of Chomsky's *Aspects of the Theory of Syntax* (1965), two years before its publication and prior to his own *Towards a Science of Translating* (1964) and had incorporated into this second book a simplified version of Chomsky's three levels of conceptualization of grammar, (1) phrase structure rules, (2) deep structure and (3) surface structure by omitting (1). Nida's work provided the foundation for a field that became known as the science of translation. Yet Gentzler calls into question the very object which translation science claims to be investigating, i.e. the fragile

48 Ibid.: 37.
49 Ibid.: 46.
50 Ibid.: 45.
51 Ibid.: 44.

theoretical premise at its center, of the *non-dit* operative "underlying message" to be translated. Nida began as a practice-oriented translator, with populist evangelical motives tempered by an anti-intellectualism and aversion to Victorian neo-classical fashion for scholarly pedantry (epitomized for him in Matthew Arnold). His formulation of a theoretical basis for his practice-oriented approach benefited from association with the terminology of Chomskian generative transformation grammar. From the point of view of a working translator, Chomskian theory was itself already idealistic and divorced from the actual problems of translation,[52] but, when mixed with Nida's own Protestant ideas about communication of the Biblical message, whereby the translation should solicit the response God intends, Nida has to appeal to rather more than a scientific theory of determining meaning, since he does not explain how "deep structure transfer" occurs. Gentzler is extremely skeptical, remarking how Nida requires in the translator the same "empathetic" spirit of the author, how he seems to equate translation with revelation, making visible that original message which now takes on archetypal status:[53]

> Nida provides an excellent model for translation which involves a manipulation of a text to serve the interests of a religious belief, but he fails to provide the groundwork for what the West in general conceives of as a 'science'.[54]

In spite of this, Nida's work has been very influential in Germany in the field of *Übersetzungswissenschaft*. Gentzler concludes his treatment of the science of translation by looking at the situation in Germany and the work of Wolfram Wilss at the University of Saarland in Saarbrücken. In short, the general conclusion is that such sciences of translation tend to proceed by universalizing and generalizing to such a degree that what is unique, different and new about ideas as expressed in language becomes obliterated, and by necessitating that the translator be the authority and disallowing the readers to interpret the text on their own. Most worryingly for the study of translation, the very investment in the notion of deep structure (which had been incorporated in order to validate their scientific and objective character), meant that the theories "tend to trivialize their own products, the works in translation, and the contributions that acts of translation may make to the development and evolution of the original text."[55] Here Gentzler puts his finger upon a problem of canonical scriptural translation with which anyone who works with such texts must wrestle. These theories remain fundamentally normative and prescriptive, which may be suited to the intra-religious domain of confessionalist translation

52 Ibid.: 50.
53 Ibid.: 56.
54 Ibid.: 60.
55 Ibid.: 67.

for missionary purposes, but which are inadequate for the academic study of religion.

Translation studies, as it exists in the early twenty-first century, traces its lineage back not to this science of translation, nor indeed to the narrowly linguistic and loosely literary modes of study which had been developing, in competition with one another, in the post-World War II period, but rather to a new movement which started in the early 1970s. The name "translation studies" was first used by James Holmes in *The Name and Nature of Translation Studies* (1972/1975)[56] in which the author distanced himself from the overly subjective theories of the past and also from linguistic and quasi-linguistic sciences of translation. Gentzler notes that translation studies had its beginnings in polyglot Netherlands and Belgium, where practical factors led scholars such as Holmes and André Lefevere to seek a new approach to translation. His description of the new field should be allowed to speak for itself:

> Translation Studies began with a call to suspend temporarily the attempts to define a theory of translation, trying first to learn more about translation procedures. Instead of trying to solve the philosophic problem of the nature of meaning, Translation Studies became concerned with how meaning travels. Most characteristic about the new field was its insistence on openness to interdisciplinary approaches: having literary scholars work together with logicians, linguists together with philosophers. Limiting distinctions such as right and wrong, formal and dynamic, literal and free, art and science, theory and practice, receded in importance. Translation as a field was no longer viewed as either literary or non-literary, but as both. New questions were posited regarding the subject of investigation, the nature of the translation process, how mediation occurs, and how the process affects both the original (redefined as source text) and received (redefined as target text) works. Even the distinction between original writer and translator was called into question. The object of study was neither an absent core of "meaning" nor deep "linguistic structure" but rather the translated text itself.[57]

Translation, then, is more than a synchronic transfer of meaning across cultures; it mediates diachronically as well, in multiple historical traditions. Gentzler is correct in pointing out the strong theoretical basis already laid out for such an approach by the school of Russian Formalism and also the work of a group of Czech scholars schooled in Russian poetics, namely Jiří Lev Levý, Anton Popovič and František Miko. There is much in this section of Gentzler's study which might be of interest to religionists, but specifically one can single out the formalist device of *ostranenie* "defamiliarization," by which is meant the resistance to the tendency to focus on meaning, and preparing the text for easy consumption by readers in the receiving culture.[58] This is a necessary feature of translating texts from non-European cultures which has long been apparent to

56 Reprinted in Toury 1987 and Venuti 2000.

57 Gentzler 1993: 76.

58 Ibid.: 80.

translators of non-European religious texts: translators of literary texts from within the European cultural-linguistic group have come relatively late to the necessity of recognizing and retaining terms, proper names, toponyms etc. which, in respect of the target language, are culturally extraneous. It is noticeable that from about this point in his book Gentzler starts to speak in the perfect or present tense about translation studies, conveying the sense of his own general agreement with what he is describing, and also that we have arrived in the extended present day, in terms of theory. It is noticeable, even at this midway stage in his description of the evolution of translation studies, that much of what happened in this field has happened in other domains of the arts and humanities, in terms of the globalization and post-colonial deconstruction of subjects and centers of knowledge. Very generally, one may say that in the coming of age of the study of translation, departing its parental home of European (and formerly Classical) literary and linguistic theory, and moving into the ideologically less prescriptive, more interdisciplinary, arena of modern translation studies, there is an analogy with the way the study of religion, in all its interdisciplinary forms, has fled its theological, philosophically well-feathered, nest. Researchers in the study of religion will recognize the parallelism in, for example, the way translation studies has had to face the many challenges of questioning the presupposition and definition of what is to be valued in a text as its literariness, as a work of art, i.e. those of modern European society. Even those core values of the Russian formalists, in their quest for impartiality and objectivity, though e.g. defamiliarization, have to be considered as belonging to a particular time and culture.

A landmark in the early development of translation studies is the work to which Gentzler himself turns in his account, namely Susan Bassnett's *Translation Studies,* first published in 1980 (revised edition 1991) as a result of work done at the University of Warwick, England and in collaboration with scholars and their students at the universities of Leuven and Amsterdam. In Gentzler's own words:

> Because she was trying to appeal to a larger audience, Bassnett was deliberately didactic and provocative in order to stimulate interest, promote discussion and clarify differences. She subscribed to two fundamental yet contradictory tenets of early Translation Studies: that there is no right way to translate a literary text, and that the interpretation of the translation be based on the comparison of the text's "function" as original and as translation.[59]

The difficulties of this period and their subsequent resolution arc, most likely, only of major interest to the those specifically interested in the history of that discipline, and as they were preoccupied with certain theoretical and hermeneutical problems arising mainly from literary translation they do not have a

59 Ibid.: 99–100.

central bearing on the translation of religious texts. Bassnett does, however, provide a useful inventory of central issues in translation studies, and also an account of the history of translation theory from Classical to modern times, though it does focus perhaps too tightly on European, indeed Anglophone tradition. Nothing is said of cultures outside Europe. Indeed this is one of the changes that has taken place in this field as in so many others in the past twenty years, that now an attempt, at least a beginning, is being made to look at the history of translation (and its equivalent) in non-European cultures.

Polysystem theory, emanating principally from two Israeli scholars, Itamar Even-Zohar and Gideon Toury since the 1970s, gives the key to the beginning of this sea change in translation studies.[60] Because of the unique character of the modern Hebrew language, the geographical and historical situation of Israel and its political and commercial relations with the rest of the world, translation has a uniquely important position in Israeli life. However, the Israeli polysystem theorists started from the opposite position from that of previous theories of translation. Previous theorists had believed in the subjective ability of the translator to derive an equivalent text that in turn influenced the literary and cultural conventions in a particular society; by contrast, Gentzler explains,

> polysystem theorists presume the opposite: that the social norms and literary conventions in the receiving culture ("target" system) govern the aesthetic presuppositions of the translator and thus influence ensuing translation decisions.[61]

With this in mind we see how this allows for the expansion of translation studies into a historical and intercultural context. Polysystem theory abandons prescriptive values and begins to see the historical contingency and social constructedness of processes of translation. This had the effect of freeing up translation studies from static, traditional cultural assumptions, and increasing interest in the translated literature of target languages. Gideon Toury, Even-Zohar's younger colleague, is credited with having successfully pushed the concept of a theory of translation beyond the margins of a model restricted to faithfulness to the original, or of single, unified relationships between the source and target texts: "Translation becomes a relative term, dependent on the forces of history and the semiotic web called culture."[62] Translation studies ceased, as a result of the influence of polysystem theory to be so fixated on source-oriented translation theories to the exclusion of the consideration of

60 No attempt will be made to describe polysystem theory here, which is the subject of a substantial chapter, "Polysystem Theory and Translation Studies," in: Gentzler 1993: 104–43. A briefer overview of polysystem theory is Mark Shuttleworth's article in Baker 1998: 176–79.

61 Gentzler 1993: 107.

62 Ibid.: 129.

target texts. For the study of religion, perhaps the most important of several insights brought to the study of translation by polysystem theory is

> the suggestion that it is more profitable to view translation as one specific instance of the more general phenomenon of inter-systemic transfer. This has the advantage not only of enabling us to examine translation within a wider context, but also of allowing those features which are genuinely peculiar to translation to stand out against the backdrop of this wider context.[63]

As well as introducing a mood of realism and pragmatism into translation theory, by drawing attention to the contextuality and locatedness of the process of translation within the polysystem, Toury and others introduce two notions[64] with which writers in the field of religion have long had to grapple. First, we see the destabilization of the notion of an original message with a fixed identity: religious orthodoxies have protected their most central notions by sacralizing them by various means, e.g. through ascription to divine revelation; and second, we see the introduction of the idea that inescapable infidelity is presumed as a normal condition of the process of translation: religious orthodoxy frequently protected itself against this by forbidding translation and retaining the "original" language as the sole medium for scripture, liturgy, etc.

It seems to be the case that in translation studies in America and Britain in the 1980s there was a shift from theory to descriptive work and a move away from what was felt to be the formalistic and restrictive polysystem model in favor of a cultural studies model. This process of development seems to have continued until the present day, to judge from publications by Bassnett, Lefevere and others, and has been accelerated by a renewed interest in literary theories of translation and deconstruction strategies. These latter challenge from everywhere, both from outside Western discourse—by what are referred to as the Third World groups—and by subgroups—gays, blacks, women, and ethnic minorities—that challenge from within.[65] Scholars within translation studies have also continued to ask tough questions about any remaining complacent assumptions in the discipline. Lefevere for example sees literary criticism and translation criticism as perpetuating a certain *status quo* of cultural values, at the expense of excluding and marginalizing others. He requires translation studies to question its own social and economic ideology and institutions of power.[66] Similarly Bassnett says that the ideological dimension, so long ignored in our investigations of translation process, has been restored and our

63 Shuttleworth, art.cit., in Baker 1998: 178.

64 Gentzler lists four, but of these only two are explicitly controversial for the study of religion: see Gentzler 1993: 134–35.

65 See further Gentzler's chapter 6, "Deconstruction," in: Gentzler 1993: 144–80.

66 Lefevere 1987: 19.

knowledge of cultural history has been enriched.[67] To some extent, those writing in the study of religion may not lag so far behind: often they are obliged by the obvious cultural and historical distances between themselves and the subjects of their studies, to take at least some account of ideological differences. No complacency is intended in saying this, for there have been, and perhaps still are, discreditable instances of jingoism and parochialism in the worst types of study in our field. However, particularly in the case of relatively remote and "exotic" languages (the extra-European), the necessary mental and emotional shifts demanded by translators working in altogether different linguistic contexts has, it is to be hoped, tended to engender a salutary understanding of cultural and ideological difference.

5. Conclusion: A New Awareness of Translation in the Study of Religion?

After more than three decades of translation studies we can no longer continue to think that translating is a simple communicative act. I hope that, both from the examples of the translations mentioned above and from the movements in theory briefly sketched, it is clear that translation is fraught with much more than the linguistic problem of reading "what the source text says." Theoreticians, however, must not lose sight of the all-important question with regard to translation: Can a translation ever communicate to its readers the understanding of the foreign text that foreign readers have?[68] The consensus seems to be: "Yes, but always only partially." This need not be seen as a failure of translation, for indeed it may be seen as part of the enriching process of intercultural exchange which has always been part of human experience. For the academic scholarly translator, translation studies need not necessarily constitute a threat to the high standards of rigor and discipline in translating by removing the goals of fidelity and scientific accuracy. The academic translator will still produce editions and translations which will be accessible to only a very small audience; there is perhaps, however, a need to provide more contextual background, including sometimes a transcribed text, for the modern student and educated reader who finds popularized paraphrases insufficient as translations. In connection with this, it is a mistake to set up the issues of fidelity, accuracy or scholarly objectivity as paramount: indeed, one of the most important insights to be gained from those who have worked on theories of translation is that for decades now they have focused not solely on the *source* text, nor on the *target* text, but instead look at how different discourses and

67 Bassnett 1989: 1; Gentzler 1993: 191.

68 See Venuti 2000: 473ff.

semiotic practices in language are *mediated through translation*. Scholars, too, have to take account of this. Gentzler used the term "interpellation" for the double movement which simultaneously interrupts our own constructed identities and propels them forward. This "interpellation" is active in every act of reading, writing and communication, it is often obscured and performed unconsciously, and is thus often difficult to observe. It is likely, though it would be difficult to prove such, that translators who come to terms with their own patterns of interpellation are better translators.

Students of religion, like those of translation, are coming to terms with both the ideological agenda of their own field[69] and also the politics of religion/translation. This latter is a point at which studies of religion and translation studies intersect. Earlier reference was made to the way in which the restriction of scriptures to a "sacred" language (Arabic, Avestan, Hebrew, Pali, Sanskrit, Tibetan etc.) may function as a kind of linguistic/cultural imperialism. A study of this area would be most timely and could be of very considerable benefit. Translation studies has pointed to many of the "sacred cows" of translation, one of which is the idea that translation is everywhere and always the same and constant. A cursory glance the history of translation and particularly at Baker 1998 (Part II, "Histories and Traditions") shows that there are very different cultural understandings of the phenomenon we know as "translation," whether they be those of actually remote cultures, or of cultures which stand at the periphery of our own societies, as marginalized groups.[70] More radically still, Harish Trivedi argues that there are fundamental differences in Indian traditional understandings of textual transmission, such as modern Indian *anuvad*, that amount to a concept closer to "retelling" of a source text in a target language, i.e. *anuvad* springs from a temporal metaphor of "saying after," from an oral context, rather than the Western term "translation" with its spatial metaphorical reference (Latin *transferre, translatio* "carry across").[71] In this case, Indianists in the study of religion will know this already: indeed this is indicative of how one field catches up with another in one respect whilst leading the way in others. As was said before, scholars in the study of religion are perhaps among the highest users and perpetrators of translation from

69 See for example T. Fitzgerald (2000), *The Ideology of Religious Studies*. Oxford: Oxford University Press.

70 Several essays in recent collections by Susan Bassnett and her colleagues have usefully addressed various aspects of this subject. Lefevere has written comparatively about Chinese and Western thinking on translation (Bassnett/Lefevere 1998: 12–40); Bassnett has argued that, after a cultural turn in translation studies, there has recently been a turn towards the study of translations in cultural studies in recognition of their pivotal importance (Ibid.: 123–39).

71 Bassnett/Trivedi 1999: 9 (Introduction); see also Ganesh Devy's essay "Translation and Literary History: An Indian View," in: ibid.

remote cultures. It would be surprising if they had not already come to terms with many of the challenges which the more European-centered traditions of translation and literary criticism have only recently embraced in the new wave of post-colonialist accounting for the past and present. However it is understood, translating and the study of translations will continue to be a central part of the study of religion. Religionists may have to ask new, philosophical and literary questions of their texts as a result of work which has gone on in translation studies. The fact that there is a field of study of translation now established across the world may be an encouragement to all translators of religious texts: e.g. that there *are* people out there writing about the things we do, and why we make the choices we do, in translating; this affords a pool of shared knowledge and theory about problems we all encounter at the "text-face," and religionists have much expertise and understanding to offer in this new field.

Bibliography

Arberry, Arthur J. (1955), The Koran Interpreted. London: Allen & Unwin; New York: Touchstone 1996.

Asín Palacios, Miguel (1931), *El Islam Cristianizado, Estudio del "Sufismo" a través de las obras de Abenarabi de Murcia*. Madrid: Editorial Plutarco.

— (1982), L'Islam christianisé, transl. from Spanish by Bernard Dubant. Paris: Trédaniel.

Baker, Mona (1992), *In Other Words: A Coursebook on Translation*. London: Routledge.

Baker, Mona/Malmkjær, Kirsten, eds. (1998), *Routledge Encyclopedia of Translation Studies*. London/New York: Routledge.

Barthes, Roland (1977), "The Death of the Author," in: Stephen Heath, ed. and transl., *Image, Music, Text*. London: Fontana: 142–49.

Bassnett, Susan (1980), *Translation Studies*. London/New York: Routledge.

Bassnett, Susan/Lefevere, André, eds. (1990), *Translation, History and Culture*. London: Pinter.

— eds. (1998), *Constructing Cultures: Essays on Literary Translation*. Topics in Translation 11. Clevedon: Multilingual Matters.

Bassnett, Susan/Trivedi, Harish, eds. (1999), *Post-colonial Translation*. Translation Studies. London: Routledge.

Behl, Aditya/Weightman, Simon, transl. (2000), *Madhumālatī: An Indian Sufi Romance*. Oxford: OUP.

Bell, Roger T. (1991), *Translation and Translating: Theory and Practice*. New York: Longman.

Belloc, Hillaire (1931), *On Translation*. Oxford: Clarendon Press.

Benjamin, Andrew (1989), *Translation and the Nature of Philosophy*. London: Routledge.

Catford, J.C. (1965), *A Linguistic Theory of Translation*. London: Oxford University Press.

The Encyclopedia of Language and Linguistics (1994), editor-in-chief: R.E. Asher. 10 Vols. Oxford: Pergamon Press.

Davis, Dick with Afkham Darbandi (1984), *The Conference of the Birds*. London: Penguin.

Dawood, N.J. (1956), *The Koran. A New Translation*. London/New York: Penguin.

Frawley, William, ed. (1984), *Translation*. Newark, Del.: University of Delaware Press.

Gentzler, Edwin (1993), *Contemporary Translation Theories*. Second revised ed. 2001. London/New York: Routledge.

Graham, William A. (1987), *Beyond the Written Word: Oral Aspects of Scripture in the History of Religion*. Cambridge: Cambridge University Press.

Hammond, Gerald (1987), "English Translations of the Bible," in: Robert Alter/Frank Kermode, eds., *The Literary Guide to the Bible*. London: Collins: 647–66.

Hickey, Leo, ed. (1998), *The Pragmatics of Translation*. Topics in Translation Series. Clevedon: Multilingual Matters.

Holmes, J. (1987), "The Name and Nature of Translation Studies," in G. Toury, ed., *Translation Across Cultures*. New Delhi: Bahri.

Jacquemond, Richard (1992), "Translation and Cultural Hegemony: The Case of French-Arabic Translation," in: Lawrence Venuti, ed., *Rethinking Translation: Discourse, Subjectivity, Ideology*. London/New York: Routledge: 139–58.

Lewis, Franklin (2000), *Rumi—Past and Present, East and West*. Oxford: Oneworld Publications.

Meisami, Julie Scott (1995), *The Haft Paykar: A Medieval Persian Romance*. Oxford: OUP.

Nicholson, R.A. (1911), *Kashf al-Mahjub of Al Hujwiri: The Oldest Persian Treatise on Sufism*. London: Luzac and Co.

— (1926), *The Mathnawī of Jalālu'ddīn Rūmī*. Vol. II. London: Luzac and Co.

Nida, Eugene A./Taber, Charles R. (1969), *The Theory and Practice of Translation*. Leiden: Brill.

Olivelle, Patrick, transl. (1996), *Upanisads*. Oxford: OUP.

Rabassa, Gregory (1984), "If This Be Treason: Translation and Its Possibilities," in: W. Frawley, *Translation: Literary, Linguistic and Philosophical Perspectives*. Newark, Del.: University of Delaware Press/Associated University Presses.

Robinson, Douglas (1993), "Decolonizing Translation," in: *Translation and Literature*. Vol. 2: 113–24.

Schroeder, Eric (1948), "Verse Translation and Hafiz," [on A.J. Arberry's 50 Poems of Hafiz] in: *Journal of Near Eastern Studies* 7 (4): 209–22.

Schulte, R./Biguenet, J. (1992), *Theories of Translation: An Anthology of Essays from Dryden to Derrida*. Chicago: University of Chicago Press.

Simms, Karl (1997), *Translating Sensitive Texts: Linguistic Aspects*. Approaches to Translation Studies. Amsterdam/Atlanta, Ga.: Rodopi.

Toury, Gideon, ed. (1987), *Translation across Cultures*. New Delhi: Bahri.

— (1995), *Descriptive Translation Studies and beyond*. Amsterdam/Philadephia, Pa.: John Benjamin's Publishing Company.

Uspensky, Boris (1973), *A Poetics of Composition: The Structure of the Artistic Text and Typology of a Compositional Form*. Transl. from Russian by Valentina Zavarin/Susan Wittig. Berkeley, Calif.: University of California Press.

Venuti, Lawrence, ed. (1992), *Rethinking Translation*. London/New York: Routledge.

— (1995), *The Translator's Invisibility*. London/New York: Routledge.

— ed. (2000), *The Translation Studies Reader*. London/New York: Routledge.

Vermes, Geza (1973), *Jesus the Jew. A Historian's Reading of the Gospels*. London: William Collins Sons & Co. Ltd.

Williams, A.V. (1990), "The Pahlavi Rivāyat Accompanying the Dadestān ī Dēnīg," in: *Historisk-filosofiske Meddelelser* 60: 1–2.

Wilt, Timothy (2003), *Bible Translation. Frames of Reference.* Manchester: St Jerome Publishing.

The Use of Electronic Media in the Study of Sacred Texts

by

GORDON D. NEWBY

Much has been written about the electronic revolution, and some writers have assumed that this revolution would sweep away old ways of reading and relating to sacred texts. If we compare the electronic revolution to the revolution of Johannes Gutenberg's movable type, we see both profound changes in the way information was disseminated and strong reinforcements of already existing modes and styles of communication. Books, including the Bible, began to be printed in vernacular languages rather than ecclesiastical Latin as part of the revolutionary, democratizing process. A wider range of subjects was printed and disseminated; the penny-dreadful novel as well as sacred texts were popularized as a result of the new print technology. One the other hand, the vernaculars in which these books were printed already abounded in Gutenberg's time, and the new technology had the effect of restricting the growth of many of those vernaculars, which, when coupled with the political ideas of nationalism, changed the linguistic ecology into a few increasingly regularized languages, each with its rules of orthography and spelling, and each with its own centers of power and authority. The Bible in German began to take on a different social valence than the Bible in English or Dutch, because it was associated with the national language and the national church. Moreover, it should be remembered, the effects of the Gutenberg transformation took centuries to be fully felt. The Ottoman Empire had printing and typewriters only several centuries after its introduction in Europe, and the Quran, that empire's sacred text, resisted and still resists the technology of moveable type. Thus sacred texts and their dissemination lie at the heart of the print revolution and at the heart of the electronic revolution.

The nature of the study of sacred texts involving electronic means has evolved along with the ecology of the study and use of sacred texts in general. By ecology, I mean the total interconnected electronic environment in which we find sacred texts, including computers, CD ROMs and the internet. Powerful desktop computers and portable hand-held wireless devices provide increasingly available means for the average person to study, analyze, and use a sacred text. More texts are available to more people, and this has transformed not only the ways in which sacred texts have been studied, but also the very notions of what is a sacred text, what are its powers of authority, and who is empowered to declare a text sacred. To some extent, questions about the electronic study of sacred texts are conjoined with the larger social and epistemological questions that have engaged scholars over the last century, including issues about what is a text and what powers do texts have to migrate from one power center to another and to colonize certain groups. If I can download a sacred text to my computer from a religious website that offers it, do I have the authority to use that text? Is it mine? Can anyone own sacred texts? This chapter will explore some of the history of the use of electronic media in the study of sacred texts, examine some illustrative examples, and ruminate on the central questions that arise from this new ecology of sacred texts. Sacred texts will be defined broadly, since issues of canon have become central to the issues of the study of sacred texts in electronic form, particularly online. References to particular versions of electronic media and websites will be found in the body of the text as well as in the notes and bibliography, although it should be noted that these versions are generally of an ephemeral nature and are regularly supplanted by newer versions.

The electronic world of computers, the Internet and other digital modes has also facilitated increased democratic dissemination of texts, both sacred and profane, and has supported demotic speech. From a worldwide perspective, however, English has become the dominant language of the Internet, and the Roman alphabet the symbol-set of choice for most computing. The Western-based ecology of computing has had a significant impact on the electronic use of sacred texts, none of which in the world's major religions began either in English or in the Roman alphabet.

Another feature of the impact of the electronic use of sacred texts is the inherent stasis in religious systems. What has become clear in the last half century of the electronic use of sacred texts is that the revolutionary ideal of a new mode of reading sacred texts is far from being realized and that computers and other electronic devices are more likely to reinforce the styles of reading and use common to a particular religion. Revolution is hard won, seldom completely transformative, even with schism, and is often lost by reassimilation into the original after several generations.[1]

One of the earliest uses of an electronic device to study sacred texts involved a means of determining authorship and authenticity of certain books of Christian scripture, chiefly those written in Greek and ascribed to the Apostle Paul. A.Q. Morton, in his *Christianity in the Computer Age,* describes an early computer method to analyze the syntactic structure and style of the letters of

1 One only has to look at the development of an ecclesial hierarchy among Baptists or the hyper-orthodoxy of some Jewish Hasidim to see that effect.

Paul to determine which ones were genuine.[2] Morton and his colleague, G.H.C. Macgregor entered the complete text of the writings of Paul on punch-tape, each punch corresponding to a letter or punctuation mark of the text. This tape was "read" by an "electric computer," which then grouped the words of the text according to the instruction program. Following the work of William Charles Wake[3] and a number of scholars of Classical Greek, they determined the frequency of the occurrence of the particle *kai* in Paul's corpus. Classicists had determined that the frequency of the use of this particle was a reliable distinguishing characteristic to separate one author from another, since previous tests using this method on over a dozen classical authors were able to identify all authentic works of that author and reject all spurious ones. They determined that Romans, First and Second Corinthians and Galatians, as well as the epistle to Philemon, could be reliably attributed to Paul. The rest of the works traditionally attributed to Paul, according to this method, should be regarded as written by different authors, reflecting a different interpretive strain in early Christianity. Morton's analysis confirmed the more subjective interpretation advanced by J.C. Baur in 1866 and regarded then as extremely radical.[4]

In this example of an early study, there is little methodological difference between the tabulation of instances of *kai* using the "electric computer" and what had been done by non-electric means. Contemporary with Prof. Morton's work, scholars were using a system from the business supply corporation, McBee, in which cards, punched with holes along all four edges were sorted by clipping out a hole that "stood for" a variable and letting those cards fall from the stack that was held up by multiple needles. Even earlier, of course, the note-card and file-box methods were used.[5]

As is increasingly clear, the underlying assumptions and, in some cases, theologies of the investigators are often more significant determinants than any new factor inherent in the electronic machine or its program. The greater power of the electronic means of counting and sorting has allowed for the possibility of analyzing greater data sets, which has meant that more elements could be included, but the general pattern that has emerged in the last half century of computing and sacred text has seemed to reinforce analytic patterns already inherent in the particular religion's assumptions about the sacred texts. From the time of Martin Luther, there has been an effort among some Protestants to separate their notion of what is authentically Christian from the rest. In the above example, seeking an authentic text of the letters of Paul, shorn of any

2 Morton/McLeman 1965.

3 Wake 1984.

4 Baur 1866.

5 It might be noted that the growth of the field of modern statistics developed with the growth of the computer, both of which, for our purposes, enhance the statistical analysis of sacred texts.

spurious additions, is a strongly Protestant Christian enterprise, arising from the notion that it is chiefly, or solely, scripture that gives authority.

A major contribution of this early machine analysis of sacred texts has been the proliferation of concordances. Such concordances have become more than just lists of locations of words. They also give word frequency counts, parallel locations of similar and identical texts, etc. One of the interesting developments as some Bible scholars are able to work with extensive Bible-text databases is the "functional" concordance that not only lists the location of the word but also marks its grammatical and syntactic function within its context. In one such project, the markers include indicators of time parsed into four types of time indicator: the time goal, the time interval or duration, the time origin and the specific time point.[6] The ability to distinguish the broad range of functions of words and phrases lies at the center of much scriptural analysis. Some concordances also indicate the putative documentary origin of certain passages according to the Documentary Hypothesis, marking the word or phrase as J, E, P, or D. This technique was first applied graphically between 1893 and 1899 in the *Polychrome Bible,* in which different colors were used to indicate different sources.[7] Some scholars are using the contextual concordance for reconstruction of missing texts. C. Fahner reports this use in comparing the methods of translating Hebrew scriptures into Aramaic and Greek used by ancient translators with the structures of the synoptic passages from the first three Gospels to gain new insights into the Aramaic sources for the synoptic Gospels.[8]

Displaying characters in alphabets or syllabaries other than the Roman alphabet remains a problem for this and other applications involving sacred texts. Solutions are still machine-specific and proprietary, in spite of the growing dominance of Microsoft's Windows software, and many of the world's sacred texts can only be represented in transliterated form. For the scholar, this presents an inconvenient but workable solution, particularly in the case of indices and concordances. Having sacred texts in transliteration presents many problems for the full use of electronic sacred texts in ritual and devotional practice.[9]

Turning to an example from Rabbinic Judaism, one of the earliest and major on-going studies of sacred text through electronic means is the "Responsa Project" at Bar Ilan University in Israel. The project, started by the Professors Schoueka and Frankel on Bar Ilan University's mainframe computer, and subsequently migrated to a PC, is one of the oldest of its type, and is producing a transgenerational Jewish library that includes texts ranging from the Bible to

---

6 Association internationale Bible et informatique 1998: 62–64.

7 Published by Dodd, Mead and Company, New York, the series was never completed because of the high cost of production. It would seem that this would be a project that could be revived on the web, were someone interested.

8 Association internationale Bible et informatique 1998: 182–83.

9 See below, p. 54.

Responsa, modern decisions by individual authorities or members of *batei-dîn,* Rabbinical courts. A central feature of this project is the hypertext linkage of all the material, with the goal to interrelate all the databases (sacred texts, commentaries on sacred texts, Rabbinic writings, etc.) at the word and topic levels. The aim here is to include as many texts as possible rather than pare the texts down to a few "authentic" ones and to be able to interrelate all the elements of each text to all the others. In other words, the project is intensifying the midrashic method of reading, in which words and fragments of texts are assumed to interrelate with the same words and fragments found in other places in the same text or in other texts. Such a method of reading, recently thrust to the center of Western literary debates, informed Rabbinic Jewish writers from a very early period. They held that texts were polysemous and capable of being taken apart and recombined to display new meanings.[10] In this example, the quest for authenticity lies in the production of as many reasonable interconnections as will help illustrate, explain, add texture, or challenge what may be the plain meaning of the text. The mode of reading is dialectic, generative of new means of understanding, and closely in tune with hypertext interactions. The point of this example is that this mode of reading comes not from the availability of electronic hypertext means to read, but from an already strongly determined Jewish way of reading that pre-dated electronic capabilities.

In another Rabbinic project, Prof. Lewis M. Barth of Hebrew Union College-Jewish Institute of Religion, Los Angeles, has started to digitize and encode the major manuscript editions of the eighth century C.E. text, *Pirqe Rabbi Eliezer.* In an article in *AJS Perspectives,* the newsletter of the Association for Jewish Studies in the United States, Barth outlines the advantages and difficulties of producing a corpus of electronic sacred texts.[11] He says that "Digitization permits the scholar to view on screen representation of original sources in a manner that is more satisfactory than either microfilm or microfiche."[12] This is because the text, once completely "marked up" and encoded will have more complete and consistent information than is available from a photographic representation of a damaged or poor manuscript. The marking depends, of course, on the care of the scholar who analyzes the manuscript as well as on the completeness and flexibility of the markup system. The one that he chose is an implementation of Standard Generalized Markup Language (SGML) known as TEI (Text Encoding

10 An interesting and accessible example of both the ancient and modern method of reading in a Jewish way can be seen at http://www.emory.edu/UDR/BLUMENTHAL/GenIntro.html. Professor Blumenthal uses hypertext to show multiple readings for Genesis. Please note that this web address and all others mentioned in this article are subject to change as servers are changed or sites are abandoned. The same content can usually be found through the use of such search engines as Google, Yahoo or Dogpile.

11 Barth 2000: 19.

12 Ibid.

Initiative).[13] When used, this markup language allows both a complete presentation of the various elements of each single text, but through hypertext links allows for an interactive comparison of all the texts in a way that the older *variorum* text editions and synoptic editions could not. The system is problematic, however, for non-Roman scripts. SGML was implemented only for the 128 lower ASCII (American Standard Code for Information Interchange) character set, a set insufficient to represent Hebrew, Arabic or similar languages. Furthermore, there is no SGML software to display and manipulate right-to-left character order. A new standard, Unicode, is being developed and implemented, but, as Barth says, "Two problems remain for serious scholarly work in right-to-left texts and especially Hebrew. First, the present Unicode fonts that have been developed for Windows only contain Modern Hebrew characters: consonants, vowels and limited punctuation. Scholars need a complete set of Unicode glyphs that will include all the signs used in Hebrew texts from the biblical period to the present. Second, XML word-processing software needs to be developed as quickly as possible that is Unicode compliant. (The potential solution of these two problems will have great commercial consequences because of the size of the Arabic and Farsi markets.) Such tools are essential for efficiently encoding, displaying and searching *Pirqe Rabbi Eliezer* or any other significant Hebrew text."[14] The problems for Hebrew, Arabic and similar alphabetic languages are compounded for syllabic and ideographicly represented languages, such as Chinese, Japanese and Nahuatl.

Among some Buddhist groups, computers have become a vehicle for the repetitive recitation of sacred texts and prayers. This is, of course, an extension of the practice among Tibetan Buddhists, who use a prayer wheel to set the syllables of the sacred text in motion.[15]

Bible translation among Christians, chiefly Protestant but Roman Catholic as well, has been enhanced and aided by the availability of electronic media. There are Bible Societies in over 125 countries overseeing translations of the Bible into more than 500 different languages, some of which have only rudimentary literary traditions. Computers provide support for morphological linguistic analyses of the languages, the production of dictionaries, and the development of orthographies specific to the phonetic systems of those languages. While not new, the adaptation of the Greek alphabet for Coptic and Slavic as examples, the use of computers and desktop publishing software has brought costs of reproducing copies of the Bible in those languages within the reach of wide distribution. Additionally, CD ROM technology has made available support material for translators in adverse condition where it is reported that prior

13 See www.uic.edu/orgs/tei.

14 Barth 2000: 19.

15 See http://dharma-haven.org/digital-wheels.htm.

to this technology, support libraries were destroyed because "the cockroaches ate the glue and the bindings and the worms and moisture ruined the books before they could be returned."[16] When the CD ROM contains software capabilities for searches and hypertext links to material related to each word or verse, the medium becomes both an invaluable research tool for the scholar and translator but also a course of study for the lay person. Additionally, the CD ROM provides multimedia possibilities for cross-cultural "translations" in more than words. There are reports of drama, rap and dance translations of the Bible on CD ROM illustrating a variety of cultural interpretations of passages of scripture.[17] Commercially available software for the study of sacred texts has proliferated for almost all platforms and operating systems, and the increasingly faster desk and laptop machines allow for complex audio and video presentations surrounding the text.

Most scripture study courses are now available on the World Wide Web from rapidly proliferating internet sites sponsored by large, well-organized groups and by individuals with particular theological and social projects.[18] These sites provide a variety of modes of presenting sacred texts, but the most complete of them offer text, commentary, audio and visual materials and often a chat-room or e-mail contact for direct communication with the group or page originator.[19] Partly in response to our more mobile society, there has been a growth of sites for the peripatetic who wants to keep in touch with scripture and religious sites. Sites such as www.goshen.net, www.cybergrace.com and www.servehim.com provide Bible search engines and connections with programmed Bible study. These claim to be non-denominational but are Protestant and Evangelical, and Roman Catholics are likely to prefer www.petersvoice.org. The Ethereal Library of Wheaton College, www.ccel.org, provides a source of downloadable Christian texts. For Jews, www.bible.ort.org, www.613.org, and www.netaxis.qc.ca/torahfax make moveable Torah study easy. The last site provides the opportunity for commemoration of the dead through the posting of the *Yartzeit* online. For Muslims, http://info.uah.edu/ msa/quran.html will give English translations of the Quran and Quran recitation, while www.islam.org/voi/ has a rich supply of audio materials. The site www.al-islam.org can be

16 Association internationale Bible et informatique 1998: 35.

17 Ibid.

18 Sometimes it is hard to distinguish which is which at first glance. I am reminded of the existence of the Church of the Bunny. Apparently started as a critique of organized religions, it was, nevertheless, taken seriously by some. See www.lucifer.com/virus/resource.html, and for an online holy war, see www.corg.org/holy1.htm.

19 A good starting place for those unfamiliar with the major sites associated with the world's religions is Bruce Lawrence's witty and informative new book *The Complete Idiot's Guide to Religions Online* (Lawrence 1999). It will guide the reader to enough places for each tradition to enable the searcher to function independently.

viewed in a number of languages including Arabic. The multilingual www.bahai.org gives the basic tenets of the Bahai faith with links to resources.

Buddhists were some of the earliest religious groups to make use of the World Wide Web, and their writings are deeply embedded in a number of sites, reflecting the varieties of Buddhism. At www.buddhanet.net one can find the Guide to the Tipitaka, which is an outline of the Pali Buddhist Canonical Scriptures of Theravada Buddhism from Burma. This is a unique work, as it is probably the only material that deals in outline with the whole of the Pali Buddhist Tipitaka. The Tipitaka includes all the teachings of the Buddha, grouped into three divisions: the Suttanta Pitaka, or general discourses; the Vinaya Pitaka, or moral code for monks and nuns; and the Abhidhamma Pitaka, or philosophical teachings. There is also an elementary Pali Course. Pali was the language spoken by the Buddha, and employed by him to expound his teachings. It is also the scriptural language used by the Theravada school of Buddhism. At www.dharmathecat.com one can find a cartoon entrance into Buddhism. While this may seem humorous to Westerners, and it is meant to be entertaining, it is another example of the interaction between indigenous religious culture and the electronic medium. Comic book representations of important religious stories are a common part of both Buddhism and Hinduism in Asia, and the migration of that medium to television and to the Web is not surprising.

There are multiple sites for Hindu sacred texts, just as there is a vast library of those texts. www.yoga.com/raw/readings/rig_veda.html and www.sacred-texts.com/hin/index.htm are two sites for finding the Rig Veda, the Upanishads, the Bhagavad Gita, the Ramayana and others, both in Sanskrit and in translations. The second site, www.sacred-texts.com, is a location for sacred texts from most of the major world religions. In most cases, as with the Sanskrit of the Rig Veda, the texts are presented in transliteration into the ASCII symbol set or are displayed as pictures of writing. While this is can be a problem for students and scholars, in the case of some Islamic sites, the depiction of the Quran as a picture of its handwritten form comes closest to its actual cultural use within Muslim circles, where a copy of the Quran used for ritual and devotional purposes should be handwritten. For Judaism, the orthographic problem is slightly different. Several commercial companies distribute programs on CD ROM as well as over the Web that contain passages from the Torah or other passages in which the name of God might occur. On one of the programs, readers are allowed to see the name of God written in Hebrew on their screens, but they are warned that if they print out the material, they must treat it with the same respect they would any holy text and dispose of it with a ritually proper burial.[20]

---

20 See the instructions accompanying the *CD ROM Judaic Classics Library*, Chicago: Davka Corporation & Institute for Computers in Jewish Life, 1993.

The development of electronic resources for the analysis, study and display of sacred texts, both on individual computers and online has led to the growth of university classes on the sacred texts of individual traditions and on comparative sacred texts. An example of the latter that has attempted to implement the positive features of electronic and particularly internet resources is the Comparative Sacred Texts project at Emory University.[21] The course is taught at both the freshman introductory level and as a doctoral seminar, with the goal of the course to produce non-reductionist, non-hierarchical interactive comparative reading of texts from the Hebrew Bible, Rabbinic Jewish, Christian, Hindu and Muslim traditions. It is grounded in the method of socio-rhetorical analysis developed by Vernon Robbins, one of the members of the team, although the course is not designed to be a training ground for that method *per se*.[22] Selected texts from each of the traditions are read around the themes of creation, end-time, sacrifice and community and daily life, with each text read first in the context of its own tradition and then compared to other traditions. The goal is to move the readers through the second-stage reading of same-and-different to a synthetic stage of interactive reading, in which questions derived from reading a text in one tradition are used to inform the questions asked about another tradition's texts without imposing a hierarchical valorization of any of the traditions. This is facilitated electronically in several ways. All of the texts are available in (English translated) word-processor compatible forms as well as in Web-based forms that preserve the specific religious and cultural context for the sacred texts. Through the use of electronically based classrooms, the class has access to the texts through projection from the local server and from the Web. Texts can be displayed side by side, and, when discussion warrants, additional texts can be called up for view from both the local server and the Web. Search engines assist the novice to find relevant passages from a tradition's larger store of sacred texts, and the scholar need not have an exhaustive set of memorized texts from more than one tradition to be able to explore the interactions. This produces a more neutral arena of inquiry by not privileging either the superior knowledge of the educated informant or the pre-prejudices of the instructor. This class is not an online class, although it could be, but is a class that meets regularly in a physical setting for discussion. All members of the class belong to an online discussion group, and daily writing assignments, questions, and discussions are available through the online means to all members of the class. The exceptions are the privileged materials, such as quizzes, tests, and other graded writing assignments, unless specific permissions have been obtained. This open, online aspect of the class has helped build community and trust among our students, who often identify with the

21 The members of the project are Laurie Patton, Vernon K. Robbins, and Gordon Newby.

22 For an explication of the method, see Robbins 1989, 1992, 1996a, 1996b.

traditions under discussion. While the positive benefits to pedagogy are beyond the scope of this chapter, the fact that this class centers on the sacred texts from four of the world's religions has stimulated broad interest and much discussion among Emory's students, who seem to want to find a way to negotiate a compatible place for their traditions in a pluralistic world.

Another dimension of the electronic use of sacred texts involves the recent growth of small hand-held devices generally termed Personal Digital Assistants (PDA's), such as those using the Palm operating system, Windows CE or miniature computers, such as the Psion. A wide variety of sacred texts and related materials is available for these devices that can be easily taken in and out of various religious and secular settings. One can find lists of downloadable texts and applications at sites like www.memoware.com/c-religion.htm and www.viaweb.com/pilotgearsw/religion.html: the *Book of Mormon,* weekday Jewish services for both the synagogue and the home, translations of the Quran into various languages, sayings of the Buddha, Baha'i prayers and the writings of Baha'ullah in English, Arabic and Persian, various translations of the Bible (both Jewish and Christian) including a Chinese version, the I-Ching, Falun Gong texts, Wiccan texts and much more. Many of the PDA's are able to be connected directly or indirectly to the Web, so that daily devotional and scripture study courses can be downloaded, shared with colleagues, often by infrared transmission (IR), and used in places where even small laptops would be difficult or inappropriate. Grace after meals in the Jewish tradition is often recited from small *Siddurîm* (prayer books). There is a growing number of observant Jews who are using Palm OS devices as portable *Siddurîm,* accessing the information in Hebrew or in Roman transliteration and scrolling through the text rather than turning pages. These electronic devices are not used by observant Jews on the Sabbath, however, since the use of electrical devices would violate the prohibitions against the use of fire, and it is interesting to note that no liturgical texts for the Sabbath are listed at http://www.PilotYid.com. Additionally, at www.ohrnet.org/ask/ask269.htm#Q3 there is a Rabbinic response that indicates that while it is permissible to carry a PDA with liturgical software into the bathroom, it would be inappropriate to turn it on.[23]

The Jewish examples of the problems of the use of sacred texts on a PDA are part of a larger and growing set of issues in the ecology of electronic sacred texts in cyberspace: Can cyberspace be sacred, and can internet connections substitute for physical community and bodily presence? These issues take this discussion beyond the bounds of this chapter, but the implications for the ritual

23 See www.pilotyid.com/faq.php, question 9. Rabbi Ephraim Zalmonovitz, the spiritual leader of Mazkeret Batia, has issued a *halachic* (Jewish law) ruling that one who has "holy" software installed on one's pilot, and drops it, must kiss it as one does to a holy book such as a prayer book or Psalms. See also http://www.jewishethicist.com/dvartorah/tamari/teshuvah.html for a *halachic* discussion about copying software.

use of sacred texts in various traditions are profound. For Christians, when two or three are gathered in God's name, God is said to be in the midst of them.[24] For Jews, the presence of ten qualified individuals is required before certain liturgical acts can be performed, and forty Muslims must be present for a congregational prayer. Tibetan Buddhists were among the first to start to sacralize cyberspace by the creation of a mandala as a digitized, three-dimensional object through Cornell's Program of Computer Graphics.[25] At http://www.mandalaproject.org, the Mandala Project has a visual demonstration of diverse individuals coming together to create something larger than themselves while maintaining their uniqueness. The Mandala Project "invites everyone to share their personal expression of common denominators by presenting an online gallery to which everyone, regardless of race, gender, location or beliefs, is invited to submit their personal mandala. The submissions become part of a collective art piece reflecting the diversity of the human race within a unified structure. Each mandala can include a message from the artist as well as email address to enable viewers to make contact."[26] For those who participate in this online practice, there is the possibility of creating collective worship through the medium of electronic communication. Churches like the Universal Life Church (http://ulc.org/ulc/index.html) exist partly online, as did the Heaven's Gate cult that resulted in the mass suicide of its members in 1997. While it is hard to predict the direction that the creation of virtual sacred communities will take, particularly as virtual reality technology enhances our abilities to have a greater sense of presence in the electronic world, we seem to be experiencing on the internet something like the proliferation of mystery religions in the Greco-Roman period. These were often secret at their core while publicly challenging the organized, public religions. They provided community and a promise of individual salvation or transcendence, and were linked with nature and animals. While it is hard to take the Church of the Bunny, mentioned above, the Church of the Shrew, or the Church of the Gerbil (http://www.corg.org/main.htm) seriously, at least the latter has claimed to have engaged in cyberspace's first holy war. Just as the television technology produced virtual congregations that have had real effects on our religious, political and moral discourse, the internet promises similar aggregations of worshippers and the possibilities of new, online sacred texts, as well as the expanded use of older sacred texts in this new setting.

In "Fire, the Kali Yuga and Textual Reading," Laurie Patton addresses the issue of the colonization and migration of texts in the context of the question,

---

24 Matthew 18:20.

25 The project is not currently online, but views of the project can be seen at www.graphics.cornell.edu/~wbt/mandala.

26 http://www.mandalaproject.org.

"Who speaks for Hinduism?"[27] After exploring her credentials and license for talking about the Rig Veda, she discusses the dilemmas of colonial and anti-colonial discourse, each locked with a death grip on the throat of the other. It has long been recognized that texts, particularly sacred texts, have been "appropriated" in the colonial manner, edited, produced in critical editions, and sold at high price to scholars and universities in ways that mean that the indigenous users of those sacred texts could not afford or did not have access to some of the most thoroughly researched and edited versions. These texts were colonized, and they changed in both their ownership and their function. To get around some of the problems posed by this situation, Patton calls for a mode of textual interpretation that would be formulated "as a transformative combination between recognizability and unrecognizability," and proposes a model of "migrancy" and "thoroughness" in textual interpretations along the lines of the classical Sanskrit *samvâda* or debate colloquy in which it is understood that the power is never equal in any conversation and that thoroughness of explication and the possibility of the ideas to migrate from one power source to another balance each other to permit the disputational conversation. In her model, she says that there should be "a textual scenario wherein the conversation partners, whose horizons only clumsily meet, if they meet at all, who are hardly ever equal in power, and who are always haunted by the ghost of the colonial past, nonetheless remain committed to the idea that textual argument matters and should take place everywhere." She argues that the "rapid and economical exchange of texts is still very much in the hands of Western economies."[28] She encourages the more powerful West to promote conversation with the less economically advantaged.

Patton's model of textual debate finds its counterparts in most other critical and analytic traditions associated with sacred texts, and the use of the internet and electronic forms of sacred texts fits into her proposal well. There are some problems, however. The text located in cyberspace can sometimes take on the dual characteristics of an oral/aural text as well as the hegemonic authority of a written text, with all the baggage that the phrase "written word" carries. It, after all, meant something to be one of the "People of the Book" under Islam, even when Muslims had "colonized" the sacred texts of Jews and Christians in the manner that Patton describes with Christian missionaries and Brahmin textualists, and as Christians had done earlier with the texts of the Hebrew bible. The ambiguity of the cyberspace sacred text can lead to some confusion, as with the students who ask if the Gospel of Thomas is one of the gospels. The answer to that question and the claims made by some that this once unknown material can reveal new information about the early Church show that the

27 Patton 2000.

28 Ibid.: 814.

dissemination of the texts in cyberspace has the potential to threaten the boundaries of the canon.[29] That means they have the power to undermine the colonial canon of possession as well. One of the promises of the increasing ability to produce, reproduce and disseminate sacred texts through electronic means is the promise of a greater democratization of access and ownership that will stimulate the use and debate about sacred texts and realize Patton's[30] dream that "textual argument matters and should take place everywhere."

The electronic use of sacred texts will continue to become a more normal part of the lives of the religious of the world. Electronic technology is becoming increasingly more affordable, even in less well developed countries, and the internet is becoming more pervasive. Cellular telephones already have miniature web browsers with the capability of accessing sites containing sacred texts. From www.netaxis.qc.ca/torahfax one can already get weekly Torah portions and commentary as e-mail on wireless PDA's and cellular telephones or one can plot one's day using Vedic astrological information at http://jyotishsoft.hypermart.net. Searchable CD ROMs have already lessened the necessity of memorizing sacred texts in order to plunder them for facts and quotes, and almost anyone can do a word or number analysis on their desktop or laptop machine, competing with ancient Rabbis and modern proponents of a Biblical number code.[31] Libraries of commentaries online or on CD ROM are available with all the ease of online ordering, many with sophisticated re-enactments of historical scenes and events. One can even perform a virtual pilgrimage online, an act long associated with sacred texts.[32]

The electronic revolution seems to be having the same impact on sacred texts as the Gutenberg technology did: more texts available to more people with a greater loss of control over the texts by established authorities. Like the environment after the Protestant Reformation, the Rise of Islam, or the beginnings of Rabbinic Judaism, we can expect a greater number of groups clustering around more and more texts, and, like those periods of ferment, we can also expect the tendency to organize and regularize the proliferation of information and groups. As stated in the beginning, the electronic revolution in the use of sacred texts will negotiate between the two poles of stasis and resistance on the one hand and proliferation and chaos on the other. In this respect, this revolution will be like many others, with the resultant change both hard won and closely tied to ways and uses of the past.

29 See http://www.thewaters.org/columns/5gospels.html.

30 Patton 2000: 816.

31 See, for example, the program at http://bible-code.com/decoder.html, which claims, "Whether a skeptic or a believer, Bible Decoder can help you research the famous ELS code phenomena since it's the only program that gives you the freedom to choose on what text or in what language the searches will be conducted."

32 See http://www.fatima.org/tour.html.

Bibliography

Association internationale Bible et informatique (1998), *Actes du cinquième Colloque international Bible et informatique: traduction et transmisssion = Proceedings of the Fifth International Colloquium Bible and Computer: Translation and Transmission = Akten des fünften Internationalen Kolloquiums Bibel und Informatik: Übersetzung und Übertragung: Aix-en-Provence, 1–4 September 1997*. Paris: Champion.

Barth, L.M. (2000), "Electronic Text Editing and Pirqe Rabbi Eliezer," in: *AJS Perspectives* 1 (2): 19.

Baur, F.C. (1866), *Paulus, der Apostel Jesu Christi, sein Leben und Wirken, seine Briefe und seine Lehre; ein Beitrag zu einer kritischen Geschichte des Urchristenthums*. Leipzig: Reisland.

Lawrence, B.B. (1999), *The Complete Idiot's Guide to Religions Online*. Indianapolis, Ind.: Alpha Books.

Morton, A.Q./McLeman, J. (1965), *Christianity in the Computer Age*. New York: Harper & Row.

Patton, L. (2000), "Fire, the Kali Yuga and Textual Reading," in: *Journal of the American Academy of Religion* 68 (4): 805–16.

Robbins, V.K. (1989), *Ancient Quotes & Anecdotes: From Crib to Crypt*. Sonoma, Calif.: Polebridge Press.

— (1992), *Jesus the Teacher: A Socio-rhetorical Interpretation of Mark*. Minneapolis, Minn.: Fortress Press.

— (1996a), *Exploring the Texture of Texts: A Guide to Socio-rhetorical Interpretation*. Valley Forge, Pa.: Trinity Press International.

— (1996b), *The Tapestry of Early Christian Discourse: Rhetoric, Society, and Ideology*. London/New York: Routledge.

Wake, W.C. (1984), *Numbers, Paul and Rational Dissent*. London: F.S. Moore.

New Approaches: Literary Theory

by

DAWNE MCCANCE

The sign, in twentieth-century theory and practice, is double. For if, as Jacques Derrida remarks, "the sign, by its root and its implications, is in all its aspects metaphysical, if it is in systematic solidarity with stoic and medieval theology," the concept of the sign also "powerfully contribute[s]" to a twentieth century turn against metaphysics (Derrida 1981: 17). In what follows, I take the sign, in both of these aspects, to be at the heart of "new approaches" to the study of religion that emerge from "literary theory." I leave to other contributors the problem of clarifying the meaning of the "new" and of delimiting what constitutes an "approach to the study of religion."[1] My task here is to outline three

1 The question of the relevance of developments in literary criticism and theory for the study of religion is one that I take up several times in this essay. At the outset, the question, as put by preeminent literary critic, Maurice Blanchot, is this: "If ... religion is etymologically that which binds, that which holds together, then what of the non-bound which disjoins beyond unity—which escapes the synchrony of 'holding together,' yet does so without breaking all the relations or without ceasing, in this break or in this absence of relations, to open yet another relation? Must one [approach] be non-religious for that?" This citation from Blanchot's *The Writing of the Disaster* opens Gil Anidjar's "Introduction" to Jacques Derrida's *Acts of Religion*, a collection of some of Derrida's many writings on religion (Anidjar: 1). To fully address the question of the relevance of the approaches I survey in this essay to the discipline of religious studies would be a major undertaking, however, one that involves consideration not only of all of the primary works in structuralism, psychoanalysis, and poststructuralism (deconstruction) that directly address the subject of "religion," but also of the enormous secondary literature on "relevance" that has come out in the past twenty years. It should be clear in this essay that I see the "new approaches" emerging from literary criticism as heralding not the demise of religion so much as its "return." On the complexity and range of this return, see Anidjar's "Introduction" to Derrida's *Acts of Religion* (Anidjar 2002). On the issue of relevance in general, several good guides and readers have come out—in structuralism, psychoanalysis, and poststructuralism, as well as in the works of the specific critics I survey in this essay; and many critical studies have been published on the question of the implications of the work of given critics for the study of religion—community, responsibility, selfhood or subjectivity, spirit, tradition, faith, and ethics. See for example: Caputo 1997; Caputo/Scanlon 1999; Crownfield 1992; Derrida/

twentieth century developments that have transformed the way we read and write "texts," religious studies texts included.[2] The approaches I overview have changed, and are changing, the discipline of religious studies.

Semiology

With the sign, we can pinpoint the emergence of linguistic science. The moment, and the constitutive concept, must be attributed to the Swiss linguist Ferdinand de Saussure. At the turn of the century, between 1907 and 1911, Saussure, at the University of Geneva, delivered a series of lectures that were published after his death from students' notes as the *Course in General Linguistics* (1916, trans. 1959). Calling for a "true science of linguistics" that would supersede the study of "grammar," the "philological" study of specific languages (primarily of Greek and Roman antiquity), and "comparative" studies (still philological and concerned with particular, mainly Indo-European, languages), Saussure in the *Course* proposes a synchronic study of language itself. "But what is language [*langue*]?" (Saussure 1959: 9). Not to be confused with speech (*parole*), or with particular "speech events," the language (*langue*) that Saussure takes as his object of study is, he says, a self-contained whole, a system made up of discrete units that stand in opposition to each other. In his suggestion that linguistics must focus on the combinatory and substitutive relations of the units within this system, Saussure introduces a significant shift, from a diachronic to a synchronic perspective, a move that, according to some, inclines structuralism, from the start, to an elision of the historical dimension, if not to an "effacement of history altogether" (Bennington/Young 1987: 1). With this shift, Saussure also introduces the notion of a pre-existing and underlying code or structure, *langue*. Rather than study the evolution of particular languages in history, as his nineteenth century predecessors had done, he proposes synchronic analysis of the rules governing the relations of units within this formal structure.

Vattimo 1998; Garber/Hanssen/Walkowitz 2000; Joy/O'Grady/Poxon 2002; Krell 2000; Oliver 1993.

2 In literary criticism post-Saussure, the text is not understood as a simple depository of meaning and it is not bounded off from its writer or reader. Structuralist conceptions of the text focus on ways in which the constituent elements of the system are brought together to form a whole; psychoanalytic conceptions of the text consider the processes by which self and text are formed in their inter-relationship; poststructuralist conceptions extend the text beyond the borders of the visible and graspable to include the "otherness" of what Heidegger called the trait. See for example, the entries on "Text," "Textuality," and "Textual Criticism" in Makaryk, ed. 1993, and Groden/Kreiswirth, eds. 1994.

The basic structural unit on which Saussure focuses is the linguistic sign. He defines this sign as a two-sided entity that combines a signified and a signifier. It is here, in the definition of the sign, that Derrida locates a solidarity of the new linguistic science with metaphysics. Saussure defines the signifier as a "sound-image, a word, for example (*arbor*, etc.)," while the signified is a concept, for example, "the concept, 'tree'" (Saussure 1959: 67), and in his diagram of the sign, he puts the signified over the signifier. Elsewhere in the *Course*, Saussure also gives primacy to the concept, the signified, and thus, according to Derrida at least, he confirms the conventional (metaphysical) notion of language as a medium or conveyer of ideas; he is also consistent here with the hermeneutic attitude, in place from Schleiermacher through Ricoeur, that takes language, and text, to be an instrument or vector of meaning. But what is metaphysical about Saussure's (and so, structuralism's) sign, according to Derrida, has to do as well with the definition of the signifier as a "sound-image." The signifier, for Saussure, is not, first of all, material, "a purely physical thing"; it is a "psychological imprint" before it is spoken or written (Saussure 1959: 66). This association between a concept, the *logos*, and a sound, this supposed "unity of sound and sense" (Derrida 1974: 29) in the prior, interior space of the self, is basic to what Derrida calls the *phonocentrism* of metaphysics. In *Of Grammatology*, *Speech and Phenomenona* and other texts, Derrida's critique of metaphysics focuses on the phonocentric and logocentric assumptions of the linguistic (and related phenomenological) concept of the sign. It is these assumptions that lead him to pose, in place of the sign, some of the terms I will discuss further below: the *grammè*, the *grapheme*, the *mark*.

But structuralism makes its start in the early years of the twentieth century by gesturing forward and backward at once. Through its link to ideal "thought-sound" (Derrida 1974: 31), Saussure's sign confirms something metaphysical. At the same time, the Saussurian sign undercuts metaphysics by introducing "arbitrariness" to the study of language. No "natural" connection ties a signifier to a signified, Saussure maintains. What brings these two together, in a given speech community at a particular place and time, is nothing but convention. This means, for one thing, that the linguistic unit "has no special phonic character" (Saussure 1959: 104). The relation of a sound to a concept is a conventional one. Language is not so much content as it is a form ("*language is a form and not a substance*" [Saussure 1959: 13]) constituted by the way its units are combined. In this combinatory system, differences, rather than essences, distinguish linguistic units one from the others. Indeed, as Saussure puts it:

> in language there are only differences. Even more important, a difference generally implies positive terms between which the difference is set up; but in language there are only differences *without positive terms*. Whether we take the signified or the signifier, language has neither ideas nor sounds that existed before the linguistic system, but only conceptual or phonic differences that have issued from the system. (Saussure 1959: 120)

In the *Course,* Saussure calls for the development of a "semiology," a general "*science that studies the life of signs within society*" (1959: 16), that includes linguistics, but that extends beyond study of language to investigate all systems of signs. The wide scope of semiology is already evident in Roman Jakobson's work. Like Saussure, by whose work he was influenced, Jakobson is one of structuralism's founding figures. A participant in Russian formalism, he was involved in establishing both the Moscow Linguistic Circle (1915) and the Prague Linguistic Circle (1926), and when he fled to the United States via Scandinavia following the Nazi invasion of Czechoslovakia in 1941, Jabobson introduced Claude Lévi-Strauss to structuralism. In Jakobson's hands, structuralism extends to the study of literature ("literariness"), visual art, comparative mythology, ritual and folklore; and even as it depends on Saussure's dyadic *langue/parole,* synchronic/diachronic model, it renders this model more dynamic and supplements it in significant ways, for example with the notion that metaphor and metonymy are the two fundamental structures of language (see Jakobson 1987). Lévi-Strauss, in turn, takes the Saussurian linguistic model (for example, the *langue/parole* distinction) into structuralist anthropology, where it becomes the basis for comparative study of kinship and marriage practices, ritual and myth. Lévi-Strauss is probably the structuralist whose work is most well-known within the field of religious studies, and primarily for his comparative analysis of myth as (a *langue*) comprised of constituent units ("mythemes") which, like Saussure's linguistic units, are organized in binary oppositions and so bespeak, not a deep truth, not essences, but a combinatory system of differences. As he puts it in the "Overture" to *The Raw and the Cooked,* Lévi-Strauss sets out "to prove that there is a kind of logic" underlying different myths (in this case "the native mythologies of the New World"); his task is to unmask this logic and to reveal the working of "its laws," thus to lay the groundwork for an all-out "science of myths" (Lévi-Strauss 1969: 1–3).

With the semiology initiated by Saussure and outlined all-too-briefly here, some "new approaches" to texts begin to emerge, approaches that religious studies cannot ignore. Language is obviously central to all of these, although it is understood now as a structure or code, something that can be studied "scientifically," some would say in isolation from its cultural context, and as an "arbitrary" system of differences rather than as a transmitter of (transcendent) ideas. Authorial intention thereby suffers a loss. Indeed, as John Sturrock sees it, "structuralism has come to stand for a way of thinking opposed to individualism, or even to humanism, for intentional human agency is given a reduced role in its interpretations of culture" (Sturrock 1979: 13). What Philip Lewis, in a 1982 essay reviewing Josué V. Harari's *Textual Strategies: Perspectives in Post-Structuralist Criticism* and Vincent Descombes's *Le Même et L'Autre: Quarante-Cinq Ans de Philosophie Française,* calls "the post-structuralist condition," has do to with this demotion of the essentialist subject. Structuralism was never an empty formalism, Lewis notes, following Descombes. It never had the meaning of a work depend simply on the arrangement of all its part in a unified whole. Structuralism has always been "strong," in Descombes's sense of that word: not organic or architectural, but a mathematical and comparative activity that "begins by constituting a model of formal relations within a given set of elements" and "then proceeds to use that model to compare the structure of the initial set to that of another one—for example, to compare the relations among the gods in one society's pantheon to the same set of relations in another society's pantheon" (Lewis 1982: 6). Importantly, such analysis does not structure "the thing itself, as literary criticism often imagines"; it structures "the set, of which this thing may be considered as one representation, in comparison with other sets" (Descombes, cited in Lewis 1982: 6). Grounded in the construction of models, rather than in representation, structuralism, in this "strong" sense, betrays a "post-structuralist" impulse from the start: "Once the communication model, positing the priority and independence of the code, determines the parameters of analysis, attention shifts away from the sender and from the content of the message toward the receiver and the medium, toward the relation of the decoder to the chain of signifiers" (Lewis 1982: 6).

What Lewis terms "post-structuralism" might then be a critical transition emanating from within structuralism, rather than a development posterior to it. Already with Lévi-Strauss and Barthes, "it is evident that sense-making is always governed by the language system and that meaning can no longer be regarded naively as the property of a perceiving subject; meaning can never be simply the direct statement of the subject's experience" (Lewis 1982: 7). Rather, with (post-)structuralism, "the possibilities for meaning are given in advance" (7). Moreover, as discussed above—and notwithstanding Saussure's privileging of the concept—the new semiology leads quickly to a shift from the signified to the signifier. With this comes a dethroning, not only of the subject, but also of the sign. This is one point that Lewis makes at the opening of his essay. He notes that Harari (along the same lines I am following here) identifies structuralism by the Saussurian account of the sign and signification, then differentiates "post-structuralism" from it by emphasizing Derrida's critique of structuralist semiology. Says Lewis, following Harari: "Derrida would go further than structuralism's attempt at 'a radical dismissal of the speaking subject' by putting the sign itself, spared in the initial assault on the subject, into question" (Lewis 1982: 4).

The question of whether Derrida's work represents "a kind of anti-structuralist structuralism" (4), I leave to my discussion of deconstruction below. The question of post-structuralism is the one I am considering here—as the matter of a transition already evident within structuralism. Perhaps the work of Roland Barthes best illustrates the critical activity that is both structuralist and post-structuralist at once. Barthes applied the methods of structural linguistics (using Saussure's binary oppositional model, especially his synchrony/diachrony pair) to the study of film, advertising (*Mythologies*), the system of fashion (*The Fashion System*), medicine, and other cultural sites, in some instances adopting a rigorously "scientific" approach. But as Barthes outlines in the opening pages of *The Semiotic Challenge*, contact in Paris the late 1960s with Julia Kristeva was "profoundly transforming" (Barthes 1988: 6), providing him with new concepts (such as paragram and intertextuality), and taking his structuralist work in a "poststructuralist" direction. Barthes also felt the influence of Derrida, whose work "vigorously displaced the very notion of sign, postulating the retreat of signifieds, the decentering of structures" (Barthes 1988: 6); of Michel Foucault, who "accentuated the problematics of the sign by assigning it an historical niche in the past" (6); and not the least, of Jacques Lacan, who "gave us a complete theory of the scission of the subject, without which science is doomed to remain blind and mute as to the place from which it speaks" (6). By the 1970s, many leading literary critics had, with Barthes, given up any belief in the "scientificity of Semiology" (Barthes 1988: 7). The recognition prevailed that science, too, must "acknowledge itself as *writing*" (8).

From late nineteenth-century philology to late twentieth-century semiology, the change in approach to language and text is great. Perhaps religious studies has felt this change most decisively in the anthropology of religion and comparative religion fields, particularly in the study of ritual and myth, where developments stemming from the work of Lévi-Strauss have had a decisive impact. Whether religious studies can, or will, contend with the signified-to-signifier shift remains to be seen. Certainly, in keeping also with "new approaches" introduced by women's studies, the so-called "subject"—an authorial presence, centered and male—has undergone displacement in religious studies as well as in literary theory.

Semanalyse

Lecturing at the Sorbonne some forty years after the *Course in General Linguistics* appeared, Jacques Lacan locates the beginning of modern linguistics in Saussure's signified/signifier formulation. Lacan, however, in what might be called a post-structuralist gesture, inverts the Saussurian signified/signifier formulation. This signifier does not represent a signified, Lacan says; indeed, the signifier does not have "to answer for its existence in the name of any signification whatever" (Lacan 1977a: 150). Suggesting that we abandon the "search for meaning" approach to language, Lacan turns our attention to the "structure of the signifier" (153), the way it functions through metaphoric and metonymic (dis)placements, and the way these result in the perpetual "veering off of signification" (160). No literal re-presentation here. Always missing the mark, sliding along the signifying chain, the signifier is caught up in what Lacan calls *méconnaissance* (162).

With Lacan, semiology meets psychoanalysis. And the *méconnaissance* of the signifier links to the status (and structure) of the Freudian unconscious. The signifier now plays a determinative role, from the start, in the constitution of subjectivity. This is the point of Lacan's seminal essay, "The mirror stage as formative of the function of the I as revealed in psychoanalytic experience" (in Lacan 1977a: 1–7). The concept of *le stade du miroir*, regarded by many as Lacan's most important contribution to psychological interpretation, is one he formulates, first of all, as a developmental moment or stage:

> This event can take place ... from the age of six months ... and its repetition has often made me reflect upon the startling spectacle of the infant in front of the mirror. Unable as yet to walk, or even to stand up, and held tightly, as he is by some support, human or artificial (what, in France, we call a '*trotte-bébé*'), he nevertheless overcomes, in a flutter of jubilant activity, the obstructions of his support and, fixing his attitude in a slightly leaning-forward position, in order to hold it in his gaze, brings back an instantaneous aspect of the image.
>
> For me, this activity retains the meaning I have given it up to the age of eighteen months ... *an identification*, in the full sense that analysis gives to the term, namely, the transformation, that takes place in the subject when he assumes an image ...
>
> This jubilant assumption of the specular image by the child at the *infans* stage, still sunk in his motor incapacity and nursling dependence, would seem to exhibit, in an exemplary situation the symbolic matrix in which the I is precipitated in a primordial form, before it is objectified in the dialectic of identification with the other (Lacan 1977a: 1–2).

The event that Lacan describes here is one of fundamental misrecognition (*méconnaissance*) in that the coherence of the specular body-image with which the child identifies is utterly discordant with the motor incoordination of this still-*infans* stage. At the same time, it is through this misrecognition that a transformation takes place, constituting the child as ego. Prior to this moment, the infant's biological drives are channeled primarily through the mother, but now, captivated by the image of coherence and desiring to coincide with this ideal, the child turns away from the mother in favor of the ideal object-other. This separation leads to another: just beginning now to use language, the child vests the specular "I" with positionality ("I am") in signification, so that, as Julia Kristeva puts it, "the specular image [becomes] the 'prototype' for the 'world of objects.' Positing the imaged ego leads to the positing of the object, which is, likewise, separate and signifiable" (Kristeva 1974: 46). Turning away from the mother in favor of her stand-in, the signifier; separating, as signifying-subject, from the signified body-object, and in the process undergoing a conscious/unconscious division, the child, at the mirror stage, incorporates signification's binary order of difference. For Lacan, this binary structure underpins not only language, but an entire socio-linguistic ("symbolic") system that he calls the *Law* or *Name-of-the-Father (le Nom-[non]-du-père)*. One becomes a subject, he says, only by taking one's place within this patriarchal, oppositional, signifying system. Entry into signification, as a unified subject, is thus an experience of *scission*. It requires a rupture from the mother; a detachment of the "I" from a world of signified objects and others; and in order that the self can hold to the misrecognition that the s/he is a unified consciousness, it entails a repression of the "unconscious" body.

What is "unconscious," in Lacan's reformulation of Freudian theory, has nothing to do with psychological interpretations of it as a negative concept, a non-concept, the "non-conscious, the more or less conscious, etc." (Lacan 1977b: 24), and it is entirely distinct from the "romantic unconscious" of Jungian psychoanalysis. For Lacan, the unconscious has not content as such (see Mitchell/Rose 1982: 32). Rather, it manifests itself as a disturbance or discontinuity produced through the split (*scission*) that signification effects in the subject. In Lacan's words, "the unconscious is always manifested as that which vacillates in a split in the subject" (Lacan 1977b: 28). From this split, the unconscious emerges as the "remainder" of the subject in language, the desire that is "left over" and that cannot "pass through" the signifier. Language, which cannot satisfy the self's demand for unity and is thus invariably marked by failure or loss, "leaves a metonymic remainder that runs under it ... absolute and unapprehensible ... unsatisfied, impossible, misconstrued (*méconnu*)" (Lacan 1977b: 154). This remainder (of the signifier) is the Lacanian unconscious. The remainder functions to show us "the gap" between what the signifying subject "is" and what it would be.

For Lacan, all signification is marked by this remainder of the subject's "*manque-à-être*," its "want-to-be" (Lacan 1977a: 311). As his work progresses, then, he comes to view the mirror stage drama not simply as an isolated event that occurs only once, and prior to the assumption of language. For one thing, such an event, by definition, would lie outside of language, in a space/place of prehistory that is theorizable only in fictional terms. But more importantly, Lacan, as a psychoanalyst, is not so much interested in developmental (or other) origins, as he is in the functioning of the subject in language, where "man's desire is the desire of the Other," that is, desire of unity or certainty that language simply cannot secure (Lacan 1977b: 38). Rather than a developmental event, the mirror stage becomes a narrative of signification, of the drama of identification/splitting that is (re)enacted each time a subject assumes a position in the *Law-of-the-Father*. This positioning is constitutive of sexual, as well as subject, identity. No more than subjectivity, is sexual identity "natural" or biologically pre-given, Lacan says: it is formed through the sign, reformed in each event of signification. Each time s/he signifies, the would-be subject has to line up on one side or other of the *Law-of-the-Father*'s binary divide: *either* one enters the patriarchal symoblic order as *homo rationalis*, a unified conscious ego for whom identity grants mastering truth; *or*, one is marginalized and excluded as "other." In Lacan's terminology, the phallus refers to the former position. As distinct from the sexual organ, the "phallus" signifies a subject-position in language, a position of unity, mastery, truth. Since, however, this position is based in *méconnaissance*, the phallic position must always be false. Moreover, since the subject's unconscious remainder cannot be completely closed off, the phallus is a cover-up that never succeeds.

With Lacan, our understanding of language, of signification, undergoes a radical change. Language, no longer separate and apart from the subject, now becomes constitutive of (sexual-subject) identity, a self-identity that is never fixed or stable, but that must be re-made with each signification. Lacan's notion of an original *méconnaissance* obviously undermines all confidence in the truth-value of the signified. And with Lacan, even as focus shifts to the signifier, signification, rather than a matter of delivering a message or meaning, turns into a repeated drama of *scission*. Approaching signification as this kind of drama changes our sense of what it is to interpret (read and write) texts. For one thing, interpretation now attends to the markings of the "unconscious" in a text; it attends to "something other" (Lacan 1977b: 24), something that, as unconscious, is un-representable but that manifests itself nonetheless through gaps, "marks, stains, spots" (35), in the text. Lacan himself gives us many examples of this new mode of interpretation in his re-reading of Freud's work on dreams.

Perhaps Lacan's work receives its most important elaboration for religious studies in the publications of Julia Kristeva, his one-time student and a practicing psychoanalyst herself. In several essays and books, Kristeva develops and tests Lacan's theories by way of analyzing religious rituals and texts. Kristeva sets the stage for this engagement with religious studies in *Revolution in Poetic Language* (1974), where she develops Lacan's concept of the mirror stage into a new theory of the subject, what she came to call *le sujet en procès*: the subject in process/on trial. Here, in an attempt "to go beyond the theatre of linguistic representations to make room for pre- or translinguistic modalities of psychic inscription" (Kristeva 1987a: 5), she borrows the term *chora* from Plato's *Timeus* and uses it to designate both *anteriority* and *heterogeneity*. The *chora* signifies a mythical space or phase "anterior" to the mirror stage and the child's acquisition of language, a pre-verbal "rhythmic space, which has no thesis and no position" (Kristeva 1974: 26); and it also designates a heterogeneousness beyond representation, an unconscious supplementarity that belongs inescapably to the process of *signifiance*. From the *chora* emanate the energy charges which Kristeva associates with the operation of the "semiotic" (*le sémiotique*). As "articulated by flow and marks: facilitation, energy transfers, the cutting up of the corporeal and social continuum as well as that of signifying material" (40), the semiotic is distinct from the (Lacanian) "symbolic" (*le symbolique*), language as representation, meaning, sign. Always "ambivalent," signification, in whatever form, involves both the semiotic and symbolic modalities: even as the metalanguage of a monological subject, signification cannot completely close off the semiotic, and neither is there any possibility of meaningful signification outside the pro-positioning of a conscious subject. The psychoanalytic *sujet en procès* is interminably in-process/on trial between the semiotic and symbolic.

Related to this distinction of the semiotic and symbolic is Kristeva's theory of the text as a production, "a process, an *engendrement*" (Lewis 1974: 30) which includes both *géno-texte* and *phéno-texte*. She uses the latter term "to denote language that serves to communicate" (Kristeva 1974: 87). The phenotext, she says, is a structure that "obeys rules of communication and presupposes a subject of enunciation and an addressee" (87). The genotext, however, is not a linguistic structure but a generative process, "a *process*, which tends to articulate structures that are ephemeral (unstable, threatened by drive charges, 'quanta' rather than 'marks') and nonsignifying (devices that do not have a double articulation)" (86), but which are nonetheless detectable in the phenotext. Although, as Christopher Johnson points out (Johnson 1988: 74), "[t]he relationship linking the geno- and pheno-texts is one of translation," Kristeva does not think of "translation" as the "zero-one" passage from an underlying original to a surface copy. There is no one-to-one correspondence between the genotext and the phenotext, the sort of correspondence which is suggested by Chomsky's Cartesian model of deep structure and surface structure, she says; and the geno-text, not an *other scene* but an *ensemble of other scenes*, is generative of signifying operations which exceed the limit of sentence-meaning (Kristeva 1969: 281–84). Through these operations, the genotext imprints its seal in the phenotext, leaves its markers to be read. *Semanalyse*, the practice of the text, always includes both semiotic and symbolic, genotext and phenotext.

In *Powers of Horror: An Essay on Abjection* (1982) Kristeva uses this theory of the subject-in-process and the text-as-practice to explores the representation of the body, particularly the female body, in the Christian West. The book begins by introducing "abjection" as the process through which the separation of subject from object, self from other, mind from body, spirit from matter, and man from woman is made. Abjection, she suggests, and demonstrates, provides a way to "read the bible." It is also, she says, a particularly useful concept for reading misogynist texts. In *Tales of Love* (1987), on the other hand, Kristeva analyzes the other pole of subject-making and text-practice, the pole of idealization. Sections of the book deal with the Christian, as distinct from the Judaic, concept of love; other sections read this "Christian love" in the writing of Thomas Aquinas and Bernard of Clairvaux. The essay "Stabat Mater" is printed on a split page, so as to juxtapose two discourses, the academic-philosophical on one side, and the connotative-poetic on the other (the symbolic, some say, on one side, the semiotic on the other). The poetic-semiotic dimension of the essay disrupts the conventional rendering of Christianity's Virgin Mary, highlighting the division of the body in language and perhaps "acting out" the "abject" status of the female body in Christian tradition. Several other of Kristeva's publications explore her theory of subject and text in a religious, particularly Christian, context—*Black Sun* (1989) a work on melancholia, is a notable example, as is *In the Beginning Was Love* (1987a). An extensive secondary literature has developed on the implications of Kristeva's *semanalyse* for the study of religion.

Grammatology

I opened this discussion of "new approaches" by referring to a 1968 interview with Kristeva, "Semiology and Grammatology" (published in English in *Positions* in 1981), in which Jacques Derrida, while acknowledging Saussure's challenge to the metaphysical tradition, puts the Saussurian sign into question. With its distinction between the signified and the signifier, the sign "leaves open the possibility of thinking *a concept signified in and of itself*," Derrida maintains (Derrida 1981: 19). As if there could be a "transcendental signified," that is, "a concept independent of language" (20), a "pure thought" of which "signifiers" are the vehicle, the signified/signifier formulation, by virtue of the distinction, the bar it places between the sign's two terms, is "problematical at its root" (20). As well, and related to the first point, Saussure in the *Course*, contradicting his own postulation of arbitrariness, privileges speech, "everything that links the sign to *phoné*. He also speaks of the 'natural link' between thought and voice, meaning and sound," Derrida writes. "He even speaks of 'thought-sound'" (21).

The sign, in short, privileges the concept and/as phonic. It thereby confirms a central tenet of metaphysics: that in the interior space of the self, an unspoken voice is tied to the concept; indeed, "the voice is consciousness itself," such that in my thought of a concept, a signified, I also hear a signifier, one "requiring the use of no instrument, no accessory, no force taken from the world" (22). The assumption is of a pure inside, an "inner speech" that reveals the identity of things without having to pass out into the world. This idealizing of voice involves a collapsing of space and time into (self-) presence, "as point [*stigmè*] of the now or of the moment [*nun*]" (Derrida 1974: 12). Indeed, in the tradition of *phonocentrism* that extends "from Plato to Husserl, passing through Aristotle, Rousseau, Hegel, etc." (Derrida 1981: 22), the inner voice presumes "a self-proximity that would in fact be the absolute reduction of space in general" (Derrida 1973: 79). The tradition places the "exterior" signifier, whether spoken or written, in a position of secondariness, Derrida claims; the spoken or written signifier represents a loss of proximity, of presence, and a "fall into the world" (Derrida 1981: 22). Derrida offers a sustained critique of this metaphysical tradition of the sign in *Speech and Phenomena and Other Essays on Husserl's Theory of Signs* (1967, trans. 1973), one of three major works (the others are *Writing and Difference* and *Of Grammatology*) he published in 1967, and the one he thought should be read first.

Insofar as "junking" the concept of the sign is impossible, one must, Derrida says in his interview with Kristeva, remain within semiology and within metaphysics (Derrida 1981: 24). "I do not believe in decisive ruptures, in an unequivocal 'epistemological break,' as it is called today. Breaks are always, and fatally, re-inscribed in an old cloth that must continually, interminably, be undone" (24). In part, Derrida's method of "un-doing" works by altering our model of structure and/or of sign. In the interview with Kristeva, for instance, he proposes "*gram*" or "*différance*" as "a new concept of writing," a concept that transposes semiology into "grammatology" (26). In another interview also published in *Positions*, Derrida adds several other new "grammatological" concepts to *gram* and *différance*: *hymen*, *mark*, *incision*, *trace*, all of these belonging to "a kind of *general strategy of deconstruction*" (Derrida 1981: 41). Derrida describes deconstruction a "strategy of the textual work" (59), where the text is "the materialist text, which has long been repressed-suppressed by logocentric discourse (idealism, metaphysics, religion)" (61). Deconstruction is always a double gesture. It first of all puts in question a number of essential premises that "are all in fact ordered around being present (*étant-present*), presence to self—which implies therefore a certain interpretation of temporality: identity to self, positionality, property, personality, ego, consciousness, will, intentionality, freedom, humanity, etc." (Derrida 1991: 109). In this first gesture, deconstruction demonstrates how this authority of being-present is at work in a given text, even as, in a simultaneous second gesture, it affirms differences, "the processes of *différance*, trace, iterability, ex-appropriation, and so on" (109), that are operating in the same text and that submit that authority to question. Deconstruction, Derrida insists, is never a matter of introducing something from the outside to the inside of a text, but only of re-marking something that is already there, a distance or absence that belongs to so-called presence from the start.

It is important to note that deconstruction transforms the sign, replaces the concept of "sign" with that of "gram." The latter never escapes exteriority or the movement/deferral that Derrida says is constitutive of language. The gram (along with the supplement, the hymen, and other related terms) is akin to the Heideggerian trait, "as a tracing incision (*entame*) of language," Derrida explains in "The *Retrait* of Metaphor" (1978b: 10). The trait is always a *retrait*, a graphic mark from which presence has already withdrawn; the suspensive "movement of withdrawal" is indissociable, for Derrida as for Heidegger, "from the movement of presence or of truth" (Derrida 1978b: 20). Instead of the sign, then, a graphics of withdrawal, "the surcharge of a supplementary trait, of a double trait (*re-trait*), of a supplementary fold" (21). The gram or the trait, unlike the sign, is, Derrida says, "structurally in withdrawal" (29). The withdrawal is not secondary to pure presence or inner speech, "the trait is *a priori* withdrawal" (29).

> Its inscription, as I have attempted to articulate it in the trace or in difference, succeeds only in being effaced (*n'arrive qu'à s'effacer*).
>
> It happens and comes about only in effacing itself. Inversely, the trait is not derived. It is not secondary, in its arrival in relation to the domains, or the essences, or

to the existences that it cuts away, frays, and refolds in their re-cut. The *re-* of *re-trait* is not an accident occurring to the trait. (Derrida 1978b: 29)

The trait, for Derrida, is the "intractable structure in which we are implicated and deflected from the outset" (Derrida 1978b: 13). Paul Ricoeur does not take the structure into consideration when he launches his attack on deconstruction in *The Rule of Metaphor*, Derrida claims. Because Derrida's work not does not take us from the signifier to the signified, or from the materialist text to the concept, as does the tradition of metaphysics and its theory of the sign, Ricoeur charges Derrida with "revers[ing] the pattern of philosophical augmentation" (Ricoeur 1977: 258–59). Derrida does not allow the sign (e.g., metaphor) to be productive of new meaning, new possibilities for philosophy, Ricoeur maintains. Rather, deconstruction moves in the opposite direction, from semantic innovation (signified) to ornament or figure (signifier). The counter-movement, Ricoeur says, is destructive. In *The Rule of Metaphor*, Derrida's work on metaphor is said to be but "one episode in a much vaster strategy of deconstruction that always consists in destroying metaphysical discourse" (Ricoeur 1977: 287). Derrida, for his part, puts into question precisely the notion of semantic or philosophical augmentation, asking whether the relation of metaphor (signifier) to concept, and the model of language as "a continuous and linearly accumulative capitalization" (Derrida 1978b: 13) of signifieds, ideas, does not reduce or efface the diversionary and discontinuous structure of the gram or the trait.

Derrida's enormous output of publications continues to change our understanding of what it is to read and write texts—as other than vehicles of signifieds. His own meticulous, text-by-text, re-reading of the European tradition of metaphysics continues, focusing recently on Heidegger and Freud and engaging the work of many traditional "religious" figures. Perhaps more directly, Derrida continues to work with specifically religious texts and figures: he has written on biblical semiotics, the Book of Revelations, for example; he has written on mysticism and negative theology; his work on Augustine and the *Confessions*, and confession, is ongoing, and was the subject of a recent major conference; he has written extensively on Emmanuel Levinas; his work on the gift, friendship and mourning as religious themes continues to be elaborated; and not the least, his work on the family is proving important for women's studies. A significant secondary literature on Derrida has developed within most religious studies fields.

Bibliography

Anidjar, Gil (2002), "Introduction," in: Jacques Derrida, *Acts of Religion*. New York: Routledge: 1–41.

Barthes, Roland (1957), *Mythologies*. Annette Lavers. London: Granada.

— (1974), *S/Z*, trans. Richard Miller. New York: Hill and Wang.

— (1983), *The Fashion System*, trans. Matthew Ward/Richard Howard. New York: Hill and Wang.
— (1988), *The Semiotic Challenge*, trans. Richard Howard. Berkeley, Calif.: University of California Press.
Bennington, Geoff/Young, Robert (1987), "Introduction: Posting the Question," in: *Post-structuralism and the Question of History*, ed. by Derek Attridge/Geoff Bennington/Robert Young. Cambridge: Cambridge University Press: 1–11.
Blanchot, Maurice (1986), *The Writing of the Disaster*, trans. Ann Smock. Lincoln, Nebr.: University of Nebraska Press.
Caputo, John D. (1997), *The Prayers and Tears of Jacques Derrida: Religion without Religion*. Bloomington, Ind.: Indiana University Press.
Caputo, John D./Scanlon, Michael J. (1999), *God, the Gift, and Postmodernism*. Bloomington, Ind.: Indiana University Press.
Crownfield, David, ed. (1992), *Body/Text in Julia Kristeva: Religion, Women, and Psychoanalysis*. Albany, N.Y.: State University of New York Press.
Derrida, Jacques (1973), *Speech and Phenomena: And Other Essays on Husserl's Theory of Signs*, trans. David Allison. Evanston, Ill.: Northwestern University Press.
— (1974), *Of Grammatology*, trans. Gayatri Spivak. Baltimore, Md.: Johns Hopkins University Press.
— (1978a), *Writing and Difference*, trans. Alan Bass. Chicago: University of Chicago Press.
— (1978b), "The Retrait of Metaphor," in: *Enclitic* 2: 4–33.
— (1981) *Positions*, trans. Alan Bass. Chicago: The University of Chicago Press.
— (1991), "'Eating Well,' or the Calculation of the Subject: An Interview with Jacques Derrida," trans. Peter Connor/Avital Ronnell, in: *Who Comes after the Subject?*, ed. by Eduardo Cadava/Peter Connor/Jean-Luc Nancy. New York: Routledge: 96–119.
— (2002), *Acts of Religion*, ed. and with an Introduction by Gil Anidjar. New York: Routledge.
Derrida, Jacques/Vattimo, Giannni (1998), *Religion*. Stanford, Calif.: Stanford University Press.
Descombes, Vincent (1979), *Le Même et L'Autre: Quarante-Cinq Ans de Philosophie Française*. Paris: Minuit.
Garber, Marjorie/Hanssen, Beatrice/Walkowitz, Rebecca L., eds. (2000), *The Turn to Ethics*. New York: Routledge.
Groden, Michael/Kreiswirth, Martin, eds. (1994), *The Johns Hopkins Guide to Literary Theory & Criticism*. Baltimore, Md.: Johns Hopkins University Press.
Harari, Josué V., ed. (1979), *Textual Strategies: Perspectives in Post-Structuralist Criticism*. Ithaca, N.Y.: Cornell University Press.
Jakobson, Roman (1987), "Two Aspects of Language and Two Types of Aphasic Disturbance," in: *Language in Literature*, ed. by Krystyna Pomorska/Stephen Rudy. Cambridge, Mass.: Harvard University Press: 95–114.
Joy, Morny/O'Grady, Kathleen/Poxon, Judith L. (2002), *French Feminists on Religion*. New York: Routledge.
Krell, David Farrell (2000), *The Purest of Bastards: Works of Mourning, Art, and Affirmation in the Thought of Jacques Derrida*. University Park, Pa.: The Pennsylvania State University Press.
Kristeva, Julia (1969). *Séméiotiké: recherches pour une sémanalyse*. Paris: Seuil.

— (1974), *Revolution in Poetic Language*, trans. Margaret Waller. New York: Columbia University Press.

— (1982), *Powers of Horror: An Essay on Abjection*, trans. Leon Roudiez. New York: Columbia University Press.

(1987a), *In the Beginning Was Love: Psychoanalysis and Faith*, trans. Arthur Goldhammer. New York: Columbia University Press.

— (1987b), *Tales of Love*, trans. Leon Roudiez. New York: Columbia University Press.

— (1989), *Black Sun: Depression and Melancholy*, trans. Leon Roudiez. New York: Columbia University Press.

Lacan, Jacques (1977a), *Écrits: A Selection*, trans. Alan Sheridan. New York: W.W. Norton.

— (1977b), *The Four Fundamental Concepts of Psychoanalysis*, trans. Alan Sheridan. New York: W.W. Norton.

— (1988a), *The Seminar of Jacques Lacan Book I: Freud's Papers on Technique 1953–1954*, trans. John Forrester. New York: W.W. Norton.

— (1988b), *The Seminar of Jacques Lacan Book II: The Ego in Freud's Theory and in the Technique of Psychoanalysis 1954–1955*, trans. Sylvana Tomaselli. New York: W.W. Norton.

Lewis, Philip (1974), "Revolutionary Semiotics," in: *Diacritics* 4: 28–32.

— (1982), "The Post-Structuralist Condition," in: *Diacritics* 12: 2–24.

Makaryk, Irena R. (1993), *Encyclopedia of Contemporary Literary Theory: Approaches, Scholars, Terms*. Toronto: University of Toronto Press.

Mitchell, Juliet/Rose, Jacqueline, eds. (1982), *Feminine Sexuality: Jacques Lacan and the école freudienne*. New York: W.W. Norton.

Oliver, Kelly (1993), *Reading Kristeva: Unraveling the Double-bind*. Bloomington, Ind.: Indiana University Press.

Ricoeur, Paul (1977), *The Rule of Metaphor*, trans. Robert Czerny. Toronto: University of Toronto Press.

Roudiez, Leon (1972), "Twelve Points from Tel Quel," in: *Esprit Createur* 14: 4 (Winter): 291–303.

Saussure, Ferdinand de (1959), *Course in General Linguistics*, trans. Wade Baskin. New York: McGraw-Hill.

Sturrock, John, ed. (1979), *Structuralism and Since: From Lévi-Strauss to Derrida*. Oxford: Oxford University Press.

Section 5

Comparative Approaches

Comparison in the Study of Religion

by

WILLIAM E. PADEN

> In many ways, the enterprise of comparison remains to this day both our greatest asset and our worst liability. On the one hand, most historians of religions would still want to argue that comparison—understood in the *strong* sense, as both cross-cultural and trans-historical—is perhaps our greatest claim to originality as an independent academic discipline, distinguished from other disciplines like theology or anthropology. But on the other hand, most would also be forced to admit that the confusion about just what comparison *is* remains perhaps our single greatest weakness and most acute source of embarrassment. It has long marked us, in the eyes of our colleagues, as a discipline that cannot define itself or defend itself against charges of crypto-theologizing, cultural imperialism or naive universalism. (Urban 2000: 340–41)

As comparison is a facet of all thought and all methodology, and hence unlimited as an issue, in this report I will focus solely on the primary site of the current debate, the problematic of cross-cultural categorization. I will also concentrate on the secular rather than the religious or dialogical forms that comparativism in religious studies has taken.

The phrase "comparative religion" typically signified the study of all forms and traditions of religious life as distinguished from the study or exposition of just one. But how to do this? With which units of comparison? Which categories of classification? In what context does one compare? Every conceivable theoretic and religious enterprise has staked out its maps of the territory.

While Mircea Eliade's "history of religions" model created influential thematic analyses of cross-cultural topics like sacred space and cosmogonic origins, it did so within a religious and ahistorical framework that has been called into question by the current generation of more sociologically oriented religious studies scholars. Thus the Eliadean lexicons, epitomized in *Patterns in Comparative Religion* (1958; first published 1949) and reflected in the Eliade-edited *Encyclopedia of Religion* (1987) have receded in their authority. Other phenomenologies have found themselves to be abandoned houses, too, but in many ways the problem of comparison has been posed as "the problem of Eliade." While the above epigraph by Hugh Urban therefore summarily states the issue, attempts at solution have also evolved. For if, on the one hand, postmodernists have eschewed comparativism as a form of hegemonizing, an extension of Eurocentric, essentialized categories that erase local and historical contextuality, then on the other hand, inspired by Jonathan Z. Smith's critical essays written from within the history of religions tradition, the very problematic nature of comparison has spurred renewed attempts at conceptual reformulation. The following report elaborates on this state of affairs.

Challenges to Comparativism

Comparativism in the last decades of the century has been surrounded and put on the defensive from several sides. One is the critical ideological climate that questions conceptual hegemonies. There are several versions of this critique, occasioned by a poststructuralist, postmodern climate combined with an age of specialization and area studies. Yet another is from the scientific side, from voices that urge more theoretically sophisticated generalization.

Comparativism as imperialistic. One argument is that the classifications of comparative religion are not neutral but have ideological, sociopolitical functions (McCutcheon 1997). To classify is to exercise the concerns of a particular culture, class, religion or gender. Cross-cultural categories therefore replace the life of other cultures with the meanings and metanarratives of one's own, suppressing the voices of others under the projected illusions of homogeneity. The objectivizing templates of the scholar thus make invisible the actual on-the-ground strategies and dispositions of the insiders (Bourdieu 1977). To compare is to abstract and to abstract is to control. Comparative thematizations can then amount to political arrogance and self-authorization.

Comparativism as religiously biased. The most obvious ideological imposition onto comparative categories has been religion itself. Comparative religion has clearly been historically allied with various religious interests and assumptions. Generic to many of these is the universalistic idea that religious histories are "expressions" of a foundational religious reality, e.g. the Divine or the Sacred. Consequently, the many forms of religious life then become automatically construed as forms of spirituality or revelation. Other, conservative religious comparativisms are more judgmental, classifying religions according to their degrees of truth or adequacy and advocating a "unique," normative religious truth as the ultimate frame of reference. In contrast, the need to distinguish the exposition of religion (even if it takes a "comparative" approach) from the critical study *of* religion has been made repeatedly (Martin 2000b; Wiebe 1999; McCutcheon 1997).

Comparativism as anti-contextual. Comparative concepts necessarily abstract from historical contexts. They therefore ignore what things "mean" to historical, religious insiders. Moreover, cultural systems function as wholes and hence their behavioral elements cannot be separately lifted out of that holistic context and meaningfully compared (Wiebe 1996: 27). That generalities cannot capture the particularities of culture has also been a longstanding axiom for many anthropologists like Clifford Geertz for whom cultures need to be understood through their own terminologies and internal signification systems. The distinctive features of a culture are what are interesting, not the generalities they have in common (Geertz 1983: 43). The critique of comparativism has therefore gone hand in hand with a renewed affirmation of social contextuality as a site for the study and explanation of religion. Thus, cultural studies, gender studies, area studies and postcolonial studies have likewise moved to define the field in opposition to the supposed synchronic, contextless, objectivizing nature of cross-cultural phenomenologies.

A variant on the problem of context is that archetypal patterns—Eliade's, for instance—are typically used to show similarity at the expense of difference. That is, when historical examples are given, it is only to illustrate a given theme, and the risk here is that from the "example" one may not learn more than what one already knew from the theme—the latter resembling a cookie-cutter mold that simply clones itself. Thus, copies of the Eliadean "world center" or "cosmic tree" could be noted around the world as replicas of the archetypes, but the sociocultural, contextual meanings and differences of these "centers" would be ignored.

Comparativism as non-theoretical. There is also criticism from an opposite direction, from those investigating new forms of scientifically grounded theory (Lawson 1996; Boyer 2001). Where postmodernism values cultural specificity and questions generalization, scientific concerns take the reverse position. The argument here is that comparativism has been too much a cultural apologetic and not theoretical enough. Hence, it is not that generalizations are bad, but that we have not learned how to give them proper, evidentiary grounding or explanatory power (Martin 2000: 48). Comparativism classically had operated solely at the level of positing and illustrating certain culturally derived themes, but this fails to ground the study of religion in infrastructural cognitive or behavioral processes that lie behind cultural meanings and it does not supply a reflexive, critical methodology of concept formation. For example, while postmodernism says that universal recurrence cannot be objectively certified, cognitivist approaches say we have not yet begun to find it at the right levels.

Jonathan Z. Smith on Comparison

Undoubtedly the prime catalyst for both challenging and reformulating the role of comparison in the study of religion has been the University of Chicago scholar, Jonathan Z. Smith (b. 1938). Among the reconstructive emphases and features of his work are: the reflexive, tactical nature of data selection in theory-driven comparison; the distinction between universals and analytic generalizations; the strategic role of "difference" in comparisons; the need to find a balance and relationship between comparative, generic forms and historical complexity; the pertinence of understanding principles of comparison in other fields, such as biology, anthropology, and the various principles of taxonomy and classification; the important difference between homological (genealogical, derivative) and analogical (similarity of function rather than of origin) comparison; and the relationship of comparison to description, generalization, and concept formation generally.

Smith's influential work has amounted to a significant second-order tradition on comparativist methodology. While paralleling some of the postmodern objections to comparativism—for example, that "facts" are not objectivities but selected "exempla" for our own imaginative productions—Smith at the same time advocates the possibility of the responsible employment of comparative patterns applied to historical materials. Since the time of his Yale doctoral thesis on comparativist issues in Frazer's *The Golden Bough*—and while relentlessly challenging pseudo-comparisons—Smith never abandoned interest in constructive issues of classification and comparativist theory.

I expand here on several of Smith's points that appear to have struck wide interest.

1) *Comparison as natural activity.* Smith directs attention to comparison as a natural mental activity.

> The process of comparison is a fundamental characteristic of human intelligence. Whether revealed in the logical grouping of classes, in poetic similes, in mimesis, or other like activities—comparison, the bringing together of two or more objects for the purpose of noting either similarity or dissimilarity, is the omnipresent substructure of human thought. Without it, we could not speak, perceive, learn or reason. (1978: 241)

The question then is not whether to compare, but how. Moreover, to fail to classify or compare "is to condemn the study of religion to an inconclusive study of individuals and individual phenomena" (Smith 1996: 402).

2) *Modes of comparison.* Smith historicized and distinguished various genres of comparison, identifying four modes: the ethnographic, encyclopedic, morphological and evolutionary (1978: 240–64; 1982: 19–35). The ethnographic is the impressionistic, subjective perception of similarities and differences relative to one's own cultural assumptions. It is the typical mode of the traveler. The encyclopedic mode, in contrast, is the mode of the reader, and arranges culled examples by topical headings, according to culturally based thematic and religious notions. Here the data simply and loosely "cohabit" the groupings. The morphological, epitomized by Eliade's *Patterns in Comparative Religion,* identifies ahistorical, archetypal forms, like the regenerative, axial "World Tree," or the "death and rebirth" pattern—forms that take variants and developments in time and space, but at base represent logical ideas. Eliade's morphology is itself genealogically connected with Goethe's ideas about "Urformen" (Smith 2000). Finally, the evolutionary type classifies persistence and

change over time. However, while fruitfully applied in biology, the human sciences illegitimately read history through previously conceived ahistorical archetypes which were then written into history as value-laden chronological developments.

Smith considered none of these adequate, though the evolutionary had potential and so would morphology if it involved "integration of a complex notion of pattern and system with an equally complex notion of history" (1982: 29) and could avoid an ontological superstructure (2000: 346–51).

3) *Controlled comparison.* "Generalizing," Smith writes, "is a comparative and taxonomic activity that intentionally focuses attention, across differences, on co-occurrences of selected, stipulated, characteristics while ignoring others" (2001: xii).

> ... there is nothing "given" or "natural" in those elements selected for comparison. Similarities and differences, understood as aspects and relations, rather than as "things," are the result of mental operations undertaken by scholars in the interest of their intellectual goals. Comparison selects and marks certain features within difference as being of possible intellectual significance by employing the trope of their being similar in some stipulated sense. (2000: 239)

In this sense, comparison is metaphoric. It is not about the way things "are," but a creative juxtaposition in order to make a point or discovery a relationship, a "disciplined exaggeration in the service of knowledge" (1990: 52).

The activity of comparison has a basic structure. First, there is a common term which makes comparison possible, and which is an expression of the scholar's area of interest; but in addition there is a second, implicit term by which differences are addressed, also a term that directs the scholar's area of interests. At the same time, because taxons (classifiers) are typically assemblages of elements rather than single features, that is, polythetic rather than monothetic, then comparativists should be careful about essentializing the taxon.

4) *Description and redescription.* Smith stresses that what might appear to the naive eye as historical data, and hence subject matter simply awaiting the hand of the comparativist, requires several stages of analysis. The four moments in the comparative enterprise include: description in two steps, comparison, redescription, and rectification (2000: 239). Description first locates a given example in the texture of the environment that gives it its significance, but *also* gives "a careful account of how *our* second-order scholarly tradition has intersected with the exemplum" (2000: 239). For example, many of the so-called data have come to us pre-filtered by Western interpretation and historical invention. Also, in the phase of description the comparativist must recognize that religious objects are always moving and always changing—over against the natural tendency of the scholar to "freeze" a phenomenon through a generalization (Smith 1990: 106–109). When this "double contextualization" is completed one can move on to a second example undertaken in the same manner.

Comparison may then be undertaken "in terms of aspects and relations held to be significant, and with respect to some category, question, theory, or model of interest to us" (2000: 239). "The aim of such a comparison is the redescription of the exempla (each in light of the other) and a rectification of the academic categories in relation to which they have been imagined" (239).

5) *Examples.* Smith's work challenged and tested received notions of patterns against closely sifted historical data. An example is his analysis of Eliade's attribution of the "center of the world" motif to the portable pole of the Australian Arunta (Smith 1987: 1–23). Smith claimed that while Eliade interpreted the pole as a kind of "world axis" that could be carried place to place, allowing the tribe to remain "at the Center" and "in its universe," a careful, descriptive examination of the matter showed that Australian notions of space (based on memorializing rather than "constructing," and on "traces" and "tracks" rather than hierarchic edifices) significantly differed from Near Eastern prototypes—prototypes that featured centralized political control, vertical relations between upper and lower worlds, and constructed places. Smith concluded that "The 'Center' is not a secure pattern to which data may be brought as illustrative; it is a dubious notion that will have to be established anew on the basis of detailed comparative endeavors" (Smith 1987: 17).

An example of Smith's own imaginative, "redescriptive" comparativism is his treatment of the theme of "canon" (1982: 36–52). Here he showed how a comparison of the biblical notion with instances like Yoruba divination systems and Australian aboriginal ancestral design systems could illuminate the common idea of an authoritative list of fixed elements that one nevertheless creatively interpreted and applied to any occasion. In each diverse case we find the hermeneutical practice of exegesis and its "ingenuity."

Smith also demonstrated the use of ideal types, coining the terms "locative" and "utopian" to clarify the language and practice of two different forms of worldview (1978: 130–42, 291–94). The first, conservative form gives sacrality to things being kept in their proper place; the second features freedom or salvation *from* place. Locative worlds feature loyalties of home and kinship; utopian ("no-place") worlds, often occasioned by diasporic situatedness, find order to be negative and turn to new or transcendent worlds (1978: xii–xiv). In the one, order and boundaries are positive; in the other, they are tyrannical or meaningless. Historical data, such as that of the early Christianities, will be construed differently depending on which of these is the operative analogy (1990: 110–15, 121–33).

In sum, for Smith comparison is not an indulgence in religious archetypes—on the whole, his interest is in "dismantling … the old theological and imperialistic impulses toward totalization, unification, and integration" (1982: 18)—but a secular, reflexive endeavor to find intelligible aspectual linkages between phenomena and to find generalizations that make sets of historical data more intelligible.

Smith's work has begun to come under some review. Hugh Urban, for example, asserts that Smith has an "unarticulated and undefended" point of view which is "essentially a neo-Enlightenment view of the human being as a rational, pragmatic agent, who cannot stand 'incongruity' or cognitive dissonance in his worlds, and who therefore tells myths and engages in rituals in order to mediate the inescapable incongruities of his world" (Urban 2000: 362). Such a rationalist view placed on the world, according to Urban, makes all other worlds rationalist enterprises (2000: 364–65). Smith's challenge to the generality of the archetype of "the center" has been responded to by the more cognitively oriented Lawrence Sullivan who argues that the notion of centering need not be limited to "the politics of empire" (2000: 228–29), but as shown in Sullivan's own work on South American religion can be a "key to hydraulic systems, color schemes, tonal scales, anatomical functions, psychic life, and artistic expression," and is also relevant in the brain sciences that address issues of attention and focus (2000: 228–29). One could also point out that at least on the surface Smith's emphasis on comparison as an act of imagination occludes potential linkages with the work of the human sciences that attempt to translate religious expressions into "real" transcultural human processes.

Rebuilding Comparativism

The issue of comparativism has of course been addressed by a range of other scholars, several of them influenced by Smith. For example, a specific response to the challenge of postmodernism is *A Magic Still Dwells: Comparative Religion in the Postmodern Age*, edited by Kimberley Patton and Benjamin Ray (2000). Fourteen historians of religion here address that theme. Smith's classic essay, "In Comparison a Magic Dwells," is reprinted at the beginning of the volume, and Smith adds an Epilogue summarizing his notion of the comparative method. The editors write:

> Recognizing that Smith used the term "magic" derogatorily, we do so, not as an act of defiance nor even one of irony, but rather to highlight a reenvisioned potential for comparative study. We reclaim the term "magic" to endorse and to extend his claim that comparison is an indeterminate scholarly procedure that is best undertaken as an intellectually creative enterprise, not as a science but as an art—an imaginative and critical act of mediation and redescription in the service of knowledge. (Patton/Ray 2000: 4)

While the essays are philosophically diverse, they all attempt to defend the prospects of comparativism in an age of relativism. Many of them distinguish between an older comparative religion that operates through commonalities and a newer comparative perspective that has the capacity to acknowledge difference as well as similarity.

Another set of papers addressing the prospect of a so-called "new comparativism" was generated by a 1994 meeting of the North American Association for the Study of Religion (Martin et al. 1996). The panel, responding to William Paden's position paper on "Elements of a New Comparativism," probed whether theoretical and methodological reformulation of the concept of comparison can accommodate such issues as the politics of otherness, the new cognitivist views of mind/brain, and issues of contextual adequacy.

Several of the emphases and directions of a contemporary comparativism may now be outlined as follows

1) *Conceptual control of comparison*. A particularly substantive statement advocating the notion of controlled selectivity is that of John Fitz Porter Poole (1986). Poole's analysis identified ways in which comparison selects analogical aspects of phenomena. By focusing on and controlling the exact point of analogy, the comparativist understands that the objects may be quite incomparable in other respects and for other purposes (414). "Comparison," he writes, "does not deal with phenomena *in toto* or in the round, but only with an aspectual characteristic of them ... Neither phenomenologically whole entities nor their local meanings are preserved in comparison" (414, 415). Nor, because two or more things do not appear "the same" on the surface, or as wholes, does it mean that they are not comparable in *some* ways. A basic example might help: It could be said of two or more dogs that they are mammals, but such a generic point of parity does not deny that the particular dogs exist in their own interactive environments and significations, which are obviously unique, or that there are differences among mammals and among canines. Only a single common feature is selected for comparison and explanation. In Catherine Bell's words, "Terms afford a useful focus on some things at the expense of other things" (2000: 11).

Jeffrey Carter's use of Bertrand Russell's theory of logical types, applied to comparativism, is a similar case in point (Carter 1998). Carter argues that description and explanation constitute different genres of comparison. The first compares by describing something as having distinguishable marks of difference from its environment and from the known categories of the describer. Its object is to point to particularity. That includes comparison between members of a class. (To pursue my example, one might say, "this particular dog is black and white, has three legs, likes raspberries, and has the name 'Zeus'".) In contrast, explanatory comparison, instead of specifying differences, connects and combines phenomenon within an overall map of some kind ("this dog is a mammal," or "this dog is a hunting dog"). The logic of the class membership of explanatory comparison is such that there is a fundamental gap or disparity between map and territory. No single map can portray the complexity of the territory.

While there is a gap between explanation and description, because the former deals with maps and the latter with particularities, and because explanation is a higher logical type than description, in both cases there is a gap between the attribution and the actual "things" described/explained. One cannot draw conclusions about a class by referring to a member of the class—for example, where the class is "religion," and the member is "Theravada Buddhism," or inversely, where one can deduce from my dog the nature of all dogs.

For Carter there is then "a certain postmodern character" to this model. Explanation, for example, is "a constructive process that is contextual and purposeful, and is not simply authoritative, constant, or universal" (143). Likewise, with regard to descriptive comparison:

> In terms of a postmodern awareness of the plurality of experience and the ambiguity of language, description cannot ... be understood as transparent, objective, or neutral. This is so because there is nothing in the world itself, in a particular object being described, that determines the differences to which a scholar will respond. Therefore, descriptions are always perspectival, necessarily incomplete, and to some degree arbitrary. During every act of description, we settle on some scale of detail, and choose a distinct perspective from which to gather it. (134–35, n. 2)

In these ways, all comparison is marked by contextuality of conceptual genre and academic circumstance. Historians of religion therefore need to always define the purpose and audience of their constructions and the level or scale of generality employed.

Benson Saler's work (1993, 2000) has addressed comparativism through prototype theory and resemblance theory. Following H.H. Price (1971) and cognitivists like Eleanor Rosch (1978), Saler postulates that the mind constructs comparative concepts in terms of prototypical resemblances. Concepts imply exemplars, that is, standard instances of the concept. Comparability, then, means closeness or distance of resemblance to the prototype. Saler offers this approach as an alternative to boundaried, essentialized views of religious subject matter, where exempla are either deemed identical members of a conceptual class or not. He writes, "... while the term 'universal' may connote something 'out there' that is independent of cognitive mediation, 'resemblance' suggests a judgment that *someone* makes, and makes within a mediating framework" (2000: 7). Because comparison cannot rid itself of its cultural conditionings, it must acknowledge them in a disciplined way. Though the term "religion" must be recognized as a cultural category that has Judeo-Christian prototypes, it still may be useful as one way of showing family relationships.

2) *Typologies of religious life.* Topical comparative studies certainly continue to be produced, and textbooks as well as encyclopedias that highlight cross-cultural forms of religion continue to reassemble synchronic ways that religious subject matters may be perceived. The *Encyclopedia of Religion* (ed. M. Eliade, 1987) became a major resource in this regard. In Ninian Smart's work (cf. Smart 1996), religious life is broken down and cross-culturally illustrated in terms of nine forms or dimensions: the ritual, doctrinal, mythic, experiential, ethical, social, material, political and economic. Similarly, Dale Cannon organizes his

text (1996) around six "ways of being religious": the ways of the mystical quest, reasoned inquiry, right action, devotion, shamanic mediation, and sacred rite (1996). *Tracing Common Themes: Comparative Courses in the Study of Religion* (Carman/Hopkins 1991) focuses on comparative ways of treating themes like pilgrimage, sacrifice, healing, scripture, ethics and mysticism. The Comparative Studies in Religion Section of the American Academy of Religion is another place to register "comparativist" thinking. In the last five years it has sponsored sessions on cross-cultural subjects such as light in mystical traditions, healing, shame and guilt, iconoclasm, nudity, ecstatic dance, food and boundaries, memory and ancestors, and secularisms. From England, edited by Jean Holm, Pinter Publishers has put out a series of texts on themes such as sacred place, worship, rites of passage, women and religion, and attitudes to nature. Nancy Jay's cross-cultural case study (1992) of the male "ownership" of sacrificial cults showed how topical comparison can generate hypotheses that have strong theoretic claims. A methodologically systematic application of Smart's typology to the comparison of symbols is Christopher Buck's *Paradise and Paradigm* (1999). Lindsay Jones' magisterial comparative study of the patterns and functions of sacred architecture brilliantly extends the Eliadean project within new conceptual frameworks (Jones 2000).

When religious materials are compared in terms of types of religious behavior rather than in terms of whole traditions believed to be essentially self-contained, then comparison brings together into a common frame what would ordinarily (or culturally) be perceived as separate. Thus, there are kinds of Christian practice that may have more in common with kinds of Buddhist practice than with other kinds of Christianities. One outcome of this point is that the old classification of Eastern vs. Western religions begins to dissolve. For example, if in the classical comparative frames those traditions were assumed to be intrinsically different genres of religion, Barbara Holdrege's comparative analysis of brahmanical "Hinduism" and rabbinic Judaism breaks down that separation. In a major study (1996) she analyzes the way the two traditions have significant affinities

> … as elite "textual communities" that have codified the norms of orthodoxy in the form of scriptural canons; as ethnocultural systems concerned with issues of family, ethnic and cultural integrity, blood lineages, and the intergenerational transmission of traditions; and as religions of orthopraxy characterized by hereditary priesthoods and sacrificial traditions, comprehensive legal systems delineated in the Dharma-Shastras and halakhic texts, elaborate regulations concerning purity and impurity, and dietary laws. (Holdrege 1996: ix)

Moreover, in each tradition, scripture (Veda and Torah) takes on a comparable cosmological function. Holdrege concludes that "the comparative study of these traditions is of significance precisely because it provides the basis for developing an alternative model of "religious tradition" founded on categories other than the Christian-based categories of interpretation that have tended to dominate our scholarly inquiries" (ix). Her work illustrates that comparative religion need not be based on historically and religiously biased folk beliefs and maps, but on common sociocultural forms of practice like "tradition" identity, purity rules, or law.

3) *Panhuman commonalities, cultural differences.* As any particular culture is self-contextualizing and to that extent incomparable, critics of comparativism have good reason to question the imposition of common intercultural "meanings." As if in response, new lines of interest have emerged to examine the species-level continuities of human behavior that lie behind any historical context or any culture. If behind all cultures are human beings, then recurrence may be found at infrastructural levels of cognition, gender and panhuman forms of sociality.

Wendy Doniger's recent work (cf. 1999, 1998), focusing largely on gender and mythology, strikes a balance in the midst of the commonality/particularity polarity. Her solution to the need to determine both similarity and difference is to take a "bottom-up" rather than a "top-down" approach. This means that instead of assuming commonalities regarding broad culturally infused topics like sacrifice or "high gods," comparativists could find certain shared panhuman factors like gendered sexuality, body, desire, procreation and their concomitant story motifs or shared human problems, and seek out individual diversity in relation to them (Doniger 2000: 70–71). This diversity is endless and includes individuality within given cultures. There is a "web" of human bonds—hence the title of one of her books, *The Implied Spider* (1998). Whether parallels in myth occur by way of historical diffusion or by independent origination, "a shared human predilection for some sorts of stories over others" may underlie either (1999: 7).

William Paden's *Religious Worlds: The Comparative Study of Religion* (1994) attempts to show that one of the functions of comparison is to exhibit cultural difference in relation to human, cross-cultural forms of world construction and world habitation. For example, all societies make pasts and form collective memories, but these pasts have different cultural contents or histories; all societies renew their pasts in periodic rites or festivals, but the content of what is renewed, that is, various social, moral, or economic values, differs; all societies make rules and boundaries, but the variation on what constitutes transgression and purity is remarkable and illuminating. Analogously, all humans are built to form and structure language, though languages themselves vary. Comparison then crystallizes around common processes and highlights salient differences and improvisations relative to them; as such, it hinges on human typicalities rather than cultural sameness or sameness of "meanings" (Paden 2001a). As well, the idea of "patterns of world construction" can help recontextualize and forward some of the thematic contributions of Mircea Eliade (Paden 2001b).

Walter Burkert's published Gifford Lectures, *Creation of the Sacred* (1996), turn to analogical relations between religious behaviors and those present in our "biological landscape," examining behavioral patterns like deference, reciprocity, hierarchy, guilt, causality and signification, in their larger evolutionary contexts. For example, regarding rituals of demonstrative submission, referring to gorilla behavior, Burkert writes that

> ... the way to avoid damage by a charging silverback was to cower to the ground, touching it with one's head, and above all to avoid staring. Assyrian reliefs show envoys to the king of Assyria assuming a strikingly similar position; the Akkadian expression was "to wipe one's nose" on the ground. (86)

The collapse of the distinction between nature and culture in cases like this invites new comparative agendas interfacing the behavioral, ethological sciences.

Thus, it may be argued that the search for commonalities can lead to issues of the patterned ways humans form social and cognitive worlds that are not contingent on any culture, and it is in these ways that comparative religion may find new inspiration from the sciences and provide a "non-ethnocentric framework for analogical religious constructs" (Martin 2000: 54). As Luther Martin puts it,

> By paying attention ... to the role that human biology, minds and social organization play in the production and constraint of cultural forms and expression, such empirical "mappings" of the architecture of human behavior and thought promise to contribute not only to our knowledge of the ubiquity of religion in human culture and its persistence in human history but to suggest also a formal framework of mental and behavioral constraints upon which might be constructed a theoretical explanation for the comparative enterprise that is so central to the way in which human beings organize their world and to academic generalizations alike. (Martin 2000: 55)

A new attention to the universals of human sociality, behavior and language holds promise for comparativism (Martin 2001; Jensen 2000; Brown 1991), and the implications of neurophysiological baselines, paralleling the deep structures of language and even the genetic code, are receiving attention from scholars pursuing the insights of cognitive science (Sullivan 2000; Boyer 2001).

Recapitulation

A "new comparativism" (Paden 1996a, 2000) does not limit the common terms of comparison to culturally constructed religious topics. Any concept, with any kind of theoretic complexity, may constellate religious data. The terms of comparison in this sense need to be as rich as the subject matter. Simply to form Western-derived catalogues and encyclopedias of religious topics and parallels has become problematic. Religion can and should be seen through the lenses of all the concepts one would use to study human culture and behavior, thus creating linkages with the theoretical capital and categories of the human sciences and the humanities generally.

Historians of religion are beginning to realize that their role is not just to repeat the insider's views or to compare one insider's view with another. It is also to seek out what the singular, culture-bound viewpoint cannot see, that is, to see what recurs in two or more cultural expressions and also how difference becomes evident relative to what recurs. Such perspective is not necessarily a suppression of "the other" but simply a different etic task that necessarily requires abstraction as all concepts do and as all science does. Comparison is therefore bilateral. It works both in the direction of similarity and difference. It requires commonality as a basis for showing difference relative to that commonality. It does not inherently imply homogenization of disparate data. William James had shown long ago that "classification does not necessarily explain away particulars, but allows careful comparison of their distinctive characteristics" (1982: 24). At the same time, comparison can uncover commonality in the midst of what might otherwise appear different or distant, discovering relationships otherwise unseen, and bringing those relationships into public view.

Comparative categories and analogies should be understood in a heuristic sense. Points or nodes of comparison are not static, essentialist entities, forever fixed but have an open, evolving texture and life. They are instruments for further discovery, perhaps leading to a pivoting succession of unanticipated thematic foci, mappings, subtypologies, problematizations, and historical analyses. As Lincoln and Grottanelli write,

> It is not enough ... simply to assemble a set of myths that display certain common themes and/or structures, although that might provide a convenient starting point for a comparative endeavor. For such an endeavor to bear fruit, however, there would have to follow a massive task of placing each myth within its total social environment and identifying its connections to other relevant dimensions of culture. Then, each of these contextualized myths would have to be considered with their proper historic moment, as part of an ongoing diachronic process marked by conflicts, contradictions, and dynamism. (Lincoln/Grottanelli 1998: 321)

A recent Boston University research endeavor, "The Comparative Religious Ideas Project," has produced a three-volume study (e.g. Neville 2000) on the themes, "The Human Condition," "Ultimate Realities," and "Religious Truth," each using materials from six religious traditions, and testing comparativist generalizations with the input of historians who are specialists in those traditions. A critical, salient factor in the entire process turned out to be the "corrigibility" of thematic material when confronted with contextual historical analysis. In Catherine Bell's phrase, "[t]erms should not predetermine where we will end up" (2001: 14).

Comparativism is clearly repositioning itself after the classical period and is attempting to avoid some of that generation's uncritical liabilities. Hence, some of the criticisms of traditional comparativism no longer apply—for example, that comparison makes everything "the same," or that it compromises contextual "territory." As well, comparison now "unavoidably involves the factor of reflexivity; self-awareness of the role of the comparativist as enculturated, classifying, and purposive subject ..., a cleaner sense of the process and practice of selectivity, and an exploratory rather than hegemonic sense of the pursuit of knowledge" (Paden 2000: 190).

The epigraph at the head of this essay mentioned that cross-cultural perspective was "perhaps our greatest claim to originality as an independent academic discipline." Whether the new approaches will be able to revive that endangered status remains to be seen.

Bibliography

Bell, Catherine (2001), "Pragmatic Theory," in: Tim Jensen/Mikael Rothstein, eds., *Secular Theories on Religion: Current Perspectives*. Copenhagen: Museum Tusculanum Press: 9–20.

Bourdieu, Pierre (1977), *Outline of a Theory of Practice*, trans. by Richard Nice. Cambridge: Cambridge University Press.

Boyer, Pascal (2001), *Religion Explained: The Evolutionary Origins of Religious Thought*. New York: Basic Books.

Brown, Donald E. (1991), *Human Universals*. New York: McGraw-Hill.

Buck, Christopher (1999), *Paradise and Paradigm: Key Symbols in Persian Christianity and the Baha'i Faith*. Albany, N.Y.: State University of New York Press.

Burkert, Walter (1996), *Creation of the Sacred: Tracks of Biology in Early Religions*. Cambridge, Mass.: Harvard University Press.

Cannon, Dale (1996), *Six Ways of Being Religious: A Framework for Comparative Studies of Religion*. Belmont, Calif.: Wadsworth Publishing Co.

Carman, John B./Hopkins, Steven P., eds. (1991), *Tracing Common Themes: Comparative Courses in the Study of Religion*. Atlanta, Ga.: Scholars Press.

Carter, Jeffrey R. (1998), Description Is Not Explanation: A Methodology of Comparison," in: *Method and Theory in the Study of Religion* 10 (2): 133–48.

Doniger, Wendy (1998), *The Implied Spider*. New York: Columbia University Press.

— (1999), *Splitting the Difference: Gender and Myth in Ancient Greece and India*. Chicago: University of Chicago Press.

— (2000), Post-Modern and -Colonial -Structural Comparison," in: Kimberley C. Patton/Benjamin C. Ray, eds., *A Magic Still Dwells: Comparative Religion in the Postmodern Age*. Berkeley, Calif.: University of California Press: 63–76.

Eliade, Mircea, ed. (1987), *Encyclopedia of Religion*. 16 vols. New York: Macmillan [a second edition, edited by Lindsay Jones, is due out in 2004].

Geertz, Clifford (1973), *The Interpretation of Cultures*. New York: Basic Books.

Holdrege, Barbara A. (1996), *Veda and Torah: Transcending the Textuality of Scripture*. Albany, N.Y.: State University of New York Press.

Holy, Ladislav, ed. (1987), *Comparative Anthropology*. Oxford: Basil Blackwell.

James, William (1982), *Varieties of Religious Experience: A Study in Human Nature*. New York: Penguin Books.

Jay, Nancy (1992), *Throughout Your Generations Forever: Sacrifice, Religion, and Paternity*. Chicago: University of Chicago Press.

Jensen, Jeppe (2000), "On Universals in the Study of Religion," in: Tim Jensen/Mikael Rothstein, eds., *Secular Theories on Religion: Current Perspectives*. Copenhagen: Museum Tusculanum Press: 51–67.

Jones, Lindsay (2000), *The Hermeneutics of Sacred Architecture: Experience, Interpretation, Comparison*. 2 vols. Cambridge, Mass.: Harvard University Press.

Lawson, E. Thomas (1996), "Theory and the New Comparativism, Old and New," in: *Method and Theory in the Study of Religion* 8 (1): 31–36.

Lincoln, Bruce/Grottanelli, Cristiano (1998), "A Brief Note on (Future) Research in the History of Religions," in: *Method and Theory in the Study of Religion* 10: 311–25.

Martin, Luther H. (2000), "Comparison," in: Willi Braun/Russell T. McCutcheon, eds., *Guide to the Study of Religion*. London: Cassell: 45–56.

— (2001), "Comparativism and Sociobiological Theory," in: *Numen* 48 (3): 290–308.

Martin, Luther H./Hewitt, Marsha/Lawson, E. Thomas/Wiebe, Donald/Paden, William E. (1996), "The New Comparativism in the Study of Religion: A Symposium," in: *Method and Theory in the Study of Religion* 8 (1): 1–49.

McCutcheon, Russell T. (1997), *Manufacturing Religion: The Discourse on Sui Generis Religion and the Politics of Nostalgia*. New York: Oxford University Press.

Neville, Robert Cummings, ed. (2000), *The Human Condition*. Albany, N.Y.: The State University of New York Press.

Paden, William E. (1994), *Religious Worlds: The Comparative Study of Religion*. Second edition. Boston, Mass.: Beacon Press.

— (1996a), "Elements of a New Comparativism," in: *Method and Theory in the Study of Religion* 8 (1): 5–14.

— (1996b), "A New Comparativism: Reply to the Panelists," in: *Method and Theory in the Study of Religion* 8 (1): 37–50.

— (2000), "Elements of a New Comparativism," in: Kimberley Patton/Benjamin Ray, eds., *A Magic Still Dwells: Comparative Religion in the Postmodern Age*. Berkeley, Calif.: University of California Press: 182–92 [revised version of Paden 1996a].

— (2001a), "Universals Revisited: Human Behaviors and Cultural Variations," in: *Numen* 48 (3): 276–89.

— (2001b), "The Concept of World Habitation: Eliadean Linkages with a New Comparativism," in: Bryan Rennie, ed., *Changing Religious Worlds: The Meaning and End of Mircea Eliade*. Albany, N.Y.: State University of New York Press: 249–62.

Patton, Kimberley C./Ray, Benjamin C., eds. (2000), *A Magic Still Dwells: Comparative Religion in the Postmodern Age*. Berkeley, Calif.: University of California Press.

Patton, Laurie L./Doniger, Wendy, eds. (1996), *Myth and Method*. Charlottesville, Va.: University of Virginia Press.

Poole, Fitz John Porter (1986), "Metaphors and Maps: Towards Comparison in the Anthropology of Religion," in: *Journal of the American Academy of Religion* 54: 411–57.

Price, H.H. (1971), "Universals and Resemblances," in: Charles Landesman, ed., *The Problem of Universals*. New York: Basic Books: 36–55.

Rosch, Eleanor (1978), "Principles of Categorization," in: Eleanor Rosch/Barbara B. Lloyd, eds., *Cognition and Categorization*. Hillsdale: Lawrence Erlbaum: 27–48.

Saler, Benson (1993), *Conceptualizing Religion: Immanent Anthropologists, Transcendent Natives, and Unbounded Categories*. Leiden: E.J. Brill.

— (2001), "Comparison: Some Suggestions for Improving the Inevitable," in: *Numen* 48 (3): 267–75.

Smart, Ninian (1996), *Dimensions of the Sacred: An Anatomy of the World's Beliefs*. Berkeley, Calif.: University of California Press.

Smith, Jonathan Z. (1978), *Map Is Not Territory: Studies in the History of Religions*. Chicago: University of Chicago Press.

— (1982), *Imagining Religion: From Babylon to Jonestown*. Chicago: University of Chicago Press.

— (1987), *To Take Place: Toward Theory in Ritual*. Chicago: University of Chicago Press.

— (1990), *Drudgery Divine: On the Comparison of Early Christianities and the Religions of Late Antiquity*. Chicago: University of Chicago Press.

— (1996), "A Matter of Class: Taxonomies of Religion," in: *Harvard Theological Review* 89 (4): 387–403.

— (2000), "Acknowledgments: Morphology and History in Mircea Eliade's *Patterns in Comparative Religion* (1949–1999), Parts 1 and 2," in: *History of Religions* 39 (4): 315–51.

— (2001), "Foreword," in: Robert C. Neville, ed., *Religious Truth*. Albany, N.Y.: The State University of New York Press: xi–xii.

Sullivan, Lawrence E. (2000), "The Net of Indra: Comparison and the Contribution of Perception," in: Kimberley C. Patton/Benjamin C. Ray, eds., *A Magic Still Dwells: Comparative Religion in the Postmodern Age*. Berkeley, Calif.: University of California Press: 206–36.

Urban, Hugh (2000), "Making a Place to Take a Stand: Jonathan Z. Smith and the Politics and Poetics of Comparison," in: *Method and Theory in the Study of Religion* 12 (3): 339–78.

Wiebe, Donald (1996), "Is the New Comparativism Really New?" in: *Method and Theory in the Study of Religion* 8 (1): 21–30.

— (1999), *The Politics of Religious Studies: The Continuing Conflict with Theology in the Academy*. New York: St. Martin's Press.

New Approaches to the Study of Syncretism

by

LUTHER H. MARTIN and ANITA MARIA LEOPOLD

Introduction

Comparative studies of religions notice both regularities and differences among the various religions but focus on, describe, and sometimes attempt to explain the regularities. Studies of a particular religion, however, assume regularity but notice irregularities. These irregularities are often described, and sometimes explained, as "syncretism," a generalization about diverse elements incorporated into some target religion from an external religious or secular source or sources. While such "syncretistic blendings" may be embraced by participants in a particular religion as an intentional strategy of historical adaptation or social inclusivity (e.g., Santeria, see Stevens-Arroyo 1995; or examples from Japan, see Pye 1994), they are more often resisted as inappropriate or corrupting influences. There is, however, considerable confusion concerning the use of this generalization among scholars of religion.

What is it exactly that is understood to be "blended" or "combined" in "religious" syncretisms? Is it a mixture of different practices? Of different beliefs? Of different symbols? And by what criteria are such thematic elements defined? Or, rather than thematic elements, might syncretism refer to contested or negotiated relationships between religious "interpenetrations" of one religious system by another (Aijmer 1995a: 11; see Bastide 1978; Droogers 1989)? Or to a mixture of divergent modes of religious expression altogether, i.e., to different ways by which people have cognized, represented and transmitted their culture (e.g., Whitehouse 2000)? Does syncretistic porosity refer to ideological or propagandistic alternatives proposed, or to attachments and commitments made?

Is there any discernible basis for syncretistic formations, or are they to be understood as random consequences of religions in contact? How might syncretisms be accounted for in light of the numerous unrealized possibilities occasioned by such contact? Does syncretism indicate dynamic processes of tension occasioning innovation? Or might syncretism refer to a strategy for employing the "new" in service of preserving or authenticating the "old"? Or, is it, perhaps, precisely the imprecision of the category that accounts for its widespread use (Anonymous 1995: 1043; Gordon 1996: 1462b)?

Any generalization is a matter of theory and the field of religious studies has been notoriously lax in its production of theories that might stipulate exactly what is constitutive of "religious" boundaries as well as those ingredients or processes that might constitute a "syncretistic" breach of those boundaries. In a culinary recipe, a successful blending together of specified ingredients, processed in a prescribed way, results in at least edible, if not necessarily gourmet, fare. Such results are at base a combination that obeys the fundamental laws of chemistry; if a recipe "fails," then some catalytic element necessary for the requisite chemical composition—whether ingredient or process—is deficient. Is there a "recipe" for successful, i.e., historically and/or anthropologically documented syncretistic formations? Are there fundamental laws or rules that might be uncovered that structure, or at least constrain, syncretistic processes? Or is syncretism merely the ubiquitous label for any random mess of potage?

Is "syncretism" an analytic category that can explain some aspects of religious formation and transformation, or is it a descriptive category that differentiates some types of religious phenomena to be explained? This essay will be concerned with clarifying the use of syncretism as a category for students of religion.

Old Approaches to the Study of Syncretism

As has oft been noted (e.g., Rudolph 1979; Martin 1983; Droogers 1989), the term "syncretism" derives from its singular usage in antiquity by Plutarch to describe conciliatory relations among the normally factious Cretans (= *syn* + *krētismoi*) in the face of aggression by foreign foes (Plutarch, *De fraterno amore* 19). The term came to be employed in religious discourse, however, only in the sixteenth and seventeenth centuries as the designation for a proposed reconciliation of diverse Protestant groups, and ultimately of all Christians (e.g., by Hugo Grotius, 1583–1645 and George Calixtus, 1586–1656), "in the manner of the Cretans" (*Oxford English Dictionary*: "syncretize"). This irenic sense of syncretism survives as the background for Christian ecumenism, on the one hand (McNeil 1964: 303–45), and in contemporary proposals for a world or global theology, on the other (e.g., W.C. Smith 1989; Reat/Perry 1991). Either of these positions may be characterized as syncretistic in the sense of diverse religious forms representing a common transcendental reality (Sharpe 1975: 252, 257).

The syncretistic proposals by Grotius and Calixtus were rejected by most Protestants as a violation of sectarian integrity, and the characterization was subsequently used largely in a pejorative sense (Schmid 1846; Moffatt 1922; McNeil 1964: 271–72). By the eighteenth century, "syncretism" had become a designation for "false" religion (Apthorp 1778: 162), especially to describe that corrupt "combination" or "mixture" of religious elements deemed characteristic of "paganism" (= *synkratizein*, "to combine," or *synkerannumi*, "to mix," neo-etymologisms that reflect this modern usage). Subsequently, biblical scholars described a pagan background for early Christianity as syncretistic and Protestants described (their) "true" religion over against what they considered to be syncretistic influences on historical developments within the expanding Roman Catholic Church (J.Z. Smith 1990: 7–27). This pejorative (and polemical) sense of syncretism was expanded in the modern world to become a description for all non-"prophetic"—especially non-Christian—religions (Kraemer 1938: 200–203), especially Eastern religions (Baird 1971: 148–51), "third-world" tribal societies (e.g., Jules-Rosette 1975: 194) and "cults" in contemporary America (Ellwood 1973: 29, 46). The modern notion of religious syncretism, then, has been primarily a category that describes the relationship between the discursive and non-discursive religious practices of an antithetically constructed "other" and those of an ethnocentric "us"—historically, some form of Christianity (Martin 1983: 134–37). Syncretism has been viewed, in other words, primarily as "a religious and missionary problem" (Kraemer 1954; Gort et al. 1989). As such, theologically defined instances of syncretism, like any theological data, can provide scholars of religion with a proper object of study (e.g., Stewart/Shaw 1994), but it offers no purchase on properly academic ways in which that object might be studied.

By the beginning of the twentieth century, historians of religion began to realize that Christianity, i.e., the ethnocentric "us," was also a syncretistic formation (Gunkel 1903: 398, 455; Showerman 1911: 293a) and subsequently to conclude that "[e]very religion ... is to a certain extent a 'syncretism'" since each "has its own previous history" (Wach 1924: 86; cited by van der Leeuw 1938 [1933]: 609; see also Baird 1971: 146). Consequently, more recent historians of religion have sought to emphasize a purely descriptive use of the category (Martin 1983; Pye 1971, 1994; Rudolph 1979) and to develop a taxonomy for the different types of syncretistic formations described (Rudolph 1979; Berner 1982). Although clarifying, such taxonomies beg the more fundamental question of what the category itself designates (Light 2000a: 163), while recent attempts to redefine syncretism as a descriptive category continue to be compromised by implicit presumptions about some pure, homogeneous or coherent character of religion which is not syncretistic (Baird 1971: 148; Stewart/Shaw 1994: 2). From the perspective of such essentialist presumptions, use of the category continues to represent a view of allegedly corrosive influences from some external source (or sources) upon a supposedly native or indigenous innocence that provides a norm against which syncretistic debasements may be judged (Bastide 1978: 284).

But if polemical intent, together with its unintended vestigia, are removed from uses of the notion syncretism and the category is recognized as a generalization to be made of all religions as a consequence of their previous histories, the term has little taxonomic value (Anonymous 1995: 1043). Simply to nominate this or that religion or this or that set of religious data as "syncretistic" contributes nothing more to the explanation—or even to the description—of that data than does the category "religion" itself. While reiterative redundancy might make for memorable lines of poetry ("a rose is a rose is a rose"), such repetition represents banal strategy as analytic method.

Old Problems and New Approaches to the Study of Syncretism

1. Historical Approaches: Syncretism as Process

Descriptive historians, and indeed even many theoretical historians, have been found lacking when it comes to the making of generalizations, though they have been quite complicit in their transmission (Gottschalk 1963: v; Starr 1963: 3). Religious syncretism is a case in point. Historians of religion continue to employ the category as a description of specific historical combinations of thematic elements: practices, beliefs, symbols, etc. These data remain impervious to generalization, however, in the absence of comparative, i.e., generalizable, data. Although societies are often characterized in terms of distinctive traditions and institutions, no known society is the pristine product of its own history, untouched by contact with other cultures. Rather, cultural change always operates on interconnected systems in which societies are variously linked within wider "social fields." "All human societies of which we have record are," in other words, "'secondary,' indeed, often tertiary, quaternary, or centenary" (E. Wolf 1982: 76). This recognition that all societies—and thus their religions—are influenced by the ubiquity of intercultural contact only becomes useful if it can be explained how or why borrowings from another culture either validate or challenge an already existing religious capital (Johnston 1999: 95, 170). Any new religious element either must align closely with an old one, in which case it cannot be so new, or its displacement of the old must be accounted for (Johnston 169–70). As such, syncretism might be employed to characterize the problematic of those "series of processes that construct, reconstruct, and dismantle cultural materials" (E. Wolf 1982: 387).

If syncretism is understood as the mode of production for each and every set of religious data rather than as deviation from some idealized ahistorical point of origin or utopian goal, then the category may have value for indicating synchronic stages in the history of a particular religious system as well as explanatory value by accounting for the ethnographic and historical particulars of their formation (Stewart 1995: 30–31; Droogers 1995: 46–52; Light 2000a: 184).

And what exactly are the "modes of production" for syncretistic formations? Cultural contact does not in and of itself imply that syncretism will necessarily take place and, conversely, syncretisms may occur apart from intercultural contact, in which apparent borrowings may represent parallel formations independently shaped by shared cultural trajectories rather than by extra-cultural influences (Colpe 1975: 25–28; J.Z. Smith 1990: 116–43). In either case, genealogies and explanations for those syncretistic formations that do occur are notoriously difficult to establish. So while historical investigations of any (and all) religious data will establish their historical antecedents (Colpe 1987), and will, consequently, instantiate them as "syncretistic," questions about the comparative value and the theoretical efficacy of that generalization remain.

2. Anthropological Approaches: Syncretism as System

Social scientists have traditionally been as diffident about generalization as have historians (Martin, 2001a) and, consequently, have employed the notion of syncretism as casually as have historians, and with the same reference to the specificities of particular societies. Recently, however, some social scientists—chiefly anthropologists—have sought to describe the relationships that pertain among those data as constitutive of more or less closed and stable sets (for proposals about syncretism as such a system, see Berner 1982: 81–114; Martin 1983). Some of these anthropologists have addressed the ubiquity of religious syncretism by specifying this generalization in structural opposition to instances of "antisyncretism" (Stewart/Shaw 1994), i.e., to the "antagonism to religious synthesis shown by agents concerned with the defense of religious boundaries" (Stewart/Shaw 1994: 7). In this view, syncretism would be a system of relationships defined and differentiated by specific antisyncretistic claims.

Participants in a religious system often contest influences perceived to be external to their system. Such believers, however, rarely describe their own religion as syncretistic (Baird 1971: 148), no matter how syncretistic the system may be viewed in historical and anthropological analysis—an observation reinforced by an insistence on the religious integrity of new religious movements by their participants. Antisyncretistic protests, in other words, would represent the apologetic stance of virtually all participants in any religious system and generalizations about syncretism defined thereby would remain as ubiquitous as that of religion itself.

Further, anthropologists have been criticized for describing systems of relationships while neglecting the historical processes of their formation. "To write of societies in a history-less way leaves the impression they sprang into being spontaneously … [T]here is no way to account for any substantial cultural change in the distant past or, *a fortiori*, in the recent past and present, because change is not what is really happening … Yet, since the present variety of cultures has not always existed—then we must assume at the very least that they must have come into being in an accountable way. *Otherwise we end up believing in a sort of miraculous virgin birth of cultures*" (Carrithers 1992: 9). Thus, as with historical studies of religious syncretism, most anthropologists have not addressed the problem of how syncretistic systems are produced.

A few anthropologists have suggested that the fundamental mode of production for syncretisms is power—that "[s]yncretism has presumably always been part of the negotiation of identities and hegemonies in such situations as conquest, trade, migration, religious dissemination and intermarriage" (Stewart/Shaw 1994: 19–20, see Benavides 1995). By this view, an imposed religious system dominates and relativizes an already existing system (or systems) creating, thereby, the problem of making sense of an incoherent surfeit of new possibilities. This problem is solved either by making a choice for one of the systems and abandoning the other(s) (conversion) or by selecting credible elements from among the systems and rejecting the remainder, constructing thereby a new system (syncretism). Perhaps the reason that revolutionary movements have so often been organized in terms of such newly integrated concepts and symbols is that native elements are too integrated into the cultural establishment to be employed effectively in processes of change (A. Wolf 1974: 145).

3. Socio-political Approaches: Syncretism as Ideology/Myth-making

Deities and cults in the context of Western antiquity which has provided the paradigm for the employment of the category syncretism in scholarly research (see e.g., Grant 1953: xiii–xv; Dunand/Lévêque 1975; Pearson 1975) largely retained their distinct identities in the face of imperialistic expansion, despite popular presumptions to the contrary. Any "syncretistic" identifications were, rather, intentional, largely "a matter of propaganda," pursuits of "magical ... power," or of philosophical theorizing (Nock 1942: 557–58; also Rudolph 1979: 208). The finding (or projection) of one's own values, whether political, religious, moral, and so forth, in (or onto) the other is the primary characteristic of propaganda, which, in the sociological sense, may be defined as the self-interested productions of any society (Merton 1968: 160, 563). And since the primary mission of any society is to maintain itself, all of its productions, including the religious, may be understood as motivated to some extent by their own ideological commitments. Classic examples of syncretism motivated by propaganda/magic/philosophy include such "intentional" syncretisms as that usually attributed to Manichaeism (Burkitt 1925: 71; Jonas 1963: 207–208; Rudolph 1983: 334), the Egyptianizations characteristic of the Greek magical papyri (Preisendanz 1956; Betz 1986: xlv–xlvi) or of the Graeco-Roman temples of Isis (Dekoulakou 1991), and the middle-Platonic essentialization by Apuleius, whose fictive, neo-Platonic "Prayer to Isis" (*Metamorphoses* xi) is often cited as the *locus classicus* for the notion of religious syncretism (Rose/Parke 1970: 1029).

A modern example of religious syncretism as ideological construction is the "invention" of a "Judeo-Christian tradition" in the United States during the

1950s as a socio-political category of American inclusiveness (Tillich 1952). This "syncretistic" category was constructed only in the aftermath of World War II on the basis of "newly-realized" perceptions among Americans about the commonalities between "modern forms of ... Judaism" and Protestantism—that most American form of the Christian religion (Tillich 1952: 107–109). Only in the 1960s, with the election of John F. Kennedy as president of the United States, were Catholics also fully included in this Judeo-Christian "Americanism," a category that continues to exclude and to excoriate non-"Judeo-Christian" groups as deviant "cults."

If religious syncretisms refer to the socio-political processes whereby religious systems are produced and maintained, then these transformations, innovations and conservations designate an ideological inversion of history, whereby a more recent, historically developed value or ideology, born of intercultural contact or of intracultural development, becomes lodged in a charter or foundation myth of a particular people. In this sense, syncretism would be a category of social formation and maintenance, legitimated by myth-making, in which "traditional" membership in a transformed or innovative social (religious) system becomes measured against and legitimated by contemporaneous values. As such, it again defines a proper object of study for the scholar of religion.

4. Semiotics: Syncretistic Formations as Cultural Construction

Semiotics is a way in which relationships might be seen between the structure of cultural systems, on the one hand, and historical and anthropological descriptions of their production, on the other. Since cultural formations, understood as systems, are both rule-governed and rule-altering, any potentially new input into a religious system is excluded or allowed by the structures of the primary religious system into which it is integrated; on the other hand, the new input will, over time, influence and alter that system (Saussure 1983: 73–78).

In semiotic analysis, the dialectic between codes and messages, whereby codes control the formation and transmission of messages but new messages can restructure the codes, is understood to provide the basis for a discussion of the creativity of religious expression and behavior. Although creativity or innovation may be viewed, from a theological (or normative) perspective, as heresy (or deviance), it may also be viewed from a semiotic point of view as conserving meaning. The gods of Rome, for example, did not relinquish their influence with the termination of their cultic practices but, changed only in name, lived on to play their same role in the framework of the Catholic Church (Schenk 1989: 83). Today's syncretistic (trans)formation is often tomorrow's truth.

On the other hand, syncretism may refer to a kind of transformative "architecture" of meaning-making which can reconstruct otherwise incompatible ideas into compatible ones at both the systemic as well as at the social level (Vroom 1989; Leopold 2001). For example, the New Age idea of reincarnation understood as "an *attractive* alternative to the essentially static heaven or hell of traditional Christianity" (Hanegraaff 1998: 378) differs from, and is even antithetical to, its Asian parallels, for example, to the tyranny of the wheel of rebirth. This reconstruction results in emergent structures of religious meaning different from the incorporated structures of the selected religious input (Fauconnier 1997; Leopold 2001).

Such examples of "inter-(con)textualizing" demonstrate a morphological and semantic range of equivalences from contiguities to deviations. What, consequently, appears to be arbitrary, outrageous or assimilatory is pragmatically established as various functions of communication: on the one hand, comparative supports for comprehensible, constructed explanations; on the other hand, the indoctrination of others on the basis of one's own ideology. In either sense, the finding of one's own in the other is the primary characteristic of syncretism (Schenk 1989: 100; Hanegraaff 1998: 377). Knowledge of the semiotic codes employed in cultural constructions and transformations might well clarify and even offer an explanation for syncretistic formations.

5. Cognitive Approaches: Syncretism as Constrained

Cognitive science is an interdisciplinary research project that seeks to document the ways by which the human brain processes various kinds of input. A number of cognitive scientists have been explicitly working on the relationship between cognition and culture (e.g., Lawson/McCauley 1990; Sperber 1996), and a few are attempting to apply the findings of cognitive research to the problem of syncretism (e.g., Martin 1996, 2001b; Light 2000a, 2000b).

Like any cultural representation, syncretistic formations are the collective product of cultural input only as that input is processed by human minds (Pinker 1994: 125). Since these cognitive processes are common to the structure of the human brain, they may be spoken of as a universal set of cognitive rules. And since the multitude of human cultures are both constructed upon these rules as well as constrained by them, it is no accident that many of the more interesting connections between cognition and culture, and especially between cognition and religion, have been made by anthropologists (e.g., Boyer 1994; Whitehouse 1995, 2000; see also Lawson/McCauley 1990; Barrett 1999).

From a cognitive perspective, the various types of syncretisms that have been identified by historians and anthropologists, including such phenomena that have been described as pluralism, eclecticism, adaptation, inculturation, and so on, are all instances of common cognitive mechanisms (Light 2000b). For example, cognitive research on category formation, i.e., the ways by which human beings select what might be included in and excluded from their cultural representations is central to any understanding of syncretistic formations (Martin 1996: 219–22), as are the ways by which these discrete representations might become "blended" (Turner 1996: 57–84, 96–100, 109–15).

Of special relevance for an understanding of syncretism is cognitive research on the transmission and transformation of (the religious) elements of culture (Aijmer 1995a: 1; Martin 2001b). The cognitive reduction of cultural representations may be explained by the hypothesis that Darwinian selection applies to replicators of any kind and not just to biological material (Dawkins 1982; Sperber 1996: 102). Since no copying process is infallible (Dawkins 1982: 85) but includes at least the possibility of a "'mutational' element" (Dawkins 1982: 112), cognitive scientists have concluded that cultural representations always transform in the process of their transmission (Sperber 1996: 101, 108). Such transformation of cultural descendants would then be the result of "a constructive cognitive process" (Sperber 1996: 101), in which "human brains use all the information they are presented with … as more or less relevant evidence with which to construct representations of their own" (Sperber 1996: 106, 108). From the perspective of the cognitive sciences, consequently, religious transmissions could not be the replication of a single parent, of some pure nonsyncretistic religious origin, as in the claims of religious orthodoxy, nor even of two parents, as in the common view of syncretistic formation as Hegelian synthesis (Préaux 1978: 7), "nor of any fixed number of parent tokens, but of an indefinite number of tokens, some of which have played a much greater 'parental' role than others" (Sperber 1996: 104). In other words, syncretism represents a *selective* blend of memetic elements that fit the cognitive map of a particular cultural collectivity. The mental representations that are inferred from this indefinite number of cultural representations are structured on the basis of "preexisting conceptual structures" (Boyer 1994: 284, see 283–94), knowledge of which would describe the architectural structure upon which all syncretisms are constructed.

Conclusion

Because of the problems of redundancy and imprecision that have characterized—and continue to characterize—use of the category "religious syncretism," might it not be better simply to dispense with its use altogether as a number of commentators have suggested (e.g., Baird 1971: 152; Lincoln 2001: 459)? Or is there something new to be said about its use?

If, first of all, "syncretism" is to be employed descriptively, the data to be described by it must be explicitly stipulated. For example, the category may name data born of missionary activity: irenic proposals, polemical charges, apologetic arguments, boundary defenses, colonial incursions, and so on; or it might name historical processes and changes with respect to a specifically defined religious tradition or to incursions into, additions to and/or deletions from a formally defined religious system; or, again, the category could indicate a semiotic translation of cultural transactions or cognitive processes of social construction and transmission.

Historians and anthropologists, because they work with data on the manifest (i.e., historical and cultural) levels, have inherited the difficulty of stipulating criteria for a category of syncretism which does not assume, at least implicitly, some emic norm. But if some norm for the measurement of syncretistic data or processes is not established, then all religions, including any normative claims they make, must be seen etically as socio-historical constructions from their beginnings. As we have seen, "syncretism" used in this latter sense describes nothing more than the historical character of "religion" itself. In other words, if any generalization is to have descriptive efficacy, it must be able to make interesting differentiations among the available data (i.e., what is not syncretism?) and not simply offer a synonym for what it purports to describe. What is required, in other words, is a theoretical basis for the category which might make it possible not only to make taxonomic differentiations among "syncretistic" sets of data but to differentiate "syncretistic" from "non-syncretistic" sets of data.

Systemic definitions of syncretism based on "antisyncretistic claims," discussed above, are theoretically suggestive if still formulated redundantly in emic terms. Other typological strategies for defining syncretisms, however, might include the historical interactions between such theoretically formulated dichotomies as routinization/charisma (Weber 1930, 1947), literate religions/oral traditions (Goody 1968, 1986), central/peripheral cults (Lewis 1971) and, most recently, doctrinal/imagistic modes of religiosity (Whitehouse 1995, 2000). All of these typologies propose historically arbitrary but theoretically formulated baselines (routinized, central/established, literate/doctrinal modes) against which "syncretisms" (charismatic innovations, peripheral indigenizations, imagistic deviations, and so on) might be defined. Although theoretically formulated, such typologies have nevertheless been developed from descriptions of manifest data and (with the exception of Whitehouse 2000) offer little or no theoretical explanation for the existence of the cultural divergences described. Consequently, further analyses of such models might well consider the cognitive and semiotic "rules" upon which all cultural structures and meanings are constructed and transmitted and by which those constructions and transmissions are also constrained.

Whereas "syncretism" might prove useful as a category that describes certain set(s) of data to be explained by scholars of religion—if it is carefully and clearly defined, it is not itself an explanatory category. Explanations for "syncretistic" data will be based on those theoretical orientation(s) (e.g., cognitive, semiotic, systemic, socio-political ...) judged finally to be most appropriate for the stipulated differentiation of that data.

Use of the category of religious syncretism, then, will prove to be useful if it can:

1. *stipulate relationships among those data* considered to be constitutive of a particular set of religious data, on both an empirical as well as on a theoretical level, at some selected historical time and place;
2. *differentiate and describe as an object of study* the incursions, additions/deletions, transformations and/or substitutions/combinations that may occur among a transmitted set of religious data between some selected historical time and place and some selected prior or subsequent time and/or different place, and the different levels (i.e., mythological, ritual, social, theological, and so on) on which these incursions, additions/deletions, transformations and/or substitutions/combinations occur; and,
3. *propose an explanation* for ways in which the described incursions, additions/deletions, transformations and/or substitutions/combinations were received (or rejected) that may be tested against comparative (historical and anthropological) data.

Ad hoc descriptions of particular historical and/or anthropological cases of what are deemed to be, in undefined ways, examples of syncretism are, as the idiosyncratic judgement of individual scholars, finally unacceptable, as are assumptive uses of the category in the pseudo-explanatory ways that have characterized—and continue to characterize—many studies. Rather, scholarly generalizations must be offered that stipulate which data might comprise particular syncretistic formations and how they might occur in just the way they do rather than in other historically possible ways. If scholars are unable—or unwilling—to bring such theoretical clarity to their generalizations about "syncretism," then perhaps it is indeed better to dispense with its use in scholarly research altogether.

References

Aijmer, Göran (1995a), "By Way of Introduction," in: *Syncretism and the Commerce of Symbols*, ed. by A. Gören. Göteborg: The Institute for Advanced Studies in Social Anthropology: 1–12.

Anonymous (1995), "Syncretism," in: *The HarperCollins Dictionary of Religion*, general ed. J.Z. Smith. San Francisco, Calif.: HarperSanFrancisco: 1042–43.

Apthorp, East (1778), *Letters on the Prevalence of Christianity before Its Civil Establishment*. London: J. Robson.

Baird, Robert (1971), *Category Formation and the History of Religions*. The Hague: Mouton.

Barrett, Justin (1999), "Theological Correctness: Cognitive Constraint and the Study of Religion," in: *Method & Theory in the Study of Religion* 11: 325–39.

Bastide, Roger (1978), *The African Religions of Brazil: Toward a Sociology of the Interpenetration of Civilizations*, transl. by H. Sebba. Baltimore, Md.: The Johns Hopkins University Press.

Benavides, Gustavo (1995), "Syncretism and Legitimacy in Latin American Religion," in: *Enigmatic Powers: Syncretism with African and Indigenous Peoples' Religions among Latinos*, ed. by A.M. Stevens-Arroyo/A.I Pérez y Mena. Program for the Analysis of Religion among Latinos 3. New York: Bildner Center for Western Hemisphere Studies: 19–46.

Berner, Ulrich (1982), *Untersuchungen zur Verwendung des Synkretismus-Begriffes*. Wiesbaden: Otto Harrassowitz.

Betz, Hans Dieter, ed. (1986), *The Greek Magical Papyri in Translation: Including the Demotic Spells*. Vol. 1: *Texts*. Chicago: The University of Chicago Press.

Boyer, Pascal (1994), *The Naturalness of Religious Ideas*. Berkeley, Calif.: University of California Press.

Burkitt, F.C. (1925), *The Religion of the Manichees*. Cambridge: Cambridge University Press.

Carrithers, Michael (1992), *Why Humans Have Cultures: Explaining Anthropology and Social Diversity*. Oxford: Oxford University Press.

Cassidy, William J., ed. (2001), *Retrofitting Syncretism, Historical Reflections/Réflexions Historiques* 27 (3) [special issue].

Colpe, Carsten (1975), "Die Vereinbarkeit historischer und struktureller Bestimmungen des Synkretismus," in: *Synkretismus im syrisch-persischen Kulturgebiet: Bericht über ein Symposium in Reinhausen bei Göttingen in der Zeit von 4. bis 8. Oktober 1971*, ed. by A. Dietrich. Göttingen: Vandenhoeck & Ruprecht: 17–30.

— (1987), "Syncretism," in: *The Encyclopedia of Religion*, ed. by M. Eliade. Vol. 14. New York/London: Macmillan: 218–27.

Dawkins, Richard (1982), *The Extended Phenotype*. Oxford: Oxford University Press.

Dekoulakou, Iphigeneia (1991), To iero tēs Isidas ston Marathōna. in: *Archaiologia* 39: 67–71.

Doležalová, Iva/Horyna, Břetislav/Papoušek, Dalibor, eds. (1996), *Religions in Contact*. Brno: Czech Society for the Study of Religions/Masaryk University.

Droogers, André (1989), "Syncretism: The Problem of Definition, the Definition of the Problem," in: *Dialogue and Syncretism: An Interdisciplinary Approach*, ed. by J.D. Gort et al. Grand Rapids, Mich.: Eerdmans: 7–25.

— (1995), "Symbolism, Power, Play," in: *Syncretism and the Commerce of Symbols*, ed. by A. Gören. Göteborg: The Institute for Advanced Studies in Social Anthropology: 38–59.

Dunand, Françoise/Lévêque, Pierre (1975), *Les syncrétismes dans les religions de l'antiquité*. Leiden: E.J. Brill.

Ellwood, Jr., Robert S. (1973), *Religious and Spiritual Groups in Modern America*. Englewood Cliffs, N.J.: Prentice-Hall.

Fauconnier, Gilles (1997), *Mappings in Thought and Language*. Cambridge: Cambridge University Press.

Goody, Jack, ed. (1968), *Literacy in Traditional Societies*. Cambridge: Cambridge University Press.

— (1986), *The Logic of Writing and the Organization of Society*. Cambridge: Cambridge University Press.

Gordon, Richard L. (1996), "Syncretism," in: *The Oxford Classical Dictionary*, third ed., ed. by S. Hornblower/A. Spawforth. Oxford: Oxford University Press: 1462b–63a.

Gort, Jerald D./Vroom, Hendrik M./Fernhout, Rein/Wessels, Anton, eds. (1989), *Dialogue and Syncretism: An Interdisciplinary Approach*. Grand Rapids, Mich.: Eerdmans.

Gottschalk, Louis (1963), "Foreword," in: *Generalization in the Writing of History*, ed. by L. Gottschalk. Chicago: The University of Chicago Press: v–xvii.

Grant, Frederick C. (1953), *Hellenistic Religions: The Age of Syncretism*. Indianapolis, Ind.: Bobbs-Merrill.

Gunkel, Hermann (1903), "The Religio-Historical Interpretation of the New Testament," transl. by W.H. Carruth, in: *The Monist*: 398–455.

Hanegraaff, Wouter J. (1998), "The New Age Movement and the Esoteric Tradition," in: *Gnosis and Hermeticism from Antiquity to Modern Times*, ed. by R. van den Broek/W. Hanegraaff. Albany, N.Y.: State University of New York Press: 359–82.

Johnston, Sarah Iles (1999), *Restless Dead: Concounters betwen the Living and the Dead in Ancient Greece*. Berkeley, Calif.: The University of California Press.

Jonas, Hans (1963), *The Gnostic Religion*. Second ed. Boston, Mass.: Beacon Press.

Jules-Rosette, Bennetta (1975), *African Apostles: Ritual and Conversion in the Church of John Maranke*. Ithaca, N.Y.: Cornell University Press.

Kraemer, Hendrik (1938), *The Christian Message in a Non-Christian World*. New York: Harper & Brothers.

— (1954), "Syncretism as a Religious and a Missionary Problem," in: *International Review of Missions* 43: 253–73.

Lawson, E. Thomas/McCauley, Robert N. (1990), *Rethinking Religion: Connecting Cognition and Culture*. Cambridge: Cambridge University Press.

Leopold, Anita (2001), "The Architecture of Syncretism: A Methodological Illustration of the Dynamics of Syncretism," in: *Historical Reflections/Réflexions Historiques* 27 (3): 401–23.

Lewis, I.M. (1971), *Ecstatic Religion*. London: Routledge.

Light, Timothy (2000a), "Orthosyncretism: An Account of Melding in Religion," in: *Perspectives on Method and Theory in the Study of Religion*, ed. by A.W. Geertz/R.T. McCutcheon. Leiden: Brill: 162–86.

— (2000b), "Transcendent Identity," unpublished paper presented at the XVIIIth Congress of the International Association for the History of Religions, Durban, South Africa, 6–12 August 2000.

Lincoln, Bruce (2001), "Response to a Panel on 'Retrofitting Syncretism,'" in: *Historical Reflections/Réflexions Historiques* 27 (3): 453–59.

Martin, Luther H. (1983), "Why Cecropian Minerva? Hellenistic Religious Syncretism as System," in: *Numen* 30: 131–45.

— (1996), Historicism, Syncretism, Comparativism, in: *Religions in Contact*, ed. by I. Doležalová/B. Horyna/D. Papoušek. Brno: Czech Society for the Study of Religion: 31–37; revised as: "Syncretism, Historicism, and Cognition," in: *Method and Theory in the Study of Religion* 8: 215–24 (version cited).

— (2001a), "Comparativism and Sociobiological Theory," in: *Numen* 48 (3): 290–308.

— (2001b), "To Use 'Syncretism,' or Not to Use 'syncretism': That Is the Question," in: *Historical Reflections/Réflexions Historiques* 27 (3): 389–400.

McNeil, John Thomas (1964), *Unitive Protestantism*. Revised ed. Richmond, Va: John Knox Press.

Merton, R.K. (1968) *Social Theory and Social Structure*. New York: Free Press.
Moffatt, James (1922), "Syncretism," in: *The Encyclopedia of Religion and Ethics*, ed. by J. Hastings. Vol. 12. New York: Charles Scribner's Sons: 155–57.
Nock, Arthur Darby (1972 [1942]), "Ruler-Worship and Syncretism," in: Arthur Darby Nock, *Essays on Religion and the Ancient World*, ed. by Z. Stewart. Cambridge, Mass.: Harvard University Press: 551–58.
Pearson, Birger A. (1975), *Religious Syncretism in Antiquity: Essays in Conversation with Geo Widengren*. Missoula, Mont.: Scholars Press.
Pinker, Steven (1994), *The Language Instinct: How the Mind Creates Language*. New York: William Morrow.
Préaux, Claire (1978), *Le Monde Hellénistique*. 2 vols. Paris: Presses Universitaires de France.
Preisendanz, Karl (1956), "Zur synkretistischen Magie im römischen Ägypten," in: *Mitteilungen aus der Papyrussammlung der Österreichischen Nationalbibliotek (Papyrus Erzherzog Rainer)*. Neue Serie, 5. Folge, ed. by H. Gerstinger. Wien: Rohrer/ Österreichische Nationalbibliothek: 111–25.
Pye, Michael (1971), "Syncretism and Ambiguity," in: *Numen* 18: 83–93.
— (1994), "Syncretism versus Synthesis," in: *Method & Theory in the Study of Religion* 6: 217–29.
Reat, N. Ross/Perry, Edmund F. (1991), *A World Theology: The Central Spiritual Reality of Humankind*. Cambridge: Cambridge University Press.
Rose, Herbert Jennings/Parke, Herbert William (1970), "Syncretism," in: *The Oxford Classical Dictionary*. Second edition, ed. by N.G.L. Hammond/H.H. Scullard. Oxford: Clarendon Press: 1029.
Rudolph, Kurt (1979), "Synkretismus—vom theologischen Scheltwort zum religionswissenschaftlichen Begriff," in: *Humanitas Religiosa: Festschrift für Haralds Biezais zu seinem 70. Geburtstag*. Stockholm: Almquist & Wiksell: 194–212.
— (1983), *Gnosis: The Nature and History of Gnosticism*, translation ed. by R. McLachlan Wilson. San Francisco, Calif.: Harper & Row.
Saussure, Ferdinand de (1983 [1915]), *Course in General Linguistics*, transl. by R. Harrise. London: Duckworth.
Schenk, Wolfgang (1989), "Interpretatio Graeca-Interpretatio Romana. Der hellenistische Synkretismus als semiotisches Problem," in: *Innovationen in Zeichentheorien: Kultur- und wissenschaftsgeschichtliche Studien zur Kreativität*, ed. by P. Schmitter/ H.W. Schmitz. Münster: Nodus Publikationen: 83–121.
Schmid, Heinrich Friedrich Ferdinand (1846), *Geschichte der syncretischen Streitigkeiten in der Zeit des Georg Calixt*. Erlangen: Carl Heyder.
Sharpe, Eric J. (1975), *Comparative Religion. A History*. New York: Charles Scribner's Sons.
Showerman, Grant (1911), "Syncretism," in: *The Encyclopædia Britannica*. Eleventh ed. Vol. 26. New York: Encyclopædia Britannnica, Inc.: 292b–93a.
Smith, Jonathan Z. (1990), *Drudgery Divine: On the Comparison of Early Christianities and the Religions of Late Antiquity*. Chicago: The University of Chicago Press.
Smith, Wilfred Cantwell (1989), *Towards a World Theology*. Maryknoll, N.Y.: Orbis Books.
Sperber, Dan (1996), *Explaining Culture: A Naturalistic Approach*. Oxford: Blackwell.
Starr, Chester G. (1963), "Reflections upon the Problem of Generalization," in: *Generalization in the Writing of History*, ed. by L. Gottschalk. Chicago: The University of Chicago Press: 3–18.

Stevens-Arroyo, Anthony M. (1995), "Introduction," in: *Enigmatic Powers: Syncretism with African and Indigenous Peoples' Religions among Latinos*, ed. by A.M. Stevens-Arroyo/A.I Pérez y Mena. Program for the Analysis of Religion among Latinos 3. New York: Bildner Center for Western Hemisphere Studies: 9–17.

Stewart, Charles (1995), "Relocating Syncretism in Social Science Discourse," in: *Syncretism and the Commerce of Symbols*, ed. by A. Gören. Göteborg: The Institute for Advanced Studies in Social Anthropology: 13–37.

Stewart, Charles/Shaw, Rosalind, eds. (1994), *Syncretism/Anti-Syncretism: The Politics of Religious Synthesis*. London/New York: Routledge.

Tillich, Paul (1952), "Is There a Judeo-Christian Tradition?" in: *Judaism* 1: 106–109.

Turner, Mark (1996), *The Literary Mind: The Origin of Thought and Language*. New York: Oxford University Press.

van der Leeuw, Gerardus (1938 [1933]), *Religion in Essence and Manifestation: A Study in Phenomenology*, transl. by J.E. Turner. London: George Allen & Unwin.

Vroom, Hendrik M. (1989), "Syncretism and Dialogue: A Philosophical Analysis," in: *Dialogue and Syncretism: An Interdisciplinary Approach*, ed. by J.D. Gort et al. Grand Rapids, Mich.: Eerdmans: 26–35.

Wach, Joachim (1924), *Religionswissenschaft: Prolegomena zu ihrer wissenschaftstheoretischen Grundlegung*. Leipzig: J.C. Hinrichs.

Weber, Max (1930), *The Protestant Ethic and the Spirit of Capitalism*, transl. by T. Parsons. New York: Charles Scribner's Sons.

— (1947), *The Theory of Social and Economic Organization*, transl. by A.R. Henderson/T. Parsons. London: W. Hodge.

Whitehouse, Harvey (1995), *Inside the Cult: Religious Innovation and Transmission in Papua New Guinea*. Oxford: Oxford University Press.

— (2000), *Arguments and Icons: Divergent Modes of Religiosity*. Oxford: Oxford University Press.

Wolf, Arthur P. (1974), "Gods, Ghosts, and Ancestors," in: *Religion and Ritual in Chinese Society*, ed. by A.P. Wolf. Stanford, Calif.: Stanford University Press: 131–82.

Wolf, Eric (1982), *Europe and the People without History*. Berkeley, Calif.: California University Press.

Performance Theory and the Study of Ritual

by

RONALD L. GRIMES

The boundaries of religious studies are increasingly permeable. Religious studies scholars are as likely to be collaborating with anthropologists or performance studies scholars as with philosophers or theologians. So it should be no surprise that "performance" has become an important conceptual bridge among disciplines. Not only does it appear in titles such as *Sacred Performance: Islam, Sexuality and Sacrifice* (Combs-Schilling 1989), *Affecting Performance: Meaning, Movement, and Experience in Okiek Women's Initiation* (Kratz 1994) and *Ritual, Performance, Media* (Hughes-Freeland 1998), it is listed as a crucial category in the recent volume, *Critical Terms for Religious Studies* (Taylor 1998).

There have been at least two important moments in the recent discussion of ritual and performance. One was epitomized by the collaboration of Victor Turner, Richard Schechner, and Erving Goffman at the turn of the decade from the 1970s to the 1980s. The other was the publication of critiques of performance theories in the 1990s. The earlier phase, which saw ritual studies emerge as a self-conscious discipline, was decisively shaped by the thinking of three very prolific writers, whose work I will summarize and only briefly analyze. Because the later phase continues into the present, I will summarize it less thoroughly and criticize it more fully.

These two moments in the history of ritual theory make the most sense against a brief historical background chronicling the emergence of so-called performance approaches to ritual. Since the myth and ritual theory of the Cambridge School was a quest for origins, specifically the origins of theater in primordial ritual, I will not summarize this late nineteenth and early twentieth century approach. Contemporary theorists have largely given up origin questions for the sake of function questions.

The Emergence of Cultural Performance as a Category

Although the use of dramatistic principles ("role," for instance) as interpretive analogs to social interaction dates back at least to the 1930s, it was not until the mid-1950s that anything resembling cultural performance theory began to emerge. In 1954 Milton Singer visited India. Not officially fieldwork, the visit was preliminary. Its goal was to determine what he might subsequently research there. In service of this aim, he traveled, observed, and interviewed. Besides his baggage, he carried a theory consisting largely of Robert Redfield's distinctions between great and little traditions, as well as the two notions: ethos and worldview. Singer assumed he knew what a civilization and a tradition were, so he thought he might study "the cultural pattern of India," but soon he began to wonder: Is this too large a unit of study? What, he asked, might be a more viable unit?

Singer's report, published a year later, in 1955–56, is remarkable not only for the grandeur of his aspiration but also for his candor in reporting how ill served he was by his theories. Staggered by India's regional variations and its bewildering linguistic and religious diversity, he figured out what every new fieldworker soon discovers: One must focus, find "the smallest manageable unit" of research (Singer 1955: 25). He quickly recognized the dissonance between units of indigenous experience and those of scholarly observation. So, he asked, how might one *discover* a unit rather than *impose* or *import* one?

When Singer asked his Indian friends and consultants how he might study the cultural pattern of India, they directed him to rites, festivals, recitations, prayers, and plays—in short, to what he called "cultural performances." These became "the elementary constituents of the culture and the ultimate units of observation" (Singer 1955: 27). He assumed rather than argued that such performances display what is central for a culture, that they more revealingly expose deeply held values than do other, non-performative aspects of the same culture.

Besides being indigenous units, performance events had the added advantage of being bounded. They had clear beginnings and endings. They existed somewhere in particular. And, unlike ideas in the head or values in the heart, they were observable, even photographable. Cultural themes and values, Singer discovered, appear in cultural performances, which utilize various cultural media such as singing, dancing, and acting. Given the limitations of human finitude and the constraints of cross-cultural field research, the only possible access to a whole culture, a "total civilization," is by way of its most revealing constituent parts.

If there is a single, modern beginning of cultural performance theory, perhaps Singer's discovery (or assumption) is it. His approach, he said, did not arise as the result of a theatrical analogy carried into the field by an ethnographer and then applied to the data. Instead, the ethnographer found his theories largely inapplicable and replaced or modified them with the notion of cultural performances, and he did so because indigenous consultants pointed him toward them. Today, we may consider him mistaken, or we may object that he has imported a Western assumption (that performances encode cultural values), but we may not accuse him of woodenly imposing theatrical analogies on other societies.

More widely known than Singer's report was the use Clifford Geertz made of Singer's idea some twenty-five years later. What student of religion has not been required to read "Religion as a Cultural System"? Some have even had to memorize its famous definition of religion, of which Geertz's article is an exposition:

> A religion is: (1) a system of symbols which acts to (2) establish powerful, pervasive, and long-lasting moods and motivations in men by (3) formulating conceptions of a general order of existence and (4) clothing these conceptions with such an aura of factuality that (5) the moods and motivations seem uniquely realistic. (Geertz 1973: 90)

Geertz attributed to ritual the power for generating religion's aura of factuality. Whatever metaphysical reality the gods may or may not have, he argued, they enter the human plane in "concrete acts," that is, in "performances" (Geertz 1973: 112–13). Explicitly following Singer, Geertz claimed that we have access to things emotional and conceptual, to a people's ethos and world view, by way of public cultural performances. Geertz was keenly aware that participants understand ritual performances differently from observers. For participants such a performance is a religious rite, while for an observer it is a mere entertaining spectacle, an aesthetic form. For observers, these performances may be "models of" what participants believe, but for participants these performances are "models for" what they believe; they have prescriptive force. "In these plastic dramas men attain their faith as they portray it" (Geertz 1973: 114).

A decade later, Geertz considered three, genre-blurring analogies: social life as game, as drama, and as text. He found the results of using the dramatic analogy (on which performance theory apparently depends) confusing for two reasons. One was that there were conflicting ways of using it; the other was the tendency to overgeneralize and to ignore cultural and historical particulars. One the one hand, he said, the symbolic action approach (represented by Kenneth Burke) emphasizes the communicative, persuasive, and political dimensions of drama. On the other, the ritual theory approach (represented by Victor Turner) emphasizes experience (rather than communication) and concentrates on the connection between religion and theater. Geertz worried about the divide between these two sub-schools and criticized their tendency to create "a form for all seasons," a theoretical construct insufficiently nuanced to discriminate among the myriad forms of social interaction (Geertz 1983: 28).

Although Geertz would later study the highly drama-oriented Balinese theater state, treating the royal palace as if it were a stage, and civil ceremony as if it were theater, he never fully subscribed to the methods and preoccupations of Burke, Turner, or Goffman even though he employed dramaturgical language, often inconclastically, in order to debunk "the pretensions upon which the society turned" (Geertz 1980: 113, 116).

The Performative Convergence

Erving Goffman

The turn to drama and performance transpires most fully in the writing of sociologist Erving Goffman, anthropologist Victor Turner, and performance studies scholar Richard Schechner. Although other writers occasionally study performative dimension of ritual or use an occasional dramatistic metaphor, these are the theorists whose writing on the topic is most sustained and prolific.

Goffman applies both ritualistic and dramatistic terminology to ordinary social interaction: Greeting and departing are "ceremonial"; serving food in a restaurant is "dramatic." As he used them, the terms "ritual," "ceremony," and "drama" often sounded interchangeable, as if there were no significant differences among them. Social performance *is* ceremonial, "an expressive rejuvenation and reaffirmation of the moral values of the community" (Goffman 1959: 35). Insofar as a performance is taken to condense reality itself (rather than being a mere simulation of it), the performance is said to be "ceremonial." Goffman's conception of ceremony, or ritual (he typically uses the terms interchangeably), was thoroughly Durkheimian.

Occasionally, Goffman discriminated between performance and ceremony. For instance, in *Frame Analysis,* he remarks, "A play keys life, a ceremony keys an event" (Goffman 1974: 58). He means that a play simulates ordinary life in general, while a ceremony strips a deed of its ordinary context in order to create a highly focused event. In plays, he says, performers pretend to be characters other than themselves, while in ceremonies performers epitomize rather than pretend.

The idea of performance is important to Goffman insofaras it gives his theory its critical edge. Actions are deemed performances when they are not only done but done to be seen. In being done to be seen, they inevitably misrepresent, thus the outcome of Goffman's theory is a hermeneutic of suspicion. The Goffman-inspired interpreter is set to searching for the backstage area, in which he or she can spy the face behind the front-stage mask. From a Goffmanian perspective, all social interaction is performance, and performance becomes ritualized when someone insists on the sacred unquestionableness of what is being presented. To ritualize is to deny or hide the discrepancy between front and back stage behavior.

Goffman is at his most ritually serious when he asserts, "The self is in part a ceremonial thing, a sacred object which must be treated with proper ritual care" (Goffman 1967: 91). In his view, a ceremony, or rite, is not merely a thing done or only an analogy for social interaction. Rather, ceremony is how the self is constituted. The ritually constituted self is essential to survival in society, a "sacred game." Goffman conflates ludic (play-driven), ritualistic, and dramatic language to present a view of contemporary, supposedly secular life in which the sacred, game-constituted self becomes a god: "The individual is so viable a god because he can actually understand the ceremonial significance of the way he is treated, and quite on his own can respond dramatically to what is proffered him. In contacts between such deities there is no need for middlemen; each of these gods is able to serve as his own priest" (Goffman 1967: 95).

Whereas the notion of performance allowed Goffman to question and expose, the notion of ceremony (or ritual) connoted the activity of tranquilizing questions, evading criticism. Thus, in his theory, the term "ritual" is suspect in a way that the word "performance" never is. This view is both the strength and weakness of his theory. On the one hand, Goffman, more than any other scholar, has helped us notice what some call ritualization and others, interaction ritual: the repetitive, stylized bits that suffuse ordinary life. On the other, he had little interest in "special" rites such as highly differentiated liturgies; the ordinary world was ritual enough. His ideas are little help in studying formal rites, since his conceptual power arose from the metaphoric move of interpreting ordinary interaction *as if* it were ritual.

Goffman would inculcate a hermeneutic of suspicion. There is nothing wrong with suspicion, since rites are means of exploitation as surely as they are of healing. But if suspicion and debunking are the only postures that observers and interpreters assume, the attitude becomes self-consuming and forecloses the possibility of genuine interaction between ritual performers and ritual theorists.

Victor Turner

If Erving Goffman was the ritual skeptic employing the idea of performance to debunk highly managed personae or expose ritual cover-ups, Victor Turner was the ritual enthusiast using the idea of drama to enhance and transform the reigning conception of ritual. By construing everyday life as performative, Goffman saw it as riddled with pretense. By considering social processes as dramatic, Turner saw it as conflict ridden but also culturally generative. For Turner, as for Goffman, society itself is inherently dramatic, creating the possibility for stage drama and the inescapability of performance in ritual.

Like Milton Singer, Victor Turner believed he had discovered drama in the field, that he did not carry the concept of drama into the field with him. However, the phenomenon he tagged "social drama" did not consist of plays and celebrations, as it had for Singer, but rather of patterned social conflicts. They follow a predicable and universal form: breach, crisis, redress, and reintegration. This sort of drama, said Turner, is prior to, and the ground of, stage drama. The two kinds of drama feed one another.

Turner was convinced that the redressive phase, in both its religious and its legal forms, is a primary source of ritual (Turner 1991: 12, 17). Since he held that the liminal phase of the ritual process gives rise to theater, the implied sequence is: social drama, ritual, theater. Turner put it another way that is perhaps truer to his intentions, because it makes the process sound less linear and more dialectical: "The processual form of social dramas is implicit in aesthetic dramas (even if only by reversal or negation), while the *rhetoric* of social dramas—and hence the shape of argument—is drawn from cultural performances. There is a lot of Perry Mason in Watergate!" (Turner 1979: 81; see also Turner 1980: 153).

The argument implied by this scheme is less a claim about what once happened long ago (as when the Cambridge school claimed that drama emerged from primordial ritual) than it is a generalization about everyone's experience in every society (Turner 1980: 149).[1] To evaluate Turner's thesis one would have to ask questions such as: Does social drama ever have *other* phases? Or *more* phases? Or *fewer*? And, does ritual ever arise from the other phases (breach, crisis, or reintegration)? Or from outside the social-drama process altogether?

From the 1950s through the 1970s "drama" was Turner's preferred term; in this period he wrote works such as "Frame, Flow, and Reflection: Ritual and Drama as Public Liminality" (Turner 1977), "Dramatic Ritual/Ritual Drama" (Turner 1979), "Social Dramas and Stories about Them" (Turner 1980), and *Dramas, Fields, and Metaphors* (Turner 1974). But by the early 1980s, influenced by Richard Schechner and the emerging field of performance studies, Turner began to speak more frequently about performance in articles such as "Performing Ethnography" (Turner/Turner 1982) and "Liminality and the Performative Genres" (Turner 1985), and *The Anthropology of Performance* (Turner 1987).

Although the terms "ritual" and "drama" were almost synonymous for Turner, the connotation of "drama" was that of patterned social conflict, while "performance" suggested role playing and the awareness of being watched. Although Turner probably wrote more about the relations between ritual and drama (or performance) than any Western scholar in the twentieth century, he showed little interest in dramatism, the extended application of the drama analogy, the systematic exposition of either ritual or of non-theatrical life *as if* they were theatrical.[2]

Turner never quite made theater an object of study in the way he did ritual. Nevertheless, he celebrated theater and attributed to it something of a privileged role as "the most forceful, *active* … genre of cultural performance"

1 Turner, however, never completely gave up the evolutionary belief that aesthetic forms of cultural performance were derived from the religious and ritualistic ones. See, for instance, Turner 1980: 161.

2 As far as I know, the only attempt at a fully dramatistic approach to ritual is David Cole's *The Theatrical Event* (Cole 1975). It uses a set of categories—script, actor, audience, scene, language, and interpretation—to explore connections between theater and a specific kind of ritualizing, shamanism.

(Turner 1982: 104). In complex industrial societies, he held, theater accomplishes many of the functions traditionally achieved in small-scale ones by rites of passage. But theater, because it depends on the liminoid rather than the liminal, has the added advantage of being "suffused with freedom" (Turner 1982: 120). However generative of creativity the liminal phase of a rite of passage may be, it is replete—especially in initiation rites—with totalitarian dangers, whereas contemporary Western theatrical experience, because it is chosen, enhances rather than obliterates individuality. Even though it often seems that Turner *liked* ritual more, he sounds like he *trusted* theater more. For instance, he worried about the mystery-laden ritualizing of Jerzy Grotowski's paratheatrical events but praised the iconoclastic theatricalizing of Richard Schechner.

In defending himself against Geertz's claims that the anthropological use of dramatistic analogies leads to overgeneralizations and that textual analogies are more nuanced, Turner replied that texts, whether social or literary, are best understood not in the abstract but in the context of the performances they inspire (Turner 1982: 107). Turner saw no good reason why anthropologists should not make use of both metaphors, as both he and Geertz, in fact, did. He remained convinced that experience is deepest when social drama and stage drama, performance and text, illumine one another, not when one is treated as more real than the other.

Because rites are essentially performative, Turner eventually felt the need to teach about them in a performative manner. What he called "performing ethnography" (Turner/Turner 1982), was an attempt to understand other cultures' rites by enacting them dramatically in classrooms and workshops. In collaboration with Richard Schechner, Erving Goffman, Edith Turner (his wife), and others he turned his ethnography of the Ndembu into a "ethnodramatic" script, for which the agonistic social drama scheme provided the basic form (Turner 1979: 84). The workshops transpired in a series of nested frames. The ethnographically constructed ritual script was nested with a play-drama frame, and the play-drama frame within a pedagogical frame. Much of the learning occurred as students in the workshops experienced frame slippage, and as they failed to enter or sustain a frame.

Although deeply influenced by Victor Turner's ideas, I also have reservations about them. It is one thing to study ritual and drama comparatively, quite another to claim that ritual universally arises from social drama. Even though there are good examples in which it does, I know of no convincing evidence that this is the usual, much less the universal, way rites emerge.

Another problem is that of building value judgements into the definition of ritual, in effect, making "ritual" mean "good ritual" or "real ritual," thus using it as a criterion.[3] Turner defined ritual and ceremony in such a way that "cere-

3 A more fully developed critique of his definition can be found in Grimes 1990.

mony" merely confirms or consolidates, while "ritual" transforms. He frequently dropped an additional adjective, "true" or "pure," in front of "ritual" to indicate that he was not talking about ceremony. "Religion," he says, like art, *lives* insofar as it is performed, that is, insofar as rituals are 'going concerns.' If you wish to spay or geld religion, first remove its rituals, its generative and regenerative processes" (Turner 1980: 167). The metaphoric identification of rites with sex organs is quite revealing.

For Turner, the primary model for transformation was the rite of passage, specifically the liminal phase of initiation. And if one examines his and van Gennep's sources, it is clear that the predominant examples are of male initiation. In the final analysis, Turner defined the whole of ritual in terms of a part, a very small one at that. Initiation furnished the original paradigm not only for ritual in general but for cultural creativity and change.

Because rites of passage, liminality, social drama, and *communitas* have become such generative ideas, and because they continue to be unreflectively cited and popularly venerated, we should recognize some of their limitations. For instance, is it really as obvious as Turner claims that rites transform? In some societies rites are not even thought to *transform*, that is, to change things fundamentally. Instead, rites of birth, coming of age, marriage and death *protect* participants, or they *celebrate* transformations that have already occurred by other means. The Bemba say their rites *purify* women at the moment of first menses. This is a view quite different from one which holds that the rite transforms girls into women. And it suggests that we cannot *assume* that rites transform any more than we can assume they conserve. In my view the most vexing problem in Turner's theory of ritual is not his dramatism (as some have claimed) but his "transformationism," the ideological assumption that rites, by definition, transform. Some do; some do not. Which do and which do not should be a matter of observation, not of definition. Not all ritual actors intend to transform, but even if they do, the intention does not guarantee the results. A group may intend to transform and fail to do so, or, as Vincent Crapanzano has shown regarding the initiation of Muslim boys in Morocco, it may say it transforms when, in fact, it does not (Crapanzano 1980).

Richard Schechner

Although Richard Schechner continues certain lines of thought developed by Turner, Schechner is far too prolific and his sources too diverse to be regarded as a mere Turnerian. In religious studies and anthropology Schechner is less well known than Turner, but Schechner not only facilitated Turner's involvement in experimental theater and nurtured his interest in performance theory, he consolidated the field of performance studies. Few other scholars or directors have Schechner's varied experience as an observer of rites and as an experimenter with dramatic and ritualistic processes.

Schechner is a theater director as well as a performance studies scholar and editor of *The Drama Review*. The Performance Group, which met in the Performing Garage under his direction, was a widely known experimental theater collective. His theatrical and theoretical research is widely studied in drama departments as well as experimental theater circles. Not a systematically theoretical writer, he is nevertheless a prolific one who cuts an impressive swath from practice to observation to theory. His writing falls into four rough categories: (1) *theatrical*—spirited, sometimes prophetic, participation in ongoing debates about contemporary experimental theater; (2) *theoretical*—schematic attempts to diagram and conceptualize the genres and dynamics of performance; (3) *ethnographic*—anecdotal writings based on field study and observation; and (4) *cultural*—essays on the modern-to-postmodern transition. For ritual studies the most important essays are "Drama, Script, Theatre and Performance" and "From Ritual to Theatre and Back" (Schechner 1977), "Restoration of Behavior" (Schechner 1985), "Performers and Spectators Transported and Transformed" (Schechner 1985) and "The Future of Ritual" (Schechner 1993).

Many of Schechner's later ideas are foreshadowed in the early piece, "Six Axioms for Environmental Theatre" (Schechner 1973; written in 1968). He treats the theatrical event as a set of related transactions in which no element (actor, text, etc.) has automatic precedence, and he rejects any attempt to predefine the uses of theater space or to establish one-dimensional theories that explain everything theatrical. What he calls "environmental" theater is poly-focused and all-encompassing, not dependent on having one place defined as "for acting" and another, "for the audience." From this basic position most of his later ideas follow.

Schechner refuses to isolate ritual from drama and play, treating all three as forms of performance, which he defines as "ritualized behavior ... permeated by play" (Schechner 1977: 52). The outcome of treating ritual as a species of performance is a theory of ritual that places it among, rather than above or outside, a large range of other cultural activities. In his discussion of "the magnitudes of performance" (Schechner/Appel 1990: 20–21), Schechner lays out a massive and impressive chart comparing sacred rites of passage with sandlot baseball, hostage crises, the Olympic games, national network television, and a host of other human activities. His aim is not to equate them but to demonstrate how they utilize the same basic temporal and spatial processes.

Defining ritual in relation to other kinds of performance, Schechner distinguishes "transformation" from "transportation" (Schechner 1985: 117ff.; Schechner 1977: 63ff.). On the one hand, rites of passage effect a transformation of social state: A dead person becomes an ancestor; a man and a woman become one flesh, and so on. On the other, Euro-American actors are transported, carried away by, and into, their roles, but they are always returned to them selves. Their performances do not effect a change of status in the way a rite of passage does. Western stage actors re-enter ordinary life at the same point they left it.

Transportation, however, is not identical with theater nor transformation with ritual. Possession rites can transport and certain kinds of theater, that of Jerzy Grotowski for instance, can transform. Ritual performance may not "go anywhere." Such is the case, for example, with the Sanskrit drama of the *Natyasastra*. It does not develop toward an Aristotelean resolution but works out variations of themes, resulting in a collective transportation rather than a goal-oriented transformation. So it seems that Schechner implicitly recognizes that ritual is not necessarily transformative.

Even though Schechner emphasizes the similarities among drama, popular entertainment, and ritual, he does not ignore the essential differences, which he plots on a continuum running from efficacy to entertainment (Schechner 1977: 75ff.). The basic opposition, he insists, is not between ritual and theater but between efficacy and entertainment. Both ritualistic and theatrical activity effect and entertain, but ritual *emphasizes* efficacy and theater, entertainment. Schechner's own theatrical values are such that he would reject a purely entertainment-oriented theater. When a performance is efficacious, he teasingly calls it a "transformance." Although this sort of transformation is traditionally attributed to rites of passage, theater has its own ways: Destructive behavior is displayed and thus rendered non-destructive; ordinary people are made into extraordinary characters transforming actors into stars.[4]

So for Schechner ritual and theater have important differences, but they are not absolute opposites. They become so only in specific cultures where aesthetic theater emerges or where ritual is shorn of its entertaining functions. In many cultures and historical periods, performance is a "braided structure" of efficacy and entertainment. Sometimes the braid is loose and sometimes, tight. When it is tight, ritualization is rife. In Schechner's thumbnail historical sketch of Western theater, this tightening occurs in fifth-century Athenian theater, late medieval and Renaissance theater, and in American experimental theater of the late 1960s and early 1970s. In all three historical moments there was noticeable ritualizing. "Efficacy," he says of experimental theater, "lies at the ideological heart of all aspects of this new theatre" (Schechner 1977: 77). Schechner's own theatrical productions have tried to overcome what he regards as the senile, ineffectual aesthetic of Western theater. His reason for arguing that No, Kathakali, Balinese Ketchak, and medieval European morality plays offer the best

4 Michelle Anderson (Anderson 1982: 106) has extended the analytical scope of Schechner's efficacy-entertainment continuum by showing how efficacious Voodoo ritual is regularly associated with closed spaces or back regions not accessible to tourists; whereas entertainment Voodoo is consistently correlated with front regions open to the public.

models for the future of theater is that they balance modes of transformation. Not mere shows, they are "showings of doings" (Schechner 1977: 66).

By insisting that the distinctive element in ritual is its transformative efficacy, Schechner illustrates his debt to the intellectual tradition that links van Gennep and Turner. Although Schechner says little or nothing about rites of passage theory, and he writes little about initiation, he considers both theater and tourism through lenses ground on rites of passage and initiation theory. For him, ritual performances *do* rather than merely mean; they *initiate* action rather than merely reflect on it.

Schechner argues that the convergence of ritual and theater is most evident in theater's workshop-rehearsal phase (Schechner 1977: 132ff.). Ritualizing is less evident in the finished production than in the preparation process. Schechner makes an important distinction between actor training and rehearsal. During rehearsal exact procedures are set in place to be repeated later, whereas actor training grows out of workshops and is not aimed at a specific production but at communicating generalized skills and bodily as well as attitudinal readiness.

In most Western acting traditions emphasis is upon rehearsal, while in Asian ones such as No the emphasis is upon preparation. Postmodern theater has witnessed a growing interest in preparation and thus Asian performance methods. One cannot rehearse transformation, only prepare for it.

In early phases of the theatrical process, says Schechner, actors and directors search for actions that work, ones they will keep for performance. In doing so, he argues, they undergo the phases of a traditional rite of passage. First, they separate themselves from ordinary street life and begin to strip away cliches; they are made "raw." Next, they undergo an initiation into the life and skills of the group in order to gather new materials. They combine personal elements with non-personal ones such as texts. They either learn by rote imitation or else master a generative code that enables them to build characters and string together actions. And finally, they reintegrate themselves into the larger society by presenting long strips of restored behavior for public viewing. They present themselves transformed, "cooked." During the rehearsal process the only audience is the group itself; it is a kind of congregation or tribe. In this respect the rehearsal process, more obviously than the theatrical product, is akin to a rite of passage.

Theatre arises when an audience emerges as a separate group, when it is accidental rather than integral (Schechner 1977: 46). Integral audiences do not pay as strict attention to the performance as accidental audiences do. In fact, not paying direct attention is one way of showing off the fact that one already knows what is going on. Relaxed inattention creates the proper conditions under which a performance can be absorbed, thereby exercising formative power over everyday life.

Applying Schechner's theory requires not only that one observe all the phases of a performative event from training through aftermath but also calls upon interpreters to notice the intensity and shape of an action. Like Turner, Schechner pays considerable attention to "flow," a state of consciousness in which actors are not separated from themselves and action seems to arise spontaneously of its own accord. Dialectically opposed to, but necessarily connected with, flow is reflexivity, a state of consciousness in which a society recognizes itself. Understanding a performance requires one to study the rhythm of movement between flow and reflexivity. Performances differ widely in the way they build toward the concentrated attention of flow and in the way they distance themselves in reflexivity.

Schechner is especially astute in his analysis of postmodern ritualizing, or what he calls "restored" behavior, events transpiring between fact and fiction (Schechner 1985: 35ff.). Unlike most religious studies scholars and anthropologists he attends to rites theatricalized for tourists in Haiti or for the cameras of Western anthropologists in India. Such performances are the results not of reaching back to some original, archaic layer but of pursuing continuous cultural reinvention.

Schechner's comparison of theme parks such as Plimoth [sic] Plantation in Plymouth, Massachusetts, with traditional rites is one of the most suggestive treatments in current scholarship. He shows how ritualists and performers cross and re-cross the lines of make-believe. The eras, costumes, settings, and behavior restored by rites and theme parks such as Williamsburg are fabrications; participants are "not not actors." The double negative is Schechner's way of suggesting how drastically immersed in ambiguity these events are. One cannot say these performers *are* actors any more than ritual actors are, but neither is it accurate to say they are *not* actors, so by describing them as "not not" actors, Schechner calls attention to their participation in both realms, fiction and reality. Although Schechner seems to revel in restored behavior, he also worries that it, in the form of international tourism, can feed into a world monoculture.

Schechner's "restored behavior," like Turner's "liminoid" and "subjunctive," is an attempt to define an emergent ritual sensibility in the postmodern world. The tone, however, is different. Schechner's emphasis falls on the fictive, contrived nature of such events. Since ritualists "rebehave," they *never* act naively: There is no first, or original, act that charters subsequent performances. Consequently, actors are able to distance themselves from their actions, which they can then treat like a strip of film consisting of frames whose sequence and number can be modified and rearranged. Because restored behavior is separable from performers, it can be composed into scenarios and directed by rubrics; it facilitates reflexivity, seeing ourselves act. Performances are not necessarily based on actual events in the past but rather on previous performances, "nonevents." Restored behavior allows performers to become someone other, or, as

Schechner, in his impish manner, puts it "to rebecome what they never were" (Schechner 1991: 443).

Schechner's and Turner's ideas are quite compatible. Since my critique of Schechner would echo much of what I said about Turner's preoccupation with transformation, I will not repeat it here. Schechner seems comfortable with Turner's view of social drama as the origin of ritual and theater, but he sometimes put the matter more bluntly by arguing that violence and sexuality are the driving, generative forces of ritual and dramatic performance (Schechner 1993). It would be difficult to deny the centrality of both themes in Western theater and film, but it also would not be difficult to find examples of ritual that evade or elide them. Even if sexuality and violence were utterly pervasive as themes, that would not be proof that they were the generative sources of ritual. I am much less inclined than either Turner or Schechner to think there is a single source of ritualizing.

Goffman, Turner, and Schechner are not the only ones to have written about the relations between ritual and performance. I have chosen to concentrate on them, because I believe that further theorizing about ritual's performative dimensions will be most effective if it elicits a thorough appreciation and critique of their work. There are many others who have written about performance and ritual: Bobby Alexander (Alexander 1997), M.E. Combs-Schilling (Combs-Schilling 1989), Margaret Thompson Drewal (Cominsky 1977), Tom Driver (Driver 1998), James Fernandez (Fernandez 1974a, 1974b, 1977), Felicia Hughes-Freeland (Hughes-Freeland 1998; Hughes-Freeland/Crain 1998), Corinne Kratz (Kratz 1994), Carol Laderman and Marina Roseman (Laderman/Roseman 1996), Gilbert Lewis (Lewis 1980), Roy Rappaport (Rappaport 1999), Edward L. Schieffelin (Schieffelin 1985), Stanley Tambiah (Tambiah 1979), and I (Grimes 1990a, 1992a, 1994). But none of us has been as consistently focused on the topic, as prolific, and as influential.

The Critical Turn

The convergence that I have sketched was characterized by enormous intellectual energy, widespread interdisciplinary collaboration, and risky experimentation. The second moment, which we are still in, is less daringly collaborative, not so energetic, and skeptical of the ritual studies in general, performance approaches in particular.

For instance, a brief but trenchant critique of Turner has been advanced by Caroline Bynum (Bynum 1984; see also Lincoln 1981). Her arguments are aimed specifically at his theory of liminality and his notion of dominant symbols. Even though her reservations are based on women's stories rather than women's rites, they imply a rejection of basic assumptions in rites of passage theory. Bynum's argument can be summarized in four related statements: (1)

Compared with men's lives, women's lives have either fewer or no turning points. Even if men's lives develop by utilizing conflict and developing in distinct stages, women's lives do not, or, if they do, women's dramas are often incomplete. (2) Women's symbols do not invert their lives; they enhance their lives. The symbols emphasize continuity, not reversal. (3) Liminality is not a meaningful category for women, because either they are permanently liminal (thus the category is meaningless) or they are never truly liminal at all. (4) Liminality is a theory from the point of view of a man looking *at* women, not a theory that assumes the point of view of women looking at the world. Thus, says Bynum, liminality is better understood as a temporary respite from obligation by élite men of power.[5]

This critique is a far cry from the Turnerian celebration of liminality as *the* engine of ritual and culture, and it should make one cautious about definitions. When Robbie Davis-Floyd, for instance, defines ritual as "a patterned, repetitive, and symbolic enactment of a cultural belief or value," adding that "its primary purpose is transformation" (Davis-Floyd 1992: 8), she risks contaminating her feminist treatment of birth ritual with a view of ritual skewed by its over-reliance on the model of male initiation rites. When claiming that rites transform, it is important not to romanticize or merely theorize. A way to avoid both errors is to specify what a rite changes and to say what degree of change transpires. In an initiation, for instance, transformation may occur in: a participant's self-perception; in restructured relationships with cosmic or divine powers; in access to power, knowledge or goods; and in re-defined kin- and other social relationships. We need to ask: What are the "before" and "after" states, and how do they compare? How significant is the change? Who is changed by a given rite of passage? What happens to ritual theory if we admit that liminality is a gender-specific category?

In addition to the transformationism and tacit sexism of Turner's and Schechner's initiation-derived models, it is not a foregone conclusion that performance theories of ritual are the best ones. Although I believe they *could* be, they will never in fact be worthwhile unless we first critique and consolidate them.

Catherine Bell has done ritual studies the service of launching the most serious and sustained critique of performance-oriented approaches to ritual. Although I consider several of her arguments to be wrong-headed, Bell has opened up an important debate. Her theoretical contribution is contained largely in two books, *Ritual Theory, Ritual Practice* (Bell 1992) and *Ritual: Perspectives and Dimensions* (Bell 1997), as well as one key article, "Performance" (Bell 1998). In all three she is ambivalent about both ritual and theory. She is concerned that rites as well as theories of ritual have assumed an aura of

5 Brief parts of this section are modifications borrowed from Grimes 2000.

unquestioned universality, thereby exercising an unwarranted domination. At times she seems to deny that she herself is presenting a definition of ritual or a theoretical alternative (Bell 1992: ix, 80, 140). The first sentence of *Perspectives* puts "ritual" in quotation marks (Bell 1997: ix); they appear and disappear throughout the book. Sometimes the word ritual is preceded by pejorative adjectives such as "so-called." Bell says she resists formal definitions and explicit theories because she thinks ritual is not "an intrinsic, universal category or feature of human behavior" (Bell 1997: ix).

If Bell's writing were more ironic and playful or consistently deconstructive, it would be pointless to engage her ambivalence. Like trying to "solve" a Zen *koan*, the exercise would be futile because the circularity and ambivalence would be infinite and thus irresolvable. But in my view, Bell *acts as if* ritual exists: She writes almost six hundred pages on the topic. In addition, she is sufficiently theoretical both to define ritual and to criticize other people's theories of it. Since one can both locate and debate her definitions and theoretical statements, it makes sense to regard her ambivalence as penultimate rather than ultimate, a rhetorical defense rather than a thoroughgoing, deconstructionist (or non-essentialist) epistemology. Likely, Bell would resist attempts to read her through her works, as well as attempts to treat her writings as a theory, but her own method invites one to "read through" her words: "Ultimately, this book will argue that talk about ritual may reveal more about the speakers than about the bespoken" (Bell 1997: xi). If this claim is true about ritual theorists in general, it is also true of Bell herself.

The Circularity of Ritualization

In concluding her first book, Bell describes her own position as one in which "ritual as such does not exist" (Bell 1992: 141). But this fact does not stop her from using the term, either when summarizing other scholars' views or when explaining her own. Despite her repeatedly expressed desire to dispense with the category of ritual, she nevertheless uses it, offering characterizations that act like definitions, for example, "The most subtle and central quality of those actions we tend to call ritual is the primacy of the body moving about within a specially constructed space, simultaneously defining (imposing) and experiencing (receiving) the values ordering the environment" (Bell 1997: 82). Bell's writing is replete with statements that sound like definitions even though she may intend them to be only descriptions: "Ritual is the medium chosen to invoke those ordered relationships that are thought to obtain between human beings in the here-and-now and non-immediate sources of power, authority and value" (Bell 1997: xi). Read in context, it is often impossible to know whose view she is representing—hers, other theorists, or ritualists themselves.

Bell's reservations about the universalizing and hegemonic pretensions of the term "ritual" lead her to prefer the term "ritualization." She hopes to avoid the twin dilemma, into which every one else falls, namely, that of too neatly and narrowly cordoning off ritual from other social behavior and that of making it a dimension of all human activity. Another outcome of Bell's argument against the circularity that she finds so characteristic of ritual theory is that it challenges the claim that ritual provides a privileged window on cultural meaning. With the loss of this privilege, she says, ritual requires a different placing or framing. It must be moved out of the realm of the paradigmatic and special and into the context of ordinary social activity. Focusing on ritualization, she believes, will help theorists avoid falsely and neatly treating ritual as special.

Bell defines ritualization formally and minimally, as "a way of acting that differentiates some acts from others" (Bell 1992: ix). But repeated reference to other qualities of action imply that they too are definitive. Ritualization is also "a strategy for the construction of a limited and limiting power relationship (Bell 1992: 8), and it aims at "the production of a ritualized body" (Bell 1992: 98). The fuller, implied definition, then, would go something like this: "Ritualization is a way of acting that differentiates itself from others, producing a ritualized body and constructing a limited and limiting power relationship."

Although Bell is hesitant to define "ritual" in a way that is cross-cultural or universal, she seems to have few such reservations about her own definition of "ritualization." Readers cannot assume that Bell's critique of "ritual's" universalizing pretensions will lead her to refrain from universalizing. She has her own way of re-importing what she casts out to sea. For example, she says, "Despite the potential for great cultural variations, however, it is still possible to point to some *basic strategies* [my emphasis] that appear to underline many ways of ritualizing" (Bell 1997: 166). She then continues describing rites and ritual-like activities with an eye to ferreting out strategies that characterize not only ritualization but ritual-like activities as well. The procedure differs little from those that inspire scholars to search for widespread ritual patterns that they label "ritual." Whether one calls them "basic" rather than "universal" hardly matters.

By the end of *Ritual Theory* Bell is summarizing the qualities of ritualization in a way that parallels other theorists' attempts to define ritual. Ritualization, she tells us, is characterized by differentiation, formalization, periodicity, bodiliness, schematization, mastery, and negotiation (Bell 1992: 220). Bell does not treat these features as definitive, but she does say they are "*very common* [my emphasis] to ritualization." They are not unique, but, in tandem with one another, they render ritualization as an identifiable, if not special, domain, a way of acting that theorists can recognize. One does not avoid universalism by using the term "common" instead of "universal."

Bell's critique of the term "ritual" does not prevent her from using it; she does not rely exclusively on the term "ritualization" as one might expect. If one tracks her globalizing statements through both books, the term "ritualization" grows considerably beyond its initial, minimal formulation. For instance, she says,

> Fundamental to *all* [my emphasis] strategies of ritualization examined previously is the appeal to a more embracing authoritative order that lies beyond the immediate situation. Ritualization is *generally* [my emphasis] a way of engaging some wide consensus that those acting are doing so as a type of natural response to a world conceived and interpreted as affected by forces that transcend it—transcend it in time, influence, and meaning, if not in ontological status. Ritualization tends to posit the existence of a type of authoritative reality that is seen to dictate to the immediate situation (Bell 1997: 169).

What Bell gives away with the right hand (a definition of ritual) she takes back with the left (a set of generalizations about ritualization). Her implied definition of ritualization is as amorphous and as universalistic as any of those she criticizes.

Bell counsels theorists not to assume their definitions will fit all the data everywhere in the world. She also counsels modesty in making claims about ritual's power. Bell hopes to formulate a balanced, realistic understanding of the power of ritualization. She insists that it *is* power, not merely a mask for, or expression of, power emanating from elsewhere, a mere functional or expressive medium (Bell 1992: 197). One the one hand, she does not elevate ritual above the jockeying for power that typifies all human interaction. On the other, she does not think ritualization has the power to achieve anything very effectively; it is "a rather blunt tool" (Bell 1992: 212, 222).

Most of what Bell conceptualizes under the rubric "ritualization," I would have discussed as "ceremony," but my disagreement with her is not merely terminological. I agree that strategizing to establish systems of domination and inscribing value-laden schemes in the body is one of the tasks that all rites engage in to some extent and that some kinds of ritual engage in almost exclusively. There are other kinds and other layers however.

The Hegemony of Theory

Just as Bell speaks of ritualization rather than ritual, she regards her writings as reflection rather than as theory. "This description of acting ritually does not necessarily add up to a neat theoretical model than can be readily applied elsewhere ..." (Bell 1992: 141). If she were merely being modest, refusing to boast that her theory is finished or complete, I would have no qualms about this and other similar disclaimers. Theories should never be allowed to rest, as if they had attained the status of neat models. But by the second book Bell is referring back to the "theoretical arguments" of her first book (Bell 1997: x), and she is applying her own insights as if they were, in fact, a model. So I read her disclaimers as serving a defensive function: She does not want to be included among the theorists she criticizes. But in my view, her classifications, descriptions, historical sketches, critiques of other theorists, as well as her definitions, explicit and implicit, constitute theorizing. And as theory, they must necessarily be "applied elsewhere" by herself and by others. Otherwise, why make generalization at all? Otherwise, how might one test their range of applicability?

It would be unfair to expect Bell's first book to be a full-blown theory, since it is a loosely related collection of essays. But the book is unmistakably theoretical in intent, and its theoretical merits deserve to be debated. Bell does, after all, claim that she has forged a framework (Bell 1992: 219), and a framework is a theoretical construct. The second book is far more systematic. Even though it pursues an introductory agenda, it also does much of what we expect of any theory: pose definitions, lay out categories, examine the history of theory, and argue for her own alternative theory. In addition, Bell is far too vigorous in her critique of previous theories for one to accept her circumspection about theory as a mere deferral or as a neutral non-position. Hers is a highly polemical theory—however piecemeal—of ritual.

Despite its title, *Ritual Theory, Ritual Practice* says little about specific ritual practices. Even when Bell is talking about practice, her focus is usually the practice of theorizing rather than the practices of ritualization. The first chapter, called "Constructing Ritual," is about the construction of *the idea* of ritual; it is not about the construction of rites. It is mainly about what scholars do, not about what ritualists do. The book is largely about the concept of ritual and about ritual theory. Even so, it is less an argument with theorists than it is a hypothesis about the social and intellectual functions of both theorizing and ritualizing. It has far more to say about the act of theorizing than about the act of ritualizing. In my opinion Bell's own most accurate summary of the book's fundamental intention is that it is "an analytical exploration of the social existence of the concept of ritual" (Bell 1992: ix).

A major difficulty in reading Bell is her tendency to bleed the boundary between rites (the specific enactments) and ritual (the general idea). My criticism is not merely that she does not use the terms in the way I use them, but that the slippage displaces agency away from human actors, notably ritualists and ritual theorists. Sometimes she is precise in making the distinctions between ritual activity and formal theories of ritual. At other times the boundaries are fuzzy or nonexistent. For instance, she remarks, "From the perspective of ritualization the categories of sacred and profane appear in a different light" (Bell 1992: 91). Does she mean from the viewpoint of ritualists (ritual actors) engaged in ritualization? Or does she mean from the point of view of theorists engaged in thinking about ritual? Probably the latter, but even if we can guess correctly in this instance, the repeated collapsing of categories, which regularly results in the deletion of either the ritual theorist or the ritual practitioner, constitutes a serious problem for readers wanting to make sense of her theory. Bell observes, "Ritual has simultaneously become an object, a method, and even something of a style of scholarship ..." (Bell 1992: 3). Although I understand her point, it is difficult to tell whether Bell is acting strategically or carelessly when "ritual" rather than "ritual studies" is construed as a style of scholarship.

Not only does Bell often rhetorically conflate rites with ritual, ritualization, or even ritual studies, she reifies them. Ritualization, she declares, occurs when "certain social actions strategically distinguish themselves in relation to other actions" (Bell 1992: 74). Do actions distinguish themselves? Or do ritualists, ritual actors, do that? Bell uses this reified, reflexive construction throughout her writing (see, e.g., Bell 1992: 90). Another example: "The term 'ritual,' which pioneered the attempt to get beyond confessional perspectives ..." (Bell 1998: 205). Here, it is the term itself, rather than theorists who use the term, that does the pioneering. It is strange that someone who emphasizes strategic purpose would eliminate ritual actors—those who strategize—in such a way that actions themselves are imagined as doing the distinguishing.

Bell too is concerned about reification; she devotes an entire section to it (Bell 1997: 253ff.). But what she means by the term is the assumption that ritual has a substantive, universal form. What I mean by it is the tendency to treat either rites or the idea of ritual rather than ritualists or ritual theorists as actors and therefore as the subjects of verbs in sentences.

To the extent that Bell wants to discriminate between the part of ritual that belongs to the theorist and the part that belongs to the phenomenon itself, one would expect her to be fastidious about the distinction between rites and scholarly theorizing about ritual. Bell anticipates this sort of a critique by admitting that her treatment may not be entirely free of the circularity that she locates in other theorists (Bell 1992: 219). I would say that it is not at all free of such circularity.

The fact that her treatment is so strongly marked by circularity raises an interesting question: Why is it so hard for all of us, Bell included, to avoid the circularity that she both describes and illustrates? Is it perhaps an inevitable outcome, not just of mind/body dualism, but of the academy and its need to establish "sides" and then "mediate" them? Is the rhythm of polarizing and then reconciling peculiar to the study of ritual in particular, or is it endemic to theorizing in general? To put it another way, is there something about the study of ritual specifically that induces ritualization in the minds of theorists, driving them into the circularity of differentiating and then reconciling? I do not think so. Bell blames ritual theorists for constituting the object of their study. Do theorists of other sorts do any differently? I doubt it. Is there any important term in Western scholarship—religion, matter, mind, creation, reality—that is not marked by its own history and sociology? Again, I doubt it.

All primary terms in all theories in all languages carry their own linguistic and cultural baggage. It is useful to be reminded of this fact but pointless to talk or act as if culture- or history-free terminology were a possibility. "Ritualization" no more successfully escapes Western gravity than "ritual" does. On occasion Bell suggests that dichotomizing is endemic to all theorizing (Bell 1992: 48). If so, we should not expect her own theorizing to be any exception.

In my view Bell's most important contribution is less to the study of ritual than to the study of theory-making. She shows how the notion of ritual is repeatedly used by scholars as a third term for reconciling two other, initially bifurcated terms, most notably the pairs thought—action and scholar—ritualist. Bell is at her most persuasive in showing how inevitably theory-making is a strategic activity.

Bell's argument makes theorists look very much like Levi-Strauss's "primitives" whose mythic minds are always splitting the world into polarized pieces and then gluing them together again at some supposedly higher level. Bell takes Clifford Geertz, for example, to considerable task, accusing him of treating ritual as both an activity and as the fusion of thought and activity. It is as if Ritual, a contending party in a neighborhood quarrel, were to offer him- or herself as the mediator of the very quarrel in which he or she is engaged. Bell's critique of Geertz's "expedient homologizing" amounts to an expose of the scholar's new clothes. The scholar, in effect, invents, constructs, or projects contradictions and oppositions "out there" in the ritual world in order to have some problem to solve "in here" in the intellectual world. And Bell has caught him in the act. The portrait of Geertz is both devastating and funny. But it differs little from Bell's own identification of, and slippage between, ritual activity, on the one hand, and ritual discourse, on the other.

However critical Bell may be of theorists' strategies, readers are seldom informed of the strategic aims of Bell's own theory-making, except insofar as it is to expose the designs-to-power characteristic of other theorists. Theory-making, she implies, amounts to an act of domination insofar as it is an attempt to exercise power in the arena of cultural knowledge. (If we were to read her in terms of her own principles, we would be forced to construe her denial that she has produced a theory as a way of covering up her own attempt to dominate the field of ritual studies.)

Bell is no happier with ritual studies than with ritual, but her dismissal of it depends on caricatures, for instance: "Ritual studies, as a recent mode of discourse, has claimed an odd exemption from the general critique that scholarship distorts and exploits, tending to see itself, by virtue of its interest in ritual performances per se, as somehow able to transcend the politics of those who study and those who are studied" (Bell 1992: ix). Because of her rhetorical predilection for casting abstractions as subjects of sentences, it is impossible to know whose discourse she has in mind. But I, for one, have never claimed such an exemption. In fact, I have regularly insisted that ritual studies and ritual criticism, like rites themselves, are deeply embedded in politics. And I know of no other ritual studies scholar who claims this "odd exemption." If all Bell means is we could be more aware of the politics of our categories, who could disagree? But I suspect that she is doing more, namely, disidentifying with ritual studies and identifying with practice theorists.

The Misrecognition of Performance

Bell is critical of what she calls "performance approaches" to the study of ritual. Since I consider performance theory fruitful, I take issue with her. Bell's position in *Ritual: Perspectives and Dimensions* depends in part on rejecting performance theories of ritual and accepting a practice theory instead. Among those she treats as holding performance theories of ritual are Kenneth Burke, Victor Turner, Erving Goffman, Milton Singer, Clifford Geertz, Gilbert Lewis, Stanley Tambiah, Roy Rappaport, J.L. Austin, Robert Wuthnow, and myself. By her account, Gilbert Lewis and Stanley Tambiah are the most cautious and sophisticated representatives.

In *Ritual Theory* Bell puts "performance" in quotation marks, considers performance theory "gravely disadvantaged," and dismisses it in eight and a half pages. She credits performance theorists with desiring to transcend the conventional dichotomies but thinks they fail in their attempt. She criticizes us for assuming that ritual enacts "prior conceptual entities" (Bell 1992: 38), wallowing in a vague extended analogy, conceptualizing ritual in a self-interested way, and of having no way to differentiate among ways of performing.

Dualisms, she thinks, creep in the back door of performance theory. There are always other things prior to, or more fundamental than, ritual—things that ritual seeks to express, if not a script, then a structure or a body, a tacit meaning or a social role. But she herself does not escape the dilemma. She speaks of practice as incorporating a "framework" "embedded in the act itself" (Bell 1992: 85). A framework, like a conceptual entity or text, is somehow both "in" the ritual performance and the ground of it. Given her critique of ritual theory, one would expect Bell to be better able to escape the implications of the container metaphors (e.g., "embedded in") that trap most, if not all, ritual theorists.

For the most part Bell treats the notion of performance as a mere analogy: Performance theory amounts to an extended exploration of the statement: Ritual is *like* drama. Occasionally, for instance in discussing Singer, she treats the notion of performance as more than an analogy, but the "method," if there is one, is too obscure and imprecise to be useful. Bell concludes that performance theory "rests of course on the slippery implications of an extended metaphor" (Bell 1992: 42). The performance analogy is not much improvement on that other, even more revered analogy: Ritual is like a text (that one can "read"). In fact, she believes that the drama analogy is but a variation of the text analogy, inasmuch as both require interpreters to get at tacit meanings.

Bell indicts performance theorists, especially Turner and me, for making ourselves into a peculiar kind of audience necessary to the ritual event (Bell 1992: 39). In her view we subscribe to dramatistic analogies, because, by an "expedient logic," ritual interpreters make themselves a necessary audience for ritual performances. "We textualize ... not because rites are intrinsically like texts, but because we approach both looking for meaning as something that can be deciphered, decoded, or interpreted" (Bell 1992: 45). Bell's claim is that performance theorists devalue the rite itself by positing a latent meaning that can be discerned from a close reading or observation of the surface of a rite. Why do they do so? To make themselves necessary—crassly, to keep themselves employed. She ignores the obvious fact that for Turner drama is both a *source* of ritual and a *part* of ritual, not merely an analog to it. She overlooks the fact that for me drama is less an *analog* to ritual than an *object of study*, which I compare to ritual.

In her later volume, *Ritual: Perspectives and Dimensions*, Bell's portrait of performance theory is a bit more descriptive and a little less polemical. She expresses appreciation for performance theorists' ability to conceptualize active rather than passive roles for ritualists and to articulate ritual's role in creativity and social change. She suggests that performance theory construes ritual as (1) a sensuous event (2) framed by the use of stylization, metaphor, and rhythm and (3) capable of transformative efficacy, and (4) characterized public reflexivity (Bell 1997: 74–75). But in the end, Bell still considers performance theory a "welter of confusing emphases and agendas" (Bell 1997: 73) imposed upon other cultures without attempting to grasp participants' ways of classifying ritual and other types of human activity. She adheres to her earlier preference for practice theory rather than performance theory, and she continues to construe the latter as an exercise in extended analogy-making, to interpreting one unknown (ritual) in terms of another unknown (drama), a criticism that applies to Goffman but only partly to Turner and not at all to Schechner.[6]

In "Performance" (Bell 1998: 209ff.) Bell summarizes the contribution of performance theorists in a somewhat different way. They (1) emphasize human agents as active creators; (2) attend to the emotional, aesthetic, physical, and sensory aspects of religion; and (3) have a greater awareness of the scholar's own position in relation to observed action. In "Performance," Bell is kinder to performance theorists. Even though she still thinks practice theorists have a "surer focus" on the deployment of power in ritual, she appears less inclined to

6 Clifford Geertz (Geertz 1983, chapter 1), Max Gluckman (Gluckman 1977), and Raymond Firth (Firth 1974) all previously expressed reservations about drama as an anthropological concept.

polarize performance theory and practice theory. Instead she emphasizes their continuity: "By virtue of a shared concern to deal with action as action, all of these theoretical orientations [performance theory and practice theory] can be loosely grouped as 'performance approaches' to the study of religion" (Bell 1998: 205). She no longer accuses performance theorists of imposing predetermined categories. Rather the theorists try to "disclose the holistic dynamics of the phenomenon in its own terms" and to "let the activities under scrutiny have ontological and analytic priority" (Bell 1998: 211, 215). Instead of blaming performance theorists with hegemonic strategies, she credits them with "negotiating less reductive and arrogant relationship between the people who study and the people who are studied" (Bell 1998: 220). Her main reservation seems to be that metaphors of performance, systematically applied, might become so dominant that they occlude the object of study.

My main disagreement with Bell's attempt to characterize performance in her article for *Critical Terms for Religious Studies* is with her suggestion that using performance approaches may, in fact, undermine the usefulness of the concept of ritual (Bell 1998: 218). Apparently, she believes—and I do not—that those who use the notion of performance in performance studies are less universalistic in their aspirations than those who use the notion of ritual in ritual studies. Essentialism and universalism are temptations of every theorist, and they plague every theory.

Practice Theory

Bell, having rejected performance theory and its reliance on the notion of action, nevertheless repeatedly uses the notion of action when she turns to practice theory, which she considers a better alternative. Practice theorists include Karl Marx, Marshal Sahlins, Frederic Jameson, Antonio Gramsci, and Pierre Bourdieu. Though Bell has some reservations about these writers, she find the idea of ritual practice a more fruitful starting place than that of ritual performance. By doing so, she believes that she focuses on the "irreducible act itself" (Bell 1997: 81) rather than on something else behind or below ritual. If ritual is practice rather than performance, it is, in her view, (1) situational, (2) strategic, (3) fraught with misrecognition, and (4) committed to reproducing or reconfiguring the order of power in the world. "Ritual *necessarily* [my emphasis] shares these four features of practice" (Bell 1997: 88). In short, ritual, understood from a practice perspective, aims at "redemptive hegemony" (Bell 1997: 81); it attempts to save the world by dominating it.

Bell identifies three traits common to practice theories: (1) their insistence that ritual is a central arena in the historical process whereby patterns are both reproduced and transformed; (2) their assumption that rituals do not merely mean but also construct and inscribe power relationships; and (3) their attempt to jettison the category of ritual altogether (Bell 1997: 83). Since all three traits typify her own position, and since she summarizes her own work under the heading of practice theory, it is fair, I think, to treat her own theorizing as a variant of practice theory.

Despite her polemics against performance theory for its supposed universalism, Bell regularly makes statements about practice and practice theory that radiate universalistic aspirations. Often they are implied in phrases such as this: "Human practice *in general* [emphasis mine] has some common features ...," and these features, naturally, perfectly match those of practice theory. Not only does Bell regularly make tacit, universalistic claims, she makes judgments that are reductionistic, and they do not echo claims made by ritual participants, whose understanding of ritual Bell would defend from hegemonically inclined performance theorists. For instance, she says, "The ritual principles of ritual practice are *nothing other* [emphasis mine] than the flexible sets of schemes and strategies acquired and deployed by an agent who has embodied them" (Bell 1997: 82). This claim may be true, but it does not arise directly from rites studied or ritualists consulted. Rather it is an axiom of practice theory, as is the statement, "The agents of ritualization *do not see* [my emphasis] how they project this schematically qualified environment or how they reembody those same schemes through the physical experience of moving about within its spatial and temporal dimensions. The goal of ritualization as such is completely circular" (Bell 1997: 81).

Perhaps ritualization is circular, but it is no more circular than the theoretically driven argument that the purpose of ritual is to produce ritualized bodies. If we ask who has the insight necessary to notice and expose this projection, the answer is obvious: the practice theorist herself. Apparently, performance theorists and ritualists, unlike practice theorists, are blind to its existence. According to Bell, the practice-oriented ritual theorist's job is "to formulate the unexpressed assumptions that constitute the actor's strategic understanding of the place, purpose, and trajectory of the act" (Bell 1992: 85). Bell, who so regularly objects when interpreters search for meanings "behind" ritual acts, and who so regularly assumes that she needs to protect ritualists from theorists and interpreters, now assumes a privileged position whereby she can spy a ritualist's strategies even though that ritualist does not know he or she even has a strategy.

The fact that "misrecognition" is defined into the phenomenon of practice (and thus ritual), insures that scholarly theorists and observers now have a role, namely, recognizing misrecognitions and unmasking "strategic blindness." In Bell's view "scholars, ritual inventors, and ritual participants do not usually see how scholarship has constructed this notion of ritual or the type of authority it has acquired. *They* [emphasis mine] think of 'ritual in general' as something that has been there all along ..." (Bell 1997: 263). The we/they opposition set up here and elsewhere in Bell's writings is not between practitioners and theorists but between her theory, on the one side, and ritualists and other theorists on the other. Apparently, she is not subject to the same blindness as they. Thus, Bell's own strategy emerges, and it does not seem much different from the strategies of ritual studies scholars. It is driven by the same oppositions and mediations and the same projections of researchers' interests onto the ritual phenomenon itself.

I have no quarrel with the notion that ritualization (to use the term in Bell's sense) needs to be seen in cultural context and thus as strategic. And I agree that "acting ritually is first and foremost a matter of nuanced contrasts and the evocation of strategic, value-laden distinctions" (Bell 1992: 90). This kind of statement is virtually a consensus position among students of ritual. There is nothing new and little controversial in it. The fact that ritual actions are privileged by virtue of their differences from other ways of acting implies that ritualization is a domain of some sort, whether permeable or firmly demarcated. So Bell hardly escapes from treating ritual as something special. In her view ritualization is activity that "regards itself" not only as different but as superior, which is to say, dominant. The implication seems to be that by definition ritual amounts to a group's self-serving activity, a kind of practiced pretension. Sometimes Bell implies a contrast between "normal" and "strategic" activity (Bell 1992: 91) in which ritual is identified with the strategic. At other times she puts ritualization and other activities in the same class by virtue of their shared strategic intentions.

I have no objection to saying that people use ritual means to create social differentiation, but when the sheer act of ritual differentiation is said to create the sacred (Bell 1992: 91), Bell (like Smith, who holds a similar view) has entered the realm of metaphysics and is engaged in theological discourse, though not of the churchly kind. The view is Durkheimian in its emphasis on the social origin of sacrality, although unlike Durkheim, Bell emphasizes the priority of ritual rather than that of myth. Why ritual, if it is a particularly "mute" activity (Bell 1992: 93) as she claims, should have such power is not at all obvious to me.

Bodies, Inscribed and Blind

Bell, who stridently argues against dualism in theorizing about ritual, nevertheless treats ritual as designed to avoid discourse and systematic thinking (Bell 1992: 93). She implies an obvious dualism, the very one she identifies as central to the theories she rejects. The dualism gets amplified by the claim that the tacit aim of ritualization—one that ritualists are apparently not aware of—is the production of ritualized bodies.

One could easily produce counter examples, traditions in which teachers of ritual are explicitly aware that the formation of ritualized bodies, both social and physical, is one of their aims. Even so, it is likely true, as Peter Berger and others have said, that cultural life is replete with "things" we create and then, having forgotten that we created them, we treat them as objectively "out there."

So I agree that ritualists can "misrecognize" ritual and that ritual theorists too may miscrecognize what they are doing. But I know of no evidence showing that ritual, due to its inherent bodiliness, is more regularly misrecognized than any other cultural activity.

Ritual sensibilities are only sometimes, and only partly, matters of implicitly cultivated dispositions. They are not always, as Bell implies, completely tacit. Some ritual knowledge is self consciously and critically held by participants. No doubt, we embody much more than we know, including the hierarchical assumptions about power embedded in our own culture, but this fact hardly warrants defining ritualization as a kind of blindness that only theorists, practice theorists in particular, are capable of seeing.

When Bell discusses the importance of the body to ritual, she repeatedly speaks of the body as a kind of repository which is "invested" with a sense of ritual. A reader imagines the body as a kind of soft material upon which strategic "schemes" are "impressed" (Bell 1992: 98), thus implying the priority of the schemes and passivity of the body. The ritualizing body is characterized by Bell as containing "socially instinctive automatisms" (Bell 1992: 99) of which it is not aware and the circularity of which it necessarily "misrecognizes." In my view "automatisms" suggests that ritual action is mindless, and thus that Bell reintroduces the mind/body split that she discovers and rejects in writings by others theorists.

In my view some of the body's functions are obviously beyond the grasp of consciousness, but probably not beyond articulation, and other bodily functions are clearly obvious to consciousness. By certain kinds of ritual practices it is possible to become aware of many of them. So neither ritual nor the body should so unequivocally be associated with misrecognition and lack of self-awareness. This association verges on implying that ritual is irrational, a view Bell castigates. The association is further reinforced by Bell's deconstructionist argument that ritual is not only empty of signification but that it is a never-never land in which problems are deferred by being "endlessly retranslated in strings of deferred schemes" (Bell 1992: 106). She implies that ritual not only does not solve problems, it perpetuates them by promising resolutions while never supplying them. I would accept this view as a characterization of one kind of ritual infelicity, but not as a definition of ritual's only function.

I do not accept the view that the sole purpose of ritual (or ritualization) is to generate ritualized bodies. Some kinds of ritual have the power to do that; others do not. Everything depends on what kind of rite one is considering and how deeply and thoroughly it is practiced. Rites vary greatly in the degree to which they are capable of driving their meanings into the bone.

Bell's attitude toward ritual is what Paul Ricoeur has called a "hermeneutic of suspicion." In one respect Bell's suspicion and my call for "ritual criticism" are very much alike. One of our aims is to demystify orders of domination so it is not so easy for rites to be drafted into replicating the status quo and propping up prejudicial hierarchies. A primary difference between us, however, is my dramatistically-inspired desire to ask: *Who* is inscribing the values that we find suspect? Bell's deconstructionist-inspired tendency is to attribute strategic purpose to ritual itself. "The purpose of ritualization," she says, "is to ritualize persons, who deploy schemes of ritualization in order to dominate (shift or nuance) other, nonritualized situations to render them more coherent with the values of the ritualizing schemes and capable of molding perceptions" (Bell 1992: 108). In statements like this she posits a paradigmatic function for ritual, even though she elsewhere rejects treating rites as paradigms. Whereas she is content to have ritualization do the purposing, I want to know who, specifically, entertains what purposes. Bell's deconstructionist rhetoric leads her into volatilizing not just the proverbial "author" but the ritualist and the theorist as well. This strategy, it seems to me, only further mystifies the ritual process by attributing agency to the act itself rather than to specific ritual agents. The only fortunate consequence I can see in this rhetorical tactic is that it sometimes avoids making ritualists themselves sound stupid:

> [Ritualization] is a way of acting that sees itself as responding to a place, event, force, problem, or tradition. It tends to see itself as the natural or appropriate thing to do in the circumstances. Ritualization does not see how it actively creates place, force, event, and tradition, how it redefines or generates the circumstances to which it is responding. It does not see how its own actions reorder and reinterpret the circumstances so as to afford the sense of a fit among the main spheres of experience—body, community, and cosmos. (Bell 1992: 109)

Since ritualists, not ritualization, "see," it is revealing to imagine this statement with "ritualists" rather than "ritualization" as its subject. And then further specify these ritualists: Such-and-such a medicine person in such-and-such a tribe, such-and-such a rabbi in such-and-such a synagogue. Surely, there are priests and shamans and rabbis who do, in fact, know that they are actively creating place and tradition, just as there are some who do not. But do we really want to attribute complete blindness to every act of ritualization, a blindness that only we observers and theorists see?

I am quite willing to acknowledge, even point out, the blindness, the strategic misrecognition, of ritual practitioners. But such blindness is not peculiar to ritual practice, and it implicates the practice of theorizing as much as it does that of ritualizing. I do not believe we can afford the arrogance, conscious or unconscious, of defining unwitting, yet strategic, manipulation into every ritual act of every individual or group—which is the effect of making such claims as a matter of definition and theory rather than as geographically and socially located acts of ritual criticism. Such a view not only displaces ritual actors, it privileges theorists who believe themselves capable of seeing ritualists' misrecognitions.

Bell's position is strong in several important respects. She is perceptive in exposing the circularity of ritual theory and ritual practice. She shows how ritual oppositions (black/white, male/female, left/right, etc.) are rooted in social distinctions and then inscribed in the body. She makes readers aware of the asymmetrical nature of such oppositions: They usually establish one party as dominant. And she notices how loosely systematic a ritual system really is. The strengths of her position lie in the cogency with which she has argued these points. But in the last analysis Bell does not avoid the traps she most wants to avoid: bifurcating and mediating, theorizing about ritual, positing functions and defining qualities of ritual, and constructing privileged positions for theorists themselves.

In my view, we scholars of ritual have little choice but to define and theorize about it. If we do not do it explicitly, it will happen tacitly. It is true, as Bell complains, that performance approaches are piecemeal and confusing, but this is reason for more systematic, more critical theory rather than less. I agree that we should resist creating privileged positions for theorists and that we should be wary of creating false dualisms which we then resolve by appeals to ritual as some kind of magical mediator. But, unlike Bell, I do not find practice theories any more precise or coherent than performance theories; they too are fragmentary. They add an increased awareness of strategic bids for power that co-opt rituals into service, but there is no inherent incompatibility between the two kinds of theory. Mainly, ritual studies needs consolidation and critique—consolidation of fragmentary theories and critique of major and emergent ones.

Bibliography

Alexander, Bobby C. (1997), "Ritual and Current Studies of Ritual: Overview," in: Stephen D. Glazier, ed., *Anthropology of Religion: A Handbook*. Westport, Conn.: Greenwood: 139–60.

Anderson, Michelle (1982), "Authentic Voodoo Is Synthetic," in: *The Drama Review* 26 (2): 89–110.

Bell, Catherine (1992), *Ritual Theory, Ritual Practice*. New York: Oxford University Press.

— (1997), *Ritual: Perspectives and Dimensions*. New York: Oxford University Press.

— (1998), "Performance," in: Mark Taylor, ed., *Critical Terms for Religious Studies*. Chicago: University of Chicago Press: 205–23.

Bynum, Caroline Walker (1984), "Women's Stories, Women's Symbols: A Critique of Victor Turner's Theory of Liminality," in: Robert L. Moore/Frank E. Reynolds, *Anthropology and the Study of Religion*. Chicago: Center for the Scientific Study of Religion: 105–25.

Cole, David (1975), *The Theatrical Event: A Mythos, a Vocabulary, a Perspective*. Middletown, Conn.: Wesleyan University Press.

Combs-Schilling, M.E. (1989), *Sacred Performances: Islam, Sexuality, Sacrifice*. New York: Columbia University Press.

Crapanzano, Vincent (1980), "Rite of Return: Circumcision in Morocco," in: Werner Muensterberger, ed., *The Psychoanalytic Study of Society* 9. New Haven, Conn.: Yale University Press: 15–36.

Davis-Floyd, Robbie E. (1992), *Birth As an American Rite of Passage*. Berkeley, Calif.: University of California Press.

Drewal, Margaret Thompson (1992), *Yoruba Ritual: Performers, Play, Agency*. Bloomington, Ind.: Indiana University Press.

Driver, Tom F. (1998), *Liberating Rites: Understanding the Transformative Power of Ritual*. Boulder, Colo.: Westview.

Fernandez, James W. (1974a), "The Mission of Metaphor in Expressive Culture," in: *Current Anthropology* 15 (2): 119–45.

— (1974b), "Persuasion and Performances," in: Clifford Geertz, ed., *Myth, Symbol, and Culture*. New York: Norton: 39–60.

— (1977), "The Performance of Ritual Metaphors," in: J. David Sapir/J. Christopher Crocker, *The Social Use of Metaphor: Essays on the Anthropology of Rhetoric*. Philadelphia, Pa.: University of Pennsylvania Press: 100–31.

Firth, Raymond (1974), *Society and Its Symbols. Times Literary Supplement*, September 13.

Geertz, Clifford (1973), *The Interpretation of Cultures*. New York: Basic Books.

— (1980), *Negara: The Theatre State in Nineteenth Century Bali*. Princeton, N.J.: Princeton University Press.

— (1983), *Local Knowledge: Further Essays in Interpretive Anthropology*. New York: Basic Books.

Gluckman, Max (1977), "On Drama and Games and Athletic Contests," in: Sally Falk Moore/Barbara Myerhoff, *Secular Ritual*. Assen, Holland: Van Gorcum: 227–43.

Goffman, Erving (1959), *The Presentation of Self in Everyday Life*. Garden City, N.Y.: Doubleday Anchor.

— (1967), *Interaction Ritual: Essays on Face-to-Face Behavior*. Garden City, N.Y.: Doubleday Anchor.

— (1974), *Frame Analysis: An Essay on the Organization of Experience*. New York: Harper & Row.

Grimes, Ronald L. (1990a), *Ritual Criticism*. Columbia, S.C.: University of South Carolina Press.

— (1990b), "Victor Turner's Definition, Theory, and Sense of Ritual," in: Kathleen M. Ashley, ed., *Victor Turner and the Construction of Cultural Criticism: Between Literature and Anthropology*. Bloomington, Ind.: Indiana University Press: 141–46.

— (1992a), *Symbol and Conquest: Public Ritual and Drama in Santa Fe, New Mexico*. Albuquerque, N.Mex.: University of New Mexico.

— (1992b), "Reinventing Ritual," in: *Soundings* 75 (1): 21–41.

— (1994), *Beginnings in Ritual Studies*. Revised ed. Columbia, S.C.: University of South Carolina Press.

— (2000), "Ritual," in: Willi Braun/Russell T. McCutcheon, *Guide to the Study of Religion*. London: Cassell: 259–70.

Hughes–Freeland, Felicia, ed. (1998), *Ritual, Performance, Media*. London: Routledge.

Hughes–Freeland, Felicia/Crain, Mary M., eds. (1998). *Recasting Ritual: Performance, Media, Identiy*. London: Routledge.

Kratz, Corrine A. (1994), *Affecting Performance: Meaning, Movement, and Experience in Okiek Women's Initiation*. Washington, D.C.: Smithsonian Institution.

Laderman, Carol/Roseman, Marina, eds. (1996), *The Performance of Healing*. New York: Routledge.

Lewis, Gilbert (1980), *A Day of Shining Red: An Essay on Understanding Ritual*. Cambridge, England: Cambridge University Press.

Lincoln, Bruce (1981), *Emerging from the Chrysalis: Studies in Rituals of Women's Initiation*. Cambridge, Mass.: Harvard University Press.

Rappaport, Roy A. (1999), *Ritual and Religion in the Making of Humanity*. Cambridge: Cambridge University Press.

Schechner, Richard (1973), *Environmental Theater*. New York: Hawthorn.

— (1977), *Essays on Performance Theory, 1970–1976*. New York: Drama Book

— (1985), *Between Theater & Anthropology*. Philadelphia, Pa.: University of Pennsylvania Press.

— (1991), "Restoration of Behavior," in: Ronald L. Grimes, ed., *Readings in Ritual Studies*. Upper Saddle River, N.J.: Prentice-Hall: 441–58.

— (1993), *The Future of Ritual: Writings on Culture and Performance*. London: Routledge.

Schechner, Richard/Appel, Willa, eds. (1990), *By Means of Performance: Intercultural Studies of Theatre and Ritual*. Cambridge, England: Cambridge University Press.

Schieffelin, Edward (1985), "Performance and the Cultural Construction of Reality," in: *American Ethnologist* 12 (4): 707–24.

Singer, Milton (1955), "The Cultural Pattern of Indian Civilization," in: *Far Eastern Quarterly* 15: 23–35.

Tambiah, Stanley J. (1979), "A Performative Approach to Ritual," in: *Proceedings of the British Academy* 65: 113–69.

Taylor, Mark, ed. (1998), *Critical Terms for Religious Studies*. Chicago: University of Chicago Press.

Turner, Victor W. (1974), *Dramas, Fields and Metaphors: Symbolic Action in Human Society*. Ithaca, N.Y.: Cornell University Press.

— (1977), "Frame, Flow, and Reflection: Ritual and Drama As Public Liminality," in: Michel Benamou/Charles Caramello, *Performance in Postmodern Culture*. Madison, Wis.: University of Wisconsin Press: 33–55.

— (1979), "Dramatic Ritual/Ritual Drama: Performative and Reflexive Anthropology," in: *The Kenyon Review* 1 (3): 80–93.

— (1980), "Social Dramas and Stories about Them," in: *Critical Inquiry* 7: 141–68.

— (1982), "Acting in Everyday Life, and Everyday Life in Acting," in: *From Ritual to Theatre: The Human Seriousness of Play*. New York: Performing Arts Journal Publications: 102–23.

— (1985), "Liminality and the Performative Genres," in: John MacAloon, ed., *Rite, Drama, Festival, Spectacle: Rehearsals toward a Theory of Cultural Performance*. Philadelphia, Pa.: ISHI: 19–41.

— (1987), *The Anthropology of Performance*. New York: Performing Arts Journal Publications.

— (1991), "Are There Universals of Performance in Myth, Ritual, and Drama?," in: Richard Schechner/Willa Appel, *By Means of Performance: Intercultural Studies of Theatre and Ritual*. Cambridge, Mass.: Cambridge University Press: 8–18.

Turner, Victor W./Turner, Edith (1982), "Performing Ethnography," in: *The Drama Review* 26 (2): 33–50.

New Approaches to the Study of Religious Dance

by

HELGA BARBARA GUNDLACH

1. Introduction

Before humans were able to express themselves with words, they arguably communicated with their environment in the form of movements, in the same way as they gave expression to their own feelings. Dance came into being by adopting natural rhythms, although it is difficult to make a clear distinction between dance and other closely related movements. A universally applicable definition of dance is also difficult to produce because of the different understandings and concepts of dance in various cultures. As one of the first (religious) forms of human expression and art, dance remains an important component of many religions, and an expression of the personal religion of many people. Its popularity has increased greatly over the last few decades. The reasons for this are many and varied, as are the forms of dance themselves.

In the Western world, a trend towards holistic thinking has reintroduced dance back into religious life. Christian churches especially are coming to feel that the experience and expression of faith in a purely spiritual, motionless form no longer meet the needs of many people. Due to the lack of any religious dance tradition of its own, recourse is often made to other cultures or to the revival and further development of older folks customs, for example, the meditative dances found in some parts of the German-speaking world. In many regions marked by past Christian missionary activity, where such dance was originally prohibited, native dance traditions have re-entered the arena of Christian religious practice.

Tourism, a growing general interest in non-Christian religions and cultures, and immigration from non-Western cultures serve to promote the spread of non-Western religious dance throughout Western cultures, primarily from Oriental, Asiatic and African regions. In the case of classical Indian dance, these dances can be reproduced in their original form, thereby offering an insight into Hindu tradition. Oriental or African dance is generally adapted for public performance, and does not attempt to provide insight into the religious roots of the dance.

In former colonized areas in Asia, Africa and the Americas where there has been a strong dance tradition rooted deep in social and religious life, the process of independence and/or reassertion of the indigenous culture has been accompanied by the rediscovery and revitalization of indigenous culture and religion, bringing dance once again to the forefront of the expression of this culture, as shown for example in the case of the powwows (dance celebrations) of the North American Prairie Indians. A return to suppressed dance rituals can also be observed in Western countries, in which so-called "heathen" customs are revived. Amongst migrants of the diaspora, for example Hindus in Canada, a reinforced emphasis on dance, as well as on other religious rituals can be observed as a means of maintaining ties with the home country. Increasing cultural exchange and globalization are having a reciprocal influence throughout the world, leading to new forms and content in dance presentations. These trends apply both to religious dance in everyday life and to the representation of religious themes in professional dancing on the stage.

Religious dance as an increasingly central element of present religious culture even in Western societies presents a challenge for the modern field of religious studies. The following article will show the aspects that make up religious dance, how religious dance can change, how the approaches of other disciplines can be applied, what knowledge religious studies can derive from the examination of religious dance and what is required for further research.

2. Previous Research into Religious Dance: Overview

Religious studies research into religious dance is characterized by the Christian concept of dance, which it adopted.[1] Research into religious dance has consequently been a peripheral area of investigation until recently. Other disciplines concern themselves much more readily with dance.

1 Missionary Christianity attempted to ban dance in order to dissociate itself from its assumed "heathen" influence. Dance as an expression of faith and as a means of attaining faith were virtually inconceivable in this perspective. The appearance of stylised court dancing and its further development into classical ballet, social dancing and so forth only locates dance more emphatically in the "secular" area of life. Dance takes place not spontaneously because of inner religious needs, but on fixed, non-religious, occasions and is expressed according to established forms, and/or passively observed.

2.1. Classical and Current Research Topics

In the first half of the twentieth century, dance was discovered and described as a religious phenomenon by theologians, in particular by William Oscar Emil Oesterley (1923), Gerardus van der Leeuw (1930, 1956, 1957) and later Theodorus Petrus van Baaren (1964). These classical scholars primarily examined the dances of ancient and indigenous cultures. When they referred to Christianity, they limited themselves to quotations from the Bible and evidence from historical traditions. One of their main concerns was the classification of dance within a phenomenological perspective. Religious elements of dance in their own (Western) cultures, such as the liturgical dance movement in the United States or religious themes in German expressive dance, were not investigated, leaving the impression that religious dance was a phenomenon only found in non-Western cultures.

Religious studies work from about the 1970s onward has largely adopted the above classificatory system noted above. Comparative investigations in general have not been undertaken, and what work has been done tends to concentrate on individual elements of dance within a narrow frame of reference. The investigation of religious dance in Western societies is as a consequence increasing very slowly (e.g. *Sources Orientales* 1963; Sequeira 1977, 1978; Adams/Apostolos-Cappadona 1990; Ahlbäck 1996; Zana 1996). Ethnologists and anthropologists in the twentieth century have also primarily investigated non-Western dance. Ethnological studies concentrate mainly on the form of the dance itself. Anthropological research into dance attempts to obtain a better insight into a particular society, placing an emphasis on the functionalist and structuralist aspects of dance. The study of Western culture and the position of dance within this culture is generally left to sociologists (e.g. Klein 1992). Dance critics and specialists on the other hand devote themselves almost entirely to Western dance, and judge such dance from an aesthetic point of view.

2.2. Classical and Current Research Methods

The classical scholars above based their views of ancient and religious dance on the analysis of religious writings and archaeological findings, while descriptions of indigenous dances rely primarily on the recorded observations of others, usually Christian missionaries. The conclusions of the musicologist Curt Sachs (1933), often cited in religious studies, are also based on similar materials.

At the moment, research into "dances of the gods and ancestors" has no other sources than those previously named. This also means that there are no other starting points for future research. Reference to contemporary dances to draw conclusions about earlier forms of dance can be helpful, though it should of course always be treated with the requisite skepticism. The sometimes very worthwhile secondary literature, such as the above-mentioned missionary reports, is certainly valuable as a documentary source, although it should not necessarily be used as objective source material. Ethnologists and anthropologists enjoy a long tradition of field research, not least because no historical sources have been handed down within the cultures that they generally study. In recent years their research methods and similar empirical methods of social research have been adopted by some religious scholars like Sequeira (1977, 1978), Gaston (1982, 1996), and Combs (1992). Bearing these concerns in mind, attention will now be drawn to some problems which must be considered in research into religious dance.

3. Problems of Research into Religious Dance

Many of the problems arising in research into religious dance are the same as those found in the study of religion more generally. Confronted with a different religion/culture or religious dance, researchers often attempt to apply familiar standards from their own religious, cultural and social backgrounds, which inevitably leads to distortion and faulty interpretation. The Western concept of "dance" itself can only be applied in a restricted way to other cultures. Even in Europe there are significant distinctions, as demonstrated by the two different Spanish terms for the concept (e.g. Span. *danza* for ritual dance and *baile* for secular dance). Other terms encompass a significantly greater area (e.g. Mexican-mixtec *yaa* for dance, music and games) or always see movement in a narrow context associated with music, or ritual, for example. And just as the grammar of a spoken language cannot be applied outside a family of languages, neither can the descriptions and structures of individual dance movements be universally applied. For example, the vocabulary of classical ballet well known to some Western researchers cannot be used to describe Hawaiian dances.

Researchers encounter many different concepts of dance and the related place of dance within the society concerned. Dance can be understood as given by the gods (Hinduism, some South American indigenous religions), only danced by special individuals (shamans, professionally trained dancers in Kathakali in India), by defined groups of people (amongst the North American Hopi Indians) or by the whole community (Shakers). It may be an integral part of everyday life (some African cultures) or have been displaced into the area of the mundane as an artificial dance (classical ballet). Problems encountered by researchers outside their own cultures cannot however be taken to infer that no difficulties exist within a more familiar environment, as demonstrated by reports of field research in the researcher's home country (Giurchescu and Koutsouba in Buckland 1999: 41–54 and 186–95). Researchers can also become involved in a discussion considered obsolete in many religious studies circles, namely, the extent to which individuals must be religious, or in this instance, take part in the dance, in order to experience the same religious feeling as the dancers, an aspect which is of central importance for many dancers.

Finally, every dance has as many variations and facets as the dancers themselves, in the same way as every religion can be experienced and lived individually by its adherents. In other words, and irrespective of the representation of religious themes and their embeddedness in religious rituals, a dance may have a different religious significance for the individual dancers and spectators. In the same way, a dance that is generally regarded as secular can be of such deep significance for individual dancers and spectators, that it could for them be defined as an almost religious experience. In order therefore not to exclude any areas prematurely, the definition of religious dance (and of religion) forming the basis of any study should be as broad as possible, should conform to that of the culture in question, and should also include the environment and background to the dance.

Religious dance as a subject of research can also be clearly distinguished from research into other religious phenomena, for a number of reasons. Dance is a phenomenon of movement, and as such can initially only be understood at face value, or in its external form (Günther 1962: 8). Dance languages can also be very different, as in the case of the Indian Bharata Natyam, and can reflect essential aspects of a religion, although they can only be translated into spoken languages to a limited extent. Some styles of dance require certain physical skills and many years of training, such as Cambodian temple dancing or the Indian Bharata Natyam, which researchers will be able to reproduce only in the rarest of cases. Further, dance is not a static element, but is subject to continual change. Even when exactly defined steps are danced by later generations, it is still necessary to take into account the context of the dance, i.e. the circumstances, motivation, training requirements, the position of the dance in the society and so forth. Some dances demonstrate an astounding capacity for adaptation to external changes, such as that of the South African Zezuru (Jonas 1992: 35). Finally, indigenous dance is a popular tourist attraction. Many dances have been deliberately changed, as in Haiti or Tonga, in order not to have to reveal their religious content to outsiders (Royce 1980: 84). Obviously, this applies to researchers as well, who may find the work of breaking through this barrier laborious and very difficult.

Fundamental problems of field research can also hinder dance researchers as soon as they enter into the field. They may be met with a general skepticism with regard to scientific research, for example, if the group being studied has had negative experiences with previous researchers, and/or considered themselves to be misrepresented in their results, possibly due to the application of inappropriate methods to the phenomenon being studied. Problems may also arise due to gender, for example, in the case of female researchers in patriarchal societies, or where certain dances are only danced by one gender, for example whirling (male) dervishes in Turkey or female ritual dances in Germany.

Researchers should not let themselves be discouraged by these obstacles. On the contrary, prior awareness of such problems can save researchers a great deal of time and help offset faulty research and conclusions. Researchers will also be better prepared for other, unforeseen difficulties.

4. Systematization and Comparability of Religious Dance

4.1. Previous Approaches

The researchers Oesterley, Sachs, van der Leeuw and van Baaren systematized and compared dance in the phenomenological tradition via supposed formal structures and clear functions. Terms such as material, type, form or function are applied, but not clearly defined. These scholars refer, for example, to the following categories: rain dances, initiation dances, fertility dances, healing dances, and hunting dances. Such a list refers to particular, frequently occurring functions primarily associated with specific, concrete purposes or occasions for the dance concerned.

A dance may however appear in quite different forms. In an initiation dance, for example, the novices may take part in the dance together (Bavenda Zulu in South Africa), or the already initiated may dance around the newcomer (some Australian Aborigines). Novices may dance around the elders (tribes in New Guinea), or the candidates must dance alone for several days as a criterion of acceptance (some Indian tribes on the west coast of North America). In some circumstances, novices alternate dancing over several days (Atxuabo in East Africa), or the elders dance with the younger ones in different roles (Kalahari). Elders may also assume the role of the novice (Bemba in Zambia), or a novice may be carried around on a man's shoulders (Wan on the Ivory Coast). In addition, certain deities or mythical beings may be invoked, the dancers may play the role of such deities or even of animals, special costumes and music may be used. The dance may also consist of simple or more complex series of movements, and so forth.

These examples show that the designation "initiation dance" does not yet give any indication of *how, by whom* and *for whom* the dance is performed. It does not take into account the participants, form or method, or any other functions which are not immediately apparent. The functions listed above refer to an immediate, deliberate aim, i.e. the dance is associated with a direct event or purpose. Religious dance can however also have functions which can be described as longer term and with transcendent aims, which are not associated with any concrete events. Anthropologist Evans Pritchard, who investigated Durkheim's theory of religion via the rites of indigenous peoples, categorizes these two functional areas in this way. Evans Pritchard (1965: 102) makes the distinction between "manifest aims" and "latent function". He ranks the latent function more highly, believing that the explicit aims of the rites do not disclose the true meaning of a ritual. His categorization into two functional areas of a ritual can be applied to dance, since dance can be a component of a ritual or can function as the ritual itself. However, these scholars mix these further functions (long term transcendent aims, which are not associated with any concrete events) with other forms and methods. In addition to the direct functions noted above, they also place processional, cosmic, ecstatic or labyrinthine dance in the same category, although these distinctions take place at a completely different level.

There is also no sense in categorizing the important functions of religious dance as sacred action, causal action or fulfillment, a defined experience or representation, or the ordering and strengthening of the community, which would then be allocated to one of the above hunting or fertility dances (Graf 1964: 1291f.). A sacred action, which may be a hunting dance, can *also* represent something else, for example, animals, weapons or a particular hunting situation, and *also* have the intention of strengthening the awareness of the community. The points of transition can therefore be fluid, and many combinations are possible. A categorization made purely according to action, or representation, or any other single aspect is therefore insufficient.

The common claim that religious dance is associated in its function and appearance with the corresponding religious concepts is also too restrictive (Graf 1964: 1291). There may be forms where this holds true. In general, however, that would mean that religious dance has no creative power of its own, which in turn contradicts its repeatedly stated role as "the most original expression of life" (Schimmel 1962: 612) or "the mother of art" (Sachs 1933: 1). It should therefore be assumed at the very least that there is a reciprocal effect between the social environment of the dancers and the power of religious dance. Nor is it sufficient to refer to religious dance in its entirety using categorizations like those of anthropologist Anthony Shay (1971), who concentrates exclusively on different functions of the dance, and deliberately excludes consideration of its form. Hanna's (1995) listing of dance's various functions by means of different techniques is very informative. By placing some dances under multiple categories, she successfully conveys the impression of the great variety of religious dance, although the allocation under central headings makes it difficult to recognize the overlapping areas at first glance.

The example of the different types of initiation dances also points out the need for further differentiation according to the form and method of religious dance. Here, Sachs (1933) and later the former expressive dancer Dorothee Günther (1962) have devoted themselves particularly to the categorization of the many different forms of movement. Despite the fact that Sachs has long been regarded as outdated, and must in many respects be regarded as having been disproven, his definitions are still used. In contrast, Günther's reflections on the aspects of pictorial, symbolic, non-pictorial or non-symbolic, absolute or abstract dance, image and the differentiation of rapture and ecstasy have lost nothing of their freshness.

An indirect contribution to formal categorization is also provided by the theologian Paul Tillich (1990). Taking the example of painting, he defines four possible combinations of the existence of a religious or non-religious style and a religious or non-religious content. This model, used especially in North America in relation to religious dance (Adams/Rock in: Adams/Apostolos-Cappadona 1990: 80–91), can also be applied for example to classical ballet with religious themes (non-religious style/religious content) or to classical Indian dance, which attempts to present contemporary themes (religious style/non-religious content). His definition is too general to cover all the components of religious dance, but it does provide encouragement for differentiation into religious and non-religious dance. More recent religious studies works provide no or very few further purely systematic accounts, but rather rely on previously established frameworks and concentrate primarily on individual aspects of dance. Religious dance and dancers are described in their relevant regional, historical and social context, and from a sociological, psychological or similar point of view (*Sources Orientales* 1963; Sequeira 1977, 1978; Adams/Apostolos-Cappadona 1990; Ahlbäck 1996; Zana 1996).

All the above-mentioned attempts at definition address important aspects of religious dance. They are however incomplete, neglecting certain aspects and failing to encompass the full extent and range of religious dance. The model outlined below covers the components discussed in the areas of form, function, method and participants in the form of a quick and clear overview, thus offering a good starting point for comparative study. This also allows combinations which might not immediately occur to Western researchers.

4.2. The Four-Determinant Model

Various types of religious dance across different ages and cultures can be described with the aid of the four-determinant model outlined below. This model is based on the work of American dance historian June Layson (1994). In her so-called three-dimensional model, she attempts to present the historical development of dance in general. Layson's model explores the dimensions of dance types, dance content and dance throughout the ages.

In order to describe religious dance and present the above-named forms and functions, other categories are required. The categories defined below as determinants are: concrete function, non-immediate aim, participants and type/method of dance. The sequence of the determinants themselves and their relevant components does not imply any particular value or significance. Multiple categorizations are possible within the determinants. In contrast to previous methods of systematization, which only allowed one single function or allocated the form of the dance to a single function, this system allows an infinite range of combinations which can be more fully and easily described. Researchers who now attempt to describe a dance in terms of the components listed below, may discover areas or aspects of research that they have neglected hitherto. This model allows for a comprehensive description of a religious dance. Historical developments of a dance and any possible resulting changes with regard to individual components of the four determinants can be represented by means of several models (the inclusion of a time determinant would have complicated the model unnecessarily).

Determinant 1—Concrete function/ place

When, Where, Why I

Immediate, specific function, directly associated with the event, time dictated by concrete circumstances, e.g. hunting or healing dances, rites de passage

Determinant 2— Non-immediate aim

Why II

Indirect, longer-term, transcendent aim, not associated with concrete events, e.g. conveyance of tradition, obtaining of own experience, reinforcement of the sense of community

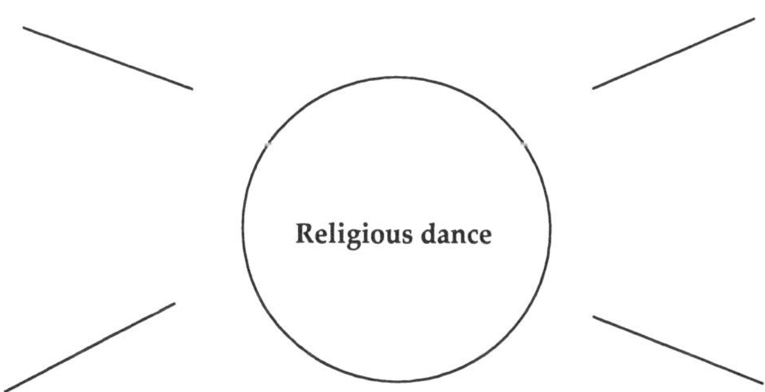

Determinant 3—Participants

Who, for whom

Performers, benefactors, spectators

e.g. one person alone, defined groups, whole community

Determinant 4—Type and Method

How

Methods, techniques

e.g. steps, costumes and props, state of awareness

Graphic representations are used in the model to provide a quick overview. More extensive explanations are given in the accompanying text. Layson chose a system of coordinates for the graphic representation of her three-dimensional model. A similar presentation did not seem suitable for the four-determinant model, since possible multiple categorizations within the individual determinants would inhibit the clarity of the presentation. The preferred means of presentation of the four-determinant model takes the form of the graphic shown above. The four determinants are allocated equal value, and can contain as many components as required, some of which are listed below by way of example. These components, taken together, describe the relevant religious dance shown in the center. For reasons of space and simplicity of presentation, a tabular presentation can also be employed, as demonstrated in the example in Section 5.

When using this or other models of systematization, it should be kept in mind that this should only be regarded as an *aid* (still using concepts with Western connotations) in the description, definition and comparison of religious dance.

4.2.1. Explanation of the Four Determinants

The components of a religious dance are summarized below under individual determinants. Many of these components have already been discussed. (For further explanation, see Gundlach Sonnemann 2000: 51–63)

First determinant—Concrete function/place: The first determinant contains the time, place and the functions mentioned repeatedly in the literature which give the reason for the performance of the dance, as perceived by the spectator. These dances have an immediate, specific function that is directly associated with an event. The time of the dance is also defined by specific circumstances. The function does not contain explicit information on the place of the dance, since in most cases it will be obvious that the dance will be performed in some place of importance to the community, such as the village square, holy places, places of worship, temples, and so forth. The dance will not normally be performed other than on the stated occasion. The dance can form part of a religious ritual or may itself be the ritual. Many of the named functions, for example hunting or rain dances, refer to the religions of indigenous cultures. More recent religious dances often lack these concrete functions, since they may be performed independently of any specific occasion. In order to be able to position such dances in place and time, the model includes the possibility of giving an arbitrarily set time and place of the performance.

Included in this category are: seasonal dances; weather dances; harvest dances; hunting dances; dances for rites of passage; initiation dances; love dances; fertility dances; healing dances; war dances; dances performed at recurring religious festivals/sacrifices/remembrance days for events/people/gods; dances associated with the court/temple; arbitrarily established places and times of performance (theatrical performances, regular groups); and training/practice in the case of particular dances.

Second determinant—Non-immediate aim: The second determinant also defines the reason for the dance (its function). In this case however, this is an indirect, latent, longer term and transcendent aim not associated with any concrete events, i.e. we now find ourselves on a completely different level. With the second determinant several aspects may occur conjointly, thus giving an almost infinite range of possible combinations both within this determinant and in combination with the first determinant.

Such aims include: obtaining religious knowledge or awareness; passing on personal religious experience; expression and demonstration of religious feelings; conveying existing religious content; honoring/invocation/appeal to deities or spirits; getting closer to/merging with supernatural beings; achievement of salvation; preparation for the afterlife; explanation of cosmology; prayer in dance form; preaching in dance form; entertainment; relaxation; education; strengthening of the sense of community; and demonstration of power.

Third determinant—Participants: The third determinant defines an aspect of the form, namely the participants: those performing the dance, the benefactors of the dance, and the spectators. If only certain persons or groups are performing the dance, the significant factors can be aspects of specific gender or age, information on the particular profession or position in the community, outstanding dance skills, or personal interest. Individual dancers, couples, groups and spectators can be defined. The transitions may be fluid, with the soloist appearing at times within a group. In most cases, reciprocal communication takes place, so that a relationship exists between the sender (dancer) and receiver (other dancers or spectators). Solo dances in front of the public are often such in name only, since they are mostly designed for show and communication, and still require the relationship with the group. Even if the dancer is performing a supposedly fixed repertoire and cannot see the spectators, s/he is still aware of their presence and reacts to their reactions. With the performance, the dancer can also act on behalf of the audience. In the case of ecstatic dance in particular, the audience can be given an active role, since it has to support and protect the dancer during the dancer's experience of ecstasy. In such cases the communication is only one-way, since the dancer is not aware of the audience. A dancer can also dance entirely alone. If several dancers are dancing together, without any additional audience, they often slip into the role of the spectator, and watch each other during the dance. Mutual, two-way communication can then take place. If several dancers dance themselves into ecstasy, they can forget their companions and thus be said to be dancing alone. The dance can also be characterized by hierarchical structures (for example, when there is a lead dancer).

Fourth determinant—Type and method: The fourth determinant defines a further element of the form, namely the methods and techniques that are used in order to achieve the desired aim. A religious dance always contains several components of this determinant, some of which are essential (for example, movement) and some of which are optional (for example, masks). These various aspects generally occur in close conjunction with each other, and can thus reinforce each other in respect to their effect on the dancers and thus also on the spectators.

Elements relevant to this category are: movement (steps, gestures, mime); formation in space; content; symbolism; mimicry/representation; external aids (such as make-up, body-painting, masks, costumes, props); internal aids (the taking of drugs); altered states of awareness (rapture/ecstasy/trance); magical techniques (analogous magic, contagious magic); rhythm/music/song; light/technical effects; and location.

All the listed components of the individual determinants can contribute to turning a dance into a religious dance. The individual components can change due to a variety of influences. An example will be given to show what sort of changes these can be, and how they can be represented in tabular form by means of several models. In addition, the example will demonstrate what role a dance can play in contemporary religious culture, and what conclusions can be drawn from research into a dance on the religion in question, its dancers, spectators and the society, all without recourse to dance notations, photographic or film material.

5. Example of an Examination and Description of a Religious Dance

The example describes one of the surely best known religious dances of all: the classical Indian dance Bharata Natyam. It is inseparable from Hinduism, it has a long tradition, and its dance language is very well defined. It has also been performed for some decades in the West, especially in England and Canada, where many Hindus now live. It is also increasingly performed in Germany, from whence the example is taken.

In addition to the study of sources and secondary literature on the historical development of Indian dance (Sequeira 1978; Gaston 1982, 1996; and others), the dance was examined by means of participatory observation carried out in Germany (consistent dance training under various German and Indian instructors, together with the author's own performances), non-participatory observation (attendance at dance performances), extensive interviews with instructors, relaxed and open discussions with other pupils, the study of numerous dance manuals and videos, and a brief period of comparative study in London and New Delhi.

The recommended expert for further study on Indian dance, Anne Marie Gaston, is representative of a the group of progressive researchers who combine the skills of a thorough dance training (in India, in all the major dance styles) with those of a university education (in Gaston's case, a Ph.D. from Oxford, 1982).

Consider the following graphic representation of Bharata Natyam according to the four determinants discussed above:

India, until approx. 17th/18th century

D1—Concrete function/place	*D2—Non-immediate aim*	*D3—Participants*	*D4—Type/method*
· daily in the temple · at religious festivals · training/instruction	· component of Indian culture · conveyance of religious (Hindu) content · strengthening of the sense of community · obtaining of own experience · expression of own religion	· dancers associated with the temple · families of instructors · the whole audience community	· traditional stylized symbolic steps, gestures, music, song, costumes and make-up · pictorial · prescribed imagery

India today

D1—Concrete function/place	*D2—Non-immediate aim*	*D3—Participants*	*D4—Type/method*
· arbitrary performance in the theatre · training/instruction · religious/cultural festivals within and outside of temples	· preservation of Indian culture · conveyance of religious (Hindu) content · obtaining of own experience · expression of own religion · current topics	· professional dancers · child hobby dancers · their instructors · interested spectators	· traditional stylized symbolic steps, gestures, music, song, costumes and make-up · pictorial · prescribed imagery · contemporary music

Germany today—danced by (Indian) Hindus

D1—Concrete function/place	*D2—Non-immediate aim*	*D3—Participants*	*D4—Type/method*
· arbitrary performance in the theatre · training/instruction · religious/cultural festivals within Hindu communities	· conveyance of Indian culture · conveyance of religious (Hindu) content · obtaining of own experience · expression of own religion · current topics	· professional dancers · small groups of interested spectators · child hobby dancers	· traditional stylized symbolic steps, gestures, music, song, costumes and make up · pictorial · prescribed imagery · contemporary music

Germany today—danced by (German) non-Hindus

D1—Concrete function/place	*D2—Non-immediate aim*	*D3—Participants*	*D4—Type/method*
· training · performances by instructors · performances by pupils	· interest in a new dance style interest in Indian culture · interest in religious (Hindu) content · obtaining of own experience · expression of own religion · current topics	· adult hobby dancers · instructors · small groups of interested spectators (acquaintances)	· traditional stylized symbolic steps, gestures, music, song, costumes and make-up · pictorial · prescribed imagery · contemporary music

Classical Indian dance comprises elements of the three cultures of the original population of India: the Mundas, the Dravidians from the Indus valley and the Aryans who migrated in from the north. Excavations provide the first evidence of dance as far back as 5,000 years ago. Its confirmable origins are over 2,500 years old. Dance can be demonstrated to be an integral component of Indian culture and religion through remnants of sculptures and references in the *Rig Veda* and the so-called fifth *Veda*, the *Natyaveda* (the knowledge of dance and drama, taken by Brahma from the four *Vedas*) and the epics (*Ramayana, Mahabharata*). Finally the classical dance manuals of the *Natyasastra* (written in the second and third centuries, C.E.) and the more refined *Abhinayadarpana* (sixth century C.E.) combine and summarize all the instructions for the dance which are still valid today.

The origin and development of the dance is closely associated with that of drama. In a country with a high rate of illiteracy, dance serves now, as it did previously, to convey a religious content. The themes of dance are traditional. Dancing gods and their histories are imitated and spiritualized. The sculpture-like poses and bodily postures (*Karanas*) can also be seen, for example, in the effigies in the Temple of Chidambaram in southern India. The connection between live dance and the dance of the gods, together with religious content, is shown most clearly in the well-known bronze statues of Shiva Nataraja. The central elements of Hinduism, the eternal cycle of coming into being and passing away, of creation and destruction, are symbolized in the individual hand gestures/postures (*Hastas*), the content and the diverse symbols of the "King of the dancers", which is reproduced precisely in many dances. The enormous eloquence of the gestures and mime serves to convey the sense of the dance. For the dancers themselves, the dance can be a form of self-realization. The *Adavus* (basic types of movement), *Karanas*, *Hastas*, mime and themes are all prescribed. The choreography can be further developed at any time, or existing choreography can be used. There are no stage settings or props. Everything is created by the dance itself. The songs, sung in Sanskrit or in living languages, for example Tamil or Telugu in southern India, originate from the *Vedas*, the *Gitagovinda*, the *Mahabharata* and contemporary poets. The music is set to prescribed *Ragas* (notations) and *Talas* (rhythms), though the musicians are otherwise free to perform their own compositions. In other words, everything that has been handed down is preserved and reproduced in its original form, while the rest is improvised. Great value is placed on external appearance. Becoming perfectly made up for the performance, with hand- and foot-painting, a coiffure, the wearing of a sari or dance costume, foot-bells and jewelry, can take up to two hours. For training, a plain dancing sari or *Salvarkamis* is worn.

For classical Indian dance, many years of training are required, together with a profound knowledge of Indian mythology and a high degree of empathy and devotion. "A disciplined body is not the aim of the training, but merely the tool, by means of which one achieves freedom during the dance," explains Kapila Vatsyayan (1993) of the Indira Gandhi National Centre for the Arts. The famous dancer Malavika Sarukkai (1999) adds: "The dance is something greater than oneself. The dancer is only the instrument. One must purify the body and cleanse the thoughts, and allow the spirit of this energy of beauty, aesthetics and eternity to flow through one." Technically brilliant and charismatic dancers could and still do command great respect.

On the basis of the *Natyasastra*, various styles of dance developed, of which the best known is the Bharata Natyam. Although the lack of a comprehensive dance history is regrettable, at the same time this can be seen as evidence of the uniformity and vitality of the classical Indian dance tradition. The above sources are still used today as training manuals. With regard to the fourth determinant, great continuity can be established. The contents of the first and third determinants have changed continually, especially in the last centuries. The dance was traditionally taught by male dance teachers from real dynasties. They were a sort of Guru for their pupils, the female *Devadasis* (literally "servants of God", usually translated as "temple dancers"). The earliest *Devadasis* can be traced back as far as 300 B.C.E. They were ritually married to one of the deities, and dedicated to the temple in which they served. Their livelihood was financed by the royal households. They enjoyed more rights than other women, and were often held in respect as persons of noble station. They danced daily in the temple, where any member of the community could come to watch at any time, and also at special religious festivals. With the establishment of the Mogul empires, the institution of temple dancing began to fall into decay, and the *Devadasis* were increasingly forced to earn their living by prostitution. Their dances took on a distinctly erotic character. Finally, dance came to be scorned, particularly amongst the higher castes, and it was forbidden to higher caste women in order to protect their reputations. Classical Indian dance had already experienced the loss of its religious-artistic significance once before, under the rising influence of Buddhism. At that time it was regarded as no more than entertainment for the nobility, while in the noble families it was considered unseemly to dance oneself. Due to the influence of social reformers, women's movements and conservative moral attitudes, a law was eventually passed in Madras in 1947 which prohibited the temple dance of the *Devadasis*, and only allowed its performance at weddings or similar occasions. At the same time, academics and artists such as Rukmeni Devi were making efforts to rehabilitate Indian dance.

As yet, it has not regained its original significance; *Devadasis* in the earlier sense of the term no longer exist. Even if contemporary Indian society has theoretically grown up with the themes and representational forms of classical Indian dance, many people understand only the typical, more easily understandable elements. Very few now understand the content or the Sanskrit language of the accompanying songs. Above all however, the great mass of people no longer have much interest in it. Performances take place in rented theatres, and are attended only by a small, educated stratum of society. The law forbidding the dance in temples is not honored in practice. Dances are still performed in many temples today on the occasion of religious festivals, although rarely in front of the images of deities, and not as part of the religious service. There are however efforts underway to incorporate it more prominently in the rituals, and formally to repeal the law. Classical Indian dance is today considered by the majority of the Indian population as nothing more than "art," although according to earlier Indian conceptions, religion and art, especially temple art, were inseparable, and art was held to be something holy. Dance has lost its decisive function as an expression of faith and an integral part of religion and religious worship. Young girls are sent to newly established dance schools in order to be brought up with an appreciation of music and a gracious posture, in much the same way as girls are sent to ballet school in the West.

On the other hand, the learning and practice of classical Indian dance is now open to a broad section of the population, and to interested non-Indians. It is no longer reserved exclusively for the *Devadasis*. The few professionally trained dancers (the majority of whom are female), who frequently still have a sort of Guru-relationship with their instructors, are taught and encouraged to preserve the tradition, to maintain and uphold the spiritual atmosphere of the temple and to convey this on stage. The first public appearance of a dancer (*Arangetram*) is still, as it always was, an important celebration for the dancer, and often an expensive one for her parents, accompanied by many religious rituals. It is considered the climax of the daughter's upbringing and a precondition for good marriage prospects. Few professional dancers in India earn their entire living from dancing. Performances as a rule have to be financed by the dancers themselves, since admission charges are either very low or non-existent. Almost all of them earn extra money from teaching or find employment in the film industry. Many also learn another profession. Within families, and especially those of the future parents-in-law, dancing is not regarded very highly as a profession for a woman. A woman's dancing career thus often ends with her marriage, and successful professional female dancers are often unmarried as a consequence. In addition to the preservation and reinforcement of traditional classical Indian dance, for some time there has been a trend in India toward the portrayal of non-Hindu (e.g. Christian), contemporary and social themes (e.g. the position of women in society) through the use of classical Indian dance techniques.

In Germany a distinction must be made as to whether the dancers come from India and are giving guest performances, or perhaps live in Germany, or whether (German) non-Hindus, generally adult women, are learning classical Indian dance as a hobby. Some of these eventually turn their hobby into a second job, in which they both give performances and teach. In addition there are Indian girls who, as in their home country, are sent for dancing lessons by their parents. Depending on the degree to which an Indian way of life is practiced within the family, this can be an important bond to the culture and religion of their ancestors. In Hindu communities, for example, Tamil refugees, dances are performed on the occasion of religious festivals. As a general observation, customs and traditions in the diaspora are often more faithfully preserved than in the home country, so that Indian dance outside India is subject to less experimentation and development than in India itself. The *Arangetram* as an essential social event in the culture of the home country is only preserved outside India in the case of the daughters of wealthy parents.

Outside of these groups, accessible to the German public, performances are given by professional Indian or German dancers and local school groups, either in theatres or at multi-cultural festivals. The times and the places of the performance are arbitrarily selected. Indian musicians and singers often have to be dispensed with for organizational reasons and cost, so recorded music is used. The audience in general has a fairly high level of education and is interested in foreign countries, cultures and religions. Since the audience does not understand the language of Indian dance, relevant notes or commentaries are given in the program or by a presenter. Naturally not every *Hasta* can be explained individually, only the basic concept of the dance. For this reason it is possible for the audience to read something else into the dance or the actions of the dancers. Under certain circumstances the dancers can bring them unintentionally to the realization of something which has nothing to do with Indian dance. In this way spectators can still feel that the dancer has something to say to them, and in return, the dancer feels understood by the spectators. They nevertheless still move on different planes, since they come from different cultural and religious backgrounds. The majority of the public will probably perceive only the external form of the dance, especially if they are not specifically attending a performance of Indian dance, but encounter it only as an "exotic tidbit" at a town festival, or as belly dancing in a restaurant.

People starting to take lessons in Indian dance might do so purely for reasons of training and to keep fit, perhaps because they might want to get to know other dance styles than ballet or jazz dance. Aesthetic and exotic Indian dance is also attractive to many non-dancers, who then seek to copy it. Others may already be interested in India and its culture in general, or may have seen Indian dance performed in India while on holiday. Occasionally, cultural exports such as the film "Kamasutra" may prompt people to become interested in Indian dance. It is also possible that dance is selected as a further means of access to Indian religion. The latter is however rare, as is interest from an esoteric standpoint. The overwhelming majority of dance pupils are female, with the average age being between the late twenties and early thirties.

There is probably one such teacher for every larger city in Germany. These may be professional dancers from India living in Germany, German non-Hindus trained in India or second generation Hindus who have grown up in Germany. In addition, guest performances and workshops may be performed by Hindu dancers from India. One thing applies in all cases, that they do not only perform themselves, and do not only teach, but generally have to do both for financial reasons. Introductory instruction in the dance is given, with guest experts at weekend workshops and ongoing regular instruction in small groups, which usually meet once a week. The instruction itself differs little or not at all from that given in India. It strongly resembles a religious ritual. To begin with, prayers are said or danced, such as the *Namaskara* and the *Dhyana Shloka*, and the backgrounds of the individual *Hastas* are explained. The pupils thus are immediately given an experience of Indian culture and Hindu religion. Whether and to what extent this knowledge is regarded purely as information on a different culture, or has any influence on the individual religious sentiments of the pupil, can vary, and depends in part on the personality and the intentions of the teacher. In the case of those who take part in the dancing lessons for an extended period of time, it is often possible to detect external changes in the style of dress and eating habits, together with the desire to travel to India, and more extensive interest in the religious and mythological background of the dance.

Classical Indian dance plays an important role in interreligious/intercultural dialogue. In professional stage dancing as early as the beginning of the twentieth century, the American dancer Ruth St. Denis, whose picture of the Orient sprang mainly from her own imagination, performed such dances as the Radha. At the same time, the famous ballerina Anna Pavlova was working in Europe in conjunction with the Indian dancer Uday Shankar, and this still influences parts of the Indian dance scene in England today. In the church too, both in India (Barboza 1990) and in Germany (Sequeira 1978) there have been attempts to present Christian religious material using the technique of the Bharata Natyam. Such cross-fertilization is taking place with increasing frequency, a fact which some dancers and researchers see as confirmation of the universality of dance, although this point is open to debate (Gundlach Sonnemann 2000: 128–35).

6. Comparative Studies

Examination of classical Indian dance in the context of its historical development in its country of origin and in its diaspora gives rise to a wealth of pronouncements on, and conclusions about, faith and religion, society and politics, social conditions and gender studies and the overall position of dance as an art form. The changes can easily be discerned by using the four-determinants model.

If the field of religious studies claims to study faith and religion(s) broadly, further comparative studies are required. There is however little sense in arbitrary comparison of very different fields, such as the Bharata Natyam and the dances of the Danis in Irian Jaya (highly specialized stage dances and simple folk dances from different religions, cultures, regions and population groups). Of course it will be possible to establish areas of common ground, such as the relationship to the ground in the movements, or the accompaniment of the dances by song, and also differences in the differentiation of the movements, the formation in space, the relationship of the dancers to the spectators, the embodiment of deities or the presentation of the mythological content. The question is what relevance such conclusions might have, especially since there is still too little data available on dance in general in order able to classify such results properly.

It is therefore only appropriate to take into account comparable elements and points of reference, as in the following anthropological examples: for example similar functions and position of the dance within the society e.g. Hopi Indians and Polynesians (Kealiinohomoku 1967), similar types of dance e.g. trance dance (Bourguignon 1968) or the manifestation of a certain character in different dances e.g. La Malinche in south-western USA and in Mexico (Saldaña 1966).

Let us return to the example of the Bharata Natyam. In order to come to further conclusions with respect to the current religious culture of India, a comparison can be made with folklore dances (simpler movements, performed by a wider section of the population at many festivals, particularly in rural areas). It is possible to make supplementary statements or conclusions about the religion of a particular stratum of the population in Germany if the comparison is made with other non-Western dances such as African or Oriental dance (for example, a different target group, greater popularity, less interest in the original religion/culture, less differentiated movements and statements of content, and/or heavy adaptation of the dance to German needs). Finally, conclusions can be drawn about relevant social conditions and cultures on the basis of the changes in classical Indian dance, in comparison to other diaspora countries. All postulations have one thing in common, that there is one connective element: one culture/religion which is expressed in different dances, one people that is interested in different religious dances, and one religious dance which is performed in different countries.

7. Importance and Prospects of Research into Religious Dance for Religious Studies

Humans express themselves in different forms and on different levels. Dance—and religious dance in particular—is an important source for research work, in the same way as written and verbal expression (sacred scriptures, verbally transmitted mythologies, testaments of believers, etc.), fleeting expression (improvised/non-recorded music) and non-fleeting artistic expression (composed/recorded music, poetry, painting, architecture etc.). Only when all forms of expression are taken together we do obtain a full picture of a society or a religion, in which (religious) dance has a role to play.

It is not without reason that quotations such as "one should not speak of dance, one should let it speak for itself" (Otto 1956: 9) are found again and again in the literature of dance. In the process of doing research, researchers might be asked repeatedly by dancers why they want to write about it, when they should really experience it themselves. In order to express themselves verbally, humans have certain, defined words available. In the case of dance, it is possible to express oneself beyond these conventions on a non-rational level.

Intensive research, if possible participatory observation, and also hermeneutic approaches are necessary in order to be able to develop at least some partial understanding of the significance of religious dance and the religion of the dancers. Nevertheless, religious dance can only be subjected to a certain degree of scientific study, especially in the area of its second determinant. Here, there is a danger in taking dancers' statements as purely objective description. Dancers are forced to translate unreflected feelings and experiences from one plane to another, in order to frame them in words in a way that they think will be understandable for the scientist. But dancers' statements can complete the description of a dance and are—apart from the researchers' own experiences—the only way to approach the (religious) feelings the dance can cause.

Many of the points raised in section 4.2.1. can contribute toward understanding dance in a religious context. In addition to the clearly definable, externally visible, components (masks, costumes or dance poses which symbolize a deity, the presentation of religious content and themes, dance as a component of a religious festival), the significance for the individual dancers and the effect on the individual spectators can be quite different from that of scholars doing research (Gundlach Sonnemann 2000: 122–27). However, by means of the *existence* of the varied forms and functions of religious dance, research can draw conclusions about the nature of a society, as shown by the example of Indian dance.

There are many and varied influences that affect the popularity of religions in the cultural marketplace, such as the increasing level of education, new media, tourism, globalization, the breaking away from traditional values and social/political structures, technology, unemployment, saturation, isolation, pluralism of values, lack of orientation, religious diversity, transience, loss of traditions, rediscovery of religious roots, recollection of naturopathy, magic, occultism and shamanism, the trend toward holism, recourse to spiritual and esoteric themes, interdisciplinarianism, fragmentation, multi-culturality, the urge toward individualization, and/or the search for new forms of expression. All these aspects can be found in religious dances. The researcher's investigation can therefore in the first instance confirm a picture of a society, secondly enrich and complete that picture, and thirdly be instrumental in pointing out new trends and tendencies.

For a newly established, and for an already existing religion, the various elements listed above provide sufficient reason for using dance as a medium for conveying a religion and strengthening the community, and as a means of personal, controlled, religious experiences, or for obtaining and preserving the same, so that contemporary, secular styles can also be included.[2] Active in-

2 For example "Dance & Praise—Hiphop to Christian Songs" was a topic presented at the German Catholic Congress 2000.

volvement is arguably one means to obtain knowledge of a phenomenon, and for religions, it can serve as a form of "buy-in" to the group. Such considerations must not be forgotten by religions which have to survive in an increasingly complex market.

All these aspects indicate and confirm that a further growth in religious dance can be anticipated and that religious studies must prepare itself for a growing area of research. A priority is religious studies research into current religious dance in Western societies and new influences in classical dance cultures. We may both expect and hope that the different disciplines will blend and overlap, due not only to the changes described in the current religious dance scene, but also to the increasing self-reflection of dance researchers, their interdisciplinary co-operation and the exchange of research methods.

8. Summary

Research into (religious) dance has until now been a peripheral area for religious studies. The need for a more intensive concern with dance arises not least from the current growth of religious dance itself. Religious studies can benefit from the preparatory work of other disciplines, and should also strive in future for interdisciplinarity, in part because the subject demands special skills and specializations that do not form part of conventional religious studies training. Religious dance is encountered in numerous and quite different variations. The components that turn a dance into a religious dance are equally varied. The choice of the research methods should be determined by this fact, just as much as by the origin and dance skills and knowledge of the researcher. The skills and knowledge that can be gained from the investigation of (religious) dance are in no way restricted to the formal description of the dance, its significance in the religion of the individual and its functions within a religion. Dance can be seen as a living record of the overall social conditions and historical development of a society.

Bibliography

Adams, Doug/Apostolos-Cappadona, Diane, eds. (1990), *Dance as Religious Studies*. New York: Crossroad.

Ahlbäck, Tore, ed. (1996), *Dance, Music, Art, and Religion. Based on Papers Read at the Symposium on Dance, Music, and Art in Religions, Held at Åbo, Finnland on the 16th–18th of August 1994*. Turku/Stockholm: Almqvist & Wiksell.

Baaren, Theodorus Petrus van (1964), *Selbst die Götter tanzen*. Gütersloh: Gütersloher Verlagshaus G. Mohn.

Backman, E. Louis (1952), *Religious Dances in the Christian Church and in Popular Medicine*. London: George Allen & Unwin.

Barboza, Francis Peter (1990), *Christianity in Indian Dance Forms*. Delhi: Sri Satguru Publications.

Berger, Teresa (1985), *Liturgie und Tanz. Anthropologische Aspekte, Historische Daten, Theologische Perspektiven*. St. Ottilien: Eos Verlag.

Bounaventura, Wendy (1983), *Belly Dancing: The Serpent and the Sphinx*. London: Virago Press.

Bourguignon, Erika (1968), "Trance Dance," in *Dance Perspectives* 35. Brooklyn, N.Y.: Dance Perspectives Foundation.

— (1998), "Trance Dance," in: Selma Jeanne Cohen, ed., *International Encyclopedia of Dance*. Vol. 6. New York: Oxford University Press: 184–88.

Buckland, Theresa J., ed. (1999), *Dance in the Field. Theory, Methods and Issues in Dance Ethnography*. London: Macmillan Press Ltd.*

Combs, Jo Anne (1992), *Christian Sacred Dance: An Ethnography of Performance and Symbolic Interactionism*. Los Angeles, Calif.: UMI Dissertation Service.

Evans Pritchard, Edward E. (1965), *Theories of Primitive Religion*. Oxford: Oxford University Press.

Friedland, LeeEllen (1995), "Popular and Folk Dance," in: Mircea Eliade, ed., *Encyclopedia of Religion*. Vol. 3. New York: Simon & Schuster Macmillan: 212–21.

Gagne, Ronald/Kane, Thomas/VerEecke, Robert (1984), *Introducing Dancing in Christian Worship*. Washington: Pastoral Press.

Gaston, Anne-Marie (1982), *Siva in Dance, Myth and Iconography*, Delhi: Oxford University Press.

— (1996), *Bharata Natyam. From Temple to Theatre*. New Delhi: Manohar.

Graf, W. (1964), "Tanz, I. Religionswissenschaftlich," in: *Lexikon für Theologie und Kirche*. Vol. 9. Freiburg: Herder: 1291–92.

Gundlach Sonnemann, Helga Barbara (2000), *Religiöser Tanz. Formen, Funktionen, aktuelle Beispiele*. Marburg: Diagonal Verlag.*

Gundlach, Helga Barbara (2002), "Tanz als Gegenstand religionswissenschaftlicher Forschung in Deutschland," in: Gabriele Klein/Christa Zipprich, eds., *Tanz Theorie Text. Jahrbuch für Tanzforschung*. Vol. 12. Münster: LIT-Verlag: 173–91.*

Günther, Dorothee (1962), *Der Tanz als Bewegungsphänomen*. Reinbek bei Hamburg: Rowohlt.*

Hanna, Judith Lynne (1995), "Dance and Religion," in: Mircea Eliade, ed., *Encyclopedia of Religion*. Vol. 3. New York: Simon & Schuster Macmillan: 203–12.*

Hoffmann, Kaye (1986), *Tanz, Trance, Transformation*, München: Knaur.

Iyer, Alessandra, ed. (1997), *South Asian Dance. The British Experience*. Choreography and Dance. An International Journal. Volume 4. Part 2. Amsterdam: Harwood Academic Publishers.

Jonas, Gerald (1992), *Dancing. The Pleasure, Power and Art of Movement*. New York: Harry N. Abrams.*

Kaeppler, Adrienne L. (1999), "The Mystique of Fieldwork," in: Theresa J. Buckland, ed., *Dance in the Field. Theory, Methods and Issues in Dance Ethnography*. London: Macmillan Press Ltd.: 13–25.

Kealiinohomoku, Joann Marie Wheeler (1967), "Hopi and Polynesian Dance: A Study in Cross-Cultural Comparisons," in: *Ethnomusicology* 11. Middletown. Conn.: : 343–58.

— (1976), *Theory and Methods for an Anthropological Study of Dance*. Indiana University: Umi Dissertation Service.

— (1998), "Primitive Dance," in: Selma Jeanne Cohen, ed., *International Encyclopedia of Dance*. Vol. 5. New York: Oxford University Press: 252–53.

Khokar, Mohan (1987), *Dancing for Themselves. Folk, Tribal and Ritual Dance of India*. Delhi.

Klein, Gabriele (1992), *FrauenKörperTanz. Eine Zivilisationsgeschichte des Tanzes*. Berlin: Quadriga.*

Kurath, Gertrude (1995), "Dance," in: *Man, Myth & Magic. The Illustrated Encyclopedia of Mythology, Religion and the Unknown*. New York: Marshall Cavendish: 528–40.

Layson, June (1994), "Historical Perspectives in the Study of Dance," in: Jane Adshead-Landsdale/June Layson, eds., *Dance History. An Introduction*. London/New York: Routledge: 5–1[illegible]

Leeuw, Gerardus van der (1930), *In dem Himmel ist ein Tanz…* München: Dornverlag.

— (1956), *Phänomenologie der Religion*. Tübingen: Mohr.*

— (1957), *Vom Heiligen in der Kunst*. Gütersloh: Bertelsmann.

Nola, Alfonso M. di (1970), "Danza," in: *Enciclopedia Delle Religioni*. Firenze: Vallecchi editore: 582–91.

Novack, Cynthia J. (1998), "Ritual and Dance," in: Selma Jeanne Cohen, ed., *International Encyclopedia of Dance*. Vol. 5. New York: Oxford University Press: 354–57.

Nürnberger, Marianne (1994), *Tanz ist die Sprache der Götter. Eine Kulturwandelsstudie der Tänzer Sri Lankas*. Frankfurt: Peter Lang Verlag.

Nürnberger, Mariannne/Schmiederer, Stephanie, eds. (1996), *Tanzkunst, Ritual und Bühne. Begegnungen zwischen Kulturen*, Frankfurt: IKO.

Oesterley, William Oscar Emil (1923), *The Sacred Dance. A Study in Comparative Folklore*. Cambridge (reprinted 1968 Brooklyn, N.Y.: Dance Horizons).

Otto, W.F. (1956), *Menschengestalt und Tanz*. München: Hermann Ring Verlag.

Padfield, Marsha Lou (1991), *An Examination of the Type and Function of Movement in the Angelican Church*. The Graduate School of the Union Institute: UMI Disertation Service.

Projektgruppe "Tanzen" am Ludwig-Uhland-Institut für Empirische Kulturwissenschaft der Universität Tübingen (1998), *Tanzlust. Empirische Untersuchungen zu Formen alltäglichen Tanzvergnügens*. Tübingen: Tübinger Vereinigung f. Volkskunde.

Randell, Janet (1999), *In Him we Move. Creative Dancing in Worship*. Carlisle: Solway.

Reed, Carlynn (1978), *And We Have Danced: A History of the Sacred Dance Guild 1958–1978*. Richmond: The Sharing Company.

— (1998), "Liturgical Dance," in: Selma Jeanne Cohen, ed., *International Encyclopedia of Dance*. Vol. 4. New York: Oxford University Press: 212–13.

Ricard, Matthieu (1999), *Moines Danseurs du Tibet*. Paris: Éditions Albin Michel.

Royce, Anya Peterson (1980), *The Anthropology of Dance*. Bloomington/London: Indiana University Press.*

Rust, Ezra Gardner (1996), *The Music and Dance of the World's Religions: A Comprehensive Annotated Bibliography of Materials in English Language*. Westport/London: Greenwood Press.*

Sachs, Curt (1933), *Eine Weltgeschichte des Tanzes*. Berlin: Dietrich Reimer Verlag. (1937 translated by B. Schönberg: *World History of the Dance*. New York: W.W. Norton & Co.).*

Sakakibara, Kiitsu (1992), *Dances of Asia*. Chandigarh: Bharat Bushan Mahndiratta.

Saldaña, Nancy (1966), "La Malinche: Her Representation in Dances of Mexico and the United States," in: *Ethnomusicology* 10. Middletown, Conn.: 298–309.

Sarukkai, Malavika (1999), in: *Shivas Töchter, Indischer Tanz zwischen Tradition und Moderne*. Film by Angela Boëti/Norbert Buse. ZDF/Arte.
Sax, William (2001), *Dancing the Self. Personhood and Performance in the Pandav Lila*. New York: Oxford University Press.
Scheier, Helmut (1995), "'Primitive Mysteries' und 'Tänze vor Gott'—sakraler Bühnentanz im 20. Jahrhundert," in: *Choreae* 2. Willich: Choros: 112–26.
Schimmel, Annemarie (1962), "Tanz, I. Religionsgeschichtlich," in: *Religion in Geschichte und Gegenwart*. Vol. 6. Tübingen: Mohr: 612–14.
Schott-Billmann, France, ed. (1999), *Danse et Spiritualité*. Paris: Éditions Noêsis.
Sequeira, A. Ronald (1977), *Spielende Liturgie. Bewegung neben Wort und Ton im Gottesdienst am Beispiel des Vaterunsers*. Freiburg: Herder.
— (1978), *Klassische indische Tanzkunst und christliche Verkündigung*. Freiburg: Herder.
Shay, Anthony (1971), *The Functions of Dance in Human Societies: An Approach Using Context (Dance Event) not Content (Movements and Gestures) for Treating Dance as Anthropological Data*. MA Thesis. Los Angeles, Calif.: California State College.
Sherman, Jane (1983), *Denishawn: the Enduring Influence*. Boston, Mass.: Twayne Publishers.
Sorell, Walter (1981), *Dance in Its Time*. Garden City/New York: Anchor Press/Doubleday.*
Sources Orientales VI (1963), *Les Danses Sacrées. Égypte Ancienne, Israël, Islam, Asie Centrale, Cambodge, Bali, Java, Chine, Japon*. Paris: Éditions du Seuil.*
St. Denis, Ruth (1989), *The Divine Dance*. San Francisco: Peace Works Press.
Stewart, Iris J. (2000), *Sacred Woman, Sacred Dance. Awakening Spirituality through Movement & Ritual*. Rochester: Inner Traditions.
Tillich, Paul (1990), "Existentialist Aspects of Modern Art," in: M. Palmer, ed., *Writings in the Philosophy of Culture*. Berlin: de Gruyter: 269–80.
Vatsyayan, Kapila (1993), in: *Dancing—Der göttliche Atem*. Film by Geoff Dunlopp, based on the book by Gerald Jonas (Thirteen/WNet/RM Arts/BBC).
Vogler, Gereon/Sudbrack, Josef/Kohlhaas, Emmanuela, eds. (1995), *Tanz und Spiritualität*. Mainz: Matthias Grünewald-Verlag.
Wosien, Maria-Gabriele (1974), *Sacred Dance. Encounter with Gods*. New York: Avon Books.*
— (1988), *Sakraler Tanz*, München: Kösel.
— (1990), *Tanz als Gebet*, Linz: Veritas.
— (1994), *Tanz: Symbole in Bewegung*, Linz: Veritas.
Youngerman, Suzanne (1995), "Theatrical and Liturgical Dance," in: Mircea Eliade, ed., *Encyclopedia of Religion*. Vol. 3. New York: Simon & Schuster Macmillan: 221–36.
Zacharias, Gerhard (1997), *Ballett. Gestalt und Wesen. Die Symbolsprache im europäischen Schautanz der Neuzeit*. Wilhelmshaven: Fischer Taschenbuch Verlag.
Zana, Elisabeth (1996), *La Danse et le Sacré*. Paris: Éditions Dervy.*

* Important works focussing on systematic and methodological aspects of dance analysis

Human Rights: An Important and Challenging New Field for the Study of Religion

by

ROSALIND I.J. HACKETT

1. Introduction: Contours and Challenges[1]

This chapter corresponds well to the mandate of the present book. It could not have been written twenty years ago, perhaps even ten years ago. That is not to say that the roots of human rights do not reach back into history as long as human beings have struggled for liberty and justice. Nor can it be argued that there has not been a voluminous output of literature on human rights, since the international movement was born out of the disasters of World War II.[2] But scholarly analysis of the promotion and protection of freedom of religion and belief, and the ambivalent relationship of human rights concepts to religious traditions, only really starts to become apparent in the 1980s—subsequent to the development of specific international human rights instruments (discussed below; see Stahnke/Martin 1998).[3]

The last decade in particular has seen the emergence of several specialized texts on what Louis Henkin calls the "vexed relationship" between religion and human rights." Arguably the most influential publication in this regard is the two-volume, *Religious Human Rights*, which resulted from a major multidisciplinary conference on this subject organized by Emory University's Law and Religion Program in 1994 (Witte/van der Vyver 1996; van der Vyver/Witte 1996). It represented the first attempt to bring together different religious traditions and scholarly disciplines to examine, from an international perspective, the various permutations of the relationship between religion and human rights

1 I wish to express my appreciation to Abdullahi An-Na'im, T. Jeremy Gunn, David Little, Mohamed Mahmoud, J.J. Rosenbaum, and Arvind Sharma for their helpful comments and suggestions on this essay.

2 There were a number of useful publications to mark the fiftieth anniversary of the signing of the Universal Declaration of Human Rights in 1948. See, for example, the special issue of the *Journal of Religious Ethics* 26 (2) 1998; also Baehr/Flinterman/Senders 1999; Evans 1998; Swedish Institute 1998.

3 I have here confined myself to literature in English.

(see Witte 2001 for an update). By the end of the 1990s it now became possible to consult reports on how freedom of religion is understood, protected or denied around the world.[4] These and the other texts to be discussed in this essay were long overdue given the relative neglect of freedom of religion and belief in the overall human rights regime (Lerner 2000), and, in fact, the general lack of serious treatment of the religious dimension of international relations (Casanova 1994; Haynes 1998; Johnston 1994; Rudolph 1997). The manifold reasons for this orphan status hardly need to be adumbrated for scholars of religion—secularist perceptions of religion as primitive and backward, sensitivity of religion questions, difficulty of achieving consensus and definition, and so on. Yet the rise of religion to prominence on the world stage has added impetus to the growing intellectual interest in religion from a human rights perspective and vice versa.

In this essay I shall examine the contours and contributions of the emerging scholarship on religion and human rights, while pointing to some potentially fruitful areas of investigation for scholars of religion. I am particularly concerned about generating data and analysis on the culture and ethnography of human rights. I shall also argue that the particular skills that religion scholars bring to the table in terms of what Ninian Smart called "worldview analysis," namely, the critical interpretation of sacred symbol, text, space, ritual, object, community, as well as cultural difference and identity (see, e.g. Chidester 1996, 2000: 436; Nye 2000), are highly germane in the analysis of human rights discourse and practice. We should also include here the mobilizing and authorizing power of religious rhetoric (McCutcheon 1997; O'Leary 1994), as well as arguments for the inclusion of secular ideologies (see, especially, Smart 1995). Moreover, the location of religious studies scholarship at the intersection of the humanities and social sciences, together with its focus on religious belief and practice as embedded historical and contemporary realities, can serve to complement, if not healthily challenge, the domination of these questions by legal, political, and philosophical theorists.

A number of international developments in the last few years with regard to freedom of religion and belief have been forcing the hand of scholars to pay more attention to what human rights lawyer and scholar Jeremy Gunn calls "the oldest, newest, and most controversial of rights" (Gunn forthcoming). First, the United States launched a controversial initiative to make religious freedom a central aspect of its foreign policy in the form of the International Religious Freedom Act of 1998.[5] As a result of this law there is now an

---

4 See below, note 5. Kevin Boyle's and Juliet Sheen's *Freedom of Religion and Belief: A World Report* was an earlier attempt to document and analyze understandings, protections and violations of the freedom of religion and secular thought (Boyle 1997).

5 See http:\\www.state.gov\www\global\human_rights\drl_religion.html.

Ambassador-at-Large for International Religious Freedom, an office in the State Department, an Advisory Commission, and annual report on the state of religious freedom worldwide; in addition, the President is required to resort to a range of actions against countries that are major violators of religious freedom (see Gunn 2000; Hackett 2001b; Hackett/Silk/Hoover 2000). Second, a number of European countries have in the last few years imposed or proposed restrictions on newer religious formations ("sects" and "cults") (Barker 2000; Lord 2000; Shterin 2001). These new developments have served to shift the focus onto actual violations of religious freedom by individual states, as well as bringing it closer to "home." The work of sociologist of religion and legal scholar, James Richardson, is paradigmatic in this regard, namely his analysis of state management of religious pluralities and minorities in a number of locations (see, for example, Richardson 1995, 2000).[6] It is predominantly religious minorities who continue to suffer the worst forms of human rights abuses (cf. Adams 2000).[7] This greater attention to the realities of religious freedom on the ground is further influenced by the ideas, images and texts which now circulate globally about religious persecution and martyrdom. Evangelical Christian organizations—with their effective publicity and lobbying mechanisms, as well as their growing cyberactivism—have been particularly active in shaping this discourse (see, in particular, Marshall 1997, 2000; Shea 1997).

But there are numerous other ways that the interrelationship between religion and human rights has been, and is being, addressed. As alluded to above, it is oft perceived as a conflictual relationship. In the diplomatic words of leading human rights scholar, Louis Henkin, "[t]he world of religion and the world of human rights have not always coexisted comfortably" (Henkin 2000: 29). This is not just because of the violence and rights abuses committed in the name of religion which it would be all too easy to cite, but also because the multiplicity of traditions and contexts associated with the phenomenon of religion would appear to be at odds with the universalist claims of human rights. This is commonly described as a controversy over "cultural relativism" or even civilizational conflict (Little 2001; Huntington 1993). Several scholars have therefore taken on the task of exploring particular religious traditions to see whether they contain the resources for human rights ideas implicitly or explicitly. Some of these efforts will be examined below.

---

6 See especially his guest-edited issue of *Social Justice Research*, 12 (4) 1999. The *Nova Religio* issue on "Alternative Religions, the State, and the Globe" (April 2001) and the Dutch publication, *Freedom of Religion: A Precious Human Right* (Naber 2000) also reflect this trend.

7 Although see Sharma's interesting argument that in India it is the religious majority (Hindus) who have suffered most at hands of minorities (Muslims, Christians) (Sharma 2000/2001).

Anthropologists, with whom historians of religion have enjoyed a close affinity over the years, have been far more distrustful of the universalizing discourses of human rights. This suspicion has been fueled by traditional anthropological emphasis on culture, localism, and non- or sub-state actors. Happily there are now anthropologists (see, especially, Wilson 1997), who recognize that human rights ideas are increasingly being appropriated by many indigenous peoples in their struggles for cultural and political self-determination—Sub-Commandante Marcos of Zapatista fame in Mexico being a primary case in point. Anthropologists have much to contribute on the cross-cultural applicability of human rights, and the tensions between global and local formulations of human rights. In fact, group rights, cultural self-determination, and the rights of indigenous peoples and ethnic minorities are currently some of the most hotly debated items on the human rights agenda, as will be seen in a later section.[8]

Finally, we can note another category of scholars—the area, or empirically-oriented tradition, specialists—whose work is taking on a human rights dimension in varying degrees. They tend to examine the way more internationalist conceptions of the freedom to manifest religious belief and practice can transform the dynamics of religion and state, and local power relations in particular contexts. Additionally, there are growing numbers of scholars who, by way of their interests in women's changing religious roles, adopt a human rights framework for analysis (see, e.g., Cooke/Lawrence 1996; Howland 1999).

One of the leading thinkers on religion and human rights, David Little, rejects any pretensions to a single methodological approach because of the sheer complexity of this "inchoate" and "uncertain" area of study (Little 1996). For his own methodology, Little draws on the perspectives he developed as former director of the "Religion, Nationalism, and Intolerance" project at the United States Institute of Peace.[9] The focus of this project was the free exercise of religion and freedom from discrimination based on religion or belief, as articulated in the first two articles of the 1981 UN Declaration on Intolerance discussed below.[10] His rationale for this perspective is that it highlights two fundamental interests of religious people: "being able to affirm, express, and manifest their convictions, and being able to avoid unfair discrimination or bias on account of religion" (Little 1996: 48). He further distinguishes in the latter right between fundamental belief as a *target* for intolerance as opposed to being

8 See, especially, the study by Sri Lankan anthropologist, H.L. Seneviratne, on the political involvement of Sri Lankan Buddhist monks (Seneviratne 2000). See, also Bartholomeusz/de Silva 1998.

9 Three studies have resulted so far from the conferences and focus areas: Hibbard/Little 1997; Little 1991; Little 1994; and Hackett forthcoming. See also Little's elaboration of the concept of religious militancy in human rights usage (Little 2000).

10 Resolution adopted by the General Assembly on November 25, 1981.

a *warrant* or justification for intolerance (Little 1996: 54). This analytical framework is useful for applying to a number of case materials as well as for the basic concepts it introduces, although it perhaps tends to privilege belief over practice, when the latter may more frequently be the cause of conflict between religious groups, and between groups and the state.[11]

The study of the concepts, practices, and institutions that connect or disconnect religion and human rights may be a relatively new sub-field, but it is nonetheless many-sided. I have chosen to work, in this particular overview, with the following sub-divisions since they seem to represent a certain logical clustering of ideas and approaches: theoretical, legal, theological/philosophical, cultural, contextual and thematic. However, as will be seen with the issues of cultural relativism and women, for example, the various sections should not be seen as bounded categories.

2. Determining Origins and Defining Terms

The history of the human rights movement need not detain us here, but it is interesting to note that its origins and trajectory are contested by both its proponents and opponents.[12] The voices calling for compromise or transcending of divisive interpretive paradigms, viz. East/West, North/South, secular/religious, universalist/relativist are getting stronger—as we shall see in succeeding sections (e.g. An-Na'im 2000d; Booth 1999; Ignatieff 1999; Ong 1999).[13] Lauren finds a more constructive way of talking about the evolution of the human rights vision by referring to the many "tributaries" of the "ever expanding and evolving river of human rights" (Lauren 1998: 9).

More than fifty years after the drafting and adoption of the historic Universal Declaration of Human Rights in 1948, with its purpose of establishing a "common standard of achievement for all peoples and all nations," human rights parlance has now achieved the status of a "moral *lingua franca* for global politics" (Barbieri 1999: 907; see also Power/Allison 2000: xiii). Although

---

11 However, Little rightly notes that religious groups frequently formulate and sharpen their beliefs when under attack (Little 1996: 53, n. 20).

12 Good overview articles on the nature and history of the human rights idea can be found under "human rights" at www.britannica.com. Also highly recommended is Lauren 1998.

13 For a good example of the secular vs. religious debate over the "ownership" of human rights, see Henkin 1999; Stackhouse 1999. Tergel's study focuses rather on the cross-fertilization of ideas between the worlds of human rights and religion. He examines the way that particular Christian churches (Lutheran, Catholic, and Reformed) in the second half of the twentieth century have responded creatively to the human rights paradigm, and, in turn, influenced it through their own greater emphasis on social and economic rights (Tergel 1998).

it is worth recalling here the trenchant observation of Michael Ignatieff, one of the most lucid authors and commentators in this area, as to why we live with a "divided consciousness" in relation to human rights: "[w]ithout the Holocaust then, no Declaration. Because of the Holocaust, no unconditional faith in the Declaration either" (Ignatieff 1999: 59; see, also, Ignatieff 2001b).

David Little seeks to offer some conceptual clarity regarding the modern understanding of human rights (Little 1996). He defines a "human right" as (and I summarize his more detailed version) 1) a moral right advanced as a legal right; 2) protecting something of indispensable human importance; 3) ascribed naturally; 4) non-derogable (if primary), or subject to limitations under prescribed conditions; 5) universally claimable by all people against all others, or by certain generic categories of people such as "women" or "children" (Little 1996: 57, n. 34). Martha Nussbaum, who has written extensively on the difference between the language of rights and capabilities or human functioning, does accept that rights possess "a moral resonance that is hard to avoid in contemporary political discourse" (Nussbaum 1997a: 1). But she is far less sanguine about the theoretical and conceptual clarity of rights language. Similarly, Barbieri writes graphically of "the tortured state of contemporary human rights discourse" as "Straussians, neo-Kantians, liberals, critical theorists, pragmatists, and skeptics of various stripes continue to butt heads over the nature of human rights" (Barbieri 1999: 3). He attributes this head-butting of Western scholars to a persistent proclivity for depoliticized, foundationalist ideas, dichotomous interpretations of the universalist/relativist character of human rights, and individualist rather than more communal understandings of the *humanum*. In his widely used textbook on *International Human Rights*, Jack Donnelly goes to the other extreme, preferring to eschew the confusing array of philosophical theories proposed to account for human nature and human rights (Donnelly 1998: 20–22). He describes, in more concrete fashion, human rights as "the social and political guarantees necessary to protect individuals from the standard threats to human dignity posed by the modern state and the modern markets" (and, he could have added, failing states). But it is unlikely that such social scientific minimalism can escape philosophical inquiry. Ecological and environmental rights, which are gradually being edged in by some proponents as a category of human rights, illustrate this type of multi-faceted debate (Rasmussen 1999; Tergel 1998: 23–24).

3. Legal Protection and Interpretation

A number of legal scholars with particular interest in the religion question have helped illuminate the theory and practice of the freedom of thought, conscience, religion and belief in international law. We can simply sketch the main developments here. Details of the fascinating semantic, political, and theological wranglings that shaped the emergent legal discourse on these issues can be found in the sources cited below (see, especially, Glendon 2001).

Four major modern instruments are concerned with the protection of freedom and belief. The first is the 1948 Universal Declaration of Human Rights (UDHR), with its most crucial provision, Article 18:

> Everyone has the right to freedom of thought, conscience and religion; this right includes the freedom to change his religion or belief, and freedom, either alone or in community with others and in public or private, to manifest his [*sic*] religion or belief in teaching, practice, worship and observance.[14]

The first clause guarantees the right to freedom of thought (and the inclusion of theistic, non-theistic, and atheistic belief is a feature of these international documents), and the second enumerates the specific rights therein. Interestingly, Kevin Boyle and Juliet Sheen aver that this article constitutes a paradigm of the widespread debates over the nature of human rights in general, because it "raises the issue of the universality and indivisibility of rights, of the primacy of international law over national law and religious codes, of individual, minority and collective rights and of the relationship between rights, duties and community" (Boyle 1997: 4).

Then followed the much-cited study in 1959 by Arcot Krishnaswami from India who was appointed by the Subcommission on Prevention of Discrimination and Protection of Minorities to study rights pertaining to religion and belief and to draw up a program of action to eradicate religious discrimination.[15] He concludes that the collective aspect of the freedom to manifest religion or belief was especially important, as it was prone to state intervention and regulation. He notes the particular vulnerability of minorities in this regard (endorsed by Adams 2000). The International Covenant on Civil and Political Rights (ICCPR) and the International Covenant on Economic, Social and Cultural Rights (ICESCR) were adopted in 1966 and ratified in 1976. The ICCPR is the only global human rights treaty with articles on religion and belief that contains measures of implementation (Lerner 2000: 19).[16]

---

14 All of the key documents pertaining to freedom of religion and belief can be found in the helpful publication from the Center for the Study of Human Rights, Columbia University (Stahnke/Martin 1998).

15 Study of Discrimination in the Matter of Religious Rights and Practices, U.N. Sales No. 60. XIV. 2 (1960).

16 Lerner also notes the importance of the General Comment on Article 18 of the Human Rights Committee (HRC) in charge of implementing the ICCPR for the clarification and influence it brings to the issue of freedom of thought, conscience, religion and belief. See Report of the Human Rights Committee, U.N. GAOR 48th Sess., Supp. No. 40, Annex VI, U.N. Doc. A/48/40 (1993).

Finally, in 1981, after years of intensive lobbying and complicated negotiations, came the landmark Declaration on the Elimination of All Forms of Intolerance and Discrimination Based on Religion or Belief. It served to elaborate what the 1966 Convenant adumbrated (Witte 2001: 771). Once again the definitional problem emerged, and to placate the non-religious believers the word "whatever" was inserted before the word "belief" in Article 1 (1). Another area of controversy was that of religious conversion, and explicit references to "changing one's religion" were deleted from the text at the behest of Muslim delegations, [illegible] (cf. Sullivan 1988). This key issue will receive further discussion in the section on proselytization below.

Bahiyyih Tahzib, as international legal scholar, is also concerned with detailing the standards regarding freedom of religion or belief in international human rights instruments (Tahzib 1996). Her particular contribution is to assess whether the adoption of a more legally binding convention would offer more effective protection. She concludes that arguments for a separate convention with its own supervisory body have grown less compelling, and prefers the solution of strengthening existing norms and mechanisms (cf. also Lerner 2000: 51–79). Boyle and Sheen acknowledge the considerable agreement that has been reached on the content of these freedoms in international law, notwithstanding the remaining disputes, chiefly over the interpretation of the requirements of these international standards (Boyle 1997: 4–5). They see the more serious reality as the "open repudiation in practice" of norms accepted by the majority of states in the United Nations in binding international agreements. These violations are documented annually in the reports by the U.N. Special Rapporteur on freedom of religion and belief (Evans 1997: 245–61; Lerner 2000: 29–32). For W. Cole Durham it is the nature of the relationship between religion and the state (persistently and problematically described by many scholars in exclusive language as "church-state") which is so formative in accounting for the substantive differences in the achievement of religious freedom around the world (Durham 1996).

There is a growing body of literature on Europe in matters of freedom of religion and belief which is not surprising given its historical significance and a surge of cases in recent times raising difficult questions under Article 9 of the European Convention on Human Rights (ECHR) (C. Evans 2001; M.D. Evans 1997). Europe presents an interesting case because of the emergence of new possibilities of misusing or reducing the constitutionally guaranteed freedom of religion and belief either by governments or by religious groups.[17] Jeremy Gunn regards the Organization for Security and Co-Operation in Europe

17 Many of these violations, in Europe and beyond, are tracked by Human Rights Without Frontiers, www.hrwf.org and the Centre for the Study of New Religions, www.cesnur.org.

(OSCE) as a "trendsetter" for the way it has raised the profile of religious freedom on the international agenda of participating states and focused critical international attention on their respective practices (Gunn 2001). He attributes this in part to the unique nature of the Helsinki process, as it is known, which allows participating states to criticize each other on their human rights performances.

In closing this section we can return to the landmark U.S. International Religious Freedom Act of 1998, referred to above, for it raises the intriguing question of whether religious freedom is different from, or more special than, other rights. Little finds legal and historical reasons for assigning some kind of special status to religious freedom, while not denying its interdependence with other rights, such as freedom of association, freedom of expression, for example (Little 2001). He points out that it is included among the nonderogable rights contained in Article 4 of the ICCPR. Moreover, he also discusses the special deference that the Human Rights Committee has afforded to the *forum internum* or sovereignty of conscience.[18]

4. Compatibility/Incompatibility Arguments

A large portion of the scholarship on the relationship between religion and human rights addresses the issue of their compatibility or incompatibility. For Louis Henkin the idea and morality of religions differ from the human rights ideology principally in terms of sources and bases of authority (Henkin 1998). While acknowledging the shared concept of human dignity, he highlights key differences in contemporary interests and concerns, namely the areas of freedom of religion and religious choice, equality and nondiscrimination, gender distinctions, and capital punishment. He recognizes and hopes for a certain growing *rapprochement* of religion and human rights in the areas of freedom, justice, and peace, but counsels against confusing the functions of religious and human rights organizations. Religious traditions are more totalizing as ideologies, and oriented (notably smaller, minority religions) toward the rights of their own adherents (see also Everett 1996). Henkin further accuses some religious groups as being too narrowly focused on religious rights. There

18 General Comment No. 22 (48), Article 18. See Stahnke/Martin 1998: 92–94. In fact, Little links the more specific notion of freedom of conscience and religion in Western thought with the intensifying of inner, personal experience in the early Christian church (Little/Kelsay/Sachedina 1988: 13–32; cf. also Reynolds/Durham 1996; Tierney 1996). It was from this point on that the struggle between the conscience and the state began to take shape. He argues that this distinction between the spiritual and the civil or material, the inner and the outer, is foundational to many religions and is constitutive of the response by religious traditions to modern claims about human rights.

is, however, an important parallel, if not correlation, between religious and human rights groups that he does not signal—the fact that both are in the business of juggling ideals and realities, and seek to mediate the dissonance between theory and practice through their various discourses.

The strong foundationalist orientation of the compatibility approach is epitomized in the words of legal historian and law and religion specialist, John Witte, "[h]uman rights are, in substantial part, the modern political fruits of ancient religious beliefs and practices" (Witte 1998: 258). So a favored methodology is the historical plumbing of religious traditions for homologues or proximate categories of thought. Witte makes a strong pitch for a "new human rights hermeneutic" involving:

> fresh methods of interpreting ... sacred texts and traditions that will allow [religious communities] ... both to reclaim the long-obscured roles that their traditions have played in the cultivation of human rights in the past and to lay claim to familiar principles and practices within these traditions that are conducive to the development of human rights in the future (Witte 1998: 258).

As outlined above, in terms of theories of origins of the human rights concept, the Protestant tradition is a popular site of investigation. For example, Witte even goes as far to say that the Protestant Reformation was, in part, "a human rights movement" (Witte 1998: 258). But fortunately this hermeneutic exercise has been nothing if not comparative—whether in the form of an ecumenical vision that glosses over differences and adopts the Golden Rule approach (e.g. Tierney 1996: 44), or a variety of religion-specific case studies. These are too numerous to treat here, but some of the general contributions can be briefly noted.

In one of the earliest comparative approaches to the subject, Arlene Swidler's *Human Rights in Religious Traditions*, the authors consider the concept of human rights from their respective traditions, followed by more general evaluations of this "primary ethical concern" (A. Swidler 1982). This was followed in 1986 by Leonard Swidler's *Religious Liberty and Human Rights*, which purports to be more centered on the problem of religious liberty "within nations, between nations, and within religions" (L. Swidler 1986). The essays in Leroy Rouner's 1988 collection, *Human Rights and the World's Religions* explore the role of religion as ground for belief in rights. There is consensus on the inherent worth and dignity of individual humans, but disagreement, notably from the Buddhist and Confucian perspectives, over whether a theory of rights is the best symbol for that value (Rouner 1988). The study also revealed that different groups emphasized different rights, and, in the case of Hinduism, the interdependence of rights and duties. The primarily European authors in *Human Rights and Religious Values: An Uneasy Relationship* critically examine the potential for religious traditions to justify and support human rights as the common core of a "universal morality" among these traditions (An-Na'im 1995). The 1996 collection of essays edited by Irene Bloom, Paul Martin and Wayne

Proudfoot offers a more nuanced discussion of the role of religion in the evolving tradition of human rights by examining comparatively traditional concepts of personhood, and the dynamic between individual and community in religious communities (Bloom/Martin/Proudfoot 1996). For a trenchant overview of Catholic, Protestant, and Orthodox theological potential for the human rights community, John Witte's article is an excellent resource (Witte 2001).

Little, Kelsay and Sachedina adopt a different approach by examining the concurrence between Islam and Western Christianity in respect to religious liberty, using a framework that distinguishes between the inner and the outer, the religious and the moral (Little/Kelsay/Sachedina 1988). The case of Islam is often viewed as particularly challenging in terms of whether Islamic law and theology support the modern notion of human rights. The Islamic legal scholar, Abdullahi An-Na'im, has been at the forefront of this exegesis (An-Na'im 1990). He seeks to resolve the tensions between Islamists and their opponents over differing visions of the state, as theocratic or democratic and constitutional, by arguing that "since Shari'a is a historically conditioned *human* interpretation of the fundamental sources of Islam, alternative modern interpretations are possible" and, moreover, imperative (An-Na'im 1996: 353). For an excellent overview of the complex, yet evolving, discourse on Islam and human rights see Mayer 1998, 1999; cf. also Dwyer 1991). Several leading African scholars have also contributed to the debate on the interrelationship of religion and human rights more generally, with their examinations of the concepts of dignity, duties and community in African traditional cultures, and the positive and negative implications of these values for the protection of human rights (see, for example, Deng 1990; Gyekye 1998; Ilesanmi 1995; Wiredu 1990).

5. Culture Matters

Culture both complicates and enriches the whole question of human rights theory and implementation. An-Na'im has been one of the most prominent advocates of the need for human rights to seek cultural legitimacy through internal and cross-cultural dialogue (An-Na'im 1992). The truth-claims and traditions of religious and ethnic groups, large and small, feed into, even exacerbate, the unending debates about universalism and relativism (Steiner/Alston 2000: 323–402; Tilley 2000) or cultural domination and subordination (Mignolo 2000). As legal scholar, S. James Anaya, rightly observes, the growing concern within the international system for peoples or populations identified as indigenous "has arisen as part of a larger concern for those segments of humanity that have experienced histories of colonization and have continued to suffer the legacies of those histories" (Anaya 1996: 43). For example, Kenyan human rights scholar, Makau Mutua, demonstrates forcefully the ongoing discriminations perpetuated by African states against their indigenous religious cultures

(Mutua 1999). Of interest here is the protection offered by Articles 18 and 27 of the ICCPR to ethnic minorities to maintain their language, culture, and religion (although, see Hannum 1996: 69–70; Pritchard 1998: 192, 113).[19] This frequently involves the control of sacred sites, skeletal remains, burial artifacts, and other items of religious and cultural significance.

For some scholars it is the challenge that these indigenous peoples, along with other ethnic minorities, are mounting to the individualistically oriented human rights paradigm that is more preoccupying. The particularism of group [illegible] (Kroes 2000: 75), though Ted Gurr's study indicates that growing respect for minority rights worldwide is reducing the incidence of ethnopolitical conflict (Gurr 2000). Contemporary debates about citizenship have some valency here (Turner 1997). There is a rich body of literature emerging on "group rights," some of it framed within current discourse on multiculturalism and cultural self-determination, in which religious identity often features prominently—whether it is about Sikhs and crash helmets or Orthodox Jewish rabbis and employment (see, especially, Kymlicka 1995). Hannum points sagaciously to the particular problematic of religious rights since they constitute classic "civil" or "individual" rights and yet are fundamental to the protection of the rights of minority, indigenous, and other groups (Hannum 1996: 110). An-Na'im realistically sees both complementarity and contradiction between individual and collective rights which is to be expected, he avers, "among all rights as instruments of negotiation and mediation of competing claims" (An-Na'im 1998; see also Little 1999).

The polarized universalist vs. relativist view of human rights has been sustained in large part by the proponents of "Asian values" who argue that the communitarianism, authoritarianism, and emphasis on economic development in Asian societies are antithetical to Western liberal conceptions of human rights (see, e.g., Bauer/Bell 1999; De Bary 1998). Daniel Bell tries to chart a middle ground between Western liberal democracy and Asian values of communitarianism and authoritarianism (Bell 2000). Some have rather wanted to expose these cultural reservations for being a "smokescreen" for human rights violations and for not taking account of the dynamic character of the human rights movement (Kelsay 1994: 31–59). Arvind Sharma questions the univocality of the term "universal" (Sharma 2000). He suggests that Eastern religions have a more accepting understanding of the term in contrast to the Western formulation which privileges the missionary religion and yet manages to posit its parochialism as universal. Similarly, An-Na'im stresses the contingency of universalist projects to date while calling for more global participation in the

19 See also the UN Draft Declaration on the Rights of Indigenous Peoples, UN Doc. E/CN.4/Sub.2/1994/2/Add.1, 20 April 1994 (Steiner/Alston 2000: 1302–1304).

construction of the human rights ideal (An-Na'im 2000c). He sees one of the greatest challenges as how to be sensitive to believers' positions, while not conceding to their relativist arguments.

A creative contribution to these contentious debates comes from a volume of work by feminist scholars, *Women, Citizenship and Difference*, where they seek to develop models of citizenship as dialogical and relational, and embedded in cultural and associational life, rather than positing an opposition between individualist and communitarian models (cf. also Ong 1999; Yuval-Davis/Werbner 1999). This is described by one contributor as "differentiated universalism" (Lister 1997; cf. Mignolo's notion of "critical cosmopolitanism," Mignolo 2000). The authors argue that the national discourses of citizenship and international discourses of human rights both imply one another; their political and jural instability points to the ongoing negotiation of difference and belonging. Several of the contributions discuss how religious ideas can disguise biased and exclusionary understandings of citizenship, by locating women in the private sphere, for example. Yet they also provide evidence of Muslim women living in diasporic communities carving out new gendered, public spaces for themselves—proclaiming the rights of their persecuted Muslim sisters in Bosnia or Kashmir. In general, it is clear that further study is required of the way many minority groups are factoring religious and cultural rights into their political agendas (cf. Hannum 1996: 72–73), or, in some cases, recasting those claims in religious rights language whether it is Muslims in Europe (Barbieri 1999) or Uzbekistan (An-Na'im 2000a), or revivalist ethnic groups in Kenya (Hackett 2004).

6. Current Topics

6.1. Patterns and Sites of Violation

For a more empirical perspective on the failures and successes of the freedom of religion and belief around the world there are several useful sources to consult, such as Boyle and Sheen's *Freedom of Religion and Belief: A World Report* as well as the annual reports by the U.S. State Department and the U.S. Commission on International Religious Freedom, and the U.N. Special Rapporteur on freedom of religion and belief. Alternatively one could turn to the special reports by human rights organizations such as Amnesty International or Human Rights Watch, or the regular monitoring by organizations such as Human Rights Without Frontiers, Freedom House, or the *Religious Freedom Reporter*.[20]

20 See, in this regard, the excellent set of reports by Human Rights Watch on religious repression in China, e.g. *China: State Control of Religion* (Human Rights Watch/Asia 1997).

These reports reveal the patterns of violation as well as the recurring targets and sites, namely religious minorities, proselytization, women, media and educational institutions. Some of these receive more elaboration in this section.

6.1.1. Proselytization

International law scholar Johan van der Vyver claims that "[t]he right to engage in missionary activity is perhaps the most controversial aspect of religious freedom" (van der Vyver 1999: 128). This is closely linked to the disputed right of changing and exiting one's religion (cf. Barry 2001; Lerner 1998: 482). Sharma argues that we must consider alternative understandings of religious freedom and conversion as in India and Japan, for example, with their differing historical and cultural contexts (Sharma 2000/2001). What is not in dispute is the fact that the religious growth that has accompanied political transformation in many parts of the world has brought in its wake clashes over conversion—whether between rival local groups or between foreign and indigenous groups. This new "war for souls" must be seen in the context of the globalizing forces of democracy and capitalism—perceived as invasive and unwelcome by many communities. It became the focus of a project conducted by Emory Law School's Law and Religion Program. Several valuable publications resulted from a series of meetings and conferences which focused on different regions of the world.

I want to focus briefly on the Africa volume, since that was the one I was involved with and because it illustrates well some of the issues at stake here (An-Na'im 1999b). Arguably the most problematic issue which emerged was the clash between the right of an individual to promote, teach or propagate his or her religion or belief, and the right of a group or people to cultural self-determination and to resist such disruptive incursions (although it should be noted that missionary activity the world over is becoming noticeably more multilateral, multidimensional, and multi-directional). In his introduction, An-Na'im rightly insists on the asymmetrical power relations generally inherent in the proselytization exercise in Africa, although he is prepared to admit that this type of interreligious encounter can stimulate cultural exchange and self-critique (An-Na'im 1999a). Casting these disputes in human rights terms leads An-Na'im to posit that an exclusively individual-rights approach is inadequate in such situations and must be complemented by an understanding of collective or group rights. He also suggests that the state should play a mediating role in resolving conflicts between the parties, although non-state actors, such as ecumenical associations, may be instrumental in this regard (see Hackett 1999b on Christian-Muslim relations in Nigeria). Influenced by the record of African states and missionary organizations in "delegitimating" traditional religious cultures, Mutua opts for the primacy of the right of self-determination (Mutua

1999). However, he does not engage the technicalities, nor the problems, of cultural protection.[21]

In the UN Declaration against Intolerance (1981) article 6 (e) details the freedom "to teach a religion or belief in places suitable for these purposes." The interpretation of a suitable location to teach or propagate one's religion has broadened with the growth of religious revivalism and militancy across Africa, and the expansion of the mass media. Public spaces such as hospitals, offices, and public transport are now regarded as fair game by active proselytizers. The schools are a particularly sensitive site. Tensions often erupt over religious bias and discrimination; states are frequently unable or unwilling to fulfill their obligations to children of minority religions (see, e.g. Hackett 1999a; cf. Evans 1997: 342–62 on the challenges of religious education in Europe). As regards the media, it is their liberalization which has caused an escalation in tensions. Government-controlled print and broadcast media are subject to guidelines ensuring interreligious civility. The commercial radio stations springing up over Africa, and the burgeoning informal media sector (audio and video cassettes, tracts, booklets, etc) are market-driven and thrive on difference (Hackett 1998). They tend to be dominated by evangelical and pentecostal Christians. The human rights community is finally waking up to the influence of the media in promoting both tolerance and intolerance (International Council on Human Rights Policy 2001).

6.1.2. Women's Rights

Turning to the specific, but no less controversial, case of women within the overall picture of religion and human rights, a strong focus of the scholarship has been on the religious traditions themselves. This is hardly surprising given the denial of their rights that many women experience both as citizens and as members of religious communities, and the fact that religious norms frequently underpin social practices of exclusion and domination. This is expressed well by South African feminist theologian, Denise Ackermann, "no freedom *of* religion without freedom *in* religion" (cited in Villa-Vicencio 1996: 535). Women's rights to equality under state and international human rights law frequently clash with the rights of religious collectivities to self-determination (cf. Sullivan 1992). There are several useful essays which explore religion as source of liberation or repression for women from a variety of textual, historical, legal, cultural and social perspectives (see, for example, Hassan 1996 and Arat 2000 on the rights of women in Islamic communities; also Berger and Lipstadt on Judaism,

21 Little notes that the right to disseminate religion is protected by both individual and group rights. Personal communication, June 24, 2001.

Berger/Lipstadt 1996. For a more general approach, see Cook 1994). The particular challenge of religious fundamentalism is addressed in an excellent collection, *Religious Fundamentalisms and the Human Rights of Women* (Howland 1999).

Several authors consider the possibilities of the human rights framework for women. Martha Nussbaum, in her latest book, *Women and Human Development*, emphasizes the importance of freedom of choice for women within religious systems, but not at the expense of their basic human capabilities (Nussbaum 2000; Hackett 2001a; see, also, Nussbaum 1997b). An-Na'im addresses the conflicts that frequently arise between religious and customary laws and international human rights norms over the equality and freedom of women in matters of land allocation, inheritance, marriage, and divorce (An-Na'im 1994). He suggests that conformity of communal norms with state and international standards is more likely to be achieved through the gradual processes of internal and cross-cultural dialogue. Bahia Tahzib focuses on alleged violations of the right to freedom of religion or belief that are primarily directed against women, concentrating on external freedoms, or the public manifestation of religion (Tahzib-Lie 2000). She examines the traditional practice of female genital mutilation (FGM), and dress codes for women in secular and non-secular societies, and carefully weighs the competing interests of the state and the woman, particularly the "dissenting woman."

6.1.3. Conflict Resolution

While conflict resolution is not always a human rights issue, in that it may not pertain to the rights of individuals or groups with regard to the state, the work of some scholars demonstrates an inclination toward viewing religion as a positive resource for peace and human rights implementation. For example, Arvind Sharma and Harvey Cox suggest that religions can a) enlarge the scope of human rights, particularly with the right to life, b) highlight the interrelations between the various articles of the UDHR, and c) strengthen the concept of human rights (Kelsay 1994: 61–79). John Clayton argues for the capacity of religions to accommodate "defensible difference" and for the capacity of the human rights concept to accommodate "differing views" (Clayton 2000: 125). In his opinion, the language of rights provides a public frame within which disparate communities of interest, religious and nonreligious alike, can differentiate and negotiate "the defensible from the indefensible in our behavior toward others" (Clayton 2000: 124).

Abdullahi An-Na'im has been exploring a more synergistic and interdependent approach to human rights, religion, and secularism—"an overlapping consensus among multiple foundations." He considers this to be more effective in the sustainable realization of human rights in practice than the usual secular versus religious dichotomy (An-Na'im 2000b). Scott Appleby, in his important work on religion, violence, and reconciliation, sees in human rights discourse a bridge linking the particular to the universal. He considers that "[r]eligious actors engaged in conflict transformation have in 'rights talk' a powerful tool for defusing the explosive elements of first-order religious language and lifting memory, testimony, and experience beyond the merely sectarian" (Appleby 1999: 280). Charles Villa-Vicencio, one of South Africa's most prominent theologians, advocates the need for the (mutual) engagement of cultures and religions in post-apartheid South Africa (Villa-Vicencio 1996: 469). Conflict resolution specialist, Marc Gopin, urges caution in pushing secular, universalist discourses preferring "methods of dealing with religious actors *as they currently define themselves*" (Gopin 2000: 18). Sumner Twiss, drawing on his skills as comparative religious ethicist, interestingly suggests that consensus among religious traditions over the need for human rights can be translated back into those traditions without requiring the formal language of rights (Twiss 1998: 163). Swidler and Mozjes, both experienced in interreligious dialogue, are more insistent about the need for a formally articulated global ethic to deepen and confirm human rights claims (Swidler/Mojzes 2000). This burgeoning area of conflict resolution and peace studies calls for closer examination of the role of religious actors and the deployment of religious and human rights concepts. It also represents a broadening and a grounding of the field of interreligious dialogue.

7. Conclusion: Lingua Franca, Lingua Sacra?

In closing let me reiterate the salience of our subject matter. One can simply consider claims regarding the persistence of religious intolerance. For example, human rights scholar Hurst Hannum, claims that "state or majority intolerance of religious diversity has perhaps surpassed racial prejudice as the primary motivation behind human rights violations in the world today" (Hannum 1996: 110). Similarly, the United Nations Special Rapporteur on freedom of religion and belief, Abdelfattah Amor, in his 2000 Report, informs us that religious discrimination worldwide has reached "alarming" levels. These developments surely beckon religion scholars of all disciplinary persuasions.

By way of summation, and influenced, in part, by Ken Booth's call to "anthropologize and historicize human rights" (Booth 1999), I propose the following areas for further critical analysis:

a) Language: definitions of religion and its component parts, whether "belief" or "manifestation," "individual," "personhood," "group," "community," "freedom"; critique of use of problematic terms, such as "faith," "sect," "cult," "syncretist," in human rights discourse;

b) History: knowledge of patterns of intra- and interreligious conflict and conflict management/resolution may inform current situations (e.g. rituals of reconciliation and remembering);
c) Cultural practice: different translations and appropriations of human rights discourses pertaining to religion and belief, privileging of (particular) religious rights;
d) Symbolic capital: repatriation of cultural property, religious art/literature/performance as expression of human rights (abuses);
e) Identity: disentangling ethnicity and religion, assessing claims of religious identity/discrimination, new strategies of defining difference and staking claims to the public sphere and resources, challenges of religious militancy and fundamentalism to human rights;
f) Power relations: how the normative framework of human rights is reconfiguring religion and state relations at domestic, regional and international levels, (de)differentiating, (de)privatizing or (de)territorializing religious formations;
g) Globalization: how transnational and translocal forces challenge state protection of freedom of religion or belief (e.g. religious hate speech on the Internet, mass mediated messages, movements of peoples, refugees), global flows of information, rights talk, and civil society;
h) Modernity: how human rights ideas might displace traditional religious explanations of inequality and lack of development (e.g. denial of political and economic rights as opposed to witchcraft/satanism accusations);
i) Survival: how religious notions of human dignity and welfare may strengthen the case of the human right to development (e.g. Jubilee 2000);
j) Agency: how human rights ideas and institutions may empower new religious publics, challenging old orders of community and authority (e.g. women, Dalits, indigenous peoples, diasporic communities, apostates, dissenters);
k) State practice: new patterns of state regulation of or support for religious plurality (e.g. state regulation of religious growth and freedom from religious exploitation, religious state creation, civil religion, interreligious dialogue groups);
l) Civil society: new modalities and legitimacies of engagement for religious NGOs, religious critiques of excessive political cooptation to preserve individual and collective rights.

There remains the troubling question of human rights *qua* religion. Are "inflexible attitudes" among believers themselves giving rise to an understanding of "freedom of religion" that does not permit "the right to adhere to a religion which is intolerant of the beliefs of others," as Malcolm Evans argues? He laments further that "'[h]uman Rights' has itself become a 'religion or belief' which is in itself as intolerant of other forms of value systems which may stand in opposition to its own central tenets as any of those it seeks to redress" (Evans 1997: 260). We do not have to look far to find additional characterizations of the human rights movement as a new "civic faith" and "world religion" (Ignatieff

2001a; cf. Küng 1990; Witte 2001: 727–28). Elie Wiesel refers to it as a "world-wide secular religion" (Wiesel 1999: 3). Scholar and advocate of human rights Ken Anderson, acerbically indicts the movement for being governed by an internationalized elite or global New Class which proclaims a transcendent universal order, but whose goal is premised on the interests of global capital. For him, the global NGO movement is nothing less than a "Sunday School of the nations" schooling them in their moral duties (Anderson 1999; cf. rebuttal by Ignatieff 1999).

My goal in this overview has been to try to encourage scholars of religion to contribute to this type of critique, or some of the areas outlined above, in this new and exciting field. If we have human rights not because we are human but to make us human, Ken Booth suggests, then clearly scholars of religion should be paying more attention to this revolutionary discursive and normative strategy of our time.

Bibliography

Adams, IV, Nathan A. (2000), "A Human Rights Imperative: Extending Religious Liberty Beyond the Border," in: *Cornell International Law Journal* 33 (1): 1–66.

Anaya, S. James (1996), *Indigenous Peoples in International Law*. New York: Oxford University Press.

Anderson, Kenneth (1999), "Secular Eschatologies and Class Interests of the Internationalized New Class," in: *Religion and Human Rights: Competing Claims?*, ed. by C. Gustafson/P. Juviler. Armonk, N.Y.: M.E. Sharpe.

An-Na'im, Abdullahi A. (1990), *Toward an Islamic Reformation: Civil Liberties, Human Rights and International Law*. Syracuse, N.Y.: Syracuse University Press.

— ed. (1992), *Human Rights in Cross-Cultural Perspectives: Quest for Consensus*. Philadelphia, Pa.: University of Pennsylvania Press.

— (1994), "State Responsibility under International Human Rights Law to Change Religious and Customary Law," in: *Human Rights of Women: National and International Perspectives*, ed. by R.J. Cook. Philadelphia, Pa.: University of Pennsylvania Press.

— (1996), "Islamic Foundations of Religious Human Rights," in: *Religious Human Rights in Global Perspectives: Religious Perspectives*, ed. by J.J. Witte/Johan D. van der Vyver. Boston, Mass.: Martinus Nijhoff Publishers.

— (1998), "Human Rights and the Challenge of Relevance: The Case of Collective Rights," in: *The Role of the Nation-State in the 21st Century: Human Rights, International Organizations and Foreign Policy*, ed. by M. Castermans-Holleman/F. v. Hoof/J. Smith. The Hague: Kluwer Law International.

— (1999a), "Competing Claims to Religious Freedom and Communal Self-Determination in Africa," in: *Proselytization and Communal Self-Determination in Africa*, edited by A.A. An-Na'im. Maryknoll, N.Y.: Orbis.

— ed. (1999b), *Proselytization and Communal Self-Determination in Africa*. Maryknoll, N.Y.: Orbis Books.

— (2000a), "Human Rights and Islamic Identity in France and Uzbekistan: Mediation of the Local and the Global," in: *Human Rights Quarterly* 22: 906–41.

—— (2000b), "Human Rights, Religion and Secularism: Does It Have to Be a Choice?" Paper read at Keynote Address, 18th Quinquennial World Congress of the International Association of the History of Religions, August 5–12, at Durban, South Africa.

—— (2000c), *Human Rights, Religion, and the Contingency of Universalist Projects*. Syracuse, N.Y.: Program on the Analysis and Resolution of Conflicts, Maxwell School of Citizenship and Public Affairs, Syracuse University.

—— (2000d), "Islam and Human Rights: Beyond the Universality Debate," in: *ASIL Proceedings*: 95–101.

An-Na'im, Abdullahi A./Gort, J.D./Jansen, H./Vroom, H.M., eds. (1995), *Human Rights and Religious Values: An Uneasy Relationship?* Grand Rapids, Mich.: William B. Eerdmans.

Appleby, R. Scott (1999), *The Ambivalence of the Sacred: Religion, Violence, and Reconciliation*. New York: Rowman and Littlefield.

Arat, Zehra F. (2000), "Women's Rights in Islam: Revisiting Quranic Rights," in: *Human Rights: New Perspectives, New Realities*, ed. by A. Pollis/P. Schwab. Boulder, Colo.: Lynne Rienner.

Baehr, Peter/Flinterman, Cees/Senders, Mignon, eds. (1999), *Innovation and Inspiration: Fifty Years of the Universal Declaration of Human Rights*. Amsterdam: Royal Netherlands Academy of Arts and Sciences.

Barbieri, William (1999), "Group Rights and the Muslim Diaspora," in: *Human Rights Quarterly* 21 (4): 907–26.

Barker, Eileen (2000), "The Opium Wars of the New Millennium: Religion in Eastern Europe and the Former Soviet Union," in: *Religion on the International News Agenda*, ed. by M. Silk. Hartford, Conn.: The Leonard E. Greenberg Center for the Study of Religion in Public Life.

Barry, Brian (2001), *Culture and Equality: An Egalitarian Critique of Multiculturalism*. Cambridge, Mass.: Harvard University Press.

Bartholomeusz, Tessa J./de Silva, Chandra Richard, eds. (1998), *Buddhist Fundamentalism and Minority Identities in Sri Lanka*. Albany, N.Y.: State University of New York Press.

Bauer, Joanne R./ Bell, Daniel A., eds. (1999), *The East Asian Challenge for Human Rights*. New York: Cambridge University Press.

Bell, Daniel A. (2000), *East Meets West: Human Rights and Democracy in East Asia*. Princeton, N.J.: Princeton University Press.

Berger, Michael S./Lipstadt, Deborah E. (1996), "Women in Judaism from the Perspective of Human Rights," in: *Religious Human Rights in Global Perspective: Religious Perspectives*, ed. by J.J. Witte/J.D. van der Vyver. The Hague: Martinus Nijhof.

Bloom, Irene/Martin, J. Paul/Proudfoot, Wayne L., eds. (1996), *Religious Diversity and Human Rights*. New York: Columbia University Press.

Booth, Ken (1999), "Three Tyrannies," in: *Human Rights in Global Politics*, ed. by T. Dunne/N.J. Wheeler. New York: Cambridge University Press.

Boyle, Kevin/Sheen, Juliet, eds. (1997), *Freedom of Religion and Belief: A World Report*. London: Routledge.

Casanova, José (1994), *Public Religions in the Modern World*. Chicago: University of Chicago Press.

Chidester, David (1996), *Savage Systems: Colonialism and Comparative Religion in Southern Africa*. Chalottesville, Va.: University of Virginia Press.

— (2000), "Colonialism," in: *Guide to the Study of Religion*, ed. by W. Braun/R.T. McCutcheon. New York: Cassell.

Clayton, John (2000), "Common Ground and Defensible Difference," in: *Religion, Politics, and Peace*, ed. by L.S. Rouner. Notre Dame, Ind.: University of Notre Dame Press.

Cook, Rebecca, ed. (1994), *Human Rights of Women: National and International Perspectives*. Philadelphia, Pa.: University of Pennsylvania Press.

Cooke, Miriam/Lawrence, Bruce (1996), "Muslim Women between Human Rights and Islamic Norms," in: *Religious Diversity and Human Rights*, ed. by I. Bloom/J.P. Martin/W.L. Proudfoot. New York: Columbia University Press.

Crahan, Margaret E. (1999), "Religion and Societal Change: The Struggle for Human Rights in Latin America," in: *Religion and Human Rights: Competing Claims?*, ed. by C. Gustafson/P. Guviler. Armonk, N.Y.: M.E. Sharpe.

De Bary, William Theodore (1998), *Asian Values and Human Rights: A Confucian Communitarian Perspective*. Cambridge, Mass.: Harvard University Press.

Deng, Francis (1990), "A Cultural Approach to Human Rights among the Dinka," in: *Human Rights in Africa: Cross-Cultural Perspectives*, ed. by A.A. An-Na'im/F. Deng. Washington, D.C.: The Brookings Institution.

Donnelly, Jack (1998), *International Human Rights*. Second ed. Boulder, Colo.: Westview.

Durham, W. Cole (1996), "Perspectives on Religious Liberty: A Comparative Framework," in: *Religious Human Rights in Global Perspective: Legal Perspectives*, ed. by J.D. van der Vyver/J. Witte. The Hague: Martinus Nijhoff.

Dwyer, Kevin (1991), *Arab Voices: The Human Rights Debate in the Middle East*. Berkeley, Calif./Los Angeles, Calif.: University of California Press.

Eickelman, Dale F./Anderson, Jon W., eds. (1999), *New Media in the Muslim World: The Emerging Public Sphere*. Bloomington, Ind.: Indiana University Press.

Evans, Carolyn (2001), *Freedom of Religion under the European Convention on Human Rights*. New York: Oxford University Press.

Evans, Malcolm D. (1997), *Religious Liberty and International Law in Europe*. New York: Cambridge University Press.

Evans, Tony, ed. (1998), *Human Rights Fifty Years On: A Reappraisal*. Manchester: Manchester University Press.

Everett, William Johnson (1996), "Human Rights in the Church," in: *Religious Human Rights in Global Perspective: Religious Perspectives*, ed. by J. Witte/J.D. van der Vyver. The Hague: Martinus Nijhoff.

Ewing, Katherine Pratt (2000), "Legislating Religious Freedom: Muslim Challenges to the Relationship between 'Church' and 'State' in Germany and France," in: *Daedalus* 129 (4): 31–54.

Freeman, Michael (2000), "Liberal Democracy and Minority Rights," in: *Human Rights: New Perspectives, New Realities*, ed. by A. Pollis/P. Schwab. Boulder, Colo.: Lynne Rienner.

Gitlitz, John S. (2000), "Peasant Justice and Respect for Human Rights: Peru," in: *Human Rights: New Perspectives, New Realities*, ed. by A. Pollis/P. Schwab. Boulder, Colo.: Lynne Rienner.

Glendon, Mary Ann (2001), *A World Made New: Eleanor Roosevelt and the Universal Declaration of Human Rights*. New York: Random House.

Gopin, Marc (2000), *Between Eden and Armageddon: The Future of World Religions, Violence, and Peacemaking*. New York: Oxford University Press.

Gunn, T. Jeremy (2000), "A Preliminary Response to Criticisms of the International Religious Freedom Act of 1998," in: *Brigham Young University Law Review* (3): 841–65.

— (2001), "The Organization for Security and Co-operation in Europe and the Rights of Religion or Belief," in: *The Protection of Religious Minorities in Europe: Human Rights Law, Theory and Practice*, ed. by P. Danchin. New York: Columbia University Press.

— (forthcoming), *Promoting Tolerance: International Standards for Freedom of Religion and Belief.*

Gurr, Ted Robert (2000), *Peoples versus States: Minorities at Risk in the New Century*. Washington, D.C.: USIP Press.

Gyekye, Kwame (1998), "Human Rights," in: *African Cultural Values: An Introduction for Secondary Schools*, ed. by K. Gyekye. Accra: Sankofa Publishing.

Hackett, Rosalind I.J. (1998), "Charismatic/Pentecostal Appropriation of Media Technologies in Nigeria and Ghana," in: *Journal of Religion in Africa* 26 (4): 1–19.

— (1999a), "Conflict in the Classroom: Educational Institutions as Sites of Religious Tolerance/Intolerance in Nigeria," in: *Brigham Young University Law Review*: 537–60.

— (1999b), "Radical Christian Revivalism in Nigeria and Ghana: Recent Patterns of Conflict and Intolerance," in: *Proselytization and Communal Self-Determination in Africa*, ed. by A.A. An-Na'im. Maryknoll, N.Y.: Orbis.

— (2001a), "Is Religion Good News or Bad News for Women?: Martha Nussbaum's Creative Solution to Conflicting Rights," in: *Soundings* 83 (3–4): 615–25.

— (2001b), "International Religious Freedom: The Talk of the Town," in: *Religious Studies News*.

— (2004), "Prophets, 'False Prophets' and the African State: Emergent Issues of Religious Freedom and Conflict" in: *New Religious Movements in the Twenty-first Century: Legal, Political and Social Challenges in Global Perspective*, ed. by Phillip Charles Lucas/Thomas Robbins. New York/London: Routledge.

— (forthcoming), *Nigeria: Religion in the Balance*. Washington, D.C.: United States Institute of Peace.

Hackett, Rosalind I.J./Silk, Mark/Hoover, Dennis, eds. (2000), *Religious Persecution as a U.S. Policy Issue*. Hartford, Conn.: Center for the Study of Religion in Public Life.

Hannum, Hurst (1996), *Autonomy, Sovereignty, and Self-Determination: The Accommodation of Conflicting Rights*. Philadelphia, Pa.: University of Pennsylvania Press.

Hassan, Riffat (1996), "Rights of Women within Islamic Communities," in: *Religious Human Rights in Global Perspective: Religious Perspectives*, ed. by J.J. Witte/J.D. van der Vyver. The Hague: Martinus Nijhof.

Haynes, Jeff (1998), *Religion in Global Politics*. Reading, Mass.: Addison-Wesley.

Hefner, Robert W. (2000), *Civil Islam: Muslims and Democratization in Indonesia*. Princeton, N.J.: Princeton University Press.

Hehir, J. Bryan (1996), "Religious Activism for Human Rights: A Christian Case Study," in: *Religious Human Rights in Global Perspective: Religious Perspectives*, ed. by J. Witte/J.D. van der Vyver. The Hague: Martinus Nijhoff.

Henkin, Louis (1998), "Religion, Religions, and Human Rights," in: *Journal of Religious Ethics* 26 (2 [Fall]): 229–39.

— (1999), "Human Rights: Religious or Enlightened?" in: *Religion and Human Rights: Competing Claims?*, ed. by C. Gustafson/P. Juviler. Armonk, N.Y.: M.E. Sharpe.

— (2000), "Human Rights: Ideology and Aspiration, Reality and Prospect," in: *Realizing Human Rights: Moving from Inspiration to Impact*, ed. by S. Power/G. Allison. New York: St. Martin's Press.

Hibbard, Scott W./Little, David (1997), *Islamic Activism and U.S. Foreign Policy*. Washington, D.C.: U.S. Institute of Peace.

Howard-Hassmann, Rhoda E. (2000), "Multiculturalism, Human Rights, and Cultural Relativism: Canadian Civic Leaders Discuss Women's Rights and Gay and Lesbian Rights," in: *Netherlands Quarterly of Human Rights* 18 (4): 493–514.

Howland, Courtney W. (1997), "The Challenge of Religious Fundamentalism to the Liberty and Equality Rights of Women: An Analysis under the United Nations Charter," in: *Columbia Journal of Transnational Law* 35: 271–377.

— ed. (1999), *Religious Fundamentalisms and the Human Rights of Women*. New York: St. Martin's Press.

Human Rights Watch/Asia (1997), *China: State Control of Religion*. New York: Human Rights Watch.

Huntington, Samuel P. (1993), "The Clash of Civilizations?," in: *Foreign Affairs* 72 (3): 22–49.

Ignatieff, Michael (1999), "Human Rights: The Midlife Crisis," in: *New York Review of Books*, May 20: 58–62.

— (2001a), *Human Rights as Politics and Idolatry*. Princeton, N.J.: Princeton University Press.

— (2001b), *The Rights Revolution*: House of Anansi Press.

Ilesanmi, Simeon O. (1995), "Human Rights Discourse in Modern Africa: A Comparative Ethical Perspective," in: *Journal of Religious Ethics* 23 (2): 293–320

International Council on Human Rights Policy (2001), *Accuracy and Consistency: The Media and Human Rights*. Versoix, Switzerland: International Council on Human Rights Policy.

Johnston, Douglas/Sampson, Cynthia, eds. (1994), *Religion, the Missing Dimension of Statecraft*. New York: Oxford University Press.

Juergensmeyer, Mark (1993), *The New Cold War? Religious Nationalism Confronts the Secular State*. Berkeley, Calif./Los Angeles, Calif.: University of California Press.

Kelsay, John/Twiss, Sumner B., eds. (1994), *Religion and Human Rights*. New York: The Project on Religion and Human Rights.

Kroes, Rob (2000), *Them and Us: Questions of Citizenship in a Globalizing World*. Urbana, Ill./Chicago: University of Illinois Press.

Küng, Hans (1990), "Towards a World Ethic of World Religions," in: *The Ethics of World Religions and Human Rights*, ed. by H. Küng/J. Moltmann. Philadelphia, Pa.: Trinity Press International.

Kymlicka, Will (1995), *Multicultural Citizenship: A Liberal Theory of Minority Rights*. Oxford: Clarendon Press.

Lauren, Paul Gordon (1998), *The Evolution of International Human Rights: Visions Seen*. Philadelphia, Pa.: University of Pennsylvania Press.

Lawrence, Bruce B. (1998), *Shattering the Myth: Islam Beyond Violence*. Princeton, N.J.: Princeton University Press.

Lerner, Natan (1998), "Proselytism, Change of Religion, and International Human Rights," in: *Emory International Law Review* 12 (1): 490–502.

— (2000), *Religion, Beliefs, and International Human Rights*. Maryknoll, N.Y.: Orbis.

Lister, Ruth (1997), *Citizenship: Feminist Perspectives*. London: Macmillan.

Little, David (1991), *Ukrane: The Legacy of Intolerance*. Washington, D.C.: United States Institute of Peace Press.

— (1994), *Sri Lanka: The Invention of Enmity*. Washington, D.C.: United States Institute of Peace Press.

— (1996), "Studying 'Religious Human Rights': Methodological Foundations," in: *Religious Human Rights in Global Perspective: Legal Perspectives*, ed. by J.D. van der Vyver/J. Witte. The Hague: Martinus Nijhoff.

— (1999), "Rethinking Human Rights: A Review Essay on Religion, Relativism, and Other Matters," in: *Journal of Religious Ethics* 27 (1).

— (2000), "Coming to Terms with Religious Militancy: The First T.J. Dermot Dunphy Lecture," in: *Harvard Divinity Bulletin* 29 (1): 17–22.

— (2001), "Does the Human Right to Freedom of Conscience, Religion, and Belief Have Special Status?," in: *Brigham Young University Law Review*.

Little, David/Kelsay, John/Sachedina, Abdulaziz A. (1988), *Human Rights and the Conflict of Cultures: Western and Islamic Perspectives on Religious Liberty*. Columbia, S.C.: University of South Carolina Press.

Lord, Karen S. (2000), "Growing Religious Intolerance in Western Europe," in: *Freedom of Religion: A Precious Human Right*, ed. by J.M.M. Naber. Assen, the Netherlands: van Gorcum.

Marshall, Paul (1997), *Their Blood Cries Out*. Dallas, Tex.: Word Publishing.

— ed. (2000), *Religious Freedom in the World: A Global Report on Persecution and Freedom*. New York: Broadman and Holman.

Maybury-Lewis, David (1997), *Indigenous Peoples, Ethnic Groups, and the State*. Boston, Mass.: Allyn and Bacon.

Mayer, Ann Elizabeth (1998), *Islam and Human Rights: Tradition and Politics*. Third ed. Boulder, Colo.: Westview Press.

— (1999), "Islamic Law and Human Rights: Conundrums and Equivocations," in: *Religion and Human Rights: Competing Claims?*, ed. by C. Gustafson/P. Juviler. Armonk, N.Y.: M.E. Sharpe.

McCutcheon, Russell (1997), *Manufacturing Religion: The Discourse on Sui Generis Religion and the Politics of Nostalgia*. New York: Oxford University Press.

Mendelsohn, Oliver/Baxi, Upendra, eds. (1994), *The Rights of Subordinated Peoples*. Delhi: Oxford University Press.

Mignolo, Walter (2000), "The Many Faces of Cosmo-polis: Border Thinking and Critical Cosmopolitanism," in: *Public Culture* 12 (3): 712–48.

Mutua, Makau (1999), "Returning to My Roots: African 'Religions' and the State," in: *Proselytization and Communal Self-Determination in Africa*, ed. by A.A. An-Na'im. Maryknoll, N.Y.: Orbis.

Naber, Jonneke M.M., ed. (2000), *Freedom of Religion: A Precious Human Right*. Assen, the Netherlands: van Gorcum.

Nussbaum, Martha C. (1997a), "Capabilities and Human Rights," in: *Fordham Law Review* 66: 273–300.

— (1997b), "Religion and Women's Human Rights," in: *Religion and Contemporary Liberalism*, ed. by P. Weithman. Notre Dame, Ind.: University of Notre Dame.

— (2000), *Women and Human Development: The Capabilities Approach*. New York: Cambridge University Press.

Nye, Malory (1998), "Minority Religious Groups and Religious Freedom in England: The ISKCON Temple at Bhaktivedanta Manor," in: *Journal of Church and State* 40 (2): 412–36.

— (2000), "Religion, Post-Religionism, and Religioning: Religious Studies and Contemporary Cultural Debates," in: *Method and Theory in the Study of Religion* 12 (4): 447–76.

— (2001), *Multiculturalism and Minority Religions in Britain: Krishna Consciousness, Religious Freedom, and the Politics of Location*. London: Curzon.

O'Leary, Stephen (1994), *Arguing the Apocalypse: A Theory of Millennial Rhetoric*. New York: Oxford University Press.

Ong, Aihwa (1999), "Clash of Civilisations or Asian Liberalism? An Anthropology of the State and Citizenship," in: *Anthropological Theory Today*, ed. by H.L. Moore. Cambridge: Polity Press.

Parekh, Bhikhu (1999), "Non-Ethnocentric Universalism," in: *Human Rights in Global Politics*, ed. by T. Dunne/N.J. Wheeler. New York: Cambridge University Press.

Persky, Stan, commentary (2000), *Delgamuukw: The Supreme Court of Canada Decision on Aboriginal Title*: Vancouver, B.C.: David Suzuki Foundation/Greystone Books/ Douglas and McIntyre.

Power, Samantha/Allison, Graham, eds. (2000), *Realizing Human Rights: Moving from Inspiration to Impact*. New York: St. Martin's Press.

Pritchard, S., ed. (1998), *Indigenous Peoples, the United Nations and Human Rights*. London: Zed.

Rasmussen, Larry (1999), "Human Environmental Rights and/or Biotic Rights," in: *Religion and Human Rights: Competing Claims?*, ed. by C. Gustafson/P. Juviler. Armonk, N.Y.: M.E. Sharpe.

Reynolds, Noel B./Durham Jr., W. Cole, eds. (1996), *Religious Liberty in Western Thought*. Atlanta, Ga.: Scholars Press.

Richardson, James T. (1995), "Minority Religions, Religious Freedom, and the New Pan-European Political and Judicial Institutions," in: *Journal of Church and State* 37 (1 [Winter]): 1–59.

— (2000), "Social Control of Minority Faiths and Religious Freedom in Israel," in: *Religion, Staat, Gesellschaft* 1 (1): 23–40.

Rouner, Leroy S., ed. (1988), *Human Rights and the World's Religions*. Notre Dame, Ind.: University of Notre Dame Press.

Rudolph, Susanne Hoeber/Piscatori, James, eds. (1997), *Transnational Religion and Fading States*. Boulder, Colo.: Westview Press.

Seneviratne, H.L. (2000), *The Work of Kings: The New Buddhism in Sri Lanka*. Chicago: University of Chicago Press.

Sharma, Arvind (1998), "Human Wrongs and Human Rights," in: *Human Rights: Positive Policies in Asia and the Pacific Rim*, ed. by J.D. Montgomery. Hollis, N.H.: Hollis Publishing Co.

— (2000), "Comment," in: *Journal of Religious Ethics* 28 (1): 159–64.

— (2000/2001), "Measuring the Reach of a Universal Right: From West to East, 'Freedom of Religion' is Never a Simple Concept," in: *Religion and Values in Public Life* 8 (4): 10–12.

Shea, Nina (1997), *In the Lion's Den*. Nashville, Tenn.: Broadman and Holman Publishers.

Shterin, Marat (2001), "Legislating on Religion in the Face of Uncertainty," in: *Law and Informal Practices in Russia*, ed. by J. Callaghan/M. Kurkchian. Oxford: Clarendon Press.

Sigmund, Paul E., ed. (1999), *Religious Freedom and Evangelization in Latin America*. Maryknoll, N.Y.: Orbis.

Smart, Ninian (1995), *Worldviews: Crosscultural Explorations of Human Beliefs*. Second ed. Englewood Cliffs, N.J.: Prentice-Hall.

Stackhouse, Max (1999), "Human Rights and Public Theology: The Basic Validation of Human Rights," in: *Religion and Human Rights: Competing Claims?*, ed. by C. Gustafson/P. Juviler. Armonk, N.Y.: M.E. Sharpe.

Stahnke, Todd/Martin, J. Paul, eds. (1998), *Religion and Human Rights: Basic Documents*. New York: Center for the Study of Human Rights, Columbia University.

Steiner, Henry J./Alston, Philip (2000), *International Human Rights in Context: Law, Politics, Morals*. Second ed. New York: Oxford University Press.

Sullivan, Donna J. (1988), "Advancing the Freedom of Religion or Belief through the UN Declaration on the Elimination of Religious Intolerance and Discrimination," in: *American Journal of International Law* 82: 487–520.

— (1992), "Gender Equality and Religious Freedom: Toward a Framework for Conflict Resolution," in: *New York University Journal of International Law and Politics* 24: 795–806.

Swedish Institute, ed. (1998), *A Human Rights Message*. Stockholm: Ministry for Foreign Affairs, Sweden.

Swidler, Arlene, ed. (1982), *Human Rights in Religious Traditions*. New York: The Pilgrim Press.

Swidler, Leonard, ed. (1986), *Religious Liberty and Human Rights in Nations and Religions*. Philadelphia, Pa./New York: Ecumenical Press/Hippocrene Press.

Swidler, Leonard/Mojzes, Paul (2000), *The Study of Religion in an Age of Global Dialogue*. Philadelphia, Pa.: Temple University Press.

Swidler, Leonard/O'Brien, Herbert (1988), *A Catholic Bill of Rights*. Kansas City, Mo.: Sheed and Ward.

Tahzib, Bahiyyih G. (1996), *Freedom of Religion or Belief: Ensuring Effective International Legal Protection*. International Studies in Human Rights, Vol. 44. The Hague: Martinus Nijhoff Publishers.

Tahzib-Lie, Bahia (2000), "Applying a Gender Perspective in the Area of the Right to Freedom of Religion or Belief," in: *Brigham Young University Law Review* (3): 967–88.

Tergel, Alf (1998), *Human Rights in Cultural and Religious Traditions*. Uppsala: Acta Universitatis Upsaliensis.

Tierney, Brian (1996), "Religious Rights: An Historical Perspective," in: *Religious Human Rights in Global Perspective: Religious Perspectives*, ed. by J. Witte/J.D. van der Vyver. The Hague: Martinus Nijhoff.

Tilley, John J. (2000), "Cultural Relativism," in: *Human Rights Quarterly* 22: 501–47.

Tschuy, Theo (1997), *Ethnic Conflict and Religion: Challenge to the Churches*. Geneva: World Council of Churches.

Turner, Bryan S. (1997), "Citizenship Studies: A General Theory," in: *Citizenship Studies* 1 (1): 5–17.

Twiss, Sumner B. (1998), "Religion and Human Rights: A Comparative Perspective," in: *Explorations in Global Ethics: Comparative Religious Ethics and Interreligious Dialogue*, ed. by S.B. Twiss/B. Grelle. Boulder, Colo.: Westview Press.

van Bijsterveld, Sophie C. (2000), "Religion, International Law and Policy in the Wider European Arena: New Dimensions and Developments," in: *Law and Religion*, ed. by R.J. Ahdar. Burlington, Vt.: Ashgate.

van der Vyver, Johan D. (1999), "Religious Freedom in African Constitutions," in: *Proselytization and Communal Self-Determination in Africa*, ed. by A.A. An-Na'im. Maryknoll, N.Y.: Orbis.

— ed. (2000), *The Problem of Proselytism in Southern Africa: Legal and Theological Dimensions*. Special edition of *Emory International Law Review* Vol. 14, 2 (summer). Atlanta, Ga.: Emory University School of Law.

van der Vyver, Johan D./Witte Jr., John, eds. (1996), *Religious Human Rights in Global Perspective: Legal Perspectives*. The Hague: Martinus Nijhoff.

Villa-Vicencio, Charles (1996), "Identity, Difference and Belonging: Religious and Cultural Rights," in: *Religious Human Rights in Global Perspective*, ed. by J. Witte, Jr./J.D. van der Vyver. The Hague: Martinus Nijhoff.

Warren, Kay B. (1998), *Indigenous Movements and Their Critics: Pan-Maya Activism in Guatemala*. Princeton, N.J.: Princeton University Press.

Wiesel, Elie (1999), "A Tribute to Human Rights," in: *The Universal Declaration of Human Rights: Fifty Years and Beyond*, ed. by Yael Danieli/Elsa Stamatopoulou/Clarence J. Dias. Amityville, N.Y.: Baywood.

Wilson, Richard A., ed. (1997), *Human Rights, Culture and Context*. Chicago: Pluto Press.

Wiredu, Kwasi (1990), "An Akan Perspective on Human Rights," in: *Human Rights in Africa: Cross-Cultural Perspectives*, ed. by A.A. An-Na'im/F. Deng. Washington, D.C.: The Brookings Institution.

Witte, John (1998), "Law, Religion, and Human Rights: A Historical Protestant Perspective," in: *Journal of Religious Ethics* 26 (2): 257–62.

— (2001), "A Dickensian Era of Religious Rights: An Update on *Religious Human Rights in Global Perspective*," in: *William and Mary Law Review* 42: 707–99.

Witte, John/Bourdeaux, Michael, eds. (1999), *Proselytism and Orthodoxy in Russia*. Maryknoll, N.Y.: Orbis.

Witte, John/Martin, Richard C., eds. (1999), *Sharing the Book: Religious Perspectives on the Rights and Wrongs of Proselytism*. Maryknoll, N.Y.: Orbis.

Witte, John/van der Vyver, Johan D., eds. (1996), *Religious Human Rights in Global Perspective: Religious Perspectives*. The Hague: Martinus Nijhof.

Yuval-Davis, Nira/Werbner, Pnina, eds. (1999), *Women, Citizenship and Difference*. New York: Zed Books.

Section 6

Social Sciences

A Survey of Advances in the Sociology of Religion (1980–2000)

by

LILIANE VOYÉ

Unquestionably, in the field of the sociology of religion, the 1970s and the very early 1980s were dominated by theories of secularization (Berger/Luckmann 1966; Dobbelaere 1981; Martin 1978; Wilson 1969). If the debate on that topic is far from being closed, contrary to what some authors—who sometimes misunderstand the real meaning of this concept—are thinking ... and hoping (Stark 1999), it is none the less evident that secularization is no longer "the reigning dogma in the field" (Swatos/Christiano 1999: 210). In the light of various events (i.e. the Islamic revolution in Iran, but also some rising evidence of a new spirituality), some authors—strongly supported by the media and by the prophecies of some wishful-thinking Church authorities—began to speak of the "return of the sacred" and "la revanche de Dieu" (Kepel 1991). In fact, there is no "revanche" and no "return" as such. Times have changed and, with them, the context and life conditions are transformed. Even the concept of secularization itself is actually revisited (Tschannen 1992; Dobbelaere 1999) in the light of the new circumstances, which thenceforth bring forward new themes in the sociology of religion.

The first, the most theoretical—and probably the most important—topic that has emerged since the 1980s is certainly that of the definition of religion itself. If, until then, religion had been taken for granted in a world largely dominated, politically, economically and culturally, by Western society—if not by Europe—and so by Christianity, the upheavals of geo-politics and the increasing facilities for mobility and communication at a distance, have put former evidence into question. "What is religion?" became, then, and still remains, a very central question in this scientific field.

The global circumstance is also now a very important topic for sociologists of religion who analyze the impact of globalization on the religious domain and who explore the roles religions play in such a context.

The increase of mobility and the global circumstance induce also the development of what some authors call "a religious market." Contrary to the former situation when there were (quasi) religious monopolies in every part of the world, all religions are now available everywhere. It is on this fact that the "rational choice theory" in the field of the sociology of religion is founded.

If these three topics appear to be the most important current advances in this scientific domain, other themes have also developed during the two last decades: politics and religion; women and religion; youth and religion—and certainly they do not exhaust the list. Older topics are still alive and new questions also appear. None the less, it appears that the main lines of current research are those briefly described below.

1. The Religious Object

In the past, religion appeared to be self-evident not only to "ordinary people" but also to sociologists. Religion was the set of beliefs, practices and organizational aspects corresponding to Christianity—essentially Catholicism and Protestantism—and all this was considered as obvious and unquestionable. Since the end of the 1960s but most of all since the 1980s, the self-evident character of the religious object has been disputable. Two main factors explain this change: the opening of the scientific study of religion to non-Christian religions, and the changes which appear in the—let us say here—"religiosity" of a large part of the (European) population. Furthermore, sociologists themselves have introduced different qualifications of religion, which change more or less the essential elements of its definition.

1.1. There Exist Other Religions besides Christianity…

It is only very recently that sociologists of religion have paid sustained attention to other religions. As Beyer said at the Annual Meeting of the Scientific Society for the Study of Religion/Religious Research Association (SSSR/RRA) in November 1999, in a session devoted to the fiftieth anniversary of these associations, "religions other than Christianity have received relatively little of our research attention and, when they have, it has been mostly in the context of North America. … When we have ventured outside our backyard it has been to study the religion that dominates in our backyard; and when we have looked at other religions, it has been mostly as these have manifested themselves in our backyard" (Beyer 2000: 524).

Beyer's reference is to American sociology but the same is true concerning European sociology in general. Let us for instance look at Islam, as it was (and sometimes still is) treated in the French-speaking world. Hames indicates that, after the long colonization of the countries of Islam had favored a certain concealment of the religious subject from the specific perspective of the sociology of religion, the study of Islam still seems to be preferentially entrusted to other disciplines—essentially to ethnology and above all, to Orientalism (Hames 1999: 178; Voyé/Billiet 1999: 15). Furthermore, Hames insists that the so-called first encounter of sociology and Islam—the study of the thought of Ibn Khaldun—was founded on a misunderstanding: "the European thinkers of the mid-19th century—like Comte and Marx—annex the thinkers of other cultures and of other continents who seem to them to corroborate their own views, conferring on them an appearance of general law ... So the thought of Ibn Khaldun is interpreted as being a sociologist who applies reason to the analysis of social facts—a frame of mind which frees one from the constraining and totalizing vision of Islamic theological thought ... The result then is that Ibn Khaldun is considered as a thinker who, if not atheistic or anti-religious, at least is released and freed from the weight of the dogmatic theology of Islam" (Hames 1999: 173).

This remark of Hames points out a well-known fact but one which it is worthwhile recalling here: sociology emerged as a specifically Western science, induced by the shift from an agricultural, "gemeinschaftliche" social life to an industrial, "gesellschafliche" life, and did so by the development of a particular mode of "rationality." Its concepts and paradigms are deeply colored by this origin. Since, up to the present, most sociologists have been Westerners, they have often been tempted to read exogenous societies through their own spectacles and with resort to their own tools. This certainly constitutes an obstacle to the understanding of other cultures and notably of other religions and to the reception of this discipline in other countries and parts of the world, characterized by other cultures and religions, or even by Christian religions other than Catholicism and Protestantism. Makrides explains the very limited development, if not the absence, of sociological studies of the Orthodox Churches by the continuing distrust of, even a certain hostility towards, this discipline, which, in this context, is considered to relate to an exogenous culture marked, from Comte to Marx, by an a-religious or anti-religious character (Makrides 1999: 139–40; Voyé/Billiet 1999: 12).

Concerning the Islamic context, the Western origin of sociology also signifies a link between this discipline and colonizing countries. The fact already mentioned, that a large majority of sociologists are Westerners, has consequences: thus, even today there are still very few works on Islam as such in the field of the sociology of religion: thus, scientific studies are centered on the political role Islamic religion plays in countries like Iran or Algeria; thus, studies focus on immigrant workers and the cultural gap that exists between their original culture and the culture that they are confronted with in Europe. Nevertheless, the introduction of the study of Islam to the specific field of the sociology of religion increasingly becomes a reality, in response to what Hames calls "the dechristianizing" of this field. More recently, the tensions between the Islamic and the Christian worlds have certainly also stimulated sociological studies of Islam.

The same term would have seemed no less appropriate to the sociologists of Judaism at an earlier stage in the development of the sociology of religion. But it must be emphasized that, when they were established, about fifty years ago, the main associations for sociology of religion (SSSR, RRA, ASR and CISR/SISR) were limited to Catholic or Protestant sociologists respectively, later on to both Catholic and Protestant together. It was only later still—at the end of the 1960s—that these associations were "deconfessionalized" and affirmed the strictly scientific orientation of their project (Dobbelaere 1999: 79–100). It took them a certain time to render this openness effective, to recruit sociologists specialized in other religions, and to develop exchanges which facilitated and even encouraged a certain questioning of the "Christocentric" point of view and reference. There is no doubt that the study of Judaism is very important in highlighting the complexity, plurio-vocity and the polymorphous character of the object "religion." In this sense, Azria wonders what exactly sociologists talk about exactly when they talk about Jews and Judaism: "About a confessional group? About an ethnic minority? About a nation understood in the pre-modern and/or political senses of the term? About a people? About a spiritual, social, historical entity? About a tradition? About cultures? The question is neither simple nor neutral," she concludes (Azria 1999: 155). But if this question concerning Judaism is obvious to many, none the less, it was ignored for a long time in the study of the Christian religions—and sometimes still is. Nevertheless, today, it is increasingly difficult to avoid the question of the definition of the religious object.

Indeed, there are not only "exogenous" religions effectively present in territories that previously were (quasi) exclusively Christian and these religions are daily present in the news, but one is also nowadays confronted, by so-called "sects and new religious movements," in countries and regions where Christianity was for centuries a monopolistic religion. These exogenous religions and new movements introduce into the religious landscape, practices, symbols, languages, architectural forms, etc. which disorientate and disturb the deeply rooted image of religion. If a major consequence in Europe appears to be the rejection—even by governments—of these sects and new religious movements, it is they who are challenging the traditional vision of religion (and perhaps it is precisely this fact which provokes their rejection) and who contribute to renewing the question: "What is religion?" Certainly, it has to be admitted that some of these groups are "pathological," that some of them seek official recognition as religions for financial reasons (e.g. reduction of or exemption from payment of taxes) and some are no more than businesses, based on the credulity of people. But is has also to be acknowledged, first, that some of these groups present effectively all the characteristics generally accepted as those which define religion (even for sociologists) and, secondly, that there are people who adhere to these movements, who believe in their doctrines, follow their rites and benefit from these beliefs and practices (and it is too simple to attribute that to mental manipulation). From a sociological point of view, we thus have not only to consider these groups at least as potential religions but also to reappraise a definition of religion which may owe too much to a single religion and its particular characteristics.

We will not develop here the different features of some of these groups which might be susceptible to a change in the definition of religion. Let us simply say that most of these groups present themselves as able to fulfill the same functions as traditional religions—particularly to answer the telic questions (origins of life, life after death, good and evil, ...)—but in other terms. Nevertheless, some groups "miss" one or more elements which in Christianity were looked upon as essential, e.g. a kind of transcendence and references to the existence of "god(s)." That, however, would not be enough to excuse us from reconsidering the sociological definition of religion, which until now owed too much to its Western institutional version. The challenges addressed to this religion by the decline of the institutional capacity for the regulation of the practices and beliefs of the "ordinary people" also calls on us to re-visit the definition of the religious object.

1.2. "Bricolage" and Institutional Deregulation

For a long time, the analysis of religion took as its reference the functioning and the rules of the institution(s) and the level of conformity people showed to them. The studies of secularization, which were at the core of the sociology of religion during the 1960s and 1970s, have since then emphasized the decreasing power of religious institutions in a society where functional differentiation is at work and where the individual affirms him- or herself as an autonomous being, free to decide and to choose by and for him- or herself.

Many sociological studies, then oriented themselves to the exploration of the dispersion of beliefs and practices, of their de-regulated and shifting character, and of the borrowings and reinvestments people made to produce what was then called their "religion à la carte," "bricolage," "patchwork," etc. These numerous studies induced a new question for sociologists: their concepts were first of all constructed to analyze "religion" as it was embedded in specialized institutions. Thus, Hervieu-Léger for instance affirms, "to define what is religion, sociology of religions operates from the particularistic configuration which is the one of the "great religions"; so it over evaluates what is in fact the result of an historical process, highly situated in time and space. So doing, it suppresses out of its field of learning many important facets of a religious reality which then appear unintelligible" (Hervieu-Léger 1999: 20). To support this affirmation, Hervieu-Léger recalls that anthropologists and historians have regularly shown that, in their fields, religion is something other than what, for a long time, was designated as such by sociologists.

Since approximately the 1980s, one may say that sociologists have changed their vision (the fact that they have taken distance from religious institutions and from a kind of ancillary role is certainly partly responsible for that). Their regard is more and more oriented to people and to what people consider as religions, to their practices and beliefs and to what they do with the resources derived from religious institutions and which they use for various purposes, without considering the rules of these institutions.

Approached for another point of view—no longer the normative view of the institution but rather the effective view of the actors—religion appears much more flexible and de-regulated. The totalizing and univocal character attributed to it by the institutional authorities becomes blurred. It is in this sense, for instance, that Grace Davie speaks about "believing without belonging," to describe the dominant religious situation in Great Britain (Davie 1994) and that Ole Riis considers that in Denmark, it is "belonging without believing" which best describes the situation (Riis 1996). This, then, is to say that in Britain, an increasing disparity appears between the perdurance of traditional formal beliefs, feelings and symbols, on one hand, and the decline of obedience to and respect for the rules of religious institution(s), on the other. The contrary would be true in Denmark, where fidelity to the Lutheran church is important as the expression of national identity, but where the majority of the population distances itself from the beliefs propounded by this church. In both cases, expression is given to the fact that people no longer feel an obligation of global conformity and that they choose those aspects of religion that they consider as best for themselves. It has to be added that this choice of behavior not only signifies a discrepancy between the different dimensions of religiosity, but it may go deeper; for instance, if the wording of beliefs remains stable, but the words used become polysemic. Such is the case with belief in God: many people continue to say that they believe in God but, for them, God is no longer considered as a person—as He is theologically in Christianity—but as an impersonal force, a kind of energy.

Religion appears then as a much more complex phenomenon than it was considered before, when specialized institutions assumed a monopoly of its definition, contents and rules, and had their definitions automatically accepted. Now people presume at least implicitly to define for themselves what constitutes religion. So sociologists have also to examine the connotations that people ascribe to this word. They may no longer define religion by referring exclusively to institutions, and they must also take into account how people identify themselves as religious, apart from any institutional regulation.

As an example of the hypotheses sociologists may then formulate, the work of Hervieu-Léger is particularly interesting. This French sociologist proposes that we should define religion as a "lignée croyante," a lineage of beliefs which functions as a "legitimating reference for those beliefs" (Hervieu-Léger 1993). Consequently, in this perspective, "a religion is an ideological, practical and symbolic device through which the individual and collective meaning of belonging to a particular lineage of beliefs is constituted, maintained and developed" (Hervieu-Léger 1999: 24). Each lineage may refer to different dimensions: a communitarian dimension, which distinguishes the in- from the out-group (to be baptized or circumcised for instance); an ethical dimension, which refers to values expressed by a particular tradition and message; a cultural dimension, including art, habits concerning food, clothing, etc.; and an emotional dimension, in the Durkheimian sense. For a very long time, says Hervieu-Léger, these different dimensions of each lineage were regulated and guaranteed by an institution and, to be recognized as a member of this lineage, people had to accept (or appear to accept) the conditions it imposed. Nowadays, many people tend to refuse these "ready made" notions of belonging and presume to construct for themselves their identifications through their own particular experiences (one may see here the link with the "reflexivity" described by Giddens). As a result, the different dimensions are no longer necessarily interrelated and interdependent. They may develop along different lines and the presence of one of them does not permit us to presuppose the existence of the others. So one may claim one's Christian roots without being a member of a Christian community and without believing in the Christian faith or in any faith (Hervieu-Léger 1999: 82–88). Religion may then no longer be automatically considered as a global phenomenon, clearly and exhaustively defined. It is what people think it is.

But Hervieu-Léger goes further: in a more recent book, she states that any belief may take on the form of a religion as soon as it finds its legitimation in the invocation of the authority of a tradition. Consequently for her, believing in God does not define a person as religious; only when the person "puts forward the logic of his/her affiliation which causes him/her to believe what he/she believes today" does his/her belief become "religious" (Hervieu-Léger 1999: 23). No doubt the concept of lineage is stimulating; however, how is it then possible to make a distinction between religions, ideologies and various existing "isms" such as communism, materialism, hedonism, humanism, nationalism, fascism or even science as a way of life—these "surrogate religions" as Robertson calls them (1992: 39). To solve the problem, Willaime proposes to add to the idea of lineage that of the existence of the charisma of the founder (Willaime 1995: 125). To this, Dobbelaere objects that there exist religions without a founder (such as Shintoism) and that a charismatic leader who engenders a lineage (e.g. de Gaulle in France) does not necessarily create a "religion" (Dobbelaere 1997: 231). Dobbelaere insists on the necessity of being more specific and proposes that the concept of religiosity be reserved to cases in which there is a reference to a "meta-empirical reality," e.g. deities, spirits, the "Sacred Law," a "Source of Creation," the Almighty, etc. "If a religiosity has generated a particular lineage of beliefs in a community, functioning as a legitimating reference for those beliefs, then we may call it a religion" (Dobbelaere 2000: 443). Currently different attempts exist to revisit the definition of religion and on this question debates among sociologists continue. All point out that religion, which was for so long taken for granted, appears now problematic and uncertain; it shows also that, like many sociological objects—the family, the city, work, etc.—become more or less de-substantiated, which creates a need for renewed approaches.

Both these circumstances—religious pluralism and the fact that attention focuses on the individual actors—induce sociologists to innovate and to create new concepts, seeking more adequately to describe the actual situation.

1.3. Emergence of New Concepts

In close relation to the concepts of "invisible religion" (Luckmann 1967) and of "civil religion" (Bellah 1967) which are well-known, different attempts have recently appeared to account for various phenomena which appear to some authors to have "affinities" with religion, or to express new modalities of the religious. We will not discuss all of them, but simply give examples by way of illustration.

One such concept is "implicit religion" proposed by Bailey. According to this author himself, "this concept has at least three (non exclusive) definitions: commitments or integrating foci or intensive concerns with extensive effects. The concept of implicit religion counterbalances the tendency to equate 'religion' with specialized institutions, with articulated beliefs, and with that which is consciously willed (or specifically intended)" (Bailey 1998: 235). Implicit religion refers to those aspects of ordinary life which seem to contain an inherently religious element within them—whether or not they are expressed in ways that are traditionally described as "religious." With this concept, Bailey intends, as he says, to discover religiosity and the sacred in what is generally considered as secular and profane. His thought rests on the idea that everybody has a religion of some sort "a faith by which they live, albeit as an unconscious core at the center of their way of life and being" (Bailey 1998: 236).

The same expression is used by Nesti (1985, 1993). With this concept, this Italian sociologist refers to the different modalities of a search for a sense and of a tension towards the transcendent, which are not conveyed through the forms of institutionalized religions or of a "church-religion." This quest is "structured on a complex network of symbols and conduct, inside a web, a frame of ways and of significations, which assure the subjects about the unconditional significance of their being here and now" (Nesti 1993: 27). So, implicit religion would refer to the tension which, says Nesti, inhabits every human being, but which has not necessarily a name and which may be situated at the margin of the sacred/profane, visible/invisible dichotomies. As an example, Nesti gives the experience of traveling, which is particularly relevant for contemporary people: "travel represents a tension to something unknown, the ambiguous relation which always exists between fear and quest for new experiences ... This search expresses the existence of a shortage, a lack, a dissatisfaction, and is as such a paradigm of the existential condition" (Nesti 1993: 31). With this concept of "implicit religion," Nesti focuses on the human subject and its life conditions, without referring to any kind of transcendence or to any kind of institution.

For this part, Cipriani constructs the concept of "diffuse religion" *(religione diffusa)* and then that of "religion of values" (*religone dei valori*). With the first, Cipriani seeks to express a kind of faith reference, of religious sentiment which is a part of the culture of a population and which finds continuous modalities of adaptation in relation to the changing times (Cipriani 1992: 265). Cipriani insists that the mediation of the family is fundamental for the perpetuation of the diffuse religion. He also underlines what he calls the "meta-institutional" character of this religion, even if, he says, these characteristics have a religious institutional origin. As for the "religion of values," Cipriani considers that it is more autonomous, that it takes more distance from the religious institution(s) and that it is *plus laïque,* very secular. Central to diffuse religion and religion of values are precisely different social values which were promoted, says Cipriani, by religious institutions and which, over time, were diffused throughout the population which continues to adhere to these values but now generally without specific religious motivation. Thus both these concepts refer essentially to a kind of "cultural" legacy—which derives from the Catholic context in which they were built, as is also the case with the "implicit religion" of Nesti.

A very different attempt to define religion is suggested by Demerath. This American scholar suggests that religion is just one among many possible sources of the sacred. Instead of using both definitions for religion, he proposes to restrict the substantive definition—i.e. the descriptive attributes—to religion, which is, he says "a category of activity," and to reserve the functional definition—i.e. characterization in terms of consequences—to the sacred which "is nothing if not a statement of function" (Demerath 2000: 3). This, Demerath affirms, makes the relationship between the two empirically problematic and the narrowed conception of religion becomes only one possible—albeit one very important—source of the broadened conception of the sacred. Demerath proceeds by proposing four varieties of sacred experience: the sacred as integrative, as quest, as collectivity and as "counter-culture." Religions, he says, may certainly perform these different functions, but they are not alone in being able to fulfill them. Religions integrate through holy services, catechism, rites, etc. but "there are other sacred equivalents outside the temple." If questing takes religious forms, it "may involve also new political causes and economic ideologies ... and a wide variety of therapies, especially psychoanalysis, qualify for this category. There exist 'collectivities' outside the religious field: nations have long been sacred ... and sports events have often served as sacred festivals for forming and maintaining collective identity." In what concerns the sacred as counter-culture, "the syndrome is hardly alien to religion. Here is the world of sects and cults—i.e. of old versus 'new religious movements.' But the category is also home to a wide range of non-religious counter-cultures that carry potential sacred significance for their participants. The Ku Klux Klan, Skinheads, Survivalists and Operation Rescue provide examples on the right; the left responds with radical wings of civil rights movement, anti nuclear activism, environmental conservation and the gay and lesbian cause" (Demerath 2000: 5–7). So religion might not be defined by its functions—they are not specific to it—but by its substance which is only the relation with a supra-natural.

Unlike these authors, Piette tries to review most of the different concepts which claim to capture what today is "religion" and, so doing, he proposes an interesting critical analysis of these concepts. He suggests that three types of criteria may be used to understand them. First of all, these concepts may directly rest on the functional or on the substantive definition of religion as it was defined by Dobbelaere (Dobbelaere 1981: 35–38). In the first case, different phenomena are qualified as "religious" when they appear to perform functions similar to those which religion was supposed to perform (the integration of individuals into a social system through the existence of common values). For Piette, "civil religion" enters into this category. Some new concepts may also rest on the substantive definition of religion, which concerns its particular irreducible essence. And what is irreducible in religion is, says Piette, the answer it gives to the question of death, through the affirmation that "something" exists after death. Piette considers that what is called "secular religions" are the concern of this substantive definition. Another "essence" of religion might be the relation between individuals and "suprahuman beings," whose existence is postulated by the culture. In this case, Nazism and Communism would be considered as "religions" established around the figures of Hitler or Stalin. A third possibility in relation to the substantive definition would finally be to consider that the essence of religion is the sacred, conceived as something which transcends everyday life. The given example is here the "invisible religion" of Luckmann, who calls religion everything which is supposed to have an ultimate signification and which is not regulated by an institution but is directly experienced by individuals.

New concepts of religion may also refer—continues Piette—to theoretical concepts, especially to the Durkheimian approach for which the opposition between sacred and profane is central to religion—the sacred itself finding its principle in an anonymous and diffused force, society. On this ground are based analyses emphasizing the structural homology between religion and politics (as does Rivière 1988, e.g.) or between religion and mass sport (as does Augé e.g.). In both cases, the accent is put on the feeling that a collectivity is able to inspire in its members. Augé sees also an analogy between religious effervescence as described by Durkheim and that which, e.g., football creates and which transcends the individual psyche.

The last basis on which we may be permitted to qualify different secular activities as "religious" is the reference to morphological criteria, notes Piette, in particular to the existence of rites. Here again the proposed examples are those of different kinds of discourse concerning politics or sport, which use a religious vocabulary to describe the practices in these fields (e.g. "the gods of the stadium," "the Olympic grand mass") and to express the analogies which appear to exist between the psycho-social manifestations of politics and those of religion.

All these forms are called "secular religions" by Piette. They may be called "mimetic," when there is a reappropriation of one or several religious features—one of them at least keeping its religious specificity (e.g. the death problematics of extra-terrestrial experience). They will be designed as "metonymic" when the strictly religious character does not exist but when the central question is one of sense (e.g. ecological thought). One may also distinguish analogical forms when the problem is centered on the mechanisms instituted to serve or maintain a principle (e.g. mechanisms of fear or of taboo in the technological or in the political field). Finally, Piette evokes the "metaphoric" religiosities when there is a literal use and reappropriation of features and of the structure of religion in a secular activity pretending to be a new religion (e.g. the spirits).

Motivations sustaining these constructions are diverse, remarks Piette: to absolutize politics or science; to substitute a secular vision for a religious vision; to compensate the dominant rationality; to mobilize people; to re-valorize a culture; to surmount a crisis. But in all these forms, it seems clear that it is the question of sense which becomes central and no longer that of salvation.

If the question of the definition of religion is actually a very central one for sociologists in consequence of increasing cultural pluralism, arising from the multiplication of contacts between the different religious traditions of the world and to the development of sects and new religious movements, this last aspect also gives rise to another phenomenon. As Wilson says "whether a particular ideological or therapeutic system can properly be designated a religion is an issue that is not solely academic. ... [It is also] a matter of real importance at law. New movements ... have sought to have their religious status acknowledged" (Wilson 1990: 267) and that regularly provokes the intervention of the juridical authorities. In the subsequent processes, sociologists are sometimes called, by a religious movement or by the judge, to give their opinion regarding the extent to which the character of a movement is religious. In other cases, different drama in which new religious movements were involved (Solar Temple, Aum, Waco, ...) and the media coverage devoted to them induced some governments to interfere; here again sociologists were sometimes implicated and asked to give their advice on the same point. In response to such requests, Wilson, e.g., proposes what he calls a probabilistic and very abstract inventory of twenty "features and functions that are frequently found in phenomena that in normal usage we recognize as religions" (Wilson 1990: 279–

81). He contends that: "we need not declare any of these items to be sine qua non, and we may concede that some are more probable than others, but without a considerable representation of them, we might seriously doubt whether what we had in hand was indeed a religion" (Wilson 1990: 279). Wilson argues also that "religion clearly takes on the color of the culture in which it evolves, and it undergoes change over time and distance in broad congruity with its social context. Typically, modern religions reflect concern with subjective, psychic well-being rather than with positive otherworldly objectivity ... Worship is less significant than is the acquisition of [illegible] and [illegible]" (Wilson 1990: 288). His appraisal is founded on these two aspects—a probabilistic and abstract inventory of generally accepted features of religion and the adaptation to the current environment—Wilson considers then that if "religion invariably offers men salvation"—salvation being so considered as a *sine qua non* component to have a religion—this salvation has to be proposed "in terms that they (men) can understand and which are relevant to their circumstances" (Wilson 1990: 288). Such arguments show clearly a tendency to broaden and deepen the definition of religion. What is mainly interesting in such a thought process is that it encourages the sociologist to distance himself from an ethnocentric and traditional point of view and may be to elucidate what sociologists consider the inevitable features in the definition of what is religion.

Through this search for the "religious object," two things seem clear. There exists a tendency to enlarge the concept of religion and, so doing, to lose every kind of specificity. At the same time, it appears very difficult to accept that apart from the "traditional" religions, there may be nothing in this secular world which might be considered as replacing religion.

2. Globalization

Among the many sociologists who have recently written on globalization, two appear particularly interesting with regard to religion because each of them insists on the cultural dimension of globalization. Robertson focuses his analysis on the fact that globalization at the same time signifies the development of universalism and generates many expressions of particularism. Beyer distinguishes between the specific function of religion and its potential performances.

2.1. Roland Robertson

Two main aspects of the work of Robertson are here of particular interest. One concerns the images of what, in the global circumstance, would constitute a good society. The other deals with the effective role of religions in this context.

Going back to the dichotomy *Gemeinschaft/Gesellschaft*, Robertson defines four world images i.e. "conceptions of how the intramundane world is actually and/or should be structured" (Robertson 1992: 75). He shows how different religions contribute to the construction and legitimation of each of them and how religions find or fail to find support in these various views (Robertson 1992: 78–83). Let us say immediately that Robertson sees the relation between the two "gesellschaftliche" views and religion as less possible than is the case with the two "gemeinschaftliche" conceptions. Let us see how this author develops these images.

In the first *gesellschaftliche* view (global Gesellschaft 1), Robertson sees the global circumstance as "as series of open (national) societies, with considerable sociocultural exchange among them" (Robertson 1992: 79), this exchange being either symmetrical and with reciprocally beneficial significance, or asymmetrical, some societies being dominant. As to the "global Gesellschaft 2," it is a view which claims that a world order can only be obtained "on the basis of formal, planned world organization" (Robertson 1992: 79)—whether it be a strong supranational polity or a federation at the global level. Robertson does not give "religious" examples for these views, which he sees as mainly referring to political organization. But he considers that these two world orders may be looked at as instrumental from the religious point of view—the first tending to restrain cultural contamination, the second aspiring to a kind of ideological unification (as for instance Marxism or liberalism). Reciprocally, religious resources may be used in the political field to construct one's specific identity and, on this basis, to be regarded as a demand for equal partnership on the global scene.

The two *gemeinschaftliche* views are, on the contrary, directly connected with religious orientations and projects. The first image (global Gemeinschaft 1) considers that the world might be ordered in the form of a series of relatively closed societal communities, whether equal to each other or not. Robertson illustrates this view by evocating "the large number of politicoreligious fundamentalist movements which have arisen around the world ... and which advocate the restoration of their own societal communities to a pristine condition, with the rest of the world being left as a series of closed communities posing no threat to the 'best' community" (Robertson 1992: 81). What Robertson calls "the search for fundamentals" and its partly connected theme of fundamentalism (Robertson 1992: 164–81) is, he says, widely stimulated by "globally diffused ideas concerning tradition, locality, identity, home, indigeneity, community and so on" (Robertson 1992: 166). He considers these ideas to be presented as "ways of finding a place within the world as a whole, ways that frequently involve attempts to enhance the power of the groups concerned" (Robertson 1992: 166) as far as identity is power. This quest for identity and recognition, which will manifest itself by re-invigorating traditions, values, etc. presented as intrinsic and specific to it, is linked with globalization considered as time-space compression. Even if it may take ostensibly anti-global forms, "it tends to partake of the distinctive features of globality" (Robertson 1992: 170). Religious resources play an important role in this process of re-structuring identities, in the hope of a full recognition in the global world. So, for instance, far from considering Islamic fundamentalism as anti-modern and anti-global, Robertson looks at it as the expression of efforts to struggle for recognition and to affirm the autonomous existence of Islamic countries in a world so long dominated by European and Western interests and culture. Actors are urged "to give life to themselves" and this is why "cultural pluralism is itself a constitutive feature of the contemporary global circumstance." A central topic in the work of Robertson is to consider that "globalization involves the simultaneity of the universal and the particular; … it produces itself variety and diversity … Locality is globally institutionalized" (Robertson 1992: 172). If globalization indeed refers to an increasing global interdependence and to an international convergence in diverse aspects (economic and technological primarily but also in various cultural domains as e.g. music or what is called "macdonaldization"), globalization stimulates also the (re)affirmation of and the search for different kinds of specificities because "the quotidian actors, collective or individual, go about the business of conceiving of the world, including attempts to deny that the world is one" (Robertson 1992: 26). These actors have to locate themselves and to define their specific identity in an increasingly globalized world, which tends to homogenization and to uniformity. And religions offer resources which may help the actors to realize this aim.

The second *gemeinschaftliche* view (global Gemeinschaft 2) rests, according to Robertson, on the idea of a fully globewide community *per se*. The Roman Catholic Church, says Robertson, is certainly the oldest significant globe-oriented organization, claiming that mankind is its major concern. But recently different new religious movements have also embraced this kind of global project. They tend—so Robertson maintains—to be essentially, "of East Asian origin where the idea of harmonizing different worldviews has a very long history" (examples being Soka Gakkai or the Unification Church of the Reverend Moon), but Robertson considers also that movements centered on Theologies of Liberation, as they appeared particularly in Latin America, may be examples of this search for a "world community" (Robertson 1992: 81). All these religious views are concerned with what Robertson calls the need for a global Durkheimian "conscience collective" in which mankind is the reference and where telic concerns (human rights, peace, …) are the main preoccupation.

If religious resources are useful for the actual construction of worldviews, religions may also play an active role in enhancing or reducing the capacity of countries to be active partners in the global world and to meet its requirements. To illustrate "what may be the contribution of religion to the structuring of a mode of societal involvement in the global situation" (Robertson 1992: 88), Robertson focuses on the particular case of Japan and starts his analysis by identifying what he considers to be three relatively unique features of Japanese religion: the particular nature of its syncretism, the resilience of its infrastructure; and the significance of pollution/purification rituals, central to the Shinto tradition.

In Japan, says Robertson, syncretism—considered as the mingling of two or more religious traditions—functions as an ideology (like pluralism in the USA) in the sense that these different traditions "have historically been used, often by governments, to legitimize each other" (inter-legitimation of one aspect of the society by another). Furthermore, syncretism in Japan is also linked to the fact that individuals adhere at the same time to different religions (Shinto for life, Buddhism for death, Confucianism for ethics). The resilience of the religious infrastructure rests, according to Robertson, on the polytheism of this country tradition, itself rooted in the beliefs in a multitude of "kamis," which facilitated an instrumental view of religion. Finally, the importance of the rituals of purification opposes the sacred and the profane but also marks the boundaries between inside and outside. They license the acceptance or rejection of some external ideas, and purify those that are imported to "japanize" them. These three essential characteristics of the Japanese religious landscape explain, according to Robertson, the actual orientation of Japan to the world, after a long period of isolation, and its high capacity to become one of the leaders in the global economy: "this religious background stimulates the capacity [of this country] to adapt selectively to and systematically import ideas from other societies in the global arena but also, in very recent times, to seek explicitly to become, in a specifically Japanese way, a global society" (Robertson 1992: 90). So in the line of what Weber says about Protestantism and Capitalism, but taking distance from what this author precisely says about Japan (which he sees as a purely passive receiver of imported cultural features), Robertson underlines the affinities which exist between religion and economy. He shows the way in which "the spirit" of the religious Japanese tradition—resting on an ideology of syncretism, on an instrumentalizing view of religion and on a capacity to incorporate external features while "japanizing" them—constitutes a resource which ensures that Japan "fulfils" the function of a society from which "leaders" of other societies can "learn how to learn about many societies"—which is crucial in the global circumstance (Robertson 1992: 85).

So, for Robertson, religions may play two major roles in the global circumstance. They may be a means of affirming and claiming identity in a world which at the same time stimulates universalism and particularism. The specificities of religious forms and traditions may operate to facilitate or, on the contrary, to handicap the integration into the world system.

2.2. Peter Beyer

Because authors do not often make such an effort, it is worth mentioning that Beyer starts with a definition of religion—inspired by the double affirmation of Luhmann (Luhmann 1982, 1990), who sees social structures as systems of expectations and communication and who emphasizes the functionally differentiated nature of today's society. Influenced by this reference, Beyer considers religion as a subsystem, whose "type of communication [is] based on the immanent [i.e. the perceptible reality, communicable among human beings] / transcendent [i.e. the potential solution to core problems in human life and what gives meaning to them] polarity, which functions to lend meaning to the root indeterminability of all meaningful human communication, and which offers ways of overcoming or at least managing this indeterminability and its consequences" (Beyer 1994: 6).

Using this definition, Beyer sees two roles for religion in the global society, considered as a "single place" where communication links are worldwide and increasingly dense. First, "religion is instrumental in the elaboration and development of globalization" (Beyer 1994: 3). Even where religion appears as a regressive force, it can in fact be a "proactive force," as, says Beyer, was the case in the Rushdie affair or in the Iranian revolution: "the central thrust is to make Islam and Muslims more determinative in the world system, not to negate it" (Beyer 1994: 3). Secondly, "globalization brings with it the relativization of particularistic identities along with the relativization and marginalization of religion as a mode of social communication" (Beyer 1994: 4). So the situation of religion in global circumstance is an ambiguous one: on the one side, religion is used as a means to affirm a particularistic identity and, in this way, seeks a place and a certain amount of power in the global system; on the other side, because of globalization, particularistic identities are marginalized and, in so far as religion has an affinity with particularism, it is also marginalized.

This marginalization is all the greater and easier since, because of functional differentiation, religions may no longer pretend to be the "sacred canopies" that once they were. Like Luhmann, Beyer considers religion to be one subsystem like others: its mode of communication has nothing to do with the modes of communication in other subsystems, such as economy, where it is money that plays the central role, or science, where truth is supposed to be the mode of communication. Furthermore—and here again we find the influence of Luhmann—expectations are no longer confronted by a normative mode but rather by a cognitive one. When a normative mode of response to expectations was the rule, religion was one—if not the main—normative institution. The general ethics of these societies was religiously grounded and, because it was defined by a transcendental power, it was considered to be unchangeable. Globalization corresponds to a much greater complexity, notably because communication is now worldwide, which opens increased possibilities, and that all the more since links are now numerous between various cultures, which tends to make evident the fact that cultures are human constructions and thus arbitrary and subject to change (Beyer 1994: 2). Thus, a shift appears from normative regulation to a cognitive mode, where learning and the possibilities of change are dominant. It is now more and more difficult to address expectations (and above all unsatisfied expectations) by fixed norms which maintain those expectations—whether they be met or not—; learning prevails and expectations may be changed when they are not met.

Taking all these aspects into account, Beyer understands why different sociologists consider that religion has become increasingly a private affair and why the thesis of privatization is often a part of the secularization theories. But, without rejecting this thesis, Beyer affirms that "privatization is not the whole story but rather only a part of it." Specifically, he says, "the thesis that I explore posits that the globalization of society, while structurally favoring privatization in religion, also provides fertile ground for the renewed public influence of religion" (Beyer 1994: 71).

To confront this thesis, Beyer once again has recourse to a distinction elaborated by Luhmann (Luhmann 1977: 54; 1982: 238–42): that between function and performance. While asserting the autonomy of each subsystem in a functionally differentiated context, Luhmann emphasizes the fact that all these systems operate in the same social milieu and that, because this is so, they are also conditioned. "One important logical deduction from this theoretical position," says Beyer, "is that there is a difference between how a subsystem relates to the society as a whole and how it relates to other social systems, especially other subsystems. Luhmann analyses the former in terms of function and the latter in terms of performance. In the present context, continues Beyer, "function refers to 'pure' religious communication (... the cure of souls, the search for enlightenment or salvation, ...). Function is the pure, sacred communication, involving the transcendent and the aspect that religious institutions claim for themselves, the basis of their autonomy in modern society. Religious performance, by contrast, occurs when religion is 'applied' to problems generated in other systems but not solved there or simply not addressed elsewhere. ... Through performance relations, religion establishes its importance for the 'profane' aspects of life" (Beyer 1994: 80). This is the case, for instance, when religious actors take positions against poverty or for human rights; when they protest against political oppression or against child labor; and so on.

Nevertheless, performance, Beyer suggests, is a problem for religion, because of its holism, i.e. "its effort to determine the whole of existence through the possibility of communication with a posited transcendent" (Beyer 1994: 81). Functional differentiation works against holism. Moreover, previously religions were a way of drawing boundaries between the in- and the out-group and, in that way, between good and evil because religions "linked religious communication and social problems through moral codes ... All problems (were seen) as consequences of sin, ignorance or similar contravention of religious norms" (Beyer 1994: 81). In the global circumstance, these boundaries are incessantly crosscut; the outsider person is my neighbor and it is difficult not to meet outsiders. So evil is from now on less easy to personify and the morally other is less easily negated as the outsider. A further consequence is that God, the transcendent—which, Beyer asserts, may only be talked about in the immanent terms of good and evil—, is more and more difficult to define. To confront this challenge, religious professionals have to choose between a liberal or a conservative option.

The first issue inclines to tolerance and oecumenism: evil exists but it is not specifically localized, it is the limitations which exist in everyone, and nobody may be excluded from religious benefits. This view will orient religious organizations to center their function on private choices: helping services, rites of passage, cure of souls. In all that concerns performance, these organizations will address the problems not (directly) as religious ones. "The solutions, therefore, while religiously inspired, will tend to take on the characteristics of the target system: economic solutions to economic problems, political solutions to political problems, and so forth" (Beyer 1994: 87). A good example, proposes Beyer, was the Liberation Theological movement in Latin America (Beyer 1994: 135–59). Even when affirming its religious inspiration, the aim of this movement was to work for social justice, by giving priority to the poor, and not to evangelize in favor of a particular religion or to transmit a specific and particular religious message—which led to its being reproached, mainly by Rome. The tools used by the movement were practical tools (as was well exemplified by the Basic Ecclesial Communities) and its main reference was the Marxist-Wallersteinian dependency theory.

Religious professionals may choose another option: the conservative option which reasserts tradition. In terms of function, this tradition is often explicitly proposed as a normative response to the problems of the world, described as going in an evil direction. Insistence is placed on holistic commitment and community solidarity. With regard to performance, the conservative option "champions the cultural distinctiveness of one region through a reappropriation of traditional religious antagonistic categories" (Beyer 1994: 93). In the West, which is challenged by former outsiders (the Japanese, the Arabs, ...) the aim is to restore the old Western dominance, as is the case, says Beyer, with the New Christian Right in the United States (Beyer 1994: 114–34). "Traditional moral values, combined with an emphasis on free enterprise and vigorous defense against Communism would restore America as the great nation God intended it to be" (Beyer 1994: 91). In non-Western countries, such as Iran, for instance, modernization is rejected as "an intrinsically infidel product" and religious professionals call for a holy war against the "Great American Satan" (Beyer 1994: 160–84). So, on both sides the world is divided into the religiously pure and impure and this appeal to religious mobilization is particularly strong when the economic and political responses have failed to encounter the hope of continuing to dominate the world (the West) or of achieving emancipation from Western domination (Iran and other Muslim countries). Politicization of religion becomes then a way for different regions of the world to assert themselves in the global context. As the conservative leaders are unable to gain control of the whole world, they affirm the religious purity of one world-region, presented as the expression of the will of God, and they enshrine religious norms in legislation.

If performance appears essentially on the strictly political scene, Beyer identifies another currently important way for religions to avoid being reduced to a private function. This option is related to the fact that functional differentiation leaves unsolved different "residual problems" and "a great deal of social communication undetermined, if not unaffected" (Beyer 1994: 97–99). It is for instance the case with personal or group identity, disparities in wealth and health, ecological threats, and gender inequalities. This kind of problem causes the emergence of numerous social movements which are outside or beyond currently normal institutional bounds. And these social movements are, Beyer suggests, a new potential for religions. Indeed—more or less conscientiously—they often apply religion "as a cultural resource (Beckford 1989) to serve mobilization directed at problems which are not inherently religious. These are performance-oriented religio-social movements" (Beyer 1994: 97). Religions—notably Catholicism and Protestantism—are well "culturally equipped" since, for centuries, they provided many social welfare services until modernization threw them back onto "faith alone," and because they have a holistic vision of man and society. These movements, Beyer avers, might afford, a renewed possibility "for bridging the gap between privatized religious function and publicly influential religious performance" (Beyer 1994: 107).

Beyer's conclusion then, is this: the global circumstance is characterized—as Luhmann sees it—by functional differentiation (which reduces religion to being only a subsystem) and by the shift from a normative to a cognitive mode of response to social and individual expectations (because of the increasing number of possibilities available through world-wide communication). In such an environment, particularistic identities are marginalized, and so are the religious affiliations which have traditionally a large affinity with them (Wilson 1976: 265). What is then the way out for religion ? Beyer suggests that religion considered in its specific function, is privatized and very open to the choice of actors. At the same time, to keep or to conquer a place in the global world, religious organizational leaders may play at the level of performance; then they try to enter "the public, especially the political, arena. … [Therefore, they have] two possibilities: an ecumenical option that looks to the global problems generated by a global, functionally differentiated society; and a particularistic option that champions the cultural distinctiveness of one region through a reappropriation of traditional religious antagonistic categories" (Beyer 1994:

93). In between these two possibilities—a privatized function and a political performance—there may exist a third way: the use of religion as cultural resource to confront "residual problems" with anti-systemic social movements.

3. Rational Choice Theory

Presented by its advocates as a new paradigm within the sociology of religion and as a theory able to solve many questions remaining in this field, or to put many problems in a new light, rational choice theory emerged in the 1990s. It claims to replace secularization theory, which is seen as having been the dominant frame of reference since approximately the 1970s.

Three main features characterize this theory. First, rational choice theory postulates that there exists "a universal form of religious commitment" and that "everyone has a motive for being religious" (Stark 1997: 8). It asserts that in all societies, one may find a "natural and relatively stable set of religious market niches" (Stark 1997: 20) and that there is an unchangeable level of—at least—potential religious demand. For this theory, religion is a commodity which, like all others, is constructed to meet "needs [which] really do not differ much over time and place." So, if "over time, most people modify their religious choices in significant ways, varying their rates of religious participation and modifying its character, or even switching religions altogether" (Iannaccone 1997: 27–28) or, indeed abandoning all religious expression, this is no more than a response to varying circumstances and to changing constraints. Thus, causes of transformation are not to be sought on the demand side, which tends to be stable and universal. Secondly, considering "religious economies to be like commercial economies in that they consist of a market of current and potential consumers, a set of firms seeking to serve that market, and the religious product lines offered by the various firms" (Stark 1997: 17), this theory focuses essentially on the supply side rather than on "religious consumers." Thirdly, rational choice theory affirms that where states regulate the religious economy in the direction of monopoly, firms are lazy and offer unattractive products, badly marketed and poorly able to meet the various segments of potential demand. On the contrary, it asserts that where the market is free, competitive and pluralistic, religious firms are invigorated: they try to specialize to meet the specific needs and tastes of particular market "niches" and, so doing, have the effect of increasing the levels of religious participation. So, counter to Berger, for instance, who considers that pluralism shatters the plausibility of all religions (Berger 1967), rational choice theory considers that "the unbridled competition forces all churches to vie for popular support to survive" (Finke 1997: 60). Consequently, the various religious bodies will try to offer products oriented to meet the particular expectations of various segments or "niches" of the population, differentiated on the basis of specific social markers such as ethnicity, race, region, social status, etc. Thus together "many religious bodies will be able to meet the demands of a much larger proportion of a population that can be the case when only one or very few faiths have free access" (Finke 1997: 57).

Let us develop more deeply the argument of rational choice theory. Stark suggests beginning with a rational choice axiom: in every field of their lives, "humans seek what they perceive to be rewards and avoid what they perceive to be costs" (Stark 1997: 6). But as some rewards are scarce or as humans do not know how to obtain some rewards if, indeed, they exist—for instance eternal life—they have constructed what Stark calls "compensators," i.e. proposals, about gaining the hoped for rewards. Religions are such kinds of compensators: they offer instructions about how rewards that do not exist in this life can be achieved over the long term; more precisely, they are "systems of general compensators—i.e. substitutes for a cluster of many rewards and for rewards of great scope—based on supernatural assumptions" (Stark/Bainbridge 1987). From this point of departure, Stark then works out the notion of "religious economy" which refers to all the religious activities going on in any society and consisting, as in any market, of (a) current and potential customers, (b) a set of firms, (c) religious "product lines" offered by these firms (Stark 1997: 17).

As we have already said, rational choice theory focuses on the supply side (Stark/Iannaccone 1993, 1994; Finke/Iannaccone 1993) and its main question is then: "under what conditions are religious firms able to create a demand ?" (Stark 1997: 17). The given answer is based on the opposition made between a monopolistic market and an open and thenceforth a pluralistic market. The market is monopolistic when one or a very few religions are admitted, regulated and/or sustained by the state (as it is the case in most European countries). States regulate religious economies and restrict competition in two possible ways: suppression and subsidy. Both reduce incentives for all religions. Suppression reduces the appeal of institutional change and innovation and of adaptation to renewed popular needs in existing and accepted religions. On its side, subsidy limits competition by being restricted to a few selected religions; and it undermines any motivation to mobilize popular support which the clergy might have. Furthermore "when the state subsidizes only a few religions, this subsidy inflates the cost of joining an alternative religion" (Finke 1997: 52) for instance in what concerns schools or health. So state regulations which limit competition tend, on the supply side, to reduce the incentives to dynamism: the firms become lazy, non innovative and so they are less and less attractive. On the consumer side, regulations tend to reduce the ratio of return people receive for their investments. On the contrary, where the market is free and is open to pluralism—i.e. where more religious firms freely exist—competition exists, which invigorates the firms and stimulates them to specialize in order to meet various market segments (Finke/Stark 1992). The more the environment is competitive, the more firms are urged to abandon unsuccessful products and inefficient modes of production and the more they try to offer attractive and profitable products (Iannaccone 1997: 27). All these aspects tend to increase the level of global religious participation.

On the basis of this general statement, rational choice theory claims to be able to explain many aspects of the religious life of a population. For instance, referring to what is called "the household production model," rational choice theory considers that, to meet their needs, households have to choose between devoting time or money (to prepare meals oneself or to go to the restaurant); "applied to religion, (what is called) the concept of input substitution implies that people with high monetary values of time will tend to engage in money-intensive religious practices ... and people with low monetary values of time will adopt more time intensive practices and contribute relatively less money" (Iannaccone 1997: 30). This would explain, says Iannaccone, survey results on church attendance and contributions and differences between congregations—the richer ones opting for a variety of time-saving, money-intensive practices such as shorter services, and larger more costly facilities.

The authors promoting in this theory explain also that rational choice theory may explain several "distinctive features of religious institutions" from the risky character of religious goods: indeed "most religious commodities are risky, promising large but uncertain benefits" like eternal life, unending bliss, and personal experience does not suffice to evaluate the religion's claims. This explains, affirms Iannaccone, "why the character of religious activity is so often collective and the structure of religious organizations is so often congregational": testimonies of personal acquaintance, of a respected figure or of fellow members are more trustworthy than those of strangers (Iannaccone 1997: 33–34). Rational choice theory would also explain why strict churches survive and flourish when less-demanding religions become apathetic and vulnerable to "free-riders i.e. to individuals who reap the benefits of other people's efforts without expending a corresponding effort of their own" (Iannaccone 1992, 1994). Costly demands (such as dietary or sexual prohibitions, restrictions of the use of modern technology, various kinds of stigma like, e.g., distinctive dress) discourage the free-riders who are reluctant to pay the price to take part. And as these "stigmas" make more or less difficult the participation in outside activities, the group tends to develop internal substitutes which require a high level of participation—which also mitigates the risk of free-riding. Iannaccone considers that this proposal enlightens the difference between churches—where costly demands are low and which are thus open to mainstream consumption—and sects, whose costly demands exclude free-riders and which develop internal activities resulting in a more or less closed and isolated life for the members from whom a high level of participation is required (Iannaccone 1992, 1994).

4. Other Topics

If the necessity to revisit the definition of the religious object, rational choice theory and globalization which, during the two last decades of the twentieth century, appear to be the current main streams in the sociology of religion, there are also some other topics that have taken a more or less larger place in the field.

4.1. Politics and Religion

The collapse of the Soviet Union at the end of the 1980s is certainly an event which has stimulated various studies on religion and politics in Central and Eastern Europe. Three main lines of research appeared in relation to this topic.

First, some works assess the history of the relation between religion and the Soviet system. In this connection, an essential topic is that which seeks to show how, during the seventy years of the Soviet system, the (Catholic) church, considered mainly in its organizational aspects, was evoked as a space which offered people various possibilities to meet and to express themselves: "pilgrimages, religious celebrations, assistance brought to poor and handicapped people gave opportunities, in short to have a relative sociability outside the official structures and to find room to resist and to contest the totalitarian order (Frybes 1997: 41).

Secondly, the question of the role played by religion—essentially by Christianity—in the collapse of the Soviet regime and in the process of democratization of the associated countries—induced a wider reflection on the relations between religion and democracy in general. The conclusions of such studies are often such as the following: "If the historical origins of the democratic regime are to be found in Europe or in North-America, its cultural sources come also from these parts of the world" (Hermet 1993: 58). Among these sources, the dominant European religion—Christianity, particularly its Protestant variant—is well placed to explain the emergence of democracy: it played indeed a major role in the promotion of the individual being and in the separation of state and church, insists Dieckhoff (Dieckhoff 1997: 336). But, continues this author, the development of democratic regimes has then to fight against the totalizing tendency of the Catholic Church, which for a long time rejected the liberal logic of the political autonomy. Thus, Dieckhoff concludes, "there is no univocal determination of the politics by the religious and thus, *a contrario*, no religion is, by nature, absolutely incompatible with democracy" (Dieckhoff 1997: 336).

A third topic induced by the events in eastern and central Europe is the examination of the uses that the new states make of religion. This third aspect is certainly the most studied and the majority of researchers agree on one point: "Religion is instrumentalized. A confusion is made between religion and morality, religion and culture, religion and nationality. This use of religion does not at all imply that there exists a real religious rebirth. Religion often looses its transcendental and divine dimension and, as a Soviet historian says, nationalist intellectuals have very good relations with the Church but have very bad ones with the faith" (Rousselet 1997: 26). If there exist a few exceptions (e.g. the work of Greeley) most of the researchers insist, then, on the fact that there is no religious renewal, no *retour du religieux*. On the one side, religion is instrumentalized by the political actor who becomes more and more in escheat and appears to be more and more unable to find his way (Michel 1997: 17). On the other side, religion seems to be an important means to (re)structure the quest for sense not only in the private life of individuals but also in a "public (political) space" which has loosened its capacity for mobilization (Michel 1997: 21).

If the collapse of the Soviet Union induced many studies of the relations between politics and religion, this event was not the only one to stimulate this type of research. Before the 1990s, the revolution in Iran was also an important moment when this kind of studies developed. In this case also, most studies focused on the politization of religion. But here a central topic, absent in the case of eastern Europe, was that of martyrdom (*chahâdat*) and the evolution of the understanding of this concept. The Iranian revolution also offered also an opportunity to return to the concept of charismatic authority, with the figure of Khomeyni (Keddie 1983; Khosrokhavar 1997). If Iran provides the best known instance, the Islamic countries in general aroused during recent decades many studies about religion and politics: this is particularly so in the case of Algeria (Baduel 1994, 1997) and Turkey (Kentel 1997).

The evolution in other parts of the world and the events which occurred there also induced numerous studies of the relations between religion and politics. In Latin America, for instance, the central question treated by sociologists was that of the relations between religion (and here essentially Catholicism), dictatorship and the emergence of democracy (Mainwaring 1986). The evolution of the alliances of the Catholic Church, the internal oppositions which developed between those who remained on the side of the dominant class and those who made up their mind to defend the poor in the line of Liberation Theology, has stimulated many interesting researches (Adriance 1986; Azevedo 1987; Bruneau 1982; Levine 1986). For his part, Martin explored and discussed the impact on political actions of the emergence of Pentecostalism in Latin America (Martin 1990, 1999).

If the relations between religion and politics appear to have been an important topic during the 1980s and the 1990s, it is interesting to remark that this theme has most of the time been treated in non Western European and non North American contexts. There exist of course studies on this topic in North America (Casanova 1994) and in Western Europe but, most of them have focused on the incidence of religious belonging; on elections; and on political behavior (van Deth 1995). As such, they may not be considered as a "new" approach as it is the case in the literature concerning the role played by religious actors in the process of political change or the instrumentalization of religion for political aims. Nevertheless, there is an occurrence which stimulates research on politics and religion in Western Europe and which induces a certain enlargement and renewal of the problematic: it is the development of the so-called sects and the emergence of new religious movements. Underlying the analysis of these movements—which are very numerous—the main question is that of the relation between democracy and human rights, on one side, sects and new religious movements, on the other (Champion/Cohen 1999; Arweck/Clarke 1997). If this question contributes, as we have seen, to a revisitation of the definition of religion, it also induces a certain interest concerning the juridical question of the religious and another concerning the role of the media in this problematic (Beckford 1995). If one readily understands why sociologists are interested in the relation between sects and politics in Europe in so far as this question is effectively highly politicized in some countries (notably in France and Germany), one may nevertheless wonder why researchers seem to be less interested by the relation which may exist in these countries between politics and traditional religions. One may answer that it is because secularization has been in evidence there for a relatively long time, but one has nevertheless to recognize that at least the cultural dimension of religion and its ethical orientation continue to have some political incidence, as it is shown by the European Values Study. Perhaps we have to explain this fact by a kind of "naturalization" of the relation between Christianity and European states, a naturalization which conspires to prevent this topic from emerging.

4.2. Women and Religion

Another major theme that began to appear in the 1970s (then essentially centered on the ordination of women) has developed considerably since the 1980s and became a permanent feature of conferences and publications: it is the theme of women and religion. Among the many aspects treated under this topic, three appear to predominate.

The first—and probably the oldest—considers the differences which appear in religious practice and, more generally, in the relation with the religious, which differentiate men and women—the latter showing a higher level of practice and of religiosity than men. These differences are imputed to the construction of sex roles. It is indeed shown that when women are engaged in professional activity, the level of their practice approaches that of men and is thus significantly lower than that of women who lack such professional involvement. In relation to gender differences—a topic which concerns mainly if not exclusively Christian religions—the question of the transmission of religious practices and beliefs to children is very often raised (Delumeau 1992), and it shows the major role women play in this transmission, most of all for daughters. This leads to a question: what will happen if more and more women undertake professional roles and their contacts with churches become less and less frequent (Auer 1989; Campiche 1996; De Vaus 1987; Gee 1991; Steggerda 1993).

Another important aspect is that of the representation of women in religious literature—in "founding texts" as well as in more recent publications from the religious authorities. Religions other than the Christian are also considered. Many studies concern Judaism (Biale 1984; Brenner 1985; Eisenberg/Abecassis 1979, 1981). They show, as Azria underlines, how, "in the Rabbinic Tradition, women are at the same time honored, magnified and protected but also feared, kept at a distance, marginalized, excluded" (Azria 1996: 121). The question of women in the Islamic context has arisen more recently and studies are here less numerous (Ascha 1987) and they are mainly connected with the appearance of Islam on the political scene. But in Islam as well as in Judaism and Christianity, the most interesting aspects in this literature are certainly the analysis of the re-reading of religious sources on which women are embarking, and also of their instrumentalization of religion to acquire greater prominence in the secular field and to attain emancipation from centuries of patriarchal power (Gaspard/Khosrokhavar 1995; Weibel 1995; Davidman/Tenenbaum 1994; Kaufman 1991; Dermience 1990, 1994).

Not so far from these questions emerges also the important issue of the power of women in the religious field. Observing that practically in every religion, men reserve for themselves the monopoly of power, different studies explore the foundations of that fact and the arguments that are put advanced to legitimize it (Chaves 1997; Voyé 1996; Wallace 1992; Willaime 1996). Obviously, the pontifical letter "Ordinatio Sacerdotalis" which appeared in 1994 and by which the Pope reaffirmed the definitive exclusion of women from the priesthood was an important occasion to highlight this debate, not only in the Catholic world but also more generally. Thus, the question was reactivated to determine whether religion is mainly to be seen as only the apparent guarantor of the reproduction of inegalitarian models, or whether it might be regarded as an (involuntary and non intentional?) instrument for women's promotion and for their recognition as equal partners not only in the religious field but in every field of social life (Côté/Zylberberg 1996; Kaufman 1991; Voyé 1996; Weibel 1995).

4.3. Youth and Religion

Three factors combine to induce a development on research focusing on youth and religion: the cultural importance that youth takes on nowadays; the observation that youth are deserting churches and religious institutions; the fact that a large number of studies emphasize the gap which, in the religious field distinguishes between older and younger generations (Jagodzinski/Dobbelaere 1995)—this variable appearing to be the most determinant (see also the results of the European Values Studies; Lambert 1992; Tomasi 1993; Ester 1993). Let us nevertheless add that most of the research with regard to youth and religion concerns only Europe and the USA; and such other research as exists regarding other religions and youth, generally concerns young immigrants (Anwar 1982; Babes 1997).

The parents of the youth of the 1980s and 1990s were the "babyboomers" who had distanced themselves from the religious institutions and their authorities and who had begun to adopt a religion "à la carte" and to choose for themselves from their own experience. In such conditions, the transmission of religion was no longer assured as it had been previously, when the religious affiliation of the young was mainly inherited from that of their parents (Roof et al. 1995).

In such a circumstance, it is not astonishing that the religious behavior and beliefs of contemporary youth are widely diversified. In consequence, one finds in the sociological literature diverse attempts to elaborate "socio-religious typologies" of youth and of its (eventual) links with religions and churches. For instance Hervieu-Léger shows that religious belonging may be related to one or two of four different dimensions: the dimension of identity which essentially concerns symbols, rites, and facilitates the distinction of the in- and the out-group; the ethical dimension which refers to a set of common values; the cultural dimension which corresponds to the knowledge of doctrine and history and so expresses a certain worldview; and the emotional dimension which rests on the feeling of a (transient) community (Hervieu-Léger 1993). For his part, Brechon identifies six groups within the youth population of Europe: two so-called "pure" types, the religious and the non religious youth; the youth who are "heterodox believers": they have a relatively high level of belief in traditional (Christian) religions but they modify the content of doctrinal beliefs (i.e. they believe in God but God is no longer considered as a person); the "non religious humanists" who are near the non-religious people but who consider that the churches have to play an active role in solving the main social problems; many young people are described as "irregular" or "half-hearted" and they define themselves as religious without having clear characteristics; finally, many young people are also "ritualistic" because their main feature is that they are deeply attached to the rites of passage but have no very firm beliefs (Brechon 1996).

Next to this kind of studies, others explore the question of the relations between the specificities of contemporary youth culture and the culture diffused by churches and schools in the religious field. They show notably the importance of leisure (Fornäs 1995) but also the impact of a context of economic and cultural precariousness, and question the capacity of traditional religions to confront these preoccupations of youth and to "adapt" their supply. In this perspective, the question arises why sects and new religious movements seem to have more success among the young than that recorded by the mainline religions.

Conclusion

Many other topics certainly occur in the sociological literature of the last twenty years and all the former themes persist. But those that we have briefly presented here appear to be the most significant and to be those that appear to have undergone greater development during this period. All of them express the changes which characterize the functioning of our societies and their impact on the religious field. Most of them reveal the importance of the disruption of the previous world order (the end of European supremacy and decolonization; the opening of borders by the collapse of the Soviet Union as well as the emergence of global order; the affirmation of the individual and the necessity for him/her to build his/her own identity; the shift from a society centered on labor to one where leisure has ever greater importance; the shift from a normative to a cognitive order; ...). All these changes have induced the necessity of revisiting the definition of religion itself and of enlightening it with the contributions of religions other than Christianity which have different features and different conceptions. Thus, comparative studies have become more and more important and have provoked the construction of international networks, most often emerging as spin-offs of the international associations for the sociology of religion. Nevertheless, it is clear that the religious situation in the Western world is still the most frequently studied and that non Christian religions are studied when they develop inside this world itself, where they become "less and less other" (Beyer 1999). Apart from the fact that sociology historically emerged as a Western science, this situation has also to be explained by the Western origins of a very large majority of sociologists. This "ethnocentrism" is therefore not specific to the sociology of religion: it characterizes the whole field. Nevertheless, given more recent trends, a change is certainly to be expected in the direction of an enlargement of our perspectives.

Two other features have finally to be underlined. One refers to what Swatos calls "the applied question" i.e. the extent to which the authors attempt to make some applications of their findings and so encounter one of the main—if not the main—purpose of the founders of the associations for sociology of religion and even of some academic departments: to serve the religious organizations (Swatos 1999). Considering this question, it has to be said that this preoccupation seems to be less and less evident and that the large majority of publications have an exclusively scientific purpose.

A final remark concerns methodological aspects. New techniques for quantitative methods have permitted a very high level of sophistication in this matter. Qualitative research has also improved. And it happens that both methodological approaches are used together. But it is evident that quantitative methods are privileged in Anglo-Saxon sociology; in Latin sociology, and typically in French speaking, sociology, the qualitative approach is much more developed and sociologists in these cultures appear more readily disposed to have recourse to both types of methods.

Bibliography

Adriance, Madeleine (1986), *Opting for the Poor: Brazilian Catholicism in Transition.* Kansas City, Mo.: Sheed and Ward.

Anwar, Muhammad (1982), *Young Muslims in a Multi-Cultural Society*. Leiceister: The Islamic Foundation.

Arweck, Elizabeth/Clarke Peter B. (1997), *New Religious Movements. An Annoted Bibliography*. London/Westport, Conn.: Greenwood Press.

Ascha, Ghassan (1987), *Du statut inférieur de la femme en Islam*. Paris: L'Harmattan.

Auer Falk, Nancy/Gross, Rita M. (1989), *Unspoken Worlds*. Belmont, Calif.: Wadsworth Publishing Company.

Augé, Marc (1982), "Football. De l'histoire sociale à l'anthropologie religieuse," in: *Le Débat* 19: 59–67.

Azevedo, Marcello de C. (1987), *Basic Ecclesial Communities in Brazil: The Challenge of a New Way of Being Church*. Washington, D.C.: Georgetown University Press.

Azria, Régine (1996), "Femme, tradition et modernité juives," in: *Archives de Sciences Sociales des Religions* 95: 117–32.

— (1999), "Le Judaïsme et la Sociolgie," in: *Sociology and Religions. An Ambiguous Relationship/Sociologie et Religions. Des relations ambiguës*, ed. by Liliane Voyé/Jaak Billiet. KADOK-Studies 23. Leuven: Leuven University Press: 155–70.

Babès, Leila (1997), *L'Islam positif. La religion des jeunes musulmans en France*. Paris: Ed. de l'Atelier.

Baduel, Pierre-Robert (1994), *L'Algérie incertaine*. Aix-en Provence: Edisud.

— (1997), "L'Islam dans l'équation politique au Maghreb aujourd'hui," in: *Religion et démocratie*, ed. by Patrick Michel. Paris: Albin-Michel.

Bailey, Edward I. (1997), *Implicit Religion in Contemporary Society*. Kampen, Netherlands: Kok Pharos.

— (1998), "Implicit Religion," in: *Encyclopedia of Religion and Society*, ed. by William H. Swatos. Walnut Creek, Calif./London/New Delhi: Altamira Press: 235.

Beckford, James A. (1989), *Religion and Advanced Industrial Society*. London: Unwin Hyman.

— (1995), "Cults, Conflicts and Journalists," in: *New Religions and the New Europe*, ed. by R. Towler. Aarhus: Aarhus University Press.

Bellah, Robert N. (1967), "Civil Religion in America," in: *Daedalus* 96 (1): 1–21.

Berger, Peter (1967), *The Sacred Canopy*. New York: Doubleday.

Berger, Peter L./Luckmann, Thomas (1966), "Secularization and Pluralism," in: *International Yearbook for the Sociology of Religion* 2: 73–86.

Beyer, Peter (1994), *Religion and Globalization*. London: Sage.

— (2000), "Not in My Backyard: Studies of Other Religions in the Context of SSSR/ RRA Annual Meetings," in: *Journal for the Scientific Study of Religion* 39 (4): 524–30.

Biale, Rachel (1984), *Women and Jewish Law. An Exploration of Women's Issues in Halakkic Sources.* New York: Shocken Books.

Brechon, Pierre (1996), "Identité religieuse des jeunes en Europe," in: *Cultures jeunes et religions en Europe,* ed. by Roland Campiche. Paris: Cerf: 45–96.

Brenner, Athalya (1985), *The Israelite Woman. Social Role and Literary Type in Biblical Narrative.* Sheffield: JSOTT Press.

Bruneau, Thomas (1982), *The Church in Brazil: The Politics of Religion.* Austin, Tex.: University of Texas Press.

Çakir, Rusen (1992), "La mobilization islamique en Turquie," in: *Esprit* 184: 130–42.

Campiche, Roland, ed. (1977), *Cultures jeunes et religions en Europe.* Paris: Cerf.

— (1996), "Religion, statut social et identité féminine," in: *Archives de Sciences Sociales des Religions* 95: 69–94.

Casanova, José (1994), *Public Religions in the Modern World.* Chicago, Ill./London: The University of Chicago Press.

Champion, Françoise/Cohen, Martine (1999), *Sectes et Démocratie.* Paris: Seuil.

Chaves, Mark (1997), *Ordaining Women. Culture and Conflict in Religions Organizations.* Cambridge, Mass./London: Harvard University Press.

Cipriani, Roberto (1992), *La religione dei Valori.* Roma: Salvatore Sciascia Ed.

Côte, Pauline/Zylberberg, Jacques (1996), "Théologie et théalogie: les légitimations religieuses du fait féminin en Amérique du Nord," in: *Archives de Sciences Sociales des Religions* 95: 95–115.

Davidman, Lynn/Tenenbaum Shelly, eds. (1994), *Feminist Perspectives on Jewish Studies.* New Haven, Conn./London: Yale University Press.

Davie, Grace (1994), *Religion in Britain since 1945. Believing without Belonging.* Oxford: Blackwell.

Delumeau, Jean, ed. (1992), *La Religion de ma mère. Le rôle des femmes dans la transmission de la foi.* Paris: Cerf.

Demerath, N. Jay (2000), "The Varieties of Sacred Experience: Finding the Sacred in a Secular Grove," in: *Journal for the Scientific Study of Religion* 39 (1): 1–11.

Dermience, Alice (1990), "Femmes et ministères dans l'Eglise primitive," in: *Actes de la XIième session du CREDIC, CNRS (Gréco n° 2).* Université Jean Moulin: 9–20.

— (1994), "Les questions de Dieu et la représentation de Dieu: un défi pour la théologie féministe," in: *Bulletin de l'Association de Théologie Catholique* 1: 40–50.

De Vaus, D./Mc Allister, I. (1987), "Gender Differences in Religion: A Test of the Structural Theory," in: *American Sociological Review* 52: 472–81.

Dieckhoff, Alain (1997), Logiques religieuses et construction démocratique," in: *Religion et démocratie,* ed. by Patrick Michel. Paris: Albin-Michel: 317–38.

Dobbelaere, Karel (1981), "Secularization: A Multi-dimensional Concept," in: *Current Sociology* 29 (2): 1–213.

— (1997), "Point de vue d'un marginal," in: *Les religieux des Sociologues,* ed. by Yves Lambert/Guy Michelat/Albert Piette. Paris: L'Harmattan: 227–33.

— (1999), "Towards an Integrated Perspective of the Processes Related to the Descriptive Concept of Secularization," in: *Sociology of Religion* 60 (3): 229–47.

— (2000), "From Religious Sociology to Sociology of Religion: Towards Globalisation?," in: *Journal for the Scientific Study of Religion* 39 (4): 433–47.

— (2004), "Assessing Secularization Theory," in: *New Approaches to the Study of Religion*. Vol. 2: *Textual, Comparative, Sociological, and Cognitive Approaches*, ed. by Peter Antes/Armin W. Geertz/Randi R. Warne. Berlin/New York: Walter de Gruyter: 229–53 [see following paper in this book].

Douglas, Mary/Ney, Steven (1998), *Missing Persons: A Critique of the Social Sciences*. Berkeley, Calif.: University of California Press.

Eisenberg, Josy/Abecassis, Arnaud (1979), *A Bible ouverte. Et Dieu créa la femme*. Paris: Albin-Michel.

— (1981), *A Bible ouverte. Jacob, Rachel, Léa et les autres*. Paris: Albin-Michel.

Ester, Peter/Halman, Loek/de Moor, Rund (1993), *The Individualizing Society. Value Change in Europe and North America*. Tilburg: Tilburg University Press.

Finke, Roger (1997), "The Consequences of Religious Competition: Supply-side Explanations for Religious Change," in: *Rational Choice Theory and Religion*, ed. by Lawrence A. Young. New York/London: Routledge: 45–64.

Finke, Roger/Iannaccone, Laurence R. (1993), "Supply-side Explanations for Religious Change," in: *Annals, AAPSS* 527: 27–39.

Finke, Roger/Stark, Rodney (1992), *The Churching of America: 1776–1990. Winners and Losers in Our Religious Economy*. New Brunswick, N.J.: Rutgers University Press.

Fornäs, Johan/Bolin, Göran, eds. (1995), *Youth Culture in Late Modernity*. London: Sage.

Frybes, Marcin (1997), "La question religieuse dans la sortie du communisme en Pologne," in: *Religion et démocratie*, ed. by Patrick Michel. Paris: Albin-Michel: 238–56.

Gaspard, Françoise/Khosrokhavar, Farhad (1995), *Le foulard et la république*. Paris: La Découverte.

Gee, E. (1991), "Gender Differences in Church Attendance in Canada: The Role of Labor Force Participation," in: *Review of Religious Research* 32: 267–73.

Gellner, Ernest/Vatin, Jean-Claude, eds. (1981), *Islam et politique au Maghreb*. Paris: Editions du CNRS.

Germain, Elizabeth (1986), *Des mots sur un silence. Les jeunes et la religion au Québec*. Québec: Université Laval.

Hadaway, C. Kirk/Marler, Penny L./Chaves, Mark (1993), "What the Polls Don't Show: A Closer Look at U.S. Church Attendance," in: *American Sociological Review* 58: 741–52.

Hames, Constant (1999), "Islam et Sociologie: une recontre qui n'a pas eu lieu," in: *Sociology and Religions. An Ambiguous Relationship/Sociologie et Religions. Des relations ambiguës*, ed. by Liliane Voyé/Jaak Billiet. KADOK-Studies 23. Leuven: Leuven University Press: 171–82.

Hermet, Guy (1993), *Culture et démocratie*. Paris: Unesco et Albin-Michel.

Hervieu-Leger, Danièle (1993), *La religion pour mémoire*. Paris: Cerf.

— (1999), *Le pèlerin et le converti. La religion en mouvement*. Paris: Flammarion.

Iannaccone, Laurence R. (1992), "Sacrifice and Stigma: Reducing Free-Riding in Cults, Communes and Other Collectives," in: *Journal of Political Economy* 100 (2): 271–91.

— (1994), "Why Strict Churches Are Strong," in: *American Journal of Sociology* 99 (5): 1180–1211.

— (1997), "Rational Choice. Framework for the Scientific Study of Religion," in: *Rational Choice Theory and Religion*, ed. by Lawrence A. Young. New York/London: Routledge: 25–44.

Introvigne, Massimo/Melton, J. Gordon (1996), *Pour en finir avec les sectes. Le débat sur le rapport de la Commission parlementaire*. Milan: CESNUR/Di Giovanni.

Jagodzinski, Wolfgang/Dobbelaere, Karel (1995), "Secularization and Church Religiosity," in: *The Impact of Values*, ed. by Jan W. van Deth/Elinor Scarbrough. Oxford: Oxford University Press: 76–119.

Janssen, Jacques/de Hart, Joep/den Draak, Christine (1990), "A Content Analysis of the Praying. Practices of Dutch Youth," in: *Journal for the Scientific Study of Religion* 29 (1): 99–107.

Kaufman, Debra Renée (1991), *Rachel's Daughters. Newly Orthodox Jewish Women*. New [illegible]

Keddie, Nikki R., ed. (1983), *Religion and Politics in Iran*. New Haven, Conn: Yale University Press.

Kentel, Ferhat (1997), "Turquie: les identités au pluriel," in: *Religion et démocratie*, ed. by Patrick Michel. Paris: Albin-Michel.

Kepel, Gilles (1991), *La revanche de Dieu. Chrétiens, Juifs et Musulmans à la reconquête du monde*. Paris: Seuil.

Khosrokhavar, Farhad (1995), *L'Islamisme et la mort. Le martyre révolutionnaire en Iran*. Paris: L'Harmattan.

— (1997), "Le sacré et le politique dans la révolution iranienne," in: *Religion et démocratie*, ed. by Patrick Michel. Paris: Albin-Michel.

Lambert, Yves/Michelat, Guy, eds. (1992), *Crépuscule des religions chez les jeunes?* Paris: L'Harmattan.

Levine, Daniel H. (1981), *Religion and Politics in Latin America: The Catholic Church in Venezuela and Colombia*. Princeton, N.J.: Princeton University Press.

— (1986), *Religion and Political Conflict in Latin America*. Chapel Hill, N.C.: University of North Carolina Press.

Luckmann, Thomas (1967), *The Invisible Religion*. New York: Macmillan.

Luhmann, Niklas (1977), *Funktion der Religion*. Frankfurt am Main: Suhrkamp.

— (1982), *The Differentiation of Society*, transl. by Stephen Holmes/Charles Larmore. New York: Columbia University.

— (1990), "The World Society as a Social System," in: N. Luhmann, *Essays on Self-Reference*. New York: Columbia University.

Mainwaring, Scott (1986), *The Catholic Church and Politics in Brazil 1916–1985*. Stanford, Calif.: Stanford University Press.

Makrides, Vasilios (1999), "Ambiguous Reception and Troublesome Relationship: The Sociology of Religion in Eastern Orthodox Europe," in: *Sociology and Religions. An Ambiguous Relationship/Sociologie et Religions. Des relations ambiguës*, ed. by Liliane Voyé/Jaak Billiet. KADOK-Studies 23. Leuven: Leuven University Press: 139–54.

Martin, David (1978), *A General Theory of Secularization*. Oxford: Blackwell.

— (1990), *Tongues of Fire: The Explosion of Protestantism in Latin America*. Oxford: Blackwell.

— (1999), "The Evangelical Upsurge and Its Political Implications," in: *The Desecularization of the World*, ed. by Peter L. Berger. Grand Rapids, Mich.: W.E. Eerdmans: 37–49.

Michel, Patrick (1992), *Les religions à l'Est*. Paris: Cerf.

— (1994), *Politique et religion. La grande mutation*. Paris: Albin-Michel.

— (1997), *Religion et démocratie*. Paris: Albin-Michel.

Nesti, Arnaldo (1985), *Il religioso implicito*. Roma: Ianua.

Nesti, Arnaldo/Giannoni, Paolo/Dianich, Severino (1993), *La religione implicita*. Bologna: Ed. Dehoniane.

Piette, Albert (1990), "La religiosité et la sacralité dans le monde contemporain," in: *Nouvelles idoles, nouveaux cultes: Dérives de la sacralité*, ed. by Claude Rivière/Albert Piette. Paris: L'Harmattan: 203–41.

Presser, Stanley/Stinson, Linda (1990), "Data Collection Mode and Social Desirability Bias in Self-Reported Religious Attendance," in: *American Sociological Review* 63: 137–45.

Riis, Ole (1996), "Religion et identité nationale au Danemark," in: *Identités religieuses en Europe*, ed. by Grace Davie/Danièle Hervieu-Léger. Paris: La Découverte: 113–30.

Rivière, Claude (1988), *Les liturgies politiques*. Paris: PUF.

Rivière, Claude/Piette, Albert (1990), *Nouvelles idoles, nouveaux cultes: Dérives de la sacralité*. Paris: L'Harmattan.

Robertson, Roland (1989), "Globalization: Politics and Religion," in: *The Changing Face of Religion*, ed. by James A. Beckford/Thomas Luckmann. Beverly Hills, Calif.: Sage: 10–23.

— (1992), *Globalization: Social Theory and Global Culture*. London: Sage.

— (1997), "Comments on the 'Global Triad' and 'Glocalization,'" in: *Globalization and Indigeneous Culture*, ed. by N. Inoue. Tokyo: Institute for Japanese Culture and Classic, Kokugakuin University: 217–25.

Robertson, Roland/Chirico, Jo Ann (1985), "Humanity, Globalization and Worldwide Religious Resurgence: A Theoretical Exploration," in: *Sociological Analysis* 46: 219–42.

Roof, Wade Clark/Carroll, Jackson W./Roozen, David A., eds. (1995), *The Post-War Generation: Cross-Cultural Perspectives*. Boulder, Colo.: Westview Press.

Rousselet, Kathy (1997), "L'orthodoxie et le déficit démocratique russe," in: *Religion et démocratie*, ed. by Patrick Michel. Paris: Albin-Michel: 257–274.

Smith, Tom W. (1998), "A Review of Church Attendance Measures," in: *American Sociological Review* 62: 131–36.

Stark, Rodney (1985), "From Church-Sect to Religious Economies," in: *The Sacred in a Post-Secular-Age*, ed. by Phillip E. Hammond. Berkeley, Calif.: University of California Press: 139–49.

— (1997), "Bringing Theory Back in," in: *Rational Choice Theory and Religion*, ed. by Lawrence A. Young. New York/London: Routledge: 3–23.

— (1999), "Secularization, RIP," in: *Sociology of Religion* 60 (3): 249–73.

Stark, Rodney/Bainbridge, William Sims (1987), *A Theory of Religion*. New York/Bern: Peter Lang.

— (1992), *The Future of Religion: Secularization, Revival and Cult Formation*. Berkeley, Calif.: University of California Press.

Stark, Rodney/Iannaccone, Laurence R. (1992), "Sociology of Religion," in: *Encyclopedia of Sociology*, ed. by Edgar F. Borgatta/Marie L. Borgatta. New York: Macmillan: 2029–37.

— (1993), "Rational Choice Propositions about Religious Movements," in: *Handbook on Cults and Sects in America*, ed. by David G. Bromley/Jeffrey K. Hadden. Greenwich: JAI Press: 109–25.

— (1994), "A Supply-Side Reinterpretation of the Secularization of Europe," in: *Journal for the Scientific Study of Religion* 33: 230–52.

Steggerda, M. (1993), "Religion and Social Positions of Women and Men," in: *Social Compass* 40 (1): 65–73.

Swatos, William H. (1999), "Continuities and Changes in the Review of Religious Research," in: *Journal for the Scientific Study of Religion* 39: 475–79.

Swatos, William H./Christiano, Kevin J. (1999), "Secularization Theory: The Course of a Concept," in: *Sociology of Religion* 60 (3): 309–28.

Tomasi, Luigi, ed. (1993), *Young People and Religions in Europe: Persistence and Change in Values.* Trento: Reverdito Edizioni.

Tschannen, Olivier (1992), *Les théories de la sécularisation.* Genève: Droz.

[illegible] Oxford: Oxford University Press.

Voyé, Liliane (1996), "Femmes et église catholique: une histoire de contradictions et d'ambiguïtés," in: *Archives de Sciences Sociales des Religions* 95: 11–28.

Voyé, Liliane/Billiet, Jaak, eds. (1999), *Sociology and Religions. An Ambiguous Relationship/ Sociologie et Religions. Des relations ambiguës*, ed. by Liliane Voyé/Jaak Billiet. KA-DOK-Studies 23. Leuven: Leuven University Press.

Wallace, Ruth A. (1992), *They Call Her Pastor: A New Role for Catholic Women.* Albany, N.Y.: State University of New York Press.

Weibel, Nadine (1995), "L'Islam-action au féminin ou une redéfiniton de l'identité de genre," in: *Studia Religiosa Helvetica* 1: 391–412.

Willaime, Jean-Paul (1995), *Sociologie des religions.* Paris: PUF, Que sais-je?

— (1996), "L'accès des femmes au pastorat et la sécularisation du rôle de clerc dans le protestantisme," in: *Archives de Sciences Sociales des Religions* 95: 29–45.

Wilson, Bryan R. (1969), *Religion in Secular Society. A Sociological Comment.* London: Watts.

— (1976), "Aspects of Secularization in the West," in: *Japanese Journal of Religious Studies* 3 (4): 259–76.

— (1990), *The Social Dimensions of Sectarianism. Sects and New Religious Movements in Contemporary Society.* Oxford: Clarendon Press.

Assessing Secularization Theory

by

KAREL DOBBELAERE

The evaluation of the secularization process is controversial. Some sociologists have rejected it totally, and called it a "doctrine" to be carried "to the graveyard of failed theories" (Stark 1999: 270). Others are its staunch defenders (Wallis/Bruce 1992; Wilson 1985, 1998), or allude to it when discussing things "beyond secularization," thereby implying that secularization is a fact (Voyé 1985). To understand this Babel, one must first consider just what different authors mean by secularization. Swatos and Christiano (1999) and Stark (1999) argue that the prediction of secularization was about the decline of "individual piety" citing several persons, including non-sociologists, who have predicted the demise of individual religiosity, and they reject this on the basis of historical and recent empirical data. Bruce, Wallis, and Wilson, to the contrary, stress the macro level: where religion has lost its overarching power over the secular sub-systems of society. With "a decline in the social power of once-dominant religious institutions whereby other social institutions ... have escaped from prior religious domination," Stark agrees, but he immediately adds: "[i]f this were all that secularization means, there would be nothing to argue about (1999: 252).

Is there nothing to argue about? What about the following questions: How did the secularization process on the macro level come about? What is its impact on religion and the religiosity of individuals? Is the sociologically inspired secularization perspective not also about "religious change" rather than merely about "the end of religion" (Demerath 1998: 8), a direction to which the work of Hervieu-Léger points (1998 and 1999)? And, what are the reactions of religious actors: do they endure the macro-changes or do they react against them and, if so, how? The preceding questions point to three levels of analysis: societal, organizational and individual. However, before dealing with these levels and their interrelationship, some preliminary remarks are due.

Since secularization is perceived as a process of social change, the concept predicates a "base-line." Certainly, this baseline may not be the degree of religiousness of the people, since the scholar has then to compare people in different situations: religious compulsion in the past compared to individual freedom at present (Le Bras 1963: 448–49; Delumeau 1975). The level of comparison must be the societal level: the age of religiously-prescribed social order, which, in the West, was the age of Innocent III (thirteenth century), when the Church controlled "the formal process of political, juridical, commercial, and social intercourse" (Wilson 1976: 9–10).

If secularization might produce not only the demise of religiosity but also the phenomenon of religious change, then we need an additional baseline, i.e. a definition of religion. I have argued that for the purpose of studying the process of secularization, we need a substantive, exclusive and real definition of religion which may read: a unified system of beliefs and practices relative to a supra-empirical, transcendent reality that unifies all those who adhere to it in a moral single community (Dobbelaere 1981: 35–38). Since religion itself is changing and adapting to changing social circumstances (Swatos/Christiano 1999: 224–25), we need to study the factors provoking that change: secularization might be just such a factor.

Finally, this contribution is limited to recent sociological studies on secularization. The founding fathers have not or only rarely used the term. Later generations of sociologists employed the term more frequently, but attached different meanings to it (Shiner 1967). Not until the late 1960s were several sociological *theories* of secularization developed, most prominently by Berger, Luckmann, and Wilson. These theories subsequently led to discussions about their validity and generality (e.g., Hammond 1985; Hadden 1989; Lechner 1991; Berger 1999). Since some criticisms failed to analyze the tenets, the hypotheses, the levels of analysis, the methodological issues, and the arguments of the theories, a more systematic examination was needed. Dobbelaere stressed the need to differentiate between levels of analysis—the macro or societal level, the meso or organizational level, and the micro or individual level—since the concept is multi-dimensional (1981), he indicated convergences and divergences between existing theories (1984) and discussed methodological issues involved in testing secularization theory (1989). Tschannen, on the other hand, pointed out the different "exemplars"[1] of what he calls the secularization paradigm (1992). In this contribution, I reassess the secularization theories by relating the different "exemplars,"[2] and by distinguishing between system levels, using the analytical distinction between segmentary and functional differentiation (Luhmann 1982: 262–65).

1 Exemplars or shared examples are central elements of a paradigm (Tschannen 1992: 20–21, 26; see also Kuhn 1970: 174–210).

2 To mark them, they are italicized in the text.

The Macro or Societal Level

Modern societies are primarily *differentiated* along *functional* lines and have developed different sub-systems (e.g. economy, polity, science, family, education). These sub-systems are similar—since, so to speak, society has equal need of them all—and dissimilar—since they perform their own particular function (production and distribution of goods and services; taking binding decisions; production of valid knowledge; procreation and mutual support; teaching). Their functional autonomy depends of course upon their environment and the communication with other functional systems. To guarantee these functions and to communicate with their environment, organizations have been established (enterprises; political parties; research centers; families; schools and universities). In each sub-system and in its relations with the environment, communication is based on the medium of the sub-system (money; power; truth; love; information and know-how). Each organization also functions according to the values of the sub-system (competition and success; separation of powers; reliability and validity; primacy of love; truth) and its specific norms.

Regarding religion, these organizations claim their autonomy and reject religiously prescribed rules, i.e. the *autonomization* of the sub-systems. For example, the separation of church and state; the development of science as an autonomous secular perspective; the rejection of church prescriptions about birth control and abortion; the emancipation of education from ecclesiastical authority; and the rejection of religious control over arts and literature. Diagnosing the loss of religion's influence on the secular sub-systems, members of the religious organizations were the first to talk about secularization or the emancipation of the secular. In this context, Luhmann speaks about secularization in the sense of a specifically religious conception of society as the environment of the religious sub-system (Luhmann 1977: 225–32). In other words, secularization describes the effect of functional differentiation for the religious sub-system and expresses the interpretation of this experience by religious personnel.

Thus, the sociological explanation of secularization starts with the process of functional differentiation: religion becomes a sub-system alongside other subsystems, losing in this process its overarching claims over the other sub-systems. In fact, it is only the particularization of the general process of functional differentiation in the religious subsystem. If secularization is only that, should we then retain the term? Since it points toward a specific social conflict, i.e. a religiously based resistance to functional differentiation, we may keep it as a purely *descriptive* concept (see also Chaves 1997: 443). Furthermore, modern, functionally highly differentiated societies, may have very different levels of secularization, i.e. different levels of differentiation between religion and the other sub-systems. Indeed, traditional structures may survive like churches functioning as civil religion, e.g. Anglicanism in England and Lutheranism in some Scandinavian countries; or the state may continue to pay directly the salaries of church personnel (Belgium for example); or, in a laicised[3] country like France continue to have an extensive Catholic school system.

Berger and Luckmann stressed a consequence of the process of functional differentiation and the autonomization of the secular spheres, to wit, the *privatization of religion*. According to Luckmann (1967: 94–106), the validity of religious norms became restricted to its "proper" sphere, i.e., that of private life. Berger (1967: 133) stressed the "functionality" of this "for the maintenance of the highly rationalised order of modern economic and political institutions," to wit, the public sphere. This dichotomy, private/public, carries with it at least two shortcomings (Dobbelaere 1981: 79–84). It suggests that secularization was limited to the so-called public sphere which is incorrect: family life was also secularized. This became very clear in the reactions of lay Catholics to the encyclical *Humanae Vitae* (1968). Married couples objected to the rules enunciated in the papal encyclical. They rejected the claim of the Church to define the goals of the family and to dictate the acceptable means to achieve these goals, in other words, they defended the differentiation of family and religion. Second, it is the adoption in sociological discourse of "ideological concepts" used by liberals and socialists in the nineteenth century to legitimate functional differentiation and the autonomization of so-called secular institutions: "religion is a private matter!"

Clearly, the dichotomy private/public is not a structural aspect of society. It is not a societal sub-system with institutionalized roles (professional versus public), as for example is the case in the economy (producers versus consumers), the educational system (teachers versus students), the polity (politicians versus voters), and the judicial system (magistrates and lawyers versus clients). It is rather a legitimizing conceptualization of the secular world, an ideological pair used in conflicts between opponents. Sociologists should, of course, study the use of this dichotomy in social discourse and conflicts, to analyze its strategic application by groups wanting to promote or to counter the secularization of the social system. These concepts were for example used by employees to defend their political, religious, or family options against possible sanctions and eventual dismissal by the management of Christian organizations, e.g., schools or hospitals, if they failed to behave according to ecclesiastical rules in matters of family life, politics or religion. Employees defended their "private" options, their "private" life, in what the managers of ecclesiastical organizations called the "public" sphere, since, according to them, these private options

3 Laicization is the process that manifestly secularizes the social system, secularization may also be a latent consequence, e.g. the result of the professionalization of the medical sector (Dobbelaere 1979).

were publicly known. The outcome of these conflicts was that managers had to accept the right to privacy of employees (Dobbelaere 1979: 54–55; 1982: 117–18, 121–23).

The private/public dichotomy is not a sociological conceptualization. In sociological discourse, this ideological pair should be replaced by Habermas' conceptual dichotomy: system versus life-world (1982: 229–93), used in a purely descriptive sense. It is in the systemic relations that societalization occurred, these relationships became secondary: formal, segmented, and utilitarian. By contrast, in the life-world—family, friends and social networks—primary relations are still the binding force, they are personal, total, sympathetic, trustful and considerate. The trend toward societalization is, for example, very clear in the distribution sector: neighborhood stores are more and more replaced by large department stores, where the interactions between customers and employees are limited to short informative questions and exchanges of money for goods. We will discuss below the process of societalization and its possible impact on the religiosity of individuals.

The Mesolevel: Functional Rationality and Its Consequences

The declining religious authority over the other sub-systems, i.e. their autonomization, allowed the development of *functional rationality*. The economy lost its religious ethos (Weber 1920: 163–206). Goals and means were evaluated on a cost-efficiency basis. This typical economic attitude implying observations, evaluations, calculation and planning—which is based on a belief that the world is calculable, predictable and controllable (Wilson 1976 and 1985)—is not limited to the economic system. The political system was also rationalized, leaving little room for traditional and charismatic authority. Economic production and distribution developed large-scale economic organizations in which Taylorism and Fayolism[4] were extensively applied, and modern states developed their rational administration. Since these structures needed more and more people who had been trained in science and rational techniques, the educational curriculum changed. A scientific approach to the world and the teaching of technical knowledge increasingly replaced a religious-literary formation. The development of scientifically-based techniques also had their impact

4 Frederic W. Taylor (1856–1915) promoted the scientific organisation of industrial work (taylorism) which is based on the specialisation of tasks and the elimination of unnecessary movement. His innovations led to the development of the assembly line. Henri Fayol (1841–1925) initiated reforms in the management of enterprises (fayolism), an aspect of modern business organisations that Taylor had neglected.

on the life-world: domestic tasks became increasingly mechanized and computerized. Even the most intimate human behavior, sexuality, became governed by it. This is also the case of the so-called natural method of birth control which the Catholic Church accepted. The Ogino-Knaus method, for example, is based on the basal temperature of the woman which she must register when she wakes up in the morning and then plot on a chart. On the basis of the temperature-curve, the fertile and infertile periods can be calculated. Clearly, it was on the basis of observation, calculation and evaluation that sexual intercourse could be planned to prevent pregnancy. Another example in the field of sexuality was the Masters and Johnson research to "enhance" sexual pleasure. It was based on experimentation, calculation, and evaluation, and sought to produce guidelines to ensure and augment sexual pleasure: sexuality became a technique which one could improve by better performances according to the published "technical rules." The consequences of these developments were the *disenchantment* of the world and the *societalization* of the sub-systems.

First, the disenchantment of the world. The world and the human body being increasingly considered to be calculable and man-made, the result of controlled planning (for example, by in vitro fertilization and through plastic surgery), engendered not only new roles, but also new, basically rational and critical, attitudes and a new cognition. Theses are replaced by hypotheses, the Bible by encyclopedia, revelation by knowledge. According to Acquaviva (1979), this new cognition has been objectified in a new language that changed the image of reality, thus eliminating "pre-logical," including religious, concepts. The mass media, using this new language, have radicalized this development and made it a social phenomenon. This suggests a possible impact of the changes in the social system on the micro level, i.e. the consciousness of the individual. People having internalized this new language, which produced a certain vision of the world, may, to a certain degree, have lost the vision of a sacred reality. For example when artificial insemination is shown on TV: technical interventions produce life and are discussed in a secular, technical language, reducing the sacredness of life.

Second, sub-systems were also societalized or became more *gesellschaftlich*. The organized world is "based on impersonal roles, relationships, the co-ordination of skills, and essentially formal and contractual patterns of behavior, in which personal virtue, as distinguished from role obligations, is of small consequence" (Wilson 1982: 155). In such systems, according to Wilson, control is no longer based on morals and religion, it has become impersonal, a matter of routine techniques and unknown officials—legal, technical, mechanized, computerized, and electronic—e.g. speed control by unmanned cameras and video control in department stores. Thus religion has lost one of its important latent functions: as long as control was interpersonal, it was founded on religiously-based mores and substantive values, e.g. sexual mores are now replaced by condoms. In Wilson's view, there is another argument why "secularization is a concomitant of societalization": since religion offers "redemption," which is personal, total, an "indivisible ultimate" unsusceptible to rational techniques or "cost-efficiency criteria," it has to be offered in a "community" (Wilson 1976), and the *Vergesellschaftung* has destroyed communal life.

The Meso Level: Reactions and Changes in the Religious Sub-system

Confronted with the secularization of the social system, some churches and sects have reacted with a counter-offensive. At the end of the nineteenth century, adapting to the modern world, a process of pillarization became institutionalized in the Western world to protect believers from the secular world, and in the twentieth century new religious movements also established pillars, even in social contexts existing beyond the Western world.[5] Pillars are organizational complexes that are religiously or ideologically legitimized, striving toward autarky or self-sufficiency. It is a form of segmental differentiation in a functionally differentiated society, which promotes exclusiveness and an in-group mentality. In the Netherlands, a Catholic and a Protestant pillar emerged, and Catholic pillars were gradually established in Austria, Belgium, Germany, Italy and Switzerland (Righart 1986). However, in the early second half of the twentieth century, the Dutch Catholic pillar started to totter, partly because of the internal crisis in the Dutch Catholic Church (Laeyendecker 1987, 1989), but, also under external pressures, among others, financial needs, which required mergers between Catholic, Protestant and non-religious schools, hospitals and welfare services, and state aid, that resulted in legal regulations and the professionalization of services (Thurlings 1978; Coleman 1979). The de-sacralization of the Christian pillars was a direct consequence of this evolution.

In Belgium, in response to the same internal and external causes, the Catholic pillar had to adapt to the changing situation. Mergers were not possible because of the antagonism between the Catholic, socialist and liberal pillars. To survive as a complex organization the Catholic pillar generalized its collective consciousness. Research has demonstrated that the core philosophy no longer consists of the strict religious rules of the Catholic Church, but rather refers to so-called typical values of the gospel such as social justice, a humane approach toward clients and patients, well-being, solidarity between social classes with special attention to marginal people, and *Gemeinschaftlichkeit*. These are values that have a universal appeal, and which are not specifically Chris-

5 Good examples are the Seventh-Day Adventist Church for the sectarian movements, and Scientology and Soka Gakkai (a non-Western new religious movement) for the new religious movements (Dobbelaere 2000a and 2000b: 233–56).

tian. However, by backing them up with a religious source, the gospels, and occasionally solemnizing them with religious ritual, they acquired a sacred aura. This new collective consciousness is still symbolized by a "C," referring to Christian, that is evangelical, instead of to Catholic, the latter being considered to have a more restricted appeal and to be more confining. This "Sociocultural Christianity" functions now as the sacred canopy for the segmented Catholic world of olden days (Dobbelaere/Voyé 1990: 6–8; Laermans 1992: 204–14). Here we have an example of what Chaves calls an ongoing process of *organizational secularization*, i.e. secularization on the meso level, which should be differentiated from *societal* secularization, the macro level, and *individual* secularization, the micro level (1994, and 1997: 445–47). However, the Catholic Church did not give up and still fights secularization. In recent years, it has called for a second evangelization of Europe, and Opus Dei, an organization which endeavors to de-secularize the different sub-systems, became a personal prelature. This special status relates Opus Dei directly to the Vatican, and where it operates, confers on it independence of local bishops.

Another major change in the religious sub-system has been the growing *pluralization* of religious organizations which has resulted in a religious market, where different religions either compete for the souls of the people or make agreements not to proselytize, as the Anglican church has agreed with the Catholic Church in Belgium. Such pluralism and competition augment the relativity of the respective religious messages, or in Berger's terms "it relativises their religious contents," their religious message is "de-objectivated," and more generally, "the pluralistic situation … *ipso facto* plunges religion into a crisis of credibility" (1967: 150–51). We will return to this issue when discussing the micro level.

The emergence of new religious movements is related to the process of globalization and intercontinental mobility, but also, as I have argued before (Dobbelaere 1999: 235–36), to the process of secularization that undermined the credibility of the "Christian collective consciousness." The slowly perceived lack of impact of Christian religions on the societal level, expressed in the loss of status and power of its representatives, allowed exotic religions to improve their position on the religious market. Some new religious movements, such as the Unification Church, the Family, and ISKCON, wanted to re-sacralize the world and its institutions by bringing God back into the different groups operating in different sub-systems like the family, the economy, and even the polity. Wallis (1984) has called these "world rejecting new religions." However, the vast majority are of another type, they are "world affirming." They offer their members esoteric means for attaining immediate and automatic assertiveness, heightened spirituality, recovery, success and a clear mind. Mahikari provides an "omitama" or amulet; Transcendental Meditation (TM) a personal mantra for meditation; Scientology auditing with an e-meter; Human Potential movements offer therapies, encounter groups or alternative health and spiritual centers; Soka Gakkai promotes chanting of an invocation before a mandala, the Gohonzon; while Elan Vital offers the knowledge revealed by Maharaji or one of his appointed instructors.

Luckmann has rightly argued that in many new religious movements the level of transcendence was lowered, they had become *"this worldly"* or *mundane* (1990). The historical religions, to the contrary, are examples of "great transcendences," referring to something other than everyday reality, notwithstanding the fact that they were also involved in mundane or "this-worldly" affairs. However, the reference was always transcendental, e.g. the incantations for healing, for success in examinations or work, or for "une ame soeur." Most world-affirming new religious movements appear to reach *only* the level of "intermediate transcendences." They bridge time and space, promote inter-subjective communication, but remain at the immanent level of everyday reality. Consequently, some, like TM, claim to be spiritual rather than religious movements. Calling new religious movements spiritual or religious, is not important, what matters is that we register a change: the ultimate has become "this-worldly."

Referring to my baseline definition of religion, the registered change should be conceived as a form of organizational secularization: in these religious organizations, the sacred is no longer a "great transcendence." Contrary to my definition of religion, the substantive element in the implicit definition of religion used by Swatos and Christiano is the "sacred" (1999). They suggest that reason was the sacred element of the "new religion" that "emerged in the Enlightenment" and suggest that post-modernity expresses "the disenchantment of that sacrality the Enlightenment gave to Reason." Following Marsden, they call that "the secularization of secularism" (Swatos/Christiano 1999: 225). So they call the "new religion" of reason "secularism" and the emergence of the "new spirituality today," e.g. the new religious movements, its secularization. In so doing, they confirm my position, although they seek to distance themselves from secularization theory. Even when we take a functional definition of religion, we may come to the same conclusion. Luhmann stated that "the problem of simultaneity of indefiniteness and certainty" is the typical function of religion (1977: 46). Indeed, most of these world-affirming new religions are not concerned with the problems of *simultaneity* of transcendence and immanence since they focus only on the immanent, on everyday life, on the secular. They are adapted to the secular world.

Mundane orientations of religion are not new. Berger and Luckmann have suggested that the higher church attendance in America compared to Europe might be explained by the mundane orientation of religion in America. Luckmann (1967: 36–37) called it internal secularization; "a radical inner change in American church religion … today the secular ideas of the American Dream pervade church religion." In asserting that American churches were "becoming highly secularized themselves" (Berger 1967: 108) these authors sought to reconcile empirical findings at the individual level, i.e. church attendance, which appeared to conflict with secularization theories, by pointing out changes at the organizational level, i.e. within the churches. The point of interest for our argument is that the idea of organizational secularization is not new: the concept of "internal secularization" was its predecessor.

Pluralization and Generalization: The Macro and Meso Level in Relationship

Parsons (1967) has argued that pluralization, or the segmentary differentiation within the sub-system religion, was possible in the Western world only once the Christian ethic was institutionalized in the so-called secular world, in other words, once the Christian ethic was generalized. Consequently, this would imply that pluralization may not be taken as an indicator of secularization, quite the contrary (see also Lechner 1991: 1109–10). However, this relationship is not unidirectional: growing pluralization may augment the necessity for generalization. Indeed, Parsons, Bellah (1967) and Martin have stressed the need for a civil religion, i.e. "a national myth which represents a common denominator of all faiths: one nation under God" (Martin 1978: 36) to preserve the unity of the nation. Such myths, such legitimations are not always religious: civil religion is one possibility, there are also secular myths like the French myth based on *la laïcité* which legitimizes the French republic, its schools and laws. A reversal is also possible: a religion replacing a secular myth: the role of the Russian Orthodox Church in rebuilding the nation after the implosion of the communist myth. However, is a myth always needed? Secular laws overarching divergent religiously inspired mores in pluralistic countries may suffice, for example secular laws overarching the Islamic (Shari'a) and Christian mores as far as family life is concerned.

What explains the emergence or re-emergence of a "religious" rather than a "secular" myth, and vice versa? And, more generally, what explains how such a secular or religious myth emerges? Fenn (1978: 41–53) suggests that this is possible only when a society conceives itself as a "nation," as a "really 'real'"— typical examples are USA, Japan (Dobbelaere 1986), and France—, to the contrary, the myth is rather seen as a cultural "fiction" to the extent that a society sees itself as an arena for conflicting and co-operative activities of various classes, race, groups, corporations, and organizations. Another issue for inquiry is how, and to what extent, a conventional religion may, in certain religiously pluralistic societies, function as civil religion, e.g., Anglicanism in England and Lutheranism in some Scandinavian countries. What degree of pluralism is congruent with a church fulfilling the role of civil religion? And how is the disestablishment of a conventional religion, e.g., Lutheranism in Sweden, which traditionally functioned as a civil religion, to be explained?

The Micro Level: The Impact of Secularization on the Individual

Many researchers refer to the micro-level when they argue against typifying modern society as secularized. They oppose the United States to Europe or refer to the global society, i.e. the world (Hadden 1989; Stark 1999). However, if one takes the sociological point of view seriously, i.e., that sociological analysis starts at the macro level, then church practice is not a valid indicator with which to evaluate the process of secularization. Berger is right: "secularization on the societal level is not necessarily linked to secularization on the level of individual consciousness" (1999: 3). The sociological analytic question should be: what is the impact of societal secularization on church practice, orthodoxy and the ethical opinions of individuals? Can we isolate the impact of societal secularization from other factors—such as individualism—on individual church behavior? Further, what is the impact of societal secularization on religious organizations? And, are the so-called conflicting theories: secularization and rational choice discordant or are they rather complimentary?

Let me start by comparing these two theoretical perspectives since this question is very much alive and informative papers have been published on the topic, dealing, for example, with the value of deductive-predictive versus descriptive-explanatory theorizing (Beyer 1998). I would like to take the opportunity to suggest a bridge between rational choice and secularization theories, both of which I call theoretical since deductive theorizing is not the standard of good theory, contrary to Stark's position (1997: 4–6). If, in order to stimulate religious responses by active competition between religious firms on the supply side, rational choice theory, extended in a supply and demand perspective, needs a de-regulated market which promotes pluralism (Stark 1997: 17–18), then it is simply suggesting that it only functions in a secularized society. This is, namely, a circumstance in which religion is differentiated from the state, i.e. where the state regulates the religious market less and less by no longer suppressing rival religions (which is the reverse of what is going on now in France, see Introvigne/Melton 1996) and by stopping subsidizing selected religious groups (which is contrary to the actual situation in Belgium where the state subsidizes six recognized religions)—in other words, where the state does not limit the supply-side (Finke 1997: 50–52). However, in order to work, the rational choice theory seems to assume a latent or implicit stable religious demand in humans which the supply-side may make manifest by competition. Actual research does not permit us to evaluate that assumption. To test it, we need more research and to differentiate conceptually between participation in institutional religion—as manifested in practice, beliefs and ethics—and the latent variable religiosity or spirituality conceived as a latent demand for religion, which, according to rational choice theory, will become manifest by strongly competing religious firms. However, the type of religiosity we should document should be based on transcendental beliefs, since it has to offer "general compensators" (Stark 1997: 7). Thus, we need a definition the substantive element of which is transcendental (cf. supra pp. 230 and 237) and not the "sacred," as found in the definition of Swatos and Christiano (1999), since outside religion there are many sacred things (Demerath 2000): indeed, the sacred is also immanent.

The connection between rational choice and secularization theories can be seen in the study by Chaves and Cann (1992). The supply approach hypothesis that established church state relations promotes monopolistic laziness, since direct state subsidies and benefits diminish the need for competition between religion organizations to grow or survive; to the contrary, when state-church relations are de-established, i.e. functionally differentiated, or the state is secularized, religious institutions have to compete for "scares goods," i.e. believers who support them. In their study, Chaves and Cann measured de-regulation of the religious market in eighteen Western countries and related it to church practice. They demonstrated that "the mechanisms specified by religious market theory are *not* limited to Protestant countries but are operative in Catholic countries as well" (1992: 287–88). However, they register a higher level of church participation in Catholic than in Protestant countries even after controlling for the degree of state regulation, which leaves room for non-economic variables. This is true for the case of France for which the model predicts an attendance rate of 38 percent compared to an observed rate of 12 percent. Referring to Martin's *General Theory of Secularization* (1978) they stressed political factors to explain the French case (1992: 288). Indeed, typical of France is the process of laicization, i.e. a manifestly enforced process of secularization during at least two centuries by the republicans against the reactionaries with whom the Church allied. This conflict produced a profound split over religion per se in the country, on the national level as well as on the local and family level: republicans versus *intégristes*, schoolmaster against *curé*, father against mother (Martin 178: 36–41). Chaves and Cann's study clearly indicates that the two theories are complementary and not contradictory.

Other studies have directly tried to test the secularization theory: some are more qualitative case studies, and consequently restricted to particular communities or regions, others are surveys and cover one or several countries facilitating comparisons between regions, countries and religions. The first type permits an analysis of individual and group actions in studying the issues involved. The second type facilitates the investigation of system differences and the analysis of the impact of structural and cultural differences. I will discuss them in the two following paragraphs.

Human Actions on the Micro Level

Hiernaux and Voyé directed a study of Catholics in French speaking Belgium who intended to have a religious burial. About one hundred in depth interviews were carried out with men and women, ranging from 25 to 65 years of age. Part of the interviews centered around the religious ritual, and these interviews were further supplemented by participant observation (Voyé 1998: 288–96). According to these observations and interviews, "the priest is no longer the grand commander of the rite faced with a passive congregation," he "is now very often relegated to the role of performer." "Either he just carries out the orders of the funeral director,[6] or when the families have a relatively high socio-cultural status, the priest performs in a scenario designed by the closest relatives of the deceased" (Voyé 1998: 291). According to Voyé, this shows that the deceased is first and foremost a member of a close emotional network and not of the Christian community, which is confirmed by the fact that the overwhelming majority of persons present at the ritual were family, friends and colleagues of the deceased and of his or her close family members, and no longer, as was the case in the past, members of the parish community.

It is also very interesting to note that the traditional Catholic rite has changed, which was partly favored by the recourse to the vernacular. When Latin was used in ritual and hymns, the priest had the central role. He used standardized formulae, which he knew and understood, creating a distance between daily life and afterlife: the ritual was centered upon the life to come and the mystery surrounding it. Now the ritual is centered upon the deceased: his life, his loves and friendships, his accomplishments. the texts read, the songs and the music played, are chosen by the family with reference to the deceased. If religious texts and hymns are used, they are chosen to express the qualities of the deceased and not because they refer to God. Quite often, "God is never brought up—except in the rare sacramental words pronounced by the priest" (Voyé 1998: 292–93). The change here was favored by the use of the vernacular, but the authors of the changes that are occurring, are not the professionals of the religious institution, but the funeral directors or the close family, who de-sacralize the ritual and bring about organizational secularization.

A study by Demerath and Williams (1992) allows us to point towards the actors, the composition of the movement and the tactics used, in a sacralizing counterthrust in a New England city where secularization was however the dominant tendency. Homelessness, black neighborhood development, abortion and sex education were the three instances in which religion played a critical

6 The funeral director "'tells me what to do and say ... and he's the one who pays me', said a priest in Brussels" (Voyé 1998: 291).

role. The sacralizing counterweight within the community's political arena was provided by minority movements, which were "more likely to share a basic ecumenism rather than a zealous religious particularism." They "took up specific issues in a kind of single-interest politics," and were rather "*ad hoc* movements" and, consequently, "smaller, more flexible" but also "less enduring" than the "established church structures," which served "as staunch bulwarks of the mainstream and the status quo." In fact, none of the conventional churches, synagogues, or other religious organizations were involved as major protagonists in the different issues. The Catholic religious personnel and clergy of various faiths were "acting more on their own initiative than as formal representatives of their basic communities," and in one of the issues "several of these clergy found themselves at odds with home congregations over their tactics and belligerent behavior." Indeed, they "are far more likely than their secular opponents to take on the shrill tone and extreme tactics of the true believer." The "resources mobilized" for effective action in taking the issues to the public, were "cultural" rather than "structural," to wit "sacred cultural images and arguments which had retained some currency even in a secularizing religious economy" and "moral fundamentals" (Demerath/Williams 1992: 201–205).

This study also allows us to emphasize that secularization is not a mechanical, evolutionary process. It is quite often the result of conflicts over particular issues in which opposing movements with religious, a-religious or anti-religious ideologies are involved. However, the changes, in one or the other direction, are not always the result of manifest actions, they may also come about as the result of certain actions which latently produce a secularizing effect. A good example of this is shown in a study done by Voyé on Christmas decorations in a Walloon village in Belgium (1998: 299–303). Two decades ago, Isambert had already underscored the increasing slide from "the scriptural and liturgical basis of the Nativity, which is altogether oriented towards the Incarnation and Redemption, which it precedes" toward "the Christchild" (1992:196). Indeed, the Christchild is placed at the center of the familial Christmas-celebrations and also in the decorations displayed by the city authorities. In this Walloon village, however, the decorations evoke a further sliding away: signboards, many meters square, erected on the lawns in front of the houses and illuminated in the evening, represented Walt Disney cartoon characters. "It is for the children," said the couple who started it all, "December is the children's month, with [the feast of] St-Nicolas [early December] and Christmas" (Voyé 1998: 299). At the time of Voyé's interviews, when she asked why they didn't set up a manger scene, the couple who initiated the display of signboards and who tried to co-ordinate it, answered: "some neighbors are thinking about it … but we told them 'If we put a manger scene, we've got to find among the Disney characters a couple of animals who have a little one. Because we, well we want to stick with the Walt Disney characters. Or at least with characters of the same type ... we don't want to do like in X, the first village in which this type of thing was done: they put up Walt Disney characters too; but last year, they changed the theme, they took film characters ... " (Voyé 1998: 300). Here Christmas is not only child oriented, but as Voyé rightfully underscores: "With the Disney characters, we are no longer in History, but in the fairytale and the domain of the marvelous. [Fairytales] peopled with fictive beings" (1998: 302). These decorations convey implicitly the idea that Christmas is a marvelous fairytale, a nice story (in the village that uses film characters), far removed from the original Incarnation-Redemption idea that the religious message of Christmas carries. By putting up these decorations, people latently secularize the Christian message.

The preceding studies indicate different types of actors—professionals and rank and file citizens—who are manifestly or latently involved in the process of promoting secularization and sacralization. The sacralizing forces may be religious individuals who are not backed by the mainline religions. Such studies, also evidence that, to have a direct or indirect effect on the process of secularization, the issues do not have to be religious, e.g. homelessness and a black neighborhood development. More such studies, and studies not merely from the Western world, are needed before we will be able to make a synthesis of individual and group actions implied in issues that have a (de-)secularizing effect on our societies.

The Impact of Social and Structural Differences on the Micro Level

Functional differentiation causing the autonomization of the subsystems promoted the development of functional rationality, which, as was argued above, promoted the societalization of systemic relations. What is the impact of these processes on the religiosity of the people?

Empirical research records a growing unbelief and a decline in the belief in the Christian notion of "God as a person" (see Halman/de Moor 1993; Dobbelaere/Jagodzinski 1995: 210–14). Durkheim's sociology of religion and knowledge gives us a clue to relate these features of individual religiosity—the micro-level—to the meso and macro changes. It is my contention (Dobbelaere 1995: 177–81)—in keeping with Durkheim (1915), Swanson (1960), and other sociologists and anthropologists—that people develop a concept of personified supernatural beings directly from the model which their society provides. But, as Swanson added, any satisfactory explanation should not only account for faith, it should explain disbelief as well. He suggests, among other factors, that "[t]he assumption that all, or the most significant features of ... [primordial and constitutional] structures [of society], are knowable and controllable by human effort," will produce disbelieve (Swanson 1960: 188–89).

Well then, functional rationality promoted an attitude in people that either they themselves or specialists could solve their problems, as they took command of their physical, social, and psychological worlds, which removed God more and more from those worlds and stimulated unbelief. However, if for some people the notion of God lingers on, God is more and more conceived of as a general power and not as "person," a spirit, "something" vague and general, a "higher power" and not as a "personal God." How could God be thought of as a "personal God" if, outside the life-world, people experience fewer and fewer "personal relationships", systemic interactions being based on impersonal roles? If they can no longer believe in "God as a person," they drop out of Christian rituals, since these rituals are centered on a relationship with "God as a person"—the Father and the Son. Consequently, with growing unbelief, the number of unchurched people augments, and the involvement in the churches of believers diminishes if they can not believe any more in "God as a person." These consequences have been clearly established in our contribution to the study *Beliefs in Government* (Jagodzinski/Dobbelaere 1995: 87–95).

Another approach to the analysis of the impact of the macro- and meso-level on the micro-level was used by W. Jagodzinski in one of our contributions to the study *Beliefs in Government* (Jagodzinski/Dobbelaere 1995). We hypothesized that in more rationalized countries church disengagement would be more advanced. The study was based on interview data gathered in 1981 and 1990 by the European Values Studies (in Belgium, France, West Germany, Great Britain, Ireland, Italy, the Netherlands and Spain), and in Denmark and Norway. Four alternative measures of level of church integration were computed: the percentage of unaffiliated people; the percentage of nuclear church members; the median integration; and the logarithm of the geometric mean (mean integration), which was calculated from a metric version of the church attendance scale. As an indirect indicator of rationalization we took the Gross Domestic Product (GDP) per capita, correcting for different inflation and exchange rates by measuring the GDP per capita in standard Purchasing Power Units (PPU). The relationship was examined with the help of a regression analysis. Warning that this regression analysis should be taken as a parsimonious description of the relationship and not as a statistical test, we stated that the comparison between countries and the aggregate level analysis provided evidence in favor of the rationalization hypothesis. The signs of the regression coefficients were always in the expected direction: "church integration declines with economic rationalization." Therefore, we concluded, that "in our view, these comparisons … offer the most convincing evidence in favor of the Weberian secularization hypothesis," i.e. the rationalization hypothesis (Jagodzinski/Dobbelaere 1995: 101).

Halman (1991: 258–59) also tested the impact of secularization on individuals, however, his approach was different. He calculated the degree of correlation between, on the one hand, the religious values of a person, and, on the other hand, his or her political and moral values and those related to the life-world, in reference to the level of structural modernization in ten European countries, Canada, and the USA. The data used were collected with the questionnaire of the European Values Study. In general, the political and moral values, and those related to the life-world of individuals were the most independent of religious values in the more modern countries.

My hypothesis deduced from the work of Durkheim and Swanson was never rigidly tested, and the other approaches have worked with proxies and have never directly tested the hypothesized effect of a secularized societal environment on religious attitudes, beliefs and behavior of people. Such an analysis should imply a comparison between countries according to their level of functional differentiation of the different sub-systems from religion, i.e. according to their level of secularization. Mark Chaves' scale of de-regulation, measuring the differentiation of Church and State in a country, is a very good example of the type of measures that should be developed (Chaves/Cann 1992: 280). One might then check if higher levels of secularization on the country level produce higher degrees of *compartmentalization* of religious values as against the other values: this is what Halman did. Thus, one might measure whether there is a higher degree of segregation on the level of the individual conscience of religious values and political, economic, familial, scientific, and other values in countries with a higher degree of secularization. In other words, do individuals think and act along the same functionally differentiated lines as the functionally differentiated social system is structured? Empirically one should then be able to differentiate people along a scale of a more or less compartmentalized worldview. Such a scale might then be used to measure the impact of compartmentalization on the different dimensions of personal religiosity: religious practices, beliefs, experiences and ethical views. This would enable researchers to measure the impact of the process of secularization on the religiosity of the people by way of compartmentalization. The causal line sequence of reasoning along this line is: different degrees of societal secularization produce different degrees of compartmentalized personal worldviews, and these in turn produce different degrees of religious involvement. However, one should be aware that an inverse relationship may also exist: less religious people compartmentalizing their worldviews, which in turn may incite them to stimulate the disappearance of so-called vestiges from the past: persisting links between religion and some of the other subsystems—for example, a religious educational network in a laicized country such as France where an extensive network of Catholic schools still exists. Consequently, research is able to demonstrate only a functional and not a causal relationship. It seems to me that this is the functional nexus which might still be demonstrated along the lines of secularization theory (Dobbelaere 2002: 169–72).

With the recent comparative studies undertaken in *Europe (Religious and Moral Pluralism* conducted in eleven countries, and the *European Values Study* concluded in almost all European countries), researchers should be able to test this functional nexus. Up to the present, I have been able to test only the impact of compartmentalization on religious beliefs, practices and attitudes with the Belgian European Values Study-data of 1999 (Dobbelaere/Voyé: 2000: 146–49, 152). In order to do this, a composite index, called normative integration in the Catholic Church, was constructed on the basis of church involvement, religiosity, orthodoxy, and rites of passage; compartmentalization was measured with the answers to questions expressing the person's view of the relationship of religion and politics.[7] This analysis shows that individuals with a more compartmentalized view on religion and politics were the least integrated in the Catholic Church, confirming our theoretical line of reasoning. Second, and very important, independently of compartmentalization, other factors—generation, work situation combined with gender, and post-materialism—also had a negative, all in all lesser impact on church integration. This indicates that there are factors other than secularization that influence the level of church integration, which allows us to restate convincingly that church integration is not a valid indicator of secularization since other factors also have a negative impact on church integration: it is at best a proxy.

The Micro Level: Conservatism and Religious Bricolage

Secularization does not always lead to unbelief and irreligiosity: orthodox, fundamental, or traditional religion "are on the rise almost everywhere": Evangelicalism, not only in the United States, orthodoxy, and conservatism in the major religions (Berger 1999: 6), indicate that counter-secularization is an important phenomenon to be analyzed. In the Muslim world, the Islamic resurgence opposes modern ideas, and seeks to restore a distinctive Islamic life-style that is strongly anti-modern. To the contrary, the fast spreading Evangelical Protestantism in Latin America has characteristics that may stimulate modernization: rejecting subservience to the hierarchy (typical of traditional Catholicism) and traditional *machismo*, women are often in charge of congregation; advancing literacy to promote reading of the Bible; and acquiring the skills necessary for leading a congregation. Pentecostalism in Latin America may promote the integration of lower classes in the mainstream of society as sectarian movements have done in the past, in the United States, Africa and elsewhere (Johnson 1961; Wilson 1974).

7 "Politicians who do not believe in God are unfit for public office" (q. 39, A); "It would be better for Belgium if more people with strong religious beliefs held public office" (q. 39, C); "Religious leaders should not influence how people vote" (q. 39, B), and "should not influence government decisions" (q. 39, D). People could answer strongly agree, agree, neither agree nor disagree, disagree, and strongly disagree.

Some interesting research questions emerge here. How is it to be explained that some anti-modernist movements have a religious overtone and others not? How may we explain the origin of the resurgence of conservative religion world-wide? Berger suggests two possible answers. The uncomfortable state of uncertainty following the emergence of modernity that undermines the "taken-for-granted certainties by which peopled lived through most of history," and the resentment by many who are not part of the elite which carries this "purely secular view of reality," but who feel nevertheless its influence, "most troublingly, as their children are subjected to an education that ignores or even directly attacks their own beliefs and values" (1999: 11). This promotes a further intriguing question: will such movements survive if the coming generations are integrated in the main culture? Of course, there always will be a category of non-integrated citizens whom these religious movements may help, but then, their latent function may well be to comfort the disinherited and to help some to climb the social ladder who ultimately may become very secular. The study of secularizing and counter-secularizing forces is only in its early stages and requests in-depth studies rather than impressionistic commentaries which are at the most hypotheses.

Another consequence of secularization is religious *bricolage* (Luckmann 1979: 134–36). Although bricolage or religion *à la carte* is not entirely new: patchwork of institutional and popular religious beliefs and practices mixed with superstitions has existed since time immemorial in the Western world (see e.g. Verlinden 1999: 133–36), however, the character of the bricolage, the patchwork, or the recomposition has changed. In olden times, the churches were able to impose their doctrines, at least publicly. What people thought we may only guess, but they would never publicly proclaim a religion *à la carte*. Now bricolage is publicly accepted, notwithstanding the official opposition of churches. Indeed, with the shift from class to functional differentiation, there was at the same time a switch in dominance from a *normative* to a *cognitive* mode of responding to "disappointed expectations." In a class society the upper strata, supported by the churches, could normatively control the lower strata, in a functionally differentiated society this is no longer possible (Luhmann 1975).

A cognitive mode imposes reflexivity which forces people to reformulate their beliefs and to adapt their practices in function of new circumstances and new knowledge. Religious pluralism offers new insights, while at the same time undermining the credibility of all religions. Consequently, people construct their religious worldview, if they still do, by mixing, on the one hand, institutional and popular religious beliefs and practices, and superstitions (as in former times), and, on the other hand, beliefs (e.g. reincarnation) and practices (e.g. yoga) from other religions (see for a typical example: Verlinden 1999: 83–98). Bibby has described such a mixture in Canada (1987: 62–85), and a similar situation has been recorded in, among other countries, Switzerland (Krüggeler 1992), France (Hervieu-Léger 1995: 159–60), and Nordic countries (Sundbach

1995: 100). In a study of Belgian Christians *"am Rande,"* Voyé suggested that individual religiosity is characterized by the "end of Great Narratives," a "mixing of codes" and a certain "re-enchantment of the World." The mixing of codes is reflected in the religious field in a threefold manner: references and practices blending the institutional and the popular; occasional borrowings from scientific discourses as well as from religious sources; and inspiration sought in diverse religions, notably, oriental religions (1995: 199–204, esp. 201).

Secularization—a Western Phenomenon?

It is sometimes suggested that secularization is a typical Western phenomenon. A synthetic study by Pace demonstrates that secularization on the societal level is also occurring in the Muslim world (1998). He distinguishes two processes: "secularization from above, and that which stems from a drive towards modernization especially on the part of the younger generation" (Pace 1998: 168). In the first process, the unyoking of politics from religious factors started at the end of last century and gained momentum from the 1950s on, after the end of colonial domination. There was either a complete and traumatic break with the religious tradition—e.g. as caused by Kemal Atatürk and the Ba'th party in Syria and Iraq, which provoked the development of strong fundamentalist movements—or, a transfer of functions of religion to the field of politics—e.g. in North Africa and the Indian sub-continent. "A variety of political solutions were adopted. ... But they all boil down to the same basic problem of modernity: how to build a modern state with an economy capable of competing in the international market, an independent administrative apparatus (public offices, schools, social services, hospitals etc.), a power basis for the leaderships founded on what is traditionally regarded as 'political' ... The ultimate goal is to turn the religious unity of the *Umma* (the community of the believers) into a resource for establishing political consensus, by secularizing, so to speak, the religious capital accumulated over time and which forms an integral part of the collective consciousness" (Pace 1998: 168–69).

In the second process—secularization from below—there is a change in attitudes towards the Islamic tradition, which has been fossilized since the fifteenth century. The process of modernization as regards this fossilization of mentality and customs is being promoted by four conflicts, which have produced a secularization of customs among the younger generation (Pace 1998: 170–73). First, the conflict between country and city: the latter having created new classes, who have a different attitude to religious traditions and who are more willing to accept new choices and values. Second the conflict over the patriarchal model contested by sons and daughters, especially in North Africa. Third, the access of women to professions, which has weakened "ancient bonds which limited women's social activity to the confined space of the home or the *hammam* (the public baths)," however, without liberating them from their ancient submission, "in many cases, the 'double presence' has resulted in a double burden and a duplication of subservient roles at home and at work" (Pace 1998: 171). Finally, emigration has affected the Islamic models of family, reproduction, education, society and religion of both the emigrants and of those who stayed behind who compare themselves with their emigrated children, relatives or friends (Pace 1998: 171–72).

Pace's study allows us to see the interrelationship between "secularization from above," the macro level, and "secularization from below," the micro level: each is supportive of the other. His study also points out that secularization does not seem to be limited to the Christian world. However, more studies from beyond the Western world are needed to validate this point.

Conclusions

In re-assessing secularization theories from a sociological point of view, I stressed the need to differentiate between levels of analysis. This enables us to see that secularization is only the particularization of the process of functional differentiation for the religious sub-system and a macro-level phenomenon. This approach allows us also to discuss the processes involved on each level and to analyze on the intra- and interlevel the interrelationships between the processes. Finally, it allows us to see the different types of studies that are still needed in order to evaluate the consequences of a secularized social system on the micro- or individual level. The stringent test of the theory can be made only on the basis of international comparative research extending beyond the Western world, which, however, as has been pointed out, does not exclude the need for qualitative research on the level of local communities.

Bibliography

Acquaviva, S.S. (1979), *The Decline of the Sacred in Industrial Society*. Oxford: Blackwell.

Bellah, R.N. (1967), "Civil Religion in America," in: *Daedalus* (96) 1: 1–21.

Berger, P.L. (1967), *The Sacred Canopy: Elements of a Sociological Theory of Religion*. Garden City, N.J.: Doubleday.

— (1999), "The Desecularization of the World. A Global Overview," in: P. Berger, ed., *The Desecularization of the World*. Grand Rapids, Mich.: Eerdmans: 1–18.

Beyer, P. (1998), "Sociological Theory of Religion between Description and Prediction: A Weberian Question Revisited," in: R. Laermans/B. Wilson/J. Billiet, eds., *Secularization and Social Integration*. Leuven: Leuven University Press.

Bibby, R.W. (1987), *Fragmented Gods: The Poverty and Potential of Religion in Canada*. Toronto: Irwin Publishing.

Chaves, M. (1994), "Secularization as Declining Religious Authority," in: *Social Forces* (72) 3: 749–74.

— (1997), "Secularization: A Luhmannian Reflection," in: *Soziale Systeme* (3) 2: 439–49.

Chaves, M./Cann, D.E. (1992), "Regulation, Pluralism, and Religious Market Structure: Explaining Religion's Vitality," in: *Rationality and Society* (4) 3: 272–90.

Coleman, J.A. (1978), *The Evolution of Dutch Catholicism: 1958–1974*. Berkeley, Calif.: University of California Press.

Delumeau, J. (1975), "Déchristianisation ou nouveau modèle de christianisme?," in: *Archives de sciences sociales des religions* (20) 4: 3–20.

Demerath III, N.J. (1998), "Secularization Disproved or Displaced?," in: R. Laermans/B. Wilson/J. Billiet, eds., op. cit.: 7–9.

— (2000), "The Varieties of Sacred Experience: Finding the Sacred in a Secular Grove," in: *Journal for the Scientific Study of Religion* (39) 1: 1–11.

Demerath II, N.J./Williams, R.H. (1992), "Secularization in a Community Context: Tensions of Religion and Politics in a New England City," in: *Journal for the Scientific Study of Religion* 31 (2): 189–206.

Dobbelaere, K. (1979), "Professionalization and Secularization in the Belgian Catholic Pillar," in: *Japanese Journal of Religious Studies* (6) 1–2: 39–64.

— (1981), "Secularization: A Multi-dimensional Concept," in: *Current Sociology* (29) 2: 1–213.

— (1982), "Contradictions between Expressive and Strategic Language in Policy Documents of Catholic Hospitals and Welfare Organizations: Trials Instead of Liturgies as Means of Social Control," in: *The Annual Review of the Social Sciences of Religion* 6: 107–31.

— (1984), "Secularization Theories and Sociological Paradigms: Convergences and Divergences," in: *Social Compass* (31) 2–3: 199–219.

— (1986), "Civil Religion and the Integration of Society: A Theoretical Reflection and an Application," in: *Japanese Journal of Religious Studies* (13) 2–3: 127–46.

— (1989), "The Secularization of Society? Some Methodological Suggestions," in: J.K. Hadden/A. Shupe, eds., *Religion and the Political Order*. Vol. 3: *Secularization and Fundamentalism Reconsidered*. New York: Paragon House: 27–44.

— (1995), "The Surviving Dominant Catholic Church in Belgium. A Consequence of Its Popular Religious Practices?," in: W.C. Roof/J.W. Carroll/D.A. Roozen, eds., *The Post-war Generation and Establishment Religion: Cross-cultural Perspectives*. Boulder Colo.: Westview Press: 171–90.

— (1999), "Towards an Integrated Perspective of the Processes Related to the Descriptive Concept of Secularization," in: *Sociology of Religion* (60) 3: 229–47.

— (2000a), "The Rationale of Pillarization: The Case of Minority Movements," in: *Journal of Contemporary Religion* (15) 2: 181–99.

— (2000b), "Toward a Pillar Organization?," in: D. Machacek/B. Wilson, eds., *Global Citizens: The Soka Gakkai Buddhist Movement in the World*. Oxford: Oxford University Press: 233–56.

— (2002), *Secularization: An Analysis at Three Levels*. Bruxelles: Peter Lang.

Dobbelaere, K./Jagodzinski, W. (1995), "Religious Cognitions and Beliefs," in: J.W. van Deth/E. Scarbrough, eds., *Beliefs in Government*. Vol. 4: *The Impact of Values*. Oxford: Oxford University Press: 197–217.

Dobbelaere, K./Voyé, L. (1990), "From Pillar to Postmodernity: The Changing Situation of Religion in Belgium," in: *Sociological Analysis* (51) S: 1–13.

— (2000), "Religie en kerkbetrokkenheid: ambivalentie en ververvreemding," in: K. Dobbelaere et al., eds., *Verloren zekerheid: de Belgen en hun waarden, overtuigingen en opvattingen*. Tielt: Lannoo: 119–51.

Durkheim, E. (1915), *The Elementary Forms of the Religious Life*, translated by J.W. Swain. NewYork: Macmillan.

Fenn, R.K. (1978), *Toward a Theory of Secularization*. Storrs, Conn.: Society for the Scientific Study of Religion.

Finke, R. (1997), "The Consequences of Religious Competition: Supply-side Explanations for Religious Change," in: L.A. Young, ed., *Rational Choice Theory and Religion: Summary and Assessment*. New York: Routledge: 47–61.

Habermas, J. (1982), *Theorie des kommunikativen Handelns*. Vol. 2: *Zur Kritik der funktionalistischen Vernunft*. Frankfurt: Suhrkamp.

Hadden, J.K. (1989), "Desacralizing Secularization Theory," in: J.K. Hadden/A. Shupe, eds., op. cit: 3–26.

Halman, L. (1991), *Waarden in de westerse wereld*. Tilburg: Tilburg University Press.

Halman, L./Moor, R. de (1993), "Religion, Churches, and Moral Values," in: P. Ester et al., eds., *The Individualizing Society: Value Change in Europe and North America*. Tilburg: Tilburg University Press: 37–65.

Hammond, P.E., ed. (1985), *The Sacred in a Secular Age*. Berkeley, Calif.: University of California Press.

Hervieu-Léger, D. (1995), "The Case of French Catholicism," in: W.C. Roof/J.W. Caroll/D.A. Roozen, eds., op. cit.: 151–69.

— (1998), "The Future of the Converted as Descriptive Figure of Religious Modernity: A Reflection Based on the File of Conversions to Catholicism in France," in: R. Laermans/B. Wilson/J. Billiet, eds., op. cit.: 77–286.

— (1999), *La Religion en Mouvement: Le Pélerin et le Converti*. Paris: Flammarion.

Introvigne, M./Melton, J.G., eds. (1996), *Pour en finir avec les sectes: Le débat sur le rapport de la commission parlementaire*. Milano: Di Giovanni.

Isambert, F.-A. (1982), *Le sens du sacré. Fête et religion populaire*. Paris: Ed. de Minuit.

Jagodzinski, W./Dobbelaere, K. (1995), "Secularization and Church Religiosity," in: J.W. van Deth/E. Scarbrough, eds., op. cit.: 79–119.

Johnson, G.B. (1961), "Do Holiness Sects Socialize in Dominant Values?," in: *Social Forces* 39 (4): 309–16.

Krüggeler, M. (1992), "Les 'îles des bienheureux': les croyances religieuses en Suisse," in: R.J. Campiche et al., eds., *Croire en Suisse(s): Analyse des résultats de l'enquête menée en 1988/1989 sur la religion des Suisses*. Lausanne: Editions l'Age d'Homme.

Kuhn, T.S. (1970), *The Structure of Scientific Discoveries*. Chicago, Ill.: University of Chicago Press.

Laermans, R. (1992), *In de greep van de "Moderne Tijd": Modernisering en verzuiling, individualisering en het naoorlogs publiek discours van de ACW-vormingsorganisaties: een proeve tot cultuursociologische duiding*. Leuven: Garant.

Laeyendecker, L. (1987), "Du Cardinal Alfrink au Cardinal Simonis: vingt ans de catholicisme hollandais," in: P. Ladrière/R. Luneau, eds., *Le retour des certitudes*. Paris: Le Centurion: 122–41.

— (1989), "Beweging binnen de R.K. Kerk in Nerderland," in: L.W. Huberts/J.W. van Noort, eds., *Sociale bewegingen in de jaren negentig*. Leiden: DSWO Press: 117–36.

Le Bras, G. (1963), "Déchristianisation: mot fallacieux," in: *Social Compass* (10) 2: 445–52.

Lechner, F.J. (1991), "The Case against Secularization: A Rebuttal," in: *Social Forces* (69) 4: 1103–19.

Luckmann, T. (1967), *The Invisible Religion: The Problem of Religion in Modern Society*. New York: Macmillan.

— (1979), "The Structural Conditions of Religious Consciousness in Modern Societies," in: *Japanese Journal of Religious Studies* (6) 1–2: 121–37.

— (1990), "Shrinking Transcendence, Expanding Religion," in: *Sociological Analysis* (51) 2: 127–38.

Luhmann, N. (1975), "Die Weltgesellschaft," in: N. Luhmann, *Soziologische Aufklärung*. Vol. 2: *Aufsätze zur Theorie der Gesellschaft*. Opladen: Westdeutscher Verlag: 51–71.

— (1977), *Funktion der Religion*. Frankfurt: Suhrkamp.

— (1982), *The Differentiation of Society*. New York: Columbia University Press.

Martin, D.A. (1978), *A General Theory of Secularization*. Oxford: Blackwell.

Pace, E. (1998), "The Helmet and the Turban: Secularization in Islam," in: R. Laermans/ B. Wilson/J. Billiet, eds., op. cit.: 165–75.

Parsons, T. (1967), "Christianity and Modern Industrial Society," in: E.A. Tiryakian, ed., *Sociological Theory: Values and Sociocultural Change*. New York: Harper and Row: 33–70.

Righart, H. (1986), *De katholieke zuil in Europa: Een vergelijkend onderzoek naar het ontstaan van verzuiling onder katholieken in Oostenrijk, Zwitserland, België en Nederland*. Meppel: Boom.

Shiner, L. (1967), "The Concept of Secularization in Empirical Research," in: *Journal for the Scientific Study of Religion* (6) 2: 207–20.

Stark, R. (1997), "Bringing Theory back in," in: L.A. Young, ed., op. cit.: 3–23.

— (1999), "Secularization, R.I.P.," in: *Sociology of Religion* (60) 3: 249–73.

Sundback, S. (1995), "Tradition and Change in the Nordic Countries," in W.C. Roof/ J.W. Caroll/D.A. Roozen, eds., op. cit.: 151–69.

Swanson, G.E. (1960), *The Birth of The Gods: The Origin of Primitive Beliefs*. Ann Arbor, Mich.: University of Michigan Press.

Swatos Jr., W.H./Christiano, K.J. (1999), "Secularization Theory: The Course of a Concept," in: *Sociology of Religion* (60) 3: 209–28.

Thurlings, J.M.G. (1978), *De wankele zuil: Nederlandse katholieken tussen assimilatie en pluralisme*. Second ed. Deventer: Van Lochum Slaterus.

Tschannen, O. (1992), *Les théories de la sécularisation*. Genève: Librairie Droz.

Verlinden, A. (1999), *Het ongewone alledaagse: over zwarte katten, horoscopen, miraculeuze genezingen*. Leuven/Amersfoort: Acco.

Voyé, L. (1985), "Au-delà de la sécularisation," in: *Lettres pastorales: informations officielles du diocèse de Tournai* (21) 1: 253–74.

— (1995), "From Institutional Catholicism to 'Christian Inspiration': Another Look at Belgium," in: W.C. Roof/J.W. Carroll/D.A. Roozen, eds., op. cit.: 191–223.

— (1998), "Death and Christmas Revisited," in R. Laermans/B. Wilson/J. Billiet, eds., op. cit.: 287–305.

Wallis, R. (1984), *The Elementary Forms of the New Religious Life*. London: Routledge and Kegan Paul.

Wallis, R./Bruce, S. (1992), "Secularization: The Orthodox Model," in: S. Bruce, ed., *Religion and Modernization: Sociologists and Historians Debate the Secularization Thesis.* Oxford: Clarendon Press: 8–30.

Weber, M. (1920), *Gesammelte Aufsätze zur Religionssoziologie.* Tübingen: Mohr.

Wilson, B.R. (1974), "Jehovah's Witnesses in Kenya," in: *Journal of Religion in Africa* 6 (2): 129–49.

— (1976), *Contemporary Transformations of Religion.* Oxford: Oxford University Press.

— (1982), *Religion in Sociological Perspective.* Oxford: Oxford University Press.

— (1985), "Secularization: The Inherited Model," in: Ph. Hammond, ed., *The Sacred in a Secular Age.* Berkeley, Calif.: University of California Press: 9–20.

Wilson, B. (1998), "The Secularization Thesis: Criticisms and Rebuttals," in: R. Laermans/B. Wilson/J. Billiet, eds., op. cit.: 45–65.

Urbanization and Religion

by

ROBERT KISALA

In a recent essay Harvey Cox, the author of *The Secular City* (1965), proclaimed the demise of secularization, "the single most comprehensive explanatory myth" of the twentieth century (Cox 2000: 4). As the title of his earlier work indicates, secularization was often seen as a corollary of urbanization, itself one of the processes of modernization. It was commonly assumed that migration to urban areas involves the fracturing of social ties, leading to an increase in anonymity and individualization, and exposure to a plurality of ideas and beliefs—all of which attenuate religious belief and practice. In his recent essay Cox highlights developments that belie the expected retreat of religious influence: the rise of fundamentalist movements, the appearance of new religious movements, and the spread of Pentecostalism. To these we might add New Age, or new spirituality movements.[1] All of these can be characterized as urban movements, testifying to a religious ferment in the very locale that was to lead to religion's demise.

As indicators of a religious revival, or the transformation of religion itself, these movements and their connection with modernization have been the focus of considerable academic interest in the last twenty years, one aspect of recent research on urbanization and religion we will need to consider here. However, theoretical and methodological developments in the study of urbanization and religion have not been limited to research on the movements highlighted above. Indeed, research on the effects of urbanization on traditional and historical religions has generated significant developments, especially regarding the questions of pluralism, migration/mobility, and social networks and their impact on religious vitality.

In this chapter we will first undertake a consideration of these theoretical and methodological developments. Here we will pay special attention to market-model analysis (also known as supply-side theory or rational choice

1 "New spirituality movements" is a term coined by Shimazono Susumu, a Japanese scholar of religion, and refers to movements such as New Age that mediate an increasingly eclectic and individualistic spirituality to many in the contemporary world (Shimazono 1996).

theory), social network analysis, comparative-historical research or a historical sociology of religion, studies of religious belief and practice among migrants and other minority groups. Following a presentation on these theoretical/ methodological developments, we will explore the phenomenon of the contemporary resurgence of religion as fundamentalisms, Pentecostalism, new religious movements, and new spirituality movements, particularly in the urban environment.

Market-model Analysis

The emergence of market-model analysis is arguably the most important development in the recent study of religion, to the extent that it has been called a "paradigm shift in process" (Warner 1993: 1044). This approach emerged as a theory primarily to explain the so-called "American exceptionalism," the fact that studies consistently show a high level of both religious affiliation and religious attendance in the United States, in contrast to the low levels of attendance in most of the Western European countries that has been taken as evidence of secularization. The proponents of market-model analysis argue that it is the plurality of religions in the United States that accounts for this difference, a direct challenge to previous perceptions that saw pluralism as a threat to religious belief.

The perception of pluralism as problematic, especially when associated with the expansion of urban environments, can be traced back to the foundations of the modern science of sociology; Émile Durkheim, in his work on suicide, identified urban pluralism with a breakdown in moral and social integration. In the contemporary period the clearest representative of this position has been Peter Berger, who, in his famous work, *The Sacred Canopy*, identifies pluralism with religious and social disintegration.

> One of the most obvious ways in which secularization has affected the man in the street is as a "crisis of credibility" in religion. Put differently, secularization has resulted in a widespread collapse of the plausibility of traditional religious definitions of reality ... Subjectively, the man in the street tends to be uncertain about religious matters. Objectively, the man in the street is confronted with a wide variety of religious and other reality-defining agencies that compete for his allegiance or at least attention, and none of which is in a position to coerce him into allegiance. (1969: 127)

Roger Finke and Rodney Stark, two of the leading proponents of market-model analysis, argue that Berger reflects a European perception that is itself suffused with nostalgic yearnings for a universal piety that in fact never existed (1992: 19). It is not pluralism that leads to a decline in religious faith or practice, but rather the situation of religious "monopolies" breeds indifference, or even hostility towards the religious establishment. Thus, it is the established churches of Western Europe that report declines in affiliation and attendance, while the denominations competing for "market-share" in the United States have more success in generating religious interest, even enthusiasm.

As is already clear from some of the terminology, Finke and Stark propose the use of economic models in order to analyze religious growth and decline. Religious groups are compared to commercial firms, believers to customers, and the pool of believers and potential believers to the market. Just as the success of commercial firms depends on their internal structure, their sales representatives, their product, and their marketing strategy, the success of religious bodies will be determined by their polity, clergy, doctrines, and evangelization techniques. In a "free market," religious bodies will want to hone their marketing skills, and there is a greater chance that a plurality of doctrines will attract different segments of the market, leading to a higher overall participation in religion. This latter supposition is the reason why this model is sometimes called the supply-side theory, imagery apparently introduced into the discussion by a historian, Terry Bilhartz, in a book on religion in post-Revolutionary Baltimore (1986). On the other hand, religious monopolies in a protected market, indicating the established churches in Western Europe, will generate less excitement, and tend to be lazy, satisfied with their control of the market long after consumers have abandoned their product.

Much research has been provided both in support of and in opposition to the main thesis of the market model, that pluralism promotes religious participation. Perhaps the most comprehensive attempt to argue for the thesis is Finke and Stark's study on American religion, *The Churching of America, 1776–1990* (1992). There the authors draw on a variety of statistical sources and extrapolations to compensate for the fact that religious affiliation has not always been included in official census data. Such calculations lead them to believe that religious affiliation and church attendance was relatively low in the early post-Revolutionary period and has generally been increasing ever since. The reason offered for this initial low performance was the presence of established churches in many of the former colonies, and it was only with the arrival of Baptists and Methodists, "upstart sects," that religious adherence took off (1992: 46). Even following formal disestablishment, some of the older congregations would try to form "cartels" to protect their market share (1992: 60). While these efforts introduced local changes in the overall pattern of church growth, in the end, it is argued, that they only offer further support for the thesis that the proliferation of religious groups encourages enhanced religious affiliation and participation.

In an earlier article, Finke and Stark (1988) make explicit claims regarding the positive correlation between urbanization and religious participation. Using data from a 1906 census of religious groups in the United States, they find a significantly higher level of religious adherence in urban areas with a population over 50,000 than in rural areas (55% vs. 50%). To explain this result they suggest a reason that is related to the issue of religious pluralism: with the larger market of the urban area more denominations will be able to sustain churches, offering more people the opportunity to participate in the religion of their choice (1988: 44).

Market-model analysis is also associated with rational choice theory. Rodney Stark and William Sims Bainbridge offer the most comprehensive development of this theory in their *A Theory of Religion* (1987). In this work they start with basic axioms to describe human action, and the fundamental motivation for all action is defined as the search for what is perceived as rewards and the avoidance of what are counted as costs. People are rational in pursuing these aims, making complex choices to weigh the costs and benefits, sometimes delaying rewards or accepting compensators, a concept key to their theory of religion, defined as follows:

> When humans cannot quickly and easily obtain strongly desired rewards they persist in their efforts and may often accept explanations that provide only compensators. These are intangible substitutes for the desired reward, having the character of I.O.U.s, the value of which must be taken on faith. (1987: 36)

Compensators, then, are the products that religious groups offer. These compensators might be doctrines that help make the burdens of life easier and offer the hope of reparation for earthy suffering in an afterlife; religious experiences that authenticate these compensators; prayer as a mechanism for seeking aid, confessing sin, or gaining comfort; or a sense of particularism and moral superiority, the assurance that one has been especially chosen and can be counted among the religious elite (1987: 46).

Rational-choice theory is offered as an explanation of how religious markets operate. Overall market behavior depends on the independent choices of religious consumers and producers, in much the same way that economists describe market activity. Both market-model analysis and rational-choice theory have come under criticism for their reliance on economic metaphors. For example, Steve Bruce criticizes these approaches to the study of religion as inadequate and misleading because, in the case of religion, we do not know ultimately what the rational choice would be. He argues that religious choices are not the same as buying breakfast cereal, for example, and that ultimately they are a matter of faith.

> There is a dramatic switch at the point of belief. What was previously a complete waste of space becomes an extremely rewarding activity. That switch prevents us from applying rational choice expectations, yet it is the very thing that economic models pretend to explain. (1993: 204)

James V. Spickard (1998) has argued that rational-choice theory seems to work as a model to describe the overall workings of the market, but it is less helpful in explaining individual human actions. On the individual level, often considerations of values, responsibilities, or cultural views of appropriate behavior intervene to encourage action that does not apparently maximize personal benefit and is not governed by universal preference, as reason would seem to demand.

Others argue against the market model and rational choice because there seems to be ample evidence that the theories are not supported by fact, especially as regards the correlation between religious plurality and higher levels of religion affiliation and participation. Here there have been a wealth of case studies and the evidence does seem ambiguous. Daniel Olson and C. Kirk Hadaway (1999) argue for a strong negative correlation between pluralism and religious affiliation in contemporary Canada; Steve Bruce (1995) contends that Britain has been characterized by religious plurality since the nineteenth century, with no corresponding upturn in religious affiliation or practice; using material from the European Values Study, Johan Verweij and his colleagues point out that, "the more religion is regulated by the state and the more a religious market is monopolistic, the higher the proportion of people that belongs to a church" (1997: 322). Much of the criticism has to do with the assumptions underlying the choice of statistics or indicators, or the analysis of the statistics, and that is perhaps why the evidence seems ambiguous. The lively debate, however, testifies to the importance of this new approach to the study of religion, and, as should be expected, it has led to some refinements in the theory. For example, in a study of religious pluralism in mid-nineteenth century England and Wales, Stark and his colleagues (1995) acknowledge cultural factors, such as a caste system, that act to constrain competitive forces despite the appearance of a pluralistic situation. In a more recent article Stark and Finke (1998) acknowledge that in a more "mature unregulated religious market" additional increases in pluralism do not further enhance competition, a classic case of diminishing returns.

Historical Sociology of Religion and Social Network Analysis: The Rise of Christianity

As one application of rational choice theory, Rodney Stark has also advocated the application of sociological theory to historical studies of religion. His book *The Rise of Christianity: A Sociologist Reconsiders History* (1996) serves as the culmination of this effort.

Largely a collection of essays that had been written over the course of a decade, *The Rise of Christianity* seeks to present a plausible thesis to explain the growth of Christianity until the beginning of the fourth century. Drawing on the research of historians, Stark posits a Christian population of between five and seven million people, or ten percent of the overall population of sixty million in the Roman Empire at the dawn of the fourth century. With a base number of around one thousand believers in the year 40, it would take an average of forty-percent growth each decade to achieve this development, a rate of growth, Stark points out, that corresponds with the growth of the Mormon church in the past century. Indeed, Stark's argument throughout this volume is that the rise of Christianity could plausibly be explained in terms of recent sociological research on new religious movements.

Stark begins by introducing a conversion model based on social network theory developed in cooperation with John Lofland in the 1960s (Lofland/Stark 1965). From their research on converts to the Unification Church in the early 1960s, Lofland and Stark concluded that the balance of interpersonal relationships played a crucial role in determining whether or not someone would convert to the group. Unification Church members were more likely to find potential converts among their family members, friends, and co-workers than among those who were approached at random. Correspondingly, a relatively weak social network outside the group of believers would enhance the potential to convert. This is described as an application of social deviance theory; people will be more likely to engage in deviant behavior, such as joining a new religious movement, if they have less at stake in conformity, such as interpersonal ties outside the group.

Numerous studies have confirmed that new religious movements often spread along the social networks of their believers. Kox, Meeus, and Hart (1991) cite twenty-five studies in their own review of the research on the Lofland and Stark model, and they confirm that interpersonal relations is one important factor in conversion. Social network analysis has also been found useful in studying religious affiliation in migrant groups, an important concern for researchers on urbanization and religion that we will turn to shortly.

Stark also argues, citing the work of historians who have studied early Christianity, that it was a predominantly urban religion. Continuing to describe the spread of Christianity in terms of recent research on new religious movements, Stark sides with historians who conclude that the religion spread more among the middle and upper classes than with the poor, although, as he admits, there is not enough direct evidence to make a final judgment. His reason for making the point about the class basis of early Christianity is to propose that skepticism towards established religious beliefs, and thus the predisposition to new beliefs, is higher among the more educated, and such elites are found disproportionately in urban areas. Stark points out that this proposition is supported by research on the class composition of contemporary new religious movements (1996: 33).

In Stark's view, the urban environment proved beneficial to Christianity's spread in another fundamental way. Cities in Roman times were crowded places, prone to the spread of disease and frequent epidemics. He argues that Christians had substantially higher rates of survival of these plagues, because their emphasis on the values of love and charity was expressed in better networks of community solidarity and nursing care. Furthermore, the decimation of the non-Christian population through disease left more people without a stable social network—family, friends, colleagues—and thus more open to recruitment by the new religion.

Thus Stark raises several important points regarding recent research into urbanization and religion in this short volume. His argument is not without controversy, however, perhaps more because of its scope and tone—his assertion that he will "introduce historians and biblical scholars to real social science" (1996: xii) is not taken well by some of his critics. More specifically, rational choice theory—peripheral to much of the discussion above but nonetheless central to his own understanding of religion—comes in for criticism along the lines mentioned in the previous section.[2] The work presented on social networks and conversion, however, has become central to our understanding of the spread of religion, particularly, in this context, in the urban environment. His other arguments regarding new religious movements will be pertinent to our discussion of contemporary religious movements and urbanization in the second half of this chapter.

Migrants and Minority Groups

The question of religious affiliation and belief among migrants, both internal (from rural areas to cities within a country) and external (to a foreign country), and other minority groups, has attracted much research. These studies often focus on the role of religion in maintaining cultural identity and the process of assimilation, an issue that can be addressed by a variety of methodologies.

Robert Orsi (1985) presents an anthropological study of urban ethnic religion as popular religion. Popular religion is itself a concept that has been the object of much recent research, criticism, and refinement. Although it was posited in opposition to elite or institutional religion in previous religious research from the nineteenth century, more recent studies, for example Eamon Duffy's study of medieval English Catholicism (1992), have emphasized the continuities between so-called elite religion and popular religion, pointing out that popular religion, that is the religion of the masses, draws on the liturgy and doctrines of institutional religion to express its beliefs and practices, while at the same time the so-called elite religion incorporates many elements of what is usually considered popular religion. Various terms have been proposed to replace "popular"—folk, traditional, common—but nevertheless continuing

2 See, for example, the review by Joseph Bryant (1997).

attention is given to a common or shared religious substratum expressed in practices that do not always conform to the doctrines of institutional religion.[3]

In *The Madonna of 115th Street: Faith and Community in Italian Harlem, 1880–1950*, Orsi explores the origins and development of the devotion to Our Lady of Mount Carmel among Italian immigrants in East Harlem in New York City. In the late nineteenth century, a mutual aid society named after the Madonna, the patron saint of the town of Polla in southern Italy, was formed by immigrants from the town. Such societies were common among immigrants, and served to provide unemployment and burial benefits as well as a forum for socialization. Soon an annual festival was organized in honor of the saint, and it was festivals such as this that, in time, became characteristic of the new Italian-American identity. For, as Orsi points out, these festivals were not only viewed with suspicion by the Irish-American hierarchy in the New York Catholic Church, they were also considerably more common in the United States than in Italy (1985: 55–57). In this way the festival laid bare two lines of division experienced by the immigrant community: between the religious expression of the people and the institutional church that was somewhat embarrassed and threatened by this public, independent display; and between the need of the people themselves to preserve a culture and moral code that had sustained them in their homeland and the need to assimilate in their new land. The institutional church saw the devotion as a way to keep the immigrants in the church, and wrestled with the immigrants for control of the festival, culminating in a civil law suit in the 1930s. Until the last remnant of the community left Harlem in the 1950s the festival was an occasion for the assimilating generations to remember their immigrant roots and renew, at least symbolically, their commitment to the culture and morals of their ancestors.

While Orsi thus takes an anthropological approach to the study of religious practice and belief in urban ethnic communities, other studies have focused on an analysis of their function from a sociological point of view. For example, a recent study conducted by Victoria Hyonchu Kwon and others (Kwon/Ebaugh/Hagan 1997) analyzes the structure and function of cell group ministry in a Korean Christian Church in the United States. Cell groups are an important organizational element in Korean churches that have attracted the attention of other Christian churches as an effective means of proselytization. The cell group is a subgroup of members of a church, divided residentially, that holds on a rotational basis an informal worship service once a month in a member's house. In Korean immigrant communities, these meetings provide the opportunity for more extensive mutual support, assisting in the settlement of new immigrants and promoting Korean-owned businesses in the community. Kwon

3 See Reader/Tanabe (1998: 23–32) for a useful discussion of popular religion and the various terms that have been proposed as its replacement.

and her colleagues point out that the support often begins as material aid—help in buying a vehicle and finding housing, obtaining job referrals, providing translating services, applying for citizenship, etc.—but gradually becomes more a matter of emotional support as the members become more settled in the community. The cell groups, therefore, function as a bridge into the new society, and contribute to the material prosperity of the Korean-American community as well by promoting networking within the group. Conflict arises, however, over the issue of assimilation. By promoting support within the group, the members are discouraged from making efforts at assimilation, promoting conflict with the larger society as well as between generations within the ethnic community; second-generation members express frustration at the lack of assimilation of their parents and their exclusive commitment to the church (1997: 254–55).

Mutual aid groups related to religious institutions, such as the Italian-Americans' Mount Carmel Association or the Korean-Americans' cell groups, are not limited to immigrant groups, but can also be found among ethnic groups that have moved to urban areas in their own country. For example, S.M. Michael (1989) has published the results of a comparative study of Tamil and Keralite migrants, both from southern India, who have settled in Mumbai (Bombay). Michael points out that there are multiple religious and ethnic associations among these groups, offering a variety of levels of openness across caste lines within the group as well as to other ethnic groups. For example, the Hindu associations in both groups, while primarily for the Brahmin caste, offer their facilities to other castes as well as other regional groups. These groups also serve a variety of functions, but here Michael sees a distinction in the primary function of Tamil and Keralite associations; while most Tamil associations serve to enhance cultural identity through cultural activities (music, dance, drama), Keralite associations are, in general, more concerned with economic improvement by offering help with job-seeking, education, or dispensary services. These differences could be related to the situations in their homelands and, thus, the class of people from each group that tend to migrate to the city. Kerala is relatively undeveloped economically, and so the more ambitious tend to leave in search of better opportunities elsewhere. Its society is also more fragmented, with a high level of competition among the various groups. These factors would tend to make the Keralites in Mumbai more interested in associations for economic advancement rather than maintaining cultural identity. Tamil, on the other hand, is relatively prosperous, and many of migrants to the city are less-educated, unskilled workers. Presumably this class would be more concerned with a loss of identity in the urban environment.

Finally, Helen Hardacre (1984) has presented the results of field study at Korean temples in a mountain area near Osaka, Japan. The Korean minority population in Japan has long been the victim of discrimination, which has affected their assimilation in various ways. The native language has largely been abandoned in favor of Japanese, and many immigrants have also adopted Japanese names. Intermarriage, however, often remains difficult because of discriminatory attitudes among the Japanese. There are numerous Korean ethnic associations and institutions in Japan, including, for example, schools that are still not recognized by the central government's Education Ministry. Hardacre's study of Korean ethnic religious institutions is interesting because, like Orsi's research on Italian-American practices, it indicates the development of a religious practice that differs from that of both Korea and Japan. In the temples of the [illegible] Osaka, frequented by the Korean residents of that city, we see a combination of Korean Buddhist and shamanistic symbols and practices, traditions that, while used synchronously by many in Korea, especially women, remain separate in their homeland. The practice in these temples reflects the ambiguous nature of Korean assimilation in Japan; the rites are conducted in Japanese using ritual objects made in Japan by Japanese artisans, but they offer the Korean participants the opportunity to separate themselves from Japanese society and reaffirm their Korean heritage.

While these case studies, perhaps, do not generate the same level of interest as development of broader theories, such as rational choice theories and theories on conversion, the richness of detail serves to bring us closer to religion as it is actually lived and experienced by different groups in urban environments. They can also serve as an introduction to the more general presentation on contemporary religious movements and urbanization that follows.

Contemporary Religious Movements and the City

Contemporary religious ferment, as seen in the rise of fundamentalisms, Pentecostalism, new religious movements, and the New Age and new spirituality movements, is largely an urban phenomenon. In a general sense we can say, as much of the research on these movements will point out, that it is the dislocations caused by the movement to urban areas—breaking family and presumably stronger rural cultural ties; living and working in crowded and often oppressive conditions; the pluralism in moral values and lifestyles offered, primarily by the various mass media—that encourage people either to look for new religious forms or to accept those forms when offered. However, each of these movements also has its own relationship to urbanization, and it is some of those specific processes that we will highlight here.

Fundamentalisms

Strictly speaking, fundamentalism is a late-nineteenth and twentieth century North American Christian phenomenon. It is often considered to be a reaction against modernization and the advance of science, as symbolized in the importance placed by the movement on the battle against the theory of biological evolution. The most basic of the "fundamentals" that it seeks to uphold is the inerrancy of the Bible, that the words of the Bible are true, as they are written. Since the 1970s, however, the term has been applied broadly to religious movements that display some common characteristics: revivalism, strict morality, protest against modern society, restriction on individual freedom, emphasis on authority, belief in the possession of absolute truth, and work towards the establishment of a religious state.

The most comprehensive research on the broader phenomenon of religious fundamentalism is undoubtedly that conducted by *The Fundamentalism Project* under the auspices of the American Academy of Arts and Sciences. The results of this study are contained in five volumes (Marty/Appleby 1991, 1993a, 1993b, 1994, 1995) and cover a spectrum of religious movements and themes. Focusing on urbanization, several authors offer the general explanation of anomie and displacement in a recently urbanized society as one factor in the emergence of these movements. However, we do see some variety in the actual processes described. For example, Donald Swearer (1991) points to an increase in prostitution as women move to the cities to work in a particularly unsavory part of the tourist trade, and a consequent concern with moral decline, as one factor in the emergence of Buddhist fundamentalist movements in Thailand. In India, the emergence of a new middle and lower-middle class in urban areas, and their frustration with the practice of reserving government jobs for registered castes, is seen as contributing to the development of Hindu fundamentalist movements (Tehranian 1993). In Nigeria, urbanization in recent decades was accompanied by the establishment of Islamic schools, funded by Saudi Arabia, and it was the development of Islamic education in this way that prepared the way for an Islamic fundamentalist movement in northern Nigeria (Kane 1994). Finally, Valerie Hoffman (1995) points out that a wide range of social problems accompanying the urbanization of Iranian society in the 1970s was attributed to moral laxity, thus encouraging the rise of Islamic fundamentalism in the country that first brought worldwide attention to these movements.

Migration can also contribute to the development of fundamentalist movements in a variety of ways, as Gabriel A. Almond and his colleagues argue (1995: 436–37). The depopulation of Jewish communities in Eastern Europe at the turn of the nineteenth century led to a strengthening of orthodoxy among the remnants of these groups, who then themselves migrated after the Holocaust, principally to Israel and the United States, aiding the establishment of Jewish fundamentalism in those countries. The movement of southerners into the northern cities of the United States contributed to the spread of fundamentalism there. The recruitment of Muslim guest workers into Western Europe and the aggravation of their identity problems as they began to settle in those societies encouraged the development of Islamic fundamentalism in Europe.

A further way that urbanization has contributed to the development of fundamentalist movements is through the involvement of these movements in social welfare services. Governments are often unable to provide the necessary services to alleviate social problems exacerbated by urbanization—the breakup of families and extended networks of care, poverty, disease, prostitution, and so on. Using their own organizational resources, fundamentalist movements are often able to provide relief for their members or for the wider urban population, such as the work of the Arya Samaj and Rashtriya Svayamsevak Sangh, or RSS, in India to organize labor unions and provide for widows and orphans (Gold 1991: 556, 558).

Pentecostalism

In its roots, Pentecostalism is also a twentieth-century North American Christian phenomenon. While an emphasis on the gifts and power of the Holy Spirit can be seen in some of the seventeenth and eighteenth century reform movements, such as the Huguenots in France or the Quakers in England, and the periodic religious revivals in United States, with their emphasis on individual conversion and personal religious experience, foreshadow this movement, characteristic of twentieth-century Pentecostalism is the importance given to speaking in tongues, one gift of the Holy Spirit that was taken as proof of "baptism in the Spirit," and, in some circles, a sign of the imminent end of the world.

From its beginnings in the Azusa Street Apostolic Faith Mission in Los Angeles in April 1906, the movement rapidly spread worldwide. In October of the same year, at a revival in New York there were reports of people falling down, being "slain in the Spirit," and of a woman levitating (Cox 1995: 68). In the following year the movement spread to Japan, Africa, England, and Germany, and later to Italy and Russia as well. By the end of the twentieth century the movement was said to have more than 400 million participants worldwide, and to be growing at a rate of 20 million new members a year (Cox 1995: xv).

While distinct from fundamentalism in its narrower North American Christian meaning—indeed, opposed to that movement in its emphasis on the Holy Spirit as the source and guarantor or their experience over and above the fundamentalists' belief in the paramount position of Scripture in religious life—the two movements are often conflated in popular discourse, as well as in the academic literature. Some of the material on South America contained in the volumes published by the Fundamentalism Project, for example, deal with Pentecostal movements. In fact, as some of the Pentecostal churches have become more established they have tended to downplay some of the more extreme expressions of their faith experience and have drawn closer to the fundamentalists in some of their attitudes.

From its beginning in Los Angeles, Pentecostalism has been primarily an urban movement. No study as comprehensive as the Fundamentalism Project has yet been made of Pentecostalism, although the movement in Latin America in particular has been the subject of several fine studies (e.g. Martin 1990; Cox 1995; Cleary/Stewart-Gambino 1998). As in the case of fundamentalism, general statements regarding the displacement of urban migrant populations and social problems accompanying urbanization can be employed to explain the spread of Pentecostalism. More specific to Pentecostalism's appeal would appear to be the emphasis placed on direct religious experience—speaking in tongues, being slain in the Spirit, and healing. The correlation of this emphasis with shamanistic practices or preexisting spirit beliefs would help to explain the success of Pentecostalism in attracting members in Korea and Africa respectively. Harvey Cox broadens the argument to include the urban masses in general. Recalling that, according to the secularization thesis, urbanization was presumed to enhance religious skepticism, Cox argues that we can, in fact, see a widespread disillusion with traditional religious dogmas and institutions in urban societies. What was unexpected in the 1960s when Cox was originally espousing the secularization thesis, however, was that urbanization and the problems that accompany it would also lead to a disillusionment with science and technology. Pentecostalists step into this gap, as they "rebelled against creeds but retained the mystery. They abolished hierarchies but kept ecstasy. They rejected both scientism and traditionalism. They returned to the raw inner core of human spirituality and thus provided just the new kind of 'religious space' many people needed" (Cox 1995: 105).

A further structural reason can be offered to explain the rise of Pentecostalism in Latin America. Bryan Froehle, in presenting a study of Pentecostalism in Venezuela, points out that the Catholic Church, which has enjoyed a monopolistic position throughout Latin America, was not able to commit the necessary resources to provide religious services to the burgeoning urban population, thus offering Pentecostals an opening (1998: 206). Pablo A. Deiros broadens the argument to speak of Latin America in general:

> [T]he Roman Catholic Church had been oriented to a rural ministry and suffered, in this time of dislocation, from a dearth of well-trained clergy capable of adapting to the quite different pastoral challenges of urban life ... The new urban dweller, recently arrived from a rural area, forced to adjust not only to the routines of factory labor but to crowded living conditions and to the personal and familial disorientation attendant upon displacement, was often without benefit of pastorally effective clergy. As with any crisis or moment of decision, the migrant was presented with new possibilities for creating identity. Evangelicals responded to this opportunity with notable vigor and enthusiasm. (Deiros 1991: 156)

The Catholic church in Latin America did make an effort to alleviate this situation, as well as the related problem of a chronically insufficient native clergy due to requirement to be celibate (Martin 1990: 62) through the establishment of Basic Christian Communities under lay leadership, an initiative that was part of the movement towards Liberation Theology in the 1970s and 1980s. Liberation Theology subsequently came under question by church's hierarchy, and Basic Christian Communities were often seen as a threat to the more traditional parish structure of the church, guaranteeing the failure of this effort. Pentecostalism is occasionally portrayed as a movement in opposition to the socially activist stance of Liberation Theology, and it is sometimes asserted that the spread of Pentecostalism in Latin America has been supported by the political right in North America cooperating with repressive regimes in the southern continent. The argument here is that Pentecostalism is non-political, that its followers are concerned, some would say exclusively, with spiritual matters and their attention has been taken away from social problems. The volume edited by Cleary and Stewart-Gambino (1998), however, calls into question this common perception.

New Religious Movements

New religious movements is a multivalent term that could be used to include many of the fundamentalist and Pentecostal movements addressed above. In general, it is used to refer to religious revival movements, often founded by a charismatic individual in order to respond to changing situations where traditional religious institutions are no longer seen as attractive to a part of the population. Often they emerge in colonial situations, where they might offer a mixture of native religious beliefs and practices and the Christianity brought by the colonial powers, or perhaps constitute a more direct revival of the native religion. They are not restricted to colonial or postcolonial situations, however, and significant numbers of new religious movements have developed, for example, in Western Europe, the United States and Japan.

There is no clear convention on how "new" the movements included in this category should be. Some Western researchers use the term to refer to movements that have emerged since the 1970s, often called "cults" in popular usage. In Japan, however, the term is commonly used to refer to religious groups that have emerged in the modern period, beginning from the mid-nineteenth century. Indeed, some groups that emerged in nineteenth century U.S. society, such as Christian Science and the Mormon church, are also commonly referred to as new religious movements.

As our discussion on Rodney Stark's historical reconstruction of the spread of Christianity to the year 300 indicated, new religious movements are also overwhelmingly urban movements. Here I would like to use the Japanese situation, with which I am most familiar, to illustrate how the emergence of these movements can characterize an urbanizing society.

While it is difficult to give an accurate count, there are perhaps up to one thousand new religious movements active in Japan. The vast majority are small, local groups; national movements or movements with an international outreach are relatively few. Nearly all of the mass movements, such as Sōka Gakkai with perhaps nine million members, or Risshō Kōseikai with over six million, are postwar, urban forms of Buddhism whose development paralleled the urbanization of Japanese society.

Early in the twentieth century more than eighty percent of the Japanese population was engaged in agriculture. By 1935 the urban population stood at thirty percent, a figure that rose to fifty percent by the end of the war. By 1977, however, more than eighty percent of the population lived in cities, reversing the situation of only sixty years before. For many people this meant that their ties with the local Buddhist temple were completely severed by the move to the city. This was problematic because Buddhist temples were called upon to perform funeral and memorial rites, an important role in a culture where ancestor veneration is fundamental to the common religiosity. Many of the new religious movements that became mass movements in postwar Japan offer their believers a means to venerate the ancestors in the home, without the assistance of a Buddhist priest. The believers are encouraged to purchase a Buddhist altar that can be set up in their small urban apartments, and to offer prayers before the altar daily. Interestingly enough, the observation can be made that Japanese urbanization has led to a considerable religious revival. Whereas in the past the main tie to the local Buddhist temple centered on annual memorial rites, for which a Buddhist monk was summoned and paid, the lay Buddhism that emerged in postwar urban Japan not only encouraged daily practice at home, but also resulted in more active and sustained participation in communal religious functions. A central practice here is the *hōza*, a combination of group counseling and faith-witnessing carried out by the believers, often on a weekly or monthly basis.

Thus, the postwar new religions serve a function in enhancing social cohesion. The postwar groups act as a bridge, both religiously and socially, between rural and urban Japanese society, providing an entirely new way to perform the requisite memorial rites for the ancestors, as well as becoming the focus of community for many people in the impersonal urban milieu. This function is less apparent in some of the more recent new religious movements that emerged or became popular in Japan since the 1970s, which are usually included in the final category of contemporary religious movements highlighted here, New Age or new spirituality movements.

New Age and New Spirituality Movements

In much of the West, as well as in Japan and societies as diverse as India and South Africa, since the 1970s one can see a new interest in mysticism and the occult that is normally summed up under the term New Age. This new religious ferment is often characterized as eclectic, individualistic, and result-oriented. Traditional religious institutions are shunned, in favor of imported religious traditions—Japanese Zen or Indian yogic practices in the U.S., or Tibetan Buddhism in Japan—or an interest in primal religions, such as Native American or Celtic religions. Through the use of techniques learned from these religions, either meditation or body-work, or some combination of the two, it is believed that one can achieve a personal transformation, resulting perhaps in a higher level of consciousness or the attainment of psychic powers. While often one participates in this movement by purchasing books that amount to training manuals at the local bookstore, or at best through a loose association or "network" of fellow practitioners, occasionally, as in Japan, a number of semi-organized networks of people sharing common interests, or new spirituality movements, have emerged.

These movements are oriented towards some kind of loose community or network, but they are not generally structured as religions. They often constitute an amorphous gathering of those who share the same interests, as indicated by reading the same books or participating in the same activities; occasionally a more formal, although small, association is formed. For example, Suzuki Kentarō (Suzuki 1995) has provided research on the informal communities of young people in Tokyo with an interest in divination techniques. These movements, however, do not encourage the development of either doctrine or rites, and leadership is often unclear. They stress the transformation of consciousness, believe that a spiritual existence permeates the universe and is available to us on an intimate level, speak of the imminent spiritual transformation of humanity, and often maintain that there is no opposition between religion and science and that the two are in fact one.

These networks and informal communities are themselves a product of the urban milieu. They are dependent on modern means of communication—books and magazines, television and satellite broadcasts, the internet—to propagate their beliefs and maintain contact among like-minded individuals. They gather in the dojo and "divination halls" in the young fashion quarters of Tokyo and other cities. They are also the product of contemporary social trends, often marked by cynicism and ennui. In the 1970s and 1980s in Japan, for example, a level of economic development had been achieved that would have been unthinkable a generation before. The "oil shock" in 1973, however, introduced a period of relatively low growth, which made future advancement, both for the individual and society, less certain. This trend was further acerbated by the collapse of the "bubble economy," based largely on stock and land speculation, and the decade-long recession in the 1990s. With economic or social advancement thus stymied, individual spiritual development has perhaps become more attractive. In addition, the failure of the 1960s student protest movement encouraged a turning inward; what could not be achieved through social protest was now sought through personal transformation, the reformation of society one person at a time.

Conclusion: Rational Choice Revisited

Instead of being the stage for religion's demise, it would appear that cities provide an environment for a contemporary religious revival. Contrary to the expectations of researchers of a generation ago, it now seems that displacement and pluralism could be positive factors for the spread of religious belief and practice. At least that is what the present ferment in contemporary religious movements would seem to indicate.

The positive effect of pluralism on religious affiliation and participation posited by supply-side theorists is still a matter of some dispute, as the research presented in first part of this chapter indicates. The theory continues to be modified and nuanced as it is applied to different situations, and to that extent it has served to provide us with a clearer picture of how religious affiliation and practice have undergone change and continue to change. Rational choice theory, with which supply-side theory is identified, is in fact a much broader conceptual model of religion, and it has also been the object of much criticism. The argument that it presents nothing more than a tautology—that any action by a religious participant that is seen to take place is found in some way to be rational or rewarding—is a serious criticism that would appear to undermine the whole enterprise. The value of the theory, however, is that in its attempt to present propositions to explain religious behavior it is often able to clarify hypotheses to be tested in further research. Research into the effects of religious pluralism is certainly an example of the benefits of this approach.

Many questions remain to be explored; much of today's commonly accepted wisdom will no doubt yet be found lacking. Do fundamentalist and Pentecostal movements propagate primarily among more disadvantaged classes, or are they similar to other new religious movements in attracting more of their members from the middle and upper classes? Are New Age or new spirituality movements really a post-industrial or postmodern phenomenon, or can they be found more generally in urban societies? And what effect do all of these movements have on the development of social awareness and political interest?

Finally, there is the question of traditional or established religious institutions and urbanization. Will the secularization thesis yet be proved right, at least as far as the religious establishment is concerned? Are established religions caught in an inevitable decline, or will future market-model theorists be presenting analyses of the processes of religious restructuring in these religions? Interestingly enough, perhaps the urban mega-churches are already providing us with a model for this restructuring process, contributing to a revival in more traditional religious establishments (albeit often with some combination of elements from Pentecostalism or New Age) through the concentration of resources in large-scale communities. Although they have been attracting attention for over a decade there is not yet much solid research available on the mega-churches, and it remains to be seen what their ultimate impact on the contemporary religious situation will be. It is a safe bet that this will be a major area of research on urbanization and religion in the coming years.

Bibliography

Almond, Gabriel A./Sivan, Emmanuel/Appleby, R. Scott (1995), "Explaining Fundamentalisms," in: Marty/Appleby 1995: 425–44.

Berger, Peter L. (1969), *The Sacred Canopy: Elements of a Sociological Theory of Religion*. Garden City, N.Y.: Anchor Books.

Bilhartz, Terry D. (1986), *Urban Religion and the Second Great Awakening: Church and Society in Early National Baltimore*. Rutherford, N.J.: Fairleigh Dickinson University Press.

Bruce, Steve (1993), "Religion and Rational Choice: A Critique of Economic Explanations of Religious Behavior," in: *Sociology of Religion* 54: 193–205.

— (1995), "The Truth about Religion in England," in: *Journal for the Scientific Study of Religion* 34: 417–30.

Bryant, Joseph M. (1997), "Review of *The Rise of Christianity: A Sociologist Reconsiders History*, by Rodney Stark," in: *Sociology of Religion* 58: 191–95.

Cleary, Edward L./Stewart-Gambino, Hannah W., eds. (1998), *Power, Politics, and Pentecostals in Latin America*. Boulder, Colo.: Westview Press.

Cox, Harvey (1965), *The Secular City*. London: SCM Press Ltd.

— (1995), *Fire from Heaven: The Rise of Pentecostal Spirituality and the Reshaping of Religion in the Twenty-first Century*. Reading, Mass.: Addison-Wesley Publishing Company.

— (2000), "The Myth of the Twentieth Century: The Rise and Fall of Secularization," in: *Japanese Journal of Religious Studies* 27: 1–13.

Deiros, Pablo A. (1991), "Protestant Fundamentalism in Latin America," in: Marty/Appleby 1991: 142–96.

Duffy, Eamon (1992), *The Stripping of the Altars: Traditional Religion in England 1400–1580*. New Haven, Conn.: Yale University Press.

Finke, Roger/Stark, Rodney (1988), "Religious Economies and Sacred Canopies: Religious Mobilization in American Cities, 1906," in: *American Sociological Review* 53: 41–49.

— (1992), *The Churching of America, 1776–1990: Winners and Losers in Our Religious Economy*. New Brunswick, N.J.: Rutgers University Press.

— (1998), "Religious Choices and Competition (Reply to Olson)," in: *American Sociological Review* 63: 761–66.

Froehle, Bryan (1998), "Pentecostals and Evangelicals in Venezuela: Consolidating Gain, Moving in New Directions," in: Cleary/Stewart-Gambino: 201–25.

Gold, Daniel (1991), "Organized Hinduisms: From Vedic Truth to Hindu Nation," in: Marty/Appleby: 531–93.

Hanegraaff, Wouter J. (1998), *New Age Religion and Western Culture: Esotericism in the Mirror of Secular Thought*. Albany, N.J.: State University of New York Press.

Hardacre, Helen (1984), *The Religion of Japan's Korean Minority: The Preservation of Ethnic Identity*. Berkeley, Calif.: University of California, Institute of East Asian Studies.

Heelas, Paul (1996), *The New Age Movement*. Oxford: Blackwell.

Hoffman, Valerie J. (1995), "Muslim Fundamentalists," in: Marty/Appleby: 199–230.

Kane, Ousmane (1994), "Izala: The Rise of Muslim Reformism in Northern Nigeria," in: Marty/Appleby: 490–512.

Kox, Willem/Meeus, Wim/Hart, Harm 't (1991), "Religious Conversion of Adolescents: Testing the Lofland and Stark Model of Religious Conversion," in: *Sociological Analysis* 52: 227–40.

Kwon, Victoria Hyonchu/Ebaugh, Helen Rose/Hagan, Jacqueline (1997), "The Structure and Function of Cell Group Ministry in a Korean Christian Church," in: *Journal for the Scientific Study of Religion* 36: 247–56.

Lofland, John/Stark, Rodney (1965), "Becoming a World-Saver: A Theory of Conversion to a Deviant Perspective," in: *American Sociological Review* 30: 862–75.

Martin, David (1990), *Tongues of Fire: The Explosion of Protestantism in Latin America*. Oxford: Blackwell.

Marty, Martin E./Appleby, R. Scott, eds. (1991), *Fundamentalisms Observed*. Chicago: University of Chicago Press.

— eds. (1993a), *Fundamentalism and Society*. Chicago: University of Chicago Press.

— eds. (1993b), *Fundamentalism and the State*. Chicago: University of Chicago Press.

— eds. (1994), *Accounting for Fundamentalisms*. Chicago: University of Chicago Press.

— eds. (1995), Fundamentalisms Comprehended. Chicago: University of Chicago Press.

Michael, S.M. (1989), *Culture and Urbanization*. New Delhi: Inter-India Publications.

Olson, Daniel V.A./Hadaway, C. Kirk (1999), "Religious Pluralism and Affiliation among Canadian Counties and Cities," in: *Journal for the Scientific Study of Religion* 38: 490–508.

Orsi, Robert Anthony (1985), *The Madonna of 115th Street: Faith and Community in Italian Harlem, 1880–1950*. New Haven, Conn.: Yale University Press.

Reader, Ian/Tanabe, Jr., George J. (1998), *Practically Religious: Worldly Benefits and the Common Religion of Japan*. Honolulu: University of Hawaii Press.

Shimazono, Susumu (1996), *Seishin sekai no yukue: Gendai sekai to Shinreisei Undō* [New Spirituality Movements in the Global Society]. Tokyo: Tōkyōdō Shuppan.

Spickard, James V. (1998), "Rethinking Religious Social Action: What is Rational about Rational Choice Theory?," in: *Sociology of Religion* 59: 99–115.

Stark, Rodney (1996), *The Rise of Christianity: A Sociologist Reconsiders History*. Princeton, N.J.: Princeton University Press.

Stark, Rodney/Bainbridge, William Sims (1987), *A Theory of Religion*. New York: Peter Lang.

Stark, Rodney/Kinke, Roger/Iannaccone, Laurence R. (1995), "Pluralism and Piety: England and Wales, 1851," in: *Journal for the Scientific Study of Religion* 34: 431–44.

Suzuki, Kentarō (1995), "Divination in Contemporary Japan: A General Overview and an Analysis of Survey Results," in: *Japanese Journal of Religious Studies* 22: 249–66.

Swearer, Donald K. (1991), "Fundamentalistic Movements in Theravada Buddhism," in: Marty/Appleby 1991: 628–90.

Tehranian, Majid (1993), "Fundamentalist Impact on Education and the Media," in: Marty/Appleby 1993a: 313–40.

Verweij, Johan/Ester, Peter/Nuata, Rein (1997), "Secularization as an Economic and Cultural Phenomenon: A Cross-National Analysis," in: *Journal for the Scientific Study of Religion* 36: 309–24.

Warner, R. Stephen (1993), "Work in Progress toward a New Paradigm for the Sociological Study of Religion in the United States," in: *The American Journal of Sociology* 98: 1044–93.

Religion and Diaspora

by

STEVEN VERTOVEC

Over the last ten years there has been a proliferation of literature and a mushrooming of interest, among members of ethnic minority groups as well as among academics, surrounding the notion of "diaspora." Historians and social scientists describe myriad facets of diaspora, while an ever increasing number of self-conscious communities call themselves diasporas. "Where once were dispersions," Kachig Tölölyan (1996: 3) observes, "there now is diaspora." Indeed, as James Clifford (1994: 306) writes, "[f]or better or worse, diaspora discourse is being widely appropriated. It is loose in the world, for reasons having to do with decolonization, increased immigration, global communication and transport—a whole range of phenomena that encourage multi-locale attachments, dwelling, and traveling within and across nations." Or, in other words, "diaspora" has become "one of the buzzwords of the postmodern age" (Cohen 1999: 3).

Surprisingly, religion has been the focus of relatively little attention within this growing field. The following article surveys a range of recent literature in order: (a) to outline some of the understandings of "diaspora" that have developed over the past ten years or so, (b) to argue that current "diaspora" concepts often suffer from conflation with "migration," "minority" and "transnationalism," and that each of these areas of study involve distinct—albeit related—dynamics of religious transformation, and (c) to indicate some patterns of religious change in connection with each of these concepts.

Emergent Meanings of Diaspora

Most recent works on the concept diaspora naturally commence with a few statements on etymology (for example, Tololyan 1996; Cohen 1997; Baumann 2000). The word "diaspora" derives from the Greek *diaspeirein* "to distribute"; it is a compound of *speirein* "to sow, to scatter" like seed, and *dia-* "from one end to the other." The term of course became associated with the Jewish historical experience, and hence was associated with being a dispersed people sharing a common religious and cultural heritage.

However, the Hebrew verb *galah* and noun *galut*—each expressing deportation and exile—perhaps convey the experience more accurately from the Jewish perspective. "[I]t is this close relationship between exile and consciousness of exile that is the singular feature of Jewish history; it is that which, over the centuries of migrations and vicissitudes, kept Jewish national consciousness alive" (Marienstras 1989: 120). *Galut* broadly designates the period from the destruction of the second Temple in 70 AD until the creation of the state of Israel. Hence a distinction is made by a number of scholars between *diaspora*—implying free movement, and especially pertaining to ancient Jews living among Greeks (Modrzejewski 1993)—and *galut* implying involuntary movement due to a conquest of the territory that was/is considered home (Marienstras 1989).

Nevertheless, the overall Jewish history of displacement has embodied the longstanding, conventional meaning of diaspora. Martin Baumann (1995) indicates that there have been at least three inherent, and rather different referential points with respect to what we refer to as the Jewish (or any other group's) historical experience "in the diaspora." That is, when we say something has taken place "in the diaspora" we must clarify whether we refer to (a) the *process* of becoming scattered, (b) the *community* living in foreign parts, or (c) the *place* or geographic *space* in which the dispersed groups live. The kind of conceptual muddle that may arise from the failure to distinguish these dimensions with regard to historical Jewish phenomena continues to plague the many emergent meanings of the notion of diaspora.

Academics have, in the term diaspora, found a useful concept through which to reorganize their research interests. This cuts across disciplines. The term has proliferated in conferences and publications within anthropology, sociology, cultural studies and political science. In 1999, by way of further example, the American Historical Association (AHA) held its annual conference on the theme "Diasporas and Migrations in History." The Chairman of the organizing committee, John O. Voll, said he received literally hundreds of session proposals and was surprised by their diversity: "Everywhere we looked, in almost every subfield, people wanted to talk about diasporas," he said (in Winkler 1999). However, not all of his colleagues welcomed the trendy topic: at the opening plenary of the 1999 AHA meeting, Colin A. Palmer opined that "[d]iaspora is a problem that invites a great deal of methodological fuzziness, ahistorical claims, and even romantic condescension" (in Winkler 1999: A 11).

Another account of the growing popularity of the term comes from Kachig Tölölyan, the editor of the academic journal entitled *Diaspora*. Tölölyan (1996: 3) has witnessed the fact that "[t]he rapidity of material and discursive change in the past three decades has increased both the number of global diasporas and the range and diversity of the new semantic domain that the term 'diaspora' inhabits." Once, as it were, there were three "classic diasporas" studied by social scientists—the Jewish, Greek and Armenian. By 1998 (only seven years after its launch), Tölölyan's journal had covered no less than thirty-six communities who had been identified by academics as, or who have called themselves, "diasporas" (Kachig Tölölyan, personal communication). These number pale in comparison to other examples of the discursive expansion of "diaspora" in the public sphere. At time of writing this article, a simple AltaVista search of the Internet turns up no less than 102,435 web pages concerned with the term "diaspora." Irish, "African," Chinese, Filipino, Indian, Arab, Tamil, Ukrainian, Iranian, Slovak—even Baganda, Anasazi, and Tongan—diasporas appear prominently with their own web pages along with numerous ones devoted to the "classic" Jewish, Greek and Armenian diasporas. Erica McClure (2000) found 650 websites for the Assyrian diaspora alone.

Why has there been such a shift of discursive category, particularly as a self-definition among dispersed groups? After all, drawing on the Jewish model, diaspora has arguably been a notion associated with suffering, loss, and victimization. Do contemporary, globally scattered communities opt to characterize themselves in this way?

One reason for the term's appeal to a range of groups lies in its relevance to addressing, in a summary fashion, a core dilemma faced by any dispersed or transplanted people: how to survive as a group. Here, J.D. Cohen Shaye and Ernst S. Frerichs (1993: i) underscore the nature of diaspora in the ancient world and signal its continued pertinence to the present:

> The contemporary common usage of the word "diaspora" which links the word to the experience of the Jewish people in their exile to Babylon and their dispersion throughout the Mediterranean world, is too exclusive an application. Viewed as a mass migration or movement or flight from one location or locations, diaspora could be viewed as an event in the history of several peoples of antiquity. Clearly the fact of dispersion and its many consequences have been an experience of many people, ancient and modern. Major issues for investigation include the question of whether, and how, those "dispersed" peoples maintain a sense of self-identity and a measure of communal cohesion. The central question for diaspora peoples is adaptation: how to adapt to the environment without surrendering group identity. These questions faced by the diaspora communities of antiquity are still apparent in modern times.

Further, the groups who now describe themselves as diasporas have wholly reappropriated and redefined the term as a new tool in cultural politics (Cohen 1999). Diaspora discourse has been adopted to move collective identity claims and community self-ascriptions beyond multiculturalism and beyond its related "impasse that the notions of 'racial and ethnic minorities' created with their emphasis on inter-group processes and their static notions of culture and difference" (Anthias 1998: 576). Diaspora has arisen as part of the postmodern project of resisting the nation-state, which is perceived as hegemonic, discriminatory and culturally homogenizing. The alternative agenda—now often associated with the notion of diaspora—advocates the recognition of hybridity, multiple identities and affiliations with people, causes and traditions outside the nation-state of residence. "Diasporic identity has become an occasion for the celebration of multiplicity and mobility—and a figure of our discontent with our being in a world apparently still dominated by nation-states" (Tölölyan 1996: 28).

While not necessarily embracing the nation-state, some scholars are taking a more critical view of this ground for a discursive shift. Katharyne Mitchell (1997), for one, is skeptical of the assumptions of many postmodernist theorists (especially Homi Bhabha 1994) who contend that hybrid, diasporic "third space" standpoints are inherently anti-essentialist and subversive of dominant hegemonies of race and nation. Indeed, Mary Kaldor (1996) points to the presence not only of cosmopolitans and anti-nationalists, but also hard-core, reactionary ethno-nationalists within numerous diasporas (also see Ignatieff 1993; Anderson 1995; Rajagopal 1997).

Overall, during the past few years the term diaspora has become a loose reference confusing categories such as immigrants, guest-workers, ethnic and "racial" minorities, refugees, expatriates and travelers. In fact, "the word diaspora is used today to describe any community that has emigrated whose numbers make it visible in the host community" (Marienstras 1989: 125). Among academics and "community leaders" alike, the over-use and under-theorization of the notion of diaspora threatens the term's descriptive usefulness (Safran 1991; Cohen 1995; Vertovec 1999).

In his seminal volume *Global Diasporas*, Robin Cohen (1997) seeks to clarify and typologize the relationship between the, as it were, original conceptualizations of the term as it applied to Jews and the contemporary extensions of the term often made to and by other groups who are dispersed worldwide. Cohen (1997: 21) undertakes his project with the view that "[a]ll scholars of diaspora recognize that the Jewish tradition is at the heart of any definition of the concept. Yet if it is necessary to take full account of this tradition, it is also necessary to transcend it." He accepts that there will be "inevitable dilutions, changes and expansions of the meaning of the term diaspora as it comes to be more widely applied" (1997: 22). To be sure, Jewish scholars themselves have intensively begun to re-think the category of diaspora with reference to the historical and modern development of Judaism (see, for instance, Boyarin/Boyarin 1993; Webber 1997; Tromp 1998). But drawing on a number of other key writers on the topic such as Kachig Tölölyan, Gabriel Sheffer and William Safran, Cohen suggests a set of features considered to be common among groups we might categorize together as sharing a diasporic existence. These are listed in Table 1.1 (see page 279).

In addition to these core traits outlined by Robin Cohen, it has been said that diasporic groups are characterized by a "triadic relationship" (Sheffer 1986; Safran 1991) between (1) a collectively self-identified ethnic group in one particular setting, (2) the group's co-ethnics in other parts of the world, and (3) the homeland states or local contexts whence they or their forebears came.

Table 1.1: Common Features of a Diaspora (Cohen 1997: 26, after Safran 1991)

1.	Dispersal from an original homeland, often traumatically, to two or more foreign regions;
2.	alternatively, the expansion from a homeland in search of work, in pursuit of trade or to further colonial ambitions;
3.	a collective memory and myth about the homeland, including its location, history and achievements;
4.	an idealization of the putative ancestral home and a collective commitment to its maintenance, restoration, safety and prosperity, even to its creation;
5.	the development of a return movement that gains collective approbation;
6.	a strong ethnic group consciousness sustained over a long time and based on a sense of distinctiveness, a common history and the belief in a common fate;
7.	a troubled relationship with host societies, suggesting a lack of acceptance at the least or the possibility that another calamity might befall the group;
8.	a sense of empathy and solidarity with co-ethnic members in other countries of settlement; and
9.	the possibility of a distinctive creative, enriching life in host countries with a tolerance for pluralism.

By way of an earlier review of this emerging field (Vertovec 1999a), I have proposed that current approaches to the topic can be distinguished in terms of underlying depictions of "diaspora" as a social form (concerned with the extent and nature of social, political and economic relationships, and marked by the kind of characteristics set out in Table 1.1), as type of consciousness (involving aspects of collective memory, desire and an awareness of identities spanning "here-and-there"), or as a mode of cultural reproduction (relating to the global flow of cultural objects, images and meanings).

While attempts to theorize and typologize diaspora are certainly beginning to clarify a number of significant dimensions and developments surrounding today's globally dispersed populations, it is clear that their religious elements (or sometimes, cores) have received relatively far less attention. Most writings on diaspora today have, in fact, "marginalized the factor of religion and relegated it to second place in favor of ethnicity and nationality" (Baumann 1998: 95).

Why Study Religion and Diaspora?

As a response to the above question, Ninian Smart (1999) offers three basic reasons why it is important to study the connection between religion and diaspora (or, we might further suggest, why it is important to study the religious aspects of diasporic experience). Firstly, the study of diasporas and their modes of adaptation can give us insights into general patterns of religious transformation. Secondly, diasporas may themselves affect the development of religion in the homeland: the wealth, education and exposure to foreign influences transferred from diaspora may have significant effects on organization, practice and even belief. Finally, because of the great incidence of diasporas in the modern world, "multiethnicity is now commonplace" (Smart 1999: 421). These three facets are addressed in more detail under various headings below.

In appreciating the transformative potentials of religion in diaspora, we must first recognize that this is nothing new. Jonathan Z. Smith (1978) notes that almost every religion in Late Antiquity occurred in both a homeland and in diasporic centers (see, for instance, van der Toorn 1998; Dirven 1998). In homelands during this period, religions developed intimately with local loyalties and ambitions, including as part of resistance to foreign domination.

> Each native tradition also had diasporic centers which exhibited marked change during the Late Antique period. There was a noticeable lessening of concern on the part of those in the diaspora from the destiny and fortunes of the native land and a relative severing of the archaic ties between religion and the land. Certain cult centers remained sites of pilgrimage or sentimental attachment, but the old beliefs in national deities and the inextricable relationship of the deity to particular places was weakened. (Smith 1978: xii)

In probing the meanings of religion, diaspora and change, we must also consider the implications of what we might call religious travel. James Clifford (1992) has written of "traveling cultures," suggesting how the meanings and relationships of dwelling-and-traveling displace conventional notions of culture and place (as well as challenge the ability of conventional methods of ethnography for representing cultures on the move). Since ancient times, religious travel has included pilgrimage, proselytization and the movement of students and scholars as well as exiles and migrants. Dale F. Eickelman and James Piscatori (1990a, 1990b) have underlined the importance of such travel on the development of Islam. They consider travel foremost as a journey of the mind, including an imaginary connection with many sacred centers that has a significant impact on notions of religious belonging over distance, collective identity with those elsewhere, and ritual practice that is both universal and localized. Obviously these ideas have relevance for the understanding of diasporic dynamics.

In thinking about traveling religion, however, Ninian Smart (1999) raises a caveat through the example of Hinduism. He asks us to consider

> themes such as caste, yoga, *bhakti* [devotion], pilgrimage, temple rituals, austerity (*tapasya*), wandering holy men, instruction in the scriptural traditions, regional variation, pundits, a strong sense of purity and impurity, household rituals, veneration of the cow, the practice of astrology, belief in reincarnation, the importance of acquiring merit, etc. These themes, which are woven together into the complicated fabric of Hinduism in India, do not all travel equally easily to new environments. (Smart 1999: 424)

Regarding categories and definitions, Robin Cohen (1997) questions whether religions can or should be described as "diasporas" alongside the dispersed ethnic groups which conventionally comprise the term. For Cohen, religions generally do not constitute diasporas in and of themselves. He describes religions at best as posing phenomena "cognate" to diasporas. This is largely because religions often span more than one ethnic group and, in the case of faiths that have come to be widely spread around the globe, religions normally do not seek to return to, or to recreate, a homeland. From Cohen's (1997: 189) perspective, while religions do not constitute diasporas themselves, they "can provide additional cement to bind a diasporic consciousness."

Judaism and Sikhism are the obvious exceptions, as Cohen recognizes. Dispersed members of these two traditions do represent diasporas since they are considered to comprise discrete ethnic groups, albeit especially marked by their religion, among whom many do indeed hold strong views about their conceived homelands. To these two, we should add groups like Ismailis, Alevis, Bahais, and Rastafarians whose respective religious distinctiveness usually tends to set them apart as ethnic groups. I have argued elsewhere (Vertovec 2000), too, that it is possible to talk of a "Hindu diaspora" especially because, no matter where in the world they live, most Hindus tend to sacralize India and therefore have a special kind of relationship to a spiritual homeland.

Other scholars are quicker to work with notions of "diaspora religion" (such as Smart 1999). John Hinnells (1997a: 686) defines diaspora religion as "the religion of any people who have a sense of living away from the land of the religion, or away from 'the old country'"; he even extends the term to cover situations in which a religion represents "a minority phenomenon" (Hinnells 1997a: 686). Gerrie ter Haar (1998) connects religion and diaspora through the assumption that migration means diaspora, migrants practice religion, and therefore diaspora implicates religion.

However, this is where conceptual waters begin to get muddy. Firstly, we begin to obfuscate the relationships of religion and diaspora, not to mention diaspora itself, if we regard it as involving any kind of migration or dispersal. It broadens the term far too much to talk—as many scholars do—about the "Muslim diaspora," "Catholic diaspora," "Methodist diaspora" and so forth. These are of course world traditions that span many ethnic groups and nationalities that have been spread by many other means than migration and displacement. Hinnells (1997a) himself flags up one problem with his own definition: are Muslims in Pakistan part of a diaspora religion because Islam is derived from and broadly centered on Mecca?

Secondly, to co-equate migration and subsequent minority status with diaspora also unnecessarily lumps together related yet arguably distinct conditions. "[O]ne does not announce the formation of the diaspora the moment the representatives of a people first get off the boat at Ellis island (or wherever)," Cohen quips (1997: 24). The same holds for patterns of "transnationalism," a concept that also tends to be wrongly used interchangeably with diaspora. Migration and minority status, diaspora and transnationalism are intuitively linked, of course (Vertovec/Cohen 1999). But linked does not mean synonymous.

Each of these abstract categories can be seen to comprise specific processes of socio-religious transformation.

Here, I argue that religious and other socio-cultural dynamics develop distinctively within the realms of (a) migration and minority status (of course a dual category that, given space to discuss, needs much unpacking as well), (b) diaspora, and (c) transnationalism. I consider migration to involve the transference and reconstitution of cultural patterns and social relations in new setting, one that usually involves the migrants as minorities becoming set apart by "race," language, cultural traditions and religion. I refer to diaspora here especially as an imagined connection between a post-migration (including refugee) population and a place of origin and with people of similar cultural origins elsewhere. By "imagined" I do not mean such connections might not be actual. Rather, by this I emphasize the often strong sentiments and mental pictures according to which members of diasporas organize themselves and undertake their cultural practices. This recalls Richard Marienstras' (1989: 120) definition of a diaspora as a group based on "a degree of national, or cultural, or linguistic awareness" of "a relationship, territorially discontinuous, with a group settled 'elsewhere.'" By transnationalism I refer to the actual, ongoing exchanges of information, money and resources—as well as regular travel and communication—that members of a diaspora may undertake with others in the homeland or elsewhere within the globalized ethnic community. Diasporas arise from some form of migration, but not all migration involves diasporic consciousness; all transnational communities comprise diasporas, but not all diasporas develop transnationalism.

These categories, their associated patterns and processes are discussed below. The list of themes or types of change briefly summarized under each heading is not meant to be exhaustive but suggestive, having been sieved from a variety of studies.

Patterns of Change Surrounding Migration and Minority Status

In many of the classic studies on immigrant incorporation processes, researchers have pointed to the continued salience of religion among immigrants (Herberg 1955; Glazer/Moynihan 1963; Gordon 1964). Although remaining important, the social organization and practice of religion is usually modified, nevertheless, by a variety of factors involved in movement and resettlement in a new context. Dimensions of change, and some of the factors having an impact upon them, include the following.

Organization and mobilization. Upon settling in a new environment, immigrants often soon set about collectively organizing themselves for purposes of religious worship. The formation of associations is one prominent kind of socio-religious organization, established to raise and distribute funds and coordinate activities (Rex/Joly/Wilpert 1987). Sometimes immigrant associations seek to draw upon a remembered past in an attempt to replicate as nearly as possible an old ethnic-religious community in a new setting, such as Nancy J. Wellmeier (1998) describes among Guatamalan Mayans in Los Angeles. Pre-migration social and cultural factors play important roles in the creation of immigrant religious institutions (Clarke/Peach/Vertovec 1990), as do residential patterns in the new setting (Ebaugh/O'Brien/Saltzman Chafetz 2000).

The establishment and maintenance of religious institutions among immigrants not unusually involves a high degree of conflict and contestation. John Bodnar (1985: 166–67) states that in the nineteenth century, for instance, "no institution in immigrant America exhibited more discord and division than the Church. ... Usually the church and other religious organizations were the only immigrant institutions to contain an entrenched, premodern cadre of leaders ... [who] labored feverishly to centralize authority, revitalize faith, and maintain the loyalty of their flocks in a rapidly changing world."

Processes surrounding associations and other institutions also reflect the size and development of the immigrant population itself. Aspects of this are described with reference to successive stages of community "fusion" and "fission" reflecting the size and distribution of migrants drawn from distinct caste/social status, regional and linguistic backgrounds (Dahya 1974; Bhardwaj/Rao 1990; Williams 1992).

David Bowen (1987) has described such organizational phases among Gujarati Hindus in Bradford, England. These are characterized by: (1) the establishment of homogeneity among new immigrants looking for some kind of commonality through religious lowest common denominators, (2) the emergence of specific devotional congregations based upon demographic factors (such as neighborhood) and devotional orientations (especially adherence to certain parochial traditions of a homeland), (3) the formation of caste associations as families were reunited and numbers of Gujaratis grew, and (4) the re-establishment of homogeneity by way of umbrella organizations created to interface with local government (cf. Vertovec 1994a).

The politics of recognition. Another important set of activities that immigrant associations engage concerns campaigns for legal tolerance or cultural rights surrounding specific practices, freedom from discrimination, and access to public resources offered to other groups (Vertovec/Peach 1997; Vertovec 1999b, 2001). Such needs arise not only due to immigrant but to minority status. Some areas and examples of such engagement are (Vertovec 1998): modes of practice such as religious slaughter of animals and, for Muslims, the provision of *halal* food in public institutions; aspects of education (from ensuring "modesty of dress" among female pupils through approaches to religious education to questions surrounding sex education, as well as the entire issue of separate religiously-based schools); law (especially family law governing matters including marriage, divorce and inheritance) and legal protection against religious discrimination or incitement to religious hatred; and access to public resources and social services (state funding for community activities, the recognition of special community needs in health and housing).

Women's position and roles. Following migration the position of women in families and in the wider immigrant community often undergoes considerable transformation (see Willis/Yeoh 2000). This is particularly the case if women take up post-migration employment in contrast to their pre-migration status. In many cases more significant and decisive functions of women arise in religious community associations and affairs: women often take the lead in the organization and management of collective religious activities. What remains central, or indeed may be enhanced, following migration is the key role women play in reproducing religious practice—particularly by way of undertaking domestic religious practice (for example among Hindus, see Logan 1988; McDonald 1987; Rayaprol 1997).

Generations. Issues of religious and cultural reproduction naturally raise questions concerning the maintenance, modification or discarding of religious practices among the subsequent generations born and raised in post-migration settings. Everyday religious and cultural practices, religious nurture at home and religious education at school, and participation at formal places of worship all shape the identities and activities of the so-called second and third generations (Larson 1989; Jackson/Nesbitt 1993). Some conditioning factors affecting identity and activity among second and third generation youth which sets them apart from their immigrant parents include (Vertovec/Rogers 1998): education in Western schools and the inculcation of secular and civil society discursive practices; youth dissatisfaction with conservative community leaders and religious teachers who do not understand the position of post-migrant youth; growth of "vernacular" religious traditions across Europe; compartmentalization of religion (see below); and immersion in American/European popular youth culture.

Ethnic and religious pluralism. The situation of being migrants from another place and, thereby, of being minority "others" often stimulates a mode of religious change through heightened self-awareness. As Barbara Metcalf (1996: 7) puts it, "[t]he sense of contrast—contrast with a past or contrast with the rest of society—is at the heart of a self-consciousness that shapes religious style." The process has been observed by Kim Knott (1986: 46), who states: "Many Hindus in Leeds are only too aware that their religion is one amongst others. Not only are there indigenous faiths, generally grouped together by Hindus as 'Christian', but there are also other South Asian faiths. ... In this country Hinduism is just one minority faith amongst others. An awareness of religious pluralism has affected the way Hindus think about themselves and their faith." And in Penny Logan's (1988: 124) research on culture and religion among Gujaratis in Britain, "many adults reported that they had become more aware of their religion in Britain, as a result of belonging to a minority group in a predominantly irreligious society. They could no longer take their religion and their children's assumption of it for granted."

We should not assume that religious pluralism only refers to the co-presence of different faiths. Migrants—like travelers—newly often come across, for the first time, members and practices of distinct traditions within their own religion. As Eickelman and Piscatori (1990: xv) point out, "the encounter with the Muslim 'Other' has been at least as important for self-definition as the confrontation with the European 'Other'. ... The ironic counterpart to travel broadening one's consciousness of the spiritual unity of the umma is that travel may define frontiers between Muslims and thus narrow their horizons."

The self-consciousness of migrant minorities due to a condition of pluralism relates to, and may in certain ways overlap with, the identity dynamics associated with the condition of diaspora.

Patterns of Change Surrounding Diaspora

As Shaye and Frerichs (1993) emphasized above, matters of cultural and religious adaptation-yet-continuity are foremost on the agendas of most diasporic groups. "[W]hat we have to grasp is a diasporic duality of continuity and change," suggests Martin Sökefeld (2000: 23), while we remain cognizant that "[t]he rhetoric of continuity obscures that [sic] actors constantly re-constitute and re-invent (or refuse to re-constitute) in diverse manners what is imagined as simply continuing." We must appreciate, too, that parallel forms of change may well be happening in the homeland as well, stimulated either from the diaspora or by non-diasporic factors altogether. The "diasporic duality of continuity and change" is evident in a number of socio-religious domains.

Identity and community. "[R]eligious identities," writes R. Stephen Warner (1998: 3), "often (but not always) mean more to [individuals] away from home, in their diaspora, than they did before, and those identities undergo more or less modification as the years pass." One reason this occurs, he suggests, is because "[t]he religious institutions they build, adapt, remodel and adopt become worlds unto themselves, 'congregations', where new relations among the members of the community—among men and women, parents and children, recent arrivals and those settled—are forged" (Warner 1998: 3). One example of this is to be found among Cubans in the United States who make pilgrimage to a purpose-built shrine in Miami. There, "through transtemporal and translocative symbols at the shrine, the diaspora imaginatively constructs its collective identity and transports itself to the Cuba of memory and desire" (Tweed 1997: 10).

"Identities change over time," Eickelman and Piscatori (1990b: 17) emphasize. Moreover, diasporic identification involves complexities and permutations: some people "continue to regard their land of birth as 'home', while others come to identify primarily with their land of settlement [Karpat 1990]. Others, such as Turkish workers in Germany [Mandel 1990], or indeed such intellectuals as Salman Rushdie (1988), may feel at home in neither place, at ease in neither their land of settlement nor their land of origin. There may also be multiple, co-existing identities" (Eickelman/Piscatori 1990b: 17).

Ritual practice. Complexities and permutations also often characterize processes of modifying or "streamlining" religious practices in diaspora (Hinnells 1997b). By way of illustration, in some places outside India basic Hindu ritual procedures have become truncated (as in Malaysia; Hutheesing 1983), refashioned (in Britain; Michaelson 1987), or eclectically performed (in East Africa; Bharati 1976); in others, much of the style or corpus of rites has been virtually "invented" in conjunction with social change in the community (evident in Trinidad; Vertovec 1992), and in still other places, basic rites have been mutually "negotiated" so as to provide a kind of socio-religious bridge between migrants from regionally distinct traditions (in England, Knott 1986; in Scotland, Nye 1995; and in the USA, Lessinger 1995). In most places, many rites have been popularized in order to appeal to young, diaspora-born Hindus even to the chagrin of conservative elders: in Malaysia, for instance, Hindu leaders have complained that the inclusion of India-produced music has wrought the "disco-ization" of Hindu ritual (Willford 1998)!

"Re-spatialization." Jonathan Z. Smith described how, in the ancient world of the Mediterranean and Near East,

> For the native religionist, homeplace, the place to which one belongs, was *the* central religious category. One's self-definition, one's reality was the place into which one had been born—understood as both geographical and social place. To the new immigrant in the diaspora, nostalgia for homeplace and cultic substitutes for the old, sacred center were central religious values. ... Diasporic religion, in contrast to native, locative religion, was utopian in the strictest sense of the word, a religion of "nowhere," of transcendence. (1978: xiv, emphasis in original)

Barbara Metcalf (1996) seems to recapitulate Smith through her interest in religious/diasporic "spaces" that are non-locative. "[I]t is ritual and sanctioned practice that is prior and that creates 'Muslim space,'" Metcalf (1996: 3) proposes, "which thus does not require any juridically claimed territory or formally consecrated or architecturally specific space." She extends the spatial metaphor through reference to the "social space" of networks and identities created in new contexts away from homelands, the "cultural space" that emerges as Muslims interact, and "physical space" of residence and community buildings founded in new settings. Together, these spaces comprise the "imagined maps of diaspora Muslims" (Metcalf 1996: 18).

Pnina Werbner (1996) echoes Metcalf's "imagined maps" by suggesting that Muslims in diaspora connect via a "global sacred geography." This is created anew through the ritual sacralization of space in diasporic settings—a process, Werbner describes among Pakistani Sufis in Britain, which inherently conjoins sites both at home in Pakistan and in Manchester, UK. Similarly for Senegalese Sufis (Mourides) in diaspora, their holy city of Touba is metaphorically "recreated in the routine activities of the migrants and through recurrent parallels of the migrants' lives with that of the founder of the order, Cheikh Amadu Bamba" (Carter 1997: 55).

Diasporic transformation also involves a changing sense of religious time as well as space. As Werner Schiffauer (1988: 150) recalls among Turkish Muslims in Germany:

> The specifically peasant experience of an oscillation of one's social world between states of religious community and society is no longer present. During sacred times, society no longer changes into a religious community but, rather, one leaves the society and enters the religious community—if possible, we must add, since the opposition between secular and sacred times is now determined by the more fundamental notions of the working day and leisure.

Religion/culture. The reconfigured distinctions of sacred and secular space and time that occur in diaspora are matched by the sharpening of distinctions between religion and culture. To illustrate what is meant here: David Pocock (1976) observed that in one branch (the Bochasanwasi Shri Akshar Purushottam Sanstha) of the Hindu Swaminarayan movement there has emerged a tendency to consider certain aspects of Gujarati culture (including family structure, language, diet, marriage networks, and the position of women) as quasi-religious phenomena—that is, as behavioral and ideological facets contributing to the fulfillment of *dharma*. The subsequent problem Pocock discerned for the Sanstha is that of "dis-embedding a set of beliefs and practices—a 'religion' from a 'culture' which would then be defined as 'secular'" (1976: 362). This is a critical yet common dilemma for Hindus throughout the diaspora (and, some observe, in India itself). It entails moves toward a self-conscious "rationalization of the distinction religion/culture" (Pocock 1976: 357) despite the everywhere-asserted dictum that "Hinduism is a way of life."

Processes of self-consciously distinguishing elements of religion/culture are bound to have differing results in various domains (in temples, in religious or cultural associations, in homes, in the workplace). In each case among Hindus in diaspora, such processes inherently involve both some kind of adaptation to religiously and culturally plural environments and the generation or heightening of distinct "ethnic" sentiments.

Martin Sökefeld (2000: 10) considers relevant developments among Alevis in diaspora:

> One could speak of an Alevi revival in Germany (and in Turkey) since 1989, but this revival was not a simple renewal of Alevism as it had been practiced until a few decades ago in Turkey. Instead, it implicated a serious transformation of Alevism and its rituals which can be glossed over as "folklorization": Although originally "religious" rituals were practiced, Alevism was re-constituted mainly as a secular culture. (Sökefeld 2000: 10)

The secularization of Alevism occurred, not least, due to the role of hardcore, anti-religious Marxists within the Alevi community in Germany. A further process of "desacralization" has occurred, Sökefeld notes, through the core Alevi collective ritual (*cem*) being turned into a public ritual solely to affirm identity based on symbolic cultural difference (from other Turks and Sunni Muslims).

In a similar way, both Madawi Al-Rasheed (1998) and Erica McClure (2000) detail ways in which members of the Assyrian diaspora sharply contend whether religion or ethnicity (or language) forms the basis of community identity.

Many young South Asian Muslim women interviewed by Kim Knott and Sadja Khokher (1993) are also conceptually establishing a firm distinction between "religion" and "culture"—a distinction between what, for their parents (particularly prior to migration), were largely indistinguishable realms. Further, they are rejecting their parents' conformity to ethnic traditions that the parents consider as emblematic of religiosity (such as manner of dress) while wholly embracing a Muslim identity in and of itself. Among these young women, Knott and Khokher explain, there is a "self-conscious exploration of the religion which was not relevant to the first generation" (1993: 596).

Patterns of Change Surrounding Transnationalism

"Transnationalism" refers to the existence of communication and interactions of many kinds linking people and institutions across the borders of nation-states and, indeed, around the world (see, among others, Glick Schiller/Basch/Szanton Blanc 1992; Smith/Guarnizo 1998; Portes/Guarnizo/Landolt 2000). Among immigrant groups, certainly the existence of such links does not represent a wholly new set of phenomena. One hundred years ago, for instance, immigrants to the United States maintained contact with relatives in the homeland, remitted money, supported homeland political groups, and so forth (see Bodnar 1985; Foner 1997; Gabaccia 2000). However, Nancy Foner (1997: 369) concludes: "Modern technology, the new global economy and culture, and new laws and political arrangements have all combined to produce transnational connections that differ in fundamental ways from those maintained by immigrants a century ago."

With regard to our current topic of inquiry, it is obvious transnationalism is relevant to more general processes and patterns of globalization, or an intensification of connectedness, affecting religion (Robertson 1992; Beyer 1994; Held et al. 1999; Beckford 2000). Yet this is a discussion that we must leave aside due to limitations of space.

As Susanne Hoeber Rudolph (1997: 1) reminds us, "[r]eligious communities are among the oldest of the transnationals: Sufi orders, Catholic missionaries, and Buddhist monks carried work and praxis across vast spaces before those places became nation-states or even states." Further, the transference of religion accompanied some of the modern period's earliest yet perhaps most powerful forms of globalization and transnationalism—namely mercantilism, conquest and colonial domination.

Coming back to the topic of migrants and diasporas, Peggy Levitt (1998) points to the serious dearth of research concerning the links maintained between post-migration communities and their origins, and how these links lead to globalized, everyday practices, discourses and relations. "While there is a rich body of work on immigrant incorporation," she (1998: 75) writes, "most of this research does not shed sufficient light on how continued relations between home and host-country institutions transform religious practice." Importantly, Levitt stresses how the transformations toward "globalized, everyday practices, discourses and relations" affect religious practice in both home and "host" contexts (also see Gardner 1995; Goldring 1998; Riccio 1999).

Networks: horizontal & vertical. Rudolph (1997) contrasts two prominent patterns of contemporary global socio-religious organization. On the one hand she describes many longstanding forms of organization as "hierarchy" (marked by concentration of decision making and coordination of action); these she contrasts to largely emergent forms of "self-organization" (characterized by decentralization and spontaneity). We might also describe this pair of ideal types as bureaucracy vs. networks, as well as globalization from above vs. globalization from below.

These forms are relevant to Eickelman's (1997: 27) view that "[m]odern forms of travel and communication have accelerated religious transnationalism—the flow of ideologies, access to information on organizational forms and tactics, and the transformation of formerly elite movements to mass movements—rendering obsolete earlier notions of frontier as defined primarily by geographical boundaries." Obviously, new technologies such as computer-mediated communication are now having a considerable impact on transnational religious organization and activity (Castells 1997; Eickelman/Anderson 1999; Miller/Slater 2000).

Transnational networks can function to enhance individual religiosity as well. This is exhibited by Haitian Catholic and Protestant preachers who maintain congregational ties in Haiti and to immigrants in the United States (Basch/Glick Schiller/Szanton Blanc 1994), and by Trinidadian Catholic priests who serve pastoral roles for members of the diaspora via the Internet (Miller/Slater 2000).

Bruno Riccio (1999) describes how Sufi brotherhoods (especially the Mouride) play key organizational roles (including the facilitation of trading networks) in the diasporic experience of Senegalese in Italy (also see Ebin 1996; Carter 1997). The transnational brotherhood provides members with continuous feedback in order to maintain morality. "In other words," Riccio writes,

> it is the fact that the Mouride movement is embedded in a transnational social field that makes it so successful in controlling potentially deviant behavior. Within this field Mouride transnational formations are kept alive by oral conversation, the selling of cassettes, where besides prayers and Kasaids [sacred poems] one finds information about *ndiguel* (orders, decrees) from the Kalif or from the Touba establishment. (1999: 132)

Riccio also depicts the movement of Marabouts, living saints or spiritual leaders who visit diasporic communities and provide followers with blessings and advice. The visits "reaffirm the link and the identification between the sacred place (Touba [whence the founder of the movement comes]), the Saint … and the diasporic community of Mourides" (Riccio 1999: 133).

A final example of new modes of transnational religious networks is represented by the "milk miracle" of September 1995. As reported by many news agencies, religious images or *murtis* in Hindu temples around Britain (London, Leicester, Birmingham and Leeds) and around the world (including New York, Delhi, Hong Kong and Bangkok) were observed to "drink" substantial quantities of milk. News of such a "miracle" in one temple location was rapidly conveyed to another, where milk was subsequently offered: if "drank" by the *murti*, the news was immediately relayed elsewhere. Practically in the course of a day, news of similar incidents spread around the world. A South Asian religious diaspora, now connected through advanced global telecommunications, had wrought "the age of the instant miracle" (*The Guardian* 23 September 1995). As Chetan Bhatt (1997: 252) describes it, however, the event was created as the "VHP and RSS were quick to mobilize their international networks to generate the miracle globally."

Patterns of Global Religious Change

Migration and minority status, diaspora and transnationalism each relate to different, but overlapping, grounds upon which religious transformations take place. The social scientific task of comprehending and analyzing these trends calls for a high degree of clarity as to which of these realms we are addressing at any time. Fuzziness and conflation of categories will cause us to chase our theoretical tails.

With special reference to South Asian religions, for instance, useful methodological frameworks for comparative study of the factors conditioning change among religious communities through migration, diaspora and transnationalism are suggested by authors such as Jayawardena (1968, 1980), Clarke, Peach and Vertovec (1990), Knott (1991), Ballard (1994), Hinnells (1997b), and Vertovec (2000). They emphasize the need to take into mutual account premigration factors (including economic patterns, social structure and status relations), modes of migration, atmospheres and frameworks of reception and settlement, and trajectories of adaptation.

Inquiry into patterns of religious change surrounding this set of categories—migration and minority status, diaspora and transnationalism—will shine significant light on yet broader processes affecting religion in the world today. The final list of themes and short examples, below, suggest some of these.

Awareness of global religious identities. Smart (1999) points to the fact that, due in large part to migration, diasporas and transnationalism, there are now world organizations for every major religious tradition and subtradition located in most parts of the world. "Such a consciousness of belonging to a world community has grown considerably in very recent times," Smart writes (1999: 423). "Consequently, the divergences between diaspora and home communities are diminishing." Even for relatively remote groups, transnational narratives "construct and negotiate the relationships between multiple identities" by tying individuals and communities into larger common constituencies (Robbins 1998: 123). Dale F. Eickelman and Jon Anderson (1999) emphasize how such a new sense of collective awareness and connection among Muslims in various parts of the globe has especially been forged through new communication technologies.

Daniel Miller and Don Slater (2000) discovered a perceived need among many local Hindus in an out-of-the-way place like Trinidad—in a community largely cut off from India for generations—to connect with a wider, indeed global, form of Hinduism (albeit in the religious nationalist form of the Bharatiya Janata Party [BJP] and the Rashtriya Swayamsevak Sangh [RSS]).

> The Internet allows for an expansion of communication, but in this case it is used to repair a discrepancy, thereby helping communities and people come closer to a realization of who they already feel they "really" are. The mechanics involved require a sense of geography that defies the usual separation of the local and the global. In these cases the increasingly global use of the Internet across the Diaspora is a function of the re-establishment of local communications that had become sundered. (Miller/Slater 2000: 178)

Universalization v. localization. Ira Lapidus (2001) describes how there has always been inherent tension between Islamic universals and the experience of specific traditions being rooted in particular cultural contexts. Much of Islamic history has seen an "oscillation" between the two. Similar tensions are found in every world religion, and processes surrounding migration, diaspora and transnationalism continue to exercise or exacerbate them.

This is apparent in Camilla Gibb's (1998) study of Muslim immigrants from the Ethiopian city of Harar. In Harar there exists a centuries-old Islam of syncretic saints cults. Yet in diaspora (in this case, Canada) there has arisen an Islam constructed to appeal to a multi-national congregation. "As a result," Gibb (1998: 260) concludes, "what appears to be happening is a homogenization or essentialization of Islamic practices, where culturally specific aspects of Islam that are not shared with other Muslim populations are likely to disappear, since they are not reinforced by Muslims from other groups in this context." Indeed, Harari children in Canada are not taught about their heritage, and they are indeed turning against any religious practices directed toward saints cults.

Among the Bangladeshis with whom Katy Gardner worked, too, "[m]igrants to Britain and the Middle East have moved from an Islam based around localized cultures and molded to the culture and geography of the homelands, to an international Islam of Muslims from many different countries and cultures" (1993: 225). On an individual level, Miller and Slater (2000: 179) met a young Trinidadian Muslim woman who was using the Internet "to try to sort out in her own mind which aspects of her practice were orthodox and which were local."

Perhaps at the same time we are seeing a shift to global forms of religion, however, new processes of localization are taking place. In this way Raymond Williams (1988) and Diana Eck (1996) both describe the emergence of an "American Hinduism" alongside a purported process bringing about the "Americanization" of Muslims (Haddad/Esposito 2000).

What is essential in a religious tradition? As we have already seen above, the conscious disaggregation of "religion" from "culture" is sometimes prompted among people in diaspora. Raymond Williams (1984: 191) comments:

> The critical assumption here is that there are some aspects associated with past religious practice that are fundamental and essential to the continuation of the religion and others that are cultural accoutrements that are not so fundamental. Thus, the process of searching for an adaptive strategy becomes the attempt to distinguish what is essential in the religion and what is not.

Jacques Waardenburg (1988) points to the growing trend (especially among young people?) for discarding national or regional traditions and focussing upon the Qur'an and Sunna in order to distinguish what is truly Islamic—that is, normative—from what is secondary. The felt need to make this distinction is often what prompts young people in diaspora situations to join so-called "fundamentalist" movements (Schiffauer 1999).

Politico-religious activity. Religious-cum-political groups and networks that are dispersed across the borders of nation-states—or indeed, scattered globally—have in recent times developed their agendas in arguably new and distinct ways. The adoption of diverse modes of communication (including electronic and computer-mediated forms), the changing nature and manipulation of resources (channeling people, funds and information to and from a number of localities), and the maintenance of various kinds of relationships in relation to encompassing social and political contexts (including ties with people in the homeland, settlement land and elsewhere in the world) are among the factors characterizing many politico-religious movements as diasporic or transnational.

Politico-religious movements in diaspora comprise many possible types. A movement's aim may be to change a particular country's current regime or its entire political system. A diasporic group may be concerned with affecting the religion and politics of a nation-state of origin, it may be seeking to create its own autonomous region or nation-state, or it may be dedicated to the cause of "exporting" a politico-religious ideology from one place of origin to another setting. The composition of a world-wide politico-religious group may be multi-ethnic or made-up of people with a single ethnic identity. Other diasporic or transnational dimensions of politico-religious groups are represented in the following examples.

Religious nationalism in India is represented by the Vishwa Hindu Parishad (VHP), the BJP and the RSS. Such revivalist Hinduism, observes Chetan Bhatt (1997: 155), "has relied extensively on its followers in the US, Britain, Canada and Europe to generate global support and funds for its political ventures in India" (also see Rajagopal 1997; Mukta/Bhatt 2000). Yet religion often provides an ally or source for secular nationalists, too, as witnessed among Armenians (Pattie 1997). Thomas A. Tweed (1997) similarly describes how a Cuban Catholic shrine in Miami functions as a place specifically to express a very particular (anti-Castro) diasporic nationalism.

Transnational religious terrorism is now high on the agenda of many security conscious institutions (Hoffman 1998). The network-without-center manner of organization now facilitated by new technologies is ideal for groups involved in extreme forms of politico-religious activity (Eickelman/Piscatori 1990b; Castells 1997). In this way Eickelman (1997) describes links between Islamicist groups, as well as the nature of relationships within the groups themselves, as decentered, multiple, fluid and subject to severance at short notice.

Peter Mandaville (1999) finds that it is usually amongst diasporic Muslims of the Western world that we find the Internet being appropriated for political purposes.

> A more sober examination of the situation, however, reveals that very few of the Muslim groups who have a presence on the Internet are involved in this sort of activity. Moreover, there are also those who argue that the Internet has actually had a moderating effect on Islamist discourse. Sacad al-Faqih, for example, believes that Internet chat rooms and discussion forums devoted to the debate of Islam and politics serve to encourage greater tolerance. He believes that in these new arenas one sees a greater convergence in the centre of the Islamist political spectrum and a weakening of its extremes.

Such a view is reinforced by Rima Berns McGown's (1999) work with Somali refugees in Canada and England. She suggests:

> The Islamists' influence is obvious in the very way that the practice of Islam has evolved for diaspora Somalis. The old religious symbolism—the local Sufi shaykh, the dhikr, the token Qur'anic memorization—has given way to a sense of Islam as a vital force in understanding how to live in this new world, a force that might require more blatant identification (via, for instance, a beard or the hijab) or personal study (a parallel with the Jewish yeshiva might be made here). While diaspora Somalis may accept or reject one or other Islamist group's interpretation of doctrine or prescription for action, they share the sense of the religion's vitality that is the Islamists' driving force. (1999: 229)

Reorienting devotion. Smith's (1978: xiv) account of religion of Late Antiquity posits that "[r]ather than a god who dwelt in his temple or would regularly manifest himself in a cult house, the diaspora evolved complicated techniques for achieving visions, epiphanies or heavenly journeys. That is to say, they evolved modes of access to the deity which transcended any particular place." Such modes represented fundamental shifts in belief or religious orientation.

Other core shifts have been observed in connection with migration or displacement. In a study of letters written by nineteenth-century immigrants to the United States, Jay P. Dolan (1998) found it difficult to determine the religious affiliation of the letter writers. In one stirring fact, Dolan observed a complete absence of Jesus, as well as of the Virgin Mary and individual saints. Instead, the immigrants' general religious orientation was toward God as a constant companion and guide, seemingly meant to mitigate another constant theme of this-worldly suffering. The afterlife was commonly thought of as a place of joy and reunion. Dolan (1998: 153) concludes: "This understanding of the afterlife as a place of reunion mirrored the social experience of the immigrants and the sense of separation inherent in the immigrant experience."

In a slightly different look at how migrant and diasporic experience affects religious orientations, Bhikhu Parekh (1994) accounts for the centrality of one sacred text, the Ramayana, among numerous overseas Hindu communities. He does so by highlighting several themes, images, and messages conveyed by the text, relating the ways these resonate with and appeal to the diasporic condition. This includes reference to the Ramayana's themes of exile, suffering, struggle and eventual return resonated especially with the indentured migrant laborers who ventured overseas.

A reorienting of devotion is also evident in the rise of orthodox, universal forms already mentioned in a number of places above. Overall, Smart (1999: 425) reckons: "The diasporas of the Global Period [of the last twenty-five years] have become somewhat more orthodox in tone." Katy Gardner's work on the social and economic dynamics linking the Sylhet district of Bangladesh with the East End of London (1993, 1995) demonstrates ways in which transnational migration processes and practices lead to increased religious fervor, puritanism and orthodoxy based on scripturalism. As a driving force of such change, Gardner found the richest transmigrants to be most interested in enforcing orthodoxy—mainly for purposes of demonstrating status and acquiring social capital.

Compartmentalization. In assessing developments affecting religions and diasporas, Hinnells (1997b) stresses the impact of contemporary Western notions of religion on transplanted non-Western faiths. Such notions include secularization, liberal notions of inter-faith dialogue, and a broad tendency to treat religion as just another "compartment" of life. Hence it may come as no surprise that for many Hindus in Britain, Hinduism now "has the status of a 'compartment', or one of a number of aspects of life. ... Some are beginning to think of Hinduism as many people do Christianity, something to be remembered during large festivals and at births, marriages and deaths" (Knott 1986: 46).

This kind of religious shift should not be limited to non-Western traditions, however. As Susan Pattie (1997: 214) discovered, "[f]or Armenians today, especially those in London, the sphere of religion is becoming increasingly isolated and definable as a distinct category of experience." Peggy Levitt (1998) relatedly suggests that Dominicans in diaspora have developed a more formal and utilitarian relationship to their church than do their counterparts in the Dominican Republic.

The problem with the past. Pattie (1997: 231) describes the "double bind" characterizing the situation of the Armenian Apostolic Church among Armenians in diaspora:

> On the one hand, its role as a national institution, imbued with visual, linguistic, and musical traditions, forges deep psychological links with the past. Looking at their diaspora situation, Armenians in Cyprus and London place great value on this continuing, seemingly unchanging aspect of the Church. Yet at the same time the old presentation is not always understood and, worse, not even experienced, as attendance and participation dwindle with each new generation.

In the Armenian example, it would seem the past is of lessening interest to newer generations. On the other hand, "[n]ow that modern communication and travel technology brings dispersed peoples together more than ever, the usual assumption that attachment to the homeland will decline significantly after the first generation, and even more after the second, seems less self-evident" (Tweed 1997: 140). But of course—like with notions of presumed diasporic "continuity" discussed above—the idea of "attachment" to a homeland and a past signals what will most likely be a highly transformed mode and meaning of relationship.

Trajectories. A final theme of change involves the possible trajectories of collective identities and of local/regional or sectarian traditions in contexts of diaspora and transnationalism.

Possibilities for trajectories of identity are represented by Jacques Waardenburg's (1988) proposed set of "options" for Muslims in Europe (cf. Vertovec/Peach 1997; Vertovec/Rogers 1998). These can be summarized as (a) the secular option—discarding Muslim identity altogether; (b) the cooperative option—playing upon Muslim identity in the process of pursuing common goals with other groups; (c) the cultural option—maintaining particular social and cultural practices without much religious sentiment; (d) the religious option—emphasizing wholly scriptural modes of religious affiliation at the expense of cultural aspects (an option described by some as "fundamentalist"); (e) the ethnic-religious option—perpetuating a specific national or regional form of Islam (e.g. Moroccan); (f) the behavioral option—expressing Islamic tenets through moral or ritual behavior only; and (g) the ideological option—identifying with or opposing the "official" Islam of a particular home country.

The possible trajectories of specific sub-traditions, I have suggested (Vertovec 2000), come down to the following: (1) remaining intact, as represented by processes of community "fission" described earlier; (2) homogenizing parochial forms through lowest common denominators of belief and practice (as developed within Hinduism in the Caribbean; van der Veer/Vertovec 1991; Vertovec 1992, 1994b); (3) promoting a kind of ecumenism, in which a number of forms co-exist under a kind of umbrella organization (Williams 1988); (4) universalizing a specific form (such as the Hinduism of the VHP) by claiming it to be all-encompassing; and (5) cosmopolitanism, whereby the possibility of multiple, successive forms is celebrated (cf. Williams 1998).

Conclusion

The possible trajectories of identity and tradition in diaspora—like most of the themes of change suggested throughout this article—are not mutually exclusive. They are taking place simultaneously worldwide, and often within the same diaspora.

By isolating, as discrete categories, conditions surrounding migration and minority status, diaspora and transnationalism, we can gain more concise insights into processes and patterns of religious change. These tell us as much about a specific group's experience as they do about general characteristics of religious transformation on broader level of abstraction. While in most ways the rush to study diaspora is certainly welcomed—as it challenges us to reconsider fundamental concepts such as identity and community, culture, continuity and change—it should not lead us to obfuscate the very categories we wish to clarify.

References

Al-Rasheed, Madawi (1998), *Iraqi Assyrian Christians in London: The Construction of Ethnicity*. Lewiston, N.Y.: Edwin Mellen Press.

Anderson, Benedict (1995), "Ice Empire and Ice Hockey: Two Fin de Siécle Dreams," in: *New Left Review* 214: 146–50.

Anthias, Floya (1998), "Evaluating 'Diaspora': Beyond Ethnicity?" in: Sociology 32 (3): 557–80.

Ballard, Roger (1994), "Introduction: The Emergence of Desh Pardesh," in R. Ballard, ed., Desh Pardesh: The South Asian Presence in Britain. London: C. Hurst: 1–34.

Basch, Linda/Glick Schiller, Nina/Szanton Blanc, Cristina (1994), *Nations Unbound: Transnational Projects, Postcolonial Predicaments and Deterritorialized Nation-States*. Amsterdam: Gordon and Breach.

Baumann, Martin (1995), "Conceptualizing Diaspora: The Preservation of Religious Identity in Foreign Parts, Exemplified by Hindu Communities Outside India," in: *Temenos* 31: 19–35.

— (1998), "Sustaining 'Little Indias': Hindu Diasporas in Europe," in: G. ter Haar, ed., *Strangers and Sojourners: Religious Communities in the Diaspora*. Leuven: Peeters: 95–132.

— (2000), "Diaspora: Genealogies of Semantics and Transcultural Comparison," in: *Numen* 47: 313–37.

Beckford, James (2000), "Religious Movements and Globalization," in R. Cohen/S. Rai, eds., *Global Social Movements*. London: Athlone: 165–83.

Berns McGown, Rima (1999), *Muslims in the Diaspora: The Somali Communities of London and Toronto*. Toronto: University of Toronto Press.

Beyer, Peter (1994), *Religion and Globalization*. London: Sage.

Bhabha, Homi (1994), *The Location of Culture*. New York: Routledge.

Bharati, Agehananda (1976), "Ritualistic Tolerance and Ideological Rigour: The Paradigm of the Expatriate Hindus in East Africa," in: *Contributions to Indian Sociology* 10: 317–39.

Bhardwaj, Surinder M./Madhusudana Rao, N. (1990), "Asian Indians in the United States: A Geographic Appraisal," in: C. Clarke/C. Peach/S. Vertovec, eds., *South Asians Overseas: Migration and Ethnicity*. Cambridge: Cambridge University Press: 197–217.

Bhatt, Chetan (1997), *Liberation and Purity: Race, New Religious Movements and the Ethics of Postmodernity*. London: UCL Press.

Bodnar, John (1985), *The Transplanted: History of Immigrants in Urban America*. Bloomington, Ind.: Indiana University Press.

Bowen, David G. (1987), "The Evolution of Gujarati Hindu Organizations in Bradford," in: R. Burghart, ed., Hinduism in Great Britain. London: Tavistock: 15–31.

Boyarin, Daniel/Boyarin, Jonathan (1993), "Diaspora: Generation and the Ground of Jewish Identity," in: *Critical Inquiry* 19 (4): 693–725.

Carter, Donald M. (1997), *States of Grace: Senegalese in Italy and the New European Immigration*. Minneapolis, Minn.: University of Minnesota Press.

Castells, Manuel (1997), *The Information Age*. Vol. 2: *The Power of Identity*. Oxford: Blackwell.

Clarke, Colin/Peach, Ceri/Vertovec, Steven (1990), "Introduction: Themes in the Study of the South Asian Diaspora," in: C. Clarke/Peach, C./Vertovec, S., eds., *South Asians Overseas: Migration and Ethnicity*. Cambridge: Cambridge University Press: 1–29.

Clifford, James (1992), "Traveling Cultures," in: L. Grossberg/C. Nelson/P.A. Treichler, eds., *Cultural Studies*. New York: Routledge: 96–116.

— (1994), "Diasporas," in: *Cultural Anthropology* 9: 302–38.

Cohen, Phil (1999), "Rethinking the Diasporama," in: *Patterns of Prejudice* 33 (1): 3–22.

Cohen, Robin (1995), "Rethinking 'Babylon': Iconoclastic Conceptions of the Diasporic Experience," in: *New Community* 21: 5–18.

— (1997), *Global Diasporas: An Introduction*. London: UCL Press.

Dahya, B. (1974), "The Nature of Pakistani Ethnicity in Industrial Cities in Britain," in: A. Cohen, ed., *Urban Ethnicity*. London: Tavistock: 77–118.

Dirven, Lucinda (1998), "The Palmyrene Diaspora in East and West: A Syrian Community in the Diaspora in the Roman Period," in: G. ter Haar, ed., *Strangers and Sojourners: Religious Communities in the Diaspora*. Leuven: Peeters: 59–75.

Dolan, Jay P. (1998), "The Immigrants and Their Gods: A New Perspective in American Religious History," in: Jon Butler/H.S. Stout, eds., *Religion in American History: A Reader*. New York: Oxford University Press: 146–56.

Ebaugh, Helen R./O'Brien, Jennifer/Saltzman Chafetz, Janet (2000), "The Social Ecology of Residential Pattern and Memberships in Immigrant Churches," in: *Journal for the Scientific Study of Religion* 39 (1): 107–16.

Ebin, V. (1996), "Making Room versus Creating Space: The Construction of Spatial Categories by Itinerant Mouride Traders," in: B. Metcalf, ed., *Making Muslim Space in North America and Europe*. Berkeley, Calif.: University of California Press.

Eck, Diana L. (1996), "American Hindus: The Ganges and the Mississippi." Paper presented at Conference on "The Comparative Study of the South Asian Diaspora Religious Experience in Britain, Canada and the USA," School of Oriental and African Studies, London.

Eickelman, Dale F. (1997), "Trans-state Islam and Security," in: S. Hoeber Rudolph/J. Piscatori, eds., *Transnational Religion and Fading States*. Boulder, Colo.: Westview Press: 27–46.

Eickelman, Dale F./Anderson, Jon W., eds. (1999), *New Media in the Muslim World: The Emerging Public Sphere*. Bloomington, Ind.: Indiana University Press.

Eickelman, Dale F./Piscatori, James (1990a), "Preface," in: D.F. Eickelman/J. Piscatori, eds., *Muslim Travellers: Pilgrimage: Migration and the Religious Imagination*. London: Routledge: xii–xxii.

— (1990b), "Social Theory in the Study of Muslim Societies," in: D.F. Eickelman/J. Piscatori, eds., *Muslim Travellers: Pilgrimage: Migration and the Religious Imagination*. London: Routledge: 3–25.

Foner, Nancy (1997), "What's New about Transnationalism? New York Immigrants Today and at the Turn of the Century," in: *Diaspora* 6 (3): 355–75.

Gabaccia, Donna R. (2000), *Italy's Many Diasporas*. London: UCL Press.

Gardner, Katy (1993), "Mullahs, Migrants, Miracles: Travel and Transformation in Sylhet," in: *Contributions to Indian Sociology* 27 (2): 213–35.

— (1995), *Global Migrants, Local Lives: Travel and Transformation in Rural Bangladesh*. Oxford: Clarendon.

Gibb, Camilla (1998), "Religious Identification in Transnational Contexts: Becoming Muslim in Ethiopia and Canada," in: *Diaspora* 7 (2): 247–69.

Glazer, Nathan/Moynihan, Daniel P. (1963), *Beyond the Melting Pot: The Negroes, Puerto Ricans, Jews, Italians and Irish of New York City*. Cambridge, Mass.: M.I.T. Press.

Glick Schiller, Nina/Basch, Linda/Szanton Blanc, Cristina, eds. (1992), *Toward a Transnational Perspective on Migration*. New York: New York Academy of Sciences.

Goldring, Luin (1998), "The Power of Status in Transnational Social Fields," in: M.P. Smith/L.E. Guarnizo, eds., *Transnationalism from Below*. New Brunswick, N.J.: Transaction Publishers: 165–95.

Gordon, Milton M. (1964), *Assimilation in American Life: The Role of Race, Religion and National Origins*. New York: Oxford University Press.

Haddad, Yvonne Y./Esposito, John L., eds. (2000), *Muslims on the Americanization Path*. New York: Oxford University Press.

Held, D./McGrew, A./Goldblatt, D./Perraton, J. (1999), *Global Transformations: Politics, Economics, Culture*. Cambridge: Polity.

Herberg, Will (1955), *Protestant—Catholic—Jew*. New York: Doubleday.

Hinnells, John R. (1997a), "The Study of Diaspora Religion," in: J.R. Hinnells, ed., *A New Handbook of Living Religions*. Oxford: Blackwell: 682–90.

— (1997b), "Comparative Reflections on South Asian Religion in International Migration," in: J.R. Hinnells, ed., *A New Handbook of Living Religions*. Oxford: Blackwell: 819–47.

Hoffman, Bruce (1998), "Old Madness, New Methods: Revival of Religious Terrorism Begs for Broader U.S. Policy, in: *Rand Review* 22 (2): 12–17.

Hutheesing, M.O.L.K. (1983), "The Thiratee Kalyanam Ceremony among South Indian Hindu Communities of Malaysia," in: *Eastern Anthropologist* 36: 131–47.

Ignatieff, Michael (1993), *Blood and Belonging: Journeys into the New Nationalism*. London: Vintage.

Jackson, Peter/Nesbitt, Eleanor (1993), *Hindu Children in Britain*. Stoke-on-Trent: Trentham.

Jayawardena, Chandra (1968), "Migration and Social Change: A Survey of Indian Communities Overseas," in: *Geographical Review* 58: 426–49.

— (1980), "Culture and Ethnicity in Guyana and Fiji," in: *Man* (N.S.) 15: 430–50.

Kaldor, Mary (1996), "Cosmopolitanism versus Nationalism: The New Divide?," in: R. Caplan/J. Feffer, eds., *Europe's New Nationalism: States and Minorities in Conflict*. Oxford: Oxford University Press: 42–58.

Karpat, Kemal H. (1990), "The Hijra from Russia and the Balkans: The Process of Self-Definition in the Late Ottoman State," in: D.F. Eickelman/J. Piscatori, eds., *Muslim Travellers: Pilgrimage: Migration and the Religious Imagination*. London: Routledge: 131–52.

Knott, Kim (1986), *Hinduism in Leeds: A Study of Religious Practice in the Indian Hindu Community and Hindu-Related Groups*. Leeds: Community Religions Project, University of Leeds.

— (1991), "Bound to Change? The Religions of South Asians in Britain," in: S. Vertovec, ed., *Aspects of the South Asian Diaspora*. New Delhi: Oxford University Press: 86–111.

Knott, Kim/Khokher, Sadja (1993), "Religious and Ethnic Identity among Young Muslim Women in Bradford," in: *New Community* 19: 593–610.

Lapidus, Ira M. (2001), "Between Universalism and Particularism: The Historical Bases of Muslim Communal, National and Global Identities," in: *Global Networks* 1 (1): 37–56.

Larson, Heidi (1989), *Asian Children—British Childhood*. Ph.D. Thesis, University of California-Berkeley.

Lessinger, Joanna (1995), *From the Ganges to the Hudson: Indian Immigrants in New York City*. Boston, Mass.: Allyn & Bacon.

Levitt, Peggy (1998), "Local-level Global Religion: The Case of U.S.-Dominican Migration," in: *Journal for the Scientific Study of Religion* 37 (1): 74–89.

Logan, P. (1988), *Practising Hinduism: The Experience of Gujarati Adults and Children in Britain*. Unpublished report. Thomas Coram Research Unit, University of London, Institute of Education.

Mandaville, Peter (1999), "Digital Islam: Changing the Boundaries of Religious Knowledge?," in: *ISIM* [International Institute for the Study of Islam in the Modern World] *Newsletter* 2 [http://isim.leidenuniv.nl/newsletter/2].

Mandel, Ruth (1990), "Shifting Centers and Emergent Identities: Turkey and Germany in the Lives of Turkish Gastarbeiter," in: D.F. Eickelman/J. Piscatori, eds., *Muslim Travellers: Pilgrimage: Migration and the Religious Imagination*. London: Routledge: 153–71.

Marienstras, Richard (1989), "On the Notion of Diaspora," in: G. Chaliand, ed., *Minority Peoples in the Age of Nation-States*. London: Pluto: 119–25.

McClure, Erica (2000), "Language, Literacy and the Construction of Ethnic Identity on the Internet: The Case of Assyrians in Diaspora." Paper presented at the Conference on "Writing Diasporas—Transnational Imagination," University of Wales Swansea.

McDonald, Merryle (1987), "Rituals of Motherhood among Gujarati Women in East London," in: R. Burghart, ed., *Hinduism in Great Britain*. London: Tavistock: 50–66.

Metcalf, Barbara (1996), "Introduction: Sacred Words, Sanctioned Practice, New Communities," in: B. Metcalf, ed., *Making Muslim Space in North America and Europe*. Berkeley, Calif.: University of California Press: 1–27.

Michaelson, Maureen (1987), "Domestic Hinduism in a Gujarati Trading Caste," in: R. Burghart, ed., *Hinduism in Great Britain*. London: Tavistock: 32–49.

Miller, Daniel/Slater, Don (2000), *The Internet: An Ethnographic Approach.* Oxford: Berg.

Mitchell, Katharyne (1997), "Different Diasporas and the Hype of Hybridity," in: *Environment and Planning D: Society and Space* 15: 533–53.

Modrzejewski, Joseph Mélèze (1993), "How to Be a Jew in Hellenistic Egypt?," in: J.D.C. Shaye/E.S. Frerichs, eds., *Diasporas in Antiquity.* Atlanta, Ga.: Scholars Press: 65–91.

Mukta, Parita/Bhatt, Chetan, eds. (2000), "Hindutva Movements in the West: Resurgent Hinduism and the Politics of Diaspora," in: Special Issue of *Ethnic and Racial Studies* 23 (3): 401–616.

Nye, Malory (1995), *A Place for Our Gods: The Construction of an Edinburgh Hindu Temple Community.* Richmond: Curzon.

Parekh, Bhikhu (1994), "Some Reflections on the Hindu Diaspora," in: *New Community* 20: 603–20.

Pattie, Susan P. (1997), *Faith in History: Armenians Rebuilding Community.* Washington, D.C.: Smithsonian Institution Press.

Pocock, David F. (1976), "Preservation of the Religious Life: Hindu Immigrants in England," in: *Contributions to Indian Sociology* 10: 341–65.

Portes, Alejandro/Guarnizo, Luis E./Landolt, Patricia, eds. (2000), "Transnational Communities." Special Issue of *Ethnic and Racial Studies* 22 (2): 217–477.

Rajagopal, Arvind (1997), "Transnational Networks and Hindu Nationalism," in: *Bulletin of Concerned Asian Scholars* 29 (3): 45–58.

Rayaprol, Aparna (1997), *Negotiating Identities: Women in the Indian Diaspora.* Delhi: Oxford University Press.

Rex, John/Joly, Danièle/Wilpert, Czarina, eds. (1987), *Immigrant Associations in Europe.* Aldershot: Gower.

Riccio, Bruno (1999), *Senegalese Transmigrants and the Construction of Immigration in Emilia-Romagna (Italy).* DPhil. Thesis, University of Sussex.

Robbins, Joel (1998), "On Reading 'World News': Apocalyptic Narrative, Negative Nationalism and Transnational Christianity in a Papua New Guinea Society," in: *Social Analysis* 42 (2): 103–30.

Robertson, Roland (1992), *Globalization: Social Theory and Global Culture.* London: Sage.

Rudolph, S. Hoeber (1997), "Introduction: Religion, States and Transnational Civil Society," in: S. Hoeber Rudolph/J. Piscatori, eds., *Transnational Religion and Fading States.* Boulder, Colo.: Westview Press: 1–24.

Rushdie, Salman (1988), *The Satanic Verses.* New York: Viking.

Safran, William (1991), "Diasporas in Modern Societies: Myths of Homeland and Return," in: *Diaspora* 1: 83–99.

Schiffauer, Werner (1988), "Migration and Religiousness," in: T. Gerholm/Y.G. Lithman, eds., *The New Islamic Presence in Europe.* London: Mansell: 146–58.

— (1999), *Islamism in the Diaspora: The Fascination of Political Islam among Second Generation German Turks.* ESRC Transnational Communities Programme Working Paper WPTC-99-06 [www.transcomm.ox.ac.uk].

Shaye, J.D. Cohen/Frerichs, Ernst S. (1993), "Preface," in: J.D.C. Shaye/E.S. Frerichs, eds., *Diasporas in Antiquity.* Atlanta, Ga.: Scholars Press: i–iii.

Sheffer, Gabriel (1986), A New Field of Study: Modern Diasporas in International Politics," in: G. Sheffer, ed., *Modern Diasporas in International Politics.* London: Croom Helm: 1–15.

Smart, Ninian (1999), "The Importance of Diasporas," in: Steven Vertovec/Robin Cohen, eds., *Migration, Diasporas and Transnationalism*. Aldershot: Edward Elgar: 420–29.

Smith, Jonathan Z. (1978), *Map Is Not Territory: Studies in the History of Religions*. Leiden: E.J. Brill.

Smith, Michael Peter/Guarnizo, Luis Eduardo, eds. (1998), *Transnationalism from Below*. New Brunswick, N.J.: Transaction Publishers.

Sökefeld, Martin (2000), "Religion or Culture? Concepts of Identity in the Alevi Diaspora." Paper presented at Conference on "Locality, Identity, Diaspora," University of Hamburg.

ter Haar, Gerrie (1998), "Strangers and Sojourners: An Introduction," in: G. ter Haar, ed., *Strangers and Sojourners: Religious Communities in the Diaspora*. Leuven: Peeters: 1–11.

Tölölyan, Kachig (1996), "Rethinking Diaspora(s): Stateless Power in the Transnational Moment," in: *Diaspora* 5 (1): 3–36.

Tromp, Johannes (1998), "The Ancient Jewish Diaspora: Some Linguistic and Sociological Observations," in: G. ter Haar, ed., *Strangers and Sojourners: Religious Communities in the Diaspora*. Leuven: Peeters: 13–35.

Tweed, Thomas A. (1997), *Our Lady of the Exile: Diasporic Religion at a Cuban Catholic Shrine in Miami*. New York: Oxford University Press.

van der Toorn, Karel (1998), "Near Eastern Communities in the Diaspora before 587 BCE," in: G. ter Haar, ed., *Strangers and Sojourners: Religious Communities in the Diaspora*. Leuven: Peeters: 77–94.

van der Veer, Peter/Vertovec, Steven (1991), "Brahmanism Abroad: On Caribbean Hinduism as an Ethnic Religion," in: *Ethnology* 30: 149–66.

Vertovec, Steven (1992), *Hindu Trinidad: Religion, Ethnicity and Socio-Economic Change*. Basingstoke: Macmillan.

—(1994a), "Multicultural, Multi-Asian, Multi-Muslim Leicester: Dimensions of Social Complexity, Ethnic Organisation and Local Government Interface," in: *Innovation: European Journal of Social Sciences* 7 (3): 259–76.

—(1994b), "'Official' and 'popular' Hinduism in the Caribbean: Historical and Contemporary Trends in Surinam, Trinidad and Guyana," in: *Contributions to Indian Sociology* 28 (1): 123–47.

—(1997), "Accommodating Religious Pluralism in Britain: South Asian Religions," in: M. Martiniello, ed., *Multicultural Policies and the State*. Utrecht: ERCOMER: 163–77.

—(1999a), "Three Meanings of 'Diaspora,' Exemplified among South Asian Religions. *Diaspora* 6: 277–300.

—(1999b), "Introduction," in: S. Vertovec, ed., *Migration and Social Cohesion*. Cheltanham: Edward Elgar: xi–xxxvii.

—(2000), *The Hindu Diaspora: Comparative Patterns*. London: Routledge.

—(2001), "Islamophobia and Muslim Recognition in Britain," in: Y.Y. Haddad, ed., *Muslims in Western Diasporas: From Sojouners to Citizens*. Oxford: Oxford University Press: 19–35.

Vertovec, Steven/Cohen, Robin (1999), "Introduction," in: S. Vertovec/R. Cohen, eds., *Migration, Diasporas and Transnationalism*. Cheltenham: Edward Elgar: xiii–xxviii.

Vertovec, Steven/Peach, Ceri (1997), "Introduction: Islam in Europe and the Politics of Religion and Community," in: S. Vertovec/C. Peach, eds., *Islam in Europe: The Politics of Religion and Community*. Basingstoke: Macmillan: 3–47.

Vertovec, Steven/Rogers, Alisdair (1998), "Introduction," in: S. Vertovec/A. Rogers, eds., *Muslim European Youth: Re-producing Religion, Ethnicity and Culture*. Aldershot: Avebury: 1–24.

Waardenburg, Jacques (1988), "The Institutionalization of Islam in the Netherlands," in: T. Gerholm/Y.G. Lithman, eds., *The New Islamic Presence in Europe*. London: Mansell: 8–31.

Warner, R. Stephen (1998), "Immigration and Religious Communities in the United States," in: R.S. Warner/J.G. Wittner, eds., *Gatherings in Diaspora: Religious Communities and the New Immigration*. Philadelphia, Pa.: Temple University Press: 3–34.

Webber, Jonathan (1997), "Jews and Judaism in Contemporary Europe: Religion or Ethnic Group?," in: *Ethnic and Racial Studies* 20 (2): 257–79.

Wellmeier, Nancy J. (1998), "Santa Eulalia's People in Exile: Maya Religion, Culture and Identity in Los Angeles," in: R.S. Warner/J.G. Wittner, eds., *Gatherings in Diaspora: Religious Communities and the New Immigration*. Philadelphia, Pa.: Temple University Press: 97–122.

Werbner, Pnina (1996), "Stamping the Earth in the Name of Allah: Zikr and the Sacralizing of Space among British Muslims," in: *Cultural Anthropology* 11 (3): 309–38.

Willford, A. (1998), "Within and beyond the State: Ritual and the Assertion of Tamil-Hindu Identities in Malaysia." Paper presented at the conference on "Globalization from Below," Duke University.

Williams, Raymond B. (1984), *A New Face of Hinduism: The Swaminarayan Religion*. Cambridge: Cambridge University Press.

— (1988), *Religions of Immigrants from India and Pakistan: New Threads in the American Tapestry*. Cambridge: Cambridge University Press.

— (1992), "Sacred Threads of Several Textures," in: R.B. Williams, ed., *A Sacred Thread: Modern Transmission of Hindu Traditions in India and Abroad*. Chambersburg: Anima: 228–57.

— (1998), "Training Religious Specialists for a Transnational Hinduism: A Swaminarayan Sadhu Training Center," in: *Journal of the American Academy of Religion* 66: 841–62.

Willis, Katie/Yeoh, Brenda, eds. (2000), *Gender and Migration*. Cheltenham: Edward Elgar.

Winkler, Karen J. (1999), "Historians Explore Questions of How People and Cultures Disperse across the Globe," in: *Chronicle of Higher Education, 22 January*: A 11–12.

Approaches to the Study of Religion in the Media

by

ALF G. LINDERMAN

It seems appropriate to say that a new field of research is evolving at the nexus of media studies and religion scholarship. In both scholarly traditions, the focus on culture and meaning has become increasingly important. Perspectives focusing on practices involving meaning construction in contexts outside the conventionally religious sphere have supplemented perspectives according to which the primary focus of religious studies is religious structures, practices and belief systems. Likewise, what the audience does with the flow of media messages and how meaning is developed has come into focus in media studies. As Stewart Hoover and Knut Lundby put it, this nexus involves a triangulation of theories of religion, theories of culture and theories of media. In this new field of research, these three dimensions have to be looked at together and not in isolation or in any combination of which one dimension is excluded. Religion, culture, and media "should be thought of as an interrelated web within society" (Hoover/Lundby 1997: 3).

In this essay, I intend to delineate some basic characteristics of this evolving field of research. For reasons of clarity and simplicity, I will do so by pointing to a few different kinds of approaches within this field of research. Before turning to some examples, it might be appropriate to make a few observations that could serve as the background to and context of these approaches. First of all, I will make some observations regarding the cultural development of (primarily) the Western world. These observations concern the general cultural development as well as changing conditions for the relation between religion, media, and culture, and the implications of this development for scholarship. This naturally leads to the second section. Here, I want to point to some traits in media studies that have been of significance to the development of the nexus between media studies and religion scholarship. I will also turn to religion scholarship to discuss how certain trends here have come into play in the development of this new field of research. After the general discussion in the first two sections, I will briefly describe three kinds of approaches to the study of religion in the media as illustrative examples of this new field of research.

Above, I have referred to a field of research that is evolving, and it is important to note that the process described here is an ongoing process. There is no universal consensus as to the conception of the relation between religion, media, and culture. Neither is there consensus among scholars—be it religion or media scholars—when it comes to the methods appropriate to the study of religion in the media. In a concluding section, I will address a few issues relating to ongoing debates and the future study of religion in the media. Already at this point, it might be worth noting that I am using the term "media" as an inclusive concept including not only conventional mass media but also computer-based modes of communication.

Before continuing on to a general discussion of cultural development, a few words have to be said about the title of this essay. The title of this chapter mentions approaches to the study of religion *in* the media. There are two equally adequate ways of interpreting this title. First of all, a great deal of scholarly attention has been devoted to how the media deal with religion and how religion is performed and expressed in the context of the media. Religion is then typically defined with reference to those groups and movements who through their beliefs, rites and practices one way or the other fall under the religion category. However, another equally adequate way of reading the title of this essay is to direct one's attention to religion in the media as religion *of* the media. As will be seen more clearly further on in this essay, scholarly attention has lately also been directed to media content and media practices as religious in their own right. Ever since Marshall McLuhan stated that the medium is the message, there has been at least some recognition that there is no such thing as a neutral medium. Rather, mass media like radio, television, and film are value-laden both in form and content and deserve scholarly attention accordingly—not least by scholars especially qualified to study public proclamation of world-views and fundamental value systems, i.e. religion scholars. As we continue to take a look at developing approaches to the study of religion in the media, both interpretations of the title are considered equally relevant. We can now turn to the first section dealing with cultural development and cultural change.

Cultural Change

Whether one chooses to discuss the cultural development we have seen over the last few decades as the beginning of a shift from the modern to the post-modern society, or one finds it more appropriate to talk about change within the modern era (using expressions like late- or high-modernity), it is obvious that the developments of the twentieth century have significantly changed the conditions for religious life and religious expressions—as it has significantly changed the conditions for life in general. In a book intended for American business life, John Naisbitt almost twenty years ago described a set of trends developed through the analysis of twelve annual volumes of American newspapers (Naisbitt 1982). Among other things, he pointed to the development from industrial society to information society, from centralization to decentralization, from social hierarchies to the development of individually centered group-networks, and from a society in which we have been used to expecting help and support from various social institutions to a society where we have realized that the help we can expect to receive has to come from ourselves. Regarding the latter tendency, Naisbitt made the following statement.

> We revered doctors as our society's high priests and denigrated our own instincts. And in response, the medical establishment sought to live up to our misplaced expectations. Placing all their trust in the modern voodoo of drugs and surgery, they practiced their priesthood and we believed ... As we became more disillusioned we asked, 'What, or whom, can we trust?' The resounding answer was 'Ourselves.' (Naisbitt 1982: 132)

Although religion is not the focus of this reference, the use of language indicates that the help expected from medical science is at least to some degree related to religious dimensions. Furthermore, this partly religious expectation has now been transferred to people themselves. While there are good reasons to further scrutinize Naisbitt's account of the cultural change in contemporary America—both in terms of what the indications pointed to by Naisbitt and others actually stand for, and in terms of comparative analyses to explore differences between cultural, religious and economic regions—it nevertheless seems relevant to take a closer look at what this might imply for religion. The general repudiation of authorities that characterizes the present cultural situation naturally also affects institutionalized religion. Today institutionalized religion, which is typically founded on the attribution of authority to certain individuals and institutions, does not necessary appear as the obvious source of spiritual and religious guidance. Thus, the individual can become his or her own religious authority. Thomas Ziehe (1994) describes the situation of young adults today as a form of cultural exemption where the individual is no longer bound by traditional authorities and values. The individual is not bound by moral obligations established through and within social structures, but forms her or his own group-networks in which she or he decides upon whom to include (cf. Bar-Haim 1997). Moreover, the capabilities of today's mass media and various modes of computer-mediated communication release these group-networks from the constraints of time and space.

According to prevalent notions within the frustratingly vague and elusive phenomenon of postmodernism (cf. Featherstone 1991), the society and culture of tomorrow also means the end of history as we have previously conceived of it. With reference to postmodern society, the modern perspective on history, where history is portrayed as a process where one can see both continuity and progress, is no longer valid. An infinite number of different histories and a variety of different knowledges is everything there is (Giddens 1994: 314). In the postmodern society, the kind of rationality that has characterized our way of looking at history, development, and progress ever since the Enlightenment has to give way for an infinite variety of perspectives and views. And, there is no consensus as to any criteria through which these contesting perspectives and views can be scrutinized. The perspective characterized by the Enlightenment where through the study of phenomena one can obtain a deeper understanding of these phenomena and their underlying structure has to give way to a great variety of perspectives where it is no longer meaningful to try to reach behind the phenomenon itself (Morley 1996: 59). Everything becomes surface and the notion of ultimate truth becomes obsolete. According to a classic figure within postmodern theory, the French philosopher François Lyotard, grand theories have lost their relevance (Lyotard 1982). Meta-stories like those found in science, religion, philosophy, etc., i.e. stories that intend to present overarching interpretational patterns for our everyday life experiences, are no longer valid if we follow the logic of some of the more radical theorists of postmodernity.

Whether we choose to follow the postmodern line of thought, or we prefer to emphasize the continuity with the modern era, it is obvious that the cultural development indicated above has implications for religion. The character and status of being a meta-story is perhaps one of the indispensable attributes of all world religions. World religions provide overarching patterns of interpretation through which individuals and groups can make sense out of the chaos of experiences in everyday life. Birth, life, and death, as well as other significant life experiences, are contextualized in the religious meta-story and made comprehensible within a coherent structure. In the diversified and pluralistic society of today, there is less room for such meta-stories that are shared and sustained by large groups of people firmly situated in shared time and space. Arrays of different perspectives exist side by side, and it is up to each individual to decide what to adopt and what to disregard.

One of the key factors involved in the cultural development alluded to here is the development of the mass media and various modes of computer-mediated communication. The human need for communication and interaction is not reduced in the diversified and pluralistic culture of today. Drawing on a Durkheimean framework, Gabriel Bar-Haim states that people continue to participate in thinking, but they do so through processes of intermediation. "Thus a connection to mediating systems becomes a necessity, and mass media is the quintessential type among such systems" (Bar-Haim 1997: 143). As the process of collective thinking becomes mediated, each individual can "think" together with many different people in many different (mediated) contexts. This process allows for many different stories and perspectives to be available and possibly also relevant to specific individuals. Thus, where stories and meta-stories used to be shared stories in the local context, such stories can still in a sense be shared but now in a much more complex fashion. All elements of one individual's meta-story might be shared with others, but all elements do not necessary have to be shared by the same group of people. Individuals can compose their own stories by combining elements from different contexts. This is facilitated by contemporary media and the infrastructure of the information society. The media have become "industrialized institutions to-think-with" (Jensen 1995: 57). The information infrastructure of today constitutes a multitude of arenas where various symbols, notions, images, and ideas are commodified and made available for consumption. Television networks and the Internet have become sites where religious symbols and messages compete for attention in the midst of a wide array of other symbols and messages continually flooding the ether and the information highway. On the individual level, television and the computer can become sites for the reflexive negotiation of individual religious identity. Media images are one of the most pervasive means by which people in the Western world "receive representations of identity and diversity, relationships, and social arrangements and institutions" (Miles 1996: 3). As Klaus Bruhn Jensen develops the concepts of time-in and time-out culture, he makes the following statement about how and where meaning construction and reflexivity is cultivated in today's culture.

> I define *time-out culture* as the aspect of semiosis that may be designated as a separate social practice, and which can be identified by social agents as such. It places reality on an explicit agenda as an object of reflexivity, and provides an occasion for contemplating oneself in a social, existential, or religious perspective. While such contemplation has traditionally been associated with religious rituals and fine arts, mass communication, certainly in a quantitative sense, is the main ingredient of time-out culture in the modern age. Time-out culture is a practice which reflects upon the nature and representation of social reality. (Jensen 1997: 57)

Roger Silverstone develops a similar argument when he describes the media as an arena where the individual can "play" with reality. "Perhaps the play can, on occasion, be a rehearsal for the real: a practice. The flight simulator for the everyday" (Silverstone 1999: 65). Consequently, the significance and primacy of the local religious community and locally established religious traditions can no longer be taken for granted. The diversification of religion does not, however, necessarily imply that there is no need for any meta-story or structure according to which the individual can coherently interpret the flow of experiences in everyday life. In his study of the American baby boom generation, Wade Clark Roof asserts the following about where religious meaning and identity is negotiated in today's culture as opposed to previous times.

> Never before has human life been so shaped by mediated image and symbol. And never before have people been so aware that ours is a world caught up in image and symbol. Increasingly, ours is a self-reflexive world in which people ponder the meanings of their lives in a context of seeming flux and impermanence. Taste, preference, hyperreality, generic culture, style, consumption—all are a production of the media, and all convey a reality in marked contrast to what we have known in the past. (Roof 1993: 61)

Religion has become part of the consumer market, which in turn is strongly related to the media in a broad sense. Therefore, the study of religion today includes as an inherent dimension the study of religion in the media. We need to scrutinize further what the changes described there imply for religion and how and where religion is represented in contemporary society. In doing this, we need to seriously consider and analyze these changes, but we also have to take into consideration that institutional religion with traditional qualities still seems to persist, and at times even thrive, in many places. This, in turn, implies that together with a focus on change and development, our study should include comparative approaches as a vital part. Having come to this conclusion, we shall continue to make some observations of how developments in media and religion scholarship have come into play in the context of approaches to the study of religion in the media.

Converging Trends in Media and Religion Scholarship

When the American scholar Joel W. Martin set out in the early 1990s to study the religious dimension of modern film he turned to two areas of scholarship: film criticism and the academic study of religion. This is what he reports as his initial finding.

> I expected to find models of how to analyze the relationship of religion and film. What I found was disappointing. Scholars engaged in prevailing modes of film criticism have had almost nothing to say about religion. And scholars who study religion have had almost nothing to say about Hollywood film. Instead of encountering an ongoing and stimulating dialogue about religion and film, I encountered silence. (Martin 1995: 2)

Despite Martin's discouraging report on what he initially found, common ground between religion and media scholarship has evolved over the last few decades. Martin's book is in itself a contribution to this process. Within media studies, this development relates to a general shift in the field of mass communication research. From a phase where the focus was primarily on institutional processes, content analysis, and on the audience as a relatively passive recipient of structured messages, there has been a shift toward perception of the audience as an active interpretative community (Morley 1992; White 1994). The meanings such interpretive communities make out of mass media texts have been related to structural elements imbedded in these texts, aspects generated by the position of mass media institutions in modern Western society (Fiske 1987: Ch. 5). While this interest in how audiences receive, understand and use mass media content is nothing new to the field, it has until recently "been on the outskirts of the research domain" (Höijer 1990: 29). This new direction within media studies is sometimes referred to as cultural media studies (Clark/Hoover 1997: 22ff.). One often referred to example is James Carey and his view on communication as ritual.

> A ritual view of communication is directed not toward the extension of messages in space but toward the maintenance of society in time; not the act of imparting information but the representation of shared beliefs. (Carey 1988: 18)

This shift of focus taking place within media scholarship has in itself implied a closer connection between media and religion scholarship. As the construction of meaning and thereby also the construction of basic value systems become the focus of media scholarship, the object of analysis functionally acquires almost religious dimensions. The study of how audiences relate to, understand, and use the flow of messages in the mass media becomes, in part, a study of how people establish their general worldviews and ultimate values. Thus, it is a study with much in common with the sociological study of religious groups and the formation of religious identities. This shift of focus taking place within media scholarship has also been accompanied by an increased interest in qualitative methods for the study of mass communication (Jensen 1991: 1–3).

This development toward a more audience-focused perspective is also shown in recent studies of religious television. While some studies continue to rely on quantitative approaches (Gerbner et al. 1984; Pettersson 1986), other studies emphasize the capabilities and advantages of qualitative methodologies (Hoover 1988), or draw on a combination of both quantitative and qualitative methods (Linderman 1996). However, they all reflect the general development within media studies in that there is an increased interest in what the audience actively does with the messages of television. Thus, both in terms of the object of analysis and in terms of methods, developments within media scholarship have had significance for the development of the field of research addressed in this essay.

Before continuing to some examples by which some new approaches to the study of religion in the media might be described, some observations should also be made about relevant developments within religious studies.

The first phenomenon in the area of religion and the media to attract substantial attention from the scholarly community was, of course, American televangelism (see for example Horsefield 1984; Frankl 1987; Hoover 1988; Schulze 1990; and Abelman/Hoover 1990). Even if the history of religious broadcasting dates back to the beginning of broadcasting in general, it was the changes in the conditions for American broadcasting that took place in the 1960s and 1970s that laid the foundation for the so-called Electronic Church. In the earlier days of American broadcasting, radio and television networks had a sustaining time policy according to which they fulfilled the requirement to serve public interest by giving access to airtime to mainline American religious denominations. This forced evangelical groups to develop techniques to fund their broadcasting through various kinds of radio and television ministry. When the Federal Communications Commission in 1960 decided that there was no public interest basis for distinguishing between sustaining time and commercially sponsored programs in evaluating station performance, it opened the door for stations to increase their income by selling time for religious programming. In a time when stations lost significant advertising revenues from tobacco and liquor commercials, this became one way of finding new sources of income (Linderman 1993).

Together with the development of cable networks, affordable satellite and computer technology, these changes helped the televangelists to become the masters of religious broadcasting. As the phenomenon of American urban revivalism was transferred to the mass media, there were also changes as to the message that was communicated. The imagined receiver was no longer the individual only, but the society as a whole. This implied a change in which the religious challenge to the individual to some extent became a moral challenge to society. Thus, American televangelism turned political in its outreach (Lejon 1988; Gross 1990; Hadden/Swann 1981; Podesta/Kurtzke 1990; Abelman 1990). Hereby, movements like the New Christian Right and Moral Majority were conceived. This in turn stimulated the scholarly community's interest in this association between religion and the media.

As the interest in media and religion has grown, these studies have developed in line with the previous observations regarding media scholarship. Thus, the focus is not so much on how these programs and messages affect the audience, but on what the audience does with these messages. As will be seen in the next section, the present scholarly focus is typically on meaning construction as it takes place in a cultural context.

Although religion in the media was introduced to the religious studies agenda through this development, there is still no definitive consensus as to the significance of the religious dimension of popular culture and the mass media. Margaret Miles vividly demonstrates this in the preface to her book about religion and values in the movies.

> ... it is frequently difficult to convince friends and fellow religion scholars that studying film in the social and cultural context of American society is anything but a lark, a departure from 'serious' academic work, a kinky side-interest of a scholar who should be doing something else. She should, some friends believe, be studying ancient Greek or Latin theological texts. (Miles 1996: ix–x)

Miles' statement illustrates that studies of religion in the media is still under development, and that there is still some way to go before this field of research is firmly established among the various approaches in religious studies. The very fact that the present volume together with many important new approaches to the study of religion includes this area of research is in itself, however, a sign of ongoing development. In the following section, we shall take a brief look at a few scholarly approaches to the study of religion in the media.

Three Kinds of Approaches to the Study of Religion in the Media

The objective for this presentation of three kinds of approaches to the study of religion in the media is not to give a conclusive description of a few new approaches available to a religion scholar of today. Such an enterprise would be pointless as the field of research focused upon here is still evolving and new ways to explore relations between religion and the media are continuously being developed. Rather, the goal is to illustrate and characterize the development of this particular field of research. The following three kinds of approaches to the study of religion in the media will be outlined here: content analysis of popular film; the study of the reception of religion when communicated through the mass media; and the study of the religious significance of "secular" media practices.

In the section cited above, Margaret Miles states that she finds many religion scholars unconvinced of the importance of scholarly approaches dedicated to the study of religion in the media. Nevertheless, she goes on to study popular film to explore how film and popular culture contribute to the structuring of our everyday life experiences and how values and fundamental perspectives on life and reality are cultivated in the process. Thus, Miles' book becomes a significant contribution to theologians and religion scholars demonstrating the relevance of this new field of research. Margaret Miles herself has a background in theology, and she is not the only theologian and religion scholar who has undertaken content analyses of films made within the boundaries of popular culture. There are surveys of how God, Jesus and religious symbols have been depicted in the movies (e.g. Kinnard/Davis 1992; Tatum 1998) and more in-depth discussions of the symbolic properties of such symbols when set within the framework of popular film and how this compares to the meaning these symbols represent when used in a religious context (e.g. Baugh 1997). There is also work that through explorations in theology and film explicitly intends to stimulate dialogue among theologians and film scholars (e.g. Marsh/Oritz 1997), and work that discusses the use of film for explicit religious purposes (e.g. May 1997) as well as general discussions of communication and theology (for an overview, see Soukup 1991). Together with Margaret Miles, there are others who explore religion, myth, ideology and values in popular secular film (e.g. the anthology of Martin/Ostwalt 1995). Drawing on the tradition of cultural studies, the latter approach recognizes film as one voice among others in a complex social conversation. Furthermore, this voice is recognized as capable of catering to the human need of stories and myths by which the chaotic flow of experiences in everyday life can be meaningfully structured.

One now classic example of how a popular film can satisfy the human need for stories and myths by which life can be interpreted is George Lucas' film

"Star Wars" which became a box-office hit in the late 1970s. In this science fiction epic, a Jedi Knight who has supernatural powers and who reveres the Force, the power that binds the universe together, trains a young hero, Luke Skywalker. With reference to Joseph Campbell's more elaborated account of the power of myth, which describes how myths are our ties to the past and how they help us understand ourselves and our world (Campbell 1990), Andrew Gordon analyzes the mythical dimension of "Star Wars."

> In an era in which Americans have lost heroes in whom to believe, Lucas has created a myth for our times, fashioned out of bits and pieces of twentieth-century U.S. popular mythology—old movies, science fiction, television and comic books—but held together at its most basic level by the standard pattern of the adventures of a mythic hero. (Gordon 1995: 73)

Whereas it could be argued that there is a significant difference between the mythical power of world religions and the mythical potential of a science fiction movie like "Star Wars," Gordon argues that this movie provides modern Americans with a new mythology that is meaningful in our times. From the perspective of a scholarly and personal interest in mythology, Campbell expresses a similar point of view. He was pleased with how classic mythological themes and the classic story of the great hero in this film were developed in modern imagery and symbolism (Campbell 1990: 13f.). This affirmation of the movie's mythical potential is based on the assumption that the decline of institutional religion and the absence of shared contemporary myths creates a void begging to be filled, and films like "Star Wars" represent a new mythology properly composed to fill it.

It comes as no surprise that the textual analysis of film seems to be an area where theologians and religion scholars are relatively apt to take on new approaches to the study of religion. Theologians and religion scholars are typically trained in the analysis of texts, and while the popular culture material discussed above is very different to traditional religious texts, it is nevertheless easily subjected to similar kinds of analyses. Thus, together with the question of relations between media ministries and existing social and religious institutions, this is a kind of study that fits well within the scholarly community of theology and religious studies departments (cf. Hoover 1997: 288). However, as soon as this kind of approach is seriously considered and explored another set of questions arises. What do these kinds of films represent for those who actually watch them? Does a reading of the religious dimension of secular films have anything meaningful to say about how the film is actually interpreted by its audience?

Such questions are addressed by research drawing on the second kind of approach to the study of religion in the media that I want to allude to here: the study of the reception of religion when communicated through the mass media. As was stated above, there has been a development within media studies toward seeing the audience as an active interpretative community, and a similar development is found within religious studies. From early work focusing on audience behavior and satisfaction (e.g. Pettersson 1986), there has been a move toward more open approaches where the actual meaning-making of the television audience is focused upon (e.g. Hoover 1988), and theoretical frameworks for this meaning-making have been developed (e.g. Linderman 1996, 1997). While much early work on the new media is made up of various kinds of content analysis (e.g. O'Leary/Brasher 1996), reception approaches have also been applied to computer mediated communication (e.g. Linderman/Lövheim forthcoming).

In his ground-breaking study of religion in the media, Stewart Hoover studied some twenty families who were members of *The 700-Club*. This so-called club was formed by televangelist Pat Robertson primarily to facilitate the solicitation of money for his media ministry.

> All of these viewers describe a process of religious development that is undergirded by a widening of the frames of reference for their beliefs. For some of them, this came about as a result of religious television. For most, they were in a process of looking outward (they were "searching," they say) before they began to view, and their exposure to these programs has reinforced this openness. For all of them, religious television is an input in their lives on which they have a sense of perspective. Few, if any, of them can be said to be unthinking or naïve consumers of its message. (Hoover 1988: 208)

Hoover found that televised religion actually turned out to be a resource for these individuals in their formation of their understanding of religion and their view of life. It became "one voice in the complex social conversation" through which these individuals created their conception of life and reality (cf. Miles 1996: xiii). The fact that the media assumed this role also implied a widening of the audience's horizon and frame of references compared to that which was available in the local religious context. Thus, religious television became part of the transformation of viewers' religious identity.

The focus on audiences' negotiation of meaning in relation to religious television has in turn led to a more general interest in the significance of media practices. There is evidence that the quest for religious meaning is no longer confined to established religious institutions, if it ever was (Roof 1993). Subsequently we are in need of new ways to study contemporary religion and religious practices (Warner 1993). For obvious reasons (cf. the previous discussion of cultural change), the study of media practices becomes part of this needed range of new approaches to the study of religion.

> What, then, are the implications of this emerging view of religion for our study of religion and media? First, we might suggest that the primary contribution of the media sphere to contemporary religious practice, thus described, is very much in the terms of a 'marketplace.' The process of religious commodification necessarily brings the institutions, practices and texts of the media sphere to a central place. (Hoover 1997: 293)

Thus, if we want to study the cultivation and maintenance of meaning practices in contemporary life we need to look at the sphere of the media and at media practices. Hoover suggests that this implies the development of a religious anthropology of the audience. This emphasis of the role of the media sphere is reflected in studies that explore the religious significance of media practices. For example, in her ethnographic study of how young adults use the media and television as a religiously significant resource, Lynn Schofield Clark was able to affirm the cultivation of personal autonomy and the privatization of religion. Popular culture and the media proved to be resources akin to traditional religious institutions which in turn led to subtle but continuous changes in the religious beliefs of young adults (Clark 1998).

Studies of the religious dimension of popular culture, the reception of religion in the media, and the media as a religious arena and resource in its own right together make up a lively collection of new approaches to the study of religion in the media. However, this also presents for religion scholarship some significant challenges. We shall conclude with a few observations with regard to these challenges.

Some Concluding Remarks Regarding the Future Study of Religion (in the Media)

The few examples of new approaches to the study of religion in the media alluded to above demonstrate among other things a broadening of the concepts involved. This however implies an obvious problem. If all kinds of human activity can take on religious dimensions, then how meaningful is the concept of "religion"? And, if we are to study religion and religious practices, what then is the object of analysis? In concluding this discussion of new approaches to the study of religion in the media, it is clearly appropriate to briefly attend to these questions. In the concluding chapter of Ostwalt and Martin's book devoted to the study of religion, myth and ideology in popular American film, Conrad Ostwalt asserts the following.

> The present work does not try to suggest that the cinema has replaced the sanctuary nor that the screen has superseded the pulpit. Neither does it posit a reductionist theory of religion in which every element of society suddenly takes on a religious aura—where anything and everything can be religious. Nevertheless, these chapters do suggest that the power of film can allow movie theaters to become sanctuaries and the screen a pulpit, complete with their own rituals, sacred spaces, and heroes that influence a secular society. (Ostwalt 1995: 158)

There seems to be a certain tension evoked by this statement. While a reductionist theory of religion is not advocated, at the same time it is shown that secular practices can take on religious attributes akin to those of established religious institutions. Further elaboration of how the religious attributes of allegedly secular practices affect our theory of religion is needed. Such deliberations should also include comparative approaches as a vital part to explore potential differences between cultural, religious and economic regions. This is not the appropriate place to try to find solutions to conceptual and theoretical problems emanating from the field of research presented here, but it is important to draw our attention to the need for continued deliberation regarding our theory of religion as the study of religion in the media is explored further.

Religion scholarship has developed informed and versatile conceptions of religion and religious life. What the recent development in the study of religion in the media has shown is that religion scholarship represents a valuable contribution to the study of popular culture, the media and contemporary media practices. Furthermore, the discussion above shows that the study of religion in the media holds a natural place among other approaches in contemporary religion scholarship. However, as the object of analysis changes and established concepts are applied to new phenomena, religion scholarship is challenged to develop further its theoretical framework and conceptual repertoire.

References

Abelman, Robert (1990), "News on the '700 Club' after Pat Robertson's Political Fall," in: *Journalism Quarterly* 67: 157–62.

Abelman, Robert/Hoover, Stewart M., eds. (1990), *Religious Television. Controversies and Conclusions*. Norwood, N.J.: Ablex Publishing Corporation.

Bar-Haim, Gabriel (1997), "The Dispersed Sacred: Anomie and the Crisis of Ritual," in: S.M. Hoover/K. Lundby, eds., *Rethinking Media, Religion, and Culture*. Thousand Oaks, Calif.: Sage Publications.

Baugh, Lloyd (1997), *Imaging the Divine. Jesus and Christ-figures in Film*. Communication, Culture & Theology. Kansas City: Sheed & Ward.

Campbell, Joseph, with Moyers, Bill (1990), Myternas makt. Stockholm: Svenska Dagbladets förlag [org. *The Power of Myth*, 1988].

Carey, James (1988), *Communication as Culture*. Boston, Mass.: Unwin Hyman.

Clark, Lynn Schofield (1998), *Identity, Discourse, and Media Audiences: A Critical Ethnography of the Role of Visual Media in Religious Identity-construction among U.S. Adolescents*. Dissertation, School of Journalism and Mass Communication, University of Colorado.

Featherstone, Mike (1991), *Consumer Culture & Postmodernism*. Newbury Park, Calif.: Sage Publications.

Fiske, John (1987), *Television Culture*. London: Metheuen.

Frankl, Razelle (1987), *Televangelism: The Marketing of Popular Religion*. Carbondale, Ill.: Southern Illinois University Press.

Gerbner, George/Gross, Larry/Hoover, Stewart M./Morgan, Michael/Signorelli, Nancy (1984), *Religion and Television. A Research Report by the Annenberg School of Communi-*

cations, University of Pennsylvania and the Gallup Organization Inc. New York, N.Y.: Committee on Electronic Church Research.

Giddens, Anthony (1994), *Sociologi.* Vol. 2. Lund: Studentlitteratur.

Gordon, Andrew (1995), "Star Wars: A Myth for Our Time," in: Joel W. Martin/Conrad E. Ostwalt Jr., eds., *Screening the Sacred. Religion, Myth, and Ideology in Popular American Film.* Boulder, Colo.: Westview Press: 73–82.

Gross, Larry (1990), "Religion, Television, and Politics: The Right Bank of the Mainstream," in: Robert Abelman/Stewart M. Hoover, eds., *Religious Television. Controversies and Conclusions.* Norwood, N.J.: Ablex Publishing Corporation: 227–36.

Hadden, Jeffrey K./Swann, Charles E. (1981), *Prime-time Preachers.* Reading, Mass.: Addison-Wesley Publishing Company Inc.

Hoover, Stewart M. (1988), *Mass Media Religion. The Social Sources of the Electronic Church.* London: Sage Publications.

— (1997), "Media and the Construction of the Religious Public Sphere," in: Stewart M. Hoover/Knut Lundby, eds., *Rethinking Media, Religion, and Culture.* Thousand Oaks, Calif.: Sage Publications.

Hoover, Stewart M./Clark, Lynn Schofield (1997), "At the Intersection of Media, Culture, and Religion: A Bibliographic Essay," in: Stewart M. Hoover/Knut Lundby, eds., *Rethinking Media, Religion, and Culture.* Thousand Oaks, Calif.: Sage Publications.

Höijer, Birgitta (1990), "Studying Viewers' Reception of Television Programmes: Theoretical and Methodological Considerations," in: *European Journal of Communication* 5 (1).

Hoover, Stewart M./Lundby, Knut, eds. (1997), *Rethinking Media, Religion and Culture.* Newbury Park, Calif.: Sage.

Horsfield, Peter G. (1984), *Religious Television. The American Experience.* New York: Longman Inc.

Jensen, Klaus B. (1991), "Introducing the Qualitative Turn," in: K.B. Jensen/N.W. Jankowski, eds., *A Handbook of Qualitative Methodologies for Mass Communication Research.* London: Routledge.

— (1995), *The Social Semiotics of Mass Communication.* London: Sage Publications.

Kinnard, Roy/Davis, Tim (1992), *Divine Images. A History of Jesus on the Screen.* New York: Carol Publ. Group.

Lejon, Kjell O.U. (1988), *Reagan, Religion and Politics. The Revitalization of "a Nation under God" during the 80s.* Bibliotheca Historico-Ecclesiastica Lundensis 19. Lund: Lund University Press.

Linderman, Alf (1993), *Religious Broadcasting in the United States and Sweden. A Comparative Analysis of the History of Religious Broadcasting with Emphasis on Religious Television.* Lund Research Papers in Media and Communication Studies. Lund: Lund University.

— (1996), *The Reception of Religious Television. Social Semeiology Applied to an Empirical Case Study.* Acta Universitatis Upsaliensis: Psychologia et Sociologia Religionum 12. Uppsala: Almqvist & Wiksell.

— (1997), "Making Sense of Religion in Television," in: Stewart M. Hoover/Knut Lundby, eds., *Rethinking Media, Religion, and Culture.* Thousand Oaks, Calif.: Sage Publications.

Linderman, Alf/Lövheim, Mia (forthcoming), *Computer Mediated Communication, Community, and Identity*. Religionssociologiska skrifter. Uppsala: Department of Theology.

Marsh, Clive/Oritz, Gaye W., eds. (1997), *Explorations in Theology and Film: Movies and Meaning*. Oxford: Blackwell.

Martin, Joel W./Ostwalt Jr., Conrad E., eds. (1995), *Screening the Sacred. Religion, Myth, and Ideology in Popular American Film*. Boulder, Colo.: Westview Press.

May, John R., ed. (1997), *New Image of Religious Film*. Communication, Culture & Theology. Kansas City, Kans.: Sheed & Ward.

Miles, M.R. (1996), *Seeing and Believing. Religion and Values in the Movies*. Boston: Mass.: Beacon Press.

Morley, D. (1992), *Television, Audiences & Cultural Studies*. New York: Routledge.

Naisbitt, J. (1982), *Megatrends. Ten New Directions Transforming Our Lives*. New York: Warner Books.

O'Leary, Steve D./Brasher, Brenda E. (1996), "The Unknown God of the Internet: Religious Communication from the Ancient Agora to the Virtual Forum," in: Charles Ess, ed., *Philosophical Perspectives on Computer-mediated Communication*. New York: State University of New York Press.

Ostwalt, Conrad E. (1995), "Conclusions," in: Joel W. Martin/Conrad E. Ostwalt Jr., eds., *Screening the Sacred. Religion, Myth, and Ideology in Popular American Film*. Boulder, Colo.: Westview Press: 73–82.

Pettersson, T. (1986), "The Audiences' Uses and Gratifications of TV Worship Services," in: *Journal for the Scientific Study of Religion* 25 (4).

Podesta, A.T./Kurtzke, J.S. (1990), "Conflict between the Electronic Church and State: The Religious Right's Crusade against Pluralism," in: Robert Abelman/Stewart M. Hoover, eds., *Religious Television. Controversies and Conclusions*. Norwood, N.J.: Ablex Publishing Corporation: 207–26.

Roof, Wade Clark (1993), *A Generation of Seekers. The Spiritual Journeys of the Baby Boom Generation*. San Francisco, Calif.: Harper.

Schultze, Quentin J., ed. (1990), *American Evangelicals and the Mass Media*. Grand Rapids, Mich.: Zondervan Publishing House.

Silverstone, Roger (1999), *Why Study the Media?* London: Sage Publications.

Soukup, Paul A. (1991), *Communication and Theology. Introduction and Review of the Literature*. London: Centre for the Study of Communication and Culture.

Tatum, Barnes W. (1998), *Jesus at the Movies. A Guide to the First Hundred Years*. Santa Rosa, Calif.: Polebridge Press.

Warner, R. Stephen (1993), "Work in Progress toward a New Paradigm for the Sociological Study of Religion in the United States," in: *American Journal of Sociology* 98 (5): 1044–93.

White, Robert (1994), "Audience 'Interpretation' of Media: Emerging Perspectives," in: *Communication Research Trends* 14 (3).

Ziehe, Thomas (1994), *Kulturanalyser. Ungdom, utbildning, modernitet*. Stockholm: Symposion.

Beyond "Church and State"

Advances in the Study of Religion and Law

by

WINNIFRED FALLERS SULLIVAN

Introduction

During the past twenty years or so, courts and legislatures around the world have increasingly been asked to adjudicate accommodations between secular states, on the one hand, and multiple religious individuals or communities, on the other. The resulting decisions have not infrequently proved controversial and unsatisfying. As an example, Indian public opinion was galvanized in 1985 by a decision of the Supreme Court of India. In 1975, having been divorced by her husband of forty years, Shah Bano brought suit in the Indian civil courts seeking maintenance under the Indian criminal code. As a member of the Muslim minority in India, Shah Bano was entitled to bring an action either under Muslim personal law (under which she would have been entitled to return of her dowry and three months maintenance) or under the 1973 Code of Criminal Procedure. The lower criminal court awarded her 25 Rupees a month. In 1985, the award was raised by a higher court to 179.20 Rupees a month (approximately 14 US Dollars), an award that was confirmed on appeal to the Supreme Court of India.

Certain segments of the Indian Muslim community were enraged by Shah Bano's decision to sue in criminal court, rather than in Muslim court, as well as by what they perceived as the anti-Muslim complicity of the Indian government. Indian law reformers, on the other hand, saw her case as illustrating the inevitable injustice resulting from having separate legal codes for religious and ethnic minorities and took the opportunity to advocate a universal civil code. Various Indian feminist groups pursued their own agendas under her banner, some accusing her of betraying all women by asking for support at all (because such support was seen as a badge of female dependence). Subsequently, however, and to the puzzlement of many, Shah Bano repudiated the high court's award, announcing that the award was contrary to the Qu'ran and to the *hadith*. The Indian Parliament then, at the instigation of leaders of the Indian Muslim community, reconfirmed the legitimacy of Muslim personal law in the Muslim Women (Protection of Rights in Divorce) Act.

Much has been written about this case. Many of the elements of interest to both academics and lawyers concerning the intersection of law and religion, as it presents itself in the beginning of the twenty-first century, are evident in it: a complex religio-legal history reaching back many centuries; a self-proclaimed modern secular state with a secular law code; an individual apparently caught between her identity and her rights as a citizen of that state, on the one hand, and her identity and rights as a member of a religious community, on the other; a transnational religious community seeking to maintain its "traditions"; a religious minority seeking political rights of self-governance; multiple understandings of what it is to be Indian, to be modern, to be Muslim, to be religious and to be a woman. Is this case primarily about "religion" at all? Do we understand it best by talking about religion? If so, whose? Is it Shah Bano's religious freedom or that of the Muslim community that is being threatened? Religion is certainly one of the languages that is used to speak about Shah Bano's case.

Shah Bano's case is also about "law"—its possibilities and its limits. The Indian Constitution declares India to be a secular state and guarantees religious freedom, yet continues to cede special jurisdiction to religious minorities, both Muslim and others, and to recognize as deserving of special religio-legal status the so-called "scheduled castes." Indian politics, long dominated by the self-consciously secular Congress Party has in the recent past been led by an aggressive Hindu nationalism. Shah Bano's case and others like it around the globe present the challenge as to whether it is possible for a single state, in a time of increasing religious pluralism, to maintain religio-cultural national identities, to advance the rule of law and to give voice to religious minorities? Is "religion" in all its protean variety, "religion" which is now demanding recognition as a legal and political category, compatible with modern democracy?

I start with the Shah Bano case in part to emphasize that all academic work in religion and law has immediate political currency and real effects on people's lives. Those who study indigenous religious traditions find themselves caught up in political and legal contests for communal and cultural survival. Islam in its many forms and those who study it are engaged in a debate over whether an explicitly Islamic state is intrinsic to the heart and soul of the religious community. Those who study church and state in medieval and early modern Europe form a part of the ongoing debate over the nature of Western law, its history and its present challenges. "Religion" appears in constitutions, law codes, and human rights conventions. Religion everywhere today (perhaps always) is highly politicized, but it is in formal legal contexts that it has a particular and special opportunity to employ state power to its own ends. The words academics use to describe religious phenomena thus find currency in legislatures and in courts. This situation presents a heady and dangerous temptation to scholars of religion.

How should scholars of religion answer questions by lawyers and judges as to whether Muslim legal practices are "cultural" or "religious?" How should they address the question as to whether various Muslim personal codes express Muslim religious truth or a constructed religious identity owing more to the political history of those communities, including colonial rule? Should we understand Shah Bano's decision to repudiate the court's award as a political or a religious act? Zakin Pathak and Rajeswari Sunder Rajan imagine her struggling valiantly to maintain her dignity and identity among the many competing and vocal parties claiming to assign meaning to her life (Pathak/Rajan 1989).

Widening the lens now to take in a world in which "law" almost everywhere is in some sense regarded as secular, it remains important to be cautious about globalizing too rapidly. It is good to remember that secularization is a complex phenomenon in itself, one that varies from place to place and is only incompletely understood (Asad 2002). Western legal secularization looks very different in different places—in the U.S., in Europe, and in the various former colonies and beyond. While there is a great deal of writing about the religion clauses of the First Amendment to the United States Constitution and in some contexts this literature is regarded as in some senses paradigmatic, in fact the American case is quite unusual. The American arrangement with respect to religion with its fastidious attention to the separation of church and state is more the exception than the rule even among the industrialized nations. Outside the U.S. there is, on the whole, greater tolerance of the residue of pre-modern religious culture (in partnerships between religious institutions and the state, for example), even by those quite hostile to religion, and greater appreciation of the difficulty of entirely privatizing religion. (Although this tolerance takes very different forms. "La laïcité à la française," as Alain Boyer points out, is almost untranslatable and finds its origins in a hostility to the church quite uniquely French—one that is now being turned on both new religious movements and on a growing Muslim population; cf. Boyer 1993: 12).

In the U.S., for political and theological reasons, religion can never be just the cultural context. It is never just the backdrop, the vestige of an earlier time. It is either believed, or not. Within the worldview of the dominant evangelical form of Christianity in the U.S., one is a person of faith, or not. In American constitutional terms, of the twin legal pillars of secularization, that is disestablishment and freedom of religion, disestablishment is legally more significant than in many places, ironically perhaps, because there has never been a legally established church. Elsewhere, issues of religious freedom and of freedom from discrimination are more important. In other words, if one puts the American case to one side, Shah Bano can be seen to be not simply the victim of the patriarchal evils of a politicized Islam, as some would have it, but also to be the beneficiary of a genuine and democratic effort, one that is quite widespread, to accommodate minority populations by providing legal mechanisms, legal mechanisms that are considered entirely consistent with the rule of law, that allow them to live out their lives as religious persons (van der Vyver/Witte 1996).

The necessary privatization of religion is widely challenged today. And yet the alternatives are far from clearly successful. Drafters of the new South African Constitution (1993), for example, sought consciously to provide an alternative constitutional structure with respect to religion, one that would allow for a continuation of what was considered a desirable public role for religion, particularly in education. The South African Constitution thus also provides for the same kind of religiously-based personal law jurisdictions as in India. As in India, these arrangements or accommodations, are already in difficulty. Who is to say and by what authority what Muslim law is? Should a South African woman stand before a court as a Muslim or as a divorced woman? (Or, as some Indian feminists would have it, as a person regardless of gender?) And who decides? Does India (or South Africa) understand itself as a place where women receive justice or as a place where religious minorities have rights of self-governance? From an academic perspective, Shah Bano's case throws into relief the challenges of accommodating religious minorities at the end of the twentieth century and demands an exploration of the life of the individual in relation to all law, whether secular or religious, that reaches more and more into every corner of people's lives. The unraveling of legal secularization also suggests the need for a re-evaluation of past legal systems and of their relationship to religion.

Defining Terms

Given the relatively recent invention of this area of religious studies, this section will spend some time clearing space for the discussion of recent work, organized by discipline, that follows.

In an American/European context it cannot be emphasized too often that to regard "law" as written rules enforced by a state with exclusive jurisdiction, and "religion" as individually chosen, deistic, and believed, is highly anachronistic when considering many religio-legal cultures, both historic and contemporary. While no one can pretend a comprehensive knowledge of all of the legal and religious cultures of human history, this essay will endeavor to point toward the complex and contested meaning of these words and the realities to which they are understood to correspond in a global context—urging the reader to contribute through his or her scholarship to a more complete understanding of these cultural complexes and their relationship. It is to be remembered that "law" is as much up for grabs as "religion" in today's academy. The study of their intersection is a rapidly changing and sometimes chaotic endeavor.

The separation of "law" and "religion," or of "church" and "state," is foundational to a Western Christian understanding of "modernity." "Modernity" is often said to begin with the creation of the secular nation states of Europe in the sixteenth century, although historians increasingly trace the formative roots of the secular modern West back to the eleventh and twelfth centuries (Berman 1983), or earlier (Gauchet 1985). Whether they find their origins in the twelfth or the sixteenth centuries, or at an earlier time, however, modernization and secularization are frequently viewed as almost synonymous. There are competing stories—stories, for example, of an essentially Christian society refined and purified through the same period. But the progressive, even inevitable, secularization of public institutions is taken for granted by most Western academics. As is becoming more and more well understood, however, the "secular" is a much more troublesome idea and practice than the triumphal history would suggest—as troublesome perhaps as the "sacred" (Asad 2002). The line between them is at best indistinct. Whether a particular law is sacred or secular is perhaps unanswerable. Law and religion overlap to a large extent when most expansively considered. (Secularization theory itself is considered elsewhere in this volume. Attention will be given here to secularization theory as it has formed a part of the recent conversation about the study and practice of law and its intersection with religion.)

There has been a shift in the last twenty years in the countries that have understood themselves to be governed by modern secular law of the double assumptions that modern law must/can be secular and that the total separation of church and state is necessary, or even desirable. The now commonplace observation of the returned attention to religion has seriously challenged the easy assumptions of the liberal state. In addition, the almost total collapse of Marxist ideology and the breakup of the Eastern bloc has presented other challenges to the secular state. Perhaps human culture cannot exist without religion. And perhaps religion cannot be theorized today in relation to law or to the state using only the skeptical tools of the enlightenment. Speaking very broadly, there are parallel global movements—one toward extension of the "rule of law"—which is essentially dependent on classic secularization theory and the rationalization of institutions and social structures—and one of religious revival—a revival which in some of its guises attempts to re-sacralize law. One can see for example in China a simultaneous demand for legal education leading to greater legal transparency and procedural rights while some religious groups make claims for privileged legal space and self-governance. One can see in the U.S., in Israel. and in India demands to re-sacralize the understanding of citizenship.

In Europe, recent thinking about religion and law has been driven to some extent by the demands of immigrant communities for freedom from discrim ination and space to celebrate their cultural and legal traditions. The legal institutionalization of the European Union, such as in the creation of the European Court of Human Rights, has also affected issues of religion (Shadid 2002). The wearing of Muslim headscarves by school girls has been one catalyst for this discussion. Comfortable historic arrangements of limited church institutionalization are disturbed in Germany and elsewhere by demands that all religious groups be given space in schools. Americans tend to think about law and religion as a constitutional rights issue because of the iconic cultural and legal importance of what are known as "the religion clauses" of the First Amendment to the U.S. Constitution: "Congress shall make no law respecting an establishment of religion or prohibiting the free exercise thereof." In many countries it might be more useful to think of law and religion as being about the practical problem of the just regulation of religious practice.

Indigenous communities are increasingly politically connected through globalized forms of communication and transportation. Many also have diasporic extensions in other places. Legal regulation of these religious traditions is implicated in the global extension of the rule of law. Indigenous communities claim religious freedom rights under both domestic and international legal human rights regimes, regimes that are designed principally with the so-called "world" religions in mind.

One of the challenges for non-lawyers in negotiating the literature of the law, both the primary sources and academic commentary on those texts and events, is that the practical business of making and enforcing laws is often done by the same people who teach about them. Law faculties are, by and large, engaged in training lawyers and promoting law reform. They are interested in what makes law successful today, not in the disinterested study of law in relation to other social and cultural forms. There is often little direct engagement with the theoretical issues that concern other academics. The sources themselves are, however, by and large, publicly available, and vastly rewarding as objects of study. They are increasingly studied by a host of other academic disciplines, including philosophy, anthropology, history, and sociology. That research has been as affected as any other area of humanistic and social scientific inquiry by the scholarly trends of the last twenty years. The religion scholar is confronted in the study of law, therefore, with what may be at once alien and familiar, one interestingly parallel to the contemporary study of religion. One sees a division of labor between believers, lawyers as pseudo-theologians, on the one hand, and the "scientific" study of law on the other.

"Law," is theorized then by legal scholars, philosophers, anthropologists, sociologists, political scientists and others. Political philosophers such as John Rawls work to refine a universal understanding of "law," as embodying, in some sense, "justice." In this guise law appears as a natural and timeless phenomenon only waiting to be more completely discovered and understood. The social scientific and humanistic study of law brackets the universality of such concepts while seeking to explore how different societies have imagined and regulated themselves through law. Law—and justice—for these scholars, are understood as cultural products, differing substantially over space and time. There has been both extensive philosophical reflection and a flowering of legal anthropology and sociology since the early modern classics of the nineteenth and first half of the twentieth centuries.

Legal comparativists have tried out various ways of classifying the world's legal systems, evolutionary, racial, linguistic and geographic, to name a few. Parallel in some ways to the comparative study of religion, legal scholar Andrew Huxley sees a shift in comparative legal studies from a focus at the beginning of the twentieth century on "unification, evolution and taxonomy" to a current focus on "globalization, transplants, and incommensurability" (Huxley 2002). Parallel also to the study of religion, the urgent question is where to go now, having deconstructed yesterday's verities. Having retreated to area studies to refine our understanding of the specifics of different legal cultures, how now to build new taxonomies?

European derived legal systems are often divided into common law and civil law jurisdictions. Common law jurisdictions, primarily those in the Anglo-American orbit, are understood as inductive, ideally, relying on the deciding of cases by judges to build up legal rules. Civil law jurisdictions begin with legal codes, such as the Code Napoléon, that are then applied deductively in particular situations. (The Code Napoléon was enacted in France in 1804 and has been a principal influence on the nineteenth century civil codes of continental Europe and Latin America.) One challenge for legal comparativists is to re-examine these categories and inquire into their continued usefulness. Many modern legal systems are, in fact, a combination of these two forms, relying both on statutory and on judge-made law. Furthermore, most individuals and groups are subject to multiple and overlapping formal legal jurisdictions, at the local, national, and international level, jurisdictions that may include privately or publicly enforced religious law. And if one is interested more broadly in how human behavior is constrained, legal sociologists would now include a host of more or less informal systems of law, including, for example, the customs of queues.

Focusing specifically on "law" as it forms a partner of sorts in the expression "law and religion," there is a sense in which what is now typically referred to in academic contexts as "law and religion" simply refers in a culturally inclusive manner to what used to be called "church and state." "Law and religion," at least in some academic contexts, is an effort to avoid Christian exclusivism—as well as an effort to acknowledge religious pluralism—and legal pluralism. That effort has been largely unsuccessful and obfuscatory, in my view. The effort at inclusion itself can and has, at the very least, created substantial confusion. It may also mask ideological agendas. "Law" and "religion" do not refer to particular institutions with particular histories as "church" and "state" do. "Church and state" while obviously indebted to a very specific cultural-historical context has the virtue of identifying the players and a specific set of issues. "Church and state" also has the advantage of drawing attention to the cultural context of most of the scholars engaged in the study. It is not clear that that history and those issues are particularly helpful when thinking globally. As an area of academic investigation, "law and religion" is perhaps most usefully thought of rather as a very generalized gesture in the direction of a cluster of scholarly issues including legal cosmology and anthropology, the interpretation of religio-legal texts, the sources of legal authority, the history of the relationship of religious and legal institutions, various ethical questions, the identity of the individual with respect to the state, and the historical development of secular law, and structural parallels between the two, among others. While religion has played an important role in the construction of law, it is highly problematic to attempt to distinguish "religion" from "culture" in most legal systems.

Law and religion intersect, of course, not only in encounters between religious communities and the secular state, but also within religious communities. Law forms an important historic part of the world's religious communities long before modernization. What is sometimes called "religious law" then can be seen to regulate the lives of both lay and monastic communities in Christianity and Buddhism, for example, while in Islam and Judaism, religious law in some sense is often said to constitute the principal way in which orthodox practitioners orient their lives toward God. To follow the law is to obey God. Both Jewish and Islamic communities have, of course, also engaged "secular" or state law both when they have constituted religious minorities and when they have participated in international trade—in the Roman Empire for Jews, for example, and in India and elsewhere for Muslims.

Whether "religious law" is a useful category (and indeed whether it has any explanatory value at all when actual legal systems are considered) is challenged among scholars of these legal systems. The challenge arises in part because the criteria for the category are based in Christian religious concepts of transcendence and revelation—criteria that would exclude Buddhist law, among others—but also because one learns little about these legal systems through such a category. They are lumped together, in essence, as "foreign" to modern secular law. Many would say that more can be understood about these systems as "law" if the prejudice that "religious" law cannot be real law is abandoned and they are seen to function in similar ways to what are often called secular legal systems. In other words their "religiousness" is in a sense by the way. What is more important is: How is law created? From whence does it derive its authority? How are legal texts interpreted? How do legal systems accommodate jurisdictional overlap? How are disputes resolved? How are legal specialists trained? How does law change to respond to changing social realities? The religiousness of "religious law" supplies the cosmological and cultural framework but does not determine their nature and function as law. One can then turn back to secular legal systems and see them also as dependent on cosmologies and anthropologies derived from religious cultures, although that derivation is often concealed or denied. (Notwithstanding this critique, important academic work is being done at the level of area studies to further understanding of law within the various religious and religio-political communities of human history. See, for example, special issue of the *Journal of the International Association of Buddhist Studies* on *Buddhism and Law* [1995] and Huxley 2002).

Internal debates about the role of law in the identity of religious communities is also underway. Abdullahi An-Na'im, for example, speaks as a Muslim theologian seeking to reinterpret early Muslim history so as to de-emphasize the shari'a as a defining structure for Islam. He argues that the Islam of the Prophet is entirely compatible with a modern secular order and with modern understandings of religious freedom and does not require a religious state (An-Na'im 1990, 1996). Much debate about the role of Jewish law takes place around the conflict in the state of Israel—although ultra-orthodox Jewish communities in the West also challenge secularism in their efforts to create self-governing enclaves.

Feminist critiques of law and of religion, critiques that have individually revolutionized the study of each, have focused to some extent on the interaction of the two, and encouraged a reconsideration of their relationship. Although most legal feminism, like most contemporary legal scholarship, has shown a marked lack of interest in religion, some legal historians and anthropologists have studied the ways in which religious understandings of the individual and of the family, of women and of women's bodies have fundamentally shaped the language and culture of the law and of women's lives. In legal systems arising in communities formed by Judaism, Christianity and Islam, legal understandings of the nature and status of women are profoundly and variously shaped by Biblical and Qur'anic accounts of God as male, of the events of creation and of the nature of the family as modeled on that of the patriarchs. Women are frequently portrayed as incomplete and subordinate. In the traditional legal systems of South Asia, law, *dharma*, incorporates a Vedic identification of women with *samsara*, an identification that supports a view of women's marginal place in the cosmic and natural order. Confucian legal cosmology divides the universe into a dark, female force, yin, and a light male principle, yang. The role of the male was to guide and govern. The role of the female was to follow and submit. Secular legal systems that have succeeded these traditional legal systems continue, in many ways, to be founded in cosmological constructions that limit women and women's lives. Family law concepts such as those governing marriage and divorce, which are central to Western legal systems, can be traced to Christian theological reflection on sexuality and sexual difference, for example, but are now explained in terms of utilitarian and scientistic understandings of law.

For scholars of religion, the study of law is a highly fertile area of research. Historically, seeing religion in legal and political contexts helps to free religion of the sometimes autonomous free-floating quality of some scholarship and to recognize religion as both shaped by law and as a legitimating discourse for the exercise of political power. Furthermore, law today is being made and remade everywhere and everywhere is bumping up against the claims of those who individually and collectively self-identify as religiously motivated or defined. A study of these collisions can provide a scholar with a snapshot or mini-ethnography of religion in the contemporary world. At the level of international law, the universalistic language of human rights declarations has been under intense scrutiny by those seeking to promote the freedom of religious ways of life, including the freedom to discipline one's own members and to proselytize for new ones.

In the remaining half of this essay I will treat new approaches to the study of religion and law by academic location. Although there is much interdisciplinary work and influence, and there could fruitfully be much more, different academic locations may reasonably be seen to have focused on different aspects of the intersection of law and religion using different scholarly tools. This section is divided by academic discipline. (There is no section for religious studies which has, with a few notable exceptions captured here in other areas, been uninterested in law.) Valuable studies have been done of law by religious tradition—Buddhist law, Hindu law, Jewish law—but this chapter will focus on the theoretical treatment of law outside of religious studies and area studies. Each section treats a representative sample of new work. They do not attempt a comprehensive review. A more extensive listing follows in the Bibliography.

Critical Legal Studies

One of the most important and influential movement in the study of law in the last twenty years or so has been the efflorescence of critical legal studies. Challenging the claims of modern positivist law to autonomy and universality, Marxist theory, critical race theory, feminism, and linguistic and psychoanalytic theory have been brought to bear on what Peter Goodrich and others at the University of London (a center for critical legal studies) have called "the legality of the contingent" (Goodrich 1995; Douzinas 1994). The study of religion has been a significant minor player in this movement. See, for example, Peter Fitzpatrick who argues that modern law itself has its foundation in a myth largely created by H.L.A. Hart's *The Concept of Laws* (Fitzpatrick 1992) and the work of Tim Murphy (Murphy 1997).

Anthropology

Legal anthropologists strive to understand the cultural locatedness of law, both in the classic ethnographic style and in the more self consciously critical postcolonial moment of current anthropology. Anglo-American legal anthropology, or anthropology of law, has its antecedents in the work of the Victorian comparatists and evolutionists such as Henry Maine (1864), whose announcement that law moves progressively "from status to contract" set the agenda for legal anthropology. Ethnographically based study of law begins with the work of Bronislaw Malinowski in the Trobriand Islands (1926) and later with Max Gluckman in southern Africa (1967). These studies of non-Western law based on anthropological fieldwork revealed both the "universality" of law and the parochial nature of much of Anglo-American legal studies and raised questions about the adequacy of the words used by Anglo-Americans to talk about law cross-culturally. As with religion, it is not simply that the categories that were used presupposed Western institutions, the pretended neutrality and universality of those legal categories, like many categories used by scholars of religion, makes and often continues to make ontological and epistemological claims. The question as to whether certain cultural practices are "law" is freighted with ideological and practical political implications. Increasingly, as is the case with the rest of anthropology, legal anthropology examines the cultural locatedness of law in Western industrial societies as well as in the "traditional" legal cultures of an earlier anthropology.

In the last twenty years, important new studies of law by anthropologists have complicated the academic study of how law works, particularly in relation to religion. Lawrence Rosen and Rebecca French, following Clifford Geertz' important 1983 article on law in *Local Knowledge* (1983) have completed detailed cultural studies of "non-Western" legal systems showing law which is highly indebted to particular cultural and religious categories and political contexts. Rosen's *The Anthropology of Law* describes the workings of a *qadi* court in Morocco. *Qadi* decision making has a social and cultural logic that belies the European stereotype of *qadi* decision-making as the paradigmatic case illustrating the dangers of unbridled discretion (Rosen 1989). What looks arbitrary, Rosen suggests, turns out to be highly structured and predictable, focused as it is on returning the parties to what Rosen calls their capacity to "bargain for reality." French carefully delineates the legal system of pre-Communist Tibet, showing how Buddhist philosophical assumptions underlie a legal system lacking what Anglo-American lawyers would regard as foundational to law—legal finality (French 1995). Tibetan Buddhist legal decisions were apparently always open to reconsideration, reconsideration that continued indefinitely until a culturally appropriate result was achieved. Rosen and French, both trained American lawyers as well as anthropologists, show how very different legal processes can be when founded on radically different cosmological and anthropological assumptions. Similarly, Carol Greenhouse, in her *Praying for Justice*, describes a religious community in the U.S. state of Georgia (Greenhouse 1986). These Baptists, religiously committed as they were to refraining from the use of litigation, have developed their own internal process of dispute resolution. The implication of all of these studies is that law is successful when it is culturally congruent.

All three of these works only touch on the complexities of contemporary contexts of radical legal pluralism and increasing migration. What is a growing body of work focused on the anthropology of the colonial encounter and of the law of diaspora communities raises questions about the "closed" cultural systems described by Rosen, French and Greenhouse. Gloria Raheja's *The Poison in the Gift* (1988) challenges Louis Dumont's conclusion in *Homo Hierarchicus* (1970) that the relations among Indians is entirely governed by the rules of caste. She shows an India of plural and overlapping sets of rights and obligations governed by more localized structures of domination that cross-cut caste rules (Raheja 1988). Sally Falk Moore's work on Kilimanjaro gives historical depth to the legal anthropological project showing a layering of legal systems, pre-colonial, colonial (German and British), and socialist (after independence), all in a pluralistic religious context (Moore 1986). Her work challenges the sometimes romantic correspondence of interpretive anthropology with a strongly Marxist critique of the abuse of power in all systems of law. The work of John Comaroff and Simon Roberts explores the classic dichotomy of law as rules and law as process in their study of Tswana legal cases (1981). Andrew Huxley's study of law in Burma examines the destructive horror of a British colonial order, armed with positivist and utilitarian notions of law, and of Anglican notions of religion, dismantling a thriving Buddhist legal culture (Huxley 2001). Sally Merry's recent *Colonizing Hawai'i: The Cultural Power of Law* (Merry 2002) reveals the transformative power of transplanted Anglo-American law on Hawai'ian society and culture. John Bowen's new work integrates religious and legal pluralism (Bowen 2003).

Dutch legal anthropologists, known as the "Adat Law School," have developed a specialized expertise in the understanding of the development of what is called "customary law" in the former colonial nations, particularly Indonesia. What was presented by colonial rulers as a simple codification of indigenous legal rules is revealed to have been subject to a kind of rationalization and selection that resulted in the invention of whole new bodies of law. While much of this work is published only in Dutch, there is a recent edited translation into English of the classic work of Van Vollenhoven (Holleman 1981).

Attempts at comparative synthesis have been made by several anthropologists: Laura Nader in her *Law in Culture and Society* (1969), Simon Roberts *Order and Dispute: An Introduction to Legal Anthropology* (1979), and Norbert Rouland, providing a French perspective in his *Anthropologie juridique* (1994).

Sociology

Sociology of law, like sociology generally, has in the last twenty years become much more empirical. While tracing their origins to the qualitative synthetic work of Max Weber and Emile Durkheim, legal sociologists are, by and large, engaged today in quantifying and measuring legal operations and their effects on society rather than on social theory. The sociological study of law has also been highly influenced by economic theory. Major exceptions during this period, and of interest to scholars of religion and law, would include Pierre Bourdieu, Boaventura de Sousa Santos and José Casanova.

Pierre Bourdieu has argued that the human relationship to rules is very much more complex than simply one of obedience or disobedience. Human behavior is governed by a subtle and complex knowledge of how to play the game in a particular society. One who went to an unfamiliar culture and followed all the rules would, he suggests, be very foreign indeed. It is knowing when and how to bend the rules that marks the insider. Bourdieu, in a manifesto on the sociology of law, criticizes the autonomous quality of much legal scholarship (Bourdieu 1986). He suggests that law, in its effort to protect its own autonomy and power, engages in various forms of cultural production including the use of linguistic devices such as the passive tense and impersonal language, pretending to a universality and mythic continuity that conceals the particularities of time and place and power. He urges rather a study of law that sees law as embedded in history, society and culture.

Boaventura de Sousa Santos in *Toward a New Common Sense* has made a bold attempt through his research in Brazilian slums to reveal the sinister congruence between scientific and legal positivism and the resulting effect on poor Brazilian communities (Santos 1995). Santos argues that modernity has two pillars: a pillar of emancipation and a pillar of regulation. Law has become, in his mind, a handmaiden of scientific regulation. He calls for a new focus on the humanities and on what he calls common sense as a way towards emancipation.

While most sociologists, including Bourdieu and Santos, are by and large uninterested explicitly in religion, a re-evaluation of classic secularization theory has also been in progress in the last twenty years. In his *Public Religions in the Modern World*, José Casanova analyzes the apparently paradoxical reappearance of what he calls "public" religions during the 1980s (Casanova 1994). The secularization thesis, he suggests, comes in three versions, secularization as cultural disenchantment, secularization as differentiation, and secularization as privatization. The second he sees as desirable and irreversible, the other two as inaccurate descriptively. The reemergence of strong public voices by religious communities, in the Islamic world, among Christian fundamentalists and evangelicals in the U.S., and among liberation theologians of Latin America reveals, according to Casanova, the fundamental connection between secularization in the sense of privatization and prior religious establishments. The most secular countries are those in which a powerful alliance of church and state was seen to have oppressed the people. Where the religious community has been in opposition to the state, it retains its power throughout the process of modernization. Casanova's thesis might be considered to be disproved, or proved, in some sense, depending on how you see it, by the rapid decline in influence of the Catholic churches in Ireland and Poland once the church is no longer the voice of the disenfranchised.

In *Le Désenchantement du Monde*, a daring and controversial work of speculative history, Marcel Gauchet takes a much longer view of secularization. He argues that religion has been declining for the last five thousand years and that it is the emergence of the state that is responsible. More specifically he traces the development of the monotheistic religions and the gradual assumption by the state of former religious functions. Christianity, is for Gauchet, the religion that ends religion, because, among other reasons, through the doctrine of the incarnation, a primarily thisworldly focus is made possible (Gauchet 1985).

In the American context, sociologists have been driven to explain the curious fact that the disestablishment of religion seems, in contrast to France, for example, to have resulted in the flourishing of religion. Because of the importance and priority of legal structures in the construction of American religion there is a sense in which all sociology of American religion is also, indirectly, a sociology of law. Religion must find space for itself in a dominant legal culture. A signal addition to this literature is the micro-sociological study of N.J. Demerath III and Rhys Williams: *A Bridging of Faiths: Religion and Politics in a New England City* (1992).

Philosophy of Law

For philosophers law and religion come together in a number of topics in contemporary academic inquiry: the nature and possibilities of moral and ethical discourse; the sources and authority of law; the nature of human behavior and its regulation, internal and external; and the limits of language. Prior, in a sense, to all of these is the question as to whether law is to be seen as autonomous, because ultimately founded in universal structures, or as embedded in social and cultural histories. If an autonomous science is it based in utilitarian calculations of the largest amount of good for the largest number? Or should it be understood as based either in the exercise of raw power, on the one hand, or in the workings of the human heart, on the other? To what extent does religion *qua* religion—either through its practitioners or through its scholars—have a legitimate claim to participate in this conversation about the role of law in the common good? Or should it be seen as having had only an historical role?

If law is understood procedurally as a vehicle for the implementation of fairness, as most political liberals would have it, is religion relegated to a subsidiary role? A person's defining social role, for liberals, is as citizen. In this sense law itself functions as a kind of religion in the modern period. The leading philosopher of law of the last half century, John Rawls, argues that law can have its foundations in an overlapping consensus among different comprehensive philosophies (including religious ones).

Political philosophers interested in the importance of equality in contemporary democratic society have addressed the question: How should liberals reconcile their commitment to equality with their commitment to religious freedom? Should equality mean that everyone is treated the same or that different people are treated differently, according to their differences? Brian Barry, in his *Culture and Equality*, offers as an emblematic case the issue raised in the British parliament as to whether Sikhs should be required to wear motorcycle helmets (Barry 2001). Special legislation resulted exempting Sikhs from the helmet law, although there was testimony that the wearing of turbans was not religiously obligatory. Barry believes that the law was a good response to a situation of historical discrimination but concedes that the precedent is a troubling one, and, in general, rejects Charles Taylor's politics of multiculturalism (Taylor 1992). It is not clear, Barry acknowledges, that there is a principled way to distinguish the Sikh case from many other claims to religious exemption from obviously beneficial laws.

For others in the arena of political philosophy, it seems that liberal political theory is bankrupt and the answer is a return to religion. In this context, natural law has made a comeback. The answer to the secular aridity of contemporary life is a return to laws explicitly founded in religious truth (Coons/Brennan 1999).

Comparative Law

Comparative law in the European/American context has historically referred only to comparison among European legal systems. Mary Ann Glendon's comparative study *Abortion and Divorce in Western Law* (1987) is a classic example. Her focus is on European and American law and her concern is law reform. In the last twenty years comparatists have attempted to remake comparative law so as to free it both from its connection to law reform and of its eurocentric focus. New studies such as Ziba Mir-Hosseini's study of divorce laws across the Muslim world, are making important contributions to an understanding of non-Western legal systems (Mir-Hosseini 1993).

New studies have recently been published surveying and comparing Asian legal systems, and "religious" legal systems generally. Andrew Huxley's introduction to his edited volume, *Religion, Law and Tradition* reviews the history of comparative law and its traditional relegation of non-European legal systems to the category of "religious law," in other words "not law" (Huxley 2002).

Jacques Vanderlinden's very useful concluding chapter in the same volume considers the difficulties with comparing "law" taking up various terms in succession, insisting that legal systems be classified by their *legal* characteristics, in their own terms. So, he suggests, if one considers a system's own understanding of the source of law, legal systems could be classified accordingly: Buddhist law is the product of legal science, canon law and Islamic law the product of revelation, Confucian law is positivist, and Hindu law is "customary."

Legal History

Legal historians have generally had little interest in religion. But that is changing. Harold Berman is the leading revisionist American legal historian in a more general effort to reconsider the telling of Western legal history. Berman's influential but not uncontroversial *Law and Revolution* argues that an equation of modernity with secularism has obscured the religious roots of Western law and distorted law's relationship to things spiritual (Berman 1983). He places the beginning of modernity in the papal revolution of the eleventh and twelfth centuries when modern universal law was first developed.

Other new works of legal history with an interest in religion include Alan Watson's study of religion and law in ancient Rome (Watson 1992), Brian Levack's study of European witchcraft (Levack 1995), and Mitchell Merback's study of medieval forms of punishment through the examination of paintings of the crucifixion (Merback 1999). Richard Helmholz has undertaken a major study of the canon law underpinnings of the common law (Helmholz 1996, 2001).

J.G.A. Pocock, in his *Barbarism and Religion*, argues that Edward Gibbon's masterpiece, *The Decline and Fall of the Roman Empire*, is best understood in the context of plural rather than singular Enlightenments, some of which were ecclesiastical. While all regarded the Christian millennium as a time of domination by "barbarism and religion," that insistence did not belie a hostility to all religion, just to the wrong religion (Pocock 2000). He insists that the Westphalian Peace brought not secularism but liberal Protestantism.

Elizabeth Dale, in her *Debating and Creating Authority* uses the trial of Anne Hutchinson in the Massachusetts Bay Colony as a site for consideration of the early modern debate about law at a turning point in the creation of secular law in the U.S. Often interpreted as a moment of community solidarity against heresy, or against women, Dale sees a community divided at a very fundamental level about the source of law and of the role of human reason in its implementation (Dale 2001).

American Legal Studies

American legal scholars have, by and large, been interested exclusively in the reform of American law. In this context in the last twenty years the positivist notion that law can be neutral and value-free, improved by science rather than moral reflection, has been increasingly called into doubt by a host of legal scholars on the right and on the left. This situation has provided an opening for religion. If law cannot be value free, one argument has it, then religion has as great a claim to be a source for law as social science does. Law schools in the United States have during this period been dominated by their own version of the "culture wars": economic analysis of the law, a hyper-rational form of legal realism, on the one hand, and critical legal theory, exposing law's pretensions to impartiality and rationality, on the other. Should law conform to market theory or should law be a vehicle for social reform? And, if the latter, how to determine the terms of the debate? One of the centers of this debate is law and economics theorist, Richard Posner, who maintains that law should be rationalized according to economic theory (Posner 1973).

Increasingly American law schools are also influenced by the "new religionists." The new religionists on the right and the left see the separation of law and religion as an error which needs to be repaired. Influential in this movement are the writings of Robert Cover, Harold Berman, Michael McConnell, and John Witte, arguing in different ways that the reintegration of law and religion is necessary. An extreme version of this position, that of Christian reconstructionists, may be found in a manual for "Christian" law students: *Is Higher Law Common Law?* (Brauch 1999). David Saunders, in response to these critics of a secular neutral law, in his *Anti-Lawyers: Religion and the Critics of Law and the State* decries the abandonment of the secular rule of law, suggesting that in the zeal to expose the heavy hand of power, the real achievements of neutral secular law have not been sufficiently acknowledged, however fictional that neutrality and secularism might be in fact (Saunders 1997).

Citing Geertz and Foucault, Paul Kahn, in *The Cultural Study of Law*, has proposed to American legal scholars a new "cultural study of law." By analogy to a distinction that he makes between theology and religious studies, Kahn argues that American legal scholarship has, on the whole, been, like theology, implicated in the orthodoxies of a particular "religious" worldview. For lawyers that orthodoxy is the commitment to the "rule of law" and the project of law reform. Kahn offers rather a program of study that would investigate law as a cultural practice with a genealogy and architecture that should be investigated rather than taken for granted. The "rule of law" is "our" way of imagining law, a way that constructs law as a product of a unique fusion of will and reason achieved in the American Revolution. Law, he says, for Americans, is their civic religion. Kahn proposes that we investigate the space, time, and subject of this religion with the tools of cultural studies. Only then will we see violence as a part of law rather than as a failure of law (Kahn 1999).

Debates over the meaning of the First Amendment as well as the bicentennial of the American constitution have led to a flowering of research into the history of religious freedom in the U.S. Particularly helpful is Merrill D. Peterson and Robert C. Vaughan, *The Virginia Statute for Religious Freedom: Its Evolution and Consequences in American History* (1988). See also Philip Hamburger's pathbreaking *Separation of Church and State* (2001).

International Law

International law has long had a somewhat suspect status among legal scholars for whom the state is a necessary institution in the creation and maintenance of law, as well as in the protection of the rights of persons before the law. The expansion of international criminal jurisdiction caused by the creation of war tribunals, for example, raises serious questions, for them, as to whether these tribunals simply constitute "winners' justice." Nevertheless international laws continue to proliferate and are arguably developing real authority in some contexts.

Various international organizations create law relating to religion. The United Nations, regional conventions such as the European Convention on Human Rights and the African Convention on Human Rights, among others, legislate concerning the rights of religious individuals and communities. Debates about "religious human rights" form a part with a larger debate about whether human rights can/should be understood to be universal and secularly expressed or whether they should be understood to be culturally and linguistically bound to Western culture. In this context questions arise as to whether religious and cultural minorities should have rights to self-governance and whether religiously motivated individuals should enjoy exemptions from the law when the law prohibits what they regard as religious duty. This has been particularly volatile in the clashes between religious and women's rights (Shweder 2002). Useful international surveys concerning this area include recent volumes edited by Irene Bloom et al., Kevin Boyle, and John Witte. Malcolm Evans has provided a helpful overview of the development of legal protection for religious freedom in Europe in his *Religious Liberty and International Law in Europe* (Evans 1997). W.A.R. Shadid and P.S. van Koningsveld's edited volume, *Religious Freedom and the Neutrality of the State: The Position of Islam in the European Union* (Shadid 2002), provides an introduction to the European regulatory context with respect to religion that is relevant beyond issues concerning the enculturation of Islam.

Literary/Aesthetic Readings of Religion and Law

The tools of literary criticism are employed in both legal and religious scholarly contexts to explore both legal and religious rhetoric and to draw together the two for comparison. There are profound similarities between legal ways of writing and reading and religious ways of writing and reading.

Foundational to a re-reading of law and religion together are the works of Robert Cover (1983) and James Boyd White (1973). Robert Cover's influential article in the Harvard Law Review, "Nomos and Narrative," initiated a conversation about the relationship of law to narrative with a view to interrogating the coercive and violent aspects of law. James Boyd White in his *The Legal Imagination* (1973), as well as in his subsequent work, has asked law students and lawyers to consider their ethical role as producers of language. Austin Sarat and Thomoas Kearns, eds., *The Rhetoric of Law* is a useful introduction to this new work in legal rhetoric.

As an example of the uses of linguistic analysis in understanding law, Kyoko Inoue's *MacArthur's Japanese Constitution: A Linguistic and Cultural Study of Its Making* considers the displacements that occurred when the postwar Japanese Constitution, written by MacArthur's staff, was translated into Japanese over the course of one week. Unacknowledged cultural translations occurred simultaneously with the translation of words. The translation, for example, of the English construction "the state shall" into a simple declarative expresses a fundamentally different relationship of the individual to the state. This is particularly evident in the provisions regarding human rights. The Japanese Constitution presupposes a state that has a paternalistic obligation to preserve human rights rather than individuals with rights against the state (Inoue 1991).

An important work considering the textuality of Islam is Brinkley Messick's *The Calligraphic State* (Messick 1993). Using the tools of literary analysis, Ebrahim Moosa has written a fascinating article comparing the sacrality of the Muslim legal decision, the *hukm*, with the Christian Eucharist. Moosa argues that the *hukm* comes to be regarded as divine through a complex mytho-philosophical reading of the speech of God, a reading that can be compared to certain Christian understandings of the transubstantiation (Moosa 2000).

Conclusion

In the last quarter of the twentieth century one might say that law as an area of interest for scholars of religion has begun to come into its own. The work, however, is only just begun. Studying law in relation to religion requires careful attention to the particularities of legal culture and history as well as sensitivity to the myriad ways in which modernist assumptions about the secularism of law have infected our understanding of their relationship.

"Law" and "religion" are vast areas of human intellectual production. To survey the last twenty years responsibly is a daunting task. The choices made in this chapter are inevitably the product of the author's interests and perspectives, formed as they have been in a dual training in American law and in history of religions.

Selected Bibliography

Agamben, Giorgio (1998), *Homo Sacer: Sovereign Power and Bare Life*. Stanford, Calif.: Stanford University Press.

Arjomand, Said (1988), *Authority and Political Culture in Shi'ism*. Albany, N.Y.: State University of New York Press.

An-Na'im, Abdullahi (1990), *Toward an Islamic Reformation: Civil Liberties, Human Rights, and International Law*. Syracuse, N.Y.: Syracuse University Press.

— ed. (1992), *Human Rights in Cross-cultural Perspectives: A Quest for Consensus*. Philadelphia, Pa.: University of Pennsylvania Press.

Asad, Talal (2003), *Formations of the Secular: Islam, Christianity, Modernity*. Stanford, Calif.: Stanford University Press.

Baird, Robert D. (1991), "Religion and Law in Modern India," in: Robert D. Baird, *Essays in the History of Religions*. New York: Peter Lang.

Barry, Brian (2001), *Culture and Equality: An Egalitarian Critique of Multiculturalism*. Cambridge, Mass.: Harvard University Press.

Berman, Harold (1983), *Law and Revolution: The Formation of the Western Legal Tradition*. Cambridge, Mass.: Harvard University Press.

Berman, Harold (2003), *Law and Revolution*. Vol. II: *The Impact of the Protestant Reformations on the Western Legal Traditions*. Cambridge, Mass.: Harvard University Press.

Bloom, Irene/Martin, J. Paul/Proudfoot, Wayne (1996), *Religious Diversity and Human Rights*. New York: Columbia University Press.

Bourdieu, Pierre (1986), "La Force du droit: Elements pour une sociologie du champ juridique" and "Habitus, Code et Codification," in: *Actes de la recherche en sciences sociales* 64.

Bowen, John R. (2003), *Islam, Law and Equality in Indonesia*. Cambridge: Cambridge University Press.

Boyer, Alain (1993), *Le Droit des Religions en France*. Paris: Gallimard.

Boyle, Kevin/Sheen, Juliet (1997), *Freedom of Religion and Belief: A World Report*. New York: Routledge.

Brauch, Jeffrey A. (1999), *Is Higher Law Common Law?: Readings in the Influence of Christian Thought in Anglo-American Law*. Littleton, Colo.: F.B. Rothman.

Brown, Brian Edward (1999), *Religion, Law, and the Land: Native Americans and the Judicial Interpretation of Sacred Land*. Westport, Conn.: Greenwood Press.

Brundage, James A. (1987), *Law, Sex and Christian Society in Medieval Europe*. Chicago: University of Chicago Press.

"Buddhism and Law" (1995): *Journal of the International Association of Buddhist Studies* 18 [special issue].

Casanova, José (1994), *Public Religions in the Modern World*. Chicago: University of Chicago Press.

Comaroff, John L./Roberts, Simon (1981), *Rules and Processes: The Cultural Logic of Dispute in an African Context.* Chicago: University of Chicago Press.

Coons, John E./Brennan, Patrick M. (1999), *By Nature Equal: The Anatomy of a Western Insight.* Princeton, N.J.: Princeton University Press.

Cover, Robert (1983), "Foreword: *Nomos* and Narrative," in: *Harvard Law Review* 97: 4–68.

Dale, Elizabeth (2001), *Debating and Creating Authority: The Failure of a Constitutional Ideal in Massachusetts Bay, 1629-1649.* Burlington, Vt.: Ashgate.

Darian-Smith, Eve/Fitzpatrick, Peter, eds. (1999), *Laws of the Postcolonial.* Ann Arbor, Mich.: University of Michigan Press.

Demerath II, N.J./Williams, Rhys (1992), *A Bridging of Faiths: Religion and Politics in a New England City.* Princeton, N.J.: Princeton University Press.

Douzinas, Costas/Goodrich, Peter/Hachamovitch, Yifat (1994), *Politics, Postmodernity and Critical Legal Studies: The Legality of the Contingent.* London: Routledge.

Dumont, Louis (1970), *Homo Hierarchicus: An Essay on the Caste System.* Chicago: University of Chicago Press.

École Française de Rome (1991), *Théologie et Droit Dans la Science Politique de l'État Moderne: Actes de la Table Ronde Organisée par l'École Française de Rome Avec le Concours du CNRS, Rome le 12–14 Novembre 1987.* Roma: École Française de Rome.

European Consortium for Church State Research (1998), *Religions in European Union Law.* Milano: A. Giuffrè.

Evans, Malcolm D. (1997), *Religious Liberty and International Law in Europe.* Cambridge: Cambridge University Press.

Everett, William Johnson (1997), *Religion, Federalism, and the Struggle for Public Life: Cases from Germany, India, and America.* Oxford: Oxford University Press.

Falk, Ze'ev (1981), *Law and Religion: The Jewish Experience.* Jerusalem: Mesharim Publishers.

Feldman, Stephen (2000), *Law & Religion: A Critical Anthology.* New York: NYU Press.

Fitzpatrick, Peter (1992), *The Mythology of Modern Law.* New York: Routledge.

Foucault, Michel (1995), *Discipline and Punish: The Birth of the Prison.* New York: Vintage Books.

French, Rebecca (1995), *The Golden Yoke: The Legal Cosmology of Buddhist Tibet.* Ithaca, N.Y.: Cornell University Press.

Gauchet, Marcel (1985), *Le désenchantement du monde: une histoire politique de la religion.* Paris: Gallimard.

Geertz, Clifford (1983), "Local Knowledge: Fact and Law in Comparative Perspective," in: Clifford Geertz, *Local Knowledge: Further Essays in Interpretive Anthropology.* New York: Basic Books.

Glendon, Mary Ann (1987), *Abortion and Divorce in Western Law.* Cambridge, Mass.: Harvard University Press.

Goodrich, Peter (1995), *Oedipus Lex: Psychoanalysis, History, Law.* Berkeley, Calif.: University of California Press.

Greenhouse, Carol (1986), *Praying for Justice: Faith, Order, and Community in an American Town.* Ithaca, N.Y.: Cornell University Press.

Hamburger, Philip (2001), *Separation of Church and State.* Cambridge, Mass.: Harvard University Press.

Hammond, Phillip E. (1992), *Religion and Personal Autonomy: The Third Disestablishment in America*. Columbia, S.C.: University of South Carolina Press.

Hart, H.L.A. (1961), *The Concept of Law*. London: Clarendon Press.

Helmholz, Richard H. (1996), *The Spirit of Classical Canon Law*. Athens, Ga.: University of Georgia Press.

— (2001), *The Ius Commune in England: Four Studies*. New York: Oxford University Press.

Holleman, J.F., ed. (1981), *Van Vollenhoven on Indonesian Adat Law: Selections from Het Adatrecht van Nederlandsch-Indië* [Vol. I 1918; Vol. II 1931]. The Hague: M. Nijhoff.

Holmes, Stephen (1988), "Jean Bodin: The Paradox of Sovereignty and the Privatisation of Religion," in: *Religion, Morality and the Law*. Nomos XXX. New York: NYU Press.

Horwitz, Morton (1992), *The Transformation of American Law, 1870–1960: The Crisis of Orthodoxy*. Oxford: Oxford University Press.

Huxley, Andrew (2001), "Positivists and Buddhists: The Rise and Fall of Anglo-Burmese Ecclesiastical Law," in: *Law & Social Inquiry* 26.

— ed. (2002), *Religion, Law and Tradition: Comparative Studies in Religious Law*. London: Routledge/Curzon.

Inoue, Kyoko (1991), *MacArthur's Japanese Constitution: A Linguistic and Cultural Study of Its Making*. Chicago: University of Chicago Press.

Jacobsohn, Gary Jefferson (2003), *The Wheel of Law: India's Secularism in Comparative Constitutional Context*. Princeton, N.J.: Princeton University Press.

Joblin, Joseph/Tremblay, Réal (1996), *I Cattolici e la Società Pluralista: Il caso delle "leggi imperfette."* Bologna: ESD.

Kahn, Paul (1999), *The Cultural Study of Law: Reconstructing Legal Scholarship*. Chicago: University of Chicago Press.

Kang, Wi Jo (1997), *Christ and Caesar in Modern Korea*. New York: SUNY Press.

Kelsay, John/Twiss, Sumner B. (1994), *Religion and Human Rights*. New York: The Project on Religion and Human Rights.

Levack, Brian (1995), *The Witch-Hunt in Early Modern Europe*. London: Longman.

Levinson, Sanford (1988), *Constitutional Faith*. Princeton, N.J.: Princeton University Press.

Maclean, Ian (1992), *Interpretation and Meaning in the Renaissance: The Case of Law*. Cambridge: Cambridge University Press.

Maine, Henry (1864), *Ancient Law: Its Connection with Early History of Society and Its Relation to Modern Ideas*. New York: Holt.

Matthews, Victor H./Levinson, Bernard M./Frymer-Kensky, Tikva (1998), *Gender and Law in the Hebrew Bible and the Ancient Near East*. Sheffield: Sheffield Academic Press.

McConnell, Michael (1990), "The Origins and Historical Understanding of Free Exercise of Religion," in: *Harvard Law Review* 103: 1409.

Megivern, James J. (1997), *The Death Penalty: An Historical and Theological Survey*. New York: Paulist Press.

Merback, Mitchell B. (1999), *The Thief, the Cross and the Wheel: Pain and the Spectacle of Punishment in Medieval and Renaissance Europe*. Chicago: University of Chicago Press.

Messick, Brinkley (1993), *The Calligraphic State: Textual Domination and History in a Muslim Society*. Berkeley, Calif.: University of California Press.

Mir-Hosseini, Ziba (1993), *Marriage on Trial: A Study of Islamic Family Law: Iran and Morocco Compared*. New York: I.B. Tauris.

Mojzes, Paul (1992), *Religious Liberty in Eastern Europe and the USSR: Before and after the Great Transformation*. Boulder, Colo.: East European Monographs.

Moore, Sally Falk (1986), *Social Facts and Fabrications: "Customary" Law on Kilimanjaro, 1880–1980*. Cambridge: Cambridge University Press.

Moosa, Ebrahim (1998), "Allegory of the Rule (*Hukm*): Law as Simulacrum in Islam?," in: *History of Religions* 38: 1–24.

Motha, Stewart/Zartaloudis, Thanos, "Law, Ethics and the Utopian End of Human Rights," in: *Social and Legal Studies* 12: 243–68.

Murphy, Tim (1997), *The Oldest Social Science?: Configurations of Law and Modernity*. Oxford: Oxford University Press.

Nader, Laura (1969), *Law in Culture and Society*. Chicago: Aldine.

Niehaus, Isak (2001), *Witchcraft, Power and Politics: Exploring the Occult in the South African Lowveld*. London: Pluto Press.

Nussbaum, Martha (1997a), "Capabilities and Human Rights," in: *Fordham Law Review* LXVI: 273-300.

— (1997b), "Religion and Women's Human Rights," in: *Religion and Contemporary Liberalism*, ed. by Paul J. Weithman. Notre Dame, Ind.: University of Notre Dame Press.

Nye, Malory (2001), *Multiculturalism and Minority Religions in Britain: Krishna Consciousness, Religious Freedom, and the Politics of Location*. Richmond: Curzon Press.

Obiora, Leslye (1997), "The Issue of Female Circumcision: Bridges and Barricades: Rethinking Polemics and Intransigence in the Campaign against Female Circumcision," in: *Case Western Reserve Law Review* 47: 275–378.

Pathak, Zakia/Rajan, Rajeswari Sundar (1989), "Shahbano," in: *Signs*.

Pocock, J.G.A. (2000), *Barbarism and Religion*. Cambridge: Cambridge University Press.

Posner, Richard (1973), *Economic Analysis of Law*. Boston, Mass.: Little, Brown & Co.

Poulter, Sebastian (1998), *Ethnicity, Law, and Human Rights: The English Experience*. Oxord: Clarendon Press.

Raheja, Gloria Goodwin (1988), *The Poison in the Gift: Ritual, Prestation, and the Dominant Caste in a North Indian Village*. Chicago: University of Chicago Press.

Rawls, John (1999), *The Law of Peoples*. Cambridge, Mass.: Harvard University Press.

Richardson, James (2004), *Regulating Religion: Case Studies from around the Globe*. New York: Kluwer Academic Publishers.

Roberts, Simon (1979), *Order and Dispute: An Introduction to Legal Anthropology*. New York: St. Martin's Press.

Rose, Gillian (1996), *Mourning Becomes the Law: Philosophy and Representation*. Cambridge: Cambridge University Press.

Rosen, Lawrence (1989), *The Anthropology of Justice: Law as Culture in Islamic Society*. New York: Cambridge University Press.

Rouland, Norbert (1988), *Anthropologie juridique*. Paris: Presses universitaires de France.

Rouner, Leroy S., ed. (1988), *Human Rights and the World's Religions*. Notre Dame, Ind.: University of Notre Dame Press.

Sajo, Andras/Avineri, Shlomo (1999), *The Law of Religious Identity: Models for Post Communism*. The Hague: Kluwer Law International.

Sarat, Austin/Kearns, Thomas R., eds. (1994), *The Rhetoric of Law*. Ann Arbor, Mich.: University of Michigan Press.

Saunders, David (1997), *Religion and the Critics of Law and State*. New York: Routledge.

Shadid, W.A.R./van Koningsveld, P.S., eds. (2002), *Religious Freedom and the Neutrality of the State: The Position of Islam in the European Union*. Leuven: Peeters.

Shweder, Richard A./Minow, Martha/Markus, Hazel R., eds. (2002), *Engaging Cultural Differences: The Multicultural Challenge in Liberal Democracies*. New York: Russell Sage Foundation.

Sousa Santos, Boaventura de (1995), *Toward a New Common Sense: Law, Science and Politics in the Paradigmatic Transition*. New York: Routledge.

Sullivan, Winnifred Fallers (1994), *Paying the Words Extra: Religious Discourse in the Supreme Court of the United States*. Cambridge, Mass.: Harvard University Center for the Study of World Religions.

Sullivan, Winnifred Fallers (forthcoming 2005), *The Impossibility of Religious Freedom*. Princeton, N.J.: Princeton University Press.

Sullivan, Winnifred Fallers/Reynolds, Frank (2001), "Symposium: Religion, Law and Identity," in: *Law and Social Inquiry* 26: 1.

Sullivan, Winnifred Fallers/Yelle, Robert A. (forthcoming), "Overview to Law and Religion," in: *Encyclopedia of Religion*, second ed. New York: Macmillan.

Taylor, Charles (1992), *Multiculturalism and "The Politics of Recognition."* Princeton, N.J.: Princeton University Press.

Tierney, Brian (1982), *Religion, Law and the Growth of Constitutional Thought, 1150–1650*. Cambridge: Cambridge University Press.

Vyver, Johan D. van der/Witte, Jr., John, eds. (1996), *Religious Human Rights in Global Perspective: Legal Perspectives*. The Hague: Martinus Nijhoff Publishers.

Watson, Alan (1992), *The State, Law and Religion: Pagan Rome*. Athens, Ga.: University of Georgia Press.

White, James Boyd (1973), *The Legal Imagination: Studies in the Nature of Legal Thought and Expression*. Boston, Mass.: Little, Brown & Co.

Williams, Robert A., Jr. (1990), *The American Indian in Western Legal Thought: The Discourses of Conquest*. Oxford: Oxford University Press.

Section 7

Cognition and Cross-Cultural Psychology

Cognitive Approaches to the Study of Religion

by

ARMIN W. GEERTZ

One of the most exciting developments in the study of religion during the past fifteen years is the application of cognitive theory. Many scholars are inspired by the thought that understanding human cognition can somehow help us to understand religion (and a lot of other things along the way). Others are more skeptical. What can neurophysiology possibly tell us about social and cultural phenomena? What does cognition have to do with historical processes let alone the history of ideas? How do we, in other words, get from the neuron to the Qu'ran? Furthermore, some of the daily headlines that flash around the world as ground-breaking news in the neurosciences are either so mundane that we wonder why money is being spent on such matters, such as "Sheep don't forget a face,"[1] or are seemingly so absurd that we worry about the mental health of our colleagues in the natural sciences, such as "Do whales and dolphins have culture?" (Rendell/Whitehead 2001), or are completely incomprehensible to mortal humans, such as "Ectopic expression of Olig1 promotes oligodendrocyte formation and reduces neuronal survival in developing mouse cortex."[2]

Before introducing cognitive theory and its possibilities for the study of religion, we should perhaps take a look at a few basic points. The most important point is that as mundane or absurd as they might seem, advances in the neurosciences are considered to be advances because they are based on empirical evidence. The *number* of faces that sheep can remember, and which can be confirmed by any shepherd, is not the point here. The point is that ethologists have devised clever experiments to find out *how* sheep can do this sort of thing and thus ultimately how perception works in animals and whether it is different than human perception. These are matters that are not intuitively accessible to us and therefore need scientific clarification.

Empirical study is, of course, informed by theories, hypotheses and plain guesswork, but there are concerted team efforts to prove and disprove, to test

1 *Nature* 4 (14): 165–66 (8 Nov 2001) "Brief Communication" by Keith M. Kendrick, Ana P. da Costa, Andrea E. Leigh, Michael R. Hinton, Jon W. Peirce.

2 *Nature Neuroscience* 4 (10), October 2001, "Brief Communications." The article was written by Q.R. Lu, L. Cai, D. Rowitch, C.L. Cepko and C.D. Stiles.

and debunk, to re-think and re-design chemical, biological, and behavioral tests. The field of neurosciences depends on laboratory tests ranging from chemical analyses of DNA-molecules to behavioral, chemical and surgical tests on rats, mice and monkeys, to simple reaction tests on three month-old human babies, to tests and surveys on human adult assumptions and behavior, to computer simulations of human neuronal networks, to linguistic competency tests on human children, to study of human or animal brain lesions, or to comparative ethological observations. Tests have been designed and applied not only in Western societies, but also in non-Western societies by cross-cultural psychologists, psychological anthropologists, and sociologists. And cognitive philosophers or philosophers interested in these matters as well as linguists, scholars of religion and cultural anthropologists have been making concerted efforts to gather the results of this vast experimental industry and draw conclusions about our knowledge of human cognition and culture. Those who think that this is only passing fashion are in for a surprise.

Because of this intimate link between the natural and the human sciences, many scholars who use cognitive theory are convinced that they are on the verge of a *scientific* (as opposed to hermeneutic) interpretation of religion. This is in part understandable because the evidence is experimental, but much is still hypothetical and in some cases highly speculative. This is why some scholars in the cognitive study of religion have gone on to develop their own experimental tests. They have moved, so to speak, from text exegeses to field and laboratory experiments. Whether their explanations are more scientific than other explanations is a philosophical problem that plagues the natural sciences as much as the humanities.[3]

The challenge to scholars of religion who are interested in or at least curious about cognitive theory is to find literature that is dependable and informative enough for us to develop plausible interpretations and explanations of religious thought and behavior. This is not an easy job, nor should it be taken lightly. We are too often the unknowing victims of exciting and well-written books *about* cognition. Few of us have the time, patience or knowledge to read the experimental literature. If we wish to get a handle on cognition, we need to brush up on our chemistry, neurology, endocrinology, genetic theory, zoology, ethology, physical anthropology, archaeology, and evolutionary theory. So why bother? We have enough trouble brushing up on our Pali or Greek, or trying to remember the difference between Sophists and Socratics, or just keeping track of the names of our field informants and all their relatives and kids!

3 See William O'Donohue and Richard F. Kitchener's excellent collection on the philosophical problems in psychology and the cognitive sciences (1996) and Jeppe Sinding Jensen's discussion on the study of religion and its model sciences (2003: 159–201).

I hope in the following that it will become evident why we need to do this anyway. I hope that it will become evident what kinds of questions cognitive theory can and cannot answer, and why it is essential for us to be well-versed in this field of inquiry.

Histories of Cognitive Research

Many scholars of religion wonder why cognition has become so popular during the past few years. Is it just another fad that in the meantime is preventing us from doing "the real job"? What many do not realize is that cognition and brain science are more than a century old, and the reason for all the recent fuss is that significant breakthroughs have put neuroscientists in an unprecedented position. An important point for scholars of religion to realize is that whereas human and social scientific breakthroughs are mostly due to new methods, theories and approaches, breakthroughs in the neurosciences are mostly due to the development of new instruments that can support or falsify central hypotheses such as the neuron doctrine[4] or the ionic hypothesis.[5] For example, in a highly acclaimed article on progress in neural science, Thomas D. Albright et al. cite among other things the development of patch-clamp methods[6] and high-resolution brain imaging as some of the most important breakthroughs in the neurosciences. The neurosciences have now developed instruments and techniques that not only allow them to draw useful conclusions but also to directly view a large amount of the microprocesses in the body and brain that produce cognition in animals and humans. This is why a large amount of breakthrough literature has hit the market since the 1990s. Insights gained in some areas have contributed significantly to insights gained in other areas. For instance improvements in DNA analysis have now made it possible to draw fairly solid conclusions in archaeology not only about dating but also about genetic relations.

4 The idea developed at the turn of the twentieth century by Santiago Ramón y Cajal "that neurons serve as the functional signaling units of the nervous system and that neurons connect to one another in precise ways" (Albright et al. 2000: 2).

5 Following on the insight that synaptic transmission was chemical in nature, the ionic hypothesis put forward by Alan Hodgkin, Andrew Huxley, and Bernhard Katz during the early 1950s is claimed to be one of the deepest insights in neural science, unifying the cellular study of the nervous system in general. The hypothesis explains signaling within neurons (Albright et al. 2000: 4).

6 Developed by Erwin Neher and Bert Sakmann in the late 1970s which revolutionized neurobiology by making it possible to study biophysical properties of the neurons of the brain as well as a large number of nonneuronal cells (Albright et al. 2000: 5).

In trying to determine what histories of research are relevant to the study of cognition, it may help to look at which disciplines have been involved. Each discipline has its own history of research, which is why the history of research on cognition is so complex, thus defying a simple genealogy. One thing that seems to be a common complaint is that even though it all started out so promisingly when the German psychologist Wilhelm Wundt[7] introduced experimental psychology and laboratory methods for studying mental processes during the latter half of the nineteenth century, it was unfortunately disrupted by the behaviorism of the first half of the twentieth century in terms of which the mind was denied.[8] Behaviorism in psychology was introduced by John Broadus Watson in 1913,[9] but first became the serious paradigm of Anglo-American experimental psychologists under the influence of Clark L. Hull during the 1930s.[10] In Germany, however, mentalistic terminology continued in the Gestalt movement during 1912 to 1933.[11] At the end of that period, the founding pioneers Max Wertheimer,[12] Kurt Koffka,[13] and Wolfgang Köhler[14] were forced to emigrate to the U.S., but they had little impact there until the neo-behaviorism of B.F. Skinner (1938) began to lose its influence (Murray 1995: 1).

Things changed to the better during the 1950s when studies on memory were pursued by George Miller,[15] the field of artificial intelligence (AI) was founded by John McCarthy, Marvin Minsky,[16] and Allen Newell and Herbert Simon,[17] and linguistics was trying to understand language in terms of mental grammars in the work of Noam Chomsky.[18] These six thinkers are considered to be the founders of cognitive science (Thagard 1996: 6).

7 Wundt 1874, 1894, 1896.

8 The methodology of behaviorism required the abandonment of introspection and the dependency on observable, measurable data. This meant that mental events were excluded from scientific inquiry because they could not be observed or measured by other people. Along with this attitude, behaviorists did not study internally induced sensations (called 'images' by psychologists) or use the words 'memory' and 'unconscious' (Murray 1995: 7).

9 Watson 1913, 1924, 1928.

10 Hull 1935, 1943; Hull et al. 1940.

11 The Gestalt movement is said to have begun with Wertheimer's paper of 1912 on apparent movement and reached its culmination with Koffka's book *Principles of Gestalt Psychology* (1935).

12 Wertheimer 1912, 1922a, 1922b.

13 Koffka 1915, 1921, 1922, 1935.

14 Köhler 1929, 1938.

15 Miller 1956.

16 Minsky 1957.

17 Newell et al. 1958; Newell/Simon 1972.

18 Chomsky 1957 and 1959.

The main paradigm of the cognitive sciences is the information processing metaphor. Professor of philosophy, psychology and computer science, Paul Thagard has identified at least six different and competing approaches to cognition that in part stem from independent intellectual traditions and from ways to understand different aspects of mind. These are: the mind as a logical system, a rule-based system, a concept-based system, an analogy-based system, an imagery-based system, and a connectionist system. They all draw on computer analogy in understanding the mind, and so far have failed to produce a unified theory of the mind (Thagard 1996: 128).

Scholars of cognition today are in general agreement that the main disciplines involved in the cognitive sciences are: cognitive psychology, cognitive neuroscience, computer science, linguistics, anthropology, and philosophy.[19] Cognitive psychology provides theories on and experimental strategies for studying various cognitive capacities. Cognitive neuroscience studies cognition at the neurological level. Computer science provides theoretical insight into how human and animal cognitive systems might be organized. Linguistics studies the cognitive capacity of language processing. Anthropology introduces the cultural, and especially the cross-cultural, perspective to cognitive study. Philosophy continues to contribute insight into classical philosophical problems such as the mind-body problem, consciousness, rationality, and mental representation. To this list of disciplines, neuropsychologist Howard Gardner rightly adds European ethology as a contributor even though this discipline first became acceptable rather late in the cognitive sciences (Gardner 1985: 31). European ethologists preferred to study animal behavior in their natural habitat rather than in the laboratory and thus were able to contribute significant insights into the relationships between cognition and the natural environment.[20]

Cognitive Anthropology

But before moving on, mention should be made of the development of cognitive anthropology because, as it turns out, our anthropological colleagues have been doing things with cognition that are closest to what scholars of religion would be doing, if they did it.

Anthropologists have long been interested in the dynamics of individual and culture. Many of Franz Boas' students began quite early during the first

19 See for instance Eysenck/Keane 1995: 4, and Harnish 2002: 2–3.

20 Founding fathers were Konrad Lorenz (1935) and Niko Tinbergen (1951). Significant examples of the wisdom of this interaction between ethology and cognitive psychology is the work of Terence Deacon (1997) and Michael Tomasello/Josep Call (1997).

two or three decades of the twentieth century to focus their attention on the psychological dimensions of culture. There were three phases in the culture and personality approach: 1) the pre-Freudian, which viewed culture as individual psychology writ large;[21] 2) the Freudian, which developed the concept of 'modal personality' in interaction with family and socialization;[22] and 3) the so-called New Directions. The latter arose as the Freudian approaches went into a sharp decline in the early 1950s because of attacks from anti-Freudian psychologists, cultural evolutionists and structural-functionalists, and also because of the defeat of behaviorism. A new kind of anthropology appeared variously termed 'the new ethnography,' 'cognitive anthropology,' 'componential analysis,' and 'ethnoscience' which clearly drew inspiration from the information processing movement in the mathematical sciences where computers began to serve as models for how human minds worked. Through analyses of people's discourse, the new anthropology attempted to identify how people perceive and categorize their social and natural worlds.[23]

Cognitive anthropology has since become very diversified and dispersed through the lenses of such disciplines as cross-cultural psychology, psychological anthropology, and ethnopsychology.[24] This development is much bemoaned by anthropologists who wish to depart from the Platonism of general psychology and the central processing paradigm of the cognitive sciences. They reject the research heuristics of the 1960s, because they ignore culture. The 'person' did not gain a foothold during the cognitive revolution and disappeared from ethnography. Therefore, it was felt, there is a need for a liberated cultural psychology, which to anthropological psychologist Richard Shweder is the study of the role of intentionality in "the interdependent functioning and development of coconstituting and coconstituted intentional persons and their coconstituted embodied and materialized intentional worlds" (1984).[25]

This turn of events brings us back to classical social psychology where James Mark Baldwin, George Herbert Mead, and Lev Vygotsky are towering figures. The new cultural psychology attempts to forge a synthesis between the two generic models of social psychology. The first model sees persons as relinquishing their individuality in favor of either participating with a social unit

21 For instance Ruth Benedict (1932, 1934), Margaret Mead (1928, 1959), and Paul Radin (1913, 1920, 1926).

22 For instance Géza Róheim (1925, 1945), George Devereux (1951a, 1951b, 1961, 1978), Bruno Bettelheim (1955, 1969) and Alan Dundes (1962). A broader neo-Freudian approach developed by psychoanalyst Abram Kardiner led to important cooperation with leading ethnographers (Kardiner 1939; Kardiner/Linton/West et al. 1945; Kardiner/Preble 1961; DuBois 1944; and Whiting/Whiting 1975).

23 Agar 1973; Berlin/Breedlove/Raven 1973; D'Andrade 1976.

24 Cole 1988; Spiro 1982; Colby/Colby 1981.

25 See Shweders earlier work on culture and personality theory in 1979a, 1979b and 1980.

or having communion with others. The second model sees persons as captives of the social world, forced or obligated to follow its rules and regulations. The new third model, that of cultural psychology, sees persons as both individually unique and simultaneously interacting with social units (Valsiner/van der Veer 2000: 388).

What Is Cognition?

Strangely enough, the literature is almost devoid of formal *definitions* of cognition. The literature focuses on approaches, theories, methods and models, but few authors actually define what they mean by the term. Robert M. Harnish noticed the problem as well. Cognitive scientists are in general agreement about what constitutes 'cognitive' phenomena, but there are no general definitions. He would much rather stick to what the *study* of cognition is, like everyone else, but if we modify slightly his 'broad conception of cognition,' a working definition might be: "attention, memory, learning, reasoning, problem solving, motivation, action, perception, and language." What these things all seem to have in common is what Harnish terms a 'narrow conception of cognition,' namely "cognition is the mental 'manipulation' (creation, transformation, deletion) of mental representations" (Harnish 2002: 5).

Cognitive scientists don't know yet what cognition is in its fullest sense. This is in part due to the stringent straightjacket of the information processing paradigm.

A few key anthropologists are currently rethinking the relation between cognition and culture and are coming up with results highly relevant to the study of religion. One of these scholars is Edwin Hutchins.[26] In his book *Cognition in the Wild* (1995), Hutchins argues that cognition in its natural environment draws on contexts rich in organizing resources. Cognition is not just influenced by culture and society, rather it is *fundamentally* cultural and social (Hutchins 1995: xiv). Hutchins chides cognitive anthropologists for ignoring culture, context and history. He claims that any approach to cognition that ignores these factors is fundamentally flawed. For him culture is a cognitive process "that takes place both inside and outside the minds of people" (354). Symbolic systems are not inside the head, and the boundary line of cognition is not inside the skin, rather it is inside the symbolic system. A significant portion of cognition happens in the social space of interaction between individuals where primary symbolic systems, such as language, play a dominant role. Social psychologists have for a century now argued that even our most intimate selves are basically products of social interaction and narrative. The individual

26 See also the work of Bradd Shore (1996).

consists of internal cognitive processes, interactions with the environment, and interaction with social others. The latter two directly shape the development of the brain's structure and function. In fact, according to psychologist Daniel J. Siegel, the emergence of mind from the substance of the brain is significantly effectuated through interpersonal experience (Siegel 1999: xii–xiii, 1). Interpersonal experience directly shapes the circuits responsible for memory, emotion and self-awareness. The mind has distinct modes of processing information, but an integration process occurs which is directly related to emotion. Emotion, [illegible] in a central organizing process within the brain, but is developed by interpersonal attachment experiences which shape the developing mind.

I emphasize this new approach for two reasons: 1) even hardcore neuroscientists are realizing that cognition is a *somatic and social* phenomenon as well as a neural one, however 2) most scholars of religion currently using cognitive approaches either deny or underplay the importance of culture in cognition, and, subsequently, in the cognitive study of religion. This attitude is not only wrong-headed, it is poor cognitive science. Today, it is very clear that cognition is as much a social as a biological phenomenon.[27]

Cognitive Themes for the Study of Religion

The question often arises whether insights in the microbiological levels of the brain and nervous system have any relevance at all to the study of religion. As one colleague laconically remarked, "Of course, all religion is based on biology, and then chemistry, and then physics. The variations between religions can ultimately be explained by the 'ripple effect' immediately subsequent to the big bang. I take it you're familiar with that." Another colleague wrote rather disbelievingly, "it is inconceivable that a cognitive theory would have any relevance, for instance in relation to sacred kingship." I will argue that there is a strong relation between all levels, from the neurobiological to the social, from cognition to sacred kingship. In fact much of what has been going on in the human sciences that are concerned with cognition is the on-going identification of the relations between cognition and culture.

Another colleague once asked after listening to one of my lectures on the usefulness of cognitive theory in the study of religion: "But how can it help me analyze my texts?" Here is the caveat: *the study of religion is significantly more*

27 See Ulric Neisser's excellent review of breakthroughs in the cognitive sciences in his 1994 article on multiple systems. Today we know that "babies see and know much more than we used to believe, the brain has more independent subsystems than we know how to count, behavior is both more innate and more culturally determined than anyone ever imagined" (225–26) and these insights demand a synthesis that is simultaneously developmental, modular, ecological, and cognitive.

than reading and analyzing texts. The study of religion is a theoretical project, exploring an academic construction called 'religion,' which is informed by empirical evidence perceived in terms of a whole range of ideas and assumptions. These ideas and assumptions often turn on the nature of human beings, their origins, cognition and psychology, their cultural and social needs, and so on.[28] Thus, cognitive theory seldom has toolbox usefulness for reading texts, rather, it helps us to understand the texts, behaviors, and attitudes we are confronted with in the study of religion.

In the following I will restrict this account to five themes: 1) Origins and Evolution, 2) Consciousness and Selves, 3) Narrative, Cognition, and Culture, 4) Cognitive Linguistics, and 5) Ritual and Cognition. This survey, I hope, will help interested scholars to take courage and plunge into the details on their own.[29]

1. Origins and Evolution

It's a pity that the vulgar social Darwinism of the latter half of the nineteenth century made such a negative impact on the history of religions in the twentieth century.[30] This same kind of evolutionism promoted by C.R. Hallpike in the 1970s and others more recently hasn't helped much either.[31] Is there anything more intriguing than the evolutionary history of anatomically modern humans and the role that religion may have played in that history? In other words, can the study of religion continue to claim scientific status without concerning itself with origins? I think not. Fortunately for us, the methodology of prehistoric science has improved significantly, and we are now in the unprecedented position to infer insights about our origins. Yes, much is still speculative, but what was once relegated to British progressionism is now on much firmer grounds.[32]

Professor of genetics, Bryan Sykes at the Institute of Molecular Medicine at Oxford University—known for his successful analysis of the so-called Ice Man trapped in glacial ice in northern Italy for 5,000 years—has developed a technique for analyzing and dating the mitochondrial segments of DNA

28 See A.W. Geertz 1997, 1999, 2000; and Jensen 2003: 63, 142, 159, 180, and 194–95.

29 There are not that many introductory volumes to the cognitive study of religion. Two come to mind, however: Boyer 1993 and Pyysiäinen/Anttonen 2002.

30 For instance Tylor 1865, 1871; Lubbock 1865, 1870; Herbert Spencer's ambitious 10 volume *A System of Synthetic Philosophy* dealing with biology, psychology, sociology, and ethics, the most important here being 1870 and 1897.

31 Hallpike 1979, 1986. For similar theories see Parsons 1966, 1977; Bellah 1970; and Barnes 2000. For critiques, see Harbsmeier 1983 and Kuper 1988.

32 See Bowler 1986, 1988 and 1989.

(mtDNA) extracted from human remains. Because these segments are only inherited through maternal lines, Sykes has demonstrated how scientists are now able to trace the current genetic makeup of humanity back to the "Mitochondrial Eve" who lived in Africa some 150,000 years ago and who is thought to have been the maternal ancestor of everyone in the world today (Sykes 2001: 276–77). A website now offers private individuals the possibility of having their DNA analyzed in order "to find out for themselves ... where they fit in."[33] This may sound like madness, but it is more plausible than may seem at first glance, and it should at least warrant interest from scholars who constantly deal with the claims of religious origin stories and are in need of ever better tools to draw independent conclusions based on archaeological and other evidence of time and place.

Former head of the population genetics research group at Oxford University's Wellcome Trust Centre for Human Genetics, Spencer Wells, has expanded the accuracy of genetic archaeology by introducing the results of his analyses of the Y-chromosome through male lines. This kind of analysis is particularly well-adapted to tracing the spread of populations. He has shown how humans spread around the globe from the first incursions into the Arabic Peninsula 50,000 years ago to the latest migrations to the Americas some 10,000 years ago. Combining mtDNA analysis with Y-chromosome analysis and archaeological evidence, Wells has reconstructed a fascinating story about the spread of anatomically modern humans.[34]

A whole industry has risen concerning the topic of human evolutionary psychology. This interesting literature combines the results of physical and cultural anthropology with developmental psychology, evolutionary psychology, behavioral ecology and primate ethology.[35] I will not take on this vast topic, but will review instead a few studies that either address the role of religion or are relevant to it.

1.1. Prehistory of the Mind

Several scholars have attempted either from the archaeological point of view or from the cognitive point of view to combine these two sciences in attempts to reconstruct the cognitive development of modern humans. The results have

33 http://www.oxfordancestors.com.

34 Wells 2002. Cf. also Cavalli-Sforza 2000 and Jones 2002.

35 Cronin 1991; Barkow/Cosmides/Tooby 1992; Dunbar 1996; Diamond 1997; Crawford/Krebs 1998; Fabian 1998; Hurford/Studdert-Kennedy/Knight 1998; Savage-Rumbaugh/Shanker/Taylor 1998; Parker/McKinney 1999; Carruthers/Chamberlain 2001; Whitehouse 2001; Laland/Brown 2002; Barrett/Dunbar/Lycett 2002.

been highly instructive and stimulating. There is still much discussion and a lot of disagreement, but on a more advanced foundation.[36]

In his groundbreaking book, *Origins of Modern Mind*, psychologist at Queen's University, Kingston, Ontario, Merlin Donald argues that the evolution of human culture and cognition from primitive apes to artificial intelligence occurred in three stages. The major impetus of our cognitive evolution was the discovery of symbolic reference which is widely considered to be lacking in other animals. The three phases of transition were all periods of rapid and radical change that led to complete redesigns of human culture. The first was the transition from apes and australopithecines to that of *Homo erectus*. The major breakthrough at this stage, according to Donald, was the development from an episodic culture to the ability to mime, or re-enact, events. This mimetic skill, which is still with us, gave rise to a buffer culture between apes and modern humans. The main mimetic representations in human society were then, as they are now, pantomime, (ritual) dance, and gestural drama. The second phase was from *Homo erectus* to *Homo sapiens* during which the biological evolution of modern humans was completed. This phase was marked by the development of language, "including a completely new cognitive capacity for constructing and decoding narrative" (1991: 16). The onset of language gave rise, according to Donald, to mythic culture, understood as the most elevated use of language. Mythic culture involves the "construction of conceptual 'models' of the human universe" (1991: 213). The third phase was recent and largely nonbiological. It involved the emergence of visual symbolism and external memory techniques that played a major role in the way they helped structure the human mind. The kind of culture produced in this phase is a transition from mythic to theoretic culture. These phases, Donald argues, are not simply the result of brain expansion, otherwise non-human primates, whose brains have been expanding ever since the great apes appeared, would have shown significant cognitive changes (1991: 17). The critical invention here was visuographic, or "the symbolic use of graphic devices" (1991: 275), which he dates beginning around 40,000 years ago with the proliferation of engraved bones and carved ivory. The invention of writing and our continual obsession with symbols led to theoretic culture such as logic and mathematics. The end result, as we all know, is a hybridization between the mind and electronic devices.[37]

Terrence W. Deacon, a neurobiologist, formerly at the Harvard Medical School and Boston University, currently at the Department of Anthropology, University of California, Berkeley, combines human evolutionary biology and

---

36 So much has in fact been discovered that encyclopedias are already appearing concerning human cognitive development: Lock/Peters 1996; Tattersall/Delson/Couvering 2000.

37 It is not possible in the context of this chapter to discuss archaeologist at the University of Reading, England, Steven Mithen's book *The Prehistory of the Mind* (1996).

neuroscience in the study of the evolution of human cognition. His wide-ranging approach moves from laboratory-based cellular-molecular neurobiology to the study of semiotic processes underlying animal and human communication. His book, *The Symbolic Species* (1997) clearly demonstrates the advantages of such an approach. Of special interest to the study of religion, and to the arts and humanities in general, is Deacon's ambition to develop a "scientific semiotics," as he terms it, that could contribute to both linguistic theory and cognitive neuroscience.

Deacon argues that humans are biologically just another type of ape, but mentally we constitute a new phylum (Deacon 1997: 23), *Homo symbolicus* (341). Language is not just communication, rather it is an expression of an unusual mode of thought in evolutionary terms, namely, that of symbolic representation. Without symbolic representation, virtual worlds would be inconceivable. Symbolic thought does not come innately, but develops "by internalizing the symbolic process that underlies language"—thus clearly opposing Noam Chomsky's claims, which Deacon specifically rejects in the book. The novel twist to Deacon's theory is that the extra support needed for language learning is found neither in the child's brain nor in the brains of teachers or parents. It is, instead, in language itself. This claim rests on the assumption that language is an intuitive and user-friendly interface. Children's acquisition of language is not *learned*, Deacon claims, it is *discovered* within certain constraints, like a rigged game. Languages are like living organisms or symbiotic parasites, and the basic principle of design is reproducibility rather than communicative utility: it must pass through "the narrow bottleneck" of children's minds (Deacon 1997: 110). Deacon explains symbolic competence through a novel semiotic theory of the hierarchical nature of symbolic reference. This theory deserves more detailed discussion than fits the scope of this chapter.

A further point that is of interest to scholars of religion is Deacon's persuasive arguments about how humans acquired the semiotic innovation in the first place, in other words, how language developed in a pre-linguistic environment. The first to cross the symbolic threshold, he claims, was an australopithecine "with roughly the cognitive capabilities of a modern chimpanzee" (Deacon 1997: 340). I will not reproduce the arguments concerning the archaeological evidence, the relationships between body size and brain, or the degree of prefrontalization for each hominid type. His conclusion, however, is that stone tools and symbols were the architects of the *Australopithecus-Homo* transition and not its consequences. The expansion of the brain was not the cause of symbolic language but a consequence of it (Deacon 1997: 340–48). All the competing scenarios of language origins, such as mother-infant cooperation, foraging information, hunt organization, competitive reproductive strategies, mate attraction, recruiting for warfare or defense, the social glue equivalent to primate grooming, etc. are probably significant, but not as causal scenarios. They can rather be viewed as specializations and elaborations of domains into which symbolic communication has been introduced and which subsequently introduced further selection pressures on symbolic abilities (Deacon 1997: 350).

The circumstances which tend to produce evolutionary changes in communication in other species, Deacon argues, is sexual selection. One of the techniques used to modify or specialize communicative function in ethological terms is "ritualization." Ritual procedures were all forms of sexual communication that evolved "to negotiate mate choice and pair-bond maintenance" (Deacon 1997: 380). In principle, Deacon argues, human societies shouldn't work because societies are "at the mercy of powerful social and sexual undercurrents" which both can form and destroy bonds as well as social stability (Deacon 1997: 384). The human solution to sexual reproduction is, contrary to what we many think, anomalous in comparison to other species. The difference can be formulated as the difference between mating and marriage. Mating patterns among mammals are determined by rank and competition which results in polygyny or in two individuals isolating themselves from other members of the species. Both types maintain the bonds through threats and violence, although particularly more so in polygyny. Humans, however, opted for cooperative, mixed-sex social groups with "significant male care and provisioning of offspring, and relatively stable patterns of reproductive exclusion, mostly in the form of monogamous relationships" (Deacon 1997: 388).

Such an option is highly volatile and susceptible to disintegration, but the stabilizing factor, he claims, is symbolic communication. Whatever the chosen pattern, marriage is always an expression of social consent involving both reproductive rights as well as social obligations for the bonded pair as well as their relatives. Consent is based on rules, alliances and expectations that can be characterized as reciprocal altruism. The relationships that structure reciprocal altruism cannot be represented indexically, no matter how sophisticated and complex indexical communication may be, because these relationships are symbolic. And marriage can in fact be represented by just a limited set of symbolic types and relationship classes. "Symbolic culture was a response to a reproductive problem that only symbols could solve: the imperative of representing a social contract" (Deacon 1997: 401). And redundant ritual behavior helped the first hominids to shift attention from the concrete to the abstract, in other words, to cross the symbolic threshold. Ritual involved not only demonstrating symbolic relations but also the use of individuals and actions as symbols demonstrating the redefining of social roles taken on by these individuals.

1.2. Counterintuitive Ideas

Standard explanations for the origins, meanings and functions of religion are: 1) religion provides explanations about the world, its origins, puzzling experiences and the sources of evil and suffering; 2) religion provides comfort in a mortally dangerous world; 3) religion provides social order thus keeping society together and upholding social morality; 4) religion is an illusion based on superstition and ignorance. In a book entitled *Religion Explained*, Henry Luce Professor of Individual and Collective Memory at Washington University in St. Louis, Pascal Boyer upends these four explanations and argues that the many forms of religion are *not* the outcome of diversification but of reduction. Those religious ideas that have survived the natural selection of cultural development are salient because our minds have particular mental predispositions.[38]

Religion is not explanation according to Boyer because the urge to explain the origin of the universe is not the origin of religion. People are much more interested in particular occurrences, and the explanations are not always that intelligible. Boyer is much more interested in what goes on in individual minds and how religious concepts function in relation to the brain's inference systems. Religion does not necessarily provide comfort, nor is deliverance from mortality as universal as we think. Religious ideas are connected to human emotional systems, but what is of interest here is how religious concepts relate to the evolutionary heritage of our emotional programs. Religion does not provide social or moral order. These things are already present in the brain from very early on as a necessary survival trait. Again religious ideas are closely connected with social and moral order, but these are primarily a function of the social mind. Religion is not a cognitive illusion as such. There are lots of other ideas and concepts that are just as unsupported. What is of interest here is what makes minds capable of accepting the plausibility of supernatural claims.

According to Boyer, perceiving and understanding the environment requires inferences and guesses about objects and beings in the environment. These inferences and guesses draw on specialized inference systems composed of more specialized neural structures. Inference systems keep us in tune to cues in the environment. Inference systems direct our knowledge acquisition and assist us in surviving in the world. Our minds are particularly sensitive to cultural gadgets that assist us in perceiving and understanding the world.

One of Boyer's lasting accomplishments is that in the face of a vast diversity of religious ideas, he argues that from a cognitive point of view there is only a limited catalogue of ideas. For instance, some of the basic ontological categories (or domain-concepts or conceptual templates—the terminology varies) are PERSON, ARTEFACT, ANIMAL, INANIMATE NATURAL OBJECT, and PLANT. Whenever an object is identified as belonging to one of these 'kinds,' a series of inferences and expectations are intuitively triggered without conscious awareness. What makes religious concepts interesting is that

38 In a coming publication (Geertz n.d.), I have described the development of Boyer's ideas in his books (Boyer 1990, 1994, and 2001) and will, therefore, limit my remarks here to his main evolutionary assumptions. This section is taken from Geertz n.d.

they generally contain violations of these expectations (flying beings, listening statues, conversational trees) even while they tacitly assume standard expectations (spirits are cognitively standard agents that act like we do except for their supernatural abilities). Thus according to Boyer, this model predicts that there are a small number of recurrent types or templates. Templates contain [1] pointers to a particular domain concept, [2] an explicit representation of a violation of intuitive expectations (either [2a] a breach or [2b] a transfer of expectations), and [3] a link to default expectations for the category. Since religious *concepts* are more specific than templates, they add two additional elements, namely a slot for additional encyclopedic information and a lexical label (Boyer/Ramble 2001: 537).

Thus spirits, ghosts or ancestors [1] point to the category person, [2a] assume that they have counterintuitive physical properties and [3] specify that they apply to intuitive expectations about persons. Such agents belong to a *single template* whereas listening statues, for instance, belong to another template because they represent the category *artefact* that contains a transfer of properties from the category *person*. All in all, with five ontological categories and three possible actions of default activation, violation of expectation, and transfer of properties, there are 15 possible varieties of counterintuitive assumptions. This list could be refined in terms of expanding the number of categories, but the logic behind Boyer's argument clearly provides us with a radical alternative to understanding and categorizing the variety of religious ideas.[39] It also demonstrates what he means by claiming that the many forms of religion are not the outcome of diversification but of reduction.

Religious thought and behavior are, in summary, supported by cognitive systems that operate in other, non-religious domains. These systems correspond to a variety of neural systems that are jointly activated. It is this joint activation of multiple systems that may explain why religious beliefs are considered to be plausible and natural (Boyer 2002: 8).

One of the main problems with Boyer's work is that in his attempts to get beyond the variability of cultural detail, he restricts himself to what is going on inside the brain. This heuristic device, as already mentioned, is self-defeating because the story of cognition and the manipulation of symbols is not restricted to the brain. It is not that Pascal Boyer is unaware of the significance of the social context (2001: 27–28), but he is more concerned with internal cognitive processes.

Boyer refers in passing to 'memes'. The concept was introduced by ethologist Richard Dawkins in his book *The Selfish Gene* (1976) as a kind of cultural replicator similar to genes. From the Greek term *mímēma*, 'anything imitated or copied,' Dawkins claims that it is a unit of imitation or of cultural transmission.

39 See Boyer 1999: 881.

Examples of memes are "tunes, ideas, catch-phrases, clothes fashions, ways of making pots or of building arches":

> Just as genes propagate themselves in the gene pool by leaping from body to body via sperms or eggs, so memes propagate themselves in the meme pool by leaping from brain to brain via a process which, in the broad sense, can be called imitation ... If the idea catches on, it can be said to propagate itself, spreading from brain to brain. (Dawkins 1976: 192)

An example is the idea of God, certainly one of the more successful memes in human history. It is replicated by spoken and written word, by music, architecture, art, dance, etc. Its survival value in the meme pool is psychological. It "provides a superficially plausible answer to deep and troubling questions about existence" (Dawkins 1976: 193). Dawkins' meme theory has been criticized for the imprecision of the term 'meme' and for the fact that there is no memetic parallel to the genotype-phenotype distinction in biology.[40]

1.3. Animism and Faces in the Clouds

Anthropologist Stewart Guthrie, at the Fordham University, New York, introduced his cognitive theory of religion in an article published in 1980. His argument is that humans tend to use human-like models to interpret ambiguous phenomena, thus, anthropomorphism, both spontaneous and cultural, is the basis of religion. In his book *Faces in the Clouds*, published thirteen years later (1993), Guthrie extends his argument.[41] In the 1994 preface to the paperback edition, he aptly sums up his theory:

> My own claim is simple. I hold that religion is best understood as anthropomorphism and that anthropomorphism results from a strategy of perception. The strategy is to interpret the world's ambiguities first as those possibilities that matter most. Such possibilities usually include living things and especially humans. Although the strategy leads to mistakes, it also leads to vital discoveries that outweigh them. We see shadows in alleys as persons and hear sounds as signals because if these interpretations are right they are invaluable, and if not, they are relatively harmless. The strategy is involuntary, mostly unconscious, and shared by other animals. Understanding it and the anthropomorphism to which it gives rise illuminates secular as well as religious experience. (Guthrie 1993: v)

The strategy involves, first of all, animism, which is understood here in the psychological sense as "the attribution of life to inanimate things and events" (Guthrie 1993: 5). Thus in doubtful circumstances, we tend to search for the

40 See further elaborations of meme theory in Blackmore 1999 and Aunger 2002.

41 Further elaborations are found in Guthrie 1997, 2000, 2001 and 2002.

most significant possibility, namely, something alive or humanlike. We see apparent people everywhere, "because it is vital to see actual people wherever they may be" (ibid.). Animism is a perceptual strategy: "to discover as much significance as possible by interpreting things and events with the most significant model" (Guthrie 1993: 61), thus there is no need to explain animism, as earlier scholars have, in terms of speculations about death and dreams (Tylor), or expressions of wish fulfillment (Marx) or examples of irrationality (Malinowski).

Religion, Guthrie claims, is the systematic application of anthropomorphism. Whether gods are humanlike, animal-like, or other nonhuman forms, they all interact symbolically with humans. Guthrie's argument is not that gods are humanlike, but that "religion makes nature humanlike by seeing gods there" (Guthrie 1993: 177). In principle, nothing sets religion off from other anthropomorphisms. In a recent publication, Guthrie writes that contrary to Pascal Boyer, there is nothing counterintuitive in religious anthropomorphism. Anthropomorphisms are deeply intuitive (Guthrie 2002: 41–42).[42]

Guthrie claims that the simplicity of his theory is its greatest strength, but one might ask whether it is too simple. Are there perhaps more specific reasons for why anthropomorphisms became religious and why they have had such lasting impact?

2. Consciousness and Selves

The cognitive neurosciences offer an extremely rich potential for the study of consciousness, mental states, and senses of the self. All of these aspects are central to philosophy, the philosophy of science, the comparative philosophy of religion, the psychology of religion, studies of identity and studies of meditative and other mental techniques. Whereas much of the philosophy of consciousness is based on contemplation and introspection, the abiding advantage of neurocognitive approaches is that their results concern mechanisms and processes to which we have no conscious access. With quick-freeze/deep-etch electron microscopy, electroencephalograms (EEG), Computerized Axial Tomography (CAT), recombinant DNA analysis, magnetic resonance imaging (MRI), functional MRI scan (fMRI, which measures blood flow and oxygen use), positron emission tomography (PET scan), patch-clamp method, etc., it is possible for neurologists to both induce and actually view the microscopic components of the brain and its processes. Together with the study of disease (Alzheimer's, Parkinson's, epilepsy, schizophrenia, etc.), brain damage, sensory

42 See the experimental evidence on animacy by Pascal Boyer and colleagues (Blakemore et al. 2003) and on anthropomorphism by Justin L. Barrett and Frank C. Keil (1996).

processing, perception, memory, language, learning, dreaming, etc. and a wide variety of personality and response tests, neurocognitive scientists and clinical psychiatrists have carefully accumulated fairly detailed knowledge of the brain and its processes.[43] Currently, a new atlas of the brain is also being developed.[44]

One of the mysteries which still remains unsolved, however, is how the brain leads to mind, in other words, what is the nature of consciousness. The 1990s witnessed the "consciousness wave" that signaled an upsurge of interest in consciousness in several disciplines.[45] But many of the problems and issues being faced today ultimately derive from age-old controversies in philosophy and psychology. Basically, as Ned Block et al. have pointed out in their excellent reader *The Nature of Consciousness* (1997), current debates stand at the divide between 'essentialist' and 'causal' intuitions, or between the 'consciousness is as consciousness feels' and 'consciousness is as consciousness does' explanatory models. In other words, the explanatory gap lies between conscious experiences as they are *experienced by their subjects* and conscious experiences as they are *investigated from a third-person perspective* (Block/Flanagan/Güzeldere 1997: xiv). Professor of Philosophy and Zoology at Duke University, Güven Güzeldere, argues that what is needed is to rethink epistemology and conceptual schemes that cross-fertilize the first-person and third-person perspectives rather than postulate new ontologies *a priori* (Güzeldere 1997: 45). This of course requires that philosophers and cognitive scientists listen to and learn from each other. Efforts have been made, but the going will be tough.[46]

2.1. Body, Emotion, and Consciousness

The Portuguese born neurologist at the University of Iowa College of Medicine and the Salk Institute for Biological Studies in La Jolla, Antonio R. Damasio, has argued in a number of books that studies of the brain, cognition, and

43 For excellent introductions, see Gleitman/Fridlund/Reisberg 1999 from the psychological point of view, Eysenck/Keane 1995 from the cognitive psychology point of view and Kandel/Schwartz/Jessell 2000 from the neurological point of view.

44 See the fascinating detail on how such an atlas is made. Two major problems in mapping the brain are that it is difficult to define borders between brain regions and there is variation in brain anatomy between individuals. Therefore, the new atlas, based on the study of 15 brains, will generate a 'probabilistic map' (Abbott 2003). See the website of the International Consortium for Brain Mapping at http://www.loni. ucla.edu/icbm.

45 The consciousness wave began with the seminal publications of Weiskrantz (1986), Baars (1988), Crick/Koch (1990), Dennett (1991), McGinn (1991), Flanagan (1992), Searle (1992), Davies/Humphreys (1993), Crick (1994), Churchland (1995), Tye (1995), Metzinger (1995), Velmans (1996) and Chalmers (1996).

46 See for instance Goldman 1992, Revonsuo/Kamppinen 1994, Churchland 1984, O'Donohue/Kitchener 1996 and Lakoff/Johnson 1999.

consciousness are seriously hampered because neuroscientists traditionally ignore the role and functions of emotion in the brain.[47] He claims that "it is possible that feelings are poised at the very threshold that separates being from knowing and thus have a privileged connection to consciousness" (Damasio 1999: 43). Emotions are at a fairly high level of life regulation, and when they are sensed, that is when one has 'feelings,' the threshold to consciousness has been crossed. Emotions are part of homeostasis, which is the automatic regulation of temperature, oxygen concentration or pH in the body by the autonomic nervous system, the endocrine system and the immune system. According to Damasio, homeostasis is the key to consciousness (Damasio 1999: 40).

Damasio defines consciousness as constructing knowledge about two facts: "that the organism is involved in relating to some object, and that the object in the relation causes a change in the organism" (Damasio 1999: 20). Understanding the biology of consciousness becomes, then, a matter of discovering "how the brain can map *both* the two players *and* the relationships they hold" (ibid.). The interesting thing is that the brain holds a model of the whole thing, and this may be the key to understanding the underpinnings of consciousness. His explanation for this enigma is precisely put as follows:

> I have come to conclude that the organism, as represented inside its own brain, is a likely biological forerunner for what eventually becomes the elusive sense of self. The deep roots for the self, including the elaborate self which encompasses identity and personhood, are to be found in the ensemble of brain devices which continuously and *nonconsciously* maintain the body state within the narrow range and relative stability required for survival. These devices continually represent, *nonconsciously*, the state of the living body, along its many dimensions. I call the state of activity within the ensemble of such devices the *proto-self*, the nonconscious forerunner for the levels of self which appear in our minds as the conscious protagonists of consciousness: core self and autobiographical self. (Damasio 1999: 22)

This is, indeed, a radical embodiment theory and should be of great interest to scholars of religion involved in studies of central religious concepts such as personalities, personhood, selves and souls. The very fact of the plurality of selves in Damasio's model should prove useful to the study of religions that deal with multiple selves and souls.

There are other theories about consciousness. There seems to be general agreement about the biology of consciousness, but disagreement about what brings all the neurological and other biological processes together.[48] I have

---

47 Damasio 1994, 1999. Others have been working on emotion and the brain, but I will restrict myself to Damasio. Cf. LeDoux 1998, 2002.

48 Mention should be made of Joseph LeDoux (2002), Todd E. Feinberg (2001), Walter J. Freeman (1999), and Rodolfo R. Llinás (2001). Daniel Dennett (1978, 1987, 1991, 1996) is a key figure in the debate on consciousness, but there is no room for discussion here.

dwelt somewhat on these issues because they set the stage, so to speak, and are prerequisites for much of what is to come.

2.2. Multiple Personalities, Voices, and Regression

All theorists of consciousness in the neurosciences draw on a wide variety of evidence, but especially evidence from brain diseases and brain damage. Anyone who has been exposed to the tragedy of having a family member struck by Alzheimer's or a similar debilitating disease knows how alien we become when things don't function the way they should. These diseases and symptoms allow scientists to draw highly probable conclusions about the functions and characteristics of the brain when it functions as it should.

Scholars of religion can also see in such symptoms the contours of certain types of personalities well known to the history of religions. Those who feel themselves 'possessed' by demons or deities, might be suffering from Multiple Personality Disorder (MPD). Others who 'see' visions and ghosts or obey 'voices,' could be suffering from schizophrenia or temporal lobe excitation. People claiming that they 'remember' being abducted by angels or aliens, or that they have been subjected to satanic ritual abuse as children might be suffering from False Memory Syndrome. Studies of these and other ailments are subsequently highly relevant to the study of religion. I will briefly examine some of the relevant evidence from current diagnostic nosology on dissociative disorders involving alterations in consciousness that affect memory and identity.[49]

The study of Multiple Personality Disorder (MPD) goes back more than 200 years, but the number of cases have fluctuated somewhat with an incredible upsurge (hundreds of cases in the U.S.) since the publication of *Sybil* (Schreiber 1973), a novelist account of a woman who apparently displayed 16 different personalities. In fact, it is unknown how many of these cases are iatrogenic or simply misdiagnosed. MPD can be easily confused with schizophrenia, psychosis and borderline personality.[50] Extremely few cases have been subjected to experimental analysis, and much of the evidence in recent times is based primarily or exclusively on hypnosis, which as we shall see below, is a very problematic therapeutic technique.[51] It has been demonstrated experimentally that MPDs can be created by patients in concert with therapists.

See Geertz 1999 for a discussion on the consequences of Dennett's stance for theories of religion.

49 A brief overview can be found in Kihlstrom/Tataryn/Hoyt 1990.

50 Kihlstrom et al. 1990, copy page 13.

51 Kihlstrom et al. 1990, copy page 16.

There is a good deal of work on the sociocultural contexts of MPD where the conclusions tend to view such behavior as a form of social strategy which allows an individual to disavow actions attributed to other selves or entities in the body. This approach harmonizes well with the idea that selves are co-created by the brain and interpersonal relationships. A leading scholar of this approach was Professor of Psychology and Director of the Laboratory for Experimental Hypnosis at Carleton University, Nicholas P. Spanos. His book, published posthumously, on MPDs and false memories (1996) provides insight into a number of phenomena well known to scholars of religion.

In reviewing the literature, there is a relatively high frequency of "multiple self-enactments" in the world, especially that of spirit possession. A leading scholar on the subject, anthropologist at the London School of Economics, I.M. Lewis, distinguished between central and peripheral possession. The former involves possession by major deities during public performances that confirm central religious tenets, and the latter involves possession by capricious and amoral deities or spirits who possess socially marginal and oppressed members of society.[52] The "politics of possession" extends also to the fact that in most traditional societies with possession beliefs, possession happens more frequently to women than men, and in some societies thus offers women social opportunities that they otherwise would not have.

What is important here is to determine to what extent MPD can be used to interpret spirit possession. Spanos' conclusion is that possession phenomena in traditional societies are rule-governed and generally socially sanctioned. The possessed usually have goals in mind, and these goals are pursued in public or, if not, they at least serve other social functions. Most persons who become possessed are normal, happy individuals. Only a few cases have been reported that indicate possession as being symptomatic of severe stress and accompanied by psychopathological symptoms (Spanos 1996: 155). On the other hand, it is clear that historical reports of demonic possession in Western, Christian contexts resemble the historical manifestations of MPD (Spanos 1996: 169). Also here we find the politics of possession, not only in demonic possession, but in witch hunts as well (Spanos 1996: 181–182).

Many of the humanistic and social science disciplines have long maintained a deep distrust of psychological and psychiatric explanations of ecstatic religious behavior. Such behavior, if touched upon at all by psychologists and psychiatrists, was quickly labeled neurotic or psychotic. Ethnographers have, however, not escaped from similar assumptions. Much of the ethnographic literature on Siberian Shamanism is rife with diagnoses of arctic hysteria, insanity, and lunacy.[53] The same holds for other shamanistic areas and possession

52 Lewis 1986, 1989; cf. Bourguignon 1976; Oesterreich 1974; and Smith 2001.

53 Bogoras 1907: 415; Krader 1954; Devereux 1956; Ohlmarks 1939; Radin 1937.

cultures.[54] But, as I.M. Lewis has pointed out, there is an equal number of scholars who are better informed with precisely the opposite view, namely, that most shamans are psychologically healthy, highly socialized, conventionally accepted, and important members of their communities (Lewis 1989: 165ff.).[55]

2.3. Dissociation and Altered States of Consciousness

In their book *Trance and Possession in Bali* (1995), Luh Ketut Suryani, a Balinese psychiatrist trained in the West and Gordon D. Jensen, a Western psychiatrist with wide experience of Balinese culture and mental health, are more positive in their evaluation of the relationship between Western psychiatric and brain disorders with trance and trance possession in Bali. They claim that trance and trance possession are forms of dissociation. There are dissociative phenomena that are normal and those that are abnormal. Dissociative disorders can be characterized by five core symptoms:

(1) amnesia, i.e. a specific and significant segment of time that is unavailable to memory; (2) depersonalization, i.e. a sense of detachment from self; (3) derealization, i.e. a sense that one's surroundings are unreal; (4) identity confusion, i.e. a feeling of confusion, uncertainty, or puzzlement regarding one's identity; (5) identity alteration, i.e. objective behavior that indicates a change in identity. All or some of these symptoms occur in the various types of dissociative disorders, e.g. MPD and PTSD (Suryani/Jensen 1995: 27–28).[56]

Dissociation is measured by using the Dissociative Experiences Scale (DES) which lists 28 dissociative behaviors (Bernstein/Putnam 1986). Studies indicate that over 25% report a substantial number of dissociative experiences (Ross/Joshi/Currie 1990).

But dissociation is also fairly widespread in normal behavior. Examples are driving a car and not remembering or being aware of details along the route; reading a good book or watching an exciting movie completely oblivious to one's surroundings; doing "absent-minded" things, like pouring coffee in the soup bowl, leaving your keys in the refrigerator or forgetting a dentist appointment; whiling the afternoon away daydreaming; and even dreaming during sleep. Suryani and Jensen claim that such behavior has great individual and species survival value.

Thus dissociation is a basic psychological process not only in normal behavior but also in altered states of consciousness, or ASCs, such as hypnosis, trance and possession, as well as in mental disorders such as MPD. Suryani and

---

54 Bateson/Mead 1942: xvi; Silverman 1967; Langness 1965; Yap 1969; Linton 1956: 131ff.

55 Shirokogoroff 1935; Anisimov 1963; Murphy 1964: 76; Nadel 1946; Wavell/Butt/Epton 1967: 40

56 PTSD is post-traumatic stress disorder.

Jensen conclude that the psychobiological mechanism and phenomenology of MPD is "similar if not the same" as possession both in the West and in Bali (Suryani/Jensen 1995: 219).

ASCs play an important role in a wide variety of religious behavior. Whether induced by hypnosis, hallucinogenic plants and drugs, meditation, rituals, solitude, fasting, music, chanting, singing or dancing, the symptoms are fairly uniform in psychophysiological terms. The differences one finds are due to circumstances, beliefs, role models, concepts of person, and so on. Altered states of consciousness involve modifying or distorting the monitoring and controlling functions of mental alertness and awareness. ASC can be defined by four features:

> (1) operationally, as the product of a particular induction technique; (2) phenomenologically, as an individual's subjective report of altered awareness or voluntary control; (3) observationally, as changes in overt behavior corresponding to a person's self-report; and (4) physiologically, as a particular pattern of changes in somatic functioning. (Kihlstrom 1994: 207)

Unfortunately, although the literature on ASC is voluminous, the experimental evidence that support claims made for performance-enhancing qualities, such as in meditation, are inconclusive either because the results have been negative or because positive results have come out of experiments lacking critical controls (Kihlstrom 1994: 247).

Professor of Psychology at the University of California, Davis, Charles T. Tart, was one of the pioneers in the study of ASC during the heyday of the drug revolution. Using a systems approach, he delineated ten major subsystems or collections of related structures of what he terms *discrete states of consciousness* (d-SoC). A discreet altered state of consciousness (d-ASC) is a system of its own involving a restructuring of consciousness (Tart 1975: 5).

Drawing on psychological and neuroscientific studies of dreaming, jogging, meditation, daydreaming, hypnosis, and drug-induced states, neuroscientist at the Behavioral Neuroscience Laboratory, Georgia College and State University, Arne Dietrich, concluded that the unifying neuroanatomical feature of these various ASCs is that they are due to transient prefrontal cortex deregulation. The phenomenological uniqueness of each state, he argues, "is the result of the differential viability of various frontal circuits" (Dietrich 2003: 231).

2.4. Past Life Therapy

There is a voluminous literature on memory in the cognitive sciences. Besides the very technical studies, much of the literature deals with recall abilities, and a lot of it deals with the role that memory plays in forming and maintaining identity or the self. There are a whole series of topics here that are relevant to the study of religion, such as claims of satanic ritual abuse, alien abduction narratives, and Past Life Therapy. In short, phenomena that have been brought out by therapies often dealing with victims of trauma, especially through the use of hypnosis. In newer neurological and psychiatric research, all of these fall under the category of False Memory Syndrome. This does not mean that there are no victims. It means that many of the so-called memories are creative interpretations performed by the brain (also under hypnosis) in collaboration with unprofessional therapists. In instances where there actually has been abuse, it is usually without religious or occult significance.

For a long time in psychology, brains were thought to record everything that happens to an individual like data recorded on a computer hard disc or images exposed to camera film.[57] Remembering is a matter of retrieving previously recorded information. When individuals are exposed to traumatic experiences, memories are often repressed. Some of them pop up unwillingly in nightmares or bizarre flashes. It was thought that hypnosis made it possible for victims of trauma to retrieve the raw data of their traumatic experiences, replay them, and expose them to conscious reflection. But already during the 1930s, psychologist F.C. Bartlett had proven that memory is essentially reconstructive (1932). The idea that memories lost as a result of trauma could be recovered through psychotherapy has been seriously challenged since then by memory research. We are talking here about situations in which adult patients suddenly and surprisingly remember regular abuse thought to have occurred decades earlier. However, as psychologist at the University of Bristol, Martin A. Conway, formulated the problem:

> But the techniques used by some psychotherapists, hypnosis, imagery, and other memory 'recovery' practices, coupled with a belief that the causes of current psychological distress lie in a patient's past, put in place a context that promotes memory fabrication. A vast body of research from the psychological laboratory and, increasingly, from more real-world studies demonstrates that human memories are inaccurate, incomplete, open to distortion, and wholesale fabrication … Indeed, experimentally inducing false memories in healthy young adults appears almost trivially easy …, the implication being that in the context of therapy, with a patient who is psychologically dysfunctional and actively seeking help, the probability of memory distortion and fabrication is multiplied many times over. (Conway 1997: 1)

Past life regression is a popular New Age therapy. It assumes the truth of reincarnation and claims that current maladies in a particular patient are due to traumatic events in the patient's former life. These ideas have also been made popular by actress and New Age icon Shirley MacLaine's autobiography *Danc-*

57 See the Emory symposia volume on remembering reconsidered (Neisser/Winograd 1988) for discussions on the so-called ecological approach as opposed to the traditional approach to memory.

ing in the Light (1985), which also was made into a movie with MacLaine and her real life therapist Chris Griscom playing themselves.

The social construction of past life identities has been demonstrated by Spanos et al. (1991) in several experiments with subjects who were given pre-hypnotic information. These subjects performed as expected with details not found in the control groups. It was also noted that those who believed in the reality of the results of the experiments were subjects with prior beliefs in reincarnation. After obtaining past life enactments, Kampman and Hirvenoja (1978) hypnotized their subjects and asked them where they got the information in their past life reports. They readily admitted to drawing on a variety of sources in the present life either as children or as adults. Spanos concludes:

> past-life personalities are an experimentally created form of multiple identity. These identities are contextually generated, rule-governed, goal-directed fantasies. Subjects construct these fantasies to meet the demands of the hypnotic regression situation. The suggestions used in this situation tacitly require that subjects' fantasies be framed as autobiographical historical minidramas that are narrated by a first-person-singular identity other than the subject (i.e., the past-life personality). (Spanos 1996: 141–42)

Subjects are also more likely to believe in the reality of their reports if they receive confirmation from a knowledgeable authority. Thus, a co-constituting process in which patients and therapists play out their parts, confirms and legitimizes the hypnotic experiences of past lives as being very real.

2.5. Temporal Lobe Religiosity

Professor of psychology and head of the Neuroscience Research Group at Laurentian University, Sudbury, Ontario, Michael A. Persinger, has explored the neuropsychological bases of god beliefs in a book of the same title (1987). God experiences (basically, mystical experiences), he argues, are correlated with transient electrical instabilities within the temporal lobe of the human brain. He claims that "they appear to have emerged within the human species as a means of dealing with the expanded capacity to anticipate aversive events" (Persinger 1987: x). The specific content of these experiences are due to upbringing, the use of religious language and symbolism, and social strategies.

Persinger made a startling discovery. By stimulating subjects electromagnetically on their temporal lobes, they report experiences of God or other ephemeral entities. Persinger and his team have conducted literally hundreds of experiments on human subjects as well as on rats.[58] The results are unequivocal: stimulation of the right temporal lobe quite often leads to experiences of

58 Persinger's recent publications (1997–2000), listed on his website, provide richly detailed resources.

spiritual visitation and impregnation (Persinger/Koren 2001), of sentient beings (Cook/Persinger 2001), of haunted experiences (Persinger/Koren/O'Connor 2001; Persinger/Tiller/Koren 2000), of Fortean phenomena (Persinger 2001), and sensed presences (Cook/Persinger 1997). Persinger's conclusion is that profound and meaningful experiences of God and similar experiences "are generated by electrical transients within the amygdaloid-hippocampal regions of the temporal lobes" in ways similar to epileptic seizures (Persinger 1997: 128). His proposal also takes account of environmental and meteorological phenomena in influencing human religious sensibilities.

Persinger's insights deserve to be discussed in a wide range of disciplines and especially in the academic study of religion. It should not, at least, be left to neuroscientists alone.[59] The various kinds of pulses produce different types of experience. Persinger and colleagues are already cataloguing patterns and associated experiences, with prosaic names like the Thomas Pulse, Burst X, and the Linda Genetic Pulse (Hitt 1999). Further investigations of the kinds of experiences that arise from temporal lobe stimulation need to be compared with the vast literature in the history of religions describing, interpreting, and analyzing not only mystical experiences but also every other kind of non-ordinary experience. And it should be done by academic scholars of religion.

The theological premises of experiential/phenomenological theories of the origin of religion would have to be abandoned and other explanations found. Those scholars that deny religious experience any causal relevance to theories about religion will also need to rethink their arguments. There is, it seems, a lot of work to be done on this topic.

2.6. Endorphins and Ecstasy

Other biological approaches concern themselves with the chemical aspects of religiosity, especially research on the body's natural defense mechanisms, such as the endorphin net.[60] Scientists had discovered that narcotic molecules attach themselves to receptors in certain nerve cells. They not only identified which receptors were involved but also their frequency and distribution in the body.

59 Persinger's interpretation of the resurrection of Christ for *Skeptic Magazine* http://www.skeptic.com (2002) is not worthy of his neuroscientific work. It is also worrying that a kind of religious devotion seems to have grown up around him. See Jack Hitt's article in the webjournal *Wired Magazine* 1999, associate Todd Murphy's more or less spiritual website *Spirituality & The Brain* http://www.innerworlds.50megs.com/ where various exercises are included for those who purchase an electromagnetic helmet, and the website of the Institute for Biblical and Scientific Studies http://www.bibleandscience.com/godpartbrain.htm. See also Alper 2001 and Albright/Asbrook/Harrington 2001.

60 This sub-chapter is a revised portion of an essay of mine in Danish (1990: 123–26).

In searching for the reason why the body was so receptive to opiates, a number of scientists discovered that the brain produced its own opioids. The two most common were identified as a small amino-acid molecule called *enkephalin* ("in the head") and the polypeptide *endorphin* ("the morphine within"). These opioids are responsible for loss of pain in severe injuries and the analgesic effects of acupuncture and chiropractic adjustments of the spine. These systems can be activated by artificially stimulating certain brain areas, but also by emotional excitement and intense motor activity. Furthermore, sexual stimulation, dangerous activities, the placebo effect, many types of therapies (such as massage and hydrotherapy), meditation, relaxation, and laughter have all been demonstrated to stimulate endorphin and enkephalin release.

Raymond H. Prince, MD, MSc. retired Professor of Psychiatry, McGill University; former Director of the Division of Social and Transcultural Psychiatry concluded in his study of psychotherapeutic practices that:

> since many of the healers' manipulations produced analgesia, euphoria, altered states of consciousness, amnesia, and calmed anxiety, perhaps a significant aspect of their therapeutic activities involved the ability to trigger or enhance the mobilization of these endogenous morphine and valiumlike substances. (Prince 1982a)

There are strong indications of a connection between auto-suggestion and the endorphins in fire-handler cults,[61] trance, and spirit possession,[62] however, hypnotic trance and drum-and-dance trance may depend on two different physiologies. The former produces what is called "faith analgesia" and the latter "endorphin-mediated analgesia" (Prince 1982b: 411–12).

Clinical psychiatrist from the University of British Columbia, Vancouver, Wolfgang G. Jilek investigated shamanism and the "Spirit Dance" among the Salish on Vancouver Island and concluded that the mechanisms of sensory stimulation that produce ASCs[63] have their underlying metabolic mechanism in endogenous opiates (1982: 336–41).

Other scholars have picked up on these findings, such as folklorist at the University of Helsinki, Anna Leena Siikala's 1978 publication on Siberian shamanism and anthropologist at Arizona State University, Tempe, Michael James Winkelman's comparative analysis of shamans, priests, and witches (1992).[64]

---

61 Cf. Kane 1982; Rawcliffe 1959: 291–96; Holm 1982: 23; Tinterow 1970; Barber 1958; Prince 1968.

62 Cf. Henry 1982 and Walker 1972.

63 I.e. pain stimulation, hypoglycemia and dehydration, forced hypermotility, temperature stimulation, acoustic stimulation, seclusion and restricted mobility, visual-sensory deprivation, sleep deprivation, kinetic stimulation, and hyperventilation.

64 On a completely different track, see the special issue of the *Journal of Psychoactive Drugs* on "Shamanism and Altered States of Consciousness" which explores psychopharm-

Finding the biological basis of belief does not replace the richness and texture of that belief, just as explaining the physiology of pain does not remove the actual feeling of pain. Religion and its myriad expressions are still our workplace. However, if we wish to pursue interpretations and explanations that move beyond the religious and theological terminology that religions provide, we need to pay heed to biological as well as cultural and social theories and explanatory models.

3. Narrative, Cognition, and Culture

The fascinating topics of 'transactional selves,' 'narrative selves,' 'biographical selves,' 'remembering selves,' 'constructed selves,' the 'co-narratives of personal storytelling,' 'transparent minds,' 'narrative identity,' and so on, are currently bringing us closer to understanding what 'mind' might actually be.[65] A cardinal point that most psychologists have noted is that humans are extraordinarily transparent to each other. In psychologist Jerome Bruner's words, intersubjectivity is based on the assumption that we have easy access into each other's minds, an access that cannot be explained simply by empathy (Bruner 1986: 57). Human beings, he noted:

> must come equipped with the means not only to calibrate the workings of their minds against one another, but to calibrate the worlds in which they live through the subtle means of reference. In effect, then, this is the means whereby we know Other Minds and their possible worlds. (Bruner 1986: 64)

Narrative as the 'glue,' one might say (Nair 2002), between cognition and culture, is currently being investigated in various parts of the world. Even though scientific interest in narrative is hardly new, it has been going on in highly specialized circles in diverse disciplines. A brief reminder of narrative theory since the 1950s should be sufficient. Closest to the study of religion, the disciplines of folkloristics, semiotics, structuralism, narratology, literary theory, all have had narrative, written and oral, as their main subject. Anthropology, history, and sociology have also paid some attention to narrative.[66] Linguistics has contributed to the study of language and communication, drawing on a variety of approaches to explore the subject. Developmental psychologists and psycho-

---

ocopia in shamanism, edited by Marlene Dobkin de Rios and Michael Winkelman (1989).

65 Just a few examples: Bruner 1986 (transactional self), 1994 (remembered self); Sarbin 1986; Goldschmidt 1990; Neisser/Fivush 1994 (remembering self); Ochs/Capps 1996 (narrative self).

66 Kluckhohn 1945; Colby/Cole 1973; Bloomfield 1970; White 1987; Goffman 1959, 1981; Bertaux 1981.

analysts have long been interested in the role of language, narrative and autobiography in the developing child and later adulthood. Social psychologists have studied what makes a good story and why. Neuroscientists have been interested in how language is produced in various parts of the brain and the role that narrative plays in social cognition. And philosophers have also turned to narrative and communication since the so-called linguistic turn.[67]

One could, in fact, view narrative as a focus of interest for a large variety of disciplines for any number of reasons. A sophisticated study of narrative would involve three subject areas: theory, text, and behavior. Thus any study of narrative must be informed by and take into account a wide variety of disparate sciences and disciplines. Yet, until recently, no sustained efforts have been made to integrate the findings of these fields. And very few have even considered *religious* narrative to have any interest at all. Nevertheless, 'narrative' is once again clamoring for attention not only in many scientific fields, but also in business, politics, and ethnic and cultural revitalizations. In Denmark, at my department, which has a Laboratory on Theories of Religion, we have launched a project on "Religious Narrative, Cognition, and Culture." Assuming that cognition is simultaneously biological and social and that narrative is one of the main expressions of this dynamic tool, we hope to explore and develop cohesive models of the interaction between these three factors.

A key theorist in this respect is Daniel J. Siegel. Siegel introduced an integrated developmental approach in his book *The Developing Mind* (1999), or as he formulated it elsewhere, "an interpersonal neurobiology of the developing mind" (Siegel 2001). The basic idea is that the mind develops "at the interface between human relationships and the unfolding structure and function of the brain" (Siegel 2001: 67). At the core of this development is an integration process "that secure attachments facilitate in promoting psychological well-being" (Siegel 2001: 67). Central to Siegel's thesis is a theory of the self. He distinguishes between the emerging self (birth to two months), the core self (three months to seven or nine months), the subjective self (nine months to 18 months), the verbal self (around age two) and beyond this period the narrative self "in which autobiographical narratives play a major role in defining the self" (Siegel 2001: 75). When Siegel and others speak of the development of the self through interpersonal connections, they are not just talking ordinary psychology. They are, in fact, talking about neurons and neural mapping.

An important aspect of the self is what is known as autonoesis or 'self-knowledge' as presented in autobiographical narratives. Experimental evidence shows that an infant's attachment to the parent is predicated on the parent's autobiographical narrative coherence. Autonoesis is, in other words, made possible for the child through attachment relations.

67 Wittgenstein 1933, 1953; Ricoeur 1984, 1995; Kerby 1991.

Thus we can begin to see the enormous potential of such neuropsychological insights to our study of religious narratives, autobiographies, hagiographies, myths and legends, dreams and vision narratives, and even gossip! In this light, our texts and narratives are not just hermetic containers of semantic worlds, but also and more significantly, producers of neural mappings, minds, selves, memories, histories and worlds.

4 Cognitive Linguistics

Cognitive semantics, or cognitive linguistics, began to hit the general market during the late 1970s. It seeks to apply insights from the cognitive sciences to the study of language. In other words, methodological attempts are made to coordinate linguistic theory with empirical discoveries being made about the brain and mind. But the history of research behind cognitive linguistics is circuitous and typically American. By this I mean what my colleague in Aarhus, historian of religions Jeppe Sinding Jensen, termed the "pizza effect":

> The 'pizza-effect' is an anthropological term for the fact that something 'must go to America' for approval, like pizzas that were not really known in Italy before poor immigrants from the South had taken the concept across the Atlantic. (Jensen 2003: 426, note 25)

In this context, some of the basic ideas and even some of the terminology and methodological operations of cognitive semantics arose already in early European philosophy (Raymundus Lullus, Giordano Bruno and Gottfried Wilhelm Leibniz) and in the German Gestalt psychology movement (Kurt Lewin and Fritz Heider). As German linguist Wolfgang Wildgen at the University of Bremen argues, once centers of cognition research began to accept insights from Gestalt psychology (probably via computational vision research), these strands of ideas entered mainstream theorizing. Early work by Marvin Minsky (1975) and Charles Fillmore (1968), who both introduced the concept of 'frames,' and the cognitive semantics proposed by philosopher René Thom (1968)[68] was ignored by Chomskyan linguists. One of the centers of cognition research was established in Berkeley in 1968, where Fillmore and his colleagues were members. After the middle of the 1970s cognitive semantics took off:

> In 1977 Lakoff gave a paper on linguistic Gestalts at the Summer School on Mathematical and Computational Linguistics in Pisa. In the same period Leonard Talmy wrote his articles "Rubber Sheet Cognition in Language" and "Figure and Ground in Complex Sentences",[69] and in 1979 Langacker published the first article—entitled "Grammar as Image"—on what would become 'space grammar' and later 'cognitive

68 A translation of his early work is found in Thom 1975 and 1983.

69 See Talmy 1977, 1978, and 2000.

> grammar'.[70] Thus, between 1976 and 1979 the new 'wave' of topological and dynamic semantics finally reached California and soon thereafter began to spread through Italy, Germany, and France—cultural areas in which, half a century earlier, the major trends in Gestalt theory and corresponding applications to linguistics had been created. But this 'comeback' was something more: it had inherited the missionary attitude of American linguistics after Chomsky. (Wildgen 1998, web version p. 7)

There is an enormous literature on cognitive linguistics, but there is no room here to go into detail.[71] Of all the cognitive approaches discussed in this chapter, this approach appears to be one of the most methodologically useful to the study of religious texts. It is for my students anyway. Two particular areas appear to be the most useful, and it is to these that I now turn.

4.1. The Body in the Mind

The basic idea is that neural human beings cannot have purely uncategorized and unconceptualized experience. Our categories are formed through embodied experience. Concepts are neural structures "that allow us to mentally characterize our categories and reason about them" (Lakoff/Johnson 1999: 19). Much of this reasoning is what linguist George Lakoff, at the University of California, Berkeley, and philosopher Mark Johnson, at the University of Oregon, call prototype-reasoning (typical-case, ideal-case, social stereotypes, salient exemplars). These types help us draw inferences relative to a category. But categories seldom fit perfectly and so there are graded similarities (called linguistic hedges) in relation to essence prototypes. Many of our categories are envisioned as spatial metaphors, such as containers, boundaries, and interiors. The important cognitive point here is:

> All of these conceptual structures are, of course, neural structures in our brains ... What makes concepts concepts is their inferential capacity, their ability to be bound together in ways that yield inferences. *An embodied concept is a neural structure that is actually part of, or makes use of, the sensorimotor system of our brains. Much of conceptual inference is, therefore, sensorimotor inference.* (Lakoff/Johnson 1999: 20; emphasis in the original)

This discovery indicates that the locus of reason is the same as the locus of perception and motor control, "which are bodily functions." The claims made here seem to be strongly supported by the empirical evidence concerning color concepts, basic-level concepts, and spatial-relations concepts (Lakoff/Johnson 1999: 23ff.).

Lakoff and Johnson have done considerable work in demonstrating the way language works through prototype metaphors. In their groundbreaking

70 See Langacker 1979, 1987, and 1991.

71 For introductions, see Ungerer/Schmid 1996, Lee 2001, and Croft/Cruse 2003.

book *Metaphors We Live By* (1980), they argue that conventional philosophies of meaning are inadequate in understanding the role that metaphor actually plays in everyday language and thought. Conventional theories cannot, they claim, simply be patched up in order to account for the role of metaphor. The whole idea of metaphor has to be reconceived. Their basic thesis, based primarily on linguistic evidence, is this: "the way we think, what we experience, and what we do every day is very much a matter of metaphor" (Lakoff/Johnson 1980: 3). They then set out to demonstrate the systematicity of metaphor and how it works. Lakoff and Johnson have been very prolific but there is no room here for further discussion of their work.[72]

4.2. Conceptual Blending

An interesting area of cognitive semantics that has proven to be quite useful analytically is the concept of 'conceptual blending.' Literary scholar Mark Turner, at the University of Maryland, drawing on the same cognitive evidence as Lakoff and Johnson—especially concerning image schemas and the body—focuses more specifically on story and narrative as the basic principle of the mind. And one of the main operations in storytelling is that of conceptual blending. Mark Turner elaborates the term in his *The Literary Mind* (1996), but its analytical potency was developed in cooperation with cognitive scientist at the University of California, San Diego, Gilles Fauconnier, who developed a theory of knowledge representation and linguistic processing in his book *Mental Spaces* (1985). The main tenet of this new approach to language and meaning is aptly summed up in the phrase: "Language does not carry meaning, it guides it" (Fauconnier 1985: xxii).

Fauconnier introduced the theory of mental spaces in 1978 at the Accademia della Crusca in Florence. The theory attempts to explain "the hidden, counterintuitive complexities of cognitive construction linked to language" (Fauconnier 1985: xvii). Mental spaces is a significant factor in what is happening in this hidden background. The principles of operation are apparently universal, and they make it possible for speakers to generate virtually unlimited varieties of meaning constructions. Mental spaces are defined as "small conceptual packets constructed as we think and talk, for purposes of local understanding and action" (Fauconnier/Turner 2002: 40). Mental spaces are connected to schematic knowledge called frames, and these frames structure the way elements are blended in mental spaces. The blend brings elements from different frames into relations that do not exist in the original sources and allows us to creatively imagine an unlimited range of ideas and situations.

72 See Lakoff 1987; Johnson 1987; and Lakoff/Turner 1989.

Individuals are not completely left to do blends on their own. Cultures, Fauconnier and Turner claim, "work hard to develop integration resources that can then be handed on with relative ease ... In cultural practices, the culture may already have run a blend to a great level of specificity for specific inputs, so that the entire integration network is available, with all of its projections and elaborations," such as the development of complex numbers (Fauconnier/ Turner 2002: 72). Furthermore, cultures offer their members methods for setting up a blend. In drawing on Edwin Hutchins' insight on the method of loci, i.e. associating long sequences of ideas in relation to landmarks in the physical environment, Fauconnier and Turner argue that "the method of loci invites us to create a blended space in which items to be remembered are objects along a familiar path and, as such, take on the inevitable sequence that would be perceived by a traveler along it" (ibid.). This method was also discussed by Cicero, but examples are rife in the history of religions as well.

Blending is essential in religious ritual and magic. Linguist at the University of California, San Diego, Eve Sweetser, in an article on ritual and blended spaces, has demonstrated its effect in the Baby's Ascent, where newborn babies in some Italian village communities are carried up the stairs of their parents' house to help the children advance in life and ritually determine their destiny (2000: 312). In this example, by influencing relations in the source domain (height), "the relations in the target domain (status) are to be changed" (ibid.). Magical ritual draws in complex ways on the imaginative activity of blending, as scholar of religion at the University of Southern Denmark, Odense, Jesper Sørensen, has shown in his groundbreaking work on a cognitive theory of magic (2001). The possibilities of applying blending theory to the comparative study of religion are as diverse and rich as conceptual blending is itself. Even in analyses of ancient cultures, such as Babylonian texts or Roman divination, blending theory is being creatively applied by students of religion.[73]

The basic idea of blended spaces theory is simple, but subsequent analyses of actual examples are extremely complex, and the resultant diagrams, catalogues, and mental maps are daunting. But the replicability and explanatory power of the theory is quite evident.

5. Ritual and Cognition

Ritual is perhaps one of the most ubiquitous topics in the comparative study of religion. Discussions on the relationship between myth and ritual throughout

73 Cf. Westh 2002 and Lisdorf 2003. These examples are Masters' theses in Denmark at the University of Copenhagen, but I am sure that similar studies are being carried on elsewhere in the world.

much of the history of research in the study of religion is an indication of its vital importance.[74] There is a relationship, but what is it, and which one came first? That discussion has never been resolved, but there is little doubt that cognitive theorists and scholars of the prehistory of the mind are convinced that ritual pushed us across the threshold to symbolic thought and on to human existence.

Ritual is one of the few areas where attempts have been made to apply insights from biology long before the cognitive revolution appeared in the study of religion. Much of the interest was no doubt due to the rise of sociobiology during the 1970s, having gained notoriety in Edward O. Wilson's seminal book *Sociobiology: The New Synthesis* (1975) even though he was not the first sociobiologist.[75]

Anthropologists such as Gregory Bateson (1972) and Roy A. Rappaport (1979, 1999) were also drawing on inspiration from sociobiology, ethology and other relevant disciplines as well as cybernetics in their attempts to understand religion and ritual. Interesting studies on the relations between animal and human rituals were also being conducted by anatomists and others connected to the University of Pennsylvania such as Eugene G. d'Aquili, Charles D. Laughlin, Jr., and John McManus. Unfortunately, they received the same kind of reception as the sociobiologists. In their ground-breaking books *Biogenetic Structuralism* (Laughlin/d'Aquili 1974) and *The Spectrum of Ritual* (d'Aquili/ Laughlin, Jr./McManus 1979), the authors found that the primary biological function of ritual behavior is cybernetic: "ritual operates to facilitate both intra-organismic and interorganismic coordination." Furthermore, they argue that ritual entrains and transforms the structure of neuromotor subsystems in the developing individual, in other words, a mechanism for socialization (d'Aquili/ Laughlin, Jr./McManus 1979: 35).[76]

One of the pioneers in introducing biological insights to the study of religion is the classicist and historian of religions at the University of Zürich, Walter Burkert. In his book *Homo Necans* (1972),[77] Burkert introduced the idea, quite revolutionary at the time in classical studies, that sacrifice was derived from hunting and religion from sacrificial ritual. He attempted to show that in

74 See Robert A. Segal's excellent anthology on the myth and ritual theory (1998).

75 His book became nothing less than a sensation inside and outside the academy because it challenged the integrity of culture *sui generis* as a distinctive and symbolic human creation, in the words of one of his critics, anthropologist Marshall Sahlins (Sahlins 1976, x). Cf. Wilson 1975 and 1976; Alexander 1974 and 1987; Hamilton 1964, 1970; and Williams 1966. See Sahlins (1976) and a critical response to Sahlins by Alexander 1977.

76 Cf. d'Aquili/Laughlin, Jr./McManus 1979; Laughlin, Jr./McManus/d'Aquili 1990; Laughlin, Jr./d'Aquili 1983; d'Aquili 1986.

77 The English translation (1983) won the 1992 Richard M. Weaver Award for Scholarly Letters, Ingersoll Foundation.

the formative period of European civilization, solidarity was achieved "through a sacred crime with due reparation" (Burkert 1972: xiv). Burkert drew on a number of disciplines such as prehistory, sociology, semiotics, structuralism, and psychology, especially the work of Konrad Lorenz on the nature of violence (1963), and he wrote the book before breakthroughs in ethology were commonly known. The book has received criticism from classicists and later from disciplines with various agendas that run counter to his argument, all of which he graciously acknowledges. Today, having lived through changing periods of theorizing in various disciplines, especially cognitive and prehistorical studies, his thesis seems to have found its proper place together with the work of another outstanding scholar on ritual violence, the French literature scholar René Girard.[78]

Burkert's book *Creation of the Sacred* (1996) has also attracted critical attention and was the subject of symposium reviews in the journal *Method & Theory in the Study of Religion* (1998) as well as the journal *Religion. An International Journal* (2000). Burkert attributes the creation of religion through "biological patterns of actions, reactions, and feelings activated and elaborated through ritual practice and verbalized teachings, with anxiety playing a foremost role" (Burkert 1996: 177). Religion, he claims, follows the tracks of biology, but was closely related to the invention of language. It is the creation of sense.

In the following, I will concentrate on two cognitive approaches to the study of ritual which are not concerned with origins. The first approach deals with representations of ritual action in the minds of participants, and the second approach deals with ritual transmission. These two approaches draw on the neurosciences rather than on ethology.

5.1. Bringing Ritual to Mind

Philosopher of science at Emory University, Robert N. McCauley and historian of religions at Western Michigan University, E. Thomas Lawson have in a number of publications promoted a cognitive approach to religion that focuses on believers' representations and judgments of ritual behavior.[79] In their book *Rethinking Religion* (1990), they draw on the transformation linguistics of Noam Chomsky and experimental psychology. The book focuses on the conceptual systems or implicit rules that generate responses in individuals to their ritual behavior. The focus is thus not on ritual behavior as such, rather it is on the normative assumptions and competencies of ritual participants. They claim that

78 See the excellent conference publication on violent origins edited by Hamerton-Kelly (1987). Girard's most important publications on this topic are 1972, 1982, and 1985.

79 Their book has received critical acclaim, but there are only a few people who are trying to apply their approach to the study of religion.

competency in religious ritual systems is accumulated much later than competency in language. Even though humans have a capacity to generate symbols, religious symbols are add-ons to more basic mechanisms. What makes religious ritual systems *religious* is due to symbolic-cultural systems that involve commitment to culturally postulated superhuman beings (Lawson/McCauley 1990: 123). Religion stands, in other words, on the shoulders of much more fundamental representational systems. Lawson and McCauley show how ordinary action representation systems work and how religious conceptual schemes use [illegible]

A by-product of this approach is that they introduce a new way of analyzing ritual sequences that is analogous to the way that transformational linguists analyze sentences. Throughout the book, ritual sequences are analyzed in handy but highly formalized models. These models clearly indicate the roles and positions of the participants, agents, objects, action complexes, qualities, properties, acts, and conditions whether they appear on the surface or in deep structure.

The main accomplishment of their approach and the main goal of the book is to identify what they call the "Universal Principles of Religious Ritual." There are two universal principles. The first is called "The Principle of Superhuman Agency" which states that "those rituals where superhuman agents function as the agent in the ritual ... will always prove more central to a religious system than those where the superhuman agents serve some other role" (Lawson/McCauley 1990: 125). The second is called "The Principle of Superhuman Immediacy" which states that "the fewer enabling actions to which appeal must be made in order to implicate a superhuman agent, the more fundamental the ritual is to the religious system in question" (ibid.). These two principles provide a typology of religious rituals based on their relative centrality. Lawson and McCauley identify five types, although as they note, there might be more.

Lawson and McCauley reiterate and further systematize their theory in *Bringing Ritual to Mind* (McCauley/Lawson 2002) but with a slight change of emphasis. As with the work of Harvey Whitehouse, with which they take issue and to which we shall return below, McCauley and Lawson are concerned with what it takes for participants to recall their rituals well enough to transmit and re-perform them. Some religions use frequent performance to ensure transmittal whereas others use extreme emotional stimulation. McCauley and Lawson advance the ritual form hypothesis to account for which performance type is used to ensure transmittal. This hypothesis posits that it is "participants' tacit knowledge about differences in ritual form that determines *which* religious rituals migrate to one or the other of the two attractor positions" (Lawson/McCauley 1990: 113). The two attractors are pageantry on the one hand and repetitiveness on the other. Lawson and McCauley are interested in *both* memory and motivation (as opposed to Whitehouse who restricts interest to memory), and therefore they argue for two conclusions:

> First, that those religious rituals that settle around the second attractor, containing increased sensory pageantry, stimulate participants' emotions in order not only to augment their recall for these events but also to motivate them religiously, and, second, that our general theory of religious ritual competence explains why those rituals that must produce enhanced episodic memories are precisely the rituals that must fortify religious motivation. (Lawson/McCauley 1990: 114)

Thus the ritual form hypothesis accounts for the interplay between ritual, sensory pageantry, memory and motivation.

Ultimately their goal is to reveal "larger patterns in the evolution of religious ritual systems (and of religious systems generally) that cut across cultures and historical epochs" (Lawson/McCauley 1990: 7), but let us suffice with the arguments already presented as an indication of the complexity and formality of their hypothesis.

5.2. Modes of Religiosity

Anthropologist at Queen's University of Belfast, Harvey Whitehouse, developed a theory of ritual transmission that draws its explanatory evidence from memory studies in experimental psychology. In his book *Inside the Cult* (1995), Whitehouse attempts to explain how two politico-religious regimes came to coexist within the Pomio Kivung political 'cargo cult' movement in the Eastern Province of New Britain in Papua New Guinea. Based on his fieldwork in the region from 1987–1988, he noted that the Pomio Kivung is hierarchically organized; holds frequent meetings and a long series of ceremonies; proselytizes a routinized, coherent and systematized body of beliefs; and does not maintain secrecy or mystery which so often characterizes indigenous religions in New Guinea. Furthermore, it involves the whole community and there is regular supervision by lieutenants to outlying regions to ensure that no deviations of doctrine are introduced. A splinter group, however, driven by prophetic visions from the ancestors, reintroduced some of the old rituals and eventually developed a radically different ritual regime than the Pomio Kivung by emphasizing pageantry, sensory stimulation and emotional provocation. There is also a tendency towards non-verbal transmission and analogic communication (Whitehouse 1995: 5).

In drawing on the experimental literature concerning 'flashbulb memory' (Brown/Kulik 1977; Winograd/Killinger 1983), Whitehouse argues that "a particular neural mechanism is activated in response to events which are surprising, salient, and emotionally arousing" as in the context of intense religious revelation (Whitehouse 1995: 195).[80] These memories remain and seem to become more vivid through the years (Scrivner/Safer 1988). Drawing further on the distinction between semantic and episodic memory as described by Endel Tulving (1972), Whitehouse concludes that repetitive mainstream rituals are encoded as scripts in semantic memory, whereas infrequent rituals are encoded as special events in the episodic memory. He argues that these ritual types reflect particular modes of religiosity. In his book *Arguments and Icons* (2000), Whitehouse defines modes of religiosity as "*tendencies* towards particular patterns of codification, transmission, cognitive processing and political association" (Whitehouse 2000: 1). The two modes of religiosity reflect the abovementioned two types of memory. The mode that is analogous to episodic memory is the "imagistic mode" which is:

> the tendency, within certain small-scale or regionally fragmented ritual traditions and cults, for revelations to be transmitted through sporadic collective action, evoking multivocal iconic imagery, encoded in memory as distinct episodes, and producing highly cohesive and particularistic social ties. (ibid.)

Its opposite is the doctrinal mode which is analogous to semantic memory. The doctrinal mode is:

> the tendency, within many regional and world religions, for revelations to be codified as a body of doctrines, transmitted through routinized forms of worship, memorized as part of one's 'general knowledge', and producing large, anonymous communities. (ibid.)

Whitehouse realizes that both forms can in fact appear in the same religious tradition, however, he argues that these contrastive modes can be understood as clusters of features "that tend to coalesce, all else being equal" (Whitehouse 2000: 2). He lists 13 distinguishing features of the contrastive modes of religiosity in terms of style of codification, frequency of transmission, cognitive processing, political ethos, solidarity/cohesion, revelatory potential, ideological coherence, moral character, how they are spread, scale and structure, leadership type, distribution of institutions and diachronic features (Whitehouse 1995: 197, table 5).

I will not go into detail on the criticisms that this approach has attracted. Some of it has been dealt with in his publications. One of the main problems concerns the psychological evidence on memory. Things are evidently not as clear-cut as they appear in Whitehouse's discussion, both concerning flashbulb effects and the characteristics of semantic and episodic memory.[81] Whether or

80 Cf. Herdt 1989.

81 See Scott Atran's sustained criticism of Whitehouse's use of the ethnographic and psychological evidence in 2002: 149–73. For discussions on flashbulb memory and false memory see Winograd/Neisser 1992.

not these criticisms are crucial to Whitehouse's theory remains to be seen, but the two modes of religiosity are clearly ideal types that go a long way in explaining a number of matters relevant to both religious and cognitive style.

Conclusion

The main point of this chapter is simple: there is more to cognitive theory than hitherto assumed in the comparative study of religion. Possibilities for future research are enormous. All that is required, on the one hand, is humility in the face of a sea of information and a plurality of epistemologies, and, on the other, creative application on one of humanity's most evocative and encompassing inventions. Indeed, if we succeed in understanding the most fundamental aspects of human cognition (consciousness, representation, symbolization, language, and emotion), I am convinced that we will discover how crucial a role religious ritual and religious ideas have played in making us what we are.

Bibliography

Abbott, Alison (2003), "A New Atlas of the Brain," in: *Nature* 424, 17 July 2003: 249–50.

Agar, Michael (1973), *Ripping and Running: A Formal Ethnography of Urban Heroin Addicts*. London: Academic Press.

Albright, Carol Rausch/Ashbrook, James B./Harrington, Anne (2001), *Where God Lives in the Human Brain*. Naperville: Sourcebooks.

Albright, Thomas D./Jessell, Thomas M./Kandel, Eric R./Posner, Michael I. (2000), "Neural Science: A Century of Progress and the Mysteries That Remain," in: *Cell/Neuron Millennial Review Supplement* 100 (25): 1–55.

Alexander, Richard D. (1974), "The Evolution of Social Behavior," in: *Annual Review of Ecology and Systematics* 5: 325–38.

— (1977), Review of "The Use and Abuse of Biology," in: *American Anthropologist* 79: 917–20.

— (1987), *The Biology of Moral Systems*. New York: Aldine De Gruyter.

Alper, Matthew (2001), *The "God" Part of the Brain*. 5th ed. New York: Rogue Press.

Anisimov, A.F. (1963), "The Shaman's Tent of the Evenks and the Origin of the Shamanistic Rite," in: *Studies in Siberian Shamanism*, ed. by Henry N. Michael. Toronto: University of Toronto Press.

Atran, Scott (2002), *In Gods We Trust: The Evolutionary Landscape of Religion*. Oxford: Oxford University Press.

Aunger, Robert (2002), *The Electric Meme: A New Theory of How We Think*. New York: The Free Press.

Baars, Bernard J. (1988), *A Cognitive Theory of Consciousness*. Cambridge: Cambridge University Press.

Barber, Theodore Xenophon (1958), "Toward a Theory of Pain: Relief in Chronic Pain by Prefrontal Leucotomy, Opiates, Placebos, and Hypnosis," in: *Psychological Bulletin* 56: 430–60.

Barkow, Jerome H./Cosmides, Leda/Tooby, John (1992), *The Adapted Mind: Evolutionary Psychology and the Generation of Culture*. Oxford: Oxford University Press.

Barnes, Michael Horace (2000), *Stages of Thought: The Co-Evolution of Religious Thought and Science*. Oxford: Oxford University Press.

Barrett, Justin L./Keil, Frank C. (1996), "Conceptualizing a Nonnatural Entity: Anthropomorphism in God Concepts," in: *Cognitive Psychology* 31: 219–47.

Barrett, Louise/Dunbar, Robin/Lycett, John (2002), *Human Evolutionary Psychology*. Basingstoke: Palgrave.

Bartlett, Frederic C. (1932), *Remembering: A Study in Experimental and Social Psychology*. Cambridge: Cambridge University Press.

Bateson, George/Mead, Margaret (1942), *Balinese Character: A Photographic Analysis*. New York: The New York Academy of Sciences.

Bateson, Gregory (1972), *Steps to an Ecology of Mind*. San Francisco, Calif.: Chandler Publishing Company; also: New York: Ballantine Books 1972, 1990.

Bellah, Robert (1970), "Religious Evolution," in: *Beyond Belief*. San Francisco, Calif.: Harper & Row: 20–50.

Benedict, Ruth (1932), "Configurations of Culture in North America," in: *American Anthropologist* 34: 1–27.

— (1934), *Patterns of Culture*. Boston, Mass.: Houghton Mifflin.

Berlin, B./Breedlove, D.E./Raven, P.H. (1973), "General Principles of Classification and Nomenclature in Folk Biology," in: *American Anthropologist* 75: 214–42.

Bernstein, E.M./Putnam, F.W. (1986), "Development, Reliability, and Validity of a Dissociation Scale," in: *Journal of Nervous and Mental Disease* 174: 727–35.

Bertaux, Daniel, ed. (1981), *Biography and Society: The Life History Approach in the Social Sciences*. Beverly Hills, Calif./London: Sage Publications.

Bettelheim, Bruno (1955), *Symbolic Wounds: Puberty Rites and the Envious Male*. London: Thames and Hudson.

— (1969), *The Children of the Dream*. London: Thames and Hudson.

Blackmore, Susan (1999), *The Meme Machine*. Oxford/New York: Oxford University Press; reprint 2000.

Blakemore, S.-J./Boyer, P./Pachot-Clouard, M./Meltzoff, A./Segebarth, C./Decety, J. (2003), "The Detection of Contingency and Animacy in the Human Brain," in: *Cerebral Cortex* 13: 837–44.

Block, Ned/Flanagan, Owen/Güzeldere, Güven, eds. (1997), *The Nature of Consciousness: Philosophical Debates*. Cambridge, Mass./London: The MIT Press; reprint 1998.

Bloomfield, M.W., ed. (1970), *The Interpretation of Narrative: Theory and Practice*. Cambridge, Mass.: Harvard University Press.

Bogoras, Waldemar (1907), *The Chukchee*. The Jesup North Pacific Expedition. Vol. 7. Memoir of the American Museum of Natural History 11. Leiden: Brill.

Bourguignon, Erika (1976), *Possession*. San Francisco, Calif.: Chandler & Sharp Publishers.

Bowler, Peter J. (1986), *Theories of Human Evolution: A Century of Debate, 1844–1944*. Baltimore, Md.: Johns Hopkins University Press; reprint Oxford: Basil Blackwell 1987.

— (1988), *The Non-Darwinian Revolution: Reinterpreting a Historical Myth*. Baltimore, Md./London: Johns Hopkins University Press.

— (1989), *The Invention of Progress: The Victorians and the Past*. Oxford: Basil Blackwell.

Boyer, Pascal (1990), *Tradition as Truth and Communication: A Cognitive Description of Traditional Discourse*. Cambridge: Cambridge University Press.

— ed. (1993), *Cognitive Aspects of Religious Symbolism*. Cambridge: Cambridge University Press.

— (1994), *The Naturalness of Religious Ideas: A Cognitive Theory of Religion*. Los Angeles, Calif.: University of California Press.

— (1999), "Cognitive Tracks of Cultural Inheritance: How Evolved Intuitive Ontology Governs Cultural Transmission," in: *American Anthropologist* 100 (4): 876–89.

— (2001), *Religion Explained: The Evolutionary Origins of Religious Thought*. New York: Basic Books.

— (2002), "Cognitive Science & Neuroscience of Religious Thought and Behaviour," draft version, forthcoming *Trends in Cognitive Sciences*, available on-line.

Boyer, Pascal/Ramble, Charles (2001), "Cognitive Templates for Religious Concepts: Cross-Cultural Evidence for Recall of Counter-Intuitive Representations," in: *Cognitive Science* 25: 535–64.

Brown, Roger/Kulik, James (1977), "Flashbulb Memories," in: *Cognition* 5: 73–99.

Bruner, Jerome (1986), *Actual Minds, Possible Worlds*. Cambridge, Mass.: Harvard University Press.

— (1994), "The 'Remembered' Self," in: *The Remembering Self: Construction and Accuracy in the Self-Narrative*, ed. by Ulric Neisser/Robyn Fivush. Cambridge: Cambridge University Press: 41–54.

Burkert, Walter (1972), *Homo Necans: Interpretationen altgriechischer Opferriten und Mythen*. Berlin: Walter de Gruyter; translated by Peter Bind as *Homo Necans: The Anthropology of Ancient Greek Sacrificial Ritual and Myth*. Berkeley, Calif.: University of California Press 1983.

— (1996), *Creation of the Sacred: Tracks of Biology in Early Religions*. Cambridge, Mass./ London: Harvard University Press.

Carruthers, Peter/Chamberlain, Andrew, eds. (2001), *Evolution and the Human Mind: Modularity, Language and Meta-Cognition*. Cambridge/New York: Cambridge University Press.

Cavalli-Sforza, Luigi Luca (2000), *Genes, Peoples and Languages*. New York: North Point Press; reprint London: Penguin Books 2001 [translation of *Genes, peuples et langues* by Mark Seielstad].

Chalmers, D.J. (1996), *The Conscious Mind*. New York: Oxford University Press.

Chomsky, Noam (1957), *Syntactic Structures*. The Hague: Mouton.

— (1959), "A Review of B.F. Skinner's Verbal Behavior," in: *Language* 35: 26–58.

Churchland, Paul M. (1984), *Matter and Consciousness: A Contemporary Introduction to the Philosophy of Mind*. Cambridge, Mass.: MIT Press.

— (1995), *The Engine of Reason, the Seat of the Soul*. Cambridge, Mass.: MIT Press.

Colby, Benjamin N./Colby, Lore N. (1981), *The Daykeeper: The Life and Discourse of an Ixil Diviner*. Cambridge, Mass.: Harvard University Press.

Colby, Benjamin/Cole, Michael (1973), "Culture, Memory and Narrative," in: *Modes of Thought: Essays on Thinking in Western and Non-Western Societies*, ed. by Robin Horton/Ruth Finnegan. London: Faber & Faber: 63–91.

Cole, Michael (1988), "Cross-Cultural Research in the Sociohistorical Tradition," in: *Human Development* 31: 137–57.

Conway, Martin A. (1997), "Introduction: What Are Memories?," in: *Recovered Memories and False Memories*, ed. by Martin A. Conway. Oxford: Oxford University Press: 1–22.

Cook, C.M./Persinger, Michael A. (1997), "Experimental Induction of the 'Sensed Presence' in Normal Subjects and an Exceptional Subject," in: *Perceptual Motor Skills* 85 (2): 683–93.

— (2001), "Geophysical Variables and Behavior: XCII. Experimental Elicitation of the Experience of a Sentient Being by Right Hemispheric, Weak Magnetic Fields: Interhemispheric Temporal Lobe Sensitivity," in: *Perceptual Motor Skills* 92 (2): 447–48.

Crawford, Charles/Krebs, Dennis L., eds. (1998), *Handbook of Evolutionary Psychology: Ideas, Issues, and Applications*. Mahwah/London: Lawrence Erlbaum.

Crick, Francis (1994), *The Astonishing Hypothesis: The Scientific Search for the Soul*. New York: Touchstone.

Crick, Francis/Koch, Christof (1990), "Towards a Neurobiological Theory of Consciousness," in: *Seminars in the Neurosciences* 2: 263–75.

Croft, William/Cruse, Alan D. (2003), *Cognitive Linguistics*. Cambridge: Cambridge University Press.

Cronin, Helena (1991), *The Ant and the Peacock: Altruism and Sexual Selection from Darwin to Today*. Cambridge: Cambridge University Press.

Damasio, Antonio R. (1994), *Descartes' Error: Emotion, Reason, and the Human Brain*. New York: Avon Books.

— (1999), *The Feeling of What Happens: Body, Emotion and the Making of Consciousness*. London: Heinemann; reprint London: Vintage 2000.

D'Andrade, Roy G. (1976), "A Propositional Analysis of U.S. American Beliefs about Illness," in: *Meaning in Anthropology*, ed. by R. Basso/H. Selbey. Albuquerque, N.Mex.: University of New Mexico Press.

d'Aquili, Eugene G. (1983), "The Myth-Ritual Complex: A Biogenetic Structural Analysis," in: *Zygon. Journal of Religion and Science* 18 (3): 247–69.

— (1986), "Myth, Ritual, and the Archetypal Hypothesis," in: *Zygon. Journal of Religion and Science* 21 (2): 141–60.

d'Aquili, Eugene G./Laughlin, Jr., Charles D./McManus, John (1979), *The Spectrum of Ritual: A Biogenetic Structural Analysis*. New York: Columbia University Press.

Davies, Martin/Humphreys, Glyn W., eds. (1993), *Consciousness*. Oxford: Blackwell.

Dawkins, Richard (1976), *The Selfish Gene*. Oxford/New York: Oxford University Press; reprint 1999.

Deacon, Terrence (1997), *The Symbolic Species: The Co-Evolution of Language and the Human Brain*. London: The Penguin Press.

Dennett, Daniel C. (1978), *Brainstorms*. Cambridge, Mass: MIT Press.

— (1987), *The Intentional Stance*. Cambridge, Mass.: MIT Press.

— (1991), *Consciousness Explained*. Boston, Mass./Toronto/London: Little, Brown and Company.

— (1996), *Kinds of Minds: Towards an Understanding of Consciousness*. London: Weidenfeld & Nicholson; also: London: Phoenix 1998.

Devereux, George (1951a), *Reality and Dream: Psychotherapy of a Plains Indian*. New York: International Universities Press.

— (1951b), "Cultural and Characterological Traits of the Mohave Related to the Anal Stage of Psychosexual Development," in: *Psychoanalytic Quarterly* 20: 398–422.

— (1956), "Normal and Abnormal: The Key Problem of Psychiatric Anthropology," in: *Some Uses of Anthropology: Theoretical and Applied*, ed. by Joseph B. Casagrande/ Thomas Gladwin. Washington, D.C.: Anthropological Society of Washington: 23–48.

— (1961), *Mohave Ethnopsychiatry and Suicide: The Psychiatric Knowledge and the Psychic Disturbances of an Indian Tribe*. Washington, D.C.: U.S. Government Printing Office.

Diamond, Jared (1997), *Guns, Germs, and Steel: The Fates of Human Societies*. New York/London: W.W. Norton; reprint New York/London: W.W. Norton 1999.

Dietrich, Arne (2003), "Functional Neuroanatomy of Altered States of Consciousness: The Transient Hypofrontality Hypothesis," in: *Consciousness and Cognition* 12: 231–56.

Dobkin de Rios, Marlene/Winkelman, Michael (1989), *Shamanism and Altered States of Consciousness*. Special issue of *Journal of Psychoactive Drugs. A Multidisciplinary Forum* 21 (1): 1–134.

Donald, Merlin (1991), *Origins of the Modern Mind: Three States in the Evolution of Culture and Cognition*. Cambridge/London: Harvard University Press; reprint Cambridge, Mass./London: Harvard University Press 1993.

DuBois, Cora (1944), *The People of Alor: A Socio-Psychological Study of an East-Indian Island*. Minneapolis, Minn.: University of Minnesota Press.

Dunbar, Robin (1996), *Grooming, Gossip and the Evolution of Language*. London: Faber and Faber.

Dundes, Alan (1962), "Earth-Diver: Creation of the Mythopoeic Male," in: *American Anthropologist* 64: 1032–51.

Eysenck, Michael W./Keane, Mark T. (1995), *Cognitive Psychology: A Student's Handbook*. 3rd ed. Hove/Hillsdale: Lawrence Erlbaum.

Fabian, A.C. (1998), *Evolution: Society, Science and the Universe*. Cambridge: Cambridge University Press.

Fauconnier, Gilles (1985), *Mental Spaces: Aspects of Meaning Construction in Natural Language*. Cambridge: Cambridge University Press; reprint 1998.

Fauconnier, Gilles/Turner, Mark (2002), *The Way We Think: Conceptual Blending and the Mind's Hidden Complexities*. New York: Basic Books.

Feinberg, Todd E. (2001), *Altered Egos: How the Brain Creates the Self*. Oxford: Oxford University Press.

Fillmore, Charles J. (1968), "The Case for Case," in: *Universals in Linguistic Theory*, ed. by Emmon Bach/Robert T. Harms. New York: Holt, Rinehart and Winston: 1–88.

Flanagan, Owen (1992), *Consciousness Reconsidered*. Cambridge, Mass.: MIT Press.

Freeman, Walter J. (1999), *How Brains Make Up Their Minds*. London: Weidenfeld & Nicolson; reprint London: Phoenix 2000.

Gardner, Howard (1985), *The Mind's New Science. A History of the Cognitive Revolution. With an New Epilogue by the Author: Cognitive Science after 1984*. Paperback ed.; reprint New York: Basic Books 1987.

Geertz, Armin W. (1990), "Mystik, visioner, ekstase og besættelse: En direkte linie?" ["Mysticism, Visions, Ecstasy and Possession: A Direct Connection?"], in: *Mystik—den indre vej? En religionshistorisk udfordring* ["Mysticism—the Inner Way? Challenges from the History of Religions"], ed. by Per Bilde/Armin W. Geertz. Aarhus: Aarhus University Press: 107–38.

— (1997), "Theory, Definition, and Typology: Reflections on Generalities and Unrepresentative Realism," in: *Temenos. Studies in Comparative Religion Presented by Scholars in Denmark, Finland, Norway and Sweden* 33: 29–47.

— (1999), "Definition as Analytical Strategy in the Study of Religion," in: *Historical Reflections/Reflexions Historiques* 25 (3): 445–75.

— (2000), "Analytical Theorizing in the Secular Study of Religion," in: *Secular Theories on Religion. Current Perpectives*, ed. by Tim Jensen/Mikael Rothstein. Copenhagen: Museum Tusculanum Press: 21–31.

— (forthcoming), "What Is Religion for? Theoretical Perspectives," in: *What Is Religion* [illegible] Wellington, New Zealand.

Girard, René (1972), *La violence et la sacré*. Paris: B. Grasset; translated by Patrick Gregory as *Violence and the Sacred*. Baltimore, Md.: Johns Hopkins University Press 1977.

— (1982), *Le bouc émissaire*. Paris: B. Grasset; translated by Yvonne Freccero as *The Scapegoat*. Baltimore, Md.: Johns Hopkins University Press 1986.

— (1985), *La route antique des hommes pervers*. Paris: Éditions Grasset & Fasquelle; translated by Yvonne Freccero as *Job the Victim of His People*. Stanford, Calif.: Stanford University Press 1987.

Gleitman, Henry/Fridlund, Alan J./Reisberg, Daniel (1981), *Psychology*. New York/ London: W.W. Norton; 5th ed. 1999.

Goffman, Erving (1959), *The Presentation of Self in Everyday Life*. Revised and expanded ed. Edinburgh: Social Sciences Research Centre, University of Edinburgh; reprint New York: Anchor Books 1959.

— (1981), *Forms of Talk*. Philadelphia, Pa.: University of Pennsylvania Press.

Goldman, Alvin I. (1992), *Liaisons: Philosophy Meets the Cognitive and Social Sciences*. Cambridge, Mass./London: MIT Press.

Goldschmidt, Walter (1990), *The Human Career: The Self in the Symbolic World*. Oxford: Basil Blackwell.

Guthrie, Stewart Elliott (1980), "A Cognitive Theory of Religion," in: *Current Anthropology* 21 (2): 181–203.

— (1993), *Faces in the Clouds: A New Theory of Religion*. New York/Oxford: Oxford University Press.

— (1997), "Anthropomorphism: A Definition and a Theory," in: *Anthropomorphism, Anecdotes, and Animals*, ed. by Robert W. Mitchell/Nicholas S. Thompson/H. Lyn Miles. Albany, N.Y.: State University of New York Press: 50–58.

— (2000), "Projection," in: *Guide to the Study of Religion*, ed. by Willi Braun/Russell T. McCutcheon. London/New York: Cassell: 225–38.

— (2001), "Why Gods? A Cognitive Theory," in: *Religion in Mind*, ed. by Jensine Andresen. Cambridge: Cambridge University Press: 94–111.

— (2002), "Animal Animism: Evolutionary Roots of Religious Cognition," in: *Current Approaches in the Cognitive Science of Religion*, ed. by Ilkka Pyysiäinen/Veikko Anttonen. London/New York: Continuum: 38–67.

Güzeldere, Güven (1997), "Introduction: The Many Faces of Consciousness: A Field Guide," in: *The Nature of Consciousness: Philosophical Debates*, ed. by Ned Block/ Owen Flanagan/Güven Güzeldere. Cambridge/London: MIT Press: 1–67.

Hallpike, C.R. (1979), *The Foundations of Primitive Thought*. Oxford: Clarendon Press.

— (1986), *The Principles of Social Evolution*. Oxford: Clarendon Press.

Hamerton-Kelly, Robert G., ed. (1987), *Violent Origins: Walter Burkert, René Girard, and Jonathan Z. Smith on Ritual Killing and Cultural Formation*. Stanford, Calif.: Stanford University Press.

Hamilton, W.D. (1964), "The Genetic Theory of Social Behaviour," in: *Journal of Theoretical Biology* 12: 12–45.

— (1970), "Selfish and Spiteful Behaviour in an Evolutionary Model," in: *Nature* 228: 1218–20.

Harbsmeier, Michael (1983), "The Savage and the Child: On C.R. Hallpike's Foundations of Primitive Thought," in: *Ethnos* 1–2: 91–103.

Harnish, Robert M. (2002), *Minds, Brains, Computers: An Historical Introduction to the Foundations of Cognitive Science*. Malden/Oxford: Blackwell.

Henry, James L. (1982), "Possible Involvement of Endorphins in Altered States of Consciousness," in: *Ethos* 10 (4): 394–408.

Herdt, Gilbert H. (1989), "Spirit Familiars in the Religious Imagination of Sambia Shamans," in: *The Religious Imagination in New Guinea*, ed. by Gilbert H. Herdt/M. Stephen. New Brunswick, N.J.: Rutgers University Press: 99–121.

Hitt, Jack (1999), "This Is Your Brain on God," in: *Wired Magazine*, November, 1–5, online versions at http://www.wired-com/wired/archive/7.11/persinger.html.

Holm, Nils G. (1982), "Ecstasy Research in the 20th Century—An Introduction," in: *Religious Ecstasy: Based on Papers Read at the Symposium on Religious Ecstasy Held at Åbo, Finland, on the 26th–28th of August 1981*. Stockholm: Almqvist & Wiksell: 7–26.

Hull, Clark L. (1935), "The Conflicting Psychologies of Learning—a Way Out," in: *Psychological Review* 42: 491–516.

— (1943), *Principles of Behavior*. New York: Appleton-Century-Crofts.

Hull, Clark L./Hovland, C.I./Ross, R.T./Hall, M./Perkins, D.T./Fitch, F.B. (1940), *Mathematico-Deductive Theory of Rote Learning*. New Haven, Conn.: Yale University Press.

Hurford, James R./Studdert-Kennedy, Michael/Knight, Chris, eds. (1998), *Approaches to the Evolution of Language: Social and Cognitive Bases*. Cambridge: Cambridge University Press.

Hutchins, Edwin (1995), *Cognition in the Wild*. Cambridge, Mass./London: MIT Press; 4th printing 2000.

Jensen, Jeppe Sinding (2003), *The Study of Religion in a New Key: Theoretical and Philosophical Soundings in the Comparative and General Study of Religion*. Aarhus: Aarhus University Press.

Jilek, Wolfgang G. (1982), "Altered States of Consciousness in North American Indian Ceremonials," in: *Ethos* 10 (4): 326–43.

Johnson, Mark (1987), *The Body in the Mind: The Bodily Basis of Meaning, Imagination, and Reason*. Chicago: University of Chicago Press.

Jones, Steve (2002), *Y: The Descent of Men*. London: Little, Brown; reprint London: Abacus 2003.

Kampman, R./Hirvenoja, R. (1978), "Dynamic Relation of the Secondary Personality Induced by Hypnosis to the Present Personality," in: *Hypnosis at Its Bicentennial*, ed. by Fred H. Frankel/Harold S. Zamansky. New York: Plenum Press: 183–88.

Kandel, Eric R./Schwartz, James H./Jessell, Thomas M., eds. (1991), *Principles of Neural Science*. New York et al.: McGraw-Hill; 4th ed. 2000.

Kane, Steven M. (1982), "Holiness Ritual Fire Handling: Ethnographic and Psychophysiological Considerations," in: *Ethos* 10 (4): 369–84.

Kardiner, Abram, ed. (1939), *The Individual and His Society*. New York: Columbia University Press.

Kardiner, Abram/Linton, Ralph/West, J. et al. (1945), *The Psychological Frontiers of Society*. New York: Columbia University Press.

Kardiner, Abram/Preble, E. (1961), *They Studied Man*. Cleveland: World Publishing Company.

Kerby, Anthony Paul (1991), *Narrative and the Self*. Bloomington, Ind.: Indiana University Press.

Kihlstrom, John F. (1994), "Altering States of Consciousness," in: *Learning, Remembering, Believing: Enhancing Human Performance*, ed. by Daniel Druckman/Robert A. Bjork. Washington, D.C.: The National Academies Press: 207–48, 351–64.

Kihlstrom, John F./Tataryn, Douglas J./Hoyt, Irene P., "Dissociative Disorders," undated, unedited manuscript, available on-line at http://socrates.berkeley.edu/~kihlstrm/Sutker93.htm, originally written in 1990 and published in edited form in: *Comprehensive Handbook of Psychopathology*. 2nd ed., ed. by P.B. Sutker/H.E. Adams. New York: Plenum 1993: 203–34 and updated in: *Comprehensive Handbook of Psychopathology*. 3rd ed., ed. by P.B. Sutker/H.E. Adams. New York: Kluwer/Plenum 2001: 259–76.

Kluckhohn, Clyde (1945), "The Personal Document in Anthropological Science," in: *The Use of Personal Documents in History, Anthropology, and Sociology*. New York: Social Science Research Council: 77–173.

Koffka, Kurt (1915), "Zur Grundlegung der Wahrnehmungspsychologie. Eine Auseinandersetzung mit V. Benussi," in: *Zeitschrift für Psychologie* 73: 11–90; abridged English translation in: *A Source Book of Gestalt Psychology*, ed. by W.D. Ellis. London: Routledge & Kegan Paul 1938: 371–78.

— (1921), *Die Grundlagen der psychischen Entwicklung*. Osterwieck am Harz: Zickfeldt; 2nd ed. translated by R.M. Ogden as *The Growth of Mind*. New York: Harcourt, Brace 1925.

— (1922), "Perception, an Introduction to the Gestalt-theorie," in: *Psychological Bulletin* 19: 531–85.

— (1935), *Principles of Gestalt Psychology*. London: Routledge & Kegan Paul.

Köhler, Wolfgang (1929), *Gestalt Psychology*. New York: Liveright; 2nd ed. 1947; reprint New York: Meridian 1980.

— (1938), *The Place of Value in a World of Facts*. New York: Liveright.

Krader, Lawrence (1954), "Buryat Religion and Society," in: *Southwestern Journal of Anthropology* 10: 322–51.

Kuper, Adam (1988), *The Invention of Primitive Society: Transformations of an Illusion*. London/New York: Routledge.

Lakoff, George (1977), "Linguistic Gestalts," in: *Papers from the Thirteenth Regional Meeting, Chicago Linguistic Society*, ed. by Woodford A. Beach. Chicago: Chicago Linguistic Society: 236–87.

— (1987), *Women, Fire and Dangerous Things: What Categories Reveal about the Mind*. Chicago: University of Chicago Press.

Lakoff, George/Johnson, Mark (1980), *Metaphors We Live by*. Chicago: University of Chicago Press.

— (1999), *Philosophy in the Flesh: The Embodied Mind and Its Challenge to Western Thought*. New York: Basic Books.

Lakoff, George/Turner, Mark (1989), *More Than Cool Reason: A Field Guide to Poetic Metaphor*. Chicago: University of Chicago Press.

Laland, Kevin N./Brown, Gillian R. (2002), *Sense and Nonsense: Evolutionary Perspectives on Human Behaviour*. Oxford: Oxford University Press.

Langacker, Ronald W. (1979), "Grammar as Image," in: *Linguistic Notes from La Jolla* 6: 88–126.

— (1987), *Foundations of Cognitive Grammar*. Vol. 1: *Theoretical Prerequisites*. Stanford, Calif.: Stanford University Press.

— (1990), *Concept, Image, and Symbol: The Cognitive Basis of Grammar*. Berlin/New York: Mouton de Gruyter.

— (1991), *Foundations of Cognitive Grammar*. Vol. 2: *Descriptive Application*. Stanford, Calif.: Stanford University Press.

Langness, L. (1965), "Hysterical Psychosis in the New Guinea Highlands: A Bena-Bena Example," in: *Psychiatry* 28: 258–77.

Laughlin, Charles D., Jr./d'Aquili, Eugene G. (1974), *Biogenetic Structuralism*. New York: Columbia University Press.

Laughlin, Charles D., Jr./McManus, John/d'Aquili, Eugene G. (1990), *Brain, Symbol & Experience: Toward a Neurophenomenology of Human Consciousness*. New York: Columbia University Press; reprint 1992.

Lawson, E. Thomas/McCauley, Robert N. (1990), *Rethinking Religion. Connecting Cognition and Culture*. Cambridge: Cambridge University Press.

LeDoux, Joseph (1998), *The Emotional Brain: The Mysterious Underpinnings of Emotional Life*. London: Phoenix.

— (2002), *Synaptic Self: How Our Brains Become Who We Are*. New York: Viking.

Lee, David (2001), *Cognitive Linguistics: An Introduction*. Oxford: Oxford University Press.

Lewis, I.M. (1971), *Ecstatic Religion: A Study of Shamanism and Spirit Possession*. New York: Routledge; 2nd ed. 1989.

— (1986), *Religion in Context: Cults and Charisma*. Cambridge: Cambridge University Press; reprint 1988.

Linton, Ralph (1956), *Culture and Mental Disorders*. Springfield, Ill.: Charles C. Thomas Publishers.

Lisdorf, Anders (2003), *Det romerske prodigiesystem. En analyse af den romerske prodigieindberetningspraksis fra 218–44 f.v.t.* ["The Roman Prodigie System: An Analysis of the Practice of Roman Prodigie Reports from 218–44 B.C."]. Master's Thesis, Department of the History of Religions, University of Copenhagen: 2003.

Llinás, Rodolfo R. (2001), *I of the Vortex: From Neurons to Self*. Cambridge, Mass.: MIT Press.

Lock, Andrew/Peters, Charles R., eds. (1996), *Handbook of Human Symbolic Evolution*, Oxford: Clarendon Press.

Lorenz, Konrad (1935), "Der Kumpan in der Umwelt des Vogels," in: *Journal of Ornithology* 87: 137–413.

— (1963), *Das sogenannte Böse: Zur Naturgeschichte der Aggression*. Vienna: G. Borotha-Schoeler; translated by Marjorie Latzke as *On Aggression*. London: Methuen 1981.

Lubbock, John (1865), *Pre-Historic Times, as Illustrated by Ancient Remains and the Manners and Customs of Modern Savages*. London/Edinburgh: Williams & Norgate.

— (1870), *The Origin of Civilization and the Primitive Condition of Man: Mental and Social Condition of Savages*. London/Edinburgh: Longmans, Green & Company.

MacCannell, Dean (1979), "Ethnosemiotics," in: *Semiotics of Culture*, ed. by Irene Portis Winner/Jean Umiker-Sebeok. The Hague: Mouton: 149–71.

MacLaine, Shirley (1985), *Dancing in the Light*. Thorndike: Thorndike Press.

McCauley, Robert N./Lawson, E. Thomas (2002), *Bringing Ritual to Mind: Psychological Foundations of Cultural Forms*. Cambridge: Cambridge University Press.

McGinn, C. (1991), *The Problem of Consciousness*. Oxford: Blackwell.

Mead, Margaret (1928), *Coming of Age in Samoa: A Psychological Study of Primitive Youth for Western Civilization*. New York: Morrow.

— (1959), *An Anthropologist at Work: Writings of Ruth Benedict*. Boston, Mass.: Houghton Mifflin.

Metzinger, T., ed. (1995), *Conscious Experience*. Paderborn: Ferdinand Schöningh.

Miller, George A. (1956), "The Magical Number Seven, Plus or Minus Two: Some Limits on Our Capacity for Processing Information," in: *Psychological Review* 63: 81–97.

Minsky, Marvin (1963), "Steps toward Artificial Intelligence," in: *Computers and Thought*. Ed. by Edward A. Feigenbaum/Julian Feldman. New York: McGraw-Hill [originally circulated in 1957].

— (1975), "A Framework for Representing Knowledge," in: *The Psychology of Computer Vision*, ed. by Patrick H. Winston. New York: McGraw-Hill: 211–77.

Mithen, Steven (1996), *The Prehistory of the Mind: A Search for the Origins of Art, Religion and Science*. London: Thames and Hudson; reprint London: Phoenix 1998.

Murphy, Jane M. (1964), "Psychotherapeutic Aspects of Shamanism on St. Lawrence Island, Alaska," in: *Magic, Faith, and Healing: Studies in Primitive Psychiatry Today*, ed. by Ari Kiev. New York: The Free Press: 53–83.

Murray, David J. (1995), *Gestalt Psychology and the Cognitive Revolution*. Hemel Hempstead: Harvester Wheatsheaf.

Nadel, S.F. (1946), "A Study of Shamanism in the Nuba Hills," in: *Journal of the Royal Anthropological Institute* 76: 25–37.

Nair, Rukmini Bhaya (2002), *Narrative Gravity: Conversation, Cognition, Culture*. New Delhi: Oxford University Press.

Neisser, Ulric (1994), "Multiple Systems: A New Approach to Cognitive Theory," in: *European Journal of Cognitive Psychology* 6 (3): 225–41.

Neisser, Ulric/Fivush, Robyn, eds. (1994), *The Remembering Self: Construction and Accuracy in the Self-Narrative*. Cambridge: Cambridge University Press.

Neisser, Ulric/Winograd, Eugene, eds. (1988), *Remembering Reconsidered: Ecological and Traditional Approaches to the Study of Memory*. Cambridge: Cambridge University Press.

Newell, Allen/Shaw, J.C./Simon, Herbert A. (1958), "Elements of a Theory of Human Problem Solving," in: *Psychological Review* 65: 151–66.

Newell, Allen/Simon, Herbert A. (1972), *Human Problem Solving*. Englewood Cliffs, N.J.: Prentice-Hall.

Ochs, Elinor/Capps, Lisa (1996), "Narrating the Self," in: *Annual Review of Anthropology* 25: 19–43.

O'Donohue, William/Kitchener, Richard F., eds. (1996), *The Philosophy of Psychology*. London: Sage Publications.

Oesterreich, Traugott Konstantin (1974), *Possession and Exorcism: among Primitive Races, in Antiquity, the Middle Ages, and Modern Times*, translated from German by D. Ibberson. New York: Causeway Books.

Ohlmarks, Åke (1939), *Studien zum Problem des Schamanismus*. Lund: Lund University.

Parker, Sue Taylor/McKinney, Michael L. (1999), *Origins of Intelligence: The Evolution of Cognitive Development in Monkeys, Apes, and Humans*. Baltimore, Md./London: Johns Hopkins University Press.

Parsons, Talcott (1966), *Societies: Evolutionary and Comparative Perspectives*. Englewood Cliffs, N.J.: Prentice-Hall.

— (1977), *The Evolution of Societies*, ed. by Jackson Toby. Englewood Cliffs, N.J.: Prentice-Hall.

Persinger, Michael A. (1987), *Neuropsychological Bases of God Beliefs*. New York: Praeger Publishers.

— (1997), "'I Would Kill in God's Name': Role of Sex, Weekly Church Attendance, Report of a Religious Experience, and Limbic Lability," in: *Perceptual and Motor Skills* 85: 128–30.

— (2001), "Geophysical Variables and Behavior: XC. What People Consider Strange: Change in Proportions of Reports of Fortean Phenomena Over Time," in: *Psychological Report* 88 (1): 89–90.

— (2002), "Science and the Resurrection," in: *Skeptic* 9 (4): 76–79.

Persinger, Michael A./Koren, S.A. (2001), "Experiences of Spiritual Visitation and Impregnation: Potential Induction by Frequence-Modulated Transients from an Adjacent Clock," in: *Perceptual Motor Skills* 92 (1): 35–36.

Persinger, Michael A./Koren, S.A./O'Connor, R.P. (2001), "Geophysical Variables and Behavior: CIV. Power-Frequency Magnetic Field Transients (5 Microtesla) and Reports of Haunt Experiences within an Electronically Dense House," in: *Perceptual Motor Skills* 92 (3, pt. 1): 673–74

Persinger, Michael A./Tiller, S.G./Koren, S.A. (2000), "Experimental Simulation of a Haunt Experience and Elicitation of Paroxysmal Electroencephalographic Activity by Transcerebral Complex Magnetic Fields: Induction of a Synthetic 'Ghost'?," in: *Perceptual Motor Skills* 90 (2): 659–74.

Prince, Raymond H., ed. (1968), *Trance and Possession States*. Montreal: R.M. Bucke Memorial Society.

— (1982a), "Introduction," in: *Ethos* 10 (4): 299–302.

— (1982b), "The Endorphins: A Review for Psychological Anthropologists," in: *Ethos* 10 (4): 303–16.

Pyysiäinen, Ilkka/Anttonen, Veikko, eds. (2002), *Current Approaches to the Cognitive Science of Religion*. London/New York: Continuum.

Radin, Paul (1913), "Personal Reminiscence of a Winnebago Indian," in: *Journal of American Folklore* 26: 293–318.

— (1920), *The Autobiography of a Winnebago Indian*. University of California Publications in American Archaeology and Ethnology 16/7. Berkeley, Calif.: University of California Press.

— (1926), *Crashing Thunder: The Autobiography of a Winnebago Indian*. New York: D. Appleton.

— (1937), *Primitive Religion: Its Nature and Origin*. New York: The Viking Press.

Rappaport, Roy A. (1979), *Ecology, Meaning, and Religion*. Berkeley, Calif.: North Atlantic Books.
— (1999), *Ritual and Religion in the Making of Humanity*. Cambridge: Cambridge University Press; reprint 2000.
Rawcliffe, Donovan Hilton (1959), *Illusions and Delusions of the Supernatural and the Occult*. New York: Dover.
Rendell, Luke/Whitehead, Hal (2001), "Culture in Whales and Dolphins," in: *Behavioral and Brain Sciences* 24: 309–82.
Revonsuo, Antti/Kamppinen, Matti, eds. (1994), *Consciousness in Philosophy and* [illegible]
Ricoeur, Paul (1984), *Time and Narrative*, translated by Kathleen McLaughlin/David Pellauer. Chicago: University of Chicago Press [original: *Temps et récit*. Paris: Seuil 1983–1985].
— (1995), *Figuring the Sacred: Religion, Narrative, and Imagination*, translated by David Pellauer, ed. by Mark I. Wallace. Minneapolis, Minn.: Fortress Press.
Róheim, Géza (1925), *Australian Totemism: A Psycho-analytic Study in Anthropology*. London: G. Allen & Unwin.
— (1945/1969/1971), *The Eternal Ones of the Dream: A Psychoanalytic Interpretation of Australian Myth and Ritual*. New York: International Universities Press.
Ross, C.A./Joshi, S./Currie, R. (1990), "Dissociative Experiences in the General Population," in: *American Journal of Psychiatry* 147: 1547–56.
Sahlins, Marshall (1976), *The Use and Abuse of Biology: An Anthropological Critique of Sociobiology*. Ann Arbor, Mich.: University of Michigan Press; London: Tavistock Publications 1977.
Sarbin, Theodore R., ed. (1986), *Narrative Psychology: The Storied Nature of Human Conduct*. New York: Praeger Publishers.
Savage-Rumbaugh, Sue/Shanker, Stuart G. /Taylor, Talbot J. (1998), *Apes, Language, and the Human Mind*. New York/Oxford: Oxford University Press.
Schreiber, Flora Rheta (1973), *Sybil*. Chicago: Regnery.
Scrivner, E./Safer, Martin A. (1983), "Eyewitnesses Show Hypermnesia for Details about a Violent Event," in: *Journal of Applied Psychology* 73: 371–77.
Searle, John R. (1992), *The Rediscovery of the Mind*. Cambridge, Mass.: MIT Press.
Segal, Robert A., ed. (1998), *The Myth and Ritual Theory: An Anthology*. Oxford: Blackwell Publishers.
Shirokogoroff, S.M. (1935), *Psychomental Complex of the Tungus*. London: Kegan Paul.
Shore, Bradd (1996), *Culture in Mind: Cognition, Culture, and the Problem of Meaning*. New York/Oxford: Oxford University Press.
Shweder, Richard A. (1979a), "Rethinking Culture and Personality Theory Part I," in: *Ethos* 7 (3): 255–78.
— (1979b), "Rethinking Culture and Personality Theory Part II," in: *Ethos* 7 (4): 279–311.
— (1980), "Rethinking Culture and Personality Theory Part III," in: *Ethos* 8 (1): 60–94.
— (1984), "Anthropology's Romantic Rebellion against the Enlightenment, or There's More to Thinking Than Reason and Evidence," in: *Culture Theory: Essays on Mind, Self, and Emotion*, ed. by Richard A. Shweder/Robert A. LeVine. Cambridge: Cambridge University Press; reprint 1986: 27–66.

Siegel, Daniel J. (1999), *The Developing Mind: How Relationships and the Brain Interact to Shape Who We Are*. New York: The Guilford Press.

— (2001), "Toward an Interpersonal Neurobiology of the Developing Mind: Attachment Relationships, 'Mindsight,' and Neural Integration," in: *Infant Mental Health Journal* 22 (1–2): 67–94.

Siikala, Anna-Leena (1978), *The Rite Technique of the Siberian Shaman*. Helsinki: Academia Scientiarum Fennica.

Silverman, Julian (1967), "Shamans and Acute Schizophrenia," in: *American Anthropologist* 69: 21–31.

Skinner, B.F. (1938), *The Behaviour of Organisms: An Experimental Analysis*. New York: Appleton-Century-Crofts.

Smith, Frank M. (2001), "The Current State of Possession Studies as a Cross-Disciplinary Project," in: *Religious Studies Review* 27 (3): 203–22.

Sørensen, Jesper (2001), *Essence, Schema, and Ritual Action: Towards a Cognitive Theory of Magic*. Ph.D. dissertation. Aarhus: University of Aarhus.

Spanos, Nicholas P. (1996), *Multiple Identities & False Memories: A Sociocognitive Perspective*. Washington, D.C.: American Psychological Association.

Spanos, Nicholas P./Menary, E./Gabora, N.J./DuBreuil, S.C./Dewhirst, B. (1991), "Secondary Identity Enactments during Hypnotic Past-Life Regression: A Socio-Cognitive Perspective," in: *Journal of Personality and Social Psychology* 61: 308–20.

Spencer, Herbert J. (1870), *The Principles of Psychology*. 2 volumes [Part of: *A System of Synthetic Philosophy*]. London/Edinburgh: Williams & Norgate.

— (1897), *The Principles of Sociology*. 3 volumes [Part of: *A System of Synthetic Philosophy*]. London/Edinburgh: Williams & Norgate.

Spiro, Melford E. (1982), *Oedipus in the Trobriands*. Chicago: University of Chicago Press.

Suryani, Luh Ketut/Jensen, Gordon D. (1995), *Trance and Possession in Bali: A Window on Western Multiple Personality, Possession Disorder, and Suicide*. Kuala Lumpur/Oxford. Oxford University Press.

Sweetser, Eve (2000), "Blended Spaces and Performativity," in: *Cognitive Linguistics* 11 (3/4): 305–33.

Sykes, Brian (2001), *The Seven Daughters of Eve*. New York/London: W.W. Norton.

Talmy, Leonard (1977), "Rubber-Sheet Cognition in Language," in: *Papers from the Thirteenth Regional Meeting, Chicago Linguistic Society*. Chicago: Chicago Linguistic Society.

— (1978), "Figure and Ground in Complex Sentences," in: *Universals of Human Language*. Volume 4: *Syntax*, ed. by Joseph H. Greenberg. Stanford, Calif.: Stanford University Press: 625–49.

— (2000), *Toward a Cognitive Semantics*. Volume 1: *Concept Structuring Systems*. Volume 2: *Typology and Process in Concept Structuring*. Cambridge, Mass.: MIT Press.

Tart, Charles T. (1975), *States of Consciousness*. New York: E.P. Dutton & Co.

Tattersall, I./Delson, E./Van Couvering, J., eds. (2000), *The Encyclopedia of Human Evolution and Prehistory*. New York: Garland Press.

Thagard, Paul R. (1996), *Mind: Introduction to Cognitive Science*. Cambridge: MIT Press.

Thom, René (1975), *Structural Stability and Morphogenesis : An Outline of a General Theory of Models*, translated and updated by D.H. Fowler. Reading, Mass.: W.A. Benjamin [Translation of *Stabilité structurelle et morphogénèse. Essai d'une théorie générale des modèles*].

— (1983), *Mathematical Models of Morphogenesis*, translated by W.M. Brookes/D. Rand. Chichester: Ellis Horwood.

Tinbergen, Niko (1951), *The Study of Instinct*. London: Oxford University Press.

Tinterow, Maurice M. (1970), *Foundations of Hypnosis, from Mesmer to Freud*. Springfield, Ill.: C.C. Thomas.

Tomasello, Michael/Call, Josep (1997), *Primate Cognition*. Oxford/New York: Oxford University Press.

Tulving, Endel (1972), "Episodic and Semantic Memory," in: *Organization of Memory*, ed. by Endel Tulving/Wayne Donaldson. New York: Academic Press.

Turner, Mark (1996), *The Literary Mind*. New York/Oxford: Oxford University Press; reprint 1998.

Tye, M. (1995), *Ten Problems of Consciousness*. Cambridge, Mass.: MIT Press.

Tylor, Edward B. (1865), *Researches into the Early History of Mankind and the Development of Civilization*. London: John Murray.

— (1871), *Primitive Culture: Researches into the Development of Mythology, Philosophy, Religion, Language, Art, and Custom*. 2 volumes. London: John Murray.

Ungerer, Friedrich/Schmid, Hans-Jörg (1996), *An Introduction to Cognitive Linguistics*. London: Longman.

Valsiner, Jaan/van der Veer, René (2000), *The Social Mind: Construction of the Idea*. Cambridge: Cambridge University Press.

Velmans, M., ed. (1996), *The Science of Consciousness*. London: Routledge.

Voigt, Vilmos (1986), "Ethnosemiotics," in: *Encyclopedic Dictionary of Semiotics*, ed. by Thomas A. Sebeok. Vol. 1. Berlin: Mouton de Gruyter: 235–37.

Walker, Sheila S. (1972), *Ceremonial Spirit Possession in Africa and Afro-America: Forms, Meanings, and Functional Significance for Individuals and Social Groups*. Leiden: E.J. Brill.

Watson, John Broadus (1913), "Psychology as the Behaviorist Views It," in: *Psychological Review* 20: 158–77.

— (1924), *Behaviorism*. Chicago: Chicago University Press; 2nd ed. 1930.

— (1928), *The Ways of Behaviorism*. New York: Harper.

Wavell, Stewart/Butt, Audrey/Epton, Nina (1966), *Trances*. London: Allen & Unwin.

Weiskrantz, L. (1986), *Blindsight: A Case Study and Implications*. Oxford: Clarendon Press.

Wells, Spencer (2002), *The Journey of Man: A Genetic Odyssey*. Princeton, N.J./Oxford: Princeton University Press.

Wertheimer, Max (1912), "Experimentelle Studien über das Sehen von Bewegungen," in: *Zeitschrift für Psychologie* 61: 161–265. Abridged English translation: W. Wertheimer (1961), "Experimental Studies on the Seeing of Motion," in: *Classics in Psychology*, ed. by T. Shipley. New York: Philosophical Library: 1032–89.

— (1922a), "Untersuchungen zur Lehre von der Gestalt. I. Prinzipielle Bemerkungen," in: *Psychologische Forschung* 1: 47–58. Abridged English translation in: W.D. Ellis, ed. (1938), *A Source Book of Gestalt Psychology*. London: Routledge & Kegan Paul: 12–16.

— (1922b), "Untersuchungen zur Lehre von der Gestalt. II," in: *Psychologische Forschung* 4: 301–50. Abridged English translation in: W.D. Ellis, ed. (1938), *A Source Book of Gestalt Psychology*. London: Routledge & Kegan Paul: 71–88.

Westh, Peter (2002), *Gud & natur fænomen i mesopotamisk religion. Et forskningshistorisk problem og et forslag til dets løsning med ildguden Girra som eksempel* ("God and Natural Phenomena in Mesopotamian Religion: A Problem in Research History and a Suggested Solution Exemplified by the Fire God Girra"). Master's Thesis, Department of the History of Religions, University of Copenhagen.

White, Hayden V. (1987), *The Content of Form: Narrative Discourse and Historical Representation*. Baltimore, Md.: Johns Hopkins University Press.

Whitehouse, Harvey (1995), *Inside the Cult: Religious Innovation and Transmission in Papua New Guinea*. Oxford: Oxford University Press.

— (2000), *Arguments and Icons: Divergent Modes of Religiosity*. London/New York: Oxford University Press.

— ed. (2001), *The Debated Mind: Evolutionary Psychology Versus Ethnography*. Oxford/New York: Berg.

Whiting, Beatrice/Whiting, John W.M. (1975), *Children of Six Cultures*. Cambridge, Mass.: Harvard University Press.

Wildgen, Wolfgang (1998), "From Lullus to Cognitive Semantics: The Evolution of a Theory of Semantic Fields." Paper presented at the Twentieth World Congress of Philosophy, Boston, Massachusetts, August 10–15, 1998. Published at http://www.bu.edu./ wcp/Papers/Cogn/CognWild.htm.

Williams, George C. (1966), *Adaptation and Natural Selection: A Critique of Some Current Evolutionary Thought*. Princeton, N.J.: Princeton University Press.

Wilson, Edward O. (1975), *Sociobiology: The New Synthesis*. Cambridge, Mass.: Harvard University Press.

— (1976), "Academic Vigilantism and the Political Significance of Sociobiology," in: *Bio Science* 26: 187–90.

Winkelman, Michael James (1992), *Shamans, Priests and Witches: A Cross-Cultural Study of Magico-Religious Practitioners*. Tempe, Ariz.: Arizona State University.

Winograd, Eugene/Killinger, W.A. (1983), "Relating Age at Encoding in Early Childhood to Adult Recall: Development of Flashbulb Memories," in: *Journal of Experimental Psychology: General* 112: 413–22.

Winograd, Eugene/Neisser, Ulric, eds. (1992), *Affect and Accuracy in Recall: Studies of "Flashbulb" Memories*. Cambridge: Cambridge University Press.

Wittgenstein, Ludwig (1933), *Tractatus logico-philosophicus*. New York: Harcourt, Brace.

— (1953), *Philosophische Untersuchungen*. Frankfurt a.M.: Suhrkamp; translated as *Philosophical Investigations* by G.E.M. Anscombe. Oxford: Blackwell 1953.

Wundt, Wilhelm (1874), *Grundzüge der physiologischen Psychologie*. Leipzig: W. Engelmann.

— (1894), "Über psychische Causalität und das Princip des psychophysischen Parallelismus," in: *Philosophische Studien* 10: 1–124.

— (1896), *Grundriss der Psychologie*. Leipzig: W. Engelmann; 4th revised ed. translated by C.M. Judd as *Outlines of Psychology*. New York: Gustav E. Stechart 1902.

Yap, P.M. (1969), "The Culture-bound Reactive Syndromes," in: *Mental Health Research in Asia and Pacific*, ed. by W. Caudell/T. Lin. Honolulu: East-West Center Press: 33–53.

The Naturalness of Religious Concepts

An Emerging Cognitive Science of Religion

by

JUSTIN L. BARRETT

After maintaining a stranglehold on psychological science for roughly the first half of the twentieth century, behaviorism's command of the human sciences began to weaken in the late 1950s and early 1960s. The "Cognitive Revolution" as it is sometimes called, returned the investigation of mental states and structures to respectability in the field of psychology. Together with advances in linguistics, computer science, neuroscience, and philosophy of mind, the Cognitive Revolution birthed the field of cognitive science, which grew into maturity in the 1980's and 90's. The aftershock of the Cognitive Revolution and growing prominence of cognitive science has recently been felt within the study of religion as well, particularly in the study of religious concepts, as evidenced by the growing number of scholars and international meetings identifying with the cognitive science of religion.

To the ears of religionists weaned on post-modern relativism, some of the new cognitive claims might sound outrageous. For example, it has been suggested that children might be prone to embrace Creationism regardless of upbringing (Evans 2001); that God-concepts of American Catholics are roughly the same as Shiva-concepts of North Indian Hindus (Barrett 1998); and that observers can have intuitions about what makes a religious ritual effective without understanding the meaning of the ritual within its ritual system (Barrett/Lawson 2001; Lawson/McCauley 1990). I will amplify these claims, among others, below. The central thesis of these and other lines of inquiry in the cognitive science of religion is that much of religious cognition is the product of quite ordinary, pan-cultural cognitive structures and processes. I argue that by virtue of being human and living in a common world, peoples of all traditions and languages share a certain set of mnemonic, perceptual, attentional, and conceptual biases that constrain and inform the representation, acquisition, and transmission of religious concepts. This thesis may be called the "naturalness of religion" thesis (Boyer 1994; Barrett 2000b).

Language is a helpful analog. While no one denies that the particular language people speak as their primary tongue and how they speak that language is the consequence of being reared in a certain sociolinguistic environment, culture is not the whole story. Regular, natural biases in how the mind is organized enable the rapid acquisition of language and restrict the range of possible natural languages. Likewise, *particular* religious concepts and consequent practices arise through people living in particular cultural settings. However, the range of potential religious concepts, how readily they are acquired, how successfully they are transmitted, and the sorts of inferences and actions that would be generated from these religious concepts may be highly constrained and informed by *natural, general* properties of human cognition.

In this chapter, I will discuss four ways in which religious concepts "come naturally" or are undergirded by ordinary, *natural* human cognition. First, ordinary cognition informs how religious concepts are represented or understood by people. Second, acquiring religious concepts depends on a number of pan-cultural cognitive dispositions. Third, successfully spreading or transmitting religious concepts requires an appropriate fit with conceptual structures and the mnemonic dynamics at play in various contexts. Finally, given natural intuitive causal theories and assumptions, religious concepts predictably give rise to a particular limited range of religious behaviors. The chapter concludes with some suggestions regarding future developments of this emerging sub-field.

Before proceeding, I should diffuse a potential objection: If religion is so natural, why are many people not religious? The claim that religion comes naturally because of ordinary cognitive dynamics and biases, does not entail that everyone will become religious. Acquiring and understanding numbers and arithmetic depend primarily on ordinary, pan-cultural cognition but not everyone gets their sums right or has much skill in mathematics. Similarly, the production and appreciation of music is importantly informed and constrained by garden-variety cognitive capacities, but some individuals and groups have little affinity for music. Likewise, one may have the equipment in place to become religious and never use the equipment. Many people are genetically predisposed to become alcohol dependent but never consume alcohol. The naturalness of religion thesis only maintains that ordinary people as a whole are particularly receptive to generating, maintaining, and transmitting religious concepts because of how their minds are organized and function in the sort of world we all live in. This naturalness may be why historically non-religious people are so rare. Very special circumstances are required to produce atheists (Barrett 2004).

Representing Religious Concepts

Religious concepts may be more "natural" than they seem. Though theologies around the world include enormously complex concepts, these are not the concepts that typically occupy the working minds of religious people. Much as folk science differs from true science, religious concepts often differ from theological ones in their relative conceptual simplicity (Barrett 1999; McCauley 2000). For example, even in a theological system that posits a non-temporal god, during real-time problem solving or casual reasoning, believers will represent the god as experiencing time much like any human (Barrett 1998; Barrett/Keil 1996; Barrett/VanOrman 1996).

This tendency to entertain religious concepts that are simpler than their theological counterparts is not merely an issue of expertise. The complexity of the concept used appears to vary based largely on the cognitive demands of the context in which it is used (Barrett 1999). While astronomers entertain fancy notions about the movement of celestial bodies in some contexts (such as when engaged in scholarship), they may still tacitly treat the sun as moving around the earth when trying to make rapid, informal judgments. A quantum physicists might fully believe that particles can move from one place to another without traversing the intervening space, but will wholly disregard this insight when playing weekend softball. Similarly, theologians may fully appreciate that the god Vishnu knows their every thought before conceived, but will still intuitively feel it necessary to make Vishnu aware of their thoughts through prayer. The simplification of concepts from the theological to the religious level appears to consist of a systematic distortion of features such that they more closely resemble intuitive ontological assumptions, and not simply a matter of shedding superfluous features.

Over the past twenty years, researchers in the area of concepts, categorization, and cognitive development have amassed considerable evidence supporting the position that people have a large number of often tacit, intuitive assumptions and expectations about the sorts of properties different things have based on ontological category membership (Keil 1989). For example, when encountering a completely novel animal, six-year-old children (and in some cases even toddlers and infants) make a host of assumptions about unobserved characteristics. Because it is a bounded physical object, it cannot pass directly through other solid objects and cannot occupy more than one location at a time. By virtue of being a living thing, it is automatically assumed to be composed of natural materials with parts having particular functions and to have nutritional needs. As an animal, it can move itself in purposeful ways to satisfy its desires (Sperber/Premack/Premack 1995). These intuitive assumptions allow for rapid categorization of novel things, as well as generation of predictions and explanations, and appear largely invariant across cultures (Avis/Harris 1991; Walker 1992a, 1992b). After all, these basic properties and causal operations that apply to naturally occurring objects are uniform around the world. A rose is a rose is a rose.

If this characterization of conceptual structures is accurate, these categorical intuitions also limit the sorts of religious concepts that may be successfully used to generate inferences during on-line processing. That is, people of every culture will first assume properties congruent with these intuitive expectations when representing an object, animal, or person. Because they are default assumptions, these properties are more easily activated and thus more likely to characterize a new concept. To illustrate, Barrett and colleagues found that when adults in India (Barrett 1998) and the United States (Barrett/Keil 1996; Barrett/VanOrman 1996) reflected on their theological ideas about supreme beings in the course of completing a questionnaire, they generated abstract, theologically correct, descriptions of gods having no physical or spatial properties, able to know and attend to everything at once, and not being reliant on sensory inputs to acquire information. Due to theological differences, when reflecting, the degree of commitment to these properties in the deities did differ somewhat between the two groups, with Hindus less likely to embrace infallible perception, for example. However, when reading and comprehending narratives about these deities, the same adults in both groups remembered the god of the narratives as having a single location in space, being unable to attend to multiple events at once, and needing to see and hear in order to complete otherwise fallible knowledge. In other words, the gods of theological reflection contained many violations of intuitive assumptions for intentional agents, but the god concepts used in the narrative comprehension task looked very much like an ordinary intentional agent—a person, and were thus quite uniform across cultures and faith traditions. Tacit assumptions for the ontological category of intentional agents constrained the way gods were represented in both cultural groups.

One consequence of this cognitive constraint is that in many ordinary contexts people might only represent religious concepts having a limited number of features that violate intuitive expectations. That is, despite sophisticated theology, religious concepts might only be "minimally counterintuitive" (Barrett 2000b; Boyer 1996a, 1996b, 2000). This observation also points to the importance of distinguishing between theological concepts used by special people or in special situations, and religious concepts that are functional in much ordinary life (Barrett 1999). Religious thought is to theological thought as folk knowledge is to scientific knowledge (McCauley 2000).

Acquiring Religious Concepts

The idea that religious concepts are minimally counterintuitive in the sense of violating few intuitive assumptions for their ontological categories, underlies a second sense in which religion might be deemed natural. People may have a natural receptivity to entertaining religious concepts. Why is receptivity to religious concepts interesting? As outlined in Sperber's epidemiological approach to explaining cultural representations (Sperber 1985, 1990, 1996), in the marketplace of all concepts, concepts for which there is a bias to represent or entertain are more likely to become widespread and part of shared cultural knowledge. Thus, Boyer (1994, 2001) argues that the finding that people are receptive to religious concepts begins to explain religion.

Cognitive research has revealed at least three ways in which people seem to be naturally receptive to acquiring religious concepts. First, as children, many conceptual default assumptions seem to be congruent with the properties of religious agents. Second, children and adults seem to be biased to account for states of affairs in the world to the possible activity of even unseen agents, rendering religious concepts particularly attractive. Third, many religious concepts may meet a conceptual optimum that renders them highly salient, memorable, and having great inferential potential.

Religious Concepts Meeting Childhood Default Assumptions

Researchers in child development frequently note that children easily adopt ideas about gods, ghosts, Santa Claus, superheroes and other agents possessing supernatural properties, and use ordinary conceptual resources for reasoning with these concepts (Harris 2000). Children's less developed conceptual systems might easily accommodate many of the properties that set religious entities apart from natural agents. For example, whereas adults have learned that people and animals do not perceive everything and cannot know everything, young children seem to have a default assumption that intentional agents are infallible, or at least super-human with regards to many mental properties. Most three-year-old children assume that whatever is true of the real world (at least from their own perspective) is what others believe to be the case. That is, people, animals, and gods cannot have false beliefs. By age five, most children have come to understand that people can be mistaken, but they may maintain God's infallibility (Barrett 2000a; Barrett/Richert/Driesenga 2001).

Recent developmental work examining young children's understanding of others' perceptual perspectives (i.e., what others see, smell, and hear) and others' ability to draw on background knowledge for interpreting visual displays, has demonstrated that three- and four-year-old Protestant children may actually be more able to reason accurately about God's perspectives and knowledge (theologically speaking) than that of other people (Barrett/Newman/Richert 2003; Richert/Barrett 1999). To illustrate, when presented with a "secret code" consisting of nonsense squiggles, three- to seven-year-olds were inclined to overestimate the likelihood that a parent or friend would know what the code meant, with the bulk of three- and four-year-olds assuming that their parents would know the meaning of an arbitrary secret code they had never seen before. However, even the youngest children believed God would be more likely (and a dog would be less likely) to understand the code than a parent or friend. That is, children demonstrated a bias to treat their parents as "god-like" by grossly overestimating their knowledge, but they still attributed even greater knowledge to God (Barrett/Newman/Richert 2003). These results suggest that a god-like mind may be conceptualized easily from very early on—even earlier than a human-like mind.

Not only do children seem to easily acquire some appreciation for an infallible god, they also appear to have biases to acquire a conception of the world as intentionally created by a being or beings with extraordinary power. Careful structured interviews in the American Midwest by Evans (2001) have shown that both children with parents that teach an evolutionary origin of living things and children with creationist parents are more inclined to adopt creationism than evolutionism. Congruent with this finding is that European preschoolers appear capable of understanding that God creates natural things but not artifacts, whereas humans create artifacts but not natural things (Petrovich 1997).

Although available developmental data is still limited, it appears that many concepts central to major religious traditions such as agents with special causal powers and special minds are not as opaque to young children as often thought. Indeed, it appears that when presented with such concepts, children find them very easy to acquire because of conceptual biases and default assumptions.

Hyperactive Agency Detection Device (HADD)

A second way in which people may be particularly receptive to religious concepts is inspired by the scholarship of Stewart Guthrie. Supported by ethnographic data and psychological research, Guthrie (1980, 1993) argues that people have a bias to detect human-like agency in their environment that might not actually exist. People are particularly sensitive to the presence of intentional agency and seem biased to over-attribute intentional action as the cause of states of affairs given ambiguous or sketchy data (Heider/Simmel 1944; Rochat/Morgan/Carpenter 1997). These observations suggest that whatever cognitive mechanism people have for detecting agency might be extremely sensitive. According to Guthrie, such a biased perceptual device would have been quite adaptive in our evolutionary past, for the consequences in failing to detect an agent are potentially much graver than mistakenly detecting an agent that is not there. Falsely detect an agent that is not there and the cost is a little extra anxiety and caution. Fail to detect an agent that is there and you could become tiger feed. I have termed such a biased perceptual/conceptual mechanism a hyperactive agency detection device or HADD (Barrett 2000b).

Though such a device is not a sufficient explanation for religious concepts, the implication for religion is that the HADD might lead people to posit agents, perhaps of a counterintuitive sort, that are then well-transmitted because of their easy fit with intuitive conceptual systems. Similarly, when presented with counterintuitive-agent concepts, their resonance with agency posited by HADD would make them more likely to receive attention and be transmitted than non-agent concepts. For example, someone might be told that an invisible person lives in the forest and trips intruders. This story could become salient because it reminds the person of having tripped in the forest and wondering, "Who did that?" (because of the HADD). Alternately, rarely does one wonder the more testable hypothesis, "Did I trip over an invisible rock?" and so a story about an invisible rock is less likely to be spread. Because of the human tendency to seek intentional explanations for states of affairs, counterintuitive *agents* provide ready explanations in ways that non-agents do not. In this way, selective pressure of the HADD might contribute to the prevalence of religious agent concepts over against other counterintuitive concepts. Further, when individuals talk about these agents they may cite empirical evidence consistent with the agents' existence.

Note that the suggestion is not necessarily that people acquire religious concepts because of experiences commensurate with the religious concepts. Though this may happen on occasion, more likely, the fact that people are hypersensitive to intentional agency will make accounts of unusual agents interesting, seem potentially important, and useful for accounting for experiences that activate HADD without satisfyingly identifying a natural agent. Further, contra Guthrie, it is more plausible that what HADD postulates are intentional agents that need not resemble humans. As the developmental data sketched above suggests, even young children seem able to distinguish various types of intentional agents and their respective minds. Thus, not all agent detection is anthropomorphism. What the presence of HADD in human cognitive architecture contributes is enhanced probability of acquiring intentional agent concepts that may or may not closely resemble humans.

Memorability and Inferential Potential of Religious Concepts

A third way in which ordinary cognitive resources enhance receptivity to acquiring many religious concepts is religious concepts' memorability and inferential potential. Adults appear to find minimally counterintuitive concepts, of which religious concepts are a subset, both easily represented (as discussed above) and highly memorable.

Recall that ontological category-level assumptions seem to develop early and are largely invariant across cultures. These categories probably include such groupings as *animal*, *artifact*, *natural non-living thing*, and so forth. On the other hand, so-called basic-level concepts (such as *dog*, *chair*, or *icicle*) are built up through particular experience or teaching relevant to these objects, and are some of the first words learned in essentially any language. For example, a cat weighing 16 tons is indeed unusual, probably agreeing with zero percent of any given person's experience with cats. However, the concept '16 ton cat' does not violate any category-level expectations for animals. After all, an animal may certainly weigh 16 tons and still be a perfectly good animal. However, a cat that has gears inside of it that make it go violates a category-level assumption for animals. Animals are not composed of artificial parts. Therefore 'a cat that has [illegible] here.

By measuring recall of concepts by adults from France, Gabon, and Nepal, Boyer and Ramble (2001) found that concepts that violate one of a number of category-level assumptions (e.g., a dog that passes through solid objects) are better remembered and transmitted than concepts that either satisfy assumptions (e.g., a brown dog) or that violate basic-level assumptions (e.g., a dog weighing five tons). That is, concepts with a counterintuitive feature were more memorable than either mundane or bizarre ones that do not challenge categorical assumptions. Congruently, in a series of transmission experiments with American adults, Barrett and Nyhof (2001) found that counterintuitive concepts were more likely to be remembered and transmitted successfully to others. In one of their studies, one third of a group of college students were told a story that included six counterintuitive concepts (e.g., a rose that could jump) and six bizarre but not counterintuitive concepts (e.g., a hot pink newspaper). The students then went into an adjacent room where others were waiting and each told two other people the story. Each student who was told the story told it again to two others. Once everyone had heard the story, they recorded their best account of the story, both immediately after the transmission session and three months later. At both times, participants successfully remembered more of the counterintuitive concepts than the bizarre concepts. Counterintuitive concepts had a clear transmission advantage.

Together with the finding that concepts that have too many counterintuitive features will be reduced to more intuitive forms in on-line processing (Barrett 1999), it appears that *minimally* counterintuitive concepts have a transmission advantage. Minimally counterintuitive concepts attain a *conceptual optimum* such that they are understood and represented without allocating too many cognitive resources, but also challenging enough to require extra attention to assimilate into conceptual schemes (Sperber 1994). As a class of minimally counterintuitive concepts, religious concepts are likely to enjoy this advantage as well (Boyer 1994, 1995, 1996a, 1996b).

Interestingly, the observation that religious concepts are typically minimally counterintuitive, implies a fairly small range of possible conceptual structures these concepts may employ. In the face of apparent enormous diversity in religious concepts, Boyer has argued that supernatural concepts typically share five representational similarities (2000):

[1] a lexical label

[2] implicit classification in an intuitive ontological category

[3] explicit representation of a violation of intuitive expectations for that category, either:

(3a) a breach of relevant expectations for the category, or

(3b) a transfer of expectations associated with another category

[4] implicit default expectations for the category

[5] additional encyclopedic information

For example, a [1] 'ghost' is [2] categorized as a *person,* that [3] can violate intuitive physics for solid objects by passing through walls, but [4] meets intuitive psychological assumptions for persons, and [5] might be understood as likely to return to where it once lived. What separates supernatural concepts from natural concepts is [3] a violation of intuitive expectations for a given ontological category. Supernatural concepts, therefore, are not wholly novel or determined by cultural instruction but exist as minor aberrations of natural concepts.

These violations of expectations may be in one of three intuitive knowledge domains: intuitive psychology, intuitive biology, or intuitive physics. For categories that assume a domain (e.g., *plant* assumes intuitive biology and intuitive physics), violations will consist of breaches of expectations for the domain (as in an invisible fern, a breach of intuitive physics for a *plant*). However, for categories that do not assume a domain (e.g., *plant* does not assume intuitive psychology), violations may consist of transfers of expectations from another domain (as in a pensive shrub, a *plant* having intuitive psychological properties).

Given three domains of knowledge and five primary ontological categories from which supernatural concepts are drawn, the vast majority of supernatural concepts that become part of cultural knowledge can be cataloged in a 3 x 5 matrix. The table on the following page gives examples of each of the fifteen possible types of supernatural concepts (adapted from Barrett 2000b, inspired by Boyer 2000).

Further adding to the transmission advantage of minimally counterintuitive concepts is their inferential potential. Unlike an extremely heavy dog, the existence of a dog that can readily pass directly through solid objects such as walls can generate a large number of interesting explanations and inferences. However, not all counterintuitive concepts are equal in this regard. Counterintuitive concepts such as invisible sofas rarely occupy important (if any) roles in religious systems. Counterintuitive beings or objects of commitment in religious belief systems are most often intentional agents. They may be people

Ontological Categories	Intuitive Knowledge Domain Violations		
	Psychology	**Biology**	**Physics**
person	a person who knows everything	a person requiring no nourishment	a person who is invisible
animal	a snail that uses language	a dog that is immortal	a cow that can be in many places at once
plant	a rose that listens to people's requests	Grass composed of metal	a tree that is weightless
artifact	a hammer that feels neglected	a shoe that sprouts roots	a car that can drip through a sieve
natural non-living	an icycle that enjoys music	a diamond that was born	a rock that may pass through solid objects

with unusual physical or biological properties (such as an invisible person), or non-humans with human-like psychologies (such as a statue that can listen) (Boyer 2000). Counterintuitive *agent* concepts are more common because they enjoy additional selective advantages in being remembered and transmitted such as their resonance with a HADD, as described above, and their ability to account for vastly more relationships and states of affairs in the world; that is, great inferential potential.

Transmission of Religious Concepts and Contextual Variables

Religious concepts may be easily acquired because they often fit conceptual biases that develop quite early, they play in to our concern for intentional agency, and they attain a conceptual optimum such that they are memorable and interesting. These factors lead to the relatively easy transmission of religious concepts and thus help account for their commonness within and between cultures. In short, natural cognitive mechanisms enable religious concepts to be readily transmitted. However, it would be misleading not to say something about contextual factors that might influence the transmission of religious concepts. Though research in this area is still in its infancy, drawing upon current theories of mnemonic dynamics and ethnographic data, some promising hypotheses have been developed, particularly by Whitehouse (1992, 1995, 1996a, 1996b, 2000).

Whitehouse has argued that the frequency of performance, the degree of sensory and emotional intensity (or "sensory pageantry" hereafter), the potential for producing group solidarity, the potential for encouraging spontaneous exegetical reflection, and the potential for transmitting theology of any given religious event is in part a consequence of mnemonic and other cognitive dynamics. For an event to become part of a religious system, its procedures must be repeatedly performed in such a way that various instances are identifiable as the same event. Practices without mnemonic aids that are infrequently performed are unlikely to be remembered and repeatedly practiced. In many primarily oral traditions, a key mnemonic aid is sensory pageantry. Use of elaborate sights, sounds, smells, tastes, and feelings set an event apart from mundane life as something special and worthy of memory and attention resources. Additionally, intensely arousing events, such as initiation rites that serve to terrorize initiates through physical and emotional torment, may elicit flashbulb-like memories for the participants (Brown/Kulik 1977). Such dramatic and traumatic events are unlikely to be easily forgotten (Whitehouse 1996b), a perspective shared by Whitehouse and others (Pfeiffer 1982). However, Whitehouse further argues that as flashbulb memory research has indicated, only certain components of such an event are likely to be remembered well. Participants in highly dramatic events tend to form strong imagistic and episodic memories regarding the sequence of events (thus enabling repeat performances after long delays), who was a co-participant (increasing likelihood of group cohesion), and salient visual features of the event (providing symbolic materials for later reflection) (Neisser et al. 1996). However, long theological (i.e., conceptually complex) treatises are unlikely to be remembered accurately. Consequently, events with a high degree of sensory pageantry typically include little sophisticated theological communication to justify or explain the event, and so participants are left to speculate why the event, in all its drama, was performed. Frequently repeated events need not require resource-intensive, high sensory pageantry, and may include more complicated theological communication including explicit rationale for the event.

Acting on Religious Concepts

Though this chapter is primarily about religious concepts, concepts that had no behavioral consequences would hardly be worth discussing. What makes religious concepts so rich and powerful is the fact that they often give rise to an enormous and varied body of actions including ceremonies, prayers, meditations, rites, and rituals. Religions are not merely collections of shared concepts, but also include action in response to those concepts. Indeed, religious practice often more than religious belief strikes outside observers as peculiar and needing explanation. Further, religious concepts spread in the context of shared religious actions, as Whitehouse's work suggests. Two specific areas of religious action have begun to receive attention by cognitive scientists of religion: religious ritual and petitionary prayer.

The Case of Religious Rituals

Whereas religious actions such as rituals seem quite unnatural in many respects, cognitive scientists of religion argue that, here too, ordinary cognition both structures religious practices and underlies the representation of religious actions in participants' and observers' minds, and the execution of these actions.

Whitehouse's analysis may apply to religious events generally, but when considering religious rituals in particular, the most developed cognitive theory is that of Lawson and McCauley (Lawson 1993; Lawson/McCauley 1990). Chomsky's work on tacit syntactic constraints on language production prompted E. Thomas Lawson in the 1970s to ponder whether religious ritual action was governed by conceptual structures akin to grammatical rules. This analogy with language proved fruitful and bore Lawson's and McCauley's groundbreaking *Rethinking Religion: Connecting Cognition and Culture* (1990), a book that advanced cognitively plausible and empirically testable grounds for meaningful explanation of cross-cultural regularities in religious ritual forms.

Under Lawson's and McCauley's theoretically-motivated typology, as a subclass of religious events, rituals are distinguished by being represented as an agent acting upon someone or something (a "patient") to bring about some state of affairs, by virtue of invoking supernatural causation. For most Catholics, baptism is thus an example of a religious ritual because an agent (the priest) acts (sprinkles water) upon a patient (an infant) for God to accept the child as part of the Church. In contrast, while possibly including rituals, Protestant worship services are religious events but typically not rituals.

Rather than cultural inputs wholly determining knowledge about rituals, their structures, and their potential effectiveness, Lawson and McCauley observe that the representation of religious ritual actions depends upon cognitive mechanisms for the representation of actions generally, with religious rituals being distinguished from ordinary actions by the presence of a supernatural agent concept represented in the action structure. A baptism is only a man wetting an infant except that the man is understood to be acting in the place of a superhuman agent. Because ordinary cognitive resources are drawn upon to make sense of religious rituals, little cultural knowledge is necessary for groups of people to have converging ideas about what are the important features of a ritual structure, or what makes a ritual "well-formed" and likely to be successful.

Indeed, as predicted by this account, Barrett and Lawson demonstrated that ritually naïve adults have converging intuitions that the most important components for fictitious religious ritual to be successful in bringing about the intended consequences are, first, that superhuman agency is represented in the action structure; and second, that an appropriate agent, capable of the right intentions, initiates the action (Barrett/Lawson 2001). Unlike popular conceptions of magic, having the right agent is more important than performing precisely the correct action. Note that the priority of agent over action is not characteristic of natural mechanistic causation (e.g., it does not matter who strikes a window with a hammer, the action will have the same result), but it is characteristic of social causation: being the right person with the right intentions may make more difference in the consequence of an action than the particular action. For example, an older sibling who gives the baby a marble to play with might be regarded either as a kind and considerate child or a mean and dangerous child depending on whether the child knows that a baby may choke on a marble and the intentions of the gift. What these findings suggest is that the ordinary cognitive structures that religious rituals draw upon may be those of social causal cognition, but more research is necessary on this topic.

Petitionary Prayer

Petitionary prayer in the Christian tradition, or the asking of God for something, is an excellent example of a domain of religious action informed by ordinary cognition. In Christianity, and other faiths as well, believers may ask God to act in the natural world in any number of ways. Biblical examples of petitionary prayer and instruction regarding prayer includes the faithful asking God to work in mechanistic (e.g., to burn an altar), biological (e.g., to heal an illness), and psychological ways (e.g., to change someone's attitude). It seems that as long as the petition is offered in faith and in accordance of the will of God, any mode of divine action is potentially acceptable. Thus, when God is understood as an omnipotent and omnipresent being, God can potentially act through any causal mechanisms. Theologically then, it seems that no domain of petitionary prayer (psychological, biological, or mechanical) should necessarily hold an advantage over any other when it comes to the real prayer practices of individuals. That most Christian traditions do not explicitly advocate one domain of activity for God over others leaves just the theological vacuum that cognitive biases might fill.

Through a series of studies asking American Protestants to rate hypothetical prayers for likelihood, to complete a questionnaire regarding prayer preferences, and to keep a journal of all petitionary prayers over a two week period, Protestants were found to be more inclined to ask God to act psychologically (e.g., to change someone's mind, help someone remember something, or make someone feel better) than to act mechanistically or biologically (Barrett 2001). Why might this be? As outlined above, cognitive research suggests that in many real-time, non-reflective, situations, people represent even highly abstract concepts of gods as human-like beings with psychological and physical limits including a single physical location (Barrett 1998; Barrett/Keil 1996; Barrett/VanOrman 1996). Given that during many instances of Christian petitionary prayer, God is represented as a psychosocial being with a particular location (e.g., in Heaven), petitioners might be biased to ask for God to act in ways at which agents acting at a distance are best. Human-like agents are generally poor at acting mechanistically or physically at a distance. Even infants know it takes physical contact to move a physical object (Spelke/Phillips/Woodward 1995); one must touch a chair to be able to move it. Similarly, human-like agents are not skilled at making biological intervention at a distance. What humans and similar agents do well at a distance is affecting psychological states: beliefs, opinions, desires, and emotions. If God is implicitly conceptualized as a human-like agent far away, then perhaps, in the absence of pertinent theology, God's omnipotence and omnipresence are often ignored and petitionary prayer consists disproportionately of requests for God to act psychologically as opposed to mechanistically.

Though more research is needed in this area, results thus far are suggestive and illustrate the potential cognitive approaches to the study of religion have in everyday religious concepts and behavior.

Future Directions for the Cognitive Science of Religion

Cognitive scientists of religion are making large strides in demonstrating that much of religious cognition, including the representation of god concepts, successful transmission of religious concepts, and the development of practices based on religious concepts, is largely reliant on ordinary cognition. No special domain for religious thought need be postulated. Religion is, in some ways, quite natural. However, the current story is not complete in either its coverage of issues or in its empirical support.

With few experimentalists in its ranks and inadequate ethnographic work to draw upon, the cognitive science of religion has many claims as yet insufficiently supported by rigorous empirical data. Cross-cultural investigations of many of the claims discussed above are still needed. For example, while it is plausible, the claim that people sometimes spontaneously account for events by reference to unseen agents needs systematic examination as do many of the claims regarding ritual intuitions made by Lawson and McCauley. Receiving some ethnographic support, Whitehouse's claims about how sensory pageantry and memory dynamics interact to produce different sorts of religious events have not been examined in a controlled fashion.

Apart from the current scarcity of empirical research testing these theories, researchers have yet to investigate other relevant questions. How do truth-claims interact with the representation and transmission of religious concepts and practices? Are minimally counterintuitive concepts easier or harder to believe than other concepts? How is the success of rituals evaluated and how does this evaluation play into whether or not the ritual is repeated? If religious concepts are so naturally accommodated by cognitive structures, why do they sometimes seem difficult to entertain? (For some preliminary thoughts on this issue, see McCauley 2000.) How does cognition constrain and inform other classes of religious phenomena such as worship and conversion? If children easily represent properties of superhuman agents, why do adults seem to have great difficulty in many contexts? From a cognitive perspective, does religious ritual differ (cognitively) from superstitious observances or from magic? Could recent advances in understanding social categories bear upon how religious roles and special religious people such as priests, prophets, and shamans are represented?

Insights from the cognitive science of religion are also yet to be earnestly applied to historical and comparative problems in the study of religion.

Conclusion

Concepts of gods, spirits, ghosts, ancestors, witches, shamans, priests, prophets, oracles, zombies, devils, and avatars are among the varied and colorful domain of religious thought. These concepts, in all their diversity, motivate an even greater and seemingly infinite pageant of religious rituals, ceremonies, and other actions. Given the centrality of religious concepts to religion in general, it comes as no surprise that scholars of religion are taking advantage of advances in the cognitive sciences to better understand religious beliefs, practices, and traditions. The past several decades have seen tremendous growth in the science of the mind with particularly revolutionary changes in understanding regularities of how human minds represent complex concepts. These insights have been commandeered to compare and explain the successful use and transmission of religious concepts. In brief, one of the prominent markers of the new cognitive science of religion is a tendency to emphasize the "naturalness" of religion—that religious concepts (and subsequent actions) capitalize on ordinary mental structures and regularities.

References

Avis, J./Harris, P.L. (1991), "Belief–Desire Reasoning among Baka Children: Evidence for a Universal Conception of Mind," in: *Child Development* 62: 460–67.

Barrett, Justin L. (1998), "Cognitive Constraints on Hindu Concepts of the Divine," in: *Journal for the Scientific Study of Religion* 37: 608–19.

— (1999), "Theological Correctness: Cognitive Constraint and the Study of Religion," in: *Method and Theory in the Study of Religion*.

— (2000a), "Do Children Experience God Like Adults? Retracing the Development of God Concepts," in: *Keeping Religion in Mind: Cognitive Perspectives on Religious Experience*, ed. by J. Andresen: Cambridge University Press: 171–90.

— (2000b), "Exploring the Natural Foundations of Religion," in: *Trends in Cognitive Sciences* 4: 29–34.

— (2001), "How Ordinary Cognition Informs Petitionary Prayer," in: *Journal of Cognition and Culture* 1: 259–69.

— (2004), *Why Would Anyone Believe in God?* Walnut Creek, Calif.: Alta Mira Press.

Barrett, Justin L./Keil, Frank C. (1996), "Anthropomorphism and God Concepts: Conceptualizing a Nonnatural Entity," in: *Cognitive Psychology* 3: 219–47.

Barrett, Justin L./Lawson, E.T. (2001), "Ritual Intuitions: Cognitive Contributions to Judgments of Religious Ritual Efficacy," in: *Journal of Cognition and Culture* 1: 183–201.

Barrett, Justin L./Newman, R.M./Richert, R.A. (2003), "When Seeing Is Not Believing: Children's Understanding of Humans' and Non Humans' Use of Background Knowledge in Interpreting Visual Displays," in: *Journal of Cognition and Culture* 3 (1): 91–108

Barrett, Justin L./Nyhof, M. (2001), "The Role of Category-level Knowledge in Cultural Transmission," in: *Journal of Cognition and Culture* 1: 69–100.

Barrett, Justin L./VanOrman, B. (1996), "The Effects of Image Use in Worship on God Concepts," in: *Journal of Psychology and Christianity* 15: 38–45.

Boyer, Pascal (1993), "Pseudo-Natural Kinds," in: *Cognitive Aspects of Religious Symbolism,* ed. by Pascal Boyer. Cambridge: Cambridge University Press: 121–41.

— (1994), *The Naturalness of Religious Ideas. A Cognitive Theory of Religion*. Berkeley, Calif.: University of California Press.

— (1995), "Causal Understandings in Cultural Representations: Cognitive Constraints on Inferences from Cultural Input," in: *Causal Cognition: A Multidisciplinary Debate,* ed. by Dan Sperber/David Premack/Ann James-Premack. Oxford: Claredon Press.

— (1996a), "Cognitive Limits to Conceptual Relativity: The Limiting-case of Religious Categories," in: *Rethinking Linguistic Relativity,* ed. by John J. Gumperz/Stephen C. Levinson. Cambridge: Cambridge University Press: 203–31.

— (1996b), "What Makes Anthropomorphism Natural: Intuitive Ontology and Cultural Representations," in: *Journal of the Royal Anthropological Institute* 2: 1–15.

— (2000), "Evolution of a Modern Mind and the Origins of Culture: Religious Concepts as a Limiting Case," in: *Evolution and the Human Mind: Modularity, Language and Meta-Cognition*, ed. by Peter Carruthers/Andrew Chamberlain. Cambridge: Cambridge University Press.

— (2001), *Religion Explained: The Evolutionary Origins of Religious Thought*. New York: Basic Books.

Boyer, Pascal/Ramble, C. (2001), "Cognitive Templates for Religious Concepts: Cross-cultural Evidence for Recall for Counter-intuitive Representations," in: *Cognitive Science* 25: 535–64.

Brown, R./Kulik, J. (1977), "Flashbulb Memories," in: *Cognition* 5: 73–99.

Evans, E.M. (2001), "Cognitive and Contextual Factors in the Emergence of Diverse Belief Systems: Creation versus Evolution," in: *Cognitive Psychology* 42: 217–66.

Guthrie, Stewart (1980), "A Cognitive Theory of Religion," in: *Current Anthropology* 21: 181–203.

— (1993), *Faces in the Clouds: A New Theory of Religion*. New York: Oxford University Press.

Harris, P.L. (2000), "On Not Falling down to Earth: Children's Metaphysical Questions," in: *Imagining the Impossible: The Development of Magical, Scientific, and Religious Thinking in Contemporary Society*, ed. by Karl S. Rosengren/Carl N. Johnson/Paul L. Harris. Cambridge: Cambridge University Press.

Heider, F./Simmel, M. (1944), "An Experimental Study of Apparent Behavior," in: *American Journal of Psychology* 57: 243–59.

Keil, Frank C. (1989), *Concepts, Kinds, and Cognitive Development*. Cambridge, Mass.: MIT Press.

Lawson, E. Thomas (1993), "Cognitive Categories, Cultural Forms, and Ritual Structures," in: *Cognitive Aspects of Religious Symbolism*, ed. by Pascal Boyer. Cambridge: Cambridge University Press: 188–206.

Lawson, E. Thomas/McCauley, Robert N. (1990), *Rethinking Religion: Connecting Cognition and Culture*. Cambridge: Cambridge University Press.

McCauley, Robert N. (2000), "The Naturalness of Religion and the Unnaturalness of Science," in: *Explanation and Cognition*, ed. by Frank C. Keil/R. Wilson. Cambridge, Mass.: MIT Press.

Neisser, U. et al. (1996), "Remembering the Earthquake: Direct Experience versus Hearing the News," in: *Memory* 4: 337–57.

Petrovich, O. (1997), "Understanding of Non-natural Causality in Children and Adults: A Case against Artificialism," in: *Psyche en Geloof* 8: 151–65.

Pfeiffer, John E. (1982), *The Creative Explosion: An Inquiry into the Origins of Art and Religion*. New York: Harper and Row.

Richert, R.A./Barrett, Justin L. (1999), *Perspectives in a New Sense: Children's Understanding of Natural and Supernatural Agents' Perspectives across Modalities*. Poster presentation at the Cognitive Development Society meeting, Chapel Hill, N.C., October 1999.

Rochat, P./Morgan, R./Carpenter, M. (1997), "Young Infants' Sensitivity to Movement Information Specifying Social Causality," in: *Cognitive Development* 12: 441–65.

Spelke, Elizabeth S./Phillips, Ann/Woodward, Amanda L. (1995), "Infant's Knowledge of Object Motion and Human Action," in: *Causal Cognition*, ed. by Dan Sperber et al.: 44–78.

Sperber, Dan (1975), *Rethinking Symbolism*. Cambridge: Cambridge University Press.

— (1985), "Anthropology and Psychology: Towards an Epidemiology of Representations," in: *Man* 20: 73–89.

— (1990), "The Epidemiology of Beliefs," in: *The Social Psychological Study of Widespread Beliefs*, ed. by C. Fraser/G. Gaskell. Oxford: Clarendon Press: 25–44.

— (1994), "The Modularity of Thought and the Epidemiology of Representations," in: *Mapping the Mind: Domain Specificity in Cognition and Culture*, ed. by L.A. Hirschfeld/S.A. Gelman. Cambridge University Press: 39–67.

— (1996), *Explaining Culture: A Naturalistic Approach*. Oxford: Blackwell.

Sperber, Dan/Premack, David/James Premack, Ann, eds. (1995), *Causal Cognition: A Multidisciplinary Debate*. Oxford: Clarendon Press.

Walker [Jeyifous], S. (1992a), "Developmental Changes in the Representation of Word-meaning: Cross-cultural Findings," in: *British Journal of Developmental Psychology* 10: 285–99.

— (1992b), "Supernatural Beliefs, Natural Kinds and Conceptual Structure," in: *Memory and Cognition* 20: 655–62.

Whitehouse, Harvey (1992), "Memorable Religions: Transmission, Codification, and Change in Divergent Melanesian Contexts," in: *Man* 27: 777–97.

— (1995), *Inside the Cult: Religious Innovation and Transmission in Papua New Guinea*. Oxford: Claredon Press/New York: Oxford University Press.

— (1996a), "Jungles and Computers: Neuronal Group Selection and the Epidemiology of Representations," in: *Journal of the Royal Anthropological Institute* 2: 99–116.

— (1996b), "Rites of Terror: Emotion, Metaphor, and Memory in Melanesian Initiation Cults," in: *Journal of the Royal Anthropological Institute* 2: 703–15.

— (2000), *Arguments and Icons: The Cognitive, Social, and Historical Implications of Divergent Modes of Religiosity*. Oxford: Oxford University Press.

Psychoanalyzing Prehistory

Struggling with the Unrecorded Past

by

DAVID A. WARBURTON[1]

The Discovery of the Dawn of Consciousness

In the early 1960s the archaeological excavation of an almost 10,000 year old village at Çatal Hüyük (in Anatolia, modern Turkey) revealed an unusual aspect of human culture. Although neither the first nor the largest village in human history, at 13 hectares (32 acres), Çatal Hüyük was certainly among the largest and earliest towns during the early spread of agriculture. The fact that it was an incipient agricultural town was not, however, its most curious aspect, nor the discovery that the entire town consisted of small densely packed windowless residential houses which were entered through the roof.

What attracted attention was the fact that the houses were decorated with modeled clay bulls' heads with real horns. Some of these were attached to the walls, but others stood in the middle of rooms. Movement in the dark windowless houses was thus dominated by extremely inconvenient pairs of bulls' horns at eye and groin level. Murals in the houses depicted vultures devouring headless human bodies. Some of the anthropomorphic figurines found in the houses had detachable heads. Burials were found under the floors and benches of the houses, which were presumably occupied by relatives of the deceased. Sticking from the walls of some houses were sculpted pairs of human female breasts, "containing lower jaws of boar, skulls of foxes and weasels, or of Griffon vultures—all animals associated with scavengers, hence death." Some of the "breasts" have open nipples, with the beaks of vultures, the teeth of foxes and

1 Although the article was conceived and written by the author alone, some of the ideas concerning religion and psychology incorporate thoughts developed by Ian Hodder and Trevor Watkins. Although I am grateful to them for ideas presented in lectures and discussions, they bear no responsibility for their use here.
Readers unfamiliar with the Ancient Near Eastern civilizations and archaeology in general will find articles covering most sites and subjects in Meyers 1997, Redford 2001, and Sasson 1995.

weasels, as well as the tusks of wild boars sticking out of them. Plaster reliefs also depict women giving birth to rams' heads and other bizarre scenes (Mellaart 1975: 108).

It is possible that some of the decoration at Çatal Hüyük was only intended to be temporary and on display for brief periods of time, being painted over or removed "after use." Nevertheless, the ghastly and shocking decoration was not really comparable to the wonderfully moving paintings of the prehistoric French caves, nor to the featureless walls of other Neolithic houses where paintings of apparently harmless birds adorned one of the earliest walls [illegible] built (Akkermans et al. 1978–1979: 152–54).

The decoration of the houses at Çatal Hüyük was similar in both neighboring—adjacent—houses as well as in superimposed houses, meaning that different houses had similar decoration at roughly the same time, but also that the decoration continued through time, being present in different houses used by successive generations. The houses of this ancient village were hardly spacious, yet the "living room" (with the decoration) was dominated by a platform whence the grisly decor would have dominated the view; other areas served as kitchens and storage spaces. Although parts of the houses were cleaner than others, all revealed traces of use. The houses themselves were crammed side by side and the only entrances via ladders from the roof. The houses were windowless; empty adjacent plots and abandoned houses were filled with rubbish, and animals. Only 4% of the 13 hectare mound was excavated, but at comparatively great depth (15 building levels amounting to more than 20 vertical meters of accumulation).

At the time, it was suggested that the excavator might perhaps have hit upon a priestly quarter, which would explain these peculiar decorations. Renewed excavation and research has, however, confirmed that the houses discovered in the 1960s were houses which were inhabited as such—as well as being cemeteries and settings for rituals ("multiple-use dwellings"), and not merely shrines as had been suggested. The persistency and standardization of the household furnishings was indeed typical rather than exceptional: recent work has revealed that other houses in other areas of the site may have had similar appurtenances. The most recent survey (Hodder 1996) has also indicated that at the top of the current site, which represents the final stage of the occupation, there is no trace of a recognizable public building. For those familiar with bureaucratic growth, the absence of traces of a large public structure at the top (and therefore final phase) of the site would certainly suggest that there were no others down underneath (i.e., earlier), as public institutions tend to grow rather than diminish in a large and prosperous community, which Çatal Hüyük certainly was. These findings suggest an unusual community, and also that the house decoration must have corresponded to some widely felt conscious need.

Archaeology

The contemporary archaeological community of the 1960s and 1970s did not, however, share a need to explore these issues. As the excavator, Mellaart, categorically stated that this village could not be explained exclusively in functional terms, the reaction of the archaeological community was to relegate the matter to the popular press while pursuing an archaeological agenda dominated by a functional subsistence-oriented approach to the early development of agriculture and the appearance of urbanism (e.g., Higgs 1972, 1973). These were the dominant themes of prehistoric archaeological theory at the time.

Academic scientific prehistoric archaeology is a new field. In 1800 A.D., archaeology was primarily the hobby of collectors, and in 2000 A.D., collectors still play an important role. In 1800 archaeology was dominated by Greece and Rome; in 2000 it still is. These two centuries have, however, seen a series of transformations which have created an independent field. Prehistory was separated from a discipline devoted to aesthetic tastes, and another quite different one—dominated by cultural issues, ranging from religion to economics—thus established. The last two centuries have also seen the emergence of the excavation as a conscious and deliberate method of acquiring both artifacts and information. Archaeologists excavate sites and survey regions in order to assemble artifacts and draw maps and plans which record the distribution of artifacts and structures. Such plans can be limited to the artifacts recovered from a slice of earth perhaps only a centimeter thick over a single square meter, or they can extend to the distribution of some particular phenomenon throughout the world throughout time.

These last two centuries have also witnessed the birth of Near Eastern archaeology and the birth of the discipline of prehistory. Prehistorians tend to be associated with anthropology while Near Eastern archaeology is linked to philology, art history and architecture. Prehistorians working in the Near East can be in departments associated with any of these fields, and thus exposed to very different theoretical frameworks. Choosing an appropriate model is difficult. A volume on archaeological theory published a decade ago (Yoffee/ Sherratt 1993) revealed this crisis of identity, but failed to address the issue directly. As a result, "archaeology" has no theoretical understanding of itself or its role, so that archaeologists attempt to solve problems without identifying the question, moving from one theoretical approach to another, without resolving the issues identified and highlighted by the previous theoretical approach. Among others, "typology," "climatic change," "subsistence," "social organization" and "cognitive issues" have dominated at different times.

Like "Classical Archaeology," "Archaeology" seems to understand itself as an independent discipline, but it is actually just a bundle of methods used to draw information from mute sources, without a specific focus. There is no general agreement about how to excavate or interpret, i.e., archaeology is not a science so much as a crude instrument whose purpose and value are slowly being discovered. The questions asked by archaeologists are frequently cloaked in an elaborate theoretical framework which disguises the lack of a conceptual context. Most archaeological excavations uncover materials from "historic" periods, but use methods and techniques developed for prehistoric excavations. For the prehistoric period, archaeology is the only method available: its results are the only source of information concerning extinct preliterate cultures.

Although the origins of humanity clearly lie in Africa, the origins of Western civilization can be traced back to the earliest villages, which appeared in the Levant less than 15,000 years ago. Archaeological sites in the Near East are distinguished by the use of mud brick, which was probably invented around 12,000 years ago, roughly when humankind began to settle down and farm. Mud-brick dwellings are generally short-lived, but people in the Near East have tended to remain in roughly the same places and thus numerous villages today are actually sitting upon the ruins of earlier villages, sometimes stretching back thousands of years. Mounds can be abandoned due to population movements, war, changes in the trade routes or even sheer inconvenience. Whether abandoned or not, archaeologists can excavate such a site.

The most important developments in archaeological thought are therefore not in the field of theoretical speculation, but in methodology. The endeavor to draw more information from the earth has led to advances in the analysis of animal bones and the microstratigraphic analysis of deposits. Such efforts allow the archaeologist to draw conclusions about life and diet which would have been impossible a few decades ago. The rapid expansion of rescue archaeology executed by competent archaeologists using new methods means that sites are now excavated which would otherwise have eluded a research agenda. This allows for a considerable increase in the breadth of knowledge, as well as its depth. These methodological advances are, however, not spectacular, and cannot compare with the attractions of interpreting the data acquired.

Many sites are excavated as part of a research agenda, while others are discovered and/or excavated because they are threatened by modern development. In some cases, the research agendas are dictated by a sheer lack of knowledge. In some regions (such as southern Arabia), the temporal and spatial distribution of sites is unknown and must be established. In some cases, the dating of sites and assemblages remains unclear and can only be accomplished by new surveys and stratigraphic excavations. In other regions (such as Palestine, Iraq and Syria) the distribution of sites and the dating of the artifacts is more or less familiar, but remains to be explained. Explanations are sought by examining the material from a particular theoretical viewpoint.

Until recently, research excavation projects were designed to examine issues such as subsistence, state formation or climatic and demographic change. Research publications are devoted to discussions of style or architecture.

Publication projects are dominated by catalogues of unprovenanced museum collections or small finds from current excavations. Excavations move slowly: many current projects were begun during the French mandate in Syria. Given the glacial progress of excavations, the sheer monotony of pottery and the limited scientific value of objects of unknown origin, university teaching about Near Eastern archaeology is largely dominated by the temples and palaces excavated before the Second World War.

While documentation has slowed, the last century has seen keen advances in the field of theoretical research. The initial problems lay in establishing a chronological framework within which change could be defined: in order to perceive trends it was essential to establish the sequence and distribution patterns. Once relative sequences had been established, the next priority was to synchronize events in different regions, such as the Aegean, Europe, Egypt and the Near East. This synchronization allowed the diffusion of influence to be confirmed or denied. During the 1970s, diffusion came increasingly under attack. Since the mid 1990s, diffusionism has begun something of a comeback, but it is clear that archaeological problems are still largely chronological.

The lack of certainty did not, however, prevent the emergence of processual archaeology, dedicated to understanding cultural evolution and adaptation. It was in this tradition that Cambridge developed the concept of "palaeoeconomy," influenced by the American processual archaeologist Lewis Binford who suggested that it was not worth seeking information about thought in the debris of material culture. The idea of "processual archaeology" was that one could move beyond typology, to ask questions about activity and change, but not thought. The Department of Archaeology at Cambridge University has traditionally attempted to play a leading role at the forefront of archaeological theory. Archaeological theory attempts to grapple with the meaning of "style," "development," "evolution" and other features which can be read out of typological studies of material culture. Archaeology relies upon typology (a method of classifying artifacts based on external characteristics) to distinguish both chronological and cultural groups. Needless to say, the external characteristics of a tool or a building are mute, and must be interpreted. Initially, typology was therefore employed to distinguish discrete units. Typology thus played a key role in defining the methodology of archaeology. It also threatened to lead the discipline up a blind alley, as typology left no means of interpreting the significance of stylistic distinctions. The capacity to identify a dozen different—but contemporary—types of "industry" or "culture" was a satisfactory discovery for early archaeologists. This necessarily opened the way to establishing the "cultures" or "industries" which preceded and followed, and thus revealed technological and cultural changes over time.

This capacity to literally "touch" change and temporal variation has left an important imprint in archaeological thought. Regardless of all other theoretical developments, archaeologists remain far more conscious of "evolution" than representatives of any other discipline in the humanities or social sciences. The facts of evolution and development are clear and lie at the background of every archaeological argument dedicated to "explaining change." Archaeologists are confronted with the fact of change, but cannot account for it. Andrew Sherratt (1995: 3) has inimitably described the situation:

> I am caught here, however, in something of a verbal quandary ... criticising the defects of what is commonly called social 'evolutionism' ... I once asked Kent Flannery if he didn't feel uncomfortable in using the phrase 'social evolution' to describe the emergence and collapse of civilisations. 'What else d'ya call it?' was his immediate and unanswerable reply. It is indeed hard to avoid the word evolution in this semantic field.

The material culture confirms that change takes place and that humankind has moved—painfully slowly, but nevertheless moved—from "lowly" beginnings to the "lofty" state of being able to observe its own progress. The individual archaeologist must decide whether his or her task is merely to chart that "progress" through typological classification or to account for it. But, the reality of the evolution is overwhelming for virtually every archaeologist, in contrast to those working in other disciplines.

Archaeologists are still struggling with chronological difficulties, but many have realized that additional questions can be posed, and here Cambridge can be treated as "paradigmatic" in defining its role in theoretical rather than practical terms. One of the approaches selected at universities around the world from the 1950s onwards was a link with anthropology. Rather than relying exclusively on excavations and typology, archaeologists were encouraged to examine the behavior of modern "primitive societies," on the assumption that prehistoric societies and "modern primitives" were similar. This eventually led to a "processual" approach where the typological records were interpreted in terms of process: both evolutionary process and the process of daily life.

As material culture was the only witness available, the approach was very "materialist," emphasizing "subsistence" and "economy," or rather "palaeoeconomy." Using the term "palaeoeconomy" suggested that there was a difference between economics and palaeoeconomics, and thus specific patterns of ancient economic systems were sought. Implicit in the line of thought was the assumption that material culture could somehow be used to demonstrate that economics was a significant aspect of ancient activity and thus that the ancients were materialists. It need hardly be pointed out that the discovery that the ancients were materialists would in fact have contradicted the whole line of thought since it would demonstrate that there was no difference between ancients and moderns. Intellectually, however, it was also a difficult agenda since the data did not lend itself to economic analysis.

With the technology identified, parallels were sought among primates and living human groups. Anthropologists working in Africa discovered however (a) that people spent less than one day a week working and (b) that the size of "functional" projectile points was at least partially dictated by social rather than practical or technological constraints. Behaviorialists in Africa studying baboons also discovered that they spent 20% of their time grooming, creating social networks of dependency. While this latter pattern does not bear comparison with the amount of time spent grooming in the modern academic world, the general tenor of the results was more important in revealing that allegedly "economic" foraging did not necessarily play as prominent a role in primate life as the processualists had assumed.

Concentrating on subsistence allowed prehistoric archaeology to skirt the issue of religion. Trigger (1997: 392) notes that only 6% of the publications during the period 1978–86 in the series *Advances in Archaeological Method and Theory* were concerned with "ideology, religion and scientific knowledge." Until the 1990s ideology and religion were regarded as insoluble problems, to which the study of material culture could hardly hope to contribute. Concentrating on prehistory meant that the cities of the literate world were neglected. The fact that these cities—which emerged a few thousand years after Çatal Hüyük was abandoned—were dominated by religious symbolism (and not concerns with subsistence) could thus be neglected. Monumental temples and tombs built of lasting stone in ancient times still dominate the landscape of Egypt today. Private letters and offerings indicate that "ordinary people" shared the piety of the kings on a lesser scale. The temples of ancient Egypt played political roles; ceremonial political structures in pre-revolutionary China likewise served religious roles. The Sumerians said that "kingship had come down from heaven." The Chinese emperor claimed the "Mandate of Heaven." The Egyptian king was described as "the good god, the son of the Sun-god Re." The Akkadian king Naram-Sin promoted himself to divinity. The intertwining of divine and political roles becomes more pronounced during the second millennium, when the role of divine oracles as a source of political advice will be found among the Egyptians, the Hittites, the Babylonians and the Shang Dynasty in China (representing roughly 100% of the literate cultures of the day whose languages can be read). This use of oracles thus reflects two simultaneous trends: increased reliance on divine guidance and increased independence for political power. In Egypt and Mesopotamia, literature was also exploited for political purposes, but the temples underscore the nexus of power. Inscriptions thus explain how the relationship between political power and religious belief developed and merged. Artifacts from these ancient civilizations indicate that religious beliefs antedated their appearance, and that these were not restricted to a small elite, but rather widely shared. The documentation of the relationship has been fraught with tension ever since the emergence of the written word some 5,000 years ago. Acquiring information before this date is more difficult.

The discipline of prehistory was the only one—by definition—which could approach the issue, but had deliberately avoided it. One leading theoretical archaeologist, Ian Hodder, contributed to the debate, arguing that the process of becoming sedentary was not a mere matter of transforming plants and animals, and building houses, but actually a question of "domesticating" humankind. Rituals, rules and conventions could be matched with symbols known from both archaeological sites (such as Çatal Hüyük) and modern ethnographic research. Partially as a result of his efforts, religion as such has now come to play a prominent part in planning the agendas of research excavations.

It has also become part of the research agenda. In Steven Mithen's recent *Prehistory of the Mind*, the cognitive approach was adopted, and he summarized:

> Indeed I believe that during the last two decades of research the explanation for the Middle/Upper Palaeolithic transition has been found—not by archaeologists but by the cognitive scientists ... (Mithen 1999: 153)
>
> It is not simply the introduction of new tools at the start of the Upper Palaeolithic which is important. It is how these were then constantly modified and changed ... As the climate began to ameliorate, and a wider range of game became available, hunting technology became more diverse ... Such behavior ... is markedly different from the monotony of the hunting tools of Early Humans ... (Mithen 1999: 169)

Much of Mithen's detailed archaeological reconstruction corresponds to the developments discussed by Deacon (1997: 321–432), and thus draws on current cognitive thinking and archaeological results. This would appear to indicate that a new explanation has been found for a typological break which has hitherto not been understood: the successful application of a new method. In his *European Economic Prehistory* written in another decade with a different agenda, Robin Dennell summarized the significance of the same developments at the end of the Middle Palaeolithic and the Upper Palaeolithic in economic terms:

> Motor and conceptual abilities were very different ... These differences are masked if types of stone tools or prey are studied in isolation from each other. Overall, behavioral systems after 30 000 years b.p. can be regarded as fully "modern," and radically different from that of Neanderthals. (Dennell 1983: 79)

The same data is thus clothed in a different set of unverifiable hypotheses (the phrases "I believe" and "I doubt" are common in Mithen's book). The appropriate solution is found in terms of the model proposed, but Mithen's basic conclusions are strangely similar to Dennell's. Archaeologists generally adopt methods from anthropology or other social sciences in order to develop their theories.

Like most "scientific academic disciplines" prehistoric archaeology is a product of the age of the Industrial Revolution, with few links to the "philosophy" of earlier ages. The importance of technology in the last two centuries of the second millennium A.D. therefore influenced the development of archaeological typology, providing a chronological framework for human "development."

Convinced that technology is the key to understanding human history, Mithen's theory assumes that technological development took off when the mind had emerged. His thesis is purportedly an answer to eight puzzles concerning human activity before the beginning of the Upper Palaeolithic, some 30,000 years ago. Most of his puzzles are real food for thought, but the most important is

> "Puzzle 8" Why is there no evidence for ritualized burial among Early Humans? This is a puzzle because while there is clear evidence that Neanderthals were burying some individuals in pits, there is no evidence of graveside ritual accompanying such acts, nor of the placing of artifacts within the pits/graves along with the dead, as is characteristic of Modern Humans. (Mithen 1999: 135–36)

Mithen is thus able to show that technological progress and ritual accompany one another, and that these appeared with the appearance of the mind, rather than 100,000 years ago with the first anatomically modern humans. This is a remarkable puzzle. There is however, one slight problem:

> Skhul Cave. … The remains of ten individuals were uncovered. The best known are the burial of Skhul V, with a pig's mandible incorporated into the grave; Skhul I, the skeleton of an infant; Skhul IV, a semi-flexed burial; and Skhul IX. The skeletal remains of this group served as the basis for the identification of early modern human anatomical characteristics [… and dating to …] the range of 80,000–117,000 years old. (Bar-Yosef 1997: 425)

There is thus evidence—contrary to the assumption of Mithen's "Puzzle 8"—of burials (which can be interpreted as a cemetery) and grave-offerings associated with the very earliest anatomically modern humans, and thus evidence that the technological change accelerated tens of thousands of years after the earliest known rituals. Mithen (1999: 180) also refers to this, and in fact—contrary to the interpretation advanced here—Mithen's puzzles are coherently arranged and consistent. The arrangement of puzzles is, however, only coherent if all are associated only with "early humans," as Mithen does. In fact, however, Mithen's argument is designed to advocate that the technological revolution of the Upper Palaeolithic betrays the emergence of the modern mind. However, Mithen fails to make it clear that his other seven puzzles—defined in terms of technological achievement and social behavior—applied not only to the "early humans" he specifies, but also to the anatomically modern humans prior to the disappearance of the Neanderthals. The technology and social systems of our closest ancestors did not, therefore, differ from those of the "early humans." It was only the use of ritual burials which distinguished them—from their very earliest appearance. There is thus a crucial change which can be seen in religious behavior immediately associated with the appearance of modern humans, which is not visible in the technological record.

It will be recalled that the typological approach enabled archaeologists to distinguish artifacts and assemblages of artifacts (termed "cultures" or "industries" depending upon the author's terms of reference), based upon their external appearance. It was later realized that different assemblages existed simultaneously and therefore that the record was not a mere account of technological progress. However, the approach to evolutionary development based upon technological improvement visible in the typological analysis of the material was never really banished from the archaeological mind, since "technological evolution" did—so obviously—play a major role in the story archaeologists were unraveling. However, misled by the emphasis on technological development, Mithen had missed the crucial importance of this evidence of ritual burial indicating that modern humans began burying their dead before the Neanderthals, while using the same technology as the Neanderthals.

Even more remarkable is the fact that these earliest humans were apparently buried in cemeteries. From Shanidar in Iraq to La Ferrassie in France, the Neanderthal burials are generally in pits in living sites, cut into the accumulations of debris, which continued to accumulate above the burials. The burials of the earliest anatomically modern humans are in cemetery-like precincts. There is little evidence of ordinary daily activity in the areas near the skeletons and the skeletons were found in groups. The early human burials also antedate the Neanderthal burials. It would thus appear that the early modern humans not only buried their dead in cemeteries with grave offerings, but also that the crude Neanderthal burials were an imitation of this human invention, which was the first sign of human sentiment and can be traced back to the earliest modern humans. Mithen's failure to recognize the significance of these events can be traced back to the blinding importance of technological development in archaeological thought.

Recognizing that humans were buried from 100,000 years ago, Cauvin was unable to define a technological/ritual moment in the Palaeolithic which could be linked to the appearance of the mind and religion. Cauvin (2000) also observed that none of the conventional explanations for the start of the Neolithic were really persuasive. Neither climatic change nor demographic pressure were compelling arguments once the evidence was in. It was, however, blindingly obvious that an explanation for the Neolithic must be found. After having lived as hunters and gatherers for a hundred thousand years, anatomically modern humans started to settle down some 10,000 years ago. Less than five millennia after the first settlements in the Near East, agriculture was practiced all across the Eurasian continent and the life of the wanderer became the exception rather than the rule. The transformation deserves to be termed a "revolution," and Cauvin posited that this revolution was linked to the human mind.

He, rightly, points to the explosion in the use of symbols accompanying and following the Neolithic Revolution. The existence of "skull-cults," statuary, "special buildings" and ritual are virtually indisputable. Cauvin therefore argues that the birth of the mind and religion were linked to the technological and economic innovations of the Neolithic rather than the Upper Palaeolithic. This may be correct, but all observers should be conscious of the deliberate and conscious link of the "mind" to "technological innovation" in archaeological thinking, whether in Dennell's economic approach, or the religious/cognitive approach advocated by Mithen and Cauvin.[2]

It is hardly an accident that the McDonald Institute at Cambridge University, and archaeologists such as Hodder, Mithen, and Cauvin are taking theoretical approaches from the currently popular "cognitive" model. Archaeology has a long history of theoretical experimentation, generally reflecting current intellectual trends.

Any theoretical approach adopted must, however, be coordinated with technological development, since change in the material culture is the only aspect of human activity archaeology can approach. This is a major barrier as it relies upon assumptions about the significance of technological change or its absence. Although apparently lending itself to the study of economic and technological development, it also contributes to defining the paradigm in terms of concepts which can be recognized in concrete artifacts.

In the nineteenth century, the use of typology was a logical reflection of the belief in technological change. Even when other issues arose typology still remained the primary basis for all work. The adoption of economic approaches employed the typological framework, and thus linked economic development and technology as economists have. Archaeologists generally argue that their time-depth enables them to answer questions which modern social scientists cannot. The original models employed depended upon recycled sociological and economic theory. These were based on (a) modern interpretations from the older archaeological literature and (b) modern theory unrelated to the specifics of the ancient world, and thus specifically dismissed. Since the remaining parts of the theory were derived from the archaeological source material, it should thus have led to purely circular logic, and it did. Initially, archaeological agendas based on the assumptions proved successful, as the evidence was open to several possible interpretations. On the other hand, however, the inability of archaeologists to identify and strengthen the link between "development" and "technology" did not lead them to question economic orthodoxy. When unplanned archaeological discoveries began to unravel its theoretical foundations, archaeological theory did not develop on these discoveries and evolve a new body of theory, based on the "deep-time" advantages. Instead, archaeology chose to abandon the field.

2 It should be noted that the present writer is convinced that Cauvin is correct in his appraisal of the chronological period when religious thinking achieved an unparalleled importance, and we will return to this later.

Although the approach centering on the appearance of religion and the gods during the Neolithic is probably valid, it should be evident that the currently popular cognitive approach provided a ready tool, and that the importance of the technological implications was the point of departure for the analysis. The technological emphasis was part of the previous typological and processual paradigms, but archaeology cannot escape from technology. Given the fact that archaeology is completely dependent upon the material remains (the technology), the danger that preconceptions about the importance of [illegible]. The legacies of the various approaches are left as palimpsests along with the unanswered questions. Exploring consciousness and religion with such an instrument is necessarily difficult, but there is no other means of approaching prehistory.

The Middle East

Assyriology, egyptology and Near Eastern archaeology were not only born in the context of nineteenth century evolutionary thinking, but also paradoxically in the context of Victorianism. Some hoped that archaeology could be exploited to scientifically prove the correctness of Biblical tradition, and thus religion played an important role in forming the disciplines, and not just in the monuments discovered.

Home to pyramids and ziqqurats, the Near Eastern archaeologist felt at home with religion. Near Eastern archaeology had always been resistant to the trends of European prehistory and had always been dominated by a recognition that the decoration of cylinder seals and the construction of temples could not be accounted for exclusively in the "challenge and response" terms of processual archaeology. Near Eastern archaeology was also born in the spirit of nineteenth century, however, and thus influenced both by processual evolutionism and Hegelianism. The one suggested that everything was interrelated and autarkic, the other that European civilization was the pinnacle of human cultural development. One implied that Egypt must be understood in its own terms, the other that Egypt must be understood as a step on the ladder leading to the Prussian state. Neither of these was consciously recognized, however. Simultaneously and unconsciously assuming that the Egyptians must be understood in their own terms and that they were a mere stage of evolution, Egyptologists have frequently suggested that the ancient Egyptians did not have a term for "religion" (e.g., Assmann 1991: 9). Since the field of the study of religion cannot agree on a definition of religion, the Egyptians could be forgiven for having neglected to invent a term for it. In fact, however, the Egyptians did have a word for it: "the things of the god" (*khet ntjer*), as in a sentence "Beginning of the religious spells which were made for the estate of

Amun" (which is here translated differently than the same text in Guglielmi/ Buroh 1997: 106, 137). Ultimately religion is a set of culturally developed symbols recognized by a community believing in an inexplicable transcendental mystery linking this world with the Beyond through death and ritual (my own definition). The Egyptians constantly refer to "great mysteries" with regard to both cult and death. And this gave religion an important role at a time when categories were still being formed.

Since the gods created and ran the world, they were responsible for science. Since learning about the world was therefore done in temples, they were responsible for education. Since the gods were responsible for order, they provided a king and gave him the legitimacy to rule the land in their name. Politics, science, education and piety were thus all part of religion. Early philologists also made the temples responsible for the economy; while this appears to have been exaggerated, the temples did play an economic role. The archaeologists realized that the people who built these structures were responding to the same needs as those who build cathedrals, mosques, temples, shrines, universities and banks today.

In the ancient Egyptian language, a "tomb" could be called a "house" and a "cemetery" a "town." Tombs were a major feature of the Egyptian landscape and the ancient Egyptians specified that tombs were "houses of eternity" belonging to those who were buried in them, and thus there could be no doubt. Inscriptions assured us that the deceased hoped to live in the Beyond for eternity, and the development of their post-mortal hopes can be followed over three millennia. The temples testify to the role of the gods in this world.

The architecturally oriented studied outlines and foundations. The artistically oriented examined cylinder seals and statuary. Iconography and architecture thus marked one branch of archaeology. Progress was made in the realm of iconography, where philology and archaeology met. The symbols and statuary of gods were recognized and discussed. The themes of kingship and fertility were also linked to the principal lines of research: divine kingship with temple architecture and urbanism and the state; fertility with the measure of time and harvests. Both themes could therefore be bound into the core disciplines of architecture, iconography, economics and power. Compendia and catalogues were produced, and students studied the architecture of temples and palaces at universities around the world.

Although some universities maintained "typological" systems based on artifacts and monuments, excavators and surveyors turned increasingly to the processualist models of prehistory, investigating "central places" and "climatic change." The study of religion as a phenomenon was basically assigned to philologists who read the texts rather than the explorers who discovered the temples.

The Politics of Ancient Villages

Before the Neolithic there were no villages and thus no architecture of any kind, let alone religious. Archaeological sites from the historical periods of the civilizations of ancient Egypt, Iraq, Greece, China, Italy, and Mexico (etc.) tend to be dominated by structures which are both monumental and sacred in character. The structures themselves are preserved and the texts confirm their character. Even today, mosques, temples and churches are architecturally prominent in communities around the world, and contemporary literature is filled with allusions or quotes from sacred texts. In the less literate world of antiquity, the decoration of virtually every object—utilitarian or otherwise—was dominated by a vernacular of symbolism relating to the divine and rebirth, and many such objects have been recovered from tombs dedicated to the dead and thus reflecting the struggle with the concept of death.

Those "temples" and "shrines" which lay between the emergence of the Neolithic and the rise of urban literate societies—the ten millennia between 13,000 and 3000 B.C. if you will—fell between the cracks, as they were equally foreign to the philologist and the processually oriented prehistorian investigating technology or urbanization. There being no way to study them, they were neglected. When Andrew Sherratt, Senior Assistant Keeper in the Oxford Ashmolean Museum, edited the *Cambridge Encyclopedia of Archaeology,* he felt justified in excluding Stonehenge from the volume, although it is arguably the single largest man-made structure in prehistoric Europe.

It had always been recognized that the artifacts found in archaeological excavations reflected ideas. Since ideas were culturally conditioned and would therefore differ from culture to culture depending upon the social milieux, social habits were deduced from stylistic features rather than economic statistics. A processual archaeologist might point out that Çatal Hüyük lies in a broad fertile plain with access to cultivable land and fish in the streams, with obsidian supplies not far off. Wood could be found in adjacent forests where game, including bulls and boar could also be hunted. Reeds could be found in the marshes. With a population of at least 5,000 people, labor power for hunting, fishing, farming and construction was available in the huge community, enabling a division of labor (and examination of the human bones indicates that the people were not over-exerting themselves).

It is, however, quite clear that this is of little interest, when compared to the bizarre decoration of the houses. The village is also rather strikingly alone in the plain: apparently no one else felt comfortable settling down in the neighborhood, even though there was enough room. Obviously processual archaeology failed to account for any of this, and then it gradually dawned on the processualists that climate and tool function were insufficient to account for human behavior. The result was that the new generation could turn to the cognitive approaches in vogue since the early 1990s. There is, however, always a difference between archaeology and other disciplines. "Palaeoeconomy" implied something different from "economics." Ancient warfare is somehow different from "warfare" (Carman/Harding 1999: 250). "Palaeopsychology" likewise implies a difference between psychology and palaeopsychology.

At the heart of the problem is the realization that the objective world is inherently and at least partly illusory because perception is always subjective. The archaeologist can never be objective in viewing the data, even if he or she is looking at the right thing asking the right question. The archaeologist is influenced by both the agenda and the artifact. Neither the ancient actor nor the modern archaeologist studying the material remains of culturally conditioned behavior can have been entirely free of unconscious conditioning, and most of our material is in pretty bad shape anyway. The unconscious need to identify with illusions nevertheless applies to both, as does a need for symbols and routines.

Death is the center of such research, for death has both conscious and unconscious implications for individuals while simultaneously being a social problem for those left behind. It was long recognized that material culture could be interpreted as a kind of language giving access to the conscious mind, and tombs were among the universals of human culture. Burial was a universal custom which differed from region to region—yet the archaeologist could only despair at ever understanding how the ancients viewed their rites, and thus turned to typology and distribution charts, isolating chronological horizons and social groups.

The recognition that social groups could be recognized in this fashion assumed a new significance in the trends of archaeological thought. European prehistorians recognized that Neolithic burial mounds were modeled on houses, implying that "tombs" were "houses." Archaeologists found the dead buried in pits surrounded with offerings, including food and drink as well as ritual objects and assorted tools. The European prehistorian could not, however, determine why the same architecture was used, nor why the offerings were being made.

Classical archaeology, Near Eastern archaeology and egyptology were necessarily dominated by the study of tombs and temples as well as religious texts and symbols: their presence and importance were indisputable. It could be postulated that the origins of such institutions lie in prehistoric social systems, and thus "sacred" structures could be expected in prehistoric excavations.

Interpreting finds in this manner is, however, fraught with difficulties, as the assumption itself risks a misinterpretation of the data by demonstrating its veracity through a course of reasoning which is effectively nothing but circular logic, devoid of critical analysis. Until very recently prehistoric archaeology avoided the issues of art and belief: typology, distribution and chronological correlations were a primary concern. When these appeared to be resolved, the analysis of style was still treated in a similarly utilitarian vein, and the functional roles of objects and styles emphasized, within the context of an archaeological paradigm dominated by concepts like "optimal foraging strategies." When sought, ethnographic parallels were primarily technological, and the methodology tended to play down the issue of motives and beliefs, whether political, commercial or religious. A strong tendency to deny the abstract conceptual capacities of the ancient Egyptians also subtly suggested that they could not "think profoundly." The concept that archaeology was being transformed into an objective science seemed to have led archaeologists to assume that their prehistoric subjects were likewise practical and unimaginative rather than irrational and superstitious.

It should be evident that the prehistoric village at Çatal Hüyük is mute testimony to the rise of human consciousness, and that practicality was not the primary concern of these villagers. They may have personally known some of the "first farmers," but they were hardly obsessed with the development of agricultural technology. Although the household furnishings would have been recognizable to any student of ancient Near Eastern religions, Çatal Hüyük lay on the other side of the literate divide. Preliterate archaeologists have no access to written sources which can guide them in understanding what these people thought, and speculation about such matters is fraught with peril, since there is no clear methodology or guide to understanding unknown preliterate cultures.

When attempting to identify temples at a Neolithic site, Gary Rollefson (1998: 44) pointed to the pitfalls. On the one hand, he cited one local archaeologist who pointed out that some scholars had become alarmed about the frequency with which archaeological features in the Holy Land were given a "sacred" character. On the other, he cited Colin Renfrew's remark that "there was no body of theory" which could be employed to identify religious structures on prehistoric sites. This summarizes the two different traditions which collide in Near Eastern archaeology.

Distinguishing a "temple" from a "house," "palace," "warehouse" or "shop" is a difficult matter before the Bronze Age, when philologists could aid. Difficulties are compounded as existing models were developed in a theoretical environment dominated by economic and social evolution, and much archaeological thinking still harbors the methodology if not the approach. It is assumed that the economies of the period did not yet require ordinary "warehouses" or "shops" and that communal activity may have included both "ritual" and "consultative" activities in the same building. A "temple" might be assumed to have been larger than an ordinary dwelling and perhaps distinguished from such by the lack of ordinary domestic appurtenances and the presence of unusual features, possibly architectural. By the end of the 1990s, this had become a suitable framework for debate, as cognitive approaches were introduced into archaeology.

The archaeologist who found shrines in the 1960s would be disregarded. The prehistorian who found a temple in the early 1980s was certain to be criticized, and thus very hesitant or very confident. The situation has changed today, but before the new paradigm, Mellaart and Rollefson had in fact found temples, statuary and burials.

Burials

The concept of burial indicates both the understanding of mortality and a concern for transcendence. It is thus at once human and religious. The ancestry of modern humans can be traced back to tool makers who lived more than a million years ago, but they did not build any houses, or leave any remains that can be interpreted in religious terms. Our direct ancestors are younger in any case, and even anatomically modern humans wandered around the earth for roughly 100,000 years before building any structures whatsoever. Some of the oldest of these anatomically modern human skeletons were, however, buried in what appear to be cemeteries, in the caves at Mount Carmel on the coast of Palestine. The skeletons were found reasonably complete in a group of individual interments, separate from occupational deposits, suggesting burial in a cemetery. Deliberate burial suggests a consciousness and the recognition of mortality, but it is difficult to say more than that this would thus be peculiarly human. Both modern humans and Neanderthals were buried in Palestine at this time. Humans continue to be buried there, the Neanderthals died out, for some reason. The groups were probably living separately, but may have had some contact. Social life lay in the distant future: villages did not arrive until about 100,000 years later, "yesterday" in prehistoric terms.

Mithen (1999: 133) suggests that the social group identifiable by any one person up until recent times gradually grew from slightly more than a hundred to almost 150 over the two million years ending about 50,000 years ago. Mithen (1999: 148) also argues that a kind of sub-conscious consciousness or evaporating memory might have accompanied developments at the end of this time when modern humans and Neanderthals were living together. It was during the last 100,000 years that bone tools began to be developed. Bone tools are especially useful for long range weapons, as the points do not fracture on impact. They also require highly specialized skills to create and use. Mithen links this to language, but sees language and other phenomena which emerge in the period following 50,000 B.C. as the consequences of the evolution of a creative mind.

Exactly what happened i.e., what "cause" and what "result" cannot be known. The tools being created by humans changed and long range weapons become more common, but the game did not change. It is still frequently assumed that the tools and campsites represent "subsistence strategies" (e.g., Bar-Yosef 1998: 116). The possibility that some of the tools were "weapons" and the more dangerous game was Human vs. Neanderthal cannot be excluded.

The thought that death in battle could provide a basis for ceremonial burial would not be without parallel in human history. Sudden, deliberate, violent murder would have been quite different from the deaths of the preceding million years and this could be the context of a new development. In this context, suggesting that "the Neanderthals did not survive because they could not compete" takes on a new meaning.

The survivors will have been better fitted to survive, and survival depends upon cooperation. Language could provide some aid in cooperation. Before speculating that the mere capacity for speech necessarily led to language as we know it, it should be noted, however, that neither the Indo-European nor the Semitic language families can be traced back more than 10,000 years at the very most. Although it is possible that this is a coincidence, the idea that language did not really develop until the Neolithic cannot be excluded: and any claims to the contrary remain speculative as the evidence does not suggest that language's antiquity is any greater. Even more important is the theoretical possibility (or probability) that language is primarily used to communicate on a social and not an intellectual level (a fact which is surprisingly seldom recognized in academic circles). The mere development of language need not therefore be associated with progress, but it was definitely social. The date of its origin is important as the evidence suggests that it may have come much later than some prehistorians seem to suggest.

Regardless of the issue of language, art and carving did flourish during the last 30,000 years. The beautiful cave paintings of France and the fertility figurines of the Upper Palaeolithic become part of human culture from this age, but their significance will truly remain as obscure as the caves where they are found. Evidently thought and communication were struggling to achieve expression. Social life restricted to hunting bands may not have been conducive to communication. Such art is, however, restricted to regions beyond the Near East.

The first villages were founded in Anatolia, Syria and Palestine, around 10,000–12,000 years ago, and by 6500 B.C. the earliest villages were being abandoned. During the gradual development from crude huts through early "towns" from the end of the Palaeolithic (13,000–10,000 B.C.) and the earliest Neolithic (termed the Pre-Pottery Neolithic A, PPNA, ca. 10,000–8,000 B.C.), it is unclear whether any particular architectural feature played a practical, social, military, secular, domestic or sacred role. Larger huts could have been the residences of chiefs, or they could have been meeting places, for meals, rituals and conferences, but it is nearly impossible to tell. The theoretical models could provide little guidance without preconceptions, and preconceptions are easily demonstrated when the evidence is scanty.

The earliest "religious architecture" probably dates to the very earliest Neolithic (At Göbekli Tepe, Turkey), but most can be assigned to the villagers of the following Pre-Pottery Neolithic B (PPNB, ca. 8,000–6,500 B.C.) who flourished in Palestine, Transjordan and Anatolia. These villagers developed some highly peculiar customs, the least controversial and most common being a "headless burial," with the body under a house, accompanied by special treatment of the skull. Children were usually buried complete and left undisturbed. In adult burials, however, the skull would usually be separated from the body, after burial, so that the lower jaw bone remained with the skeleton beneath the floor. The skull itself was then buried separately, either near the skeleton, or kept in a room, or even buried with other skulls, so that groups of up to four skulls have been excavated. Occasionally, skulls show signs of plaster molding, designed to reconstruct the facial features of the deceased. Burials of this type are restricted to a domestic context, i.e. a residential house in a village.

During the Neolithic, children were also buried in the walls of houses. Through the end of the Iron Age, children would be buried near thresholds as well. Over the centuries and millennia, burial customs developed in different regions differently. The ancient Egyptians pioneered the concept of a cemetery in the desert, separate from the living, while Mesopotamian cemeteries never achieved the same degree of separation. Although developments differed, concern for the dead seems to be a universal human propensity, and the earliest detectable sign of "religious" activity or belief.

Temples

In later times, concern with the transcendental has promoted architectural development, but even today, "churchyards" are frequently "cemeteries," linking death and the numinous transcendentally. Architecture was only invented in the Neolithic. The relationship between enclosed space and the numinous is of greater antiquity. The cave paintings of southern France reveal a consciousness of life and their locations suggest a high degree of secrecy and ritual, as the caves were not used as residences in general, and the paintings frequently well off the beaten track, hidden in eternal darkness, dispelled only by artificial lighting. Their meaning and role remains equally obscure, however, and social life was still a matter of the distant future even 20,000 years ago, as most people still lived in small bands.

During the earliest period of human prehistory, religious practices are virtually impossible to recognize or identify. Interpretation is clouded by problems in understanding technology and society and hindered by problems of preservation. Deliberate burials in cemeteries appear to begin at roughly the same time as anatomically modern humans, and thus to underscore the significance of consciousness and humanity, but the meaning of the burials to those involved can only be a matter of speculation. Most of the architecture assigned to the PPNB can be explained in social and military—rather than religious—terms. The earliest clearly recognizable circular, but house-like, huts date to little more than 14,000 years ago. Developments in the succeeding period moved more rapidly. Within a few thousand years, both primitive stone masonry and the manufacture of mud-bricks had been perfected so that they were soon building rectangular buildings with two floors in villages up to 15 hectares in size.

Most of these settlements were abruptly abandoned about 6000 B.C. or 8000 years ago, and archaeological theory has provided various different versions of the end of the first villages, such as (1) environmental degradation (Köhler-Rollefson 1988) or (2) climatic change which both correspond to modern concerns. Under the influence of fashionable "cognitive" studies, "magic" and "ritual" have recently assumed some importance. This has led to some discoveries of "ritual" significance. It has been suggested that a PPNB "special building" was buried (Rollefson 1998: 54–55) and even that a Bronze Age temple was "ritually buried" as well (Oates/Oates 1991: 132–34). (It has, however, not yet been suggested that either the PPNB or Bronze Age civilizations were decimated through magic.)

At this earliest—Neolithic—era, voiceless artifacts and architecture are our only source. The most important of the vague hints are some putative temples at the site of Ain Ghazal, in Jordan (Rollefson). In an era of rectangular orthogonal domestic architecture, "apsidal" and "circular" buildings are clearly exceptions. The circular buildings were themselves distinguished by a sub-floor passage and a central hole. Two rectangular buildings appear not to have any traces of "ordinary" usage, but are distinguished by three standing vertical stone slabs, which would only have been inconvenient unless they served some "special purpose."

Such architectural details are, however, not very useful as their significance is open to dispute and to several different interpretations in any case. Of particular significance, however, might be the fact that the entrance to one of the rectangular "special buildings" was shielded by a stone screen in front of the entrance, preventing a glance through an open doorway from revealing anything to a casual viewer. The idea that activities within were not intended for sight by ordinary villagers indicates that this particular building was not communal, yet the unusual fixtures suggest that it was used for "ritual" purposes.

Even this would appear to be speculative were it not for the half-life-size modeled plaster statues found in a pit at the site. These figures were mostly plaster over twigs and represented human beings or anthropomorphic deities. In one case, a female statue had molded breasts, and her hands may have been cupped beneath them, as in the numerous figures from later prehistoric and historic periods in the Near East. Again, however, the original location of the statues is unknown and their role obscure.

The end of the earliest ("Pre-Pottery") Neolithic (around 7000–6000 B.C.) was rapid. Typologically, it ended with the appearance of pottery. Politically, it meant a time of movement as people moved consciously into zones with more water and left the periphery of the deserts. Some sought out zones with more rainfall, others plains which were regularly flooded. The first settlement in the plains of southern Mesopotamia dates to the same time as the end of the Pre-Pottery Neolithic B, which marked the end of the earliest Neolithic.

One of the major symbols of the Neolithic was the arrowhead. Gopher's thesis was entitled, simply, *Arrowheads of the Neolithic Levant* (Gopher 1993). It would have been impossible to write a treatise of this type about an earlier period, for arrowheads are not characteristic of the earlier period. It would also be difficult to imagine a more characteristic artifact for the Neolithic. This should be slightly surprising, for economically, people were becoming less dependent on hunting, rather than more so. Cauvin dismisses the logical alternative explanation:

> Indeed, we might wonder whether the PPNB expansion was in fact achieved through 'force of arms'. The appearance of warfare in the Neolithic as the logical consequence of the new need to defend property is postulated by prehistorians rather than demonstrated on the basis of the available information. One arrow-head retrieved here or there stuck in a human vertebra is perhaps not as adequate a proof as has been claimed. ... This weaponry indeed has a 'symbolic' value, as Ian Hodder would say. (Cauvin 2000: 126)

The suggestion would be reasonable, but the mere selection of arrowheads as a dominant symbol of society is important, especially at a time of "skull cults" when arrowheads are found in human bones. If symbolism has any value to society, it must symbolize something. Many villages were set in inaccessible areas. Most villages were destroyed by fire several times before being ultimately abandoned, suggesting warfare (Eichmann et al. 1997). Should warfare prove to be a partial explanation for the end of the PPNB, it may be possible to associate these early burial practices with the victims of warfare and thus to link killing and burial. It is improbable that mere sedentary life would lead to the wide-spread adoption of burial practices, but the potential coincidence of burial customs appearing at a time of increasing violence and deliberate killing would provide a reasonable context for a consciousness of life and death.

This symbolism preceded the Neolithic and was simply enhanced in the millennia after people became sedentary. Cauvin explicitly eschews an economic explanation for the Neolithic, and argues that the change was cultural, and that the cultural change led to the economic change. This is arguably the case. There is, however, an additional factor to be considered. Cauvin is correct that the symbols and other "cognitive" aspects of the Neolithic Revolution can be traced back to the Epipalaeolithic, and therefore that the cultural changes preceded the economic change. The earliest settlements were not agricultural, but rather clusters of dwellings used by hunters and gatherers. These earliest villages lie on the Western rim of the fertile crescent, where the Neolithic revolution began. It is therefore clear that the sedentary life style and the symbolism of the Epipalaeolithic were gradually transformed into the agricultural revolution.

Cauvin assumes that the gods and symbols of male virility accompanied the rectangular architecture and the appearance of the mind. He then suggests that by making this leap he is separating himself from materialism, by making the mind the source of the transformation. It can be argued that this is correct, but it should not be forgotten that this was also his point of departure: he assumed that the Neolithic needed an explanation, for those offered earlier were inadequate, and concluded that the birth of the mind led to the technological change. It will be noted that this is exactly the same link as that posited by Mithen, who simply dated the development to a period several tens of thousands of years earlier. Cauvin is thus materialist in the sense that he assumes that technological innovation reflects the "mind."

There is another explanation, which can employ the same set of assumptions and the same evidence, which Cauvin had adopted, but interpreted differently. There can be no doubt that Cauvin is correct in stating that the Neolithic was based on developments in the Epipalaeolithic and that current explanations for the Neolithic are inadequate. It is true that there was no demographic pressure on people in the sense that the supply of animals threatened humankind with famine. There was, however, another development in Palestine at the end of the Epipalaeolithic. Palestine was the home to several different groups of people using their own specific tool-kits (Goring-Morris 1998). The tools are stylistically distinctive, and modern ethnographic research has shown that modern hunter-gatherers consciously and deliberately fashion tools with specific stylistic features intended to be distinctive (Carr/Neitzel 1995: 163–64). Under the circumstances, the various competing groups may simply have made it impossible for other groups to move, and thus the sedentary villages could have resulted from constrictions on movement, dictated by the competing groups. Some groups may have been shoved into marginal or desert zones, and found themselves obliged to simultaneously develop a new economic basis and a new sedentary lifestyle. Given the evidence of intensified warfare during the Neolithic, this could be traced back to the end of the Epipalaeolithic.

According to this logic, the Neolithic will therefore have had its origin in the banal fact that people simply could not move. The symbolism of the Neolithic and the emphasis on death and burial can be related to the male symbolism of the arrowheads, and the ritual linked to violent, abrupt death: killing. That people simply could not cope with this on an ordinary daily basis and thus will doubtless have contributed to the development of religion. It is a banal explanation, but one which is equally compatible with the facts, while not assuming that the dark caverns of the human mind are open to voluntary technological innovation.

In contrast to this version, Cauvin assumes that the coexistence of several different groups at the end of the Epipalaeolithic was not relevant. He assigns primary significance to the "development of imagination," and that there

> is nothing to indicate a social tension that might, following a Marxist analysis, have generated some sort of competition for available resources. There was no poverty of environment resources, no indication at this stage that individuals or minorities within these societies had acquired the ability to monopolise the products if gathering or hunting sop as to make paupers of the rest. (Cauvin 2000: 208)

He assumes that this "imagination" evolved within the period he terms the "Khiamian," a period defined by an arrowhead he links to hunting (Cauvin 2000: 22). In archaeological terms, the only distinctive feature of the Khiamian is the arrowhead. Otherwise the culture cannot be distinguished from any other. If arrowheads are found in human bones, and are recognized as symbolic at a time when there is no reason to believe that there was any reason to suspect competition for resources, to deny the obvious symbolic meaning of that arrowhead is courageous. If the arrowhead had a specific symbolic meaning, then that meaning must have been widely understood.

It will be noted that the only alternative that Cauvin offers to "imagination" is a Marxist competition for scarce resources. Part of the dominant archaeological paradigm (Carman/Harding 1999) implies that ancient warfare had "causes." It will be recalled that one modern commentator contended that "[w]ar is thus an act of force to compel our enemy to do our will" (Clausewitz 1989: 75). If ancient warfare had a cause—rather than a purpose—ancient warfare was radically different to modern warfare. This is an assumption, which corresponds to the theoretical framework of archaeology. If this assumption is open to doubt, then Cauvin's thesis is at least open to doubt.

Killing in the hypothetical eradication of the Neanderthals can be linked to burials and thus the birth of consciousness. Linking warfare to the economic and religious aspects of the Neolithic revolution could also be important. The fundamental assumption of Deacon's *Symbolic Species* (1997) is that our species is the only one which employs language to communicate. This is indisputable, but all theses based on humankind's unique capacity for "reflection" and "thought" would be fundamentally altered if it were recognized that our species is the only capable of language and symbolism precisely because we killed off the others, and not because of some freak in evolution. The "thinking" and "reflection" may be a partial response to this killing. If ritual arose as a means of confronting this aspect of reality, the origins of religion and language would be quite different. This is speculation. It is, however, Cauvin who dismisses the warfare while emphasizing the symbolic character of the arrowheads.[3]

3 The relevance of the models—that "palaeo-something" is different from the "something"—assumes importance when this effects interpretations in other disciplines,

The link between the Neolithic and the birth of religion can be argued, although the origins are debatable. Cauvin assumes that this can be traced back to the birth of "imagination," before the technological revolution. Regardless of the origins of religion, the results were apparent in that part of the Western reaches of the Fertile Crescent where the PPNB culture developed. It was here that people erected houses and lived in villages. It was here that people were buried under the floors and in the walls of the new houses. And it was here that the first unusual buildings appeared, those in which people did not live.

The clear distinction between the "larger than ordinary" structures interpreted as being "communal" and the closed entrance to the special building at Ain Ghazal indicates different types of activities, of a "ritual" kind. Given the widespread and common funerary practices involving the preparation of skulls, one would be inclined to consider the possibility that some of the "special buildings" at Ain Ghazal were actually the sites of mortuary activities. Such thoughts are pure speculation however.

Aside from the "evidence" from Ain Ghazal, the earliest "temples" recognized may be the round tower at PPNA Jericho or structures at PPNB Beidha in Jordan. The tower at Jericho may be a defensive structure, however, and the buildings at Beidha therefore of potentially greater import.

> Larger, distinct, nondomestic structures were centrally situated throughout the village's history ... Five uniquely constructed medium sized buildings off-site were also interpreted as non-domestic, possibly associated with aspects of the rich ideological and ritual tradition that flourished during the PPNB. (Byrd 1997: 292)

---

because these involuntarily reflect archaeological thinking, and this is particularly true in the case of Deacon (1997). It cannot be dealt with here, but scholars should be conscious of the influence which the distinction has on their own work, one being that "ancient" warfare had a "cause."

As long as ancient warfare is studied as a matter of "causes" and distinguished from modern war, the distinction threatens to have an impact on other aspects of cognitive thinking. The present writer's conviction that this is the case is one of the reasons that Deacon's major work is not discussed in the context of the emergence of language. Deacon avoids the issue of mortal conflict between neighboring hominid groups, dwelling on intra-group interaction, and avoids the issue of cannibalism when discussing hominid meat consumption, reaching "warfare" via ritual, and moving straight to "peace-making" rather than eradication. He can therefore conclude: "Evolution has widened the cognitive gap between the human species and all others into a yawning chasm" (Deacon 1997: 412). His conclusion depends upon the validity of the currently prevalent archaeological paradigms that "ritual" leads to peace and that "ancient warfare" was different.

The reluctance of modern scholars and philosophers to face the reality of warfare could itself be a new form of ritual designed to deal with this unpalatable truth, a secular means of expelling it.

Given such "evidence," one can share Mellaart's sentiments when he remarked that

> [a]fter this tantalizingly vague information ... the reader may well turn with relief to the site of Çatal Hüyük, 11 km north of Çumra in the alluvial Konya plain ... a large mound, approximately 600 x 350 m ... (1975: 98)

Çatal Hüyük

By 7000 B.C. the village of Çatal Hüyük had appeared. Written texts dating to the middle of the third millennium B.C. from Iraq, Syria and Egypt demonstrate that by this time—perhaps 3,000 years after Çatal Hüyük was abandoned—gods were worshiped in temples. Architectural elements currently identified as temples dominated the cities of Mesopotamia, and kings traced their right to rule back to divine sanction: "kingship was lowered from heaven" is the formula in the Sumerian King List (Oppenheim 1969: 265).

The clay modeling of skulls, elaborate burial customs, statuary and possible temples at Ain Ghazal cannot be dismissed, but none of this material has been preserved in a fashion which would allow an understanding of the customs (as opposed to identification). It is clear that by 6000 B.C. human consciousness and imagination had been allied with technology (sculpture and architecture) in a fashion that can only be described as religious. The village of Çatal Hüyük represents the next logical stage of this sequence.

Çatal Hüyük is also pivotal in another fashion. Mallaha in Palestine is slightly earlier, but plays a key role as one of the earliest known human settlements anywhere, dating to the end of the Paleolithic Natufian culture. The largest house there (9 meters in diameter, or more than twice the average) cannot be assigned a role which is unequivocally either political or religious, but the concept of a "town hall" either dominated by a "chieftain" or an "assembly" could be more easily defended than a religious one. By the same token, the pyramids of third millennium Egypt are arguably more political than religious, as are the palaces of third millennium Mesopotamia. Positing a single logical evolutionary line would imply that political structures would show a linear development between 12,000 B.C. and 2500 B.C. Çatal Hüyük demonstrates that this is not the case: clearly consciousness had briefly gained the upper hand.

In the face of archaeological theory dominated by economics and function, Mellaart noted that the decoration revealed by the excavations had uncovered plaster reliefs which

> defy materialistic interpretation. Women do not give birth to bulls' or rams' heads, and certainly not on top of a doorway from which peer the ferocious heads of three superimposed bulls ... Nor is it very usual to find 6-foot-tall Siamese female twins, one which gives birth to a huge bull's head, on top of which there appears another, smaller one. (1975: 108)

As the spectacular results did not correspond to the dominant paradigm, the excavation was thus abandoned and neglected until the appearance of "cognitive" philosophy as a dominant trend. The new methodological approach found that Çatal Hüyük was an ideal site for the exploration of "cognitive" ideas, and thus the excavations were resumed in the early 1990s. This change in emphasis to economic features during the intervening decades after the initial discovery of Çatal Hüyük meant, however, that the resumption of the excavations benefited from improvements and changes influenced by the new methods. The discoveries of the earlier and later excavations were the same, but the methods and interpretations were complementary.

Dismissed as an exception when archaeology was directed towards questions of "subsistence," Çatal Hüyük was necessarily an exception again when the Cambridge palaeopsychologists began to re-write the archaeological agenda, especially as this site did not require philologists and yet demanded attention in psychological terms: the ruins required psychoanalysts more than most people.

The community of five or ten thousand people at Çatal Hüyük was one of the largest groups of people who had ever attempted to live communally at the time, and they did it for longer than most. The largest sites of the PPNB were 12 hectares at the limit, and generally dominated by a short period of residence and large open spaces between the houses. Rollefson (1998, etc.) has suggested that buildings at Ain Ghazal may have been temples and it could be argued that the preparation of the bodies was carried out in one of the buildings. It is far from certain that these arguments can be compellingly pursued, but the idea of a temple as originating in the mortuary cult would provide a link with past practice, as burial is the only recognizable religious activity in the earlier history of humanity. (It may not be irrelevant to recall here that the architecture, rituals and paraphernalia used in the mortuary cults of ancient Egypt—several thousand years later—would appear to be the source for the material used in the divine cults.)

The Anatolian site of Çatal Hüyük may have been founded just before the end of the PPNB in Anatolia and the Levant. The village was characterized by quite different traditions. At Çatal Hüyük, the houses were crammed together with party-walls serving neighboring houses. Open spaces were merely collapsing houses filled with rubbish and animals. There were no streets or alleys and thus no doors or windows. Light, air and people apparently entered the houses via the roof. People lived in dark smoke filled rooms and those living on the edge of the settlement were constantly subjected to people and animals moving back and forth over their heads. Those living in the center had to skirt the roof-top entries and avoid the abandoned roofless houses which barred their path, meaning that they were compelled to cross the houses of the living. They can be excused for such unorthodox ways as so many (perhaps 10,000) had probably never ever been gathered in one place before, and thus the concept of city planning had to follow the experiment rather than precede it.

An archaeologist working at a PPNB site in Jordan has associated rock art depictions of gazelles as a form of "sympathetic magic" in hunting (Betts 2002). Animal figurines are also known from the contemporary site of Ain Ghazal, but the most striking feature of the Neolithic is the abundance and size of the anthropomorphic figurines. The large figurines from PPNB Ain Ghazal are generally close to sexless, as are figurines from many other sites. Recently excavated material from Nevali Çori in Turkey has shown a large proportion of sexually distinct human figurines, with both sexes represented in equal proportions, and genitalia sufficiently clear as to leave no doubt, especially in the cases of pregnant women. The same site also uses the bird in a figurative fashion, which the archaeologist linked to life and death (cf. Morsch 2002).

Anthropomorphic—or more correctly, gynaemorphic—figurines were common at both Çatal Hüyük and the later neighboring site of Haçilar. Many of those at Çatal Hüyük were crudely made, but clearly emphasized a number of different roles played by women, frequently emphasizing fertility and associations with the animal world. The emphasis on children, breasts, pregnancy and sexually provocative positions leave little room for imagination. In one case, a double figurine depicts the sexual act and then a mother and child on the other side. Some of the figurines from Haçilar leave no doubt about their explicitly human sexual character, and in one case seems to imply that the woman is more important, by portraying the female at a larger scale than the man with whom she is coupling.

Consciousness of sexuality and death will have become increasingly prominent in Neolithic communities. Archaeology cannot, however, do more than point to the fact that the context for immorality was created. The archaeologist only finds the context. In religious terms, burials are as close as archaeology can come. The dead were interred individually under the floors in a series of pits, and never buried in kitchens or storage areas. Examination of the bones of the deceased (which were carefully buried under the platforms in the houses) demonstrated that the residents of these strange houses were not working very hard. The bones also revealed that many of the residents died young. Their lungs must have been completely covered with soot, however, and thus they cannot have breathed very well if exposed to hard labor.

The architectural reconstruction of the houses suggested a conscious organization of space. The main room was the living room, and the partition separating it from the kitchen was perforated so that food could have been passed into the living room through the kitchen walls. Mats may have been laid over divisions in the floors, making symbolic distinctions visible where the dirt floor could not have served as well, although steps and ridges were also present. The floors were covered with soot, littered with fragments of wood and stone debris. Although brooms were probably used to sweep the floors regularly, the paths were defined by repeated trampling: even the movement of children must have been controlled. These conclusions logically follow analysis of the distribution of micro-debitage: they are not speculations. In the same fashion, analysis of the micro-stratigraphy revealed more than 700 layers of plaster on the walls of one house, suggesting both that the house was used for almost a century and that it was cleaned and repainted both seasonally and annually.

The paintings and sculptures were all in the houses, and may have been painted over and/or removed when no longer required. In one case, sculptures had clearly been removed from the wall and carefully buried below their original position, along with some stone debris. Inside, the houses will have been clean areas—in neighborhoods of collapsing houses and rubbish. Analysis of deposits has demonstrated that animals were actually kept on the site (Matthews et al. 1997: 302).

There was no decoration outside the buildings, and thus the interior of the house contrasted strongly with the world outside, one dominated by animals, even just outside the house. It is clear that life took place in houses which were clean and that patterns of movement within these houses were "predictable" and therefore possibly "regulated." It is difficult to imagine or describe the world revealed by the excavations at Çatal Hüyük. One can, however, perhaps see the head of the household seated on the platform in which the ancestors were buried, receiving food passed by invisible hands while relaxing in an ill-lit smoke filled room listening to the din of goat herds above and gazing at the bizarre paraphernalia decorating the living room. In the fields outside, vultures may have been devouring the flesh of a relative who would join the others in the family vault. To suggest that these people had psychological problems is to miss the point entirely: they were facing them.

A wall painting shows vultures consuming headless bodies. One idea could be that human bodies were exposed to vultures for excarnation prior to reburial. Could the vulture simply represent death taking a person away? Was this a ritual or a metaphor? Many other paintings reveal what appears to be the deliberate baiting of animals. Young men wearing leopard skins appear to run around baiting bulls, deer, boars and bear. Clearly a representation of male hunting prowess, it can represent a mythical activity, or a ritual or an initiation.

Even if fictive, the concept of the domestication of male aggression can lie at the heart of the decoration, as it brings chaos, power and conflict into the clean order of the house. It can thus define the social hierarchy of a household. If a symbolic initiation, it can imply the *rite de passage* of reaching adulthood. The use of bull's horns as interior decoration can also be understood as a system of framing, domesticating the powerful bull. It is clearly a mechanism for staging, enhancing, magnifying and taming the wild. The boar handle of a well-flaked flint dagger was both part of a boar and carved in the form of a boar's head. The boar has been tamed and mystified through art, but linked to death through the dagger. That these symbolize authority, power, violence and displacement should be clear. Such an interpretation would be confirmed by the analysis of the animal bones found in the houses. Sheep and goats were well represented on the daily menu, but not in the art, while boar and bear were not on the menu, and dominate the art.

The mere presence of boar's tusks and bull horns among the materials which are still found in the houses underlines, however, that this was no mere game. These alone suffice to argue that the leopard skins in the paintings reflected a part of reality lost in the archaeological record. Bears, bulls, leopards, boars and vultures must have been part of the landscape, and someone must have been hunting and killing bulls, boars and leopards. These remnants thus demonstrate the reality of fear and the real danger of sudden and violent death as a matter of everyday life. These people were ordinary people living ordinary lives of which—by social interaction and the quality of their leisurely lives—they were probably more conscious of than any other. They had to find a means of coping with the challenges they faced.

Concluding Remarks

Çatal Hüyük lies at the origin of many features of modern life. The town was founded just before the end of the Pre-Pottery Neolithic, and it was during the Pre-Pottery Neolithic B that pottery was invented and the first murals appeared. It was one of the largest concentrations of human beings the world had ever seen at that time, and the site of more art than any other in the preceding history of humanity. The metal found there is among the earliest in the world.

If Çatal Hüyük is known, however, it is primarily as the home of the mother goddess. The mother goddess seated on her panther throne. The mother goddess giving birth as a leopard. The female was associated with terror and nourishment as echoed in the title of George Lakoff's book *Women, Fire and Dangerous Things*. The exact meaning of the context will, however, continue to elude us, as we cannot (yet?) tell whether the "head of the household" at Çatal Hüyük was a male or female. This merely underlines our incapacity to understand who was doing what and why.

The evidence is open to many interpretations and possibilities for speculation endless. The literature is growing rapidly. Rather than follow a path of free association, one can close this discussion by noting three different trends of thought drawing on archaeological material: one popular, one archaeological, and one philological. Literally while preparing the final version of this text, the author had three revelations about the character of archaeology and religion. One was reading a popular work by Leonard Shlain, The Alphabet Versus the Goddess. Another was attending a workshop on "Magic Practices in the Near Eastern Neolithic" at the Second International Congress on the Archaeology of the Ancient Near East (Copenhagen 23 May 2000, published as Gebel et al. 2002). The third item was the appearance of a book on political theology by the Egyptologist, Jan Assmann (2000).

Shlain's argument is that the invention of writing led to the marginalization of female deities, a process which was considerably accelerated by the introduction and widespread use of the alphabet. It is impossible (and superfluous) to summarize the argument in detail. Many of the details are correct, and in many cases his argument would be buttressed with additional evidence with which Shlain was unfamiliar. This is particularly true for Egypt, where the goddess Hathor was largely marginalized by masculine deities consciously exploited to support the concept of divine kingship under male leadership. There remain, however, several crucial issues.

One question is whether there really was such a process. One could suggest that Shlain has misunderstood the message. Temples at Paestum which were originally ascribed to Poseidon by modern archaeologists are now assigned to the goddess Hera, i.e., the substitution was a mere artifact in the history of science and not a rupture in antiquity. It could also be argued that the proliferation of goddess cults actually accompanied the spread of alphabetic writing: the Virgin Mary, Artemis of Ephesus and Isis come to mind. The association of a female goddess and a feline (leopard or lion) remained alive in Anatolia long after Çatal Hüyük was abandoned. In the second millennium B.C., the Hittites incorporated an anthropomorphic female deity associated with leopards known to us as the Hurrian goddess Khepat, whom they syncretized with their Sun-goddess of Arinna as the major female deity of the Hittite pantheon (Haas 1982). And the same goddess was worshiped among the Neo-Hittite states in Anatolia during the first half of the first millennium. The Greeks and the Romans maintained *magna mater* cults in Anatolia as well, cults which lasted until the advent of Islam and Christianity. The goddess lives on: if you go to the web-site of the goddess movement, you will find that Çatal Hüyük is the main site listed under "archaeology" and that they "create rituals of gratitude and healing to honor and connect with Goddess energy."

Were one—merely for the sake of argument—to concede that such a process of marginalization actually occurred, it could be debated when this began. The vaguely familiar concept of "divine kingship" in Egypt is closely linked with urbanization, states and male rule, all of which accompanied the appearance of writing and not just the alphabet (as Shlain points out). A review of the archaeological material could, however, be used to argue that the origins of the development lie much earlier, with the Neolithic revolution and sedentary life. A strong case could be made that the eclipse of the goddess cults actually began with the end of the Palaeolithic, but the character and insufficiency of the evidence makes it difficult to be certain. Of crucial importance is, therefore, Shlain's treatment of the Palaeolithic.

Shlain's discussion of the Palaeolithic necessarily mirrors the economic character of prehistoric studies during the decades before he began writing his book. Shlain therefore relies upon arguments developed within the "optimal foraging strategy" era of prehistory when archaeologists attempted to ascribe a practical, functional significance to every find and evolutionary development. Shlain's description of female activity and roles during early prehistory is thus practical, implying that women were struggling for survival and that all activity was dedicated to the conscious exploitation of material advantages. This reflects prehistoric studies until the 1990s. If these interpretations are discarded (as is increasingly the case), the very premises of Shlain's argument are removed, and the eclipse of the goddess must be reviewed in entirely different terms. This demonstrates the difficulties inherent in interpreting archaeological evidence, and clearly reveals the dangers of the use of archaeological materials by non-archaeologists.[4]

Shlain's book is popular and thus perhaps an inappropriate target in the present discussion. It could be suggested that this is a cheap tactic, designed to protect the professional interests and competence of archaeologists. More relevant, therefore, was the scientific workshop at the conference in Copenhagen where participants and audience consisted exclusively of Near Eastern prehistorians interested in an obscure era. Virtually every paper was presented by colleagues who had excavated the sites in question and studied the actual physical objects and structures which they had unearthed. Virtually everyone listening had shared in the same experiences.

One participant presented an interpretation of the finds from his site by simply superimposing them on two intersecting circles representing this world and the beyond linked by ritual and death (Morsch 2002: 152). This was revolutionary for Near East archaeology. The source of the inspiration was not, however, the objects alone, but also the available literature. The semantic source for this interpretation was, therefore—not surprisingly—the field of the history of religions itself.

The only written literature on the subject is that produced in this field. However, whereas the study of the history of religion concentrates on evidence of belief in transcendental agents, the archaeological record clearly reveals a process of socialization, linked to the growth of society and recognition of the power of sexuality, greed and envy. Archaeology will never be able to trace the emergence of prehistoric morality: archaeology can only trace the appearance of houses, villages, burials and evidence of violence against humans. When we trace back the written records recording values, they still conform to our own

4 It is, however, important to note that virtually the same logic about foraging strategies and meat also appears in Deacon, where the discussion of early human life (Deacon 1997: 384–401) reflects current palaeontological thinking.

thinking. The moral preachings of ancient Israel, Egypt and Mesopotamia do not differ greatly from our own, discouraging, e.g., theft, murder and illicit sexual activity. Neither then nor now are they observed in practice, but the concepts still seem reasonable to us, and from the earliest times, they are discussed in religious texts; punishment for misdeeds is assigned to a transcendent deity in some religions.

Such thoughts cannot have their origins in the Palaeolithic. "Thou shalt not covet thy neighbor's wife" is a superfluous injunction when there are neither "neighborhoods" nor "neighbors" (except perhaps the neighboring band from which you capture your women?). The same terms of reference apply to respect for property and farm animals. Before the Neolithic there will have been little worth stealing. These "modern morals" must have begun to play an important role in a society as complex as that of Çatal Hüyük, where such activity will have been possible for the first time. Dealing with both the problem itself and the emotional problems ensuing from it will have been a complicated matter.

The concept of deities related to death and fertility seems to have been syncretized at Çatal Hüyük, where ordinary houses served as cemeteries and shrines. If religion is the culmination of the burial practices and mortuary beliefs of the Palaeolithic and Neolithic, then Çatal Hüyük plays a crucial role, as the deities and temples of later times developed in a world where death was less important than immortality and morality.

The fertility and allure of goddesses belongs to a world concerned with life rather than death. The sedentary society of the Neolithic provided the context for the emergence of social problems relating to immorality as well as immortality. Controlling male and female inclinations became a problem with social rather than personal implications—and society needed to react. Respect for property demanded the same. Binding fertility and morality into transcendental immortality became a social necessity. The restrictions on use of space and the "otherworldly" character of the domestic furnishings complement the omnipresence of female sexuality and fertility.

The issues of "homes" and "pregnancy" are the crucial problems here, rather than what used to be called "deviant sexual behavior." Homosexual and other recreational sex need not lead to pregnancy and therefore does not compel regulation. Male and female copulation leading to pregnancy becomes an important social issue when it is possible that the grandparents cannot be certain about the identity of the father, but care strongly about the issue. Prior to the development of settled society, groups will rarely have come into the possibility of uncontrolled contact with others, and the concepts of "relationships" and the importance of pregnancy may have been less significant. A settlement the size of Çatal Hüyük may not have required a bureaucratic government, but it is highly probable that the entire social system (including both those in the settlement and anyone living in the adjacent forests) had developed some features of social hierarchy. This meant that there were not only "homes" with families and clans but also concepts of "blood relations." It is difficult to guess where the dangers first arose, but in a settlement the size of Çatal Hüyük it will have been possible for girls/women to become pregnant with children fathered by boys/men of whom the family ("home") "did not approve" (neighbors, inappropriate social classes). Conversely, it will have been possible to increase the number of "legitimate" children born. The concept of "legitimacy" assures that the identity of the father is known, and is therefore linked to "morality." It was only through the regulation of female activity and thereby fertility that this could be controlled.

Female figurines are found in the archaeological material in the rooms. Pairs of protuberances sticking out of the walls have also been interpreted as female human breasts. Some of the "breasts" have open nipples, with the beaks of vultures, the teeth of foxes and weasels, as well as the tusks of wild boars sticking out of them. The fact that these are "breasts" can be recognized from the "holes" in the nipples of female figurines. Peculiarly, these are frequently concealed, being plastered over. As the house was clearly inhabited afterwards, it is clear that the "ceremony," "ritual" or "action" demonstrated the close of one era and the start of a new one. In another case, a house was dismantled after a special burial: after being filled with clean earth, it was burnt, ritually terminating the use of the building.

There was no decoration outside the buildings, and thus social life was clearly domestic and controlled. Detailed analysis of the composition and accumulation of the floors and debris in and on them allows patterns of movement to be identified, allowing us to literally "follow" the ancients in their daily routines. Such tracking allows us to conclude that movement in the house was highly constrained, probably largely determined by social distinctions. Routines were created and maintained through the use of space. The house was a microcosm of the universe, but domesticated: an internalization of the external world.

The symbols of female sexuality and tamed male violence dominate the rooms. The number of conceivable associations here is mind boggling. The thought that the most dangerous parts of animals are "coming through" the walls is one. That the walls were permeable interfaces separating chaos and order is another, leading to the idea that the walls and floors were also interfaces between space and time as well, with ancestors and animals as mediators.

Walls not only partitioned the houses and the neighborhoods, but also linked past and present. The continuity of Near Eastern sites is remarkable. Walls were built on walls and hearths on hearths for centuries. The same motifs appear on cylinder seals for generations. The destruction of a temple was a symbolic act, which could not avoid retribution. Most of this continuity dates to the period following the beginning of the Bronze Age, which only began three millennia after Çatal Hüyük was abandoned. Most of the sites occupied before the beginning of the Bronze Age were abandoned and never inhabited again.

Many of the sites occupied since the beginning of the Bronze Age are still inhabited today. Clearly a shift took place, yet many of the features which mark Çatal Hüyük and are still present in the world were first seen there.

The fact that the memes familiar to the cultures of the modern world all stem from the sedentary agricultural world should discourage speculation about the degree of linguistic capacity before the Neolithic. The issues of language and social life become entwined with the concept of groups and bonding. Several simultaneously converging needs may therefore have contributed to the development of language, perhaps at the same time that rituals were also being developed. The existence of large groups of people interacting socially on a permanent basis will alone have stimulated language. At the same time, the requirements of technology and moral education may have been as important as coordination of hunting strategies and warfare. The capacity of language to confine and institutionalize thoughts may have been as important as the development of ritual as a means of confronting the transcendental and the emotionally painful. Language can contribute significantly to the satisfaction of these differing needs, and its development may have been speeded up remarkably during the Neolithic. The significance of the debate is apparent from the deluge of publications on prehistoric religion and language (cf., e.g., http://www.mcdonald.arch.cam.ac.uk/Publications/publications.htm), all necessarily speculative.

The existence of ritual is speculative, as is any possible interpretation. Reducing issues as diverse as social congestion and death to formulae will doubtless have simplified their lives. It will, however, be impossible for us to grasp either the rituals themselves or what they thought. We cannot tell whether meaningless rituals were developed to create patterns, or whether specific moral codes led to the emergence of rituals which then became meaningless.

After having devoted his life to the study of ancient Egypt and particularly the religion of ancient Egypt, Jan Assmann has now produced a book (Assmann 2000) suggesting that Egyptian religion originated in the political rather than the religious sphere, i.e., the rituals and myths followed and reflected political developments. Ironically therefore, egyptology is abandoning religion at the moment when archaeology is discovering it. Assmann suggests that this is potentially revolutionary from the standpoint of the study of religion (or at least his earlier understanding of it), but Kemp (1989: 7) had already pointed out that the ancient Egyptian state used a "wealth of devices—myth, symbol and institution—to manipulate the minds" of the ancient Egyptians. Assmann's earlier work reflected an understanding of Egyptian religion as a system of belief. Kemp's more realistic approach must have been at least partially influenced by Foucault's work.

Archaeologists can only view the detritus of this dead civilization. The possibility of employing the literature of disciplines relating to religious thought in conjunction with meticulously excavated archaeological material is very promising. The danger that such methods will lead to archaeological sources apparently "confirming" existing interpretations developed by students of the history of religions should not, however, be underestimated. Interpreting mute sources means that the listener is obliged to speak, and in this case, the archaeologist himself is actually speaking for the dead. Whether the cognitive models being proposed to explore religious phenomena in archaeology will contribute to an understanding by reexamination of the evidence remains to be seen.

The creation of "meaning" cannot be traced in the archaeological record. However, the evidence of the appearance of burials and villages and the creation of symbols deserves attention: it cannot be assumed that they existed before they appeared, nor that they necessarily bore "meanings" even remotely similar to those which we now associate with them.

References

Akkermans, P./Rodenberg, J.J./van loon, M./Waterbolk, H.T. (1978–1979), "Tall Buqras," in: *Archiv für Orientforschung* 26: 152–54.

Assmann, Jan (1991), *Ägypten: Theologie und Frömmigkeit einer frühen Hochkultur*. Second ed. Stuttgart: Kohlhammer.

— (2000), *Herrschaft und Heil: Politische Theologie in Ägypten, Israel und Europa*. Darmstadt: Wissenschaftliche Buchgesellschaft.

Bar-Yosef, Ofer (1997), "Carmel Caves," in: Eric Meyers, ed., *The Oxford Encyclopedia of Archaeology in the Near East*. Vol. I. New York: Oxford University Press: 424–28.

— (1998), "The Origins of Modern Humans," in: Thomas Levy, ed., *The Archaeology of Society in the Holy Land*. London: Leicester University Press: 109–23.

Betts, Alison (2002), "Interpretations of Dhuweila Rock Art: Shamanism and Increase Rites," in: Hans Georg K. Gebel/Bo Dahl Hermansen/Charlott Hoffmann Jensen, eds., *Magic Practices and Ritual in the Near Eastern Neolithic*. Berlin: Ex Oriente: 109–18.

Byrd, Brian F. (1997), "Beidha," in: Eric Meyers, ed., *The Oxford Encyclopedia of Archaeology in the Near East*. Vol. I. New York: Oxford University Press: 291–92.

Carman, John/Harding, Anthony, eds. (1999), *Ancient Warfare*. Gloucestershire: Sutton.

Carr, Christopher/Neitzel, Jill, eds. (1995), *Style, Society, and Person*. New York: Plenum Press.

Cauvin, Jacques (2000), *The Birth of the Gods and the Origins of Agriculture*. Cambridge: Cambridge University Press.

Clausewitz, Carl von (1989), *On War*. Princeton, N.J.: Princeton University Press.

Deacon, Terrence W. (1997), *The Symbolic Species*. New York: Norton.

Dennell, Robin (1983), *European Economic Prehistory: A New Approach*. London: Academic Press.

Eichmann, R./Gebel, H.G.K./Simmons, A. (1997), "Symposium General Discussion," in: *Neo-lithics* 2: 10–11.

Gebel, Hans Georg K./Dahl Hermansen, Bo/Hoffmann Jensen, Charlott, eds. (2002), *Magic Practices and Ritual in the Near Eastern Neolithic*. Berlin: Ex Oriente.

Gopher, Avi (1993), *Arrowheads of the Neolithic Levant: A Seriation Analysis*. Winona Lake, Ind.: Eisenbrauns.

Goring-Morris, Nigel (1998), "Complex Hunter/Gatherers at the End of the Paleolithic (20,000–10,000 BP)," in: Thomas Levy, ed., *The Archaeology of Society in the Holy Land*. London: Leicester University Press: 141–68.

Guglielmi, Waltraud/Buroh, Knut (1997), "Die Eingangssprüche des täglichen Tempelrituals nach Papyrus Berlin 3055 (I, 1–VI, 3)," in: Jacobus van Dijk, ed., *Essays on Ancient Egypt in Honour of Herman te Velde*. Groningen: Styx Publications: 101–66.

Haas, Völkert (1982), *Hethitische Berggötter und Hurritische Steindämonen*. Mainz: Von Zabern.

Hays, K.A. (1993), "When Is a Symbol Archaeologically Meaningful? Meaning, Function and Prehistoric Visual Arts," in: Norman Yoffee/Andrew Sherratt, eds., *Archaeological Theory: Who Sets the Agenda?* Cambridge: Cambridge University Press: 81–92.

Higgs, E.S., ed. (1972), *Papers in Economic Prehistory*. Cambridge: Cambridge University Press.

— ed. (1973), *Palaeoeconomy: Being the Second Volume of Papers in Economic Prehistory*. Cambridge: Cambridge University Press.

Hodder, Ian (1990), *The Domestication of Europe*. Oxford: Blackwell.

— ed. (1996), *On the Surface: Çatalhöyük 1993–95*. Cambridge: McDonald Institute.

Kemp, Barry J. (1989), *Ancient Egypt: Anatomy of a Civilization*. London: Routledge.

Köhler-Rollefson, Ilse (1988), "The Aftermath of the Levantine Neolithic Revolution in the Light of Ecological and Ethnographic Evidence," in: *Paléorient* 14: 87–93.

Matthews, W./French, C.A.I./Lawrence, T. /Cutler, D.F./Jones, M.K. (1997), "Microstratigraphic Traces of Site Formation Processes and Human Activities," in: *World Archaeology* 29: 281–308.

Mellaart, James (1963), "Deities and Shrines of Neolithic Anatolia: Excavations at Çatal Hüyük 1962," in: *Archaeology* 16: 29–38.

— (1967), *Çatal Hüyük: A Neolithic Town in Anatolia*. London: Thames and Hudson.

— (1970), *Excavations at Hacilar*. 2 vols. Edinburgh: Edinburgh University Press.

— (1975), *The Neolithic of the Near East*. London: Thames and Hudson.

Meyers, Eric, ed. (1997), *The Oxford Encyclopedia of Archaeology in the Near East*. 5 vols. New York: Oxford University Press.

Mithen, Steven (1999), *The Prehistory of the Mind*. London: Thames and Hudson.

Morsch, Michael G.F (2002), in: Hans Georg K. Gebel/Bo Dahl Hermansen/Charlott Hoffmann Jensen, eds., *Magic Practices and Ritual in the Near Eastern Neolithic*. Berlin: Ex Oriente: 145–62.

Oates, David/Oates, Joan (1991), "Excavations at Tell Brak," in: *Iraq* 53: 127–45.

Oppenheim, A. Leo (1969), "Babylonian and Assyrian Historical Texts," in: James Pritchard, ed., *Ancient Near Eastern Texts*. Princeton, N.J.: Princeton University Press.

Redford, Donald, ed. (2001), *The Oxford Encyclopedia of Ancient Egypt*. 3 vols. Oxford: Oxford University Press.

Rollefson, Gary O. (1983), "Ritual and Ceremony at Neolithic Ain Ghazal (Jordan)," in: *Paléorient* 9: 29–38.

— (1986), "Neolithic 'Ain Ghazal (Jordan): Ritual and Ceremony, II.," in: *Paléorient* 12: 45–52.

— (1994), "'Ain Ghazal 1993–1994," in: *Biblical Archaeologist* 57: 239–41.

— (1998), "'Ain Ghazal (Jordan): Ritual and Ceremony III," in: *Paléorient* 24: 43–58.

Rollefson, Gary O./Kafafi, Z./Simmons, A.H. (1991), "The Neolithic Village of 'Ain Ghazal, Jordan: Preliminary Report on the 1988 Season," in: Walter E. Rast, ed., *Preliminary Reports of ASOR-Sponsored Excavations 1982–89*. Baltimore, Md.: American Schools of Oriental Research: 95–116.

Sasson, Jack, ed. (1995), *Civilizations of the Ancient Near East*. 4 vols. New York: Scribner.

Shlain, Leonard (1998), *The Alphabet versus the Goddess: The Conflict between Word and Image*. New York: Penguin.

Sherratt, Andrew (1995), "Reviving the Grand Narrative," in: *Journal of European Archaeology* 3: 1–32.

Trigger, Bruce (1997), *A History of Archaeological Thought*. Cambridge: Cambridge University Press.

Conclusion

by

PETER ANTES, ARMIN W. GEERTZ, and RANDI R. WARNE

If a single conclusion can be drawn from a two-volume work on new approaches to the study of religion, it is this: The academic study of religion has become a global endeavor that is very different from and, yet, strangely similar to the comparative *Religionswissenschaft* envisioned by Friedrich Max Müller over 150 years ago. When looking through the predecessors of the thematic series that this publication is a part of, namely Jacques Waardenburg's *Classical Approaches to the Study of Religion* and Frank Whaling's *Contemporary Approaches to the Study of Religion*, the main points of *New Approaches to the Study of Religion* become evident.

Jacques Waardenburg's volume documents the formative period of the study of religion. This period consisted of formulating the differences between the comparative study of religion and (primarily) Christian theology. The struggle was then, as it still is now in some parts of the world, a methodological and ideological demarcation process that continued into the first decades of the twentieth century. The second phase of the study of religion, as evidenced by Frank Whaling's two-volume publication, consisted in formulating the differences between the comparative study of religion and most other humanistic and social disciplines. The concern was then, as it still is now in some parts of the world, to identify the distinctive characteristics of religion and religions on their own terms, with as little "interference" from general theories as possible. As it turns out, this highly ideological attempt was doomed to fail because it violated basic principles in the philosophy of science. The third phase of the study of religion, as evidenced by the present two-volume publication, consists in what could be called "the critical turn" in the study of religion. It consists of extracting the study of religion from the vanities and wrong turns of the past and providing it with a theoretically and methodologically sound framework for a global pursuit.

The extraction process, which is evident in a large number of the chapters presented here, is very difficult. There are many problems that have been ignored in the past or provided for with inept solutions. Thus a number of chapters demonstrate that what is "new" in the study of religion can and does involve re-evaluating and reconfiguring past approaches. Other chapters indicate that some matters are best left forgotten and that the only defendable way forward is through emulating advances in other disciplines. A clear lesson that has been learned is that religion is not the exclusive domain of any particular discipline. It is a fascinating human phenomenon that challenges all of us by its sheer multiplicity of expressions and contexts. Thus, any reasonable study of religion must at least assume linguistic, historical, comparative, social, psychological, political and cognitive dimensions. Scholars from these disciplines continue to contribute to the study of religion, but scholars who specialize in the study of religion must of necessity develop inter-disciplinary competence and theoretical sophistication. As is indicated in several chapters, scholars of religion face pressures from ideological, political and religious interest groups. Resisting these pressures not only involves responsible science, but also a great deal of sensitivity to the human issues that often times lay behind these pressures. It is the hope of the editors, that this third phase of the study of religion will be more successful than the prior phases.

A theoretically and methodologically sound framework for the study of religion has become more important than ever before. The reason for this is that our discipline has become pluralistic and global. The study of religion exists in many parts of the world in quite different historical and academic contexts. The study of religion is pursued in diverse cultures and languages. It draws on diverse methods, theories and data. Thus attempts to develop universal standards are exceedingly difficult, but not entirely impossible, as many of the chapters in this publication also clearly demonstrate.

As we move into the first decade of the twenty-first century, the study of religion is becoming an inclusive discipline. Like-minded scholars from all over the world are meeting on common ground at conferences and congresses hosted by the International Association for the History of Religions and similar organizations. This publication has tried to document an important and on-going phase in the study of religion, and it is the hope of the editors that scholars of religion will reflect on past failures and achievements in order to creatively meet the challenges and possibilities that lie ahead.

List of Contributors

PETER ANTES (1942), Dr. theol., Dr. phil., Habilitation for "Religionsgeschichte und Vergleichende Religionswissenschaft," Professor and Chair of the Department for the History of Religions (Religionswissenschaft), University of Hannover, Germany. Research interests: Islamic ethics, methodology in the study of religions and world religions in education.

JUSTIN L. BARRETT (1971), Ph.D., former faculty member of University of Michigan and Calvin College; Young Life staff, Lawrence, Kansas, USA. Research topics and fields of interest: Cognitive science of religion, cognition and culture, religious development, spiritual transformation.

KAREL DOBBELAERE (1933), Doctor in political and social sciences, Professor Emeritus, Department of Sociology, Katholieke Universiteit Leuven and Universiteit Antwerpen, Belgium. Research interests: Secularization, pillarization and religious involvement.

ARMIN W. GEERTZ (1948), Dr. phil., Professor in the history of religions at the Department of the Study of Religion, University of Aarhus, Denmark. General Secretary of the International Association for the History of Religions (IAHR). Research interests: Hopi Indian religion (based on fieldwork since 1978), the religions of indigenous peoples, method and theory in the study of religion, cognitive theory in the study of religion, and new religious movements.

RONALD L. GRIMES (1943), M.Div., Ph.D., Professor, Department of Religion and Culture, Wilfrid Laurier University, Waterloo, Ontario, Canada. Research interests: Ritual studies, anthropology of religion, religion and the arts, religion in the American Southwest.

HELGA BARBARA GUNDLACH (1965), M.A.; former dancer and choreographer, lecturer in adult education, Hannover, Germany. Research interests and seminars on religious dance, women in religion, intercultural communication.

ROSALIND I.J. HACKETT, Ph.D., Distinguished Professor in the Humanities, Professor at the Department of Religious Studies and Adjunct Professor at the Department of Anthropology, University of Tennessee, Knoxville, Tennessee/ USA.

ROBERT KISALA (1957), Doctor in religious studies (University of Tokyo), Permanent Fellow at the Nanzan Institute for Religion and Culture, Nagoya, Japan.

ANITA MARIA LEOPOLD (1953), cand. phil., Ph.D. scholarship (the defense of the Ph.D. dissertation is due in October 2004), University of Aarhus, Denmark. Research interests: Syncretism including Hellenistic religions and new religious movements; the theoretical perspectives are the cognitive science of religion and semiotics.

ALF G. LINDERMAN, Ph.D. in sociology of religion, Research Assistant Professor at Uppsala University, Sweden. Former works on comparative analyses of religious broadcasting in the United States and Sweden, development of theory and methods for reception studies with a particular emphasis on semiotics and semiology, methods for analyzing newspaper editorials, and religion and the Internet.

LUTHER H. MARTIN (1937), Ph.D., Professor of religion and former chair of the department, University of Vermont, Burlington, Vermont/USA. Research interests: Hellenistic religions (including Christian origins), especially from the theoretical perspective of the cognitive science of religion.

DAWNE MCCANCE (1944), Ph.D., Professor and Head, Department of Religion, University of Manitoba, Winnipeg, Manitoba/Canada; Editor of *Mosaic: A Journal for the Interdisciplinary Study of Literature*. Research interests: Critical theory and methodology; continental philosophy; ethics; body history.

GORDON D. NEWBY (1939), Ph.D., Professor and Chair of the Department of Middle Eastern and South Asian Studies, Emory University, Atlanta, Georgia/ USA. Research interests: Early Islam; Muslim relations with Jews and Christians; comparative sacred texts.

WILLIAM E. PADEN (1939), Ph.D., Professor and Chair, Department of Religion, University of Vermont, Burlington, Vermont/USA. Research interests: Theory and method in the comparative study of religion.

WINNIFRED FALLERS SULLIVAN (1950), Ph.D., J.D., Senior Lecturer and Dean of Students, University of Chicago Divinity School, Chicago, Illinois, USA.

STEVEN VERTOVEC (1957), M.A. in religious studies, D.Phil. in social anthropology, Professor of Transnational Anthropology at the University of Oxford/UK, and Director of the British Economic and Social Research Council's Centre on Migration, Policy and Society (COMPAS). Research interests: International migration, ethnic diasporas, religious minorities and multiculturalism.

LILIANE VOYÉ (1938), Doctor in sociology, Professor, Department of Anthropology and Sociology, Catholic University of Louvain, Belgium. Research interests: Religion, values, city and urbanization.

DAVID A. WARBURTON (1956), Dr. phil., Research Fellow, Department of the Study of Religion, University of Aarhus, Denmark. Current research: Ancient Egypt and Near East (economics, warfare, religion, color terminology, stratigraphy, chronology).

RANDI R. WARNE (1952), Ph.D., Professor and Chair of the Department of Philosophy/Religious Studies, and Coordinator of Cultural Studies, Mount St. Vincent University, Halifax, NS, Canada. Research interests: Gender, religion and culture, method and theory in the study of religion.

ALAN WILLIAMS (1953), M.A. oriental studies, Ph.D. Iranian studies, Senior Lecturer in comparative religion, University of Manchester, England. Research interests: Iranian literature and religions, comparative literature, linguistic and literary criticism, poetics.

Index of Names

Index of Subjects